AF579065

Great Photographic Journeys

Dewi Lewis Publishing

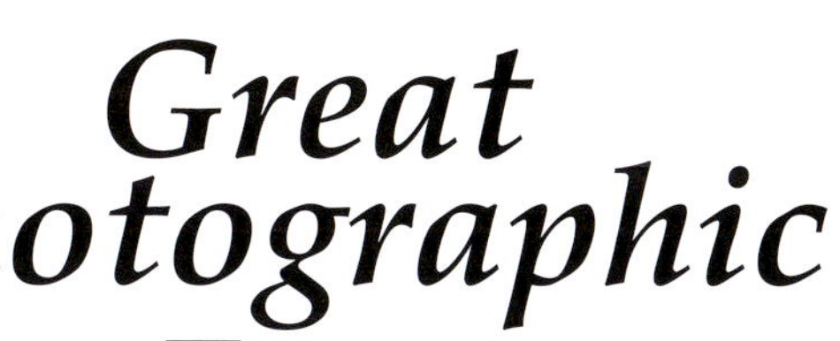

Great Photographic Journeys

in the footsteps of 19th century British photographers

John Hannavy

First published in 2007 by Dewi Lewis Publishing, 8, Broomfield Road, Heaton Moor, Stockport SK4 4ND, England

www.dewilewispublishing.com

Great Photographic Journeys*: in the footsteps of 19th century British photographers* was conceived, written, photographed and designed by John Hannavy

ISBN: 978-1-904587-54-5

Printed in China by 1010 Printing

John Hannavy was awarded a Winston Churchill Travelling Fellowship in support of this project, and the travel and research could not have been undertaken without a generous grant from the Winston Churchill Memorial Trust.

The support of Christies Ltd; Hans P Kraus Jnr. Inc.; The Metropolitan Museum of Art, New York; the National Library of Brazil; The National Museum of the History of Ukraine; and the National Media Museum, Bradford, England, in helping source Victorian images is also greatly appreciated.

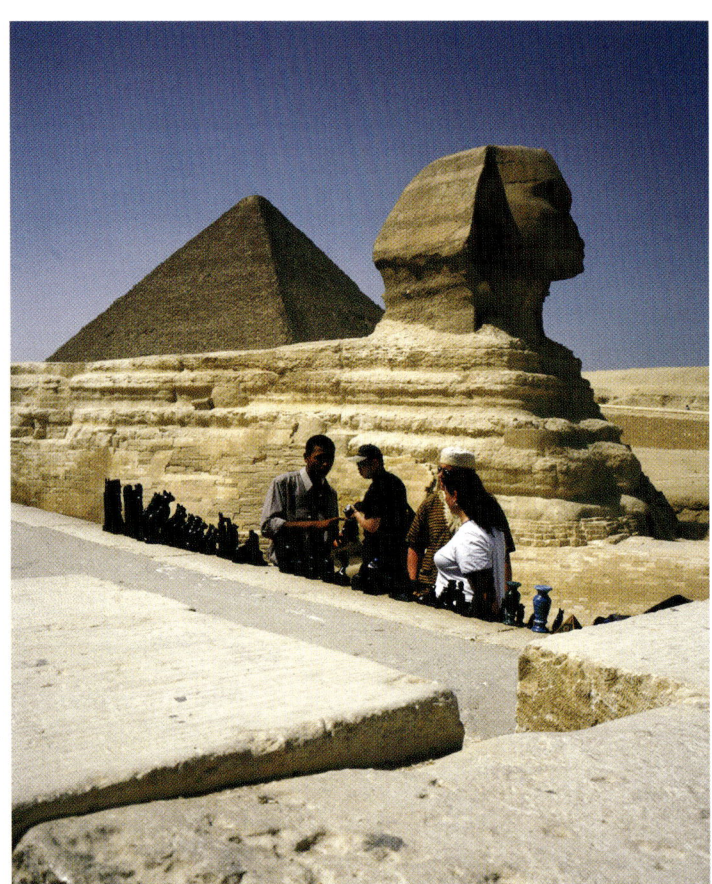

previous page: The Sphinx at Giza, photographed by the Zangaki Brothers in the 1870s. The Sphinx, then still only partially excavated from the desert, and with an intrepid 'dragoman' sitting on its head, was a magnet for early photographers. After the early travelling photographer had opened Egypt up to the camera, others fed the growing tourist market from their Nile-side studios, with commercially produced photographs available for sale at every tourist venue along the Nile.

above: The Sphinx at Giza today. The site on the edge of the desert only a few miles from the centre of Cairo, abounds with visitors, and almost as many souvenir sellers.

Contents

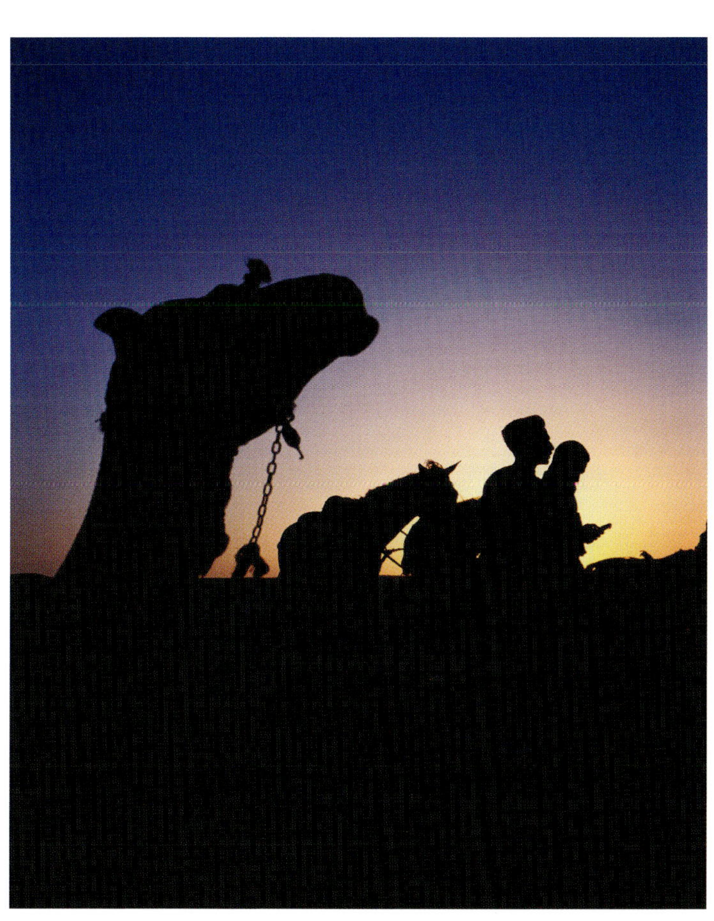

above: Desert sunset at Giza, a few miles from the pyramids – an apparently timeless image, until you notice the silhouetted figure of one of the camel handlers texting a friend from his mobile phone.

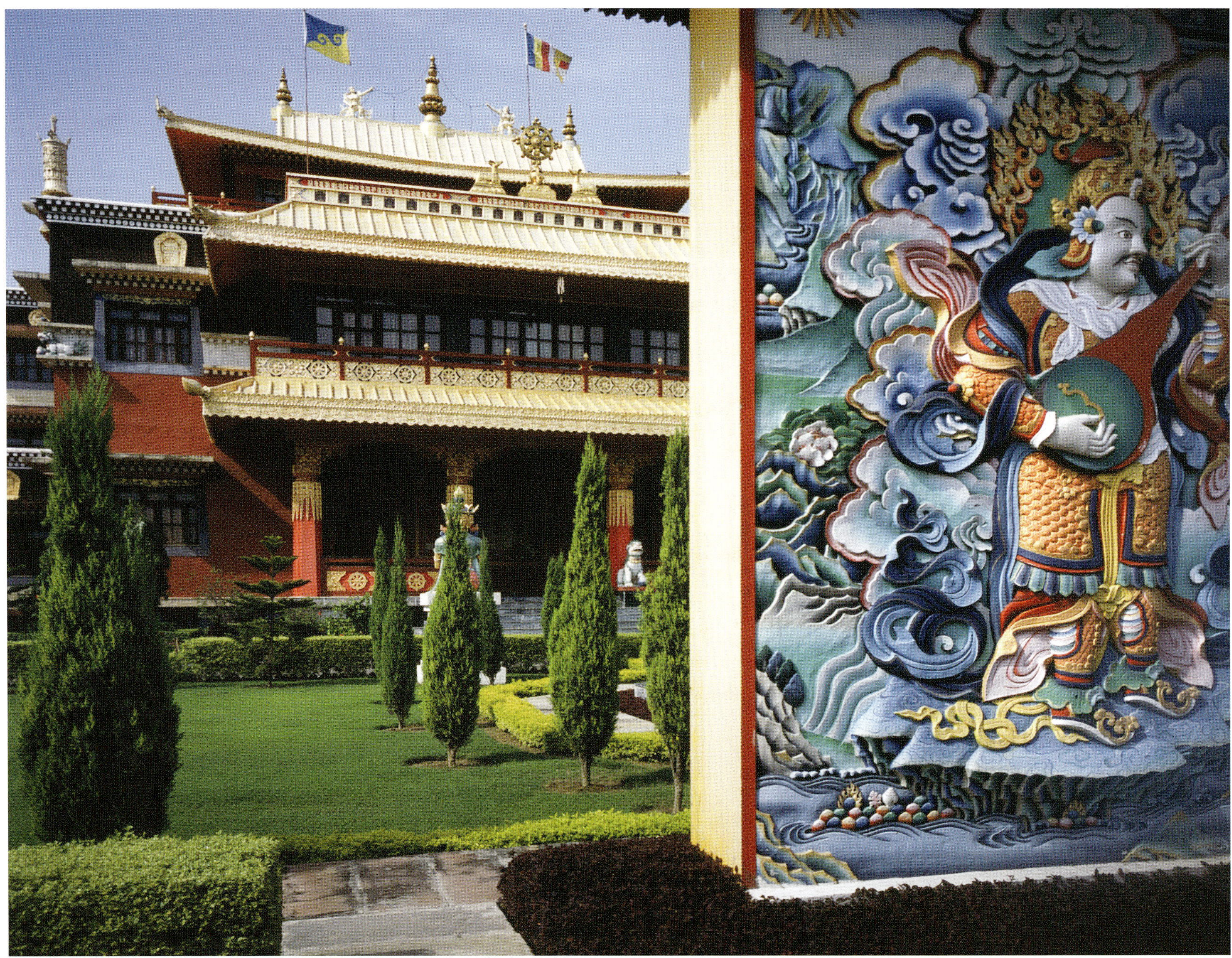

Acknowledgements

The author's name on any book merely draws the reader's attention to the person who brought all the diverse threads together. It by no means attributes to the author sole possession of the expertise and knowledge which has gone into the book's creation – and this book is no exception. The six years of its genesis have been punctuated by opportunities to meet many people throughout the world and learn about their lifestyles. With a number of them I have also been able to discuss the lives and works of the photographers whose journeys I have been privileged to recreate. Without their help, this project would have remained nothing more than a dream.

Thanks are due to more people than I can ever mention – some have answered my many questions, others have offered important information without even waiting for me to ask! Their insight has helped me greatly.

The project travel costs were met in part by the Winston Churchill Memorial Trust, to whom I owe a considerable debt of gratitude. I am also extremely grateful to my former employers, the University of Bolton, for allowing me to absent myself while undertaking the journeys which brought the idea to life.

A special thankyou is owed to Lisa Croft, Valerie Poole and their colleagues in the Ryley Library at the University who were wonderful in following up my many requests for obscure books and articles.

Many people have helped with this book, including Jayant Gandhi of Bourne & Shepherd in Kolkata; Michael Pritchard of Christies Ltd; Professor Larry Schaaf; Dr Sara Stevenson from the Scottish National Portrait Gallery; Colin Harding and Brian Liddy at the National Media Museum, Bradford; Michael Gray; Malcom Daniel at the Metropolitan Museum of Art, New York; William Schupbach at the Wellcome Library; Peter Stubbs; Roger Taylor; Dave Clark; and the staff at many museums and photographic collections throughout the world.

Just as important was assistance from the staff of the British Council offices in Beijing, Kiev and Moscow; Ms Gagarina and her colleagues in the Kremlin, Moscow; Adrian Greenhalgh; Dai Price; Hans P Kraus Jnr.; Miss Jean Maxwell-Scott, Chatelaine of Abbotsford; Vladislava Osmak of the Museum of One Street, Kiev; Olga Fedotova, National Museum of the History of the Ukraine, Kiev; Pettits India; Trailfinders, Manchester; Gordon Burnett of Interchange Travel, Croydon; the Deputy Commissioner of the Port Police, Kolkata; Hasselblad (UK) Ltd, Fuji Photo Film Co Ltd; and I must not forget the barman in the Taj Ganges Hotel in Varanasi whose interest in Indian history, especially the history of Benares, pointed me towards the work of James Prinsep. My thanks also go to the many drivers, guides and interpreters who have smoothed my way across so many countries. I hope I have made good use of everybody's help. I am also indebted to Mike Hallett who took time out from his own work to read the draft text and make some key comments and suggestions.

The Victorian photographs come, substantially, from my own collection and two private collections. To those have been added key images by John Thomson *(pp230, 234)* Samuel Bourne *(pp154, 156, 158, 166, 177, 181-182, 186-187)*, and the portraits of Frith *(p95)*, kindly provided by Christie's London, *www.christies.com.* Two images by Talbot *(pp27, 34)* came from Michael Gray. A number of other images by Talbot *(pp21-22, 28,)* and Calvert Richard Jones *(pp38-39)* came from Hans P Kraus Jnr. Inc., New York, and by Fenton *(pp81)* from a private collection courtesy of Hans P Kraus Jnr. The Fenton view of the raising of the chains on the Dnipro Bridge *(p66)* comes from the National Library of Brazil, while John Cooke Bourne's view of the same bridge *(p65)* comes from the National Museum of the History of the Ukraine. The National Media Museum, Bradford kindly supplied images by Talbot *(pp19, 25)*, and the portraits of Talbot himself *(p12)*, and Bourne *(p151)*, as well as the previously unpublished photographs by Kinnear *(pp 130, 144)* and Raven *(p149)*. The portrait of Thomson *(p189)* comes from the Wellcome Library, London, while the photographs of the Ottewill-Kinnear camera *(pp123, 137)* were kindly supplied by Rob Niederman. To them all, my sincere thanks. All the location colour photography is my own.

And finally, throughout the project I have had the constant support of my wife, Kath, whose own work commitments meant she could only accompany me on two of the journeys, but was there in spirit on the others!

John Hannavy, Great Cheverell, 2007

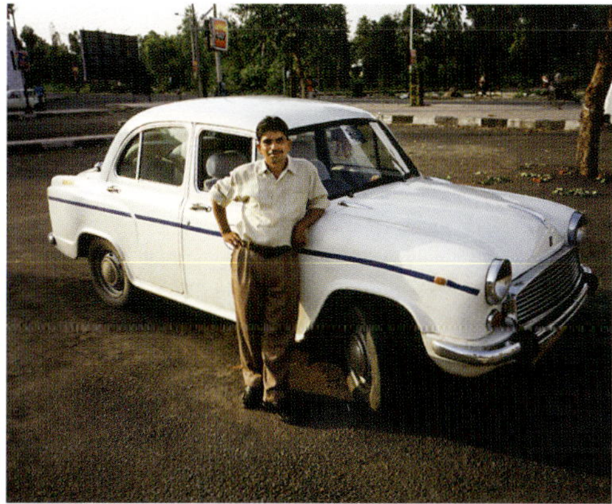

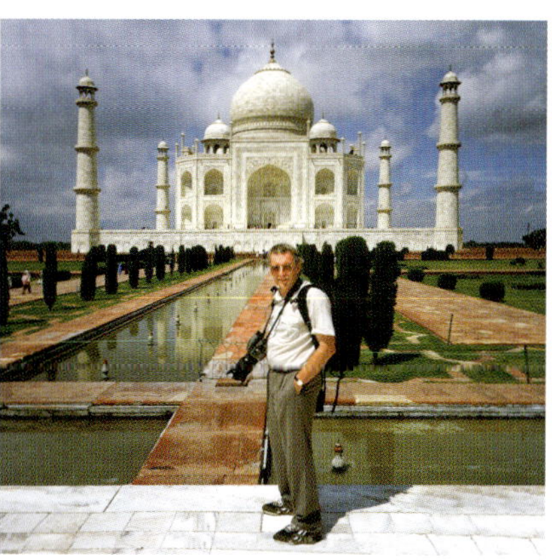

opposite page: The great Buddhist temple at Sarnath, a few miles from Varanasi, India. *above left:* Raseel Singh, my driver throughout the Indian leg of this project, standing in front of his trusty Hindustan Ambassador car in Chadigarh. Based on a Morris Oxford design over half a century old, this car is still in production, and is a workhorse across India. *above* The author photographed by a local Indian photographer in front of the Taj Mahal.

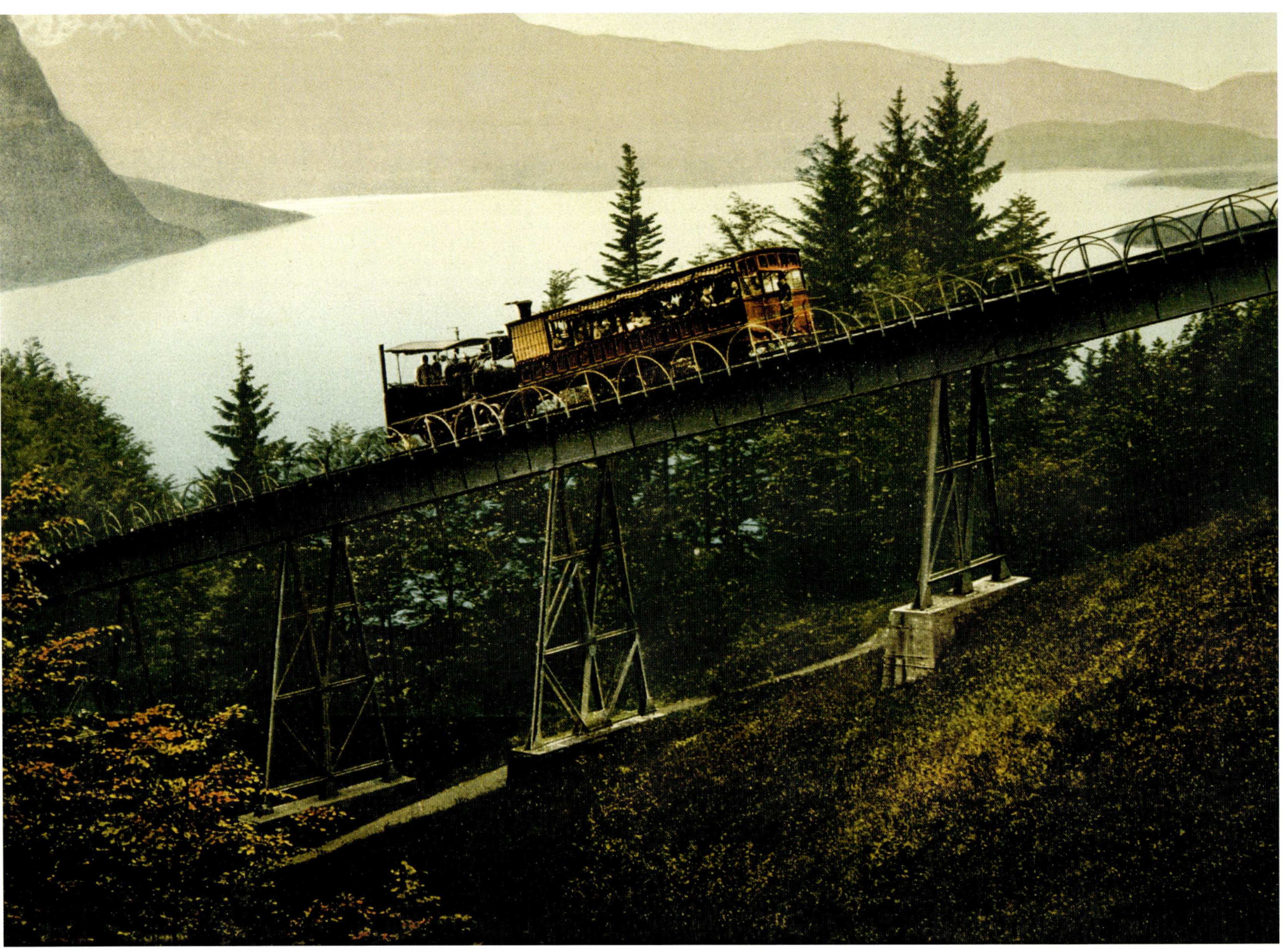

Introduction

This book had its genesis some years ago while researching a feature for a well-known French magazine. The discovery that a Victorian photographer had, some one hundred and forty years earlier, completed an almost identical journey and kept a meticulous diary led to the idea of comparing his experiences with mine.

The changes in travel, in lifestyle and in photography which had taken place between our two journeys offered an insight into photography as a mirror of history which a conventional photographic history could not. That revelation led me on a series of enlightening journeys which totally changed my view of the achievements of my Victorian predecessors.

This book, therefore, is part photographic history, part travelogue, part history of travel and part history as seen through photography.

The first Victorian travelling photographers existed in the days before package holidays – indeed their imagery did much to popularise travel. It follows, therefore, that a true comparison cannot be gained from the experience of today's package-holiday traveller.

Independent travel gave the Victorian photographers their insight into cultures, landscapes and architecture, which had been seen by few people at home. Independent travel offered me an insight into cultures throughout the world, which is as different from the modern package holiday experience as it is from the experience of the Victorian pioneers.

It is one of photography's most enduring values that it reflects and chronicles change. Ever since photography became a practical and viable recording medium for the traveller in the early 1840s, much of our understanding of

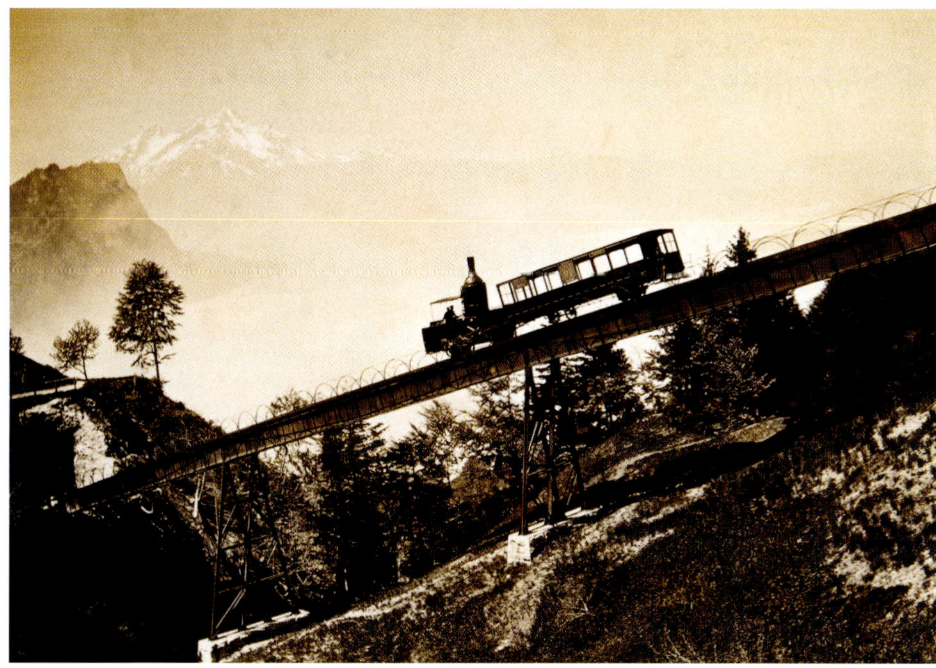

above: The mountain railway at Rigi in Switzerland, photographer unknown c.1870. Albumen print from a wet collodion negative. Images like this were sold to the growing number of travellers undertaking the Grand Tour.
opposite page: The same location photographed in 1895 by a photographer working for the Photochrom Company of Zurich. Changes to the rolling stock of the fragile-looking railway in the intervening twenty-five years gave the locomotive crew some protection from the elements. The tourist market had expanded considerably by the time this image was published, and the Photochrom Company misleadingly described it as "photography in natural colours" – their prints were, in fact, produced by colour lithographic printing over a monochrome photograph. The company's 1894 catalogue claimed that "Photochroms are bought in all countries throughout the world as mementos of excursions or journeys, and for presents of all kind." As Photoglob AG, the company is still in business today.

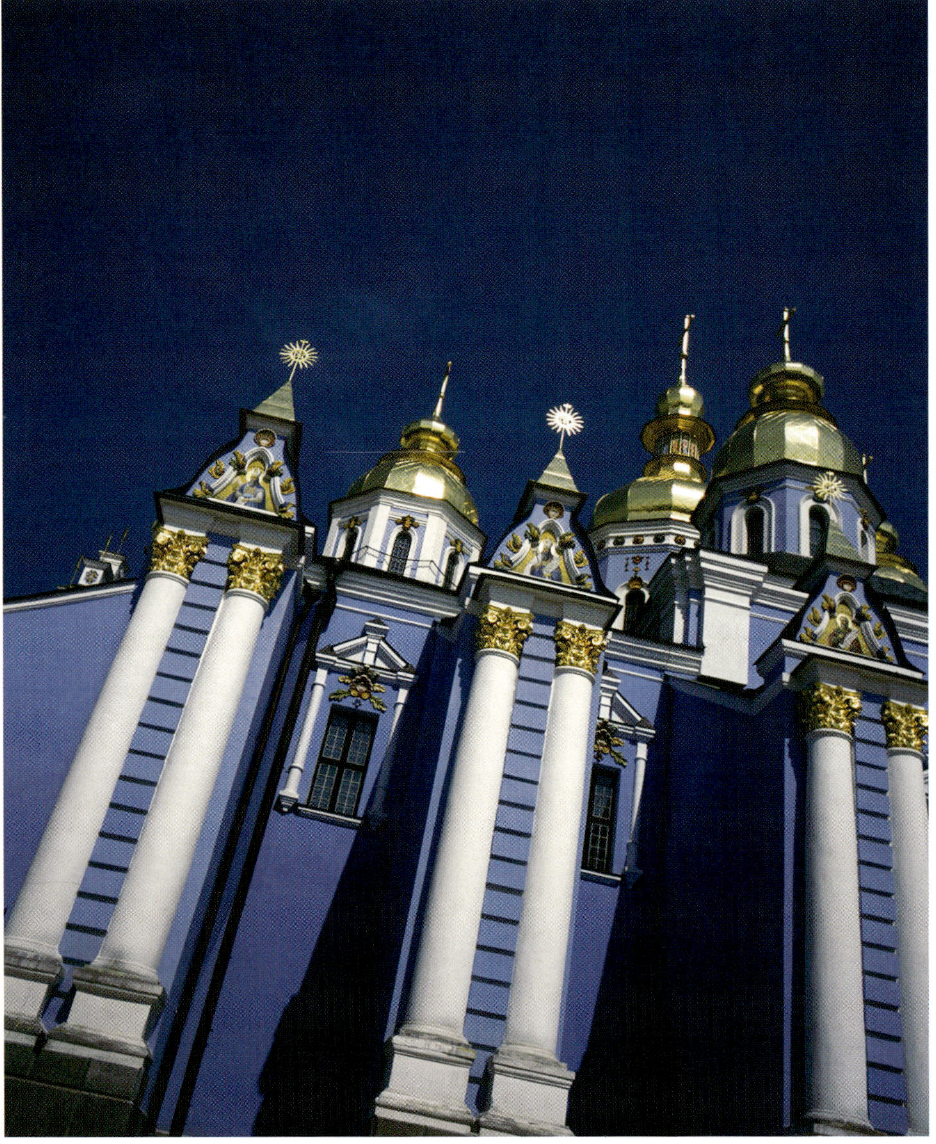

above: Since Roger Fenton photographed St Mikhail's monastery in Kiev in 1852, it had been demolished, by Stalin, and completely rebuilt after Independence.

change, progress and development has been gleaned from photographic evidence.

The photographers whose work inspired this book were all pioneers in the real sense of the word. They took their cameras further than anyone had done before, and brought back images of a world unknown at home. In so doing, they developed the art of the travel photographer, and initiated and developed the idea of the photograph as memento.

Walking in their footsteps has been a privilege, and has offered a very real insight into the scale, the challenges, and the sheer audacity of what they set out to do. The photographers and the journeys which have been selected cover photography's first four decades, and progressively take the camera further from home.

When William Henry Fox Talbot travelled to Scotland with his camera in 1844, that journey was, in every respect, a major undertaking. The only access was by coach, and the journey was slow and uncomfortable. The railway across the border from Newcastle to Edinburgh opened two years later in 1846, while the west side of the country was not served by a direct railway between Carlisle and Glasgow until 1850. In less than a decade, with the opening of the railways and the development of Thomas Cook's tours, such journeys – for both photographers and tourists – became relatively commonplace. Numerous professional photographers responded to the growth in visitors by taking and marketing countless images of Scotland – visual mementos for the visitors to take home, and the direct predecessor of today's picture postcards.

The more affluent amateur photographers had already looked further afield, and taken their cameras across mainland Europe.[1]

By the early 1850s, Roger Fenton had travelled with his cameras to Russia, visiting St. Petersburg, Moscow and Kiev. He was to return in 1855 under very different circumstances during the Crimean War.

In 1857 Francis Frith took cameras further up the Nile than any photographer before him.

Thanks to the published accounts of their journeys, we have a fascinating insight into the challenges which faced these pioneer image makers. Just how enormous the changes have been in photographic practice and style in the years since their journeys becomes illuminated by comparisons with the attitudes, styles, equipment and materials of today.

The journeys have also been selected because of the fascination of their locations and, in several cases, because of the changes which have taken place in those countries in the intervening years.

Fenton's journey in 1852 was to pre-communist, Tsarist, Russia, mine was to the post-communist Russian Federation and the recently independent Ukrainian Republic. In those intervening years, the now-independent republics of the former Soviet Union have seen change on a scale which almost defies description.

Frith's Egypt was a land where the buried remains of great temples peered tantalizingly out of the desert sand. Today's Egypt is a Mecca for travellers, historians and archaeologists alike, visiting the excavated and preserved monuments, and offering a remarkable contrast between the modern tourist economy and rural existence which has probably changed little since Frith's day.

John Thomson's journeys to China between 1862 and 1872 were his introduction to a society almost unknown in the West, while my visit to today's China was to a vast country rapidly opening its doors to the West and to visitors.

His visit to Cyprus in 1878 was to an island then only recently taken under the British flag as part of a deal with the Turkish Sultan in return for which Britain offered to protect Turkey against Russian aggression. My visits were to an island divided since 1974, and to Nicosia, the world's last divided capital city. To many British visitors today, the Cyprus they see is limited to a small number of tourist resorts, insulated from the real Cyprus, and where British food and British beer are supplied to holidaymakers who

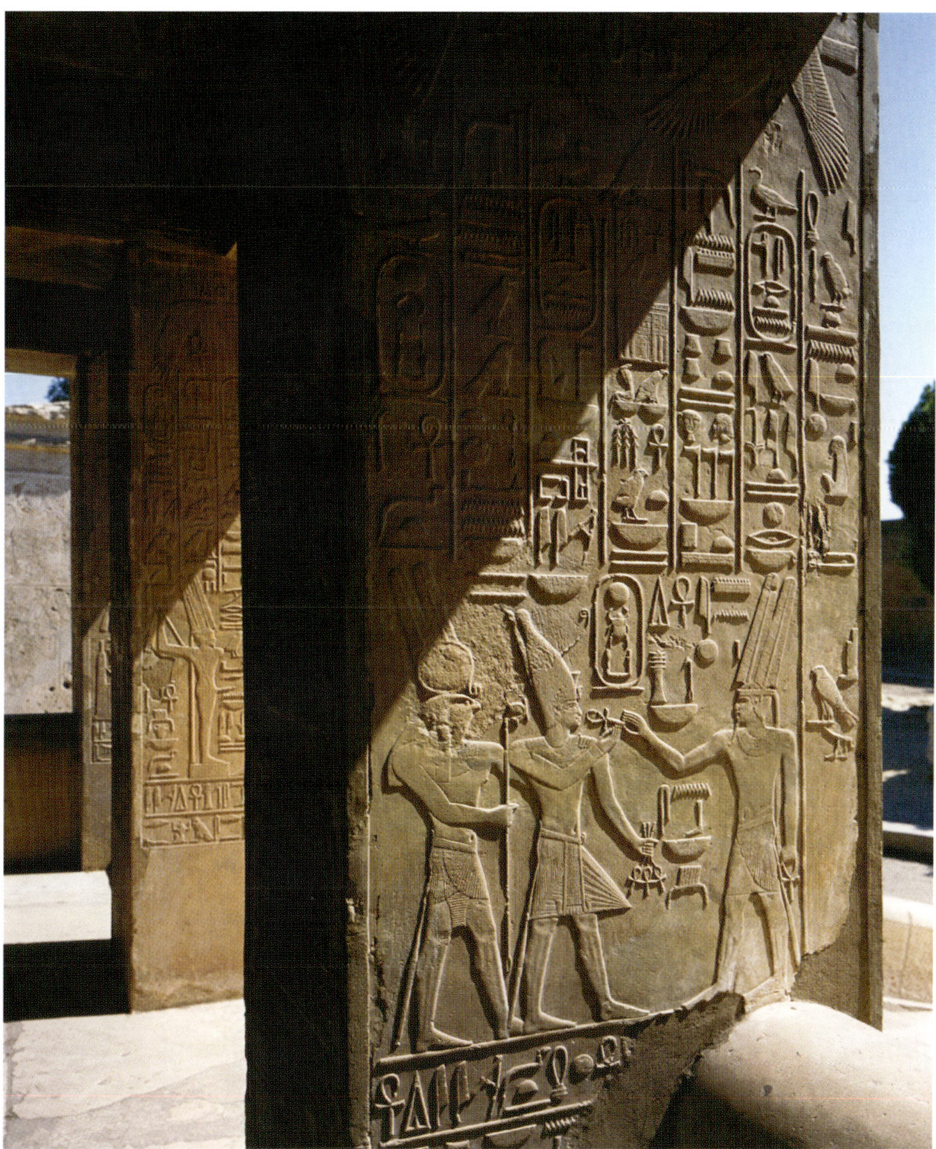

above: The White Chapel at Karnak, completely ruined and buried in Francis Frith's day, has now been restored to its former glory

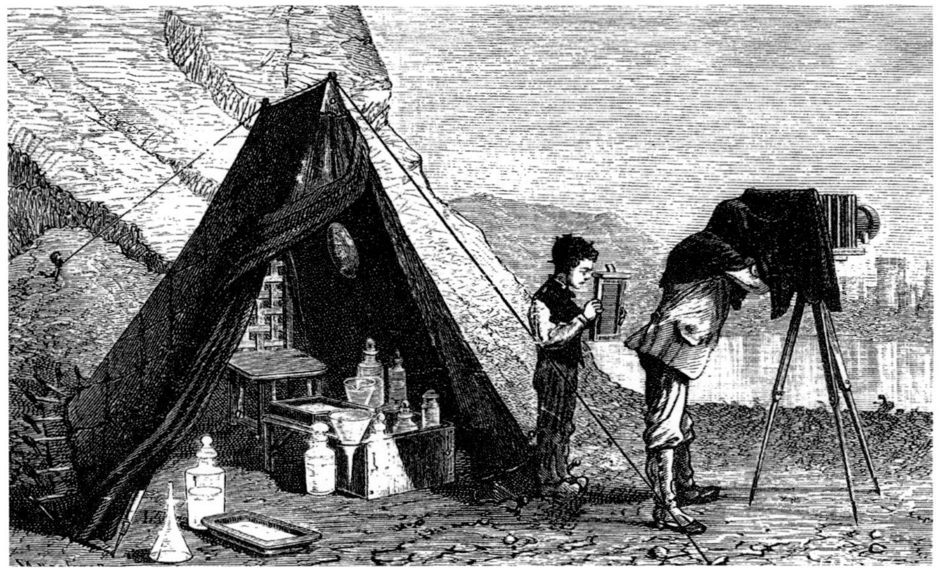

above: The wet plate photographer and his assistant at work on location – a woodcut from Gaston Tissandier's 1878 *History and handbook of Photography*, edited by John Thomson. As the words of the travelling photographers featured in this book will confirm, none of the pioneers whose stories are contained here travelled as light as the gentleman under the darkcloth here.

show little interest in engaging with the local culture! The Cyprus that John Thomson visited remains unknown to them, partly because of the border, but more because it is not location or history, but the sun, which is the attraction.

All the overseas journeys involved the pioneer photographers in long slow and often turbulent sea journeys, whereas all mine were by modern fast jets.

A writer in the *British Journal of Photography* in 1867 wrote that

the perfect accuracy of sun pictures gives them a value, which it is impossible to over estimate, as the best means we possess of illustrating scientific works and travel books.[2]

Gaston Tissandier, writing in his 1878 work *A History and Handbook of Photography* – edited for the British market by none other than John Thomson F.R.G.S. whose exploits feature heavily in these pages – saw the future of photography as record, and the value of travel photography, just as clearly, and noted

what resource in the hands of an architect, or an archaeologist, are the views of buildings in distant countries! The marvels of Athens and of Rome, the inimitable richness of the monuments of India, the bold architecture of Egyptian temples, can be kept in his portfolio, not modified or disfigured by an untrustworthy pencil, but such as they are in reality with their beauties, their imperfections, and the marks of destruction which time has engraved upon them. Photographic prints are mirrors from which are reflected the banks of the Nile and of the Indus – the buildings and the landscapes of all the countries through which the camera has passed.

The explorer furnished with his photographic apparatus, which is now constructed in such a manner that it can be used with ease in any part of the world brings back with him from his travels documents invaluable, because no one can deny their accuracy. A photograph represents an object just as it is – the landscape as nature formed it – the building as it has been seen, a broken column, a mark upon a stone.[3]

To illustrate his point, Tissandier included a delightful – and now familiar – woodcut showing the travelling photographer and his 'boy' at work, with a relatively lightweight outfit consisting of tent, 10x8 camera and chemicals. But the photographers whose journeys this book replicates were travelling in harsher times. They had to be made of sterner stuff, and had to take with them everything they might conceivably need – for they knew not what faced them, or what sort of terrain they would have to traverse with their delicate glass plates. They were the trailblazers, working in an era when cameras were bulky and the paraphernalia of travelling photography not yet refined down even to the level of limited easy portability. And even in later journeys, closer to Tissandier's time, the professional photographer sought to take more photographs, and on larger plates, than his amateur explorer counterpart – and thus carried much more weight.

As he edited Tissandier's opus, Thomson must certainly have thought back to his own years of travelling with his cameras through Vietnam, Cambodia and China, or thought ahead to the trip on which he was about to embark – his last – to what was then Britain's most recent acquisition, Cyprus.

This book, then, is a tribute to Henry Fox Talbot, Roger Fenton, Francis Frith, Charles Kinnear, John Thomson, Samuel Bourne, and the many others who excited the world about the joint pleasures of travel and photography. It was their vision that photography had a major role to play in educating us about our world, its sites, its landscape and its cultures.

But what is additionally special about these pioneers is that they wrote or lectured about their experiences, and those notes and lectures were published in the emerging photographic press, or in the texts of their books. So we know an enormous amount about what they did, why they did it, and the hardships they experienced along the way.

We can smile at their naiveté, and even at their arrogance. But we can offer only respect for their perseverance, and their talent with what was then still a youthful art. Their efforts produced, for many, the first glimpses of unknown civilisations, of sometimes alien cultures, and of foreign lands. They produced the first travel books, creating an industry which would grow to enormous proportions.

Travel books, guidebooks and picture postcards are now a more integral part of twenty-first century travel than any of these pioneers could ever have envisaged.

After he had given up globe-trotting, John Thomson, whose travel books were amongst the most successful of the era, wrote

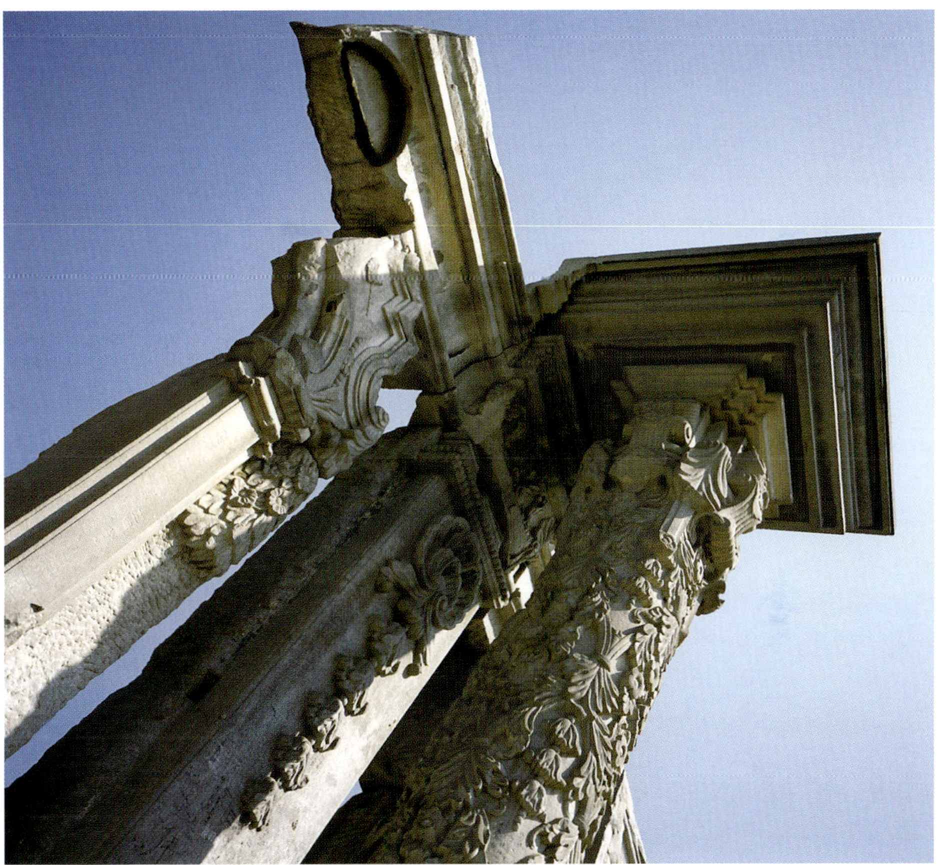

above: the ruins of the Old Summer Palace, Beijing, destroyed by the British. *A photograph represents an object just as it is, the building as it has been seen, a broken column, a mark upon the stone,* wrote Tissandier, having earlier observed that the true value of the photographic image was that it was *not modified or disfigured by an untrustworthy pencil.* Belief in the objectivity of the camera – that the camera cannot lie – although always misplaced, endures to this day.

We are now making history, and the sun picture supplies the means of passing down a record of what we are, and what we have achieved in this nineteenth century of our progress.[4]

This book picks up those challenges and progresses them by more than a century and a quarter - and in some cases a century and a half - by revisiting their journeys, those places and the challenges so ably risen to by the pioneers. The logistical challenges of getting even today's lightweight equipment into some of the more out-of-the-way places, brought the achievement of the early photographers into even sharper focus.

The challenge was never to replicate their photography, although in a few cases the opportunity to stand where a great Victorian photographer had stood and take a picture from that exact spot was too appealing to pass by - and brought me into closer contact with them.

Nor was the plan ever to attempt to use the cumbersome equipment and kitchen-sink chemistry with which they grappled. Today's photography was created very much with today's equipment and materials - thus, to reflect continuing change, the last journey, to Northern Cyprus, was captured digitally as well as on film. Thanks to the digital camera, like the pioneers, I was able to assess immediately the success of my images.[5]

The challenge was more about walking in the footsteps of the early photographers, experiencing the extremes of weather and terrain which they experienced, and seeing what photographic possibilities those journeys offered to today's independent traveller.

In many instances there were locations and views which were unavailable to the pioneers - buildings constructed long after they had returned home, and cultural photo-opportunities which would have been unknown to them.

Having now walked in the footsteps of these great men, and worked under the temperatures under which they worked - though certainly not with the pungent chemicals or in the confined darktents and darkrooms which they endured - my respect for their achievements is immense.

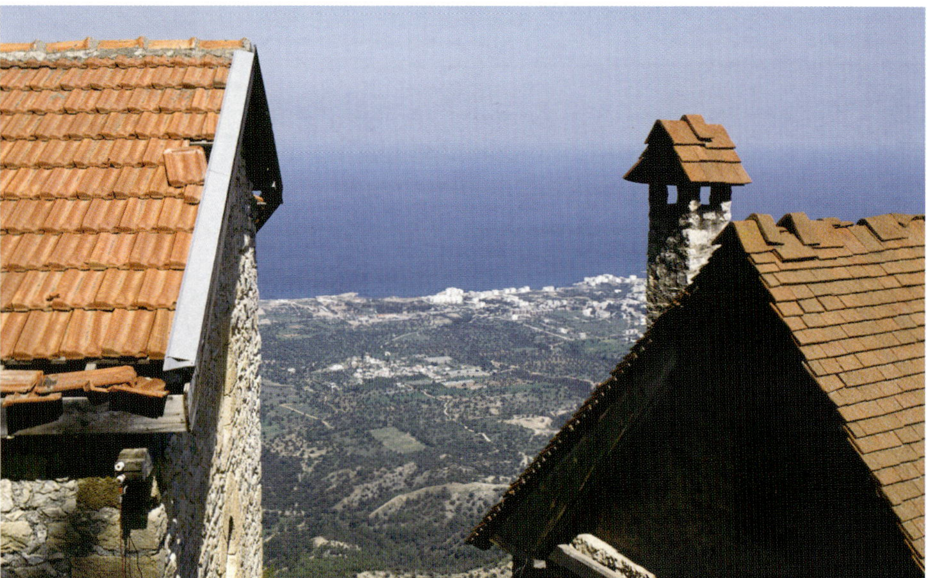

below: Kyrenia (Girne) from St Hilarion Castle, stronghold of Richard the Lionheart. In *Through Cyprus with the Camera* John Thomson wrote *as one makes the ascent of the hills, the arid appearance of the plain is exchanged for the vivid green of shrubs and pines, interspersed with flowers of brilliant hues. Pleasant glimpses of the rich plain of Kyrenia may be obtained from time to time between the hills.*

Notes

1. Several British amateur photographers travelled to Holland, Belgium, France, Italy, Malta and other Mediterranean countries during the 1840s, amongst them Robert MacPherson, George Moir, James Francis Dunlop, The Rev. George Bridges, Calvert Richard Jones. William Henry Fox Talbot himself had taken his camera abroad on a number of occasions before embarking on his Scottish journey.

2. Anon: 'Enlargements from Small Negatives', in *The British Journal of Photography*, London, 1867, p13.

3. Gaston Tissandier, *A History and Handbook of Photography*, edited by John Thomson F.R.G.S.; second and revised edition with an appendix by the late Henry Fox Talbot; London: Sampson, Low, Marston, Searle and Rivington, 1878, pp 318-319.

4. John Thomson, 'Photography and Exploration' in *Proceedings of the Royal Geographical Society*, 1891, p673.

5. For those interested in hardware, the majority of the modern photography for this book was taken on medium format Fuji. Hasselblad, Contax and Bronica cameras. All film images were taken on Fujichrome colour film. To reflect the changing times, and bring the story up to date, the final images, from Northern Cyprus, were taken using Canon digital equipment.

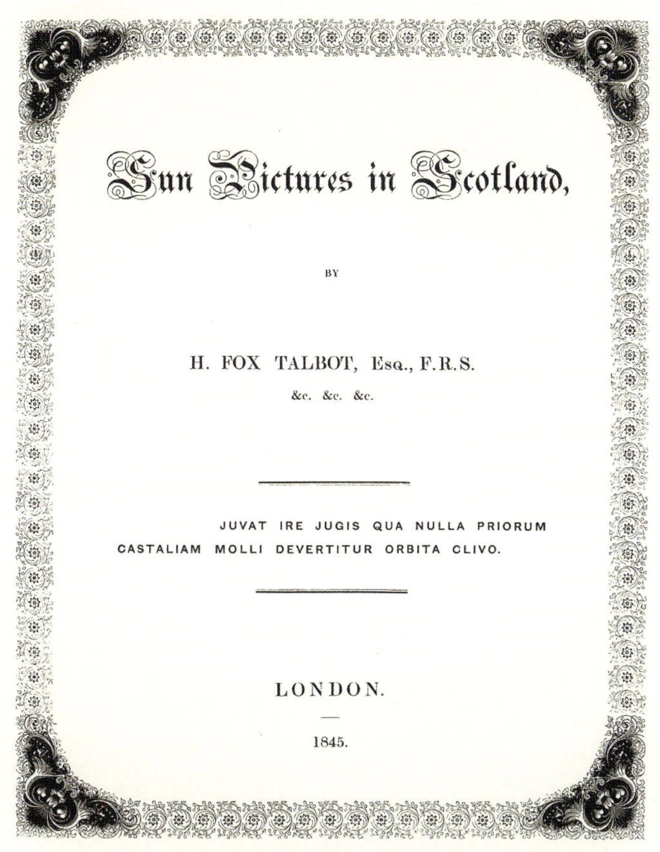
Sun Pictures in Scotland,

BY

H. FOX TALBOT, Esq., F.R.S.
&c. &c. &c.

JUVAT IRE JUGIS QUA NULLA PRIORUM
CASTALIAM MOLLI DEVERTITUR ORBITA CLIVO.

LONDON.

1845.

W. H. F. Talbot

Sun Pictures in Scotland

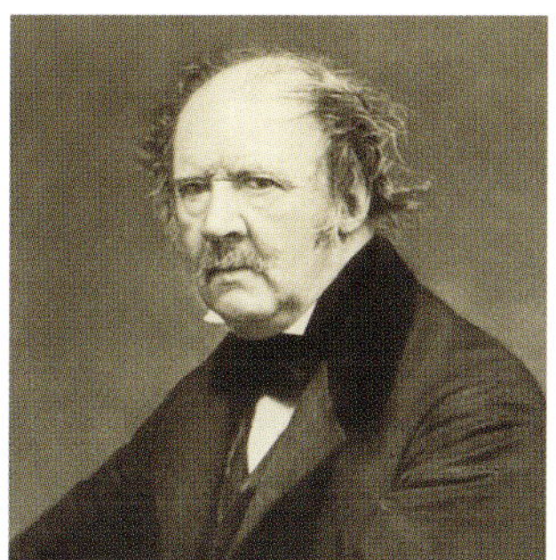

above: William Henry Fox Talbot,
from a portrait by John Moffat

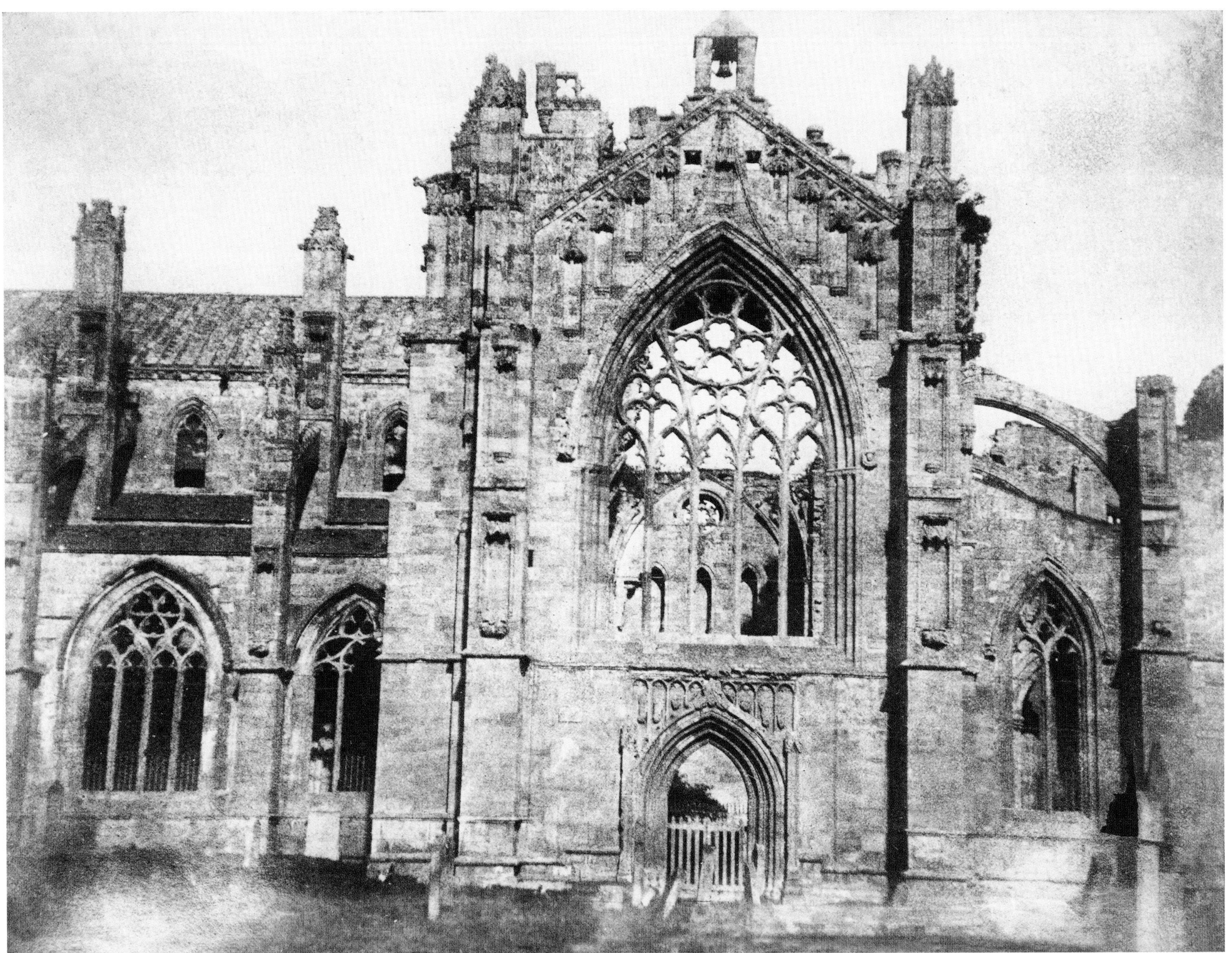

On a bleak day in October 1844, William Henry Fox Talbot set up his calotype camera to the south of one of Scotland's most beautiful mediaeval monastic ruins, Melrose Abbey. He made several negatives of the buildings, and indeed made duplicate exposures of some of his chosen views to speed up the task of making the large number of salted paper prints he knew he would need for his project.

His journey to Scotland had a clear purpose – to produce the illustrations for the world's first ever photographically illustrated book.

In a period of little more than three weeks, he travelled to a number of locations associated with Sir Walter Scott, the pre-eminent poet and novelist of early 19th century Scotland who had died twelve years earlier, on September 12th 1832.[1]

Scott had guaranteed for himself a special place in Scottish literary history – his epic poems drew on the stories of the great clans, on folklore, and on celebrated great moments in the nation's past.

He was buried in nearby Dryburgh Abbey, and the line of carriages carrying mourners to his burial in one of the aisles of the Abbey church reportedly stretched for over a mile. It was met in the ruined interior of the church by huge crowds, under one of those 'dark and lowering' skies for which Scotland is renowned.

For Henry Talbot, his projected book, *Sun Pictures in Scotland*[2] was a logical development from his photographically illustrated partwork *The Pencil of Nature*[3], publication of which had started earlier in the year.

The book was not published widely in the modern sense, but limited to a wealthy list of subscribers, including Queen Victoria, who effectively underwrote the photographic and publication costs.

The romance of Scott was a growing phenomenon in the 1840s, and the Queen's declared love of Scotland and highland scenery an added spur to the popularising of tourism. Only two years after Talbot's visit, and a year after

below: A decade after Talbot, Roger Fenton visited Melrose Abbey, and produced both large format and stereoscopic views of the romantic ruins.

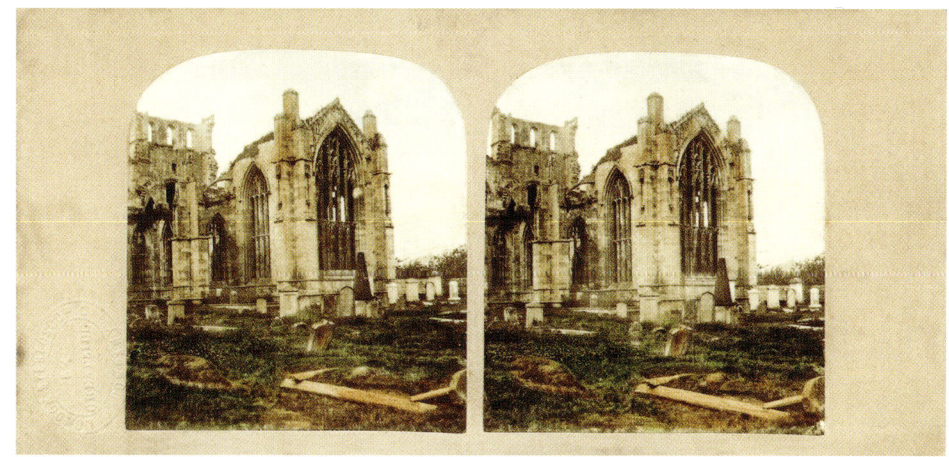

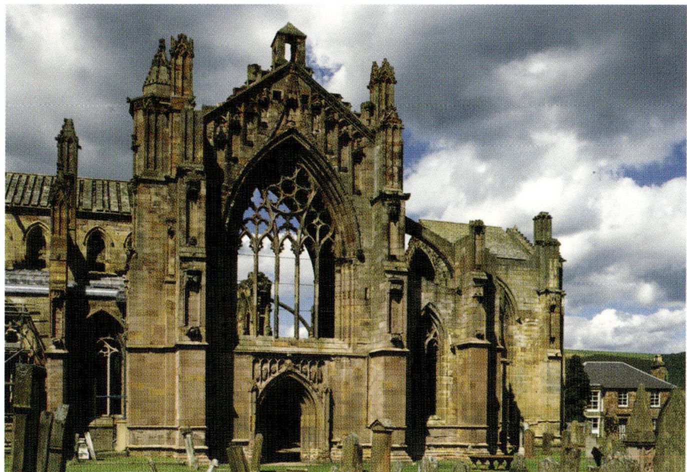

Opposite page: Melrose Abbey church from the south, a salt print from a calotype negative, taken by Talbot in October 1844 and reproduced here at actual size. Two slightly different negatives by Talbot survive of this view.
above: Roger Fenton's photographed the abbey in stereo a decade after Talbot visited the site.
left: 160 years after Talbot's visit, the Abbey is little changed – tidier and lacking a little of the romance the Victorian pioneers found there.

right: Talbot's pre-publication for *Sun Pictures in Scotland* promised a volume of views celebrating the life and work of Sir Walter Scott, at a cost of one guinea. Subscriptions were received for all one hundred copies of the book in advance of publication.

SUN PICTURES IN SCOTLAND.

Preparing for publication in 1 vol. royal 4to.

TWENTY-THREE PHOTOGRAPHIC VIEWS

IN

SCOTLAND,

BY

H. FOX TALBOT, Esq.

Price to Subscribers, One Guinea.

Subscribers names will be received by J. Rodwell, Bookseller, New Bond Street, London.

Most of the views represent scenes connected with the life and writings of Sir Walter Scott. Among them will be found—

ABBOTSFORD, | LOCH KATRINE,
MELROSE ABBEY, | DRYBURGH ABBEY,
DOUNE CASTLE, | HERIOT'S HOSPITAL,
SIR W. SCOTT'S MONUMENT, EDINBURGH.

the publication of *Sun Pictures in Scotland*, Thomas Cook organised his first ever package tour to Scotland, bringing a large party of visitors north to experience the romance of the Highlands. Their journey took them to many of the locations featured in Talbot's pioneering publication.[4]

This was not Talbot's first long-distance foray with his camera – he had been to France in May and June of the previous year, 1843, and had brought back some fine studies of Rouen, Paris, Orléans, and the surrounding countryside.

In many respects, therefore, the journey to Scotland would hold no major surprises for him in terms of the logistics of using his camera a long way from home. The poor weather and the lower than anticipated levels of light in a late Scottish autumn would, however, be in stark contrast to what he had had to work with in the early French summer. To add to the challenge, Talbot himself was unwell.

He and his associate Nicolaas Henneman left Reading on September 25th, staying overnight in Oxford to take some pictures, and in Derby before continuing north. They broke their journey to Scotland to attend the annual conference of the British Association for the Advancement of Science in York, arriving in the city on September 30th 1844. After two days there they moved north to Durham, eventually crossing the border at Berwick on October 4th.

For a journey of this complexity, he needed to take a considerable amount of materials with him. Henneman noted that they had to book a separate cab to take the cameras and other equipment from their hotel to the railway station at Derby.[5]

They got as far as Newcastle by train, before transferring everything to a carriage – or perhaps carriages – for the onward journey into Scotland. Had the two men made the expedition a few years later it would have been so much easier but in 1843 the railways to Scotland were not yet completed, so the journey involved several transfers from train to coach along the way.

The entire project was completed in less than a month. He and Henneman crossed the border again on their way south on October 27th.

Given the bulk of equipment they must have carried with them, that represented quite an onerous schedule, especially given the vagaries of the Scottish weather, and the likelihood that on the Sabbath at least - irrespective of the weather - photography would have been out of the question. It also perhaps explains the somewhat limited range of subjects Talbot attempted to photograph. Certainly the weather was not generally kind, and several of the pictures were taken under conditions which must have pushed the infant process, and Talbot's mastery of it, to the limit.

The journey from York took them across the border at Berwick, and then north west towards Kelso - where he and Henneman stayed overnight - and on to Melrose, Dryburgh, Jedburgh and Selkirk, where they boarded a train to Edinburgh on October 10th. The Selkirk to Edinburgh Railway had been open just a year! Alas, it is no more, so replicating Talbot's journey by train is not possible. The best today's railways could offer was a bus from Selkirk to Carlisle, and a train to Edinburgh - a journey time of over three and a half hours! So much for progress!

It would appear that the two men originally intended to spend two nights in Edinburgh, although Henneman's notes are a little unclear.

On his arrival in the city, Talbot took up rooms in Robert Cranston's Temperance Hotel on Princes Street, with a splendid view across to the castle and the Old Town. The hotel was ideally situated.

The closest of his chosen locations, the Scott Monument, nearing completion at that time, was just across the street from his hotel. Interestingly, the monument was 'topped out' only days after Talbot photographed it, although it would be 1846 before the finished monument, complete with Scott's marble statue, was opened. The cost was

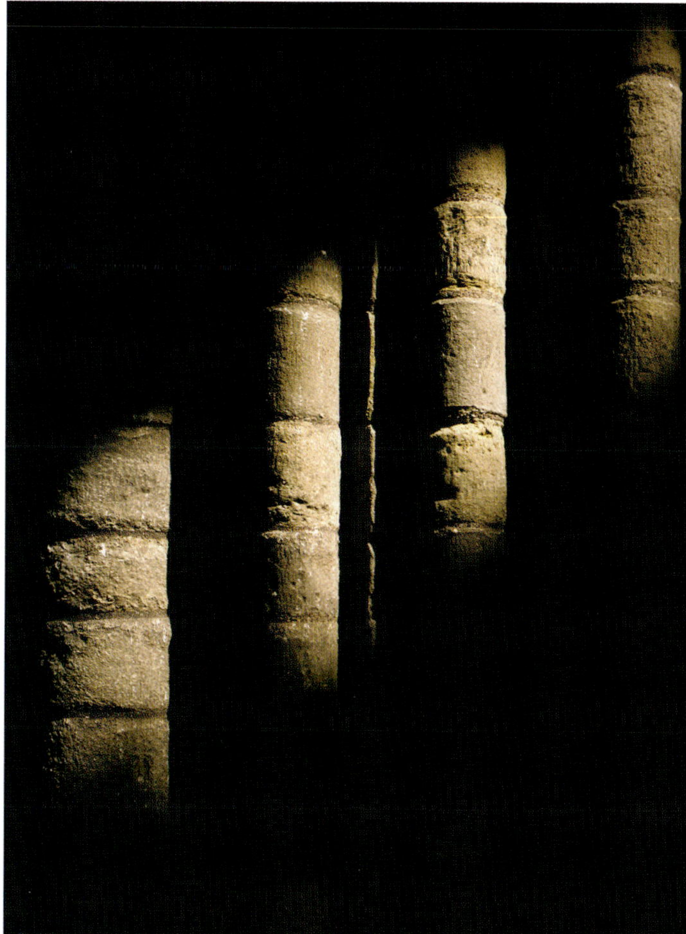

left: Late evening sunlight highlighting the detail of one of Kelso Abbey's great columns. Talbot and Henneman spent the night of October 5th 1844 in Kelso, before travelling on to Selkirk and Edinburgh.

£15000, rather more than the original estimate of £6000 for which there had been a public subscription. The fresh stone seen in Talbot's pictures - which proved very popular indeed and sold in large numbers - contrasts vividly with the blackened stonework visible today.

The design for the monument was decided by competition, the only stipulation being that a neo-Gothic structure was required. The design, by George Meikle Kemp envisaged a monument resembling a cathedral spire, surrounded by niches containing sculptures of figures from Scott's writings. At the time Talbot directed his camera towards the almost-complete structure in October 1844, the niches were still empty, and indeed all but eight remained that way at the time of the official opening. It was 1882, some thirty-six years after the monument was officially completed, before the last statues were put in place.

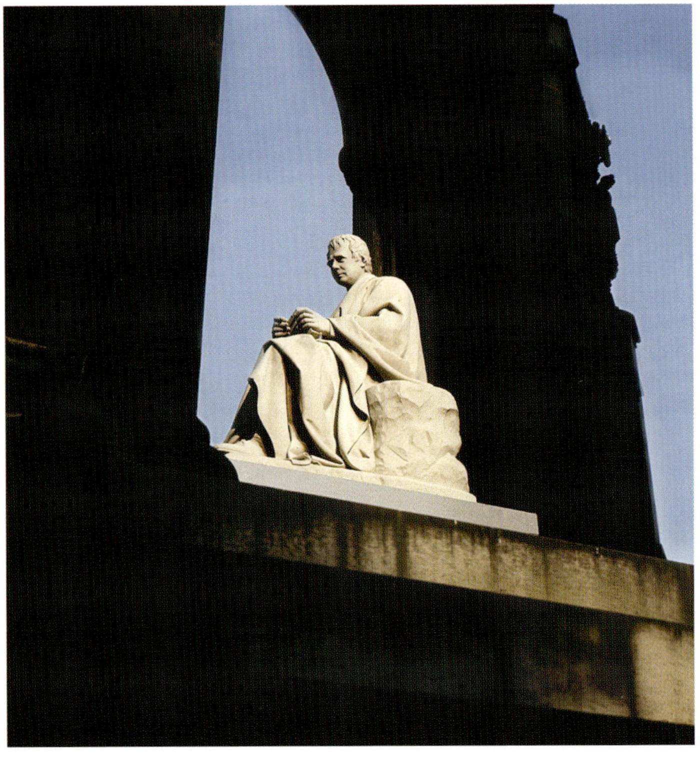

above: The marble statue of Scott was carved in a studio next door to Talbot's Edinburgh hotel - but he never saw it. The 20-ton block of uncut Carrara marble arrived just a few days after he had left for the borders. It had been carried by ship to Leith, and brought to Princes Street on a specially constructed cart pulled by a team of twenty horses. The sculptor was Sir John Steel.

Talbot's view was probably taken from his hotel window - and being able to take that view might indeed have dictated his choice of hotel.

The combination of viewpoint and available lenses, might also explain the perhaps curious crop of the Scott Monument view used in *Sun Pictures in Scotland* - with the top of the almost-completed tower missing from the plate. Or perhaps there was a symbolic reason for not defining how far the pinnacle reached up to the heavens.

Throughout the trip, he set what later became a Victorian tradition - of using his room as a makeshift darkroom.

From the 1850s, at the height of the wet collodion era, there survive several entertaining accounts of hoteliers in Britain and France either banning photographers, or giving them bed linen and towels already soiled with silver nitrate - leftovers from previous occupants of a similar persuasion! The travels of Charles Kinnear and Thomas Melville Raven in France, described later in this book, recall such instances.

The images Talbot published in *Sun Pictures in Scotland* are of three different sizes. As all prints were made by contact, at least two cameras were clearly used. The larger camera used negative papers approximately 18.5cm x 22.5cm (with some individual variations of print size). The smaller camera produced negatives approximately 10cm x 8cm – suggesting cameras approximately whole plate and quarter plate respectively.

The calotype negative was at its most sensitive to light immediately after sensitising with silver iodide, and was preferably exposed in the camera while still damp. With the Scott Monument just across the road from his Edinburgh hotel, and the camera pointed out of the window, such a practice was straightforward.

He was not, however, the first person to photograph the monument. The Scottish photographers David Octavius Hill and Robert Adamson had used Talbot's calotype process to take the first view of the partially completed monument several months earlier, though they chose a camera position further along Princes Street, setting the monument against a backdrop of the Calton Hill.

Talbot's calotype paper negatives were at least partly prepared and iodised each night in whichever hotel or inn he and Henneman stopped. At that stage they were only slightly sensitive to light, and could be preserved in a folio between sheets of blotting paper for later sensitisation and use.

In his 1841 patent No.8842, *Photographic Pictures*, he noted that

> *This second part is best deferred until the paper is wanted for use; when that time is arrived, I take a sheet of the iodized paper, and wash it with a liquid prepared in the following manner:- dissolve one hundred grains of crystallised nitrate of silver in two ounces of distilled water, to this solution add one-sixth of its volume of strong acetic acid; let this mixture be called A. Dissolve crystallised gallic acid in water as much as it will dissolve (which is a very small quantity); let this solution be called B. When you wish to prepare a sheet of paper for use, mix together the liquids A and B in equal volumes. This mixture I shall call by the name of gallo-nitrate of silver. Let no more be mixed than is intended to be used at*

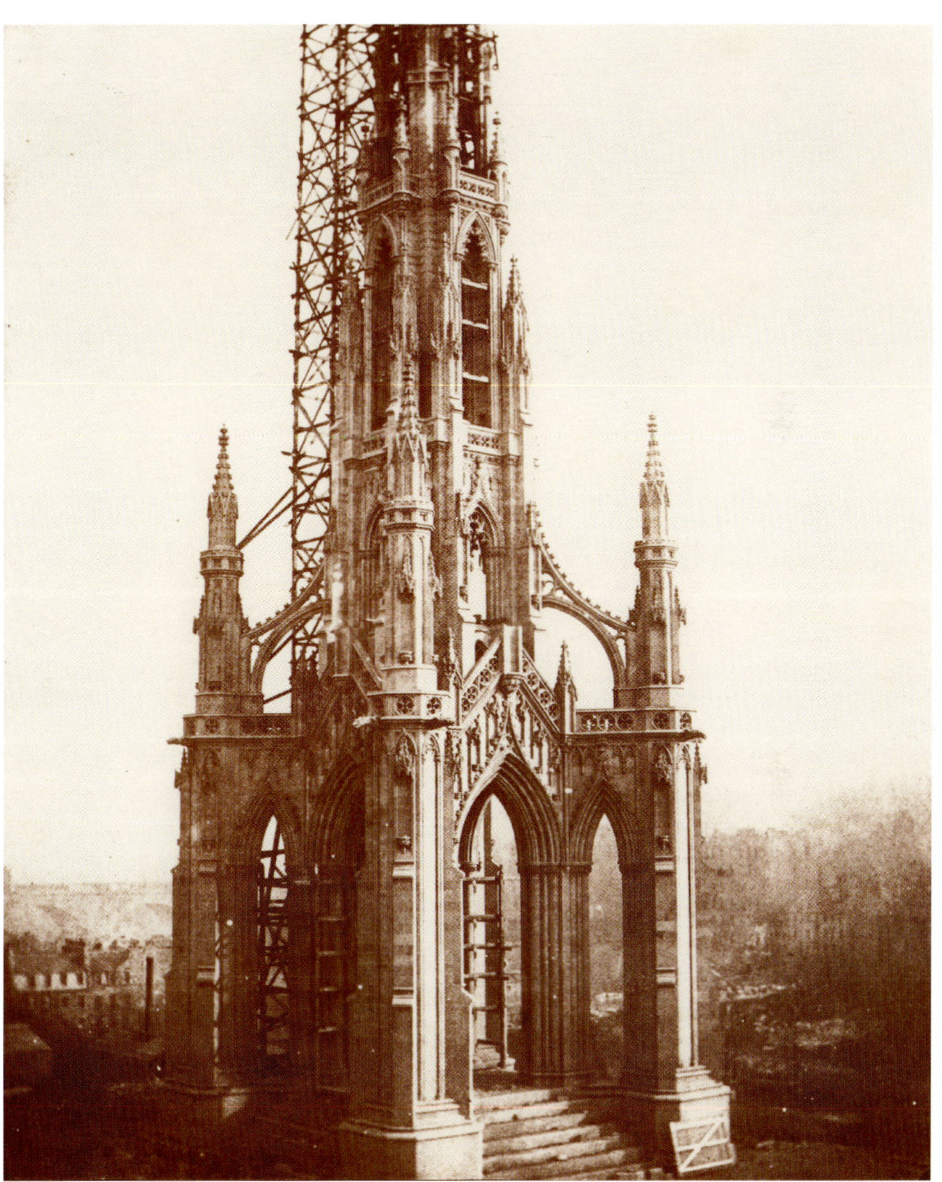

above: One of the most popular images from Talbot's Scottish tour, this view of the partially completed Scott Monument on Edinburgh's Princes Street was photographed from a first floor room in his hotel, October 1844.

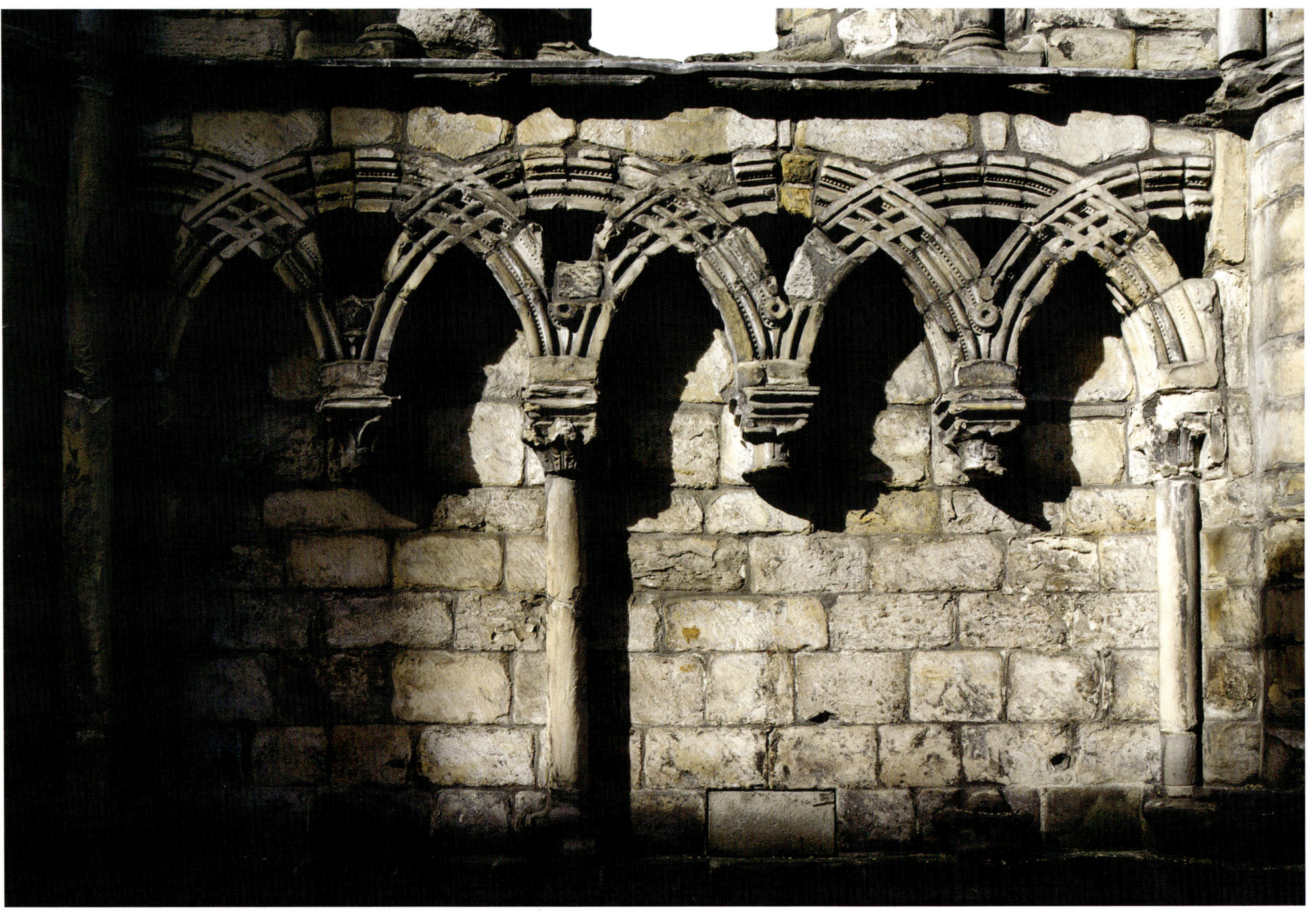

above: Despite their strong associations with Scott and his writings on Mary Queen of Scots, the Royal Palace of Holyroodhouse and the ruined Holyrood Abbey – much more attractive and architecturally interesting subjects for his camera than Heriot's Hospital – did not feature in the illustrations published in *Sun Pictures in Scotland.*

one time, because the mixture will not keep for a long period. Then take a sheet of iodized paper and wash it over with this gallo-nitrate of silver with a soft camel hair brush, taking care to wash it on the side which has been previously marked. This operation should be performed by candle-light. Let the paper rest half a minute, and then dip it into water, then dry it lightly with blotting paper, and lastly, dry it cautiously at a fire, holding it a considerable distance therefrom.

When in an ideal location like his Edinburgh hotel, the traditional wooden shutters on Georgian or Victorian windows would have rendered the room sufficiently dark to enable that sensitising stage to be performed with ease.

Once sensitised, the papers were ready for exposure in the camera, but while the drying process reduced their sensitivity, they could be kept in this state for several hours before use.

The book ultimately contained only two Edinburgh views - Plate I showed Heriot's Hospital, and Plate II was the Scott Monument - and surprisingly did not feature several other sites in the city with strong Scott connections, such as the Abbey and Palace of Holyrood, one of the settings of *Marmion*.

The following day Talbot and Henneman took a train to Glasgow, and after a night's rest, a coach south to Hamilton and the Falls of Clyde.

There is evidence in surviving correspondence that the weather played a major part in limiting photography during the early days of the journey - and perhaps also in restricting what Talbot was able to photograph in Edinburgh as well as on the Clyde. A letter from his wife Constance, dated October 29th noted

We are so glad that you have been successful at Abbotsford & Dryburgh Abbey - and we think the latter part of your tour has made amends for the disappointments at the beginning.[6]

The majority of the images which finally appeared in *Sun Pictures in Scotland* were, indeed, from the final two weeks of the trip.

From the Falls of Clyde, the men moved to Lanark and

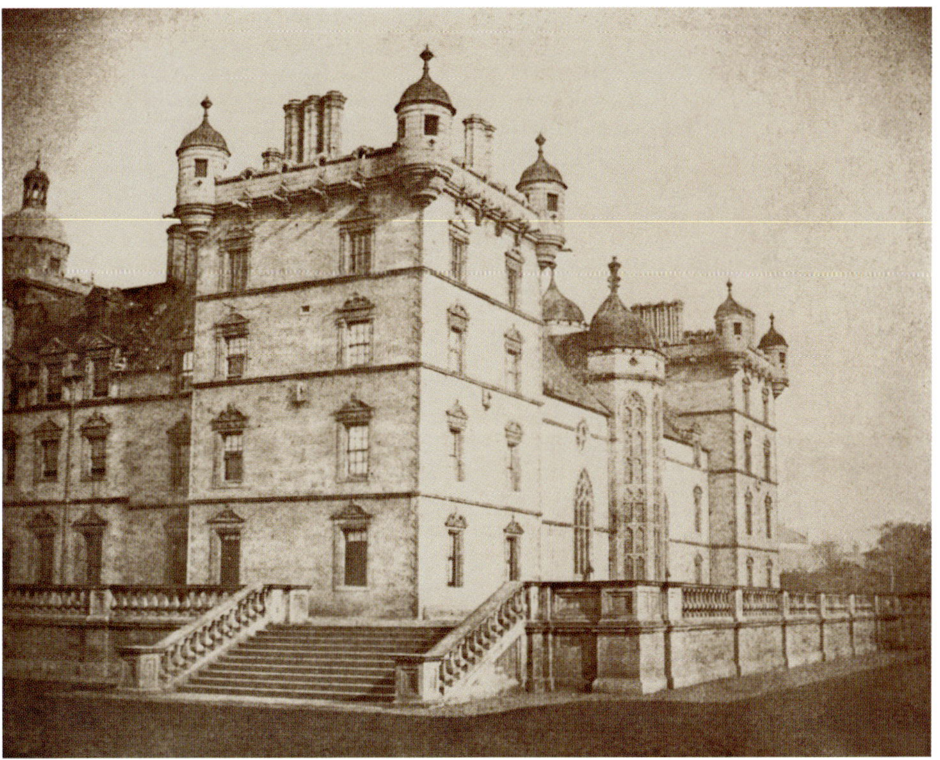

above: Plate 1 of *Sun Pictures in Scotland* was this view of the 17th century Heriot's Hospital - George Heriot's School - in Edinburgh. In the days before cameras could be equipped with a sliding lens panel to create rising front - essential if the geometry of the subject was to be reproduced accurately - the only way Talbot could include the entire building was to tilt the camera upwards - thus introducing the converging verticals we see here.

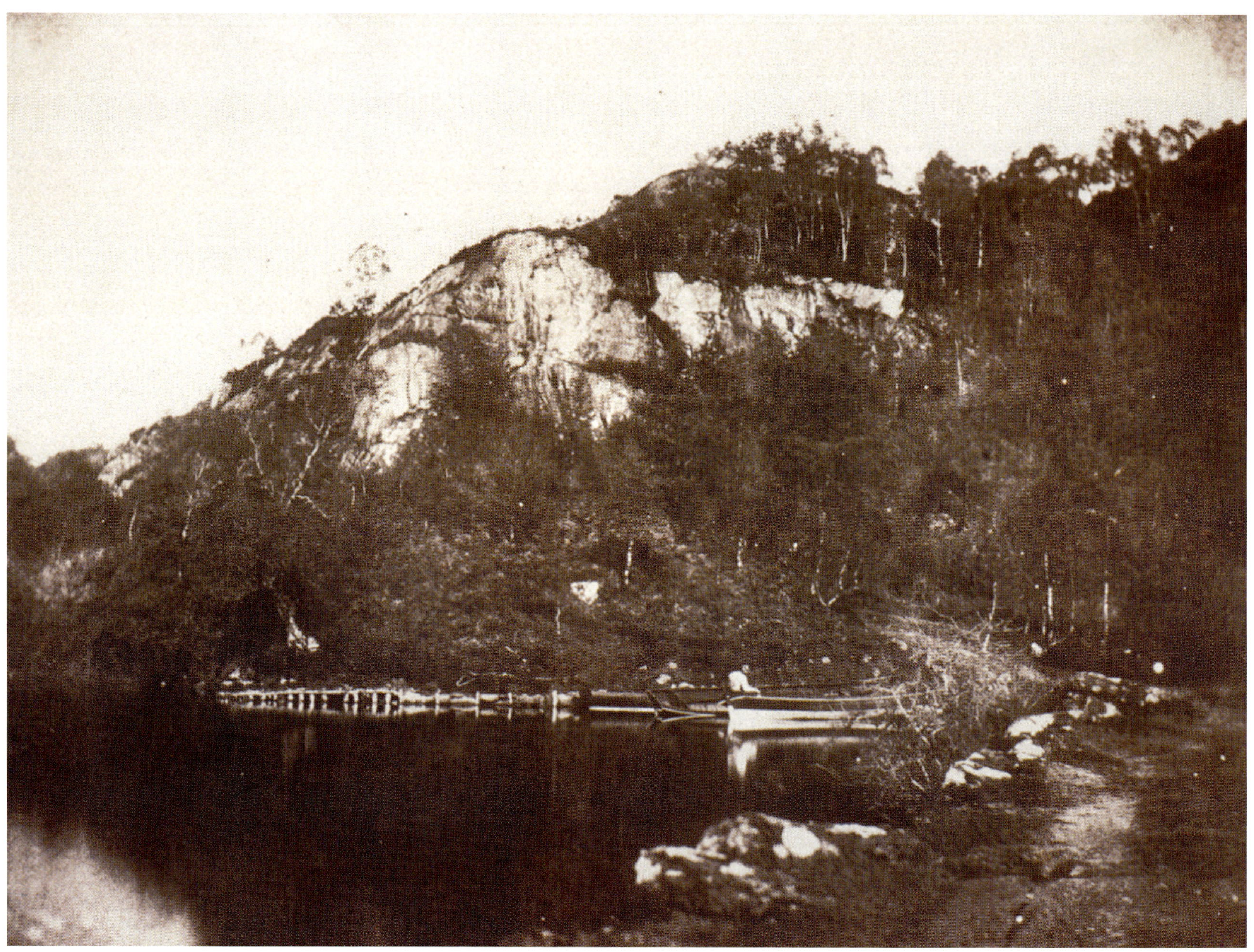

then, by carriage, back to Edinburgh where they boarded a train to Stirling.

This was the start of that part of their journey which immersed them in the heart of Scott country – the highland landscape which Scott described so vividly in his writings. From Stirling a coach took them to Callander for the night, then on into the Trossachs region of mountains and lochs where many of Scott's best known novels and epic poems were set.

A short carriage ride from Callander took Talbot and his camera to Loch Katrine, the setting for *The Lady of the Lake* – the romantic poem celebrating clan allegiances and epic rivalries set in some of Scotland's most majestic scenery.

Written in 1810, the poem was hugely influential in making the Trossachs fashionable for tourists, and for greatly increasing the number of visitors to central Scotland. In its first year, the book sold over twenty thousand copies, setting the pattern for the subsequent success of Scott's many celebrations of the landscape and history of the area.

Talbot was certainly the first to photograph the place, and was obviously impressed by what he saw. No fewer than eight images made it into the final selection of twenty three for the book – three views of the loch taken with his larger whole plate camera, three with the quarter plate camera, and two small views of a 'Highland Hut' by the loch-side, one with a figure, perhaps Nicolaas Henneman, leaning against the rugged stonework.

But the loch he saw in 1844 was very different to that which greets today's visitor. Then it was a quiet and entirely natural stretch of water, but less than twenty years after his visit, the loch was changed forever to meet the city of Glasgow's voracious demand for drinking water.

A huge waterworks project was initiated in the 1850s, which linked the loch to the city through a network of over thirty miles of tunnels and aqueducts. Queen Victoria interrupted her holiday at Balmoral to open the project in October 1859.

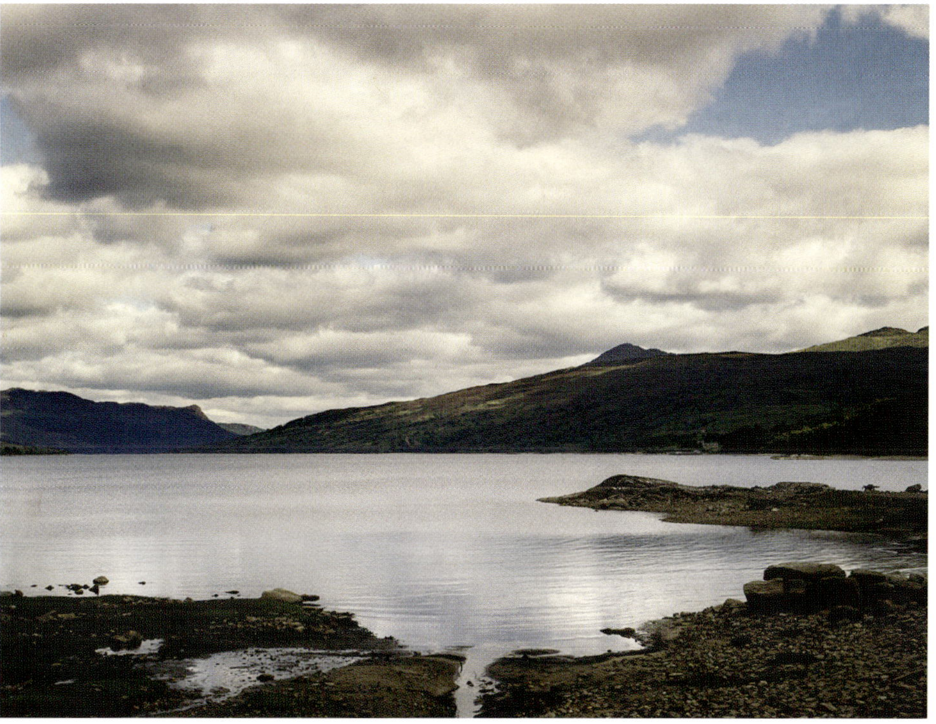

opposite page: One of Talbot's views of Loch Katrine, the setting for Scott's epic poem *The Lady of the Lake*.
above: A view of the loch today, dominated by a towering autumn sky. The blue-sensitive chemistry of Talbot's calotype process was incapable of differentiating between sky and cloud and exposures were generally too long to register moving clouds anyway. Cloudy skies would first become a feature of landscape photography towards the end of the 1850s, significantly in the works of Gustave le Gray and Roger Fenton.

"At Doune, o'er many a
spear and glaive
Two barons proud their
banners wave.
I saw the Moray's
silver star,
And mark'd the sable
pale of Mar."

The Lady of the Lake, 1810

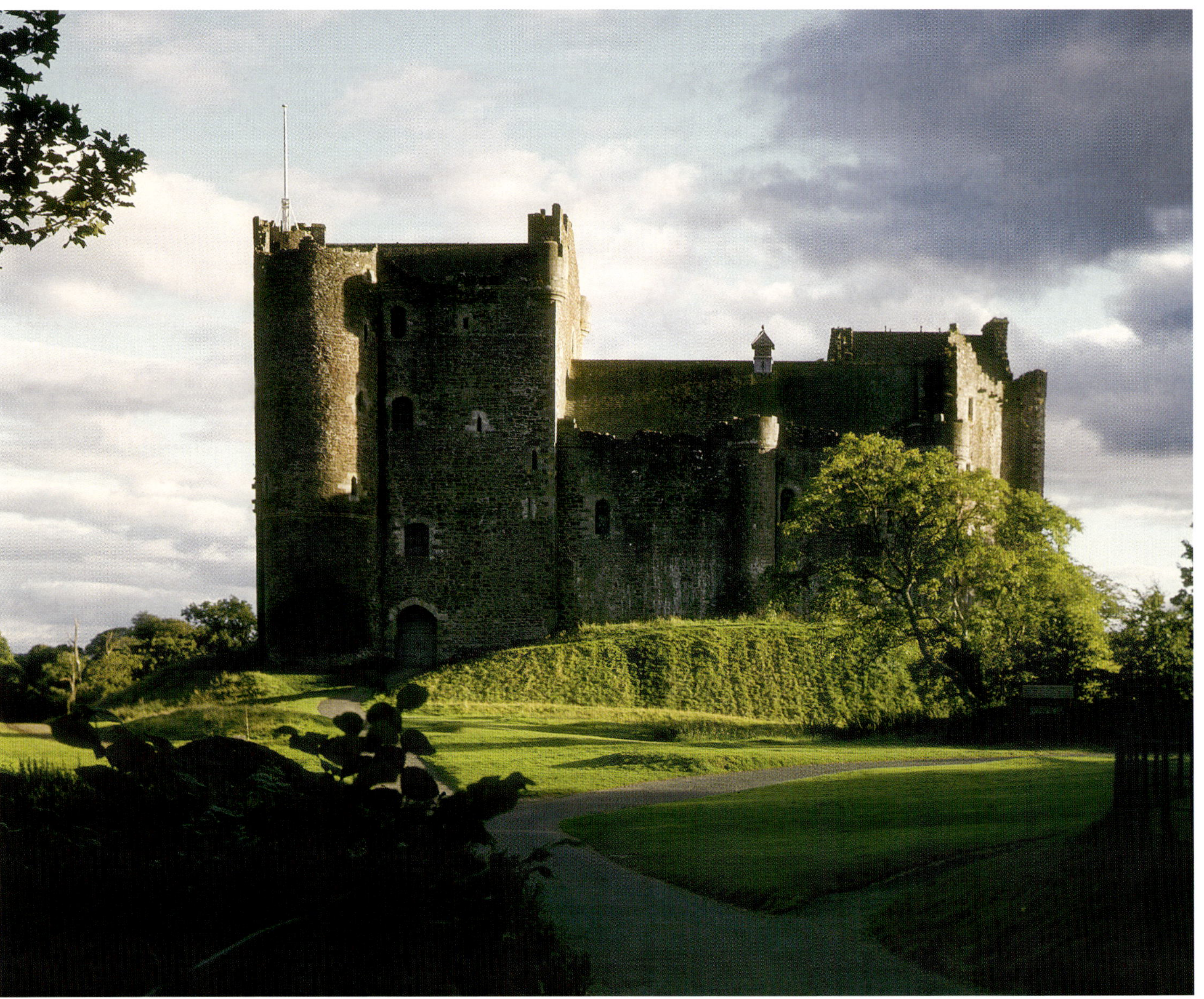

above: Doune Castle photographed under late evening sunlight.

In turning Loch Katrine into a reservoir, the water level was eventually raised by five metres, considerably enlarging the surface area, and completely redefining the perimeter shape. The Silver Strand, featured in *The Lady of the Lake* disappeared forever beneath the waters of the loch, and is remembered only in the photographs taken by early photographers, James Valentine, George Washington Wilson and others in the late 1850s. Interestingly, Wilson's pictures of the Silver Strand continued to sell well long after the subject itself had been submerged. The legend of the Lady of the Lake, already well known before Scott's epic poem, was hardly likely to disappear just because the Silver Strand was no more!

Ignoring the scenic potential of Loch Achray and several other locations from *The Lady of the Lake*, Talbot returned to Callander where he spent the nights of October 20th and 21st before moving the few miles to the village of Doune and its ancient castle. Stopping only long enough to capture at least three views - exposing two quarter plate negatives of the castle and one exposure with each of his cameras of an eloquent and richly textured landscape view which he described as *A Mountain Rivulet which Flows at the Foot of Doune Castle*. It was, in fact, the Ardoch Water, a small tributary of the River Teith. The burn and the river flow either side of the castle and meet just behind it. The paucity of foliage in the view suggests that autumn 1844 was well advanced even for Scotland in late October.

On a sunny autumn day, much of the interesting detail in the deep cutting through which the stream flows would have been in shadow, but on this occasion, the overcast weather conditions and soft lighting worked in Talbot's favour.

Doune Castle was well known to Scott's considerable and widespread readership as one of the many locations described in *The Lady of the Lake*. It was also the setting for a scene in *Waverly*, written in 1816, which described the escape of Jacobite prisoners from this dramatic 14th century keep in 1746.

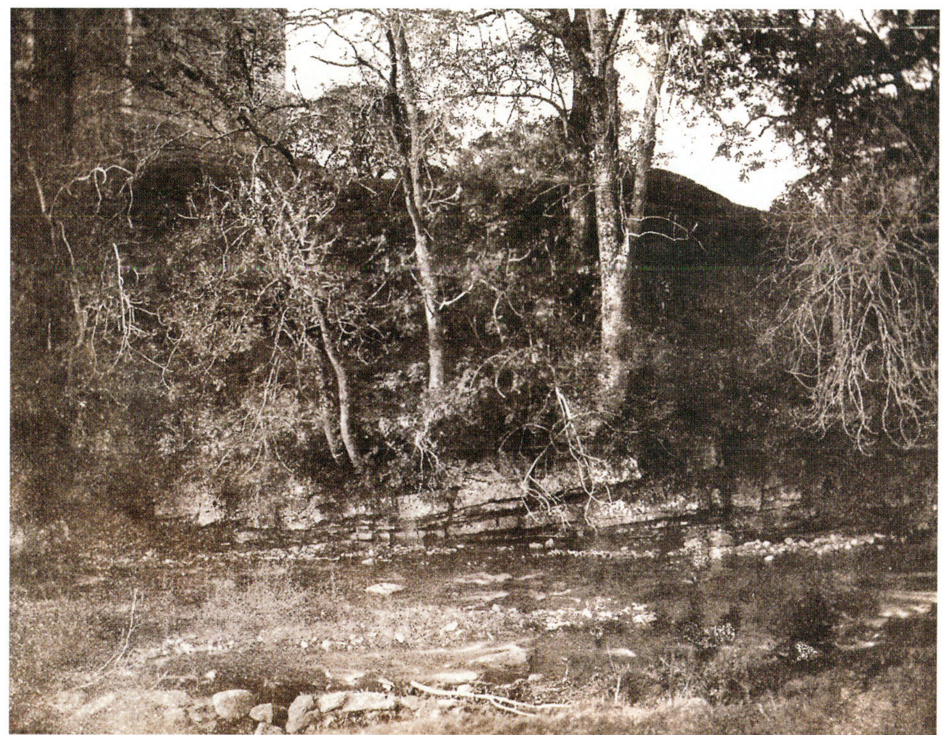

above: Talbot photographed *A Mountain Rivulet which Flows at the Foot of Doune Castle* with both of his cameras. The quarter plate version of the view - which shows more of the burn at the expense of including a fragment of the castle - was preferred by Talbot to this whole plate variant, and was included as Plate 20 in *Sun Pictures in Scotland*.

below: Sunset on Mullarochy Bay, Loch Lomond, Christmas Day. Despite a reference in Henneman's accounts to Drymen – only two miles away – there is no evidence to suggest that Talbot and Henneman visited Scotland's most celebrated loch.

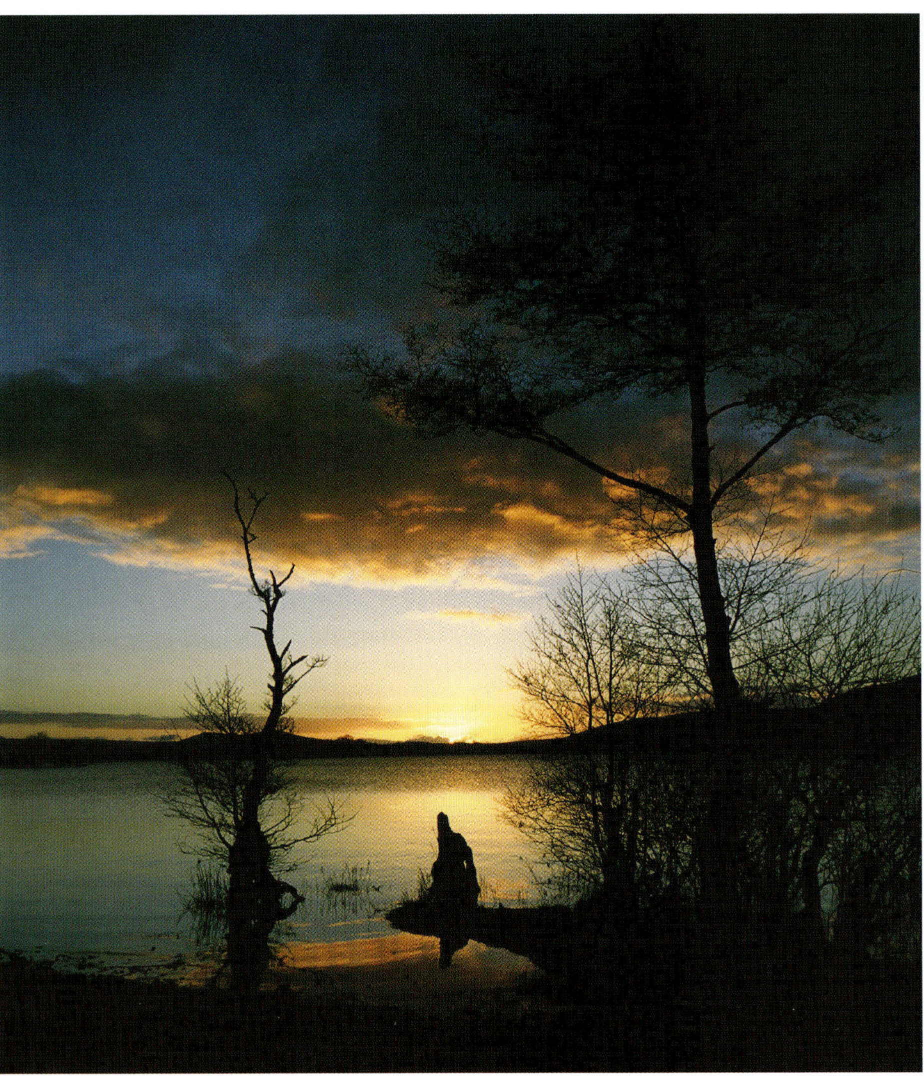

An undoubted limitation – perhaps even a failing – of *Sun Pictures in Scotland* is the absence of any text. With the exception of a title page and a list of images, there is no contextual captioning to support the images. So we are left none the wiser about the references which led Talbot to select the locations he chose to photograph, and nothing to explain the sequencing of the images.

Talbot's decision not to include views of several other easily accessible locations which have undoubted connections with Scott's life and his most famous works – such as Rob Roy's grave at Balquidder for example – is surprising. So is the duplication which is found in the published selection. Out of twenty three calotypes, Melrose Abbey is the subject of six views – two of them almost identical – Loch Katrine features seven times and Abbotsford four.

Perhaps the combination of the poor weather and Talbot's ill-health caused him to limit the locations he could visit and the time he could devote to each, restricting his ability to cover his subject adequately.

After Doune, Talbot and Henneman proceeded to Stirling, and on to Edinburgh via Falkirk. There is a strange reference to Drymen in Henneman's accounts, but no evidence that they went there – a pity, as he might have enjoyed spending a little time at nearby Loch Lomond.

Leaving Edinburgh on the morning of October 23rd – taking a cab from their hotel to meet the coach – the two men journeyed south, returning to Scott's beloved border country where he spent so many years of his life. They returned to the ruined abbeys at Melrose, Dryburgh and Kelso, and to Scott's home at Abbotsford, presumably under better weather conditions than they had experienced earlier in the month. The light, at times, was much better for photography – although never especially so in late autumn in Scotland – but they did take several calotypes and, as Constance had written in her letter to Talbot,

> *The latter part of your tour has made amends for the disappointments at the beginning.*

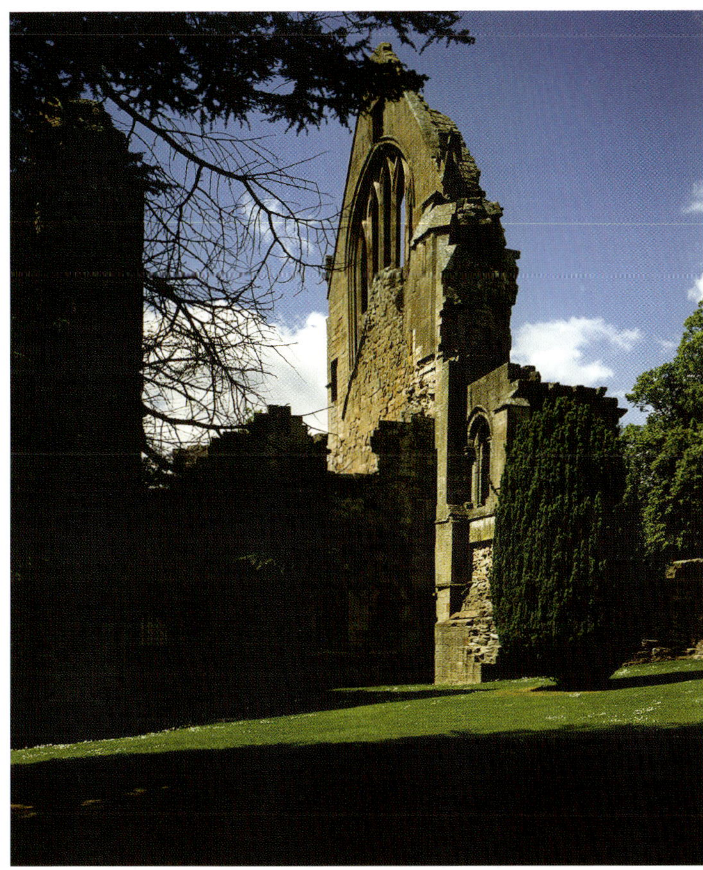

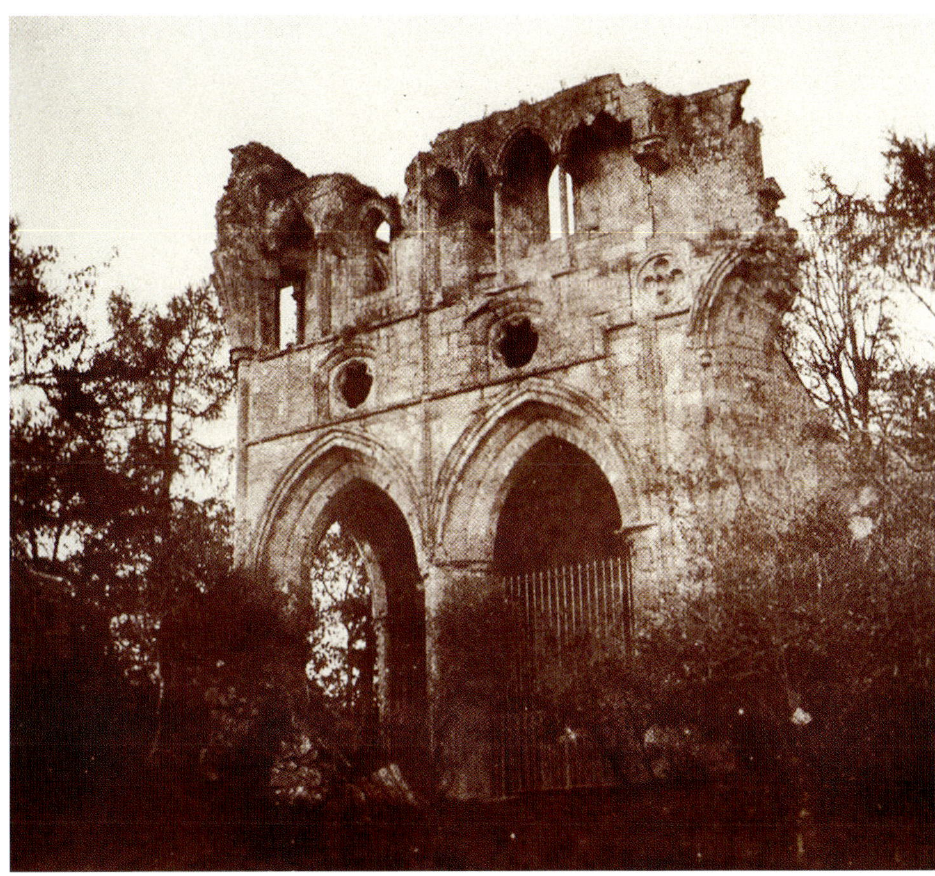

above left: Dryburgh Abbey today is a lot more accessible and a lot tidier than in Talbot's day but, as a result, offers a much less romantic experience to today's visitors than it did in Victorian times. Sir Walter Scott's tomb still attracts visitors from all over the world in their thousands, but nothing approaching the crowds who lined the six mile route from Abbotsford to the Abbey on the day of his funeral in 1832.
above right: Scott's tomb in the north transept, as photographed by Talbot in October 1844. Scott's wife, who had predeceased him by six years is also buried in the transept. Many of his descendants have also been laid to rest in the abbey, most recently – in 1998 – Patricia Maxwell-Scott, who had been Chatelaine of Abbotsford for forty-six years.

below: Talbot selected this whole plate view of the entrance gate at Abbotsford as Plate IV in *Sun Pictures in Scotland.*

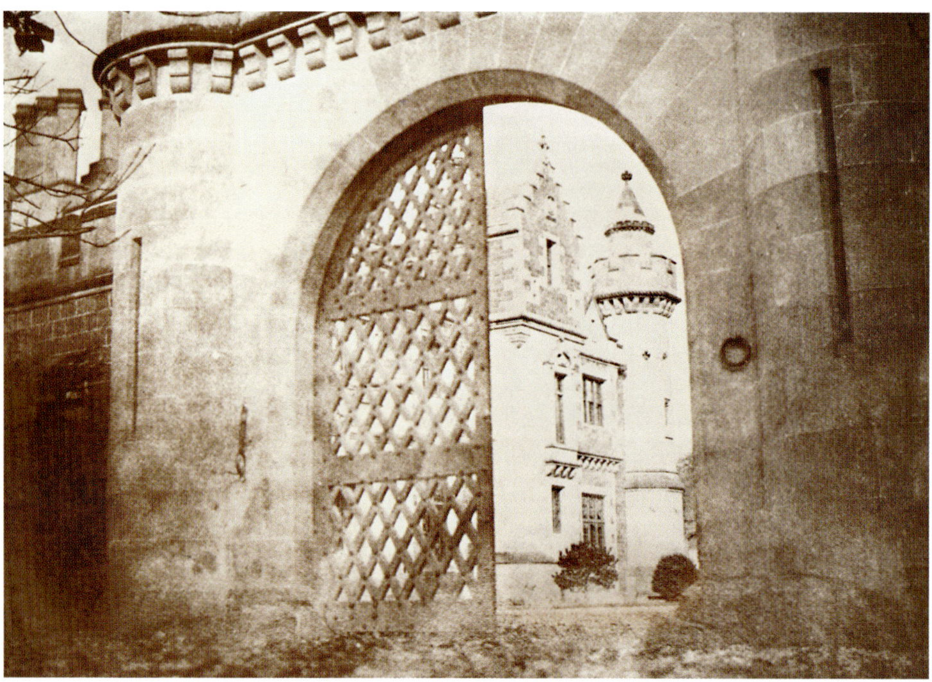

right: The statue of Maida has lain at the front door of the house since Scott himself lived at Abbotsford. Talbot published his calotype of the statue as Plate VI of *Sun Pictures in Scotland* and captioned it as *Effigy of Sir W. Scott's favourite dog, Maida, by the side of the hall door at Abbotsford.*

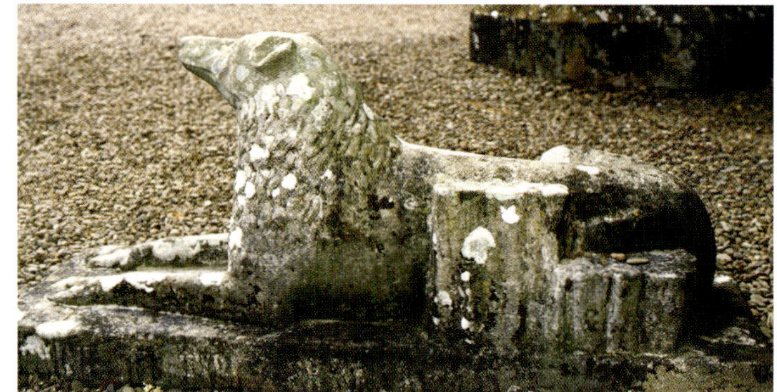

Surprisingly, only one picture from Dryburgh was included in the final selection – a sumptuously rich and brooding view of Scott's tomb in the abbey's north transept.

Despite the fact that Scott had been dead only twelve years, his tomb at Dryburgh had become something of a shrine to his readers, and was already regularly visited. In the years after the introduction of the 'Scott tour', it would acquire a popularity it retains to this day.

But while Talbot, and later photographers such as James Valentine, George Washington Wilson and Francis Frith used their cameras to celebrate the romantic image of the "broken column and the ivy-wreathed arch" – as the Manchester-based photographer James Mudd would later describe the allure of ruined castles and abbeys – today's visitor finds the ruins almost clinically manicured.

For early photographers, an attraction of exploring with their cameras was being amongst the first to photograph these sites, the excitement of discovery, of exploring the interplay of ruin, light and undergrowth. To the subscribers who acquired a copy of *Sun Pictures in Scotland*, these images were a revelation. Their previous encounters with illustrations of the great abbeys and castles of Scotland would have been through the wood or steel engravings which illustrated contemporary books. Indeed, Talbot understood the need to make the point to his subscribers that these were photographs, and every copy of *Sun Pictures in Scotland* contained a *Notice to the Reader* with the promise that

The plates of the present work are impressed by the agency of Light alone, without any aid whatsoever from the artist's pencil. They are the sun-pictures themselves, and not, as some persons have imagined, engravings in imitation.

The tangible realism which photography offered was entirely new. While engravers tended to open up shadows to clarify and simplify detail, photography captured the true sense of being there – deep and alluring shadows, shafts of bright light and, because of the blue sensitivity of the calotype and other early materials, an impenetrable, almost mystical, blackness amongst the trees and bushes.

The combination of Talbot's mastery with the camera, and Henneman's salt paper prints produced some images with a wonderful richness which in many cases survives undiminished today. Surprisingly, given the quality of prints like this, questions over the stability and permanence of Henneman's prints led to the lucritive contract for printing the illustrations for the *Reports by the Juries* at the 1851 Great Exhibition going to France.

Today's photographers still seek to capture that interplay between light and monument, and in many respects are still just as much at the mercy of the light if the true magic of the place is to be captured.

For the Abbotsford and Melrose pictures, Talbot and Henneman based themselves at Galashiels, a few miles away, and thanks to a letter from Talbot to the *Literary Gazette* in 1852,[7] we know a great deal about his *modus operandi*. We can assume that the comments he made with regard to the Abbotsford pictures are equally appropriate when considering the views of Melrose and Dryburgh Abbeys.

> *I was accustomed to prepare the paper beforehand,* wrote Talbot, *and carry it ready prepared, in closely shut paper-holders, to the scene of action. It was in this way that in September 1844 I made a series of views of Abbotsford, the residence of Sir Walter Scott.*

He continued his recollections with a description of what had undoubtedly been a considerable achievement.

> *The paper was prepared in the inn at Galashiels, several miles distant, and it retained its sensibility during some hours sufficiently well. This can readily be effected now by several methods, but at the time I speak of, eight years ago, it was more difficult of accomplishment. But this method had, in the first place, the inconvenience of being exposed to occasional failure, which required all the principal points of view to be taken in duplicate as a necessary precaution.*[8]

Well aware that his negative papers were at their most

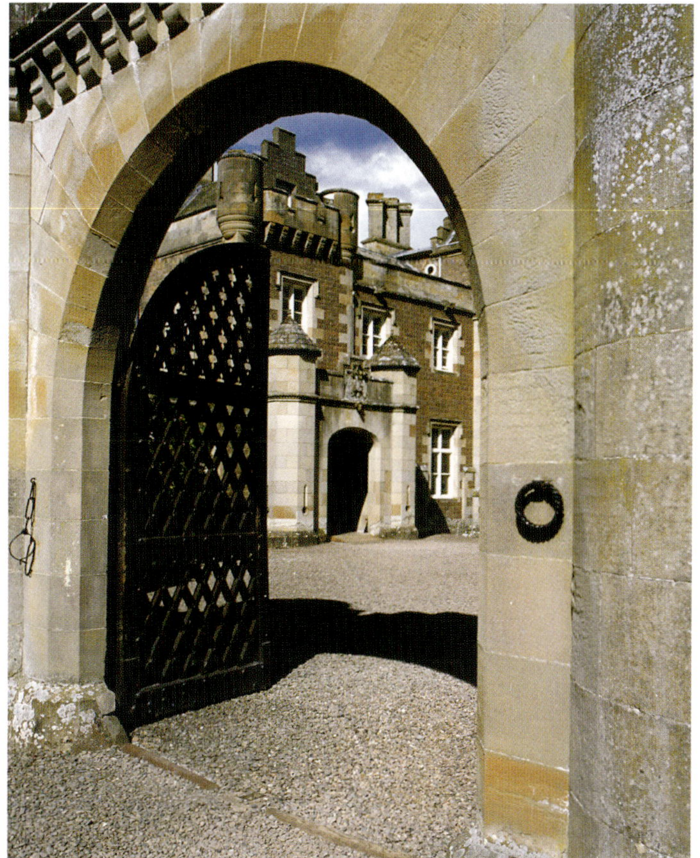

above: Talbot would have passed through this arch to reach the front door at Abbotsford. Today's visitors enter via a cellar door into the servants'quarters, but are still encouraged to sign the visitors' book.

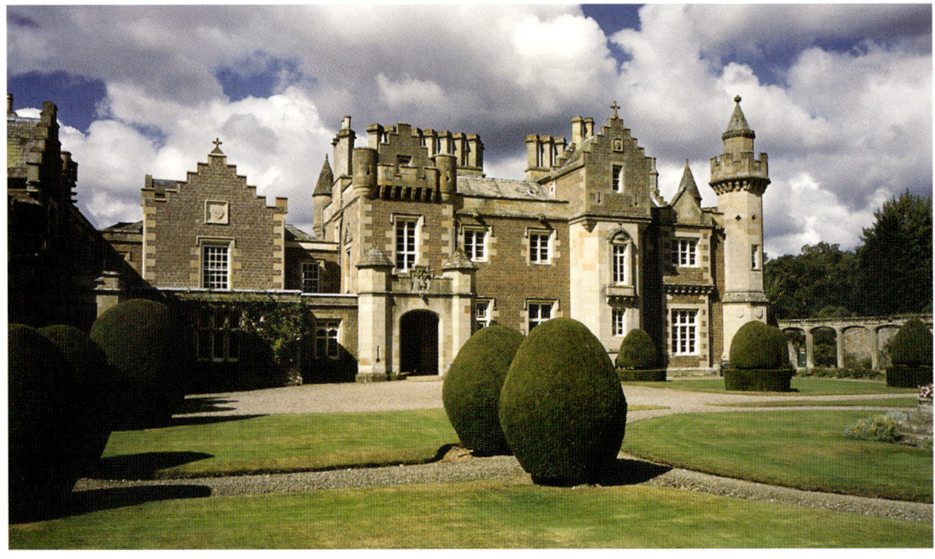

above: Abbotsford today. The house is preserved very much as Scott would have known it, and as Talbot visited it.

sensitive if exposed damp, Talbot had, however, devised an ingenious method of sensitising in the field without the need for the cumbersome darktent or portable darkroom which would burden later wet plate photographers, although it is unclear whether or not this method was available to him as early as 1844.

Some eight years after the *Sun Pictures* journey, he recalled his practice of preparing each evening for the following day's work. He then wrote of a specially designed small quarter plate 'traveller's camera' he had built for the task - although he did not say just when this camera was built.

Suspended from below the camera's tailboard, three tanks contained silver iodide to sensitise the paper immediately before exposure, developer for processing immediately after exposure, and water to keep it moist until it could be fixed and properly washed back at the hotel later that day. Might the smaller format 'duplicate' images have been taken with this innovative camera?

His description continued:-

And secondly, it required the use of as many paper holders as there were sheets of prepared paper; because on the supposition of the operator being unprovided with a tent, or some substitute for one, and of his not meeting with a shelter of any kind, it was a matter of difficulty to remove the photographic pictures from the paper holder and place fresh sheets therein, without allowing a gleam of light to fall on them during the exchange. Add to this, that in order to have a reasonable degree of security, the paper would keep good for twelve or twenty-four hours, it was found advisable to diminish its sensibility, so that it would not work well by an evening or failing light.[9]

Talbot's memory eight years after the event was a little inaccurate, for their visit to Abbotsford took place not in September, but on October 24th 1844, and he duly signed the visitors' book - one of four people to do so on that afternoon. On my visit, the present Chatelaine of Abbotsford, Miss Jean Maxwell-Scott retrieved the old book from its locked drawer in an elaborate Chinese cabinet, and we turned the pages until Talbot's name was before me - creating one of many moments in these journeys when my experience touched, albeit briefly, the experiences of those whose journeys I was recreating.

Scott had bought Abbotsford in 1811, then a farmhouse, and expanded and remodelled it. It was his home until his death in 1826 when, lying in his bed in the ground floor dining room, he asked for the window to be opened so that the last sound he might hear would be his beloved River Tweed. If he was to do that today, that last sound would be of the traffic thundering past on its way north from the border.

Weather was much more of an issue with early photography than it is today. The calotype process

Talbot was using was, by today's standards, remarkably insensitive to light, and required long exposures even in bright sunshine. Under heavy clouds, and towards evening, exposure times could lengthen into minutes, limiting photography only to those subjects which remained absolutely static.

Thus, out in the landscape, even a gentle breeze caused trees to move and blur during the several seconds exposure required. Water had to be still, or the rippling of moving water took on a cloud-like, misty and sometimes surreal appearance.

It is evident from many of the pictures Talbot created during his Scottish journey, that the weather was not generally good. That was in itself not a problem, as the calotype process favoured slightly diffuse lighting. Again because of the limited sensitivity, bright sunlight produced shadows which had no detail whatsoever in them. Early photographers favoured a thin veil of cloud as this opened the shadows up slightly, permitting a hint of detail to be recorded in all but the darkest corners of any subject. However several of the *Sun Pictures in Scotland* images have clearly been taken under conditions which stretched the infant process to its limits.

Sun Pictures in Scotland may not have been Talbot's finest photographic achievement – it is repetitive and the light was often not in his favour – but as a milestone in the evolution of photography, its publication was a landmark. It stands, of course, as the world's first 'guide book', the world's first 'coffee-table' book and the world's first 'themed' book, for it was the first self-contained publication to contain photographs – *Pencil of Nature* was a partwork whose publication started before the appearance of *Sun Pictures in Scotland* and ended after.

Those who assert it should be classified as an album rather than a book – because it has no text – overlook its pivotal importance.

In the years which followed the publication of *Sun Pictures in Scotland*, others would develop Talbot's ideas to

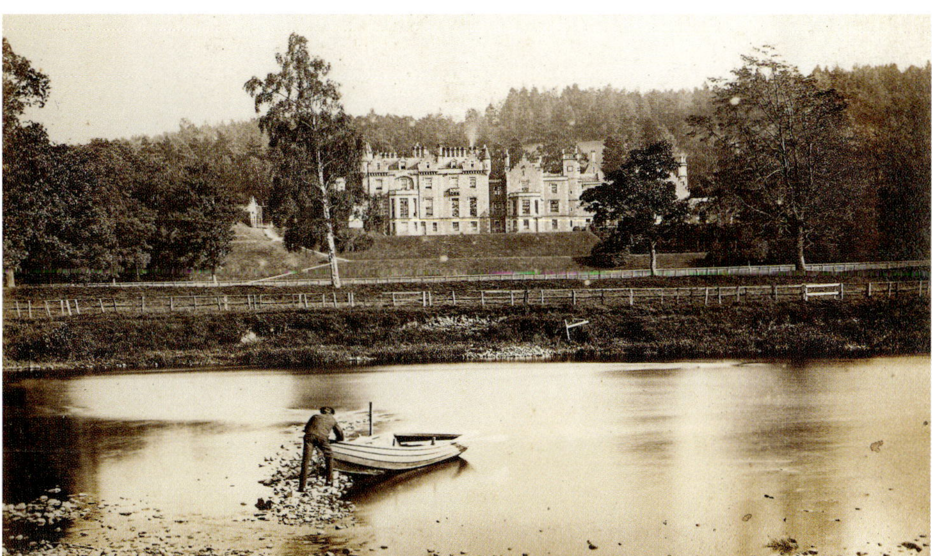

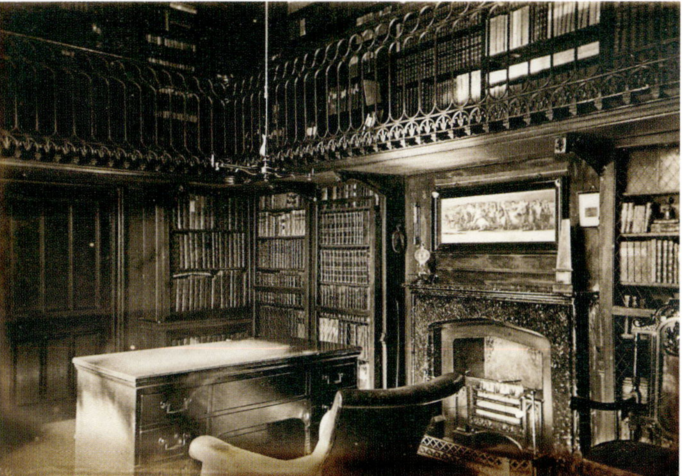

above: Abbotsford from across the River Tweed, c.1870, photographed by James Valentine of Dundee.
left: Valentine's half plate view of the interior of Scott's study sold in huge numbers to visitors to Abbotsford from the 1860s through into the 1880s. Only the use of colour separates this view from those available to today's visitors.

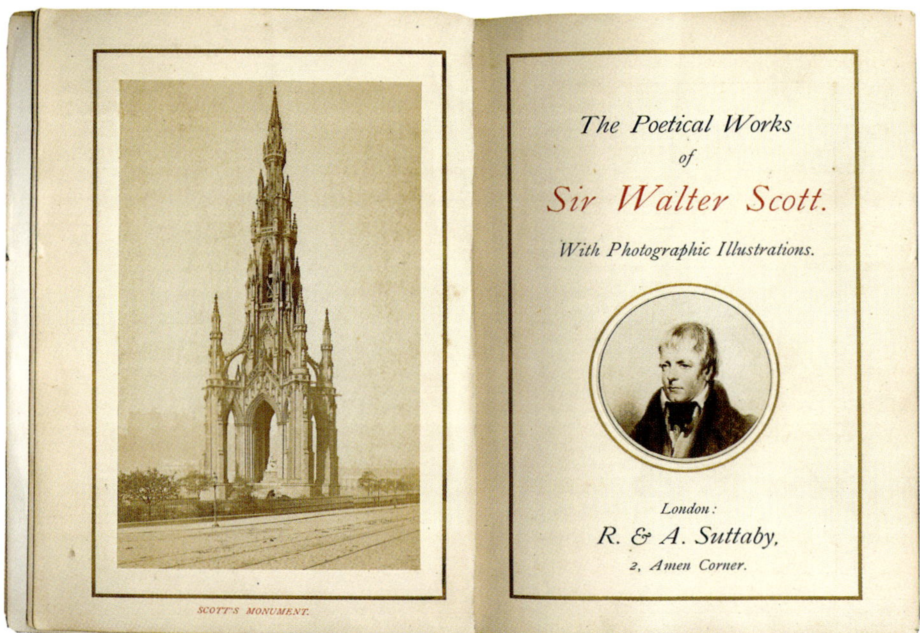

above: The huge market for Scott's work naturally led to the photographically illustrated volume, and many of them echoed and expanded Talbot's selection of views. This volume, probably published in the early 1880s, like *Sun Pictures in Scotland*, contains views of Abbotsford, the Scott Monument, Dryburgh Abbey, and Loch Katrine, with additional views of other locations featured in Scott's writings – Newark Castle, Notland Castle, Stirling Castle, and Fingal's Cave. No credit is given to the photographer or photographers.

opposite page: Loch Lubnaig, like many other locations in the Trossachs, featured in *The Lady of the Lake*. Talbot would have passed by this beautiful loch on his coach journey from Callender to Loch Katrine.

create the vast market for illustrated travel books which we enjoy today – and into which tradition this volume fits.

Once the calotype was replaced with the faster wet collodion process, and as Scott's reputation and tourist appeal grew, the great publisher-photographers – Francis Frith, James Valentine, and George Washington Wilson amongst them – commissioned photography to sell to visitors to Abbotsford, to those doing the Scottish Grand Tour, and to illustrate hundreds of books on Scott's life and work.

By October 25th, 1844, Talbot and his party were in Kelso where they spent the night – and according to their accounts, treated themselves to some chocolate, obviously a comfort food then as now! From there they took a somewhat circuitous route back to England, travelling south west to Hawick, right across the country to Carlisle, and then east again to Newcastle. From there they journeyed south to Darlington and York where they arrived by train on the night of October 28th and stayed for a couple of nights before returning to the south, the first stage of their Scottish adventure over.

Back in Reading, the real work started – the preparation of the individual hand-made salt prints – at least one hundred and twenty sets, at least two thousand seven hundred prints being needed for the published edition of one hundred copies. Some of the images were printed in larger editions. The view of the partially completed Scott Monument, for example, was a very popular image and sold in large numbers as an individual print separately from the publication. Similarly, the views of Abbotsford were also available individually.

Sun Pictures in Scotland survives in greater numbers than the better-known *Pencil of Nature*, but many copies are in poorer condition.

Its importance in the history of photographic publishing permits such shortcomings to be overlooked. Talbot's first 'Great Photographic Journey' defined one of photography's most enduring applications.

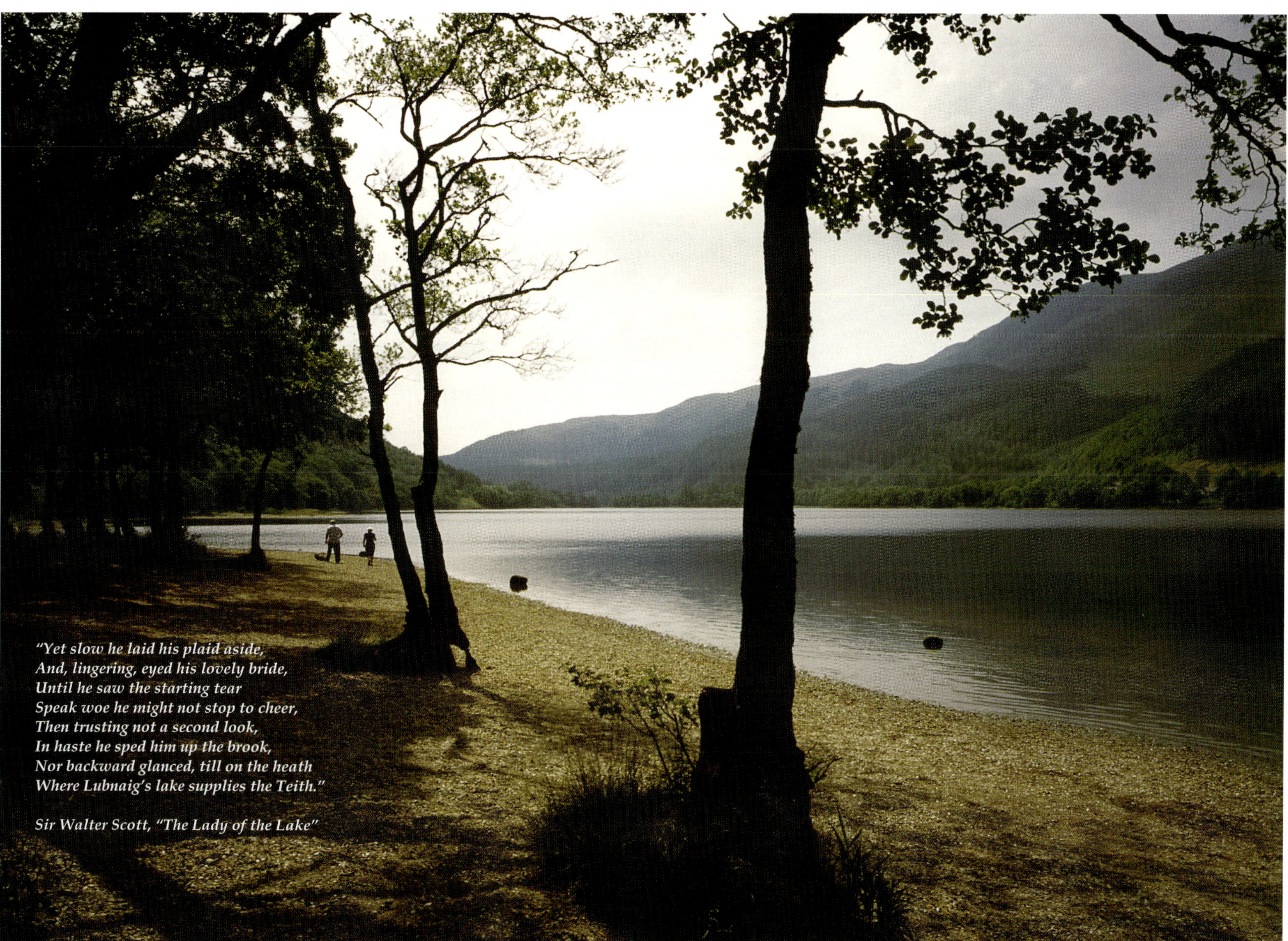
"Yet slow he laid his plaid aside,
And, lingering, eyed his lovely bride,
Until he saw the starting tear
Speak woe he might not stop to cheer,
Then trusting not a second look,
In haste he sped him up the brook,
Nor backward glanced, till on the heath
Where Lubnaig's lake supplies the Teith."

Sir Walter Scott, "The Lady of the Lake"

below: This calotype panorama, c.1845, of Talbot's printing establishment at Reading in Berkshire offers the earliest ever view of the production stages in early photography. Talbot himself is fourth from the left, Henneman on the right, and in between them several uses of photography have been depicted. On the left, a camera is being set up to copy a painting, while Talbot is preparing to make a portrait. To his right, rows of printing frames are out on their racks, pointed skywards to maximise the effect of daylight. The slow process of making contact prints from the paper negatives - always dependent on a good supply of daylight - was speeded up slightly by waxing the processed negatives before printing to make them more translucent.

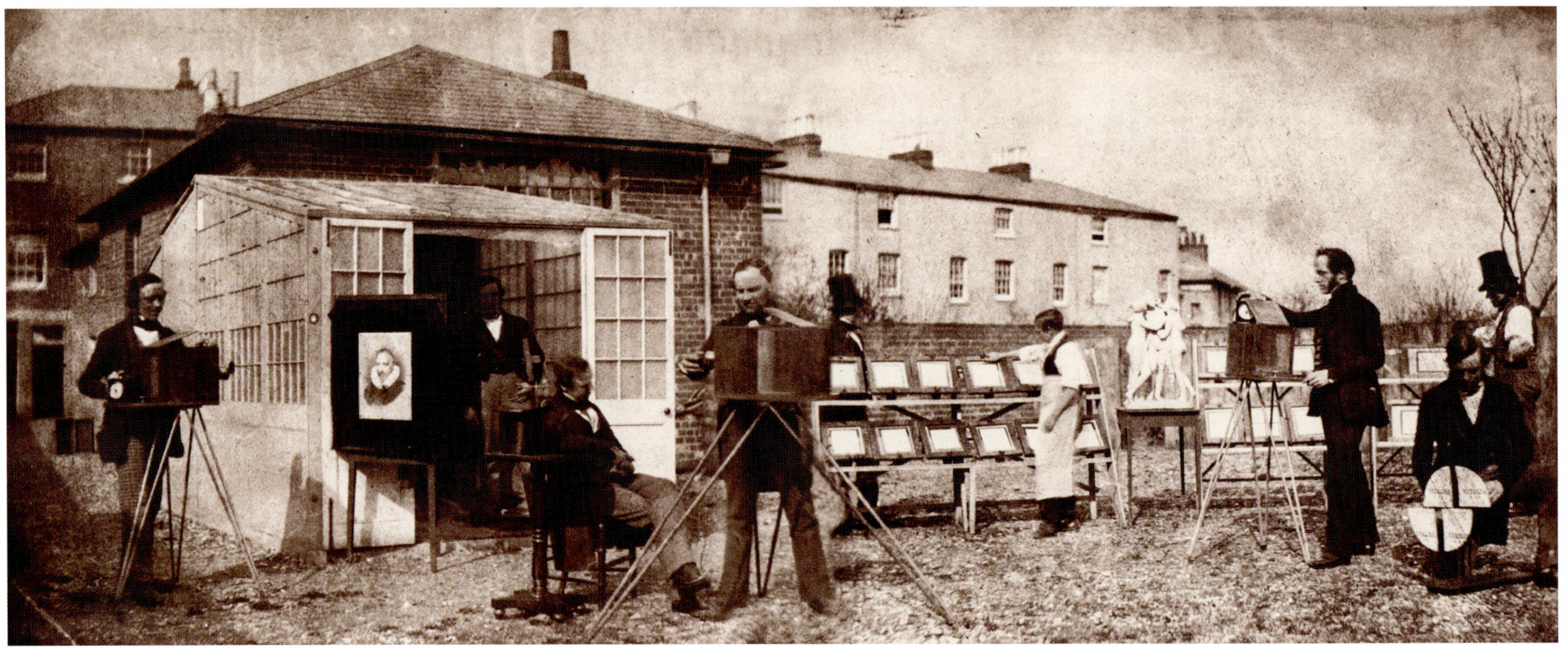

Notes

1. Sir Walter Scott (1771-1832) was without doubt the most successful novelist Scotland had ever seen. His books were sold and read in huge numbers, and his success brought him fame, fortune, a title and a mansion in the Scottish Borders. Unwise investments led to bankruptcy, and took its toll on his health as he tried to repay his creditors.
2. *Sun Pictures in Scotland* was self-published in London in summer 1845, in an edition estimated at 120 copies, and containing twenty three calotype prints - in whole plate, half plate and quarter plate sizes.
3. *The Pencil of Nature*, published in London in six parts by Longmans, Brown, Green & Longmans, between June 1844 and April 1846, contained a total of twenty four calotype illustrations.
4. Cook's first tour brought a temperance group from Leicester to Scotland, visiting Lochs Lomond and Katrine, and surrounding areas with Scott associations.
5. Henneman's notes are contained within documents housed in Glasgow University Library. I am grateful to Professor Larry Schaaf for bringing those notes to my attention.
6. Quoted in Schaaf, Larry *The Photographic Art of William Henry Fox Talbot*, Princeton University Press, Princeton and Oxford, 2000, p208.
7. *Literary Gazette*, 27th November 1852, page 876.
8. *ditto*
9. *ditto*

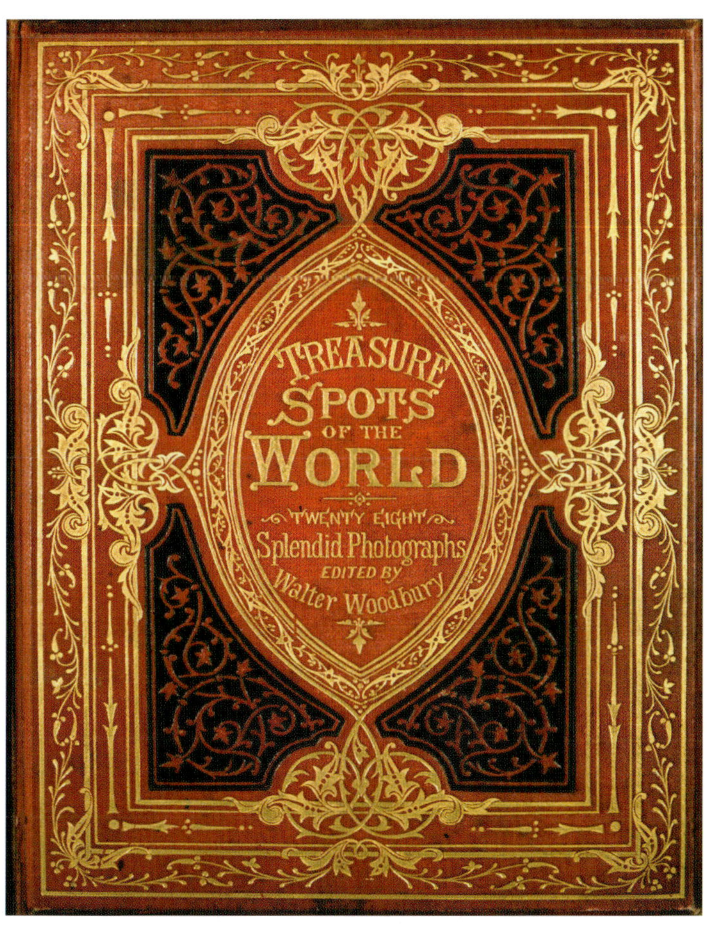

Travel Photography

Opening a Window on the World

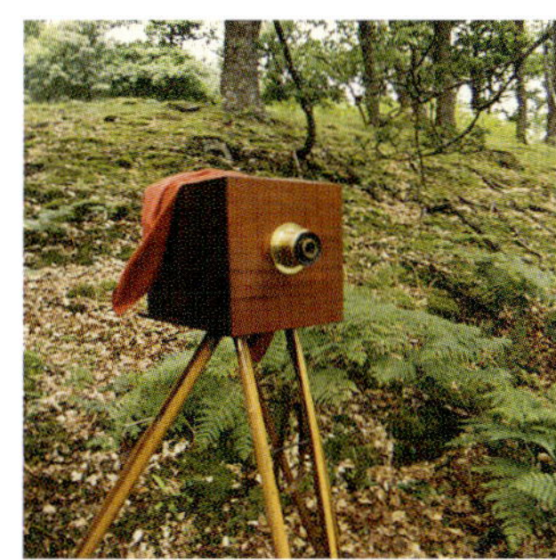

above: A replica of a typical sliding box camera design from the 1850s

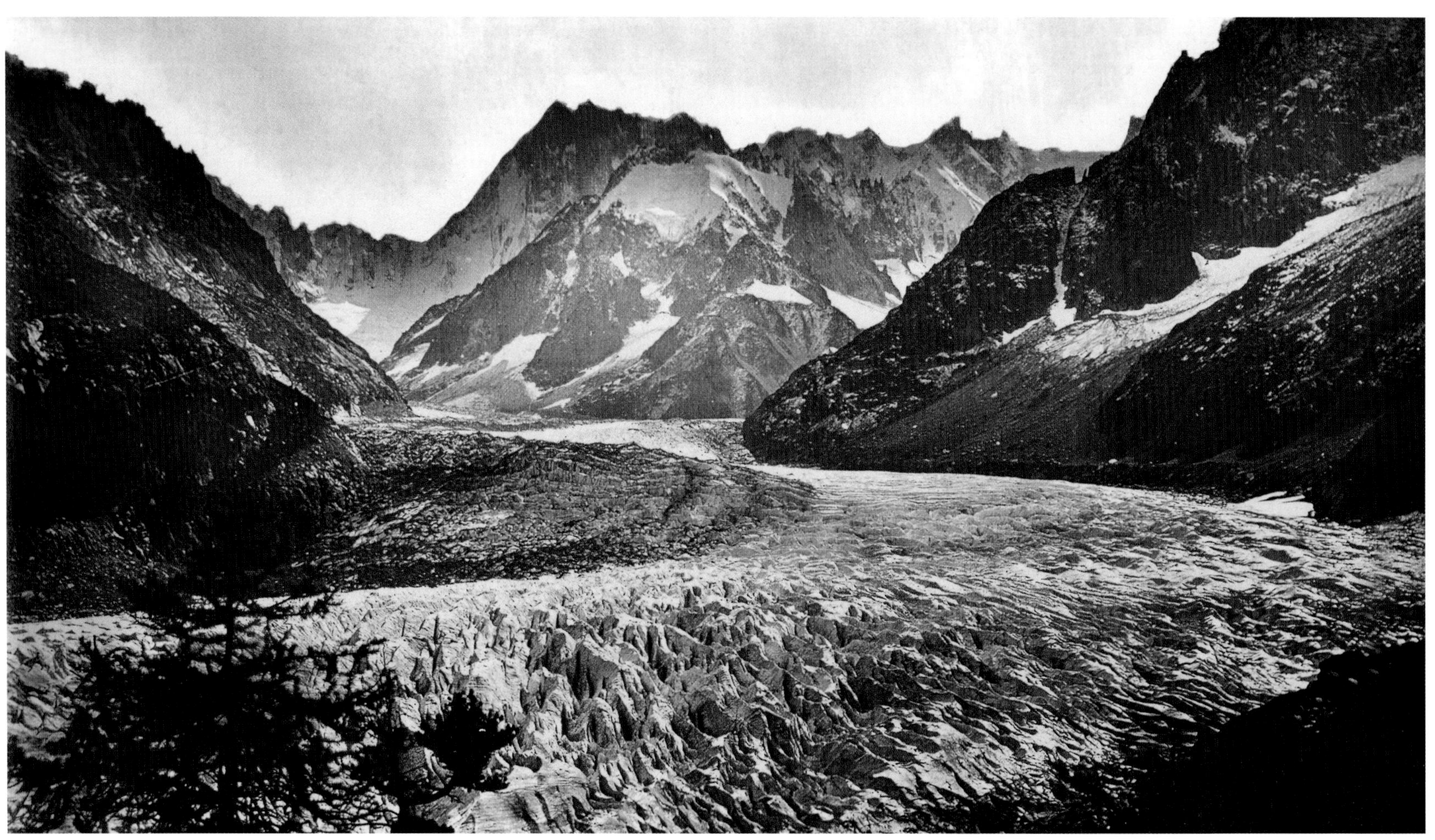

above: 'Mer de Glace, Chamouni, Switzerland' by Stephen Thompson, one of the plates from *Treasure Spots of the World*. Of this picture Thompson wrote "After scrambling for hours over precipice and moraine, past the vast masses and pyramids of ice into which the lower extremity of the Glacier de Talfrère is broken, the traveller at length reaches a rocky island set in a sea of ice... ...at an elevation of 9000 feet above the level of the sea."

With the publication of Walter Bentley Woodbury's 1875 *Treasure Spots of the World*, the use of photography as an accessible window on the world entered a new era.[1]

Illustrated with twenty-eight permanent "splendid photographs", the book offered readers "a selection of the chief beauties and wonders of nature and art." Photographs from locations as close to home as Tintern Abbey and as far away as China and Java were brought together both as a testament to the quality of Woodbury's revolutionary printing process, and to the ability of photography to bring the remote corners of the world into the Victorian drawing room.

In his introduction, Woodbury wrote that

> *The object of this, the first gift-book of its character, is to place before the public a collection of the most celebrated of the world's beauties and wonders, which being all pictures of the unerring sun's work are necessarily true to the places they represent, without any flattery.*

Since the birth of photography, the impermanence of the silver print had been a cause for concern, and early photographers had established a committee to explore the threat which that posed to the future direction of the 'new art'. The Woodburytype offered a permanent carbon-based print which could be produced mechanically and therefore had the advantage that it could be mass produced more cheaply. Silver prints, handmade by a slow and hugely labour-intensive process, had both limited the production of illustrated travel books, and maintained an unpopularly high price.

In the thirty years since Henry Fox Talbot had published *Sun Pictures in Scotland*, photography had come a long way, and so enthusiastic was Woodbury about the opportunities his process presented that he wrote

> *The endless choice of earth's beautiful scenery will enable us, should the present volume receive the esteem of the public, to present yearly a collection of the camera's choicest rendering.*

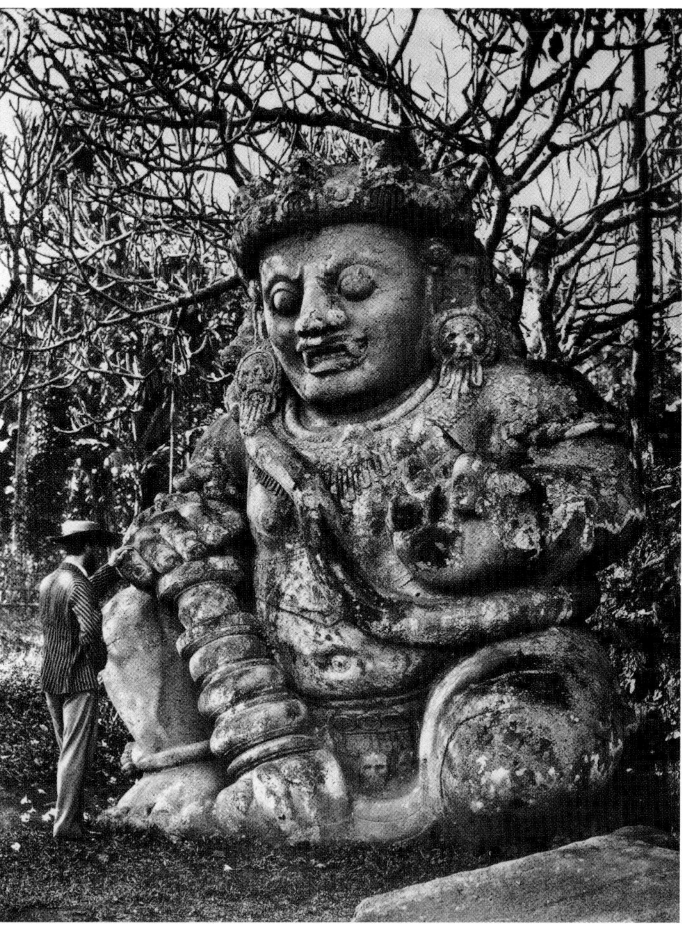

left: 'Colossal Figure at Singa-Sarie, Java', photographed by Walter Bentley Woodbury and used as one of the plates in his *Treasure Spots of the World*, published by Ward, Lock & Tyler, 1875.

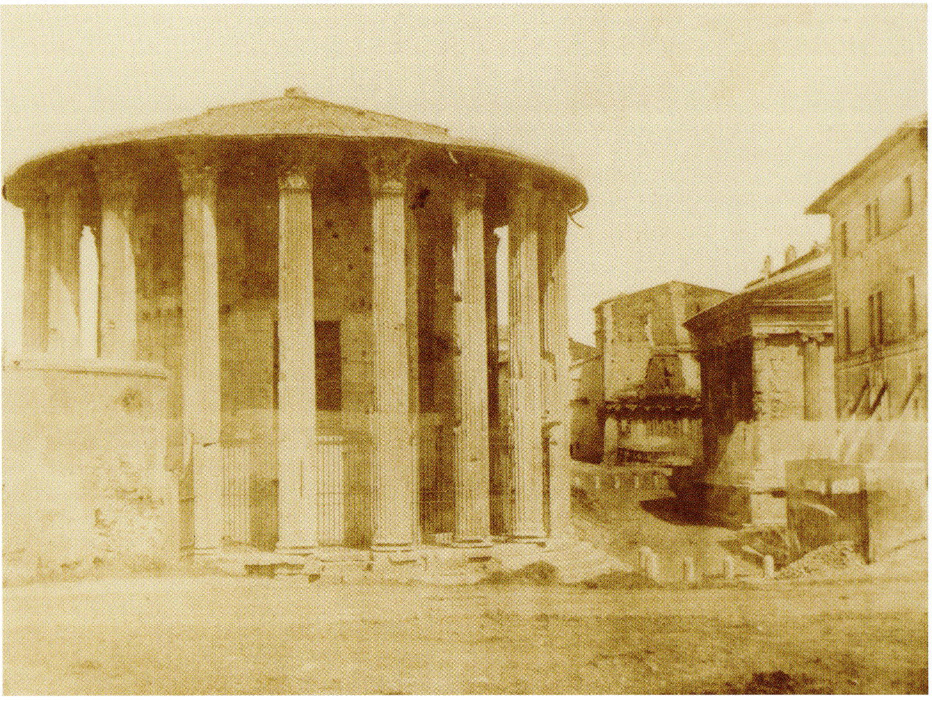

above: The Temple of Vesta, Rome, salt print from a calotype negative by the Reverend Calvert Rochard Jones, 1846. Jones, a native of Swansea, was one of a number of British photographers who took their cameras to Europe before 1850. Jones undertook an extensive photographic tour of the Mediterranean, from November 1845 through into the spring of 1846, visiting and photographing a large number of locations in Rome, Florence, Sicily, Naples and Pompeii, as well as Malta. The temple he photographed is now believed to be the Temple of Hadrian, but was formerly assumed to be dedicated to Vesta because of its similarity to other known Vestal temples.

To get to that stage, photography had undergone many changes and improvements - a thirty-year rollercoaster of developments which had taken it from being a solution in search of a problem, to a point where the photographic print had become the souvenir of choice for travellers everywhere.

Woodbury's book was, in 1875, a long way in quality from Talbot's rather crude *Sun Pictures in Scotland*, but its lineage could be traced back to 1845. It had been Talbot's vision which had inspired photographic publishing in the intervening three decades, and which would continue to do so.

Without Talbot's early appreciation of the photograph's ability to encapsulate a sense of place, a quality of light, and a new and unique perspective, who is to say what directions photography might have taken. While many early photographers simply set out to record, the medium quickly developed an innate expression which made it the ideal reminder of personal experiences.

Even in the mid 1870s, Woodbury still drew attention to the view that photographs were the unerring sun's work and necessarily true to the places they represented, without any flattery, as had Sir David Brewster twenty years earlier when he informed the inaugural meeting of the Photographic Society of Scotland that

> *photography is pre-eminently a scientific art; it requires no particular genius in its cultivators; the Painter and the Sculptor must bring into the world those high gifts which qualify them for the practice of their divine art, but there is no poetry in the pencil of the Sun.*[2]

The photographs which graced the albums of the early travellers and travelling photographers - even as early as Brewster's 1856 speech - gave the lie to such statements, but photographers laboured for decades under the unfair dismissal of their art as nothing more than a medium of record.

That they produced works of such beauty under the adverse conditions imposed on them by the cumbersome nature of early photography is little short of remarkable.

Very early in the history of photography, enthusiastic amateurs started to take their cameras abroad, bringing back their own photographic mementos in place of the engravings and sketches of earlier travellers.

Little is known of many of these early photographers except that many of them were wealthy members of the middle and upper classes. They were the most likely to have sufficient leisure time, and sufficient money, to be able to indulge both in extended periods of travel and in the not inconsiderable cost of acquiring all the paraphernalia of early photography.

Travelling with a camera in the 1840s and 1850s was a significant undertaking. The camera itself was large and heavy, and the materials and bottles of chemicals which were necessary to make the primitive processes work added significantly to the baggage.

While Talbot's 1844 journey to Scotland, and the production of all the pictures for *Sun Pictures in Scotland* in less than four weeks, is remarkable, his later travels and those of some of his contemporaries are even more so.

With a process requiring – in the case of the calotype – exposures of several minutes for a 10″ x 8″ view, the photographer was constantly at the mercy of the weather. Even in a light breeze, the movement of foliage in the scene could ruin the resulting negative.

The problems did not discourage the early enthusiasts! Driven by the promise of photography either for personal reasons or for commercial exploitation, amateur and professional photographers seemed undaunted by the logistical problems their journeys imposed.

Calvert Richard Jones travelled to Italy and Malta in 1846; Sir James Francis Dunlop travelled from Scotland to Rome; Talbot himself travelled to France and Belgium, and both George Moir and John Muir Wood travelled to Belgium. There were many others. Together, they were amongst the first to bring back to Britain original photographs from mainland Europe.

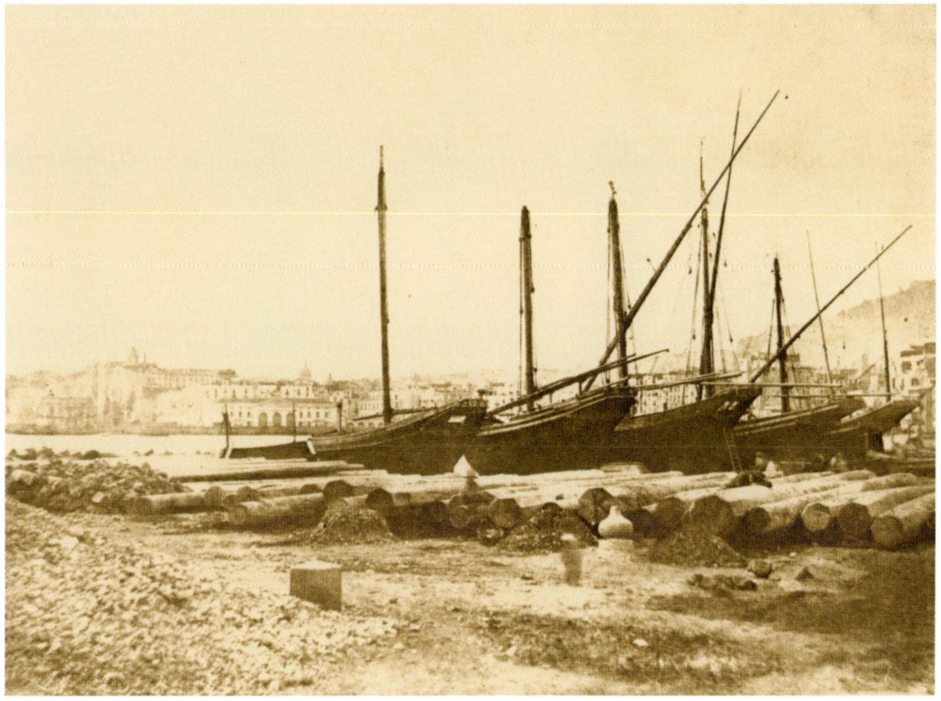

above: Naples, photographed by Calvert Richard Jones in 1846. In addition to Italy, Jones took his calotype camera to Belgium (where he had lived for a time in the 1830s), France, Malta and Italy, and later sold his negatives to Talbot. In a letter to Talbot about the commercial value of his calotypes, he wrote "this beautiful art cannot fail to gain entire admiration, and a most extensive sale, provided it is properly brought forward." With the long exposures required for the calotype, it was essential that he took this picture at low tide to ensure the boats did not move. The blurred figure of a child can be seen in the centre foreground.

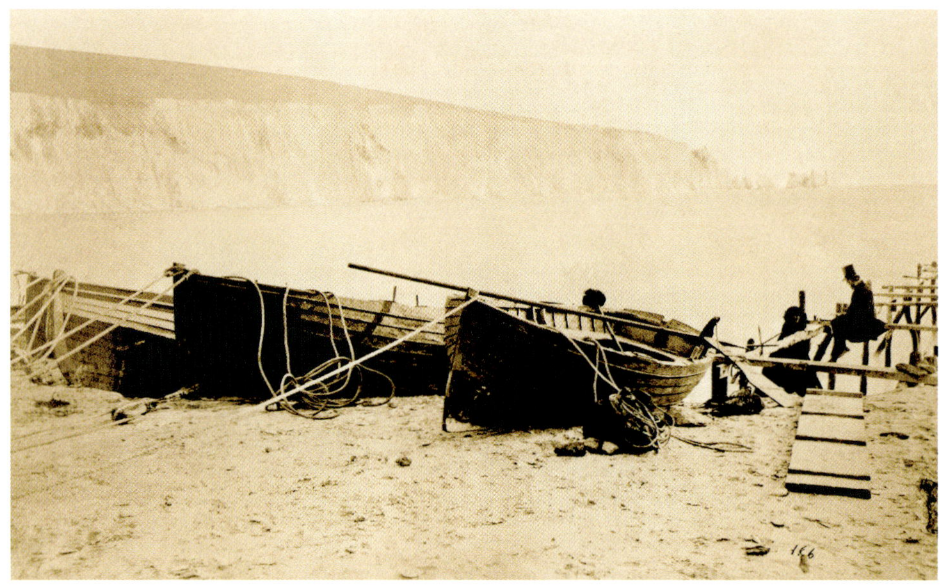

above: On the Dorset Coast, photographer unknown, 1860s. Even for a relatively short journey from home or studio, the photographer using the wet collodion process needed to carry a substantial weight of equipment, utensils and materials. For this picture, he would have needed his 10x8 camera, a supply of glass plates and the necessary chemicals for coating, sensitising, developing and fixing, a portable dark tent and a range of dishes and other utensils. A supply of clean fresh or distilled water would also have been needed.

What we now accept as commonplace, with our automatic high-performance film or digital cameras, was a challenging and demanding undertaking.

The work rate which a calotype photographer could maintain was low - a good day's output might be no more than six or eight exposures once the lengthy preparation and processing sequences had been completed.

Most calotype photographers processed their pictures on location, often in a hotel room as Talbot had done. Making the prints, of course, was left until they returned home. Then, with the processed paper negative treated with wax to render it translucent, salted paper prints were made by prolonged exposure to daylight.

For the photographer using the wet collodion process, things were a little easier in some respects, but a lot more cumbersome in others.

The glass plate of the collodion negative, being transparent, offered greatly reduced printing time - although still long - but the manipulation of the process itself was a lot more cumbersome, and required a lot more in the way of equipment.

William Sparling, writing of the process in 1856 praised it highly, because

> *the extreme sensibility of the medium itself, and the comparative ease of its manipulation, place it at the head of all photographic agents.*[3]

Many a wet plate photographer would have challenged *the comparative ease of its manipulation*, while conceding the undoubted quality of the images which could be produced with collodion.

The wet plate photographer had to coat his carefully cleaned glass plate immediately before use - using a mixture of guncotton dissolved in alcohol and ether, and potassium bromide. He then had to sensitise it in a bath of silver nitrate. As the collodion negative lost its sensitivity very quickly after sensitisation, the plate was exposed while still damp. In hot weather the plate surface often dried too quickly, and modifications were introduced to keep the light sensitive coating damp under all but the most extreme of conditions.

In order to carry out the delicate coating operation, the photographer needed a portable darkroom or darktent – the scale of which was in direct proportion to the size of plates being coated. For small images, a compact lightweight darktent which could be carried as a backpack was often sufficient. For large format glass plates, a much larger tent was needed. If the photographer was working on a very large scale, or planning to take a large number of pictures, a carriage was needed to carry the heavy equipment and materials, and this might be fitted out as a darkroom as well.

Once coated, the plate was carefully loaded into a light-tight holder and taken to the camera, which had, of course, previously been set up on its tripod and focussed.

If the photographer was fortunate enough to have an assistant, then the assistant could be doing all the preparation work in the darktent while the photographer decided on viewpoint and composed the picture. For the photographer working alone, all that had to be done before retiring into the tent.

On a bright day, an exposure of less than a second could be achieved, but under dull lighting, five to twenty seconds might be necessary. Without exposure meters, there was a degree of luck and intuition in deciding the exposure, but as the negative was processed immediately afterwards, serious errors could quickly be rectified and a second exposure made.

On bright days, the flamboyant Scottish photographer George Washington Wilson could effect an exposure of less than a fifth of a second by removing the camera's lens cap with one hand, and immediately covering the lens again with his Glengarry bonnet held in the other hand!

In Scotland, one cannot imagine that such a feat of dexterity was called into play very often!

The enthusiasm for images associated with Sir Walter Scott grew exponentially through the 1850s, 1860s and

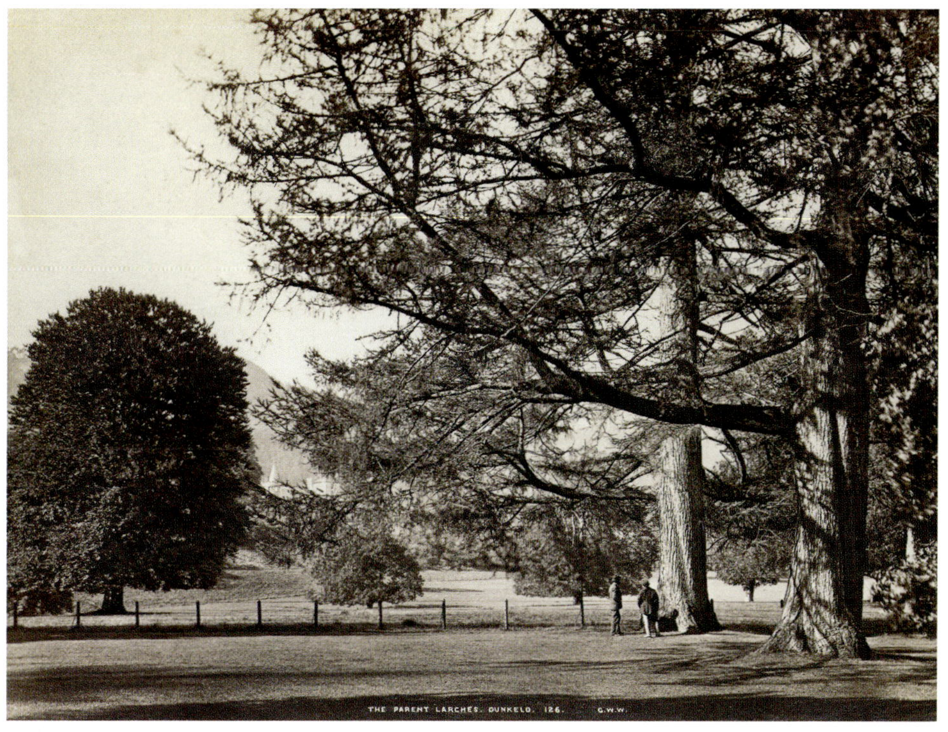

above: 'The Parent Larches, Dunkeld', George Washington Wilson, late 1860s. The photographer required very still weather for this study of trees near Dunkeld Cathedral – but even on a very calm day, the outer branches of the trees moved during the relatively short exposure of no more than a few seconds.

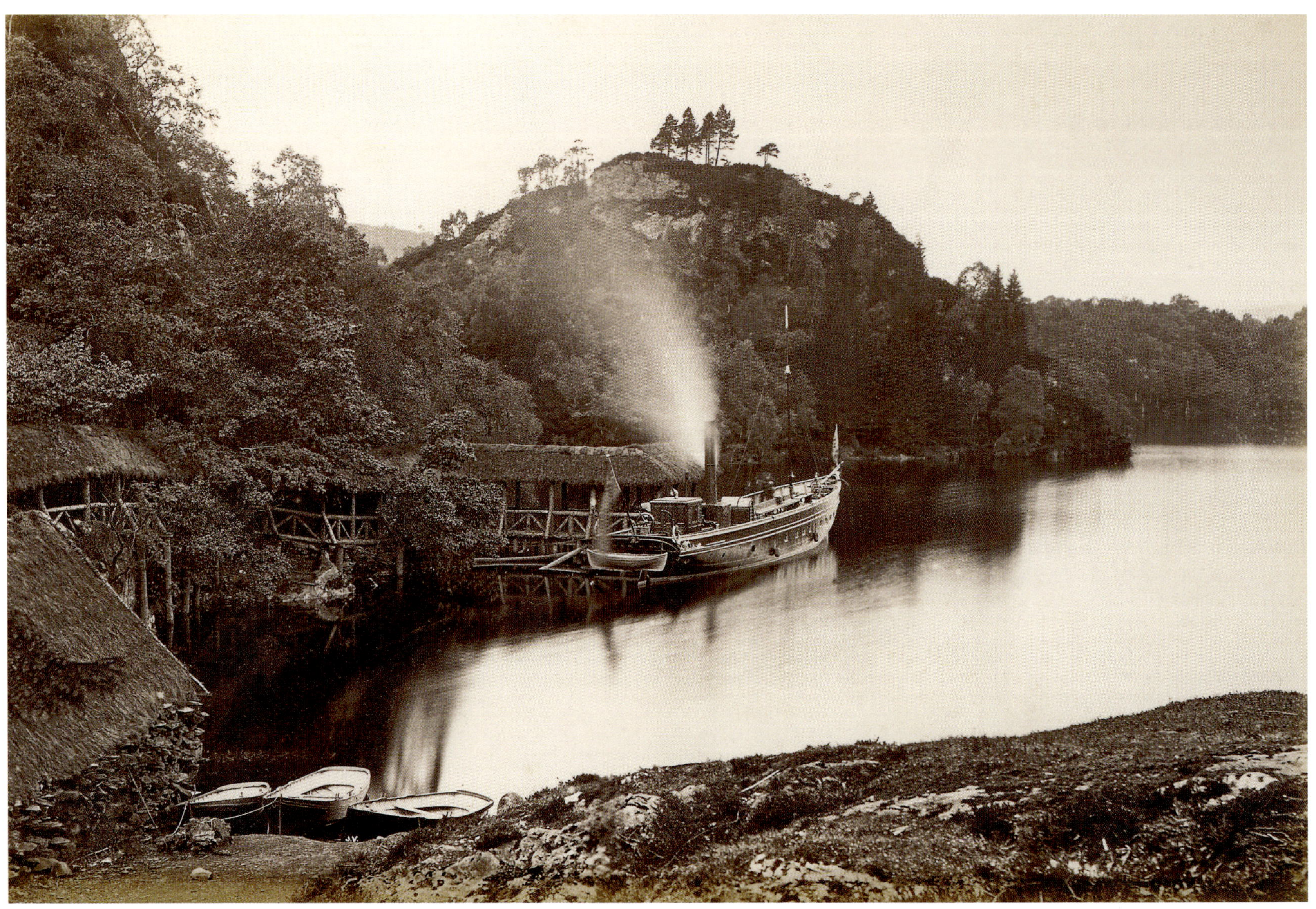

above: 'Rob Roy' getting up steam, Trossachs Pier, Loch Katrine, photographed on a still day c.1870 and published by Dundee photographer James Valentine in a lavish red leather-bound album of views of the scenery to be found on the Scott Tour. This is one of several studies of the boat and pier (*see opposite page top*) published by Valentine.

1870s. Several Scottish photographers made a handsome living out of supplying the tourists with their visual memories.

By the late 1870s, Francis Frith claimed to be able to supply photographs of every town, village and tourist attraction in Britain - sometimes taking the pictures himself, but more often commissioning local photographers with local knowledge to take the negatives for him. The one thing all these photographers had in common was a dependence on the wet collodion process, and a willingness to rise to the challenges which satisfying the tourist market placed upon them.

The public was always keen to acquire new and spectacular views, so the photographer had to carry all the heavy equipment to more and more remote locations - sometimes only to be thwarted by a sudden change from still weather to high winds, or from sunshine to torrential rain.

On one journey through the Highlands in the 1860s George Washington Wilson wrote of the problems the weather imposed

> *After breakfast Gellie and I took a walk up a footpath which leads to the corries of Ben Eay. Saw on our way down a capital view looking down a gullie towards Craig Roy. Went on to the end of a footpath about three miles and got a splendid view of Ben Eay. After going a little further over the quartz rocks, saw down the glen by the back of Ben Luigeach and Ben Alligan. We then went up a hill to the right some distance, and saw a peep of Loch Maree and had a fine view of Ben Silloch, Craig Roy and the mountain beyond... ...came on to rain... We got a soaking before reaching the inn at Kinlochewe.*[4]

It might have taken several hours to get to a location, only for a relatively slight change in the weather to render photography virtually impossible.

Working as a photographer in mid-Victorian Scotland, however, it was not only the vicissitudes of the weather with which they had to contend, as Wilson noted in his

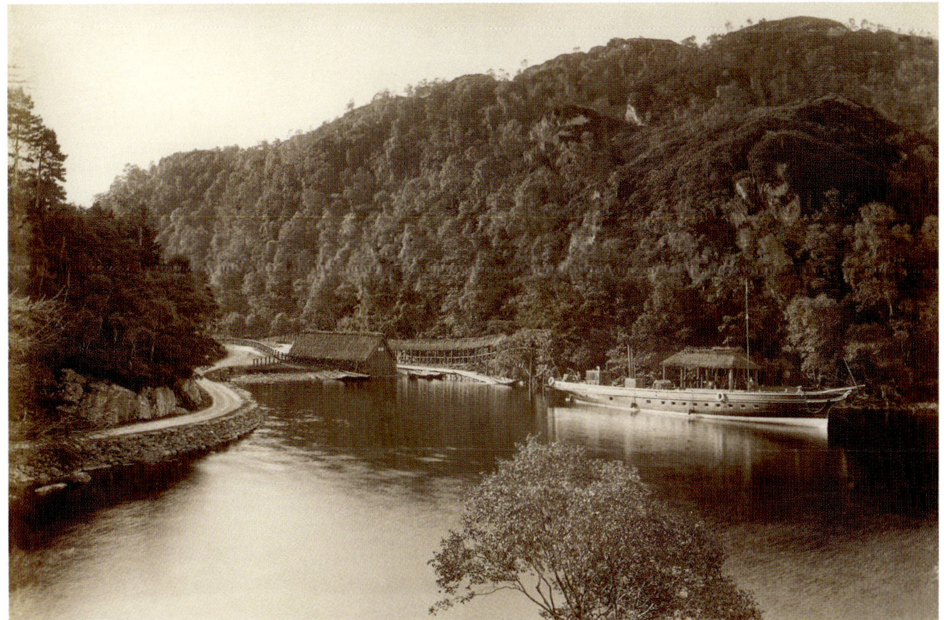

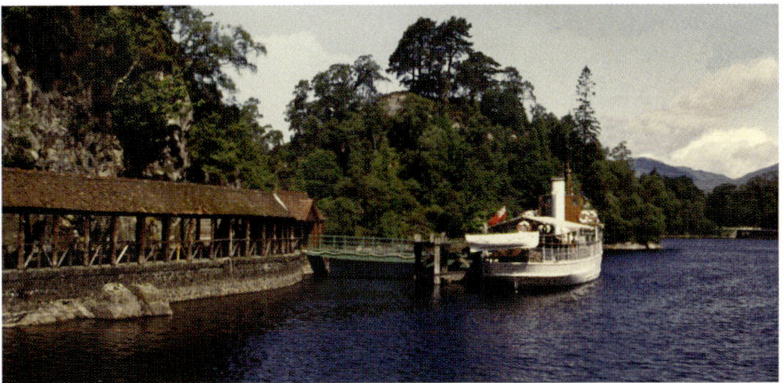

above: Today, the steamer *Sir Walter Scott,* itself now over a century old, continues the tradition of sailing on the loch

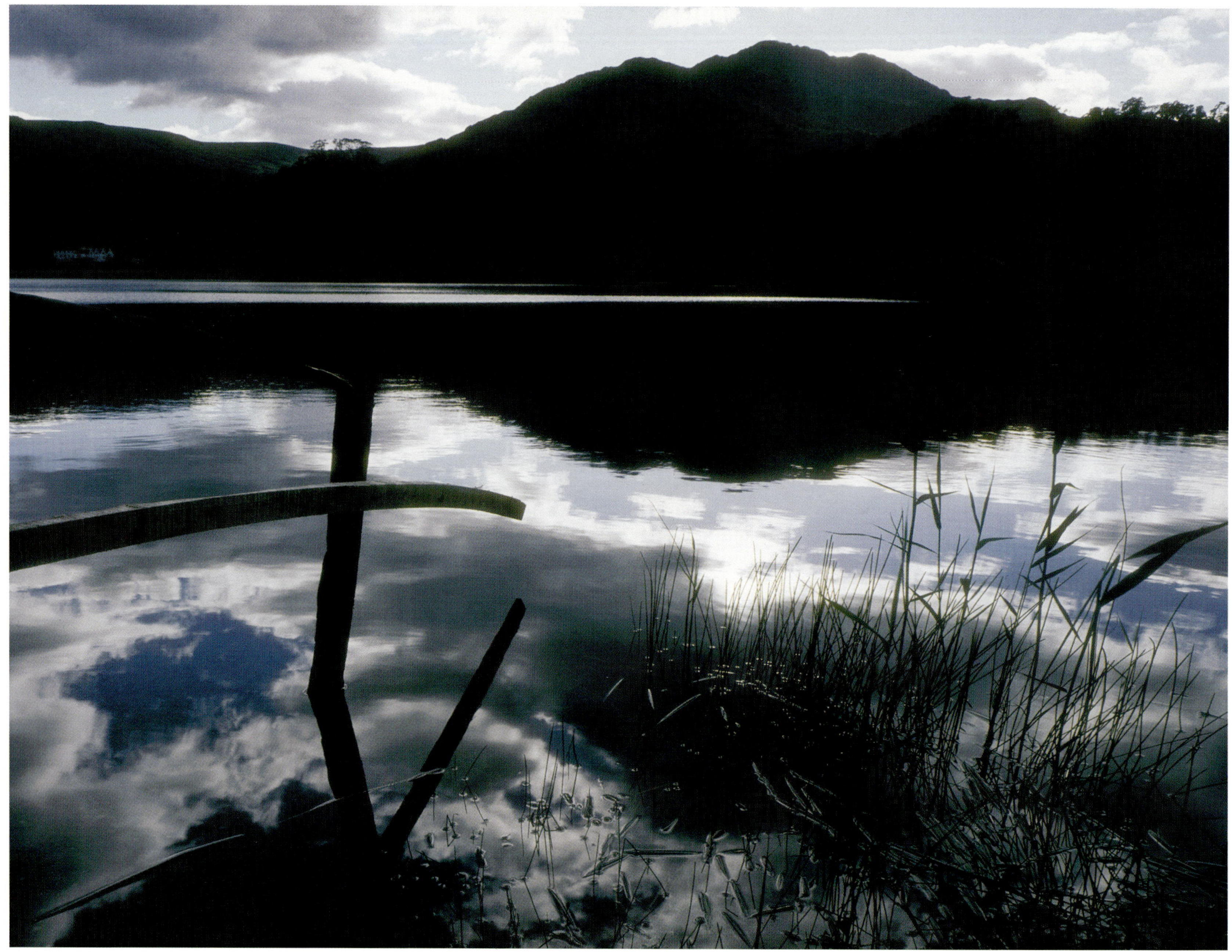

diaries. After a long and fruitless walk on a Saturday, with no pictures possible, he could then be faced with perfect weather the following day - but to work on the Sabbath was considered sinful!

Wilson and many other travelling photographers carried several cameras with them. In the days before enlargers were commonplace, all photographic prints were made by contact with the original glass negative. That meant that if a large print was required, a large negative had to be made in a large and heavy camera. The sheer weight of glass plates carried by photographers working in the largest formats must have been considerable. That in turn impacted upon the sort of transport the photographer needed to get all that weight to the intended location.

Using a smaller camera had an advantage - the shorter distance between the lens and the back of the camera meant that more light reached the negative plate. The more light, the shorter the exposure.

With small stereoscopic (3D) cameras, such as used to take the view of Loch Katrine's Silver Strand (*right*) the combination of large lens, small plate - and therefore very short distance between lens and plate - allowed photographs to be taken with very short exposures indeed. The first instantaneous exposures were made with just such a camera.

The stereoscope was a popular entertainment in the Victorian drawing room, and sets of three-dimensional views were sold widely throughout the 1860s and 1870s.

Irrespective of the format being used, the collodion photographer had to take a great deal of equipment and materials with him wherever he went.

The ingenuity of photographer-inventors in seeking to lighten the load apparently knew no bounds.

The bellows camera was the first innovation to lighten the travelling photographer's load. As well as significantly reducing the camera's weight, the bellows camera could be folded up into a compact and more portable package. The folding bellows camera design has been continuously

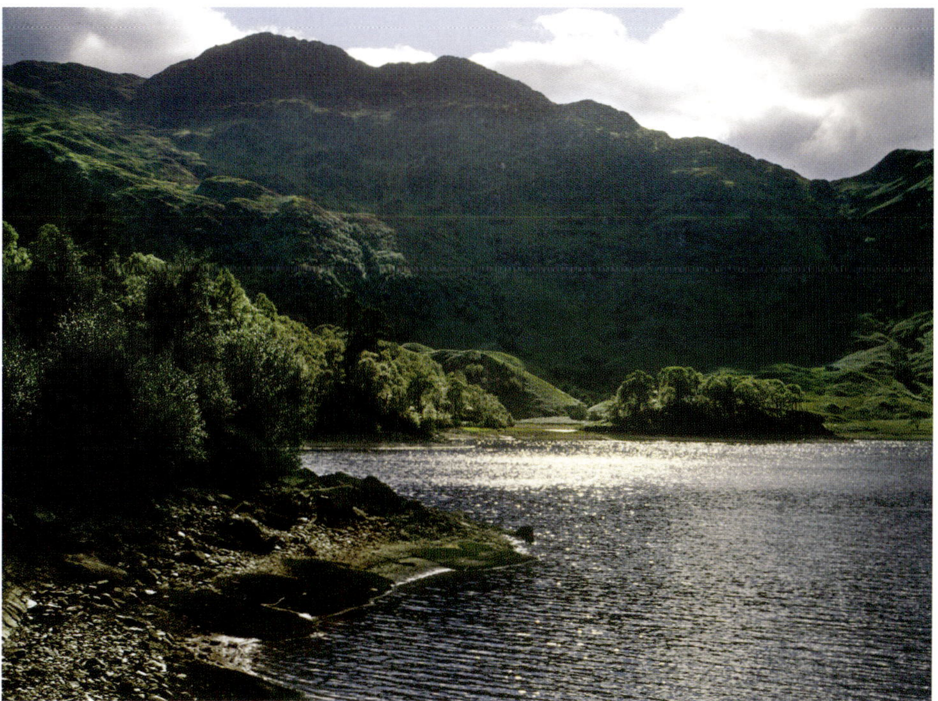

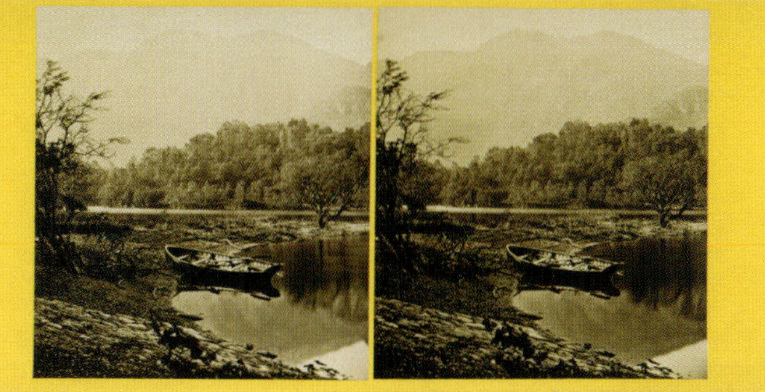

opposite page: The still waters of Loch Achray, reflecting a dramatic summer sky.
above: The silvery waters of Loch Katrine, now used as a reservoir, are higher than they were in Scott's or Wilson's days.
left: G.W.Wilson's popular stereo view of the Silver Strand on Loch Katrine, 1860s.

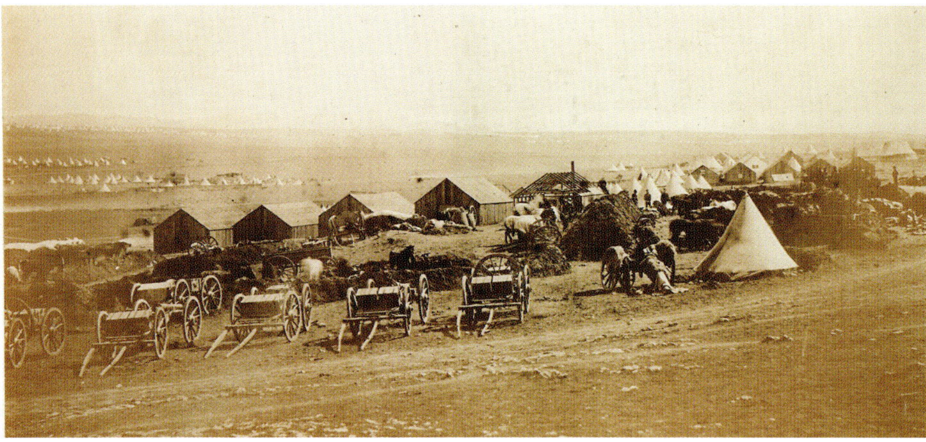

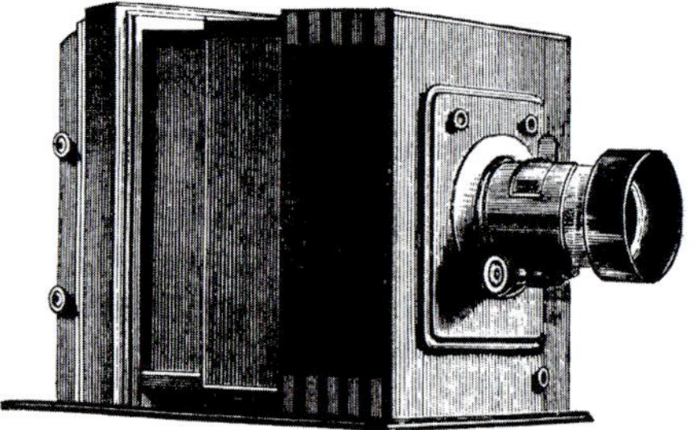

above: Artillery Wagons, Balaclava, photographed using the wet collodion process, in 1855, during the Crimean War, by Roger Fenton. It was his mastery of the wet plate process under challenging conditions which enabled him to create so many striking photographs from the war zone.
right: A contemporary illustration of a typical sliding box camera design from the 1840s and 1850s.

refined over a century and a half and is still recognisable in the modern 4x5 inch view camera of today.

The most significant weight, however, was not the camera, but the portable darkroom and all the equipment and materials needed to coat, expose and process the negatives.

The efforts of photographers to obtain landscape sketches with the collodion process have long been impeded by the weight of the apparatus and chemicals to be carried. The difficulty is now obviated by the invention of The Collodion Knapsack, which answers the three-fold purpose of the Packing case, Camera and Dark-Chamber; and enables the Photographer to manipulate out of doors without the assistance of a tent. The materials which accompany the knapsack occupy the smallest possible space.

So ran an advertisement in the May 21st 1857 edition of the *Journal of the Photographic Society.*[5] The advertisement continued:

The dimensions of the knapsack for pictures 7 inches by 5 inches are not more than 16 inches by 11, and 6 inches thickness. The following apparatus is packed in this space: - Three Gutta Percha Bottles for Water, Gutta Percha Developing Tray, Collodion Bottle, Varnish Bottle and Spirit Lamp, Lens, Nitrate Bath, Plate Box and Plates, Reserve Box with Bottles of Chemicals, Funnel, Glass Cloths, Dusters, &c. The price of the entire apparatus and fittings for pictures of the above size is £10.10s. The weight is about 18 lbs., and it has been found that from the position of the knapsack on the back a greater weight may be carried long distances without inconvenience.

This was just one manufacturer's solution to the problem. There were many others and the editorial pages of contemporary journals were filled with the ideas and inventions of individual photographers, some well known, others not.

Henry Peach Robinson, the eminent pictorialist, designed two different darktents for different plate formats. For the smallest plates, his portable darktent collapsed into

below: A reconstruction of a typical wet collodion photographer's field equipment from the early 1860s. The wicker basket carried all the chemicals, while the utensils were packed inside the collapsible dark tent. A supply of fresh or distilled water also had to be transported on location, unless a reliable local source was assured. The more remote the location, the less likely that would be!

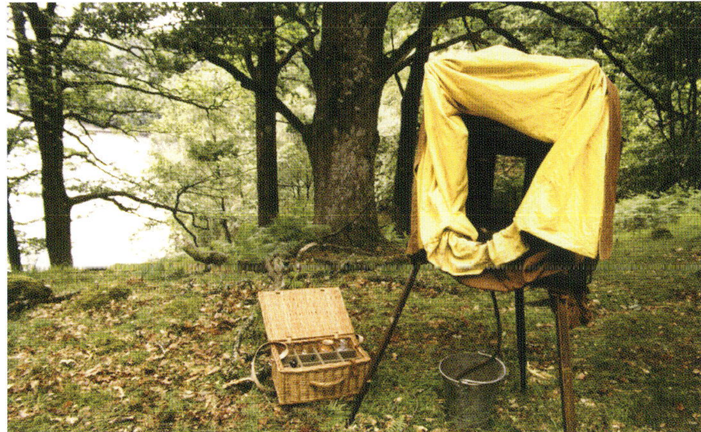

a small wooden carrying case while, for larger work, he suggested a wheelbarrow version.

Between such compact outfits and the large horse-drawn darkroom used by Roger Fenton throughout Britain and in the Crimea, were 'photographic wheelbarrows', small handcarts, and tents large and small.

James How, a well respected photographer turned equipment dealer, marketed 'How's New Photographic Tent' in the early 1860s, designed to fit into a small portmanteau measuring 24x18x6 inches and weighing about 20 lbs.

Of all the dark tent designs, perhaps the most ingenious was that designed in 1859 by a Sidmouth-based amateur photographer who revelled in the name of Mr Heineken.[6]

Alongside his description, he published two illustrations, one of the equipment packed up and ready for travel, the other of the camera in use.

In his design almost every component item of the travelling photographer's equipment had multiple uses.

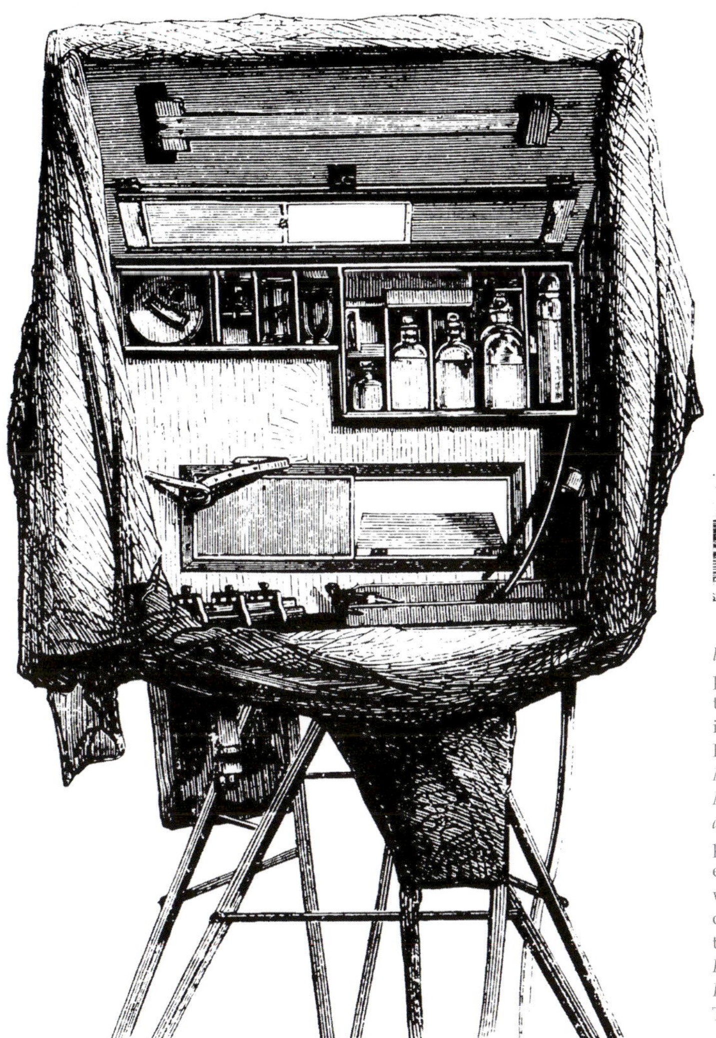

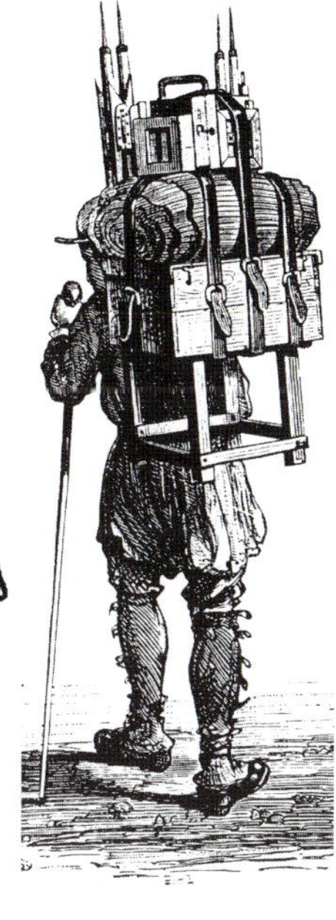

left: The interior of a photographer's dark tent, as illustrated in William Lake Price's 1868 book *A Manual of Photographic Manipulation*.
above: A travelling photographer with everything needed for wet plate photography on location strapped to his back - from *A History and Handbook of Photography* by Gaston Tissandier, 1878.

below: Bolton Castle, Yorkshire, hand-tinted stereo view, c.1854, by Roger Fenton.
below middle: Sir Walter Scott's tomb, Dryburgh Abbey, James Valentine, 1870s.
bottom centre and right: Mr Heineken's portable dark tent (*see text*)

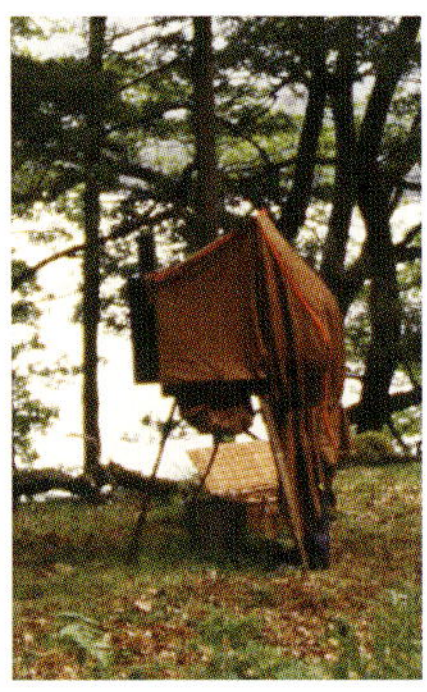

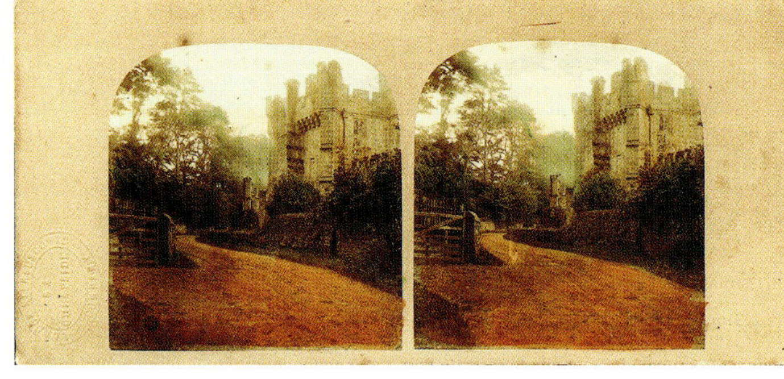

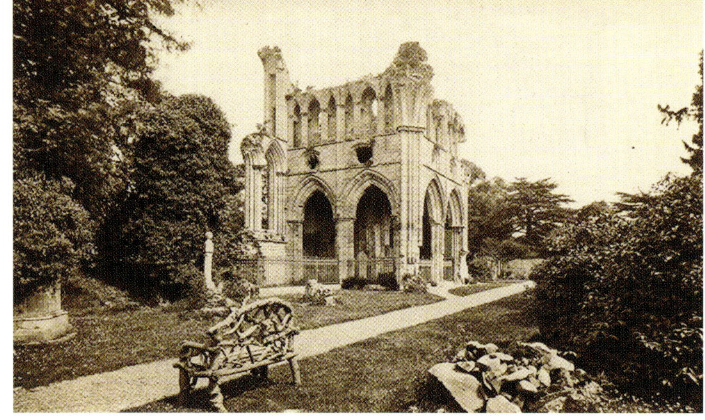

above: The photographer at work coating a plate, inside the darktent.
below: H.P. Robinson's tent designs used a yellow calico sheet draped over the arms to create the workspace. The wheelbarrow design was intended for large format work.

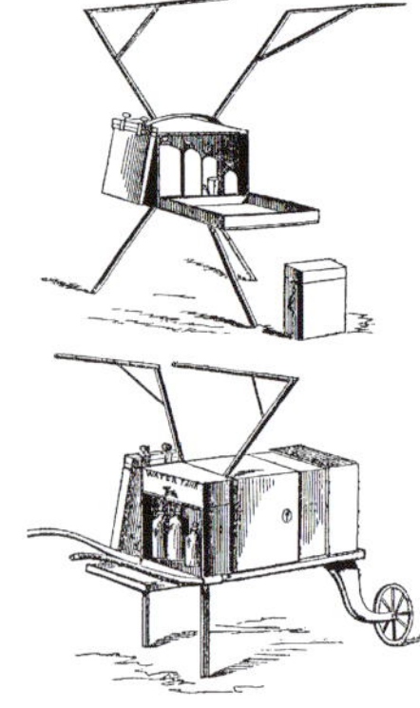

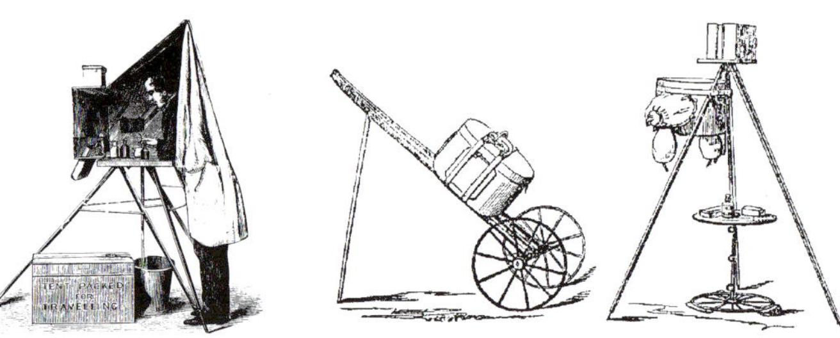

The tripod legs, when not in use to support the camera, could be strapped together to form the platform of a trolley. The trolley wheels acted as a base for the tripod, and a small ledge on which to place small items of equipment during the taking of the picture. The case, which carried the camera and lens as well as the chemicals and glass plates, doubled as a dark chamber inside which the photographer could manipulate his chemicals and coat the plate - using two light tight sleeves to gain access. A yellow glass lid to the box allowed him to see what he was doing!

In the face of all the challenges which confronted the wet collodion photographer, it is perhaps surprising that the process enjoyed such popularity.

From the professional's point of view, the ease of printing from glass negatives obviously made sense, but for amateurs, where mass production of prints was not an issue, rising to the challenges imposed by the logistics of the process made little sense. The slower Waxed Paper Process enabled the photographer to coat his paper negative materials before leaving home, and process them upon return, and ought to have been a more attractive proposition. Yet relatively few photographers adopted that process - exceptions being Roger Fenton early in his career, and several amateurs travelling in Britain and France.

Everyone else seems to have been happy to carry the heavy burden out on location, and then rise to the challenges of using the process. They also had to endure the breathing of ether fumes in the confined space of their darktents in order to produce those elusive images.

Just what impact such repeated exposure had on the health of the professional or the enthusiastic amateur has not been widely recorded, but is known to have impaired the health of many.

For some photographers, there were better reasons for eschewing the tent for something a little more substantial. Writing in the *Journal of the Photographic Society* in May 1854, one B. Jones Jun. of Cheltenham offered his fellow photographers a novel piece of advice

Sir,–I have lately accompanied a friend in some Photographic excursions, and we have adopted a plan for manipulating with collodion, which has answered admirably, but which may not have occurred to many of your readers. We fitted some yellow blinds to the windows of a fly [a small carriage], *and placed on one of the seats a large shallow box, which held all the chemicals, water, &c., and at the same time protected the cushions from stains. We had previously used a portable tent, but found it did not afford half the comfort and convenience of our darkroom on wheels, which has the additional advantage of not collecting a crowd of "gazing curious men", to say nothing of women and children, the latter of whom especially are a perfect nuisance to photographers.*

The photographic van would very soon afterwards become a common sight throughout Britain, and indeed across western Europe.

While many photographers hired carriages to carry their equipment around both in Britain and abroad, only the more successful professionals rose to the luxury of fully equipped horse-drawn darkrooms.

One solution for the photographer working not too far from the studio base was a robust handcart. This approach was suggested in 1859, the entire darkroom being contained within a wooden frame measuring 3ft x 2ft x 2ft, and supplied with a yellow calico cover to go over the photographer. A very similar design can be seen in the Italian architectural view (*right*).

Henry Peach Robinson proposed a larger version of this design in the early 1860s – intended to be pulled by a pony or a donkey if it proved too much for the assistant to manhandle!

Compare all the burden and the manipulative requirements imposed on the wet collodion photographer with those of the amateur using waxed paper!

Victorian doctor and amateur photographer Thomas Keith, lecturing to the Photographic Society of Scotland in 1856 related how he endeavoured to travel light

I sensitise my papers overnight, for in the middle of summer

below: Under the Arch of Constantine in Rome in the c.1870, an anonymous photographer set up his portable darktent to prepare and process his glass plate views of the arch itself, the Colosseum, and the nearby Arch of Titus.

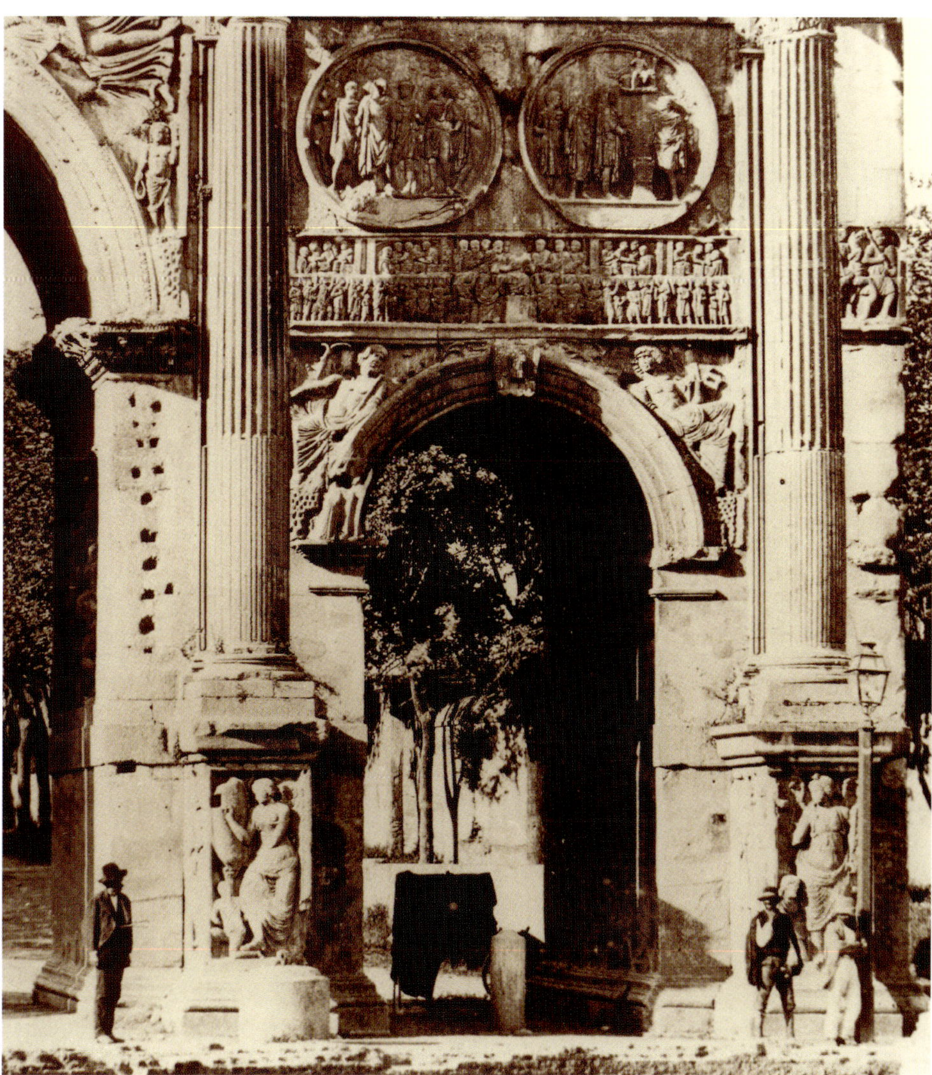

below: Watchet photographer James Date took these stereoscopic ambrotypes during extensive rebuilding of the Somerset town's harbour in 1861, after a storm. He may only have been working a few hundred yards from his Myrtle Street studio, but he would still have needed a portrable darktent on location to prepare his wet collodion plates.

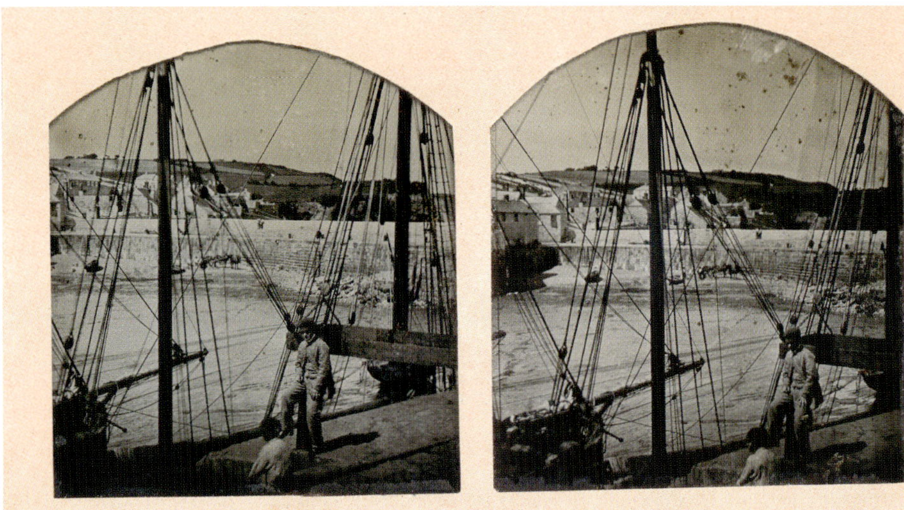

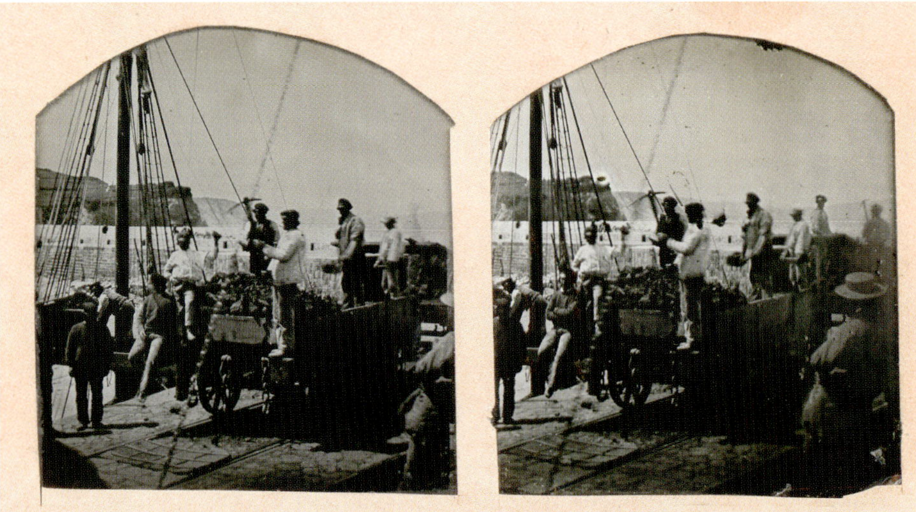

I am almost always sure of clear mornings soon after sunrise, and most of my negatives have been taken before 7 in the morning, or after 4 in the afternoon. The light is then much softer, the shadows larger, and the halftints in your pictures are more perfect, and the lights more agreeable.[7]

With all the preparatory work done at home the night before, or wherever he was staying while on holiday, the good doctor had only to carry his camera, tripod, and paper holder. In fact, he travelled only slightly heavier than a modern day photographer using a large format camera.

Processing could be carried out later that evening, or even several days or even weeks later – although few photographers left that task for more than a day, so keen were they to see the fruits of their labours.

Portability and ease of use were amongst the major attractions of the waxed paper process. Another was the early availability of roll-holders, allowing several photographs to be taken without having to carry a large number of heavy negative paper holders. Roll-holders were available for cameras taking both plain and waxed paper, greatly reducing the bulk and weight to be carried, but the longer exposures for the slower material meant that, by the early 1860s, collodion reigned supreme.

The need to prepare the wet collodion plates just before use limited any move towards 'automation', and camera backs allowing the photographer to pre-load a number of plates did not gain popularity until the introduction of the dry plate in the late 1860s.

While many of the earliest photographers were content simply to produce a record of what had been presented to their cameras, others saw that the camera offered a unique vision, and sought to understand it.

The challenge of reducing the full colour three-dimensional scene before the camera to a two dimensional monochrome image was considerable, especially when the limited colour sensitivity of the early materials was taken into consideration.

All the photographic processes in use until the 1870s

were sensitive only to blue light, causing considerable problems with the reproduction of objects of other colours. The more blue there was in any tone or colour, the darker it recorded on the negative, and the lighter on the resulting print. Trees, with their brown bark, required a long exposure before their detail could be seen on the negative – while the sky behind them needed a much shorter exposure. The green of their foliage, with a little blue in it, required somewhere in between the two.

One early photographer taking pictures in a Paris street observed that when the buildings were correctly exposed, the trees were 'not yet ready'.

That lack of sensitivity also meant that the calotype and collodion processes performed less well under bright sunlight – with dense impenetrable shadows – than it did when there was light cloud in the sky. That cloud, reflecting light into the darkest areas of the subject, opened the shadows and resulted in a more naturalistic picture.

In the earliest days of photography, few recognised the importance of the direction and character of the light, but by the later 1850s, photographic journals frequently carried letters, articles and reports of lectures by those advocating the photographer to employ the eye of the artist rather than just the skill of the scientist.

Accounts of travels, both within Great Britain and overseas, were popular lecture subjects at the growing number of photographic societies throughout the country, and many were published in contemporary magazines.

One of the most eloquent writers was Manchester photographer James Mudd, whose paper *The Artistic Arrangement of Photographic Landscapes* was read to the Manchester Photographic Society by his friend Joseph Sidebotham in spring 1858.[8]

In the introduction to his paper, Mudd summed up the appeal of architectural and landscape photography in Victorian times, and its associations with the romanticism of the age.

Landscape photography! How pleasantly the words fall upon

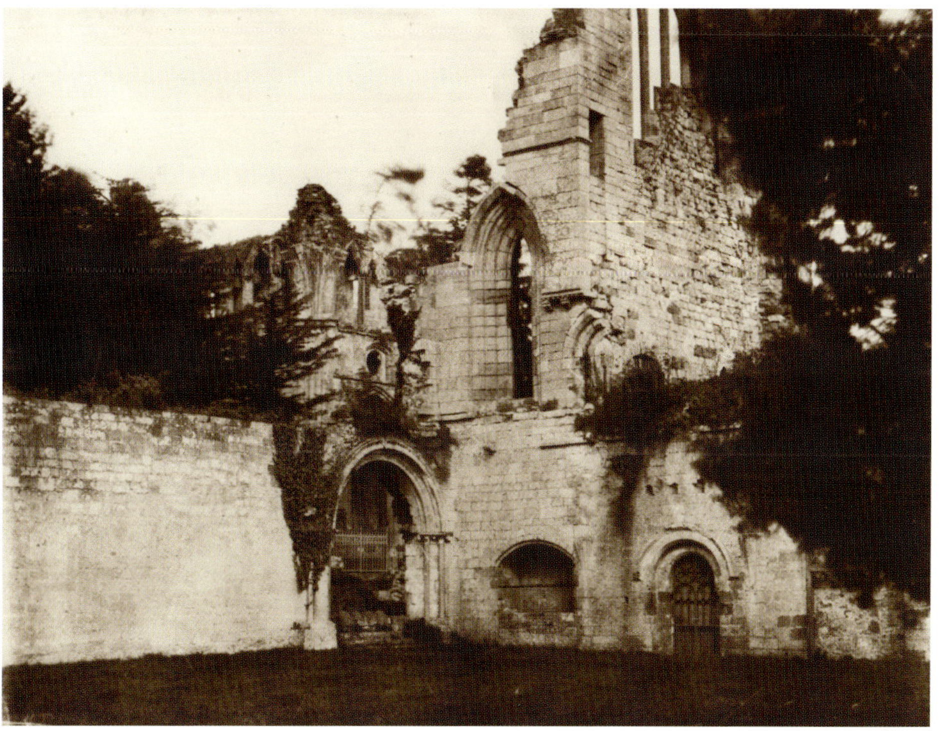

above: The Cloisters, Dryburgh Abbey, c.1855, from a waxed paper negative attributed to Thomas Keith. Even on a sunny day, the exposure time required for waxed paper was too long to freeze the movement in the foliage. The blue sensitivity of the paper negative meant that by the time the stonework was correctly exposed, the sky was grossly overexposed – solid black on the negative, light on the print. Lecturing about his technique to the Photographic Society of Scotland in 1856, Keith remarked "if you were to ask me to what circumstance more than any other I attribute my success, I should say, not any peculiarity whatever in my manipulation, or to any particular strength in the solutions I employ, but entirely to this, that I never expose my papers unless the light is first rate. This I have now made a rule, and nothing ever induces me to deviate from it."

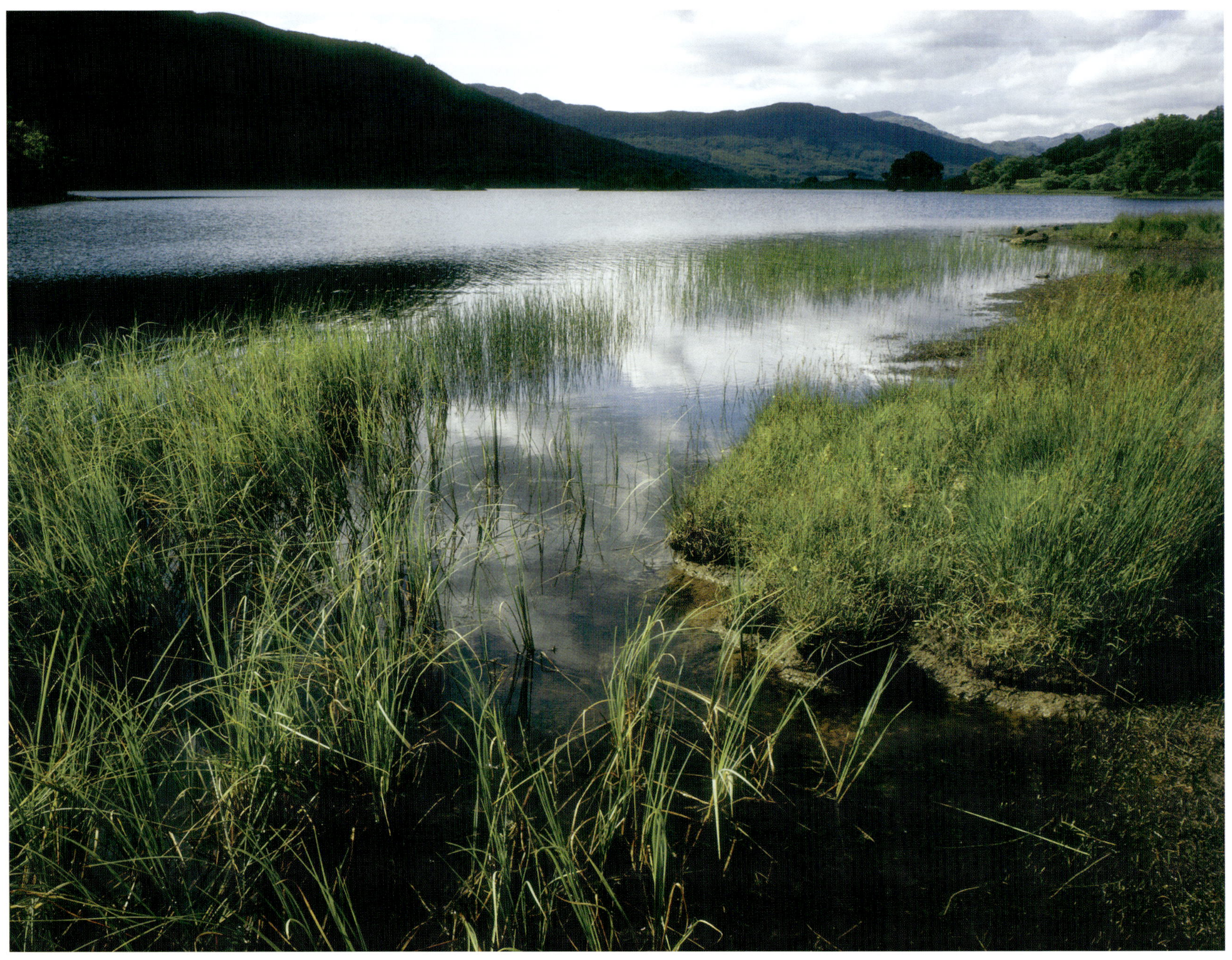

the ear of the enthusiastic photographer. What agreeable associations are connected with our excursions in the country. How often have we wandered along the rough sea-shore, or climbed the breezy hill-side, or descended into the shady valley, or toiled along the rocky bed of some mountain stream, forgetting, in the excitement of our pursuit, the burdens we carried, or the roughness of the path we trod. What delightful hours have we passed in wandering through the quiet ruins of some venerable abbey, impressing, with wondrous truth, upon the tablets we carried, the marvellous beauty of Gothic window, of broken column and ivy-wreathed arch. How pleasant our visits to moss-green old churches, and picturesque cottages, and stately castles, and a thousand pretty nooks, in the shady wood, by the river side, or in the hedge-rows, where the twining wild convolvulus, the bramble, and luxuriant fern have arrested us in our wanderings.[9]

So, Mudd would clearly not have approved of the sterile sites of ancient abbeys and castles today – the over manicured lawns, the removal of all creepers and undergrowth in the name of preservation.

In other publications, the clinical approach to preserved buildings which we endure today was almost predicted, and its effect on photography understood! Writing in the journal *Photographic Notes* on March 22nd 1857, a writer, reviewing a photograph of the Baptistry at Canterbury Cathedral noted:

What would become of our picture if the reverend authorities at Canterbury had ordered a gardener before it was taken, to fresh gravel the path, and clear away the rubbish from the lawn to the right. This would merely be putting the foreground a little tidy, and the principal object in the view would remain untouched. The Baptistry of Canterbury would still be there, with its crumbling stones and clumps of ivy and quaint old windows, and it would have a better approach and look more respectable. But would this improve our picture? Certainly not.[10]

Today, the travelling photographer searching for the 'broken column and the ivy-wreathed arch' referred to by

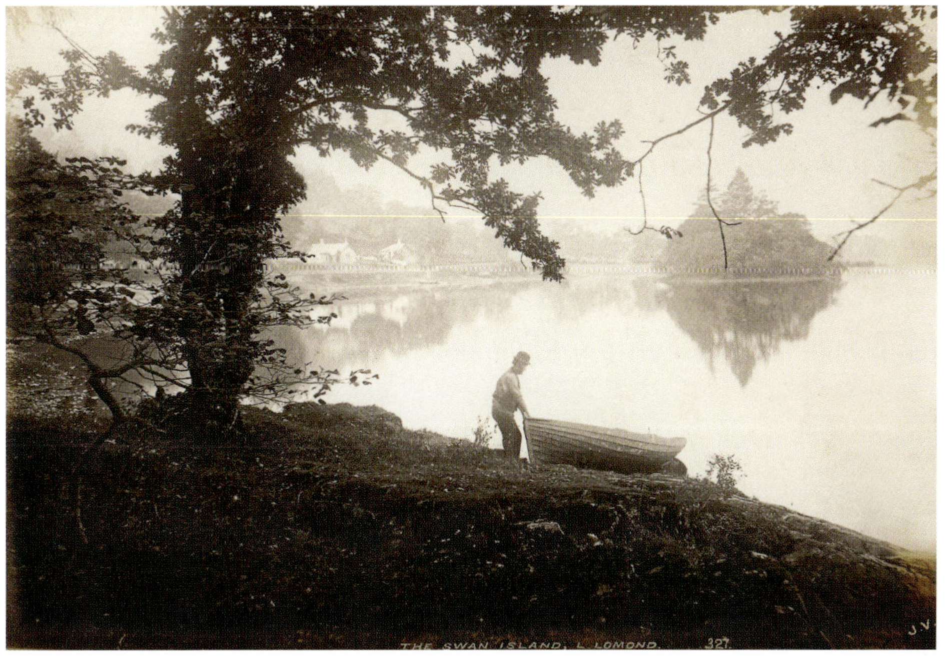

opposite page: Loch Chon, Trossachs. Soft lighting like this was preferred to intense bright sunlight by Victorian photographers, despite the length of exposure it imposed on them. However, they would have avoided the sort of foreground detail evident in this view, as any movement during the exposure would be more evident in close up. This view was taken with a modern 4x5 view camera, the direct descendant of the folding bellows camera first introduced in the 1850s.
above: The Swan Island, Loch Lomond, c.1870, by James Valentine. The use of the silhouetted figure adds depth and contrast to the image, as well as reinforcing the romantic idyll developed and perpetuated in so much Victorian writing about the landscape in general and Scotland in particular.

Mudd, is likely to be disappointed. The overgrown ruined abbey, seen by the Victorians as a romantic reminder of a past age being slowly reclaimed by nature, now survives only in a very few locations.

James Mudd, who took every opportunity to visit such places, was a great advocate of the waxed paper negative, and later for the collodion dry plate. Having eulogised about the pleasures of photography in the landscape, he observed that

> *I can scarcely imagine the same amount of pleasure in connection with the laborious duties of a tent. The constant occupation of time in preparing, exposing, and completing the plate on the spot, leaves but little leisure for enjoying the beauties of the scene around, while the demand upon the physical powers is something considerable. I have known photographers who remember, with no very pleasant sensations, their voluntary incarceration in the portable tent, or what may not inappropriately be called (remembering its Indian temperature sometimes), the photographic "black hole".*[11]

Notwithstanding Mudd's opinion, history tells us that the majority of photographers thought the manipulative demands simply the price they had to pay for the highest image quality.

One of the great qualities of early photographers was their evangelical zeal for the new process, and their willingness to share ideas, improvements, or just simple advice, with their fellows.

That advice ranged from identifying hotels willing to allow photographers to process negatives in their rooms, to recommending the best sort of boxes to pack materials in. Several photographic magazines shared stories, so advice given to French photographers in *La Lumière*, could reappear in the *Journal of the Photographic Society*. That is how advice from Monsieur F. A. Oppenheim on travelling with a camera in Spain was brought to the attention of British photographers in 1851. Oppenheim wrote

> *For taking photographs in Spain, it will be well to provide*

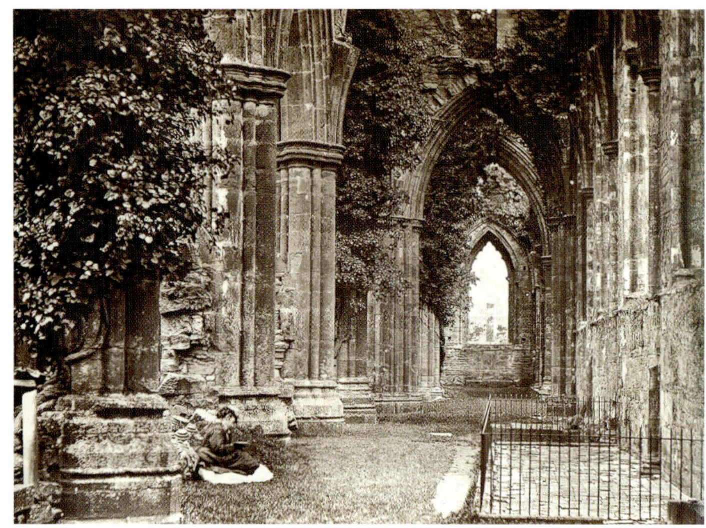

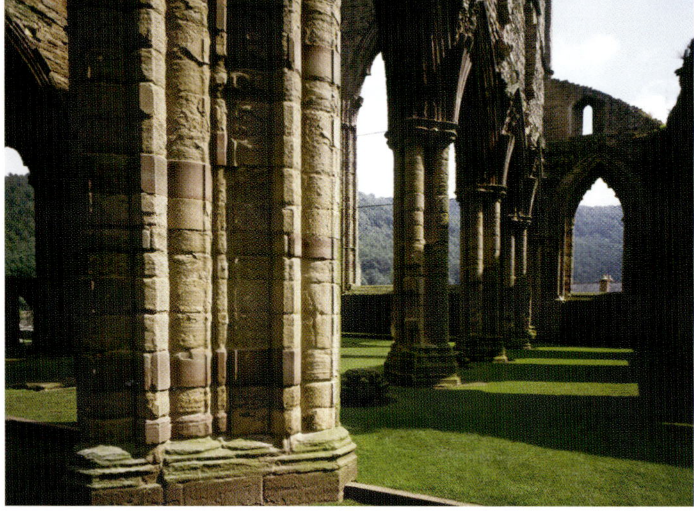

right: The South Aisle, Tintern Abbey, photographed c.1870 by the splendidly named Horatio Nelson King. When King visited Tintern it was a romantic overgrown ruin in the best tradition of the "broken column and the ivy-wreathed arch" referred to by James Mudd. *below right:* The same aisle today, manicured, cleaned and sterile by comparison. *opposite page:* Jervaulx Abbey in Yorkshire, still privately owned, presents a scene today which any Victorian travel photographer would have recognised as the norm – wild flowers grow in the ruins, cascades of colour spilling out of holes in the walls and over fallen stones.

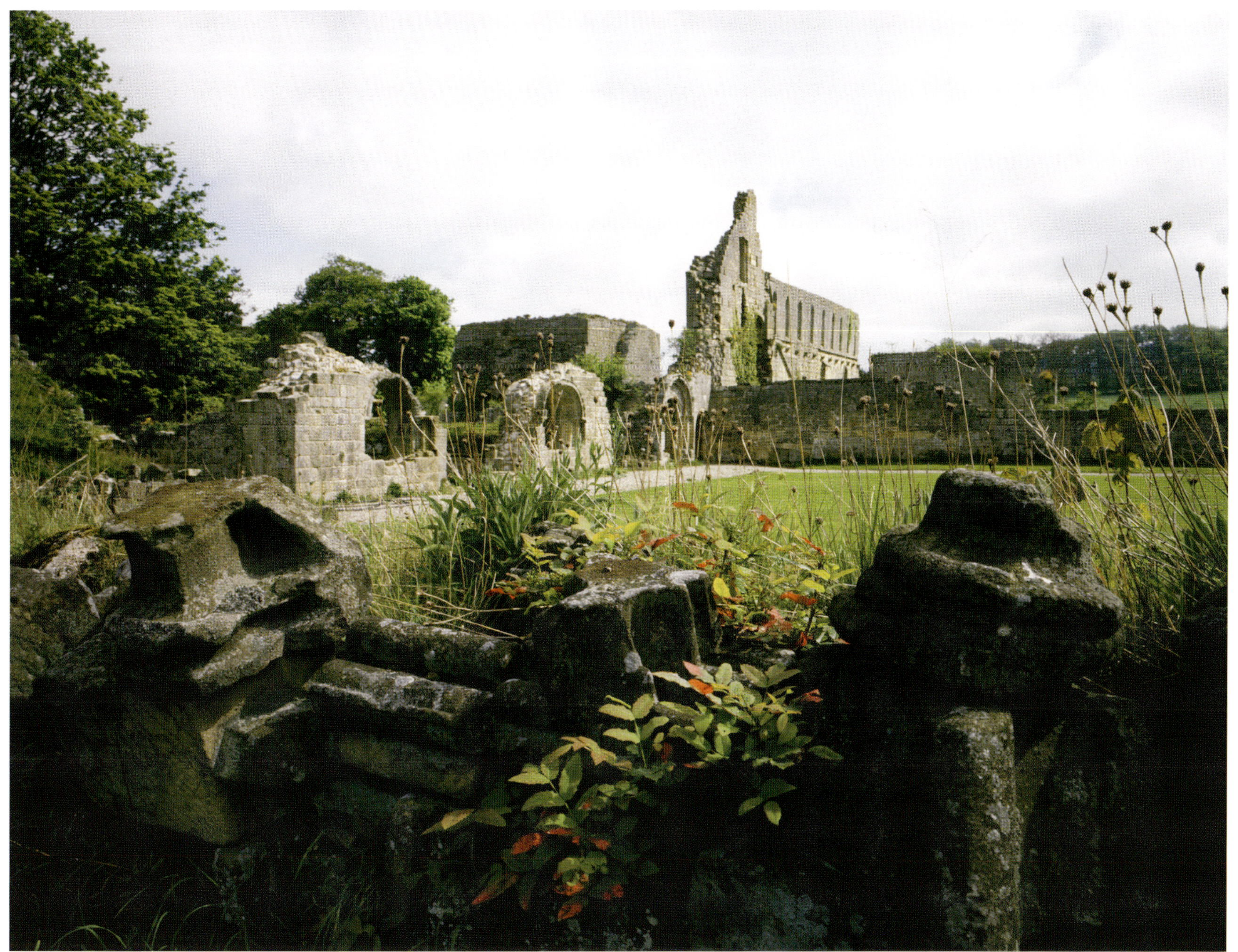

below: Alcazar, Seville, photographed by John Stuart, c.1870 and published in Walter Bentley Woodbury's *Treasure Spots of the World*. The addition of a figure to give the viewer a sense of scale had already become an established tradition. Stuart contributed views from Spain, Gibraltar and Belgium to the book

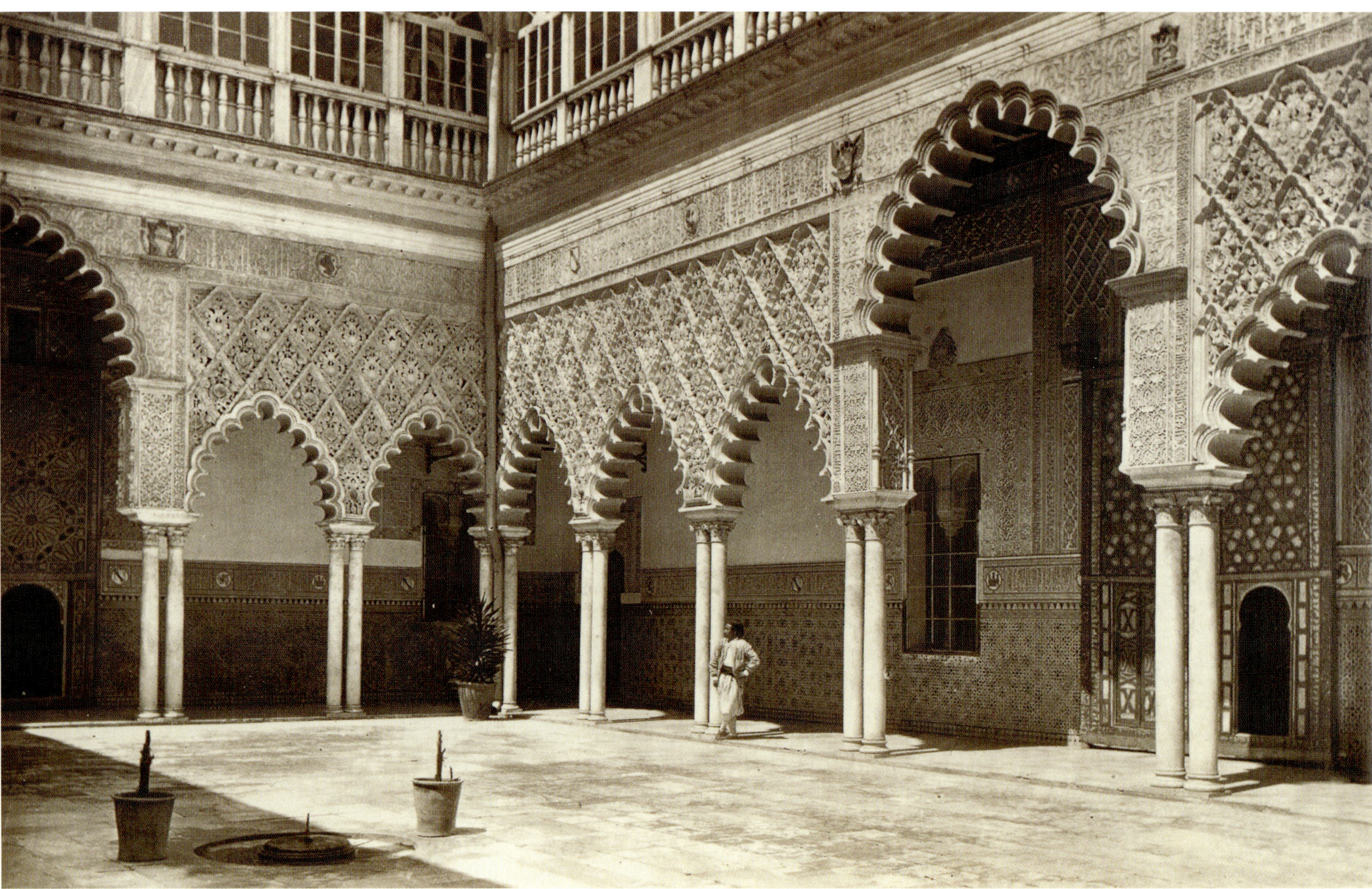

a lens of very short focus, because most of the monuments are surrounded by houses, which prevent the choice of a very distant point of view. At the same time, the complaisance of the inhabitants when one asks permission to enter their houses with one's instruments, cannot but be praised. It will also be well to learn the rules of the customs' officers, and to conform to them as much as possible. I allow readily that a better plan might be found; but I found it requisite, in each town where I wished to stay, to take all my photographic objects and show them at the custom house, both on arriving and departing.[12]

Today's photographers might think that little has changed, as it is still a good idea of declare photographic equipment on entering many countries. Today's photographers have the additional challenge of the ubiquitous airport X-ray machine. Interestingly, in all the travels for this book, hand-searching of my camera and film bags to avoid repeated passage through the X-rays has been readily agreed to everywhere except UK airports.

Oppenheim's problems were a little greater than mine when it came to materials. Keeping my film cool and away from a succession of airport scanners pales into insignificance when compared with the need to either carry every conceivable chemical across Europe, or seek a reliable supply on location.

Travellers must not expect to find good distilled water everywhere... I met with it only in Madrid and Granada. At Seville, for example, I applied to the first pharmaceutical establishment, but could not use the water they sent me; so that a little still is almost indispensable. It is still less to be expected to find chemical products fit to use.[13]

Oppenheim was using the Waxed Paper process. Later photographers using collodion found even greater problems if they did not travel fully prepared.

Travellers wrote to the photographic press with feedback on their experiences for the benefit of their fellows. One writer warned against carrying glass or porcelain utensils due to their fragility - observing that being transported

below: An old man sits in a shady corner of the square in Pienza, Tuscany, while the late evening sublight illuminates the alley behind him. With sophisticated modern film and digital cameras, today's photographer can capture the spirit of a place in ways denied to the Victorian traveller.

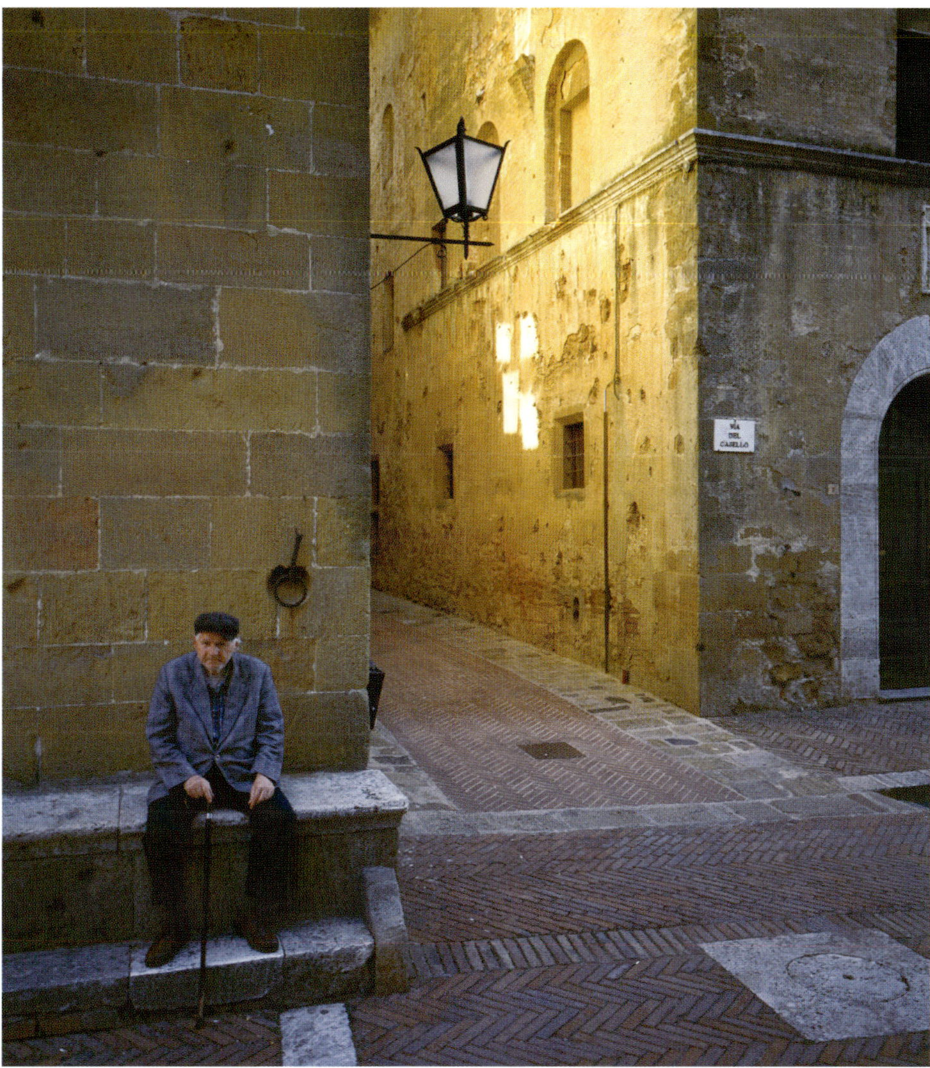

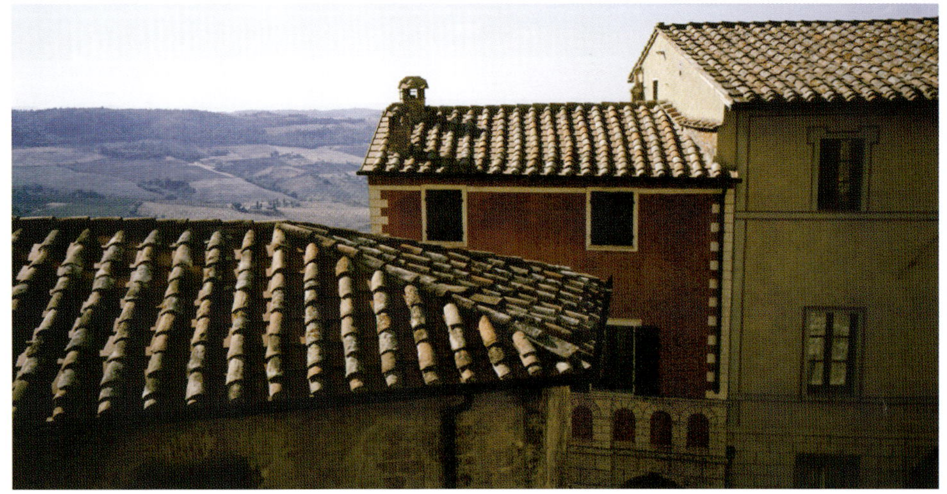

above: The subtle tints of early autumn, and the crisp oblique sunlight on the pantile rooftops of Montepulciano, combine to make an evocative statement about the architecture and landscape of Tuscany.

opposite page: The Forum, Rome, photographer unknown, late 1860s. The Victorian travelling photographer could avail himself of plenty of advice in contemporary manuals on how to compose and take a good photograph. Not only were clear instructions available for mixing and using the chemicals involved in collodion photography, but guidance on how and where to set up the camera was also offered. In Lake Price's book *A Manual of Photographic Manipulation*, the author proposed the following 'memoranda' which might almost have been describing the recommended technical requirements for taking and processing this picture - "The Forum, Rome; foreground, the Temple of Saturn within fifty yards of the lens, the Colosseum half a mile, both included in the picture; size 18x14; lens No.3, Ross orthos.; 5/8 diphragm; Thomas's collodion; bath 30 grams recrystallised nitrate, just acid, three minutes exposure; development, pyrogallic acid 1$^1/_2$ grain, when well out, the picture being large, strengthened with twenty minims nit.sol. thirty grains strength - Result fine creamy negative."

across Europe rattling about in packaging cases was not good for delicate vessels. Another reported that his porcelain dishes had been broken as a result of being too well packed - the wooden cases into which they had been tightly fitted had shrunk under the heat of a Mediterranean summer, shattering the dishes in the process!

Mass produced dry plates were introduced in the 1860s, albeit rather less sensitive initially than their wet counterparts. Photographers were, understandably, reluctant to exploit the advantages of the dry plate - of waiting until they returned home before processing their negatives. Writer and photographer William Lake Price wrote, in 1868, that

> *whilst, at the same time the photographer may, in these railway times, be several hundred miles distant from the pet subject of which he fondly imagines he has a transcript safely in his baggage, but of which illusion subsequent development proves the fallacy; the only certain way is to see the result before leaving the spot.*[14]

Waxed Paper photographers were already accustomed to processing later, but usually in their hotel rooms at night, rather than after travelling home.

The reliability of materials which we take for granted was a long time coming, and those materials earned the confidence of photographers only very slowly.

The dry plate represented a step into the dark for many photographers who modified their processing, or modified their exposures depending on the appearance of the developed plate.

Today's understanding of the importance of correct exposure, and correct development to ensure optimum image quality was still some way in the future when photographers manufactured their own materials.

The development of the wet plate negative could be observed in the darktent by the yellow light which filtered in through the calico covering. Thus the photographer could curtail the development if the plate seemed to be darkening too quickly, or extend the time if the image was appearing

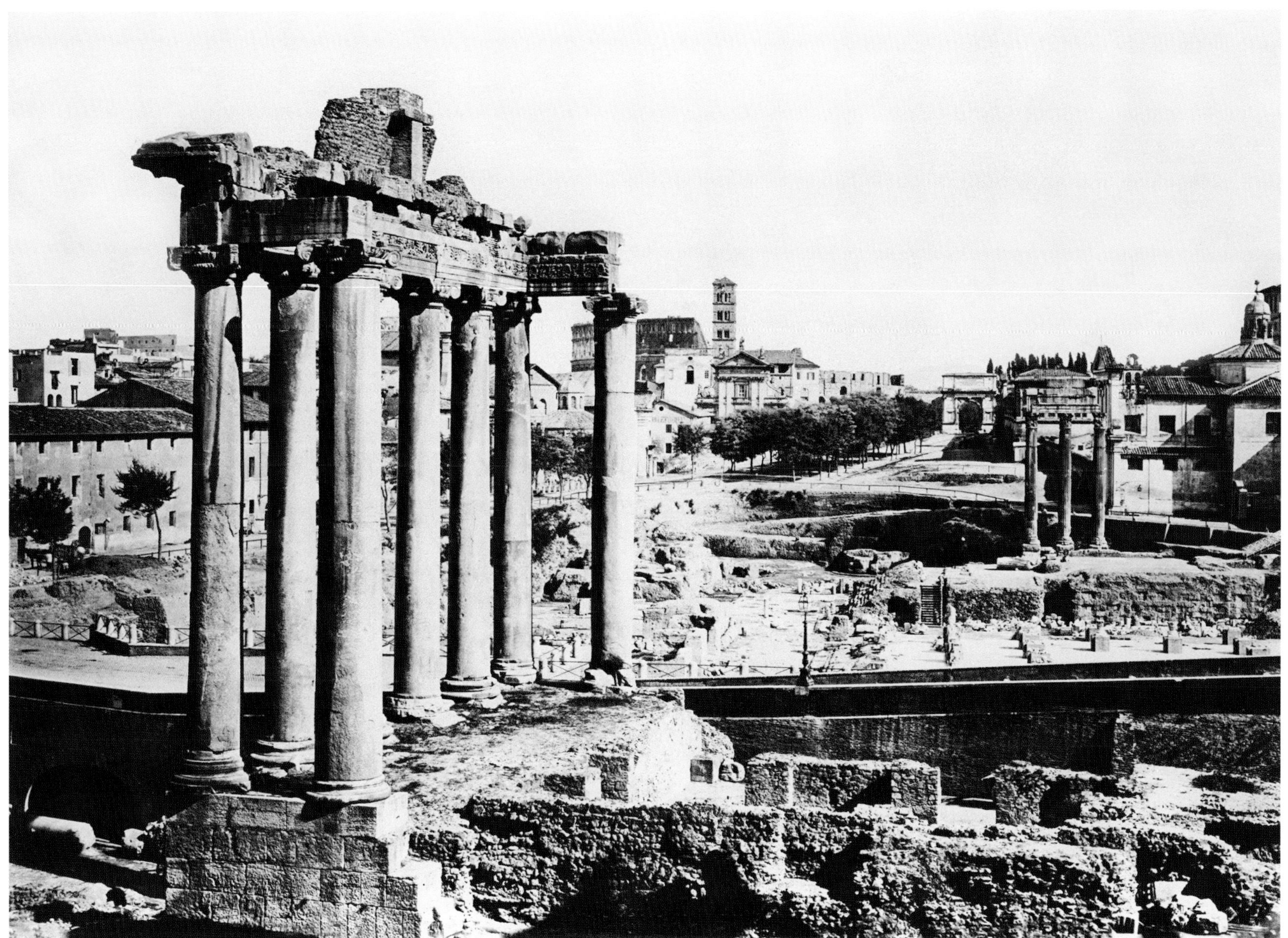

only very slowly. Only towards the end of the century would there be a full understanding of the implications of such decisions on the contrast, tonal representation and shadow or highlight detail in the negative. If the estimated exposure had been completely awry, then another negative could always be coated and exposed.

The further the photographer was away from home, the more important the need to be certain the plates were correctly exposed. Thus, while dry plates were available from the 1850s, few photographers trusted them away from home.

A notable exception was the Rome-based Scottish photographer Robert Macpherson, whose achievements with early dry plates from around 1856 were remarkable. Of course, by largely limiting his work to Rome and its environs, he was never too far away from a location should a reshoot be necessary.

It would be the 1870s before the dry plate really established itself, by which time manufacturing techniques had improved to a point where reliability could be assumed. On only one of these great photographic journeys - John Thomson's 1878 tour in Cyprus - were dry plates used.

Several of the earlier photographers travelled light with waxed paper negatives prepared before leaving home, but there is no evidence that any of them waited until returning to Britain before developing their papers. As will be recounted, the practice adopted by Henry Fox Talbot in Edinburgh of using his hotel room as a darkroom was widely emulated. The most widely used process on location was wet collodion.

That these pioneers created the vast and illuminating photographic heritage that has been passed down to us today using such complicated and fickle processes is a striking testament to their skill and perseverance.

Their achievements offer us a fresh perspective on the challenges we face when travelling with our cameras today.

Notes

1. Walter Woodbury *Treasure Spots of the World*, London, Ward, Lock & Tyler, Paternoster Row, 1875.
2. Quoted from a paper read by Sir David Brewster to the inaugural meeting of the Photographic Society of Scotland, April 8th 1856, reported in *Photographic Notes*, vol.1, no.1, p8.
3. Marcus Sparling, *Theory and Practice of the Photographic Art, Including its Chemistry and Optics*, London, Houlston and Stoneman, Paternoster Row, and Wm. S. Orr and Co., Amen Corner, 1856, p93.
4. From George Washington Wilson's diaries, October 1863, reprinted in Roger Taylor, *George Washington Wilson, Artist & Photographer*, Aberdeen: Aberdeen University Press, 1981, p100. The original diary is in the Gernsheim Collection, Humanities Research Centre, University of Texas at Austin.
5. *The Journal of the Photographic Society*, later *The Photographic Journal*, and now *The RPS Journal*, has been published continuously since 1853, making it the longest-established photographic magazine in the world.
6. N. S. Heineken's description of his dark tent was published in detail in *The Photographic Journal*, Dec 15th 1859, p109.
7. Dr. Keith's lecture was read to the monthly meeting of the Photographic Society of Scotland on June 10th 1856, and reproduced in full in *Photographic Notes*, vol.1, no.8, July 17th 1856, pp101-104.
8. Extracts from a paper read by James Mudd to the Manchester Photographic Society, reproduced in *Liverpool & Manchester Photographic Journal*, vol.2, no.4, February 15th 1858, pp43-46.
9. ibid.
10. ibid.
11. ibid.
12. F.A. Oppenheim "Notes for Travelling Photographers", originally published in *La Lumière*, April 9th 1851, revised by the writer and reproduced in *The Journal of the Photographic Society*, vol.1, no.4, May 2nd 1853, p50-53.
13. ibid. p51
14. William Lake Price, *A Manual of Photographic Manipulation*, London: John Churchill & Sons, 1868, p191

Roger Fenton

Journeys to Russia 1852 and 1855

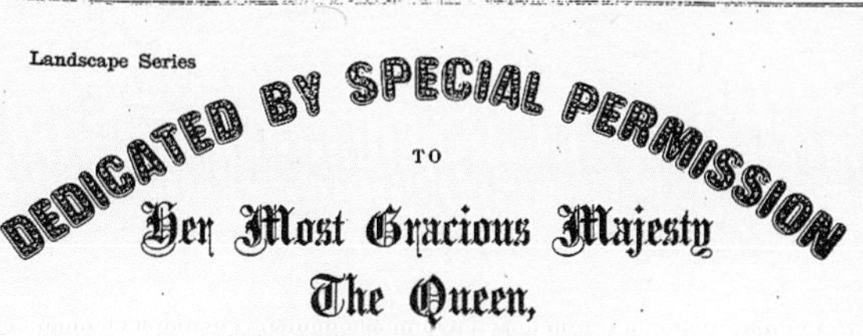

Landscape Series

DEDICATED BY SPECIAL PERMISSION

TO

Her Most Gracious Majesty

The Queen,

AND UNDER THE PATRONAGE OF

His Imperial Majesty the Emperor of the French,

AND

His Royal Highness Prince Albert.

PHOTOGRAPHS

By Roger Fenton, Esq. B.A.

OF THE

SEAT OF WAR IN THE CRIMEA.

THE Series of VIEWS, GROUPS, and PORTRAITS, was taken by Mr. FENTON during the Spring and Summer of 1855, and is intended to illustrate faithfully the Scenery of the Camps; to display prominent incidents of Military Life, as well as to perpetuate the Portraits of those distinguished Officers, who have taken part in the ever memorable SIEGE OF SEBASTOPOL.

MANCHESTER: THOMAS AGNEW AND SONS, EXCHANGE STREET,

Publishers and Printsellers to the Queen.

LONDON: P. AND D. COLNAGHI AND CO., PALL MALL EAST.

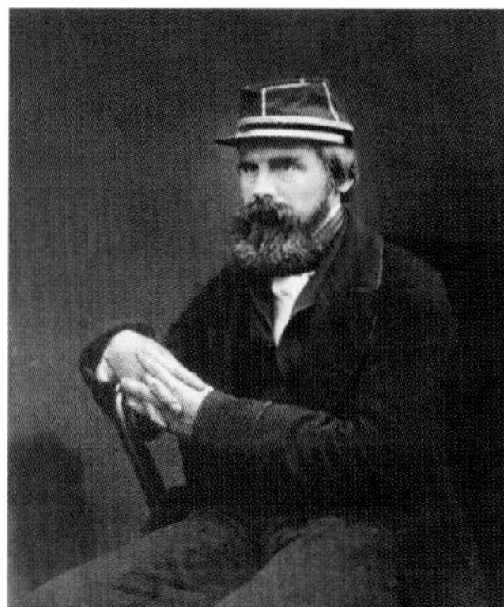

above: Roger Fenton wearing a Kepi, photographed by Dr. Hugh Diamond

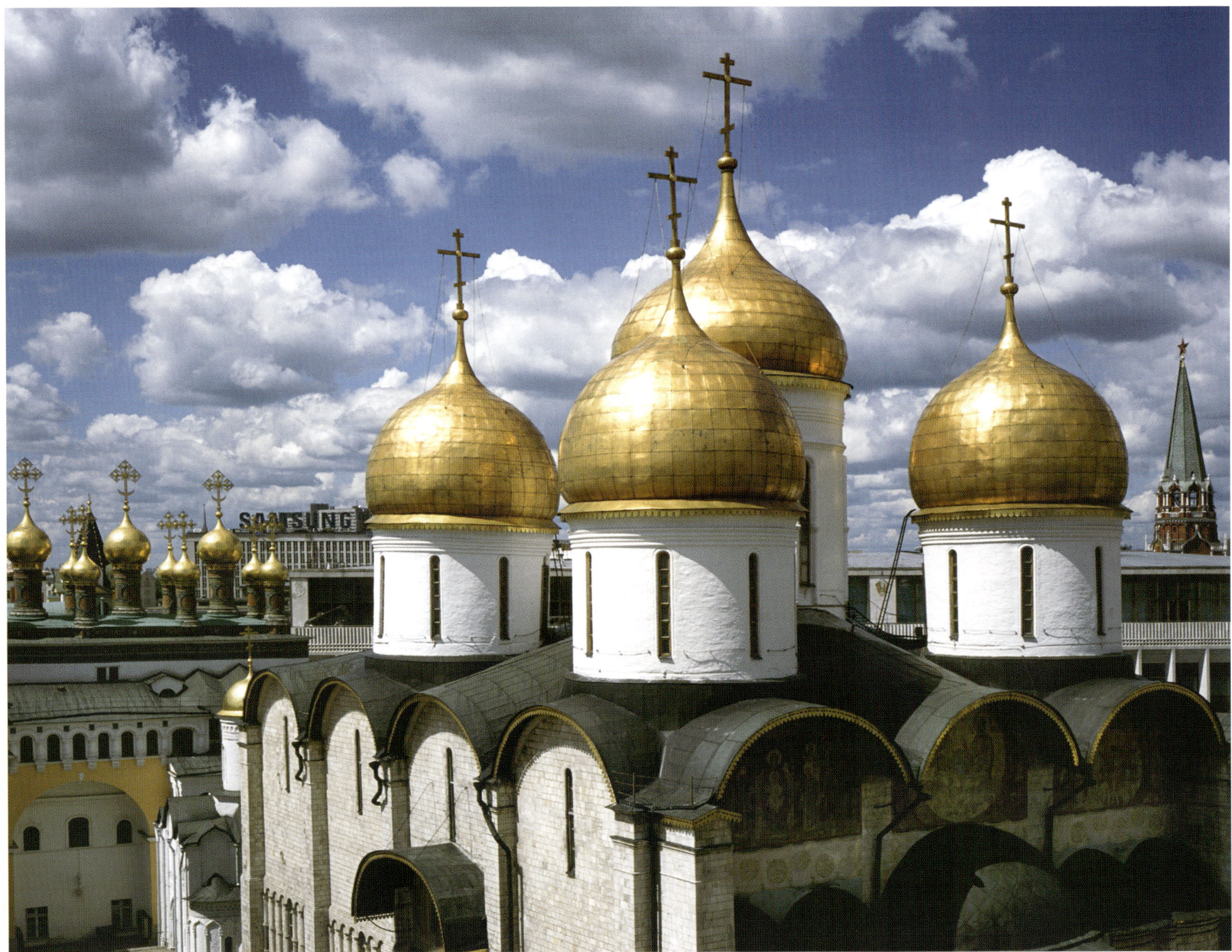

Climbing up the dark and narrow spiral staircase, my camera bag was bouncing and rubbing against the central pillar as I used my left hand to grip the worn handrail. How on earth, I asked myself, had Roger Fenton and his travelling companions got up there in 1852 with their heavy wooden whole plate cameras, tripods and other paraphernalia?

I was on my way up Ivan the Great's Gate Tower at the edge of the Kremlin's Cathedral Square, making for the ledge from which Fenton had taken his best known Russian view – of the domes of the beautiful Cathedral of the Assumption, a 15th century masterpiece of Russian church architecture.

Thanks to the Kremlin authorities who had uniquely granted me access to the tower which has long been closed to the public – albeit with an armed military escort – I was about to stand where Fenton had stood a century and a half before me. My plan was to reinterpret his famous picture using a modern camera and modern colour film.

It was not unusual, even as early as 1852, for a few special visitors to be given guided tours of the Kremlin. Fenton, the first visitor to Moscow with a camera, would certainly have been considered as just such an honoured guest. It was, perhaps, easier for him than it was for me – as he visited in the days before health and safety were important considerations. But he, like me, would have been accompanied by a member of the Kremlin staff as he made his way up the narrow staircase.

Fenton's cameras were of the large wooden sliding box design which had become familiar to British photographers during the calotype era, and were equally well suited to the more versatile waxed paper process, which gave the travelling photographer unprecedented freedom from the need to coat and prepare the paper negatives just before use. Waxed paper, where the paper was waxed before sensitising, not only allowed the material to be prepared well before use – indeed Fenton had prepared his materials before leaving London – but also restricted the light sensitive

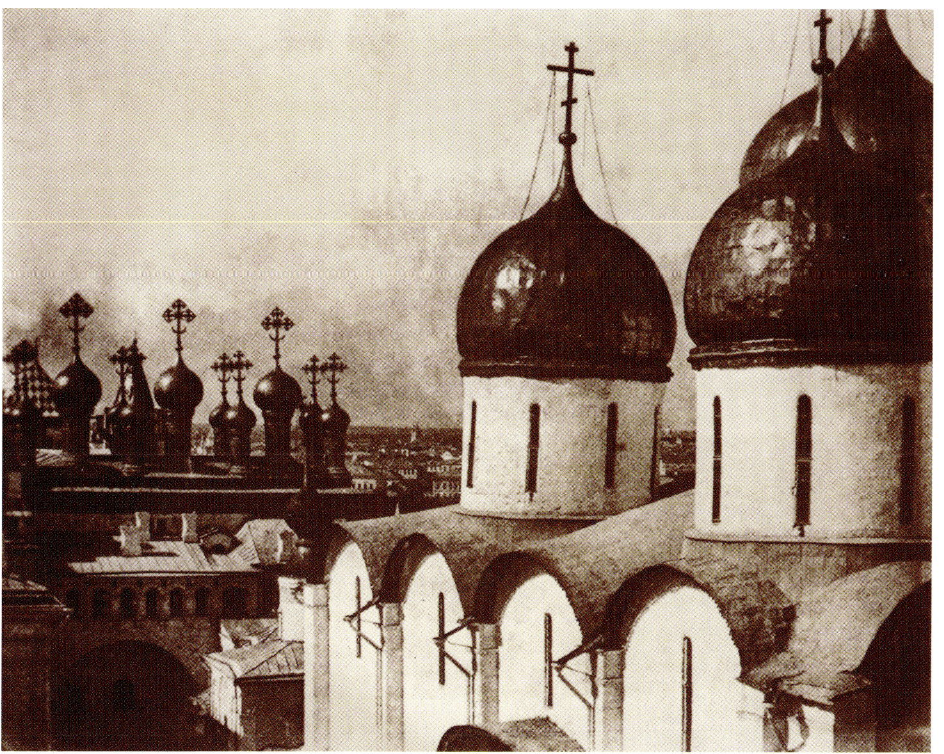

above: The most celebrated image to survive from Roger Fenton's visit to Moscow in late autumn 1852 is this view of the Cathedral of the Assumption in the Kremlin's Cathedral Square. The blue sensitive waxed paper negative material which Fenton used could not accurately reproduce the tone of the gold domes, recording only minimal exposure on the negative, and resulting in almost maximum density on the salted paper print.
opposite page: In contrast, a modern colour transparency shot from the same ledge on Ivan the Great's Bell Tower shows how little the scene has changed in the intervening century and a half. Beyond the domes, the upper floors of the 1961 Palace of Congresses can be seen, built on the site of earlier monasteries, and beyond that, a modern office block topped with a 'Samsung' advertising neon.

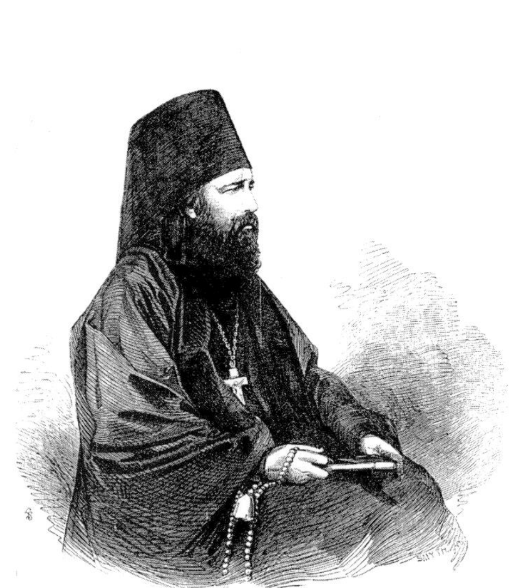

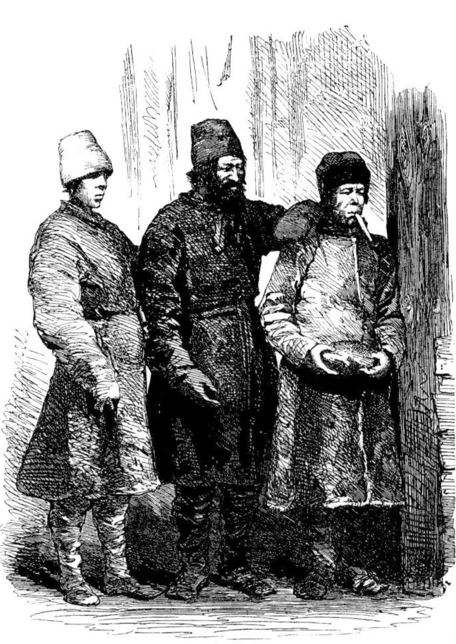

above left: 'Priest of the Greek Church' appeared as a woodcut in the *Illustrated London News* in the issue published November 19th 1853. It was described in the caption as being from a calotype by Fenton, although every surviving image from the Russian journey is described as being taken on waxed paper. Indeed, his pamphlet on the waxed paper process had been published shortly before he departed for Russia. Did Fenton use the faster calotype process for this and other portraits? This opens a whole new area of research into his early photography. Charles Vignoles exhibited a portrait by Fenton, simply entitled 'A Monk' at the Dundee Infirmary Fund exhibition in March 1854 – despite being described as 'on collodion' in the catalogue, might this be the pictures?
above right: 'Russian Peasants', based on another of Fenton's Russian portraits, appeared in the *Illustrated London News* on February 4th 1854. Given the costumes and the architectural clues in the engraving, the likely location for this portrait would be somewhere near the bridge construction site at Kiev. Neither of the original photographs upon which these engravings are based has yet been located.

chemistry to a thin surface coating, giving enhanced image sharpness and a much finer image structure than had been possible with the calotype.

In one of Fenton's pictures of St Mikhail's monastery in Kiev, an example of which survives in the RPS Collection,[1] a camera suitable for waxed paper photography can be seen. This may be a second camera for Fenton, or one belonging to his travelling companion and fellow photographer, John Cooke Bourne.

The two men were in Russia to photograph construction work on the first permanent bridge to be built over the Dnipro River in Kiev, and took the opportunity to see something of the country while they were there. Whilst they travelled by ship to St Petersburg, I flew via Frankfurt, but from then onwards we both used the train.

Fenton was in Russia not primarily as a tourist, although his visits to Moscow and St Petersburg do seem to have been purely for his own interest.

In St Petersburg, as indeed in Moscow and Kiev, Fenton indulged his passion for architecture, especially religious architecture, photographing monasteries, convents and cathedrals – all of which abounded in Czarist Russia, and still abound today. He did not ignore the locals though, and despite the long exposures needed for his waxed paper negatives, he took several images of local children, clergy and peasants. While the originals of these have long since been lost, woodblock engravings from two of them were published by the *Illustrated London News* after his return home.

Considering the fact that Fenton was in Russia to photograph the construction of Charles Vignoles' bridge over the Dnipro (Dneiper) river in Kiev, surprisingly few of his pictures of that project survive.

He had travelled to Russia with the engineer Charles Vignoles, and the photographer and eminent railway artist John Cooke Bourne.

Bourne was the official photographer on the project,[2] and Fenton had apparently been invited along because he had experience of taking stereoscopic photographs, and Vignoles was presumably interested in having a three-dimensional record of progress on the site as well as a two-dimensional one.

It is uncertain how many exposures the two men made during their visit, but only a little more than a handful of images by Fenton have been located. An important body of work by J. C. Bourne from his second visit in 1853 has recently been rediscovered, and there are tantalising suggestions that his 1852 images may still survive, albeit in a poor state of preservation.[3]

The images of the bridge construction are remarkable, not least because they represent the first industrial photography project undertaken in what was then Imperial Russia.

The bridge construction was a wholly British project. Vignoles was engineer in charge, most of the construction materials were manufactured in, and imported from, Britain, and the photographers recording the progress of the project were both British.

At 2562ft. in length, the six span chain-suspension bridge would have been a major undertaking at home. To undertake it thousands of miles from home must have been a considerable challenge.

Work started in September 1848, and it was opened to traffic on October 10th 1853. A total of 3,500 tons of ironwork were manufactured in England and shipped to Odesa on the Black Sea. The main contractors for that ironwork were Fox Henderson & Co. of London and Birmingham, with Musgrove & Sons of Bolton (then known as Bolton-le-Moors) manufacturing the remainder at their Globe Works.[4]

Kiev (the English spelling was Kief or Kieff at the time, but the preferred spelling in Ukraine today is Kyiv) was a relatively small city on the Dnipro river, and was home to a military garrison. Each year, for decades, if not centuries, when the ice on the river melted, a new wooden floating bridge had been constructed over the river to give the

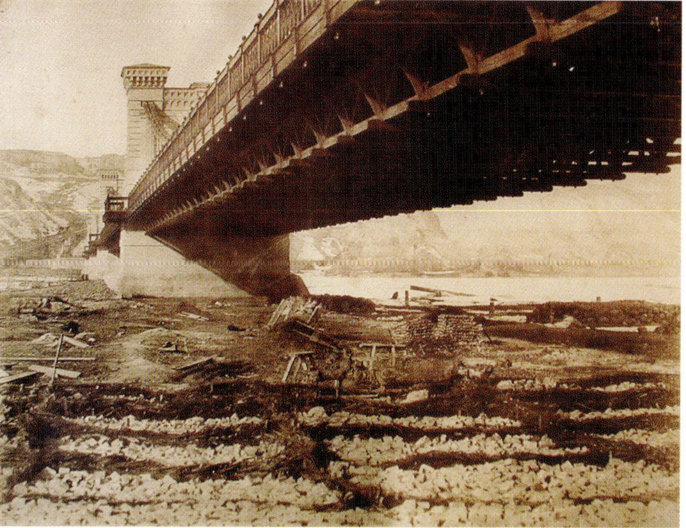

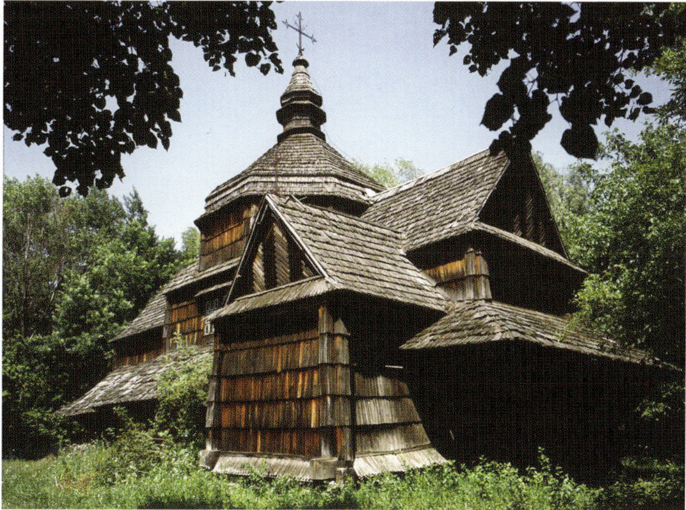

left: The Nikolaskyy Most. Vignoles bridge over the Dnipro River at Kiev photographed by John Cook Bourne during his last visit in September 1853, just a few weeks before it opened. This rare image is one of only a very few examples of Bourne's work so far discovered. For this journey, Bourne took a large format camera for paper negatives – probably calotypes – and a smaller camera for collodion glass negatives.

below left: This wooden church, now preserved in the open air museum of Ukrainian life at Pigorov, is typical of the sorts of buildings Fenton and Bourne would have encountered as they travelled in the countryside surrounding the bridge construction site.

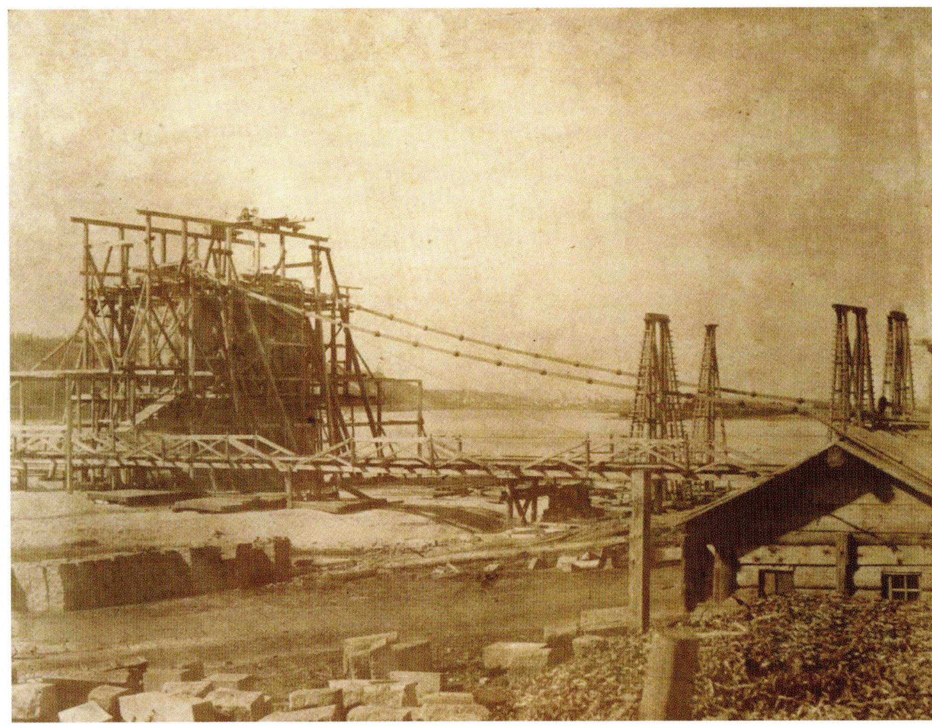

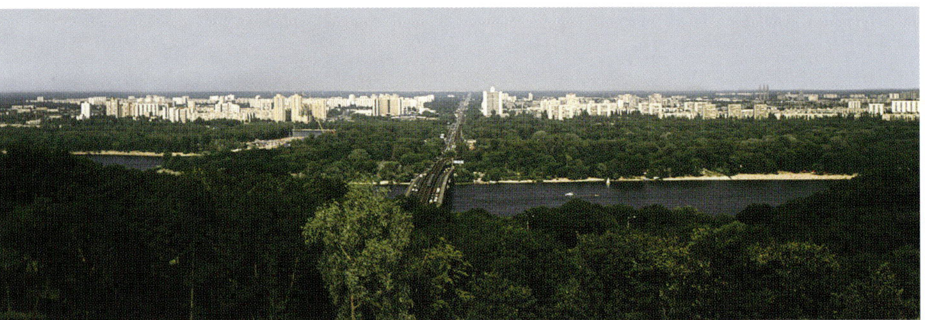

military access to the area to the east of the city. Vignoles' Bridge was the first permanent crossing of the river.

At the time of their 1852 visit, with a year to go before opening, Vignoles, Fenton and Bourne would have seen a bridge far from completion. A number of Fenton's surviving pictures show the 1852 floating bridge, while others show construction work being undertaken on the west side of the river.

The trio probably arrived in Kiev on September 25th, and started work on the photography the next day. Vignoles noted in his diary that

> *This was one of the finest days of the year – though cool in the early Morning the Weather was deliciously warm all day with a manificent Atmosphere. Arranging with Mr. Bourne and Mr. Fenton about the first subject to be taken for the Calotypes and the stereoscopic views of the Works in detail.*[5]

A number of Fenton's images were recently discovered in Rio de Janeiro, and it is conjectured that they were used by Vignoles while tendering for a bridge project in Brazil in the mid 1850s. These include views of the scaffolding surrounding the partly built bridge piers, and details of the raising of the first of the great chains which would eventually support the roadway.

A stereoscopic pair discovered recently in Britain shows a general view of the construction site, and it is hoped that continued research will help identify others.

Fenton's journey was important in the evolution of photography, as he was perhaps the first British photographer to travel abroad with pre-coated paper negatives. Earlier travellers had prepared their negatives on location, but in a talk given to the Liverpool Photographic Society in early 1853, James T. Foard confirmed that his friend had taken pre-prepared materials with him.

Fenton and Bourne seem to have shared cameras – the similarities in size in their work is too close to be coincidental – and it would appear that they were the first photographers to work in Russia. No records of locally-based studios have been traced before the very late 1850s.

While Fenton prepared his waxed paper materials in London, Bourne, using Talbot's calotype process, would certainly have had to prepare and sensitise his materials 'in the field' – but he chose not to work at night in his hotel room by the light of a candle, as Talbot had done in Scotland. Instead he took a darkroom with him, and Vignoles' own diaries confirm that when the three men travelled from St Petersburg to Moscow by train, two large coaches met the train and were filled with their luggage and equipment! For my recreation of Fenton's journey I took only one small shoulder bag containing the camera, three lenses and several dozen rolls of colour film.

In St. Petersburg, the time Fenton was able to devote to photography seems to have been limited – for very few images of the city survive. Those that do reflect his interest in architecture in general, and religious architecture in particular.

He photographed the Smolnoyy Monastery, then on the outskirts of the city, and the great Admiralty buildings, the Alexander Column, and the exterior of the Little Hermitage – but not the great Hermitage Palace next door.

With few exceptions, his photography in St. Petersburg lacks the compositional accomplishment which became his trademark, and none of the images rivals the style or quality of some of the views taken in Moscow only a few days later.

His grasp of Russian was obviously limited, for he mis-captioned several of his pictures. Indeed he got the cities wrong with a small number of images, which might suggest that some of his negatives remained undeveloped until he returned home – by which time, presumably, he had forgotten their precise locations. One view, simply captioned 'Monastery, St Petersburg' turned out to be St Mikhail's Monastery in Kiev![6]

The Russia he visited has changed dramatically in the century and a half since he returned home. Czarist Russia was replaced by the Soviet Union, and now that has split up into the many independent republics, the names of

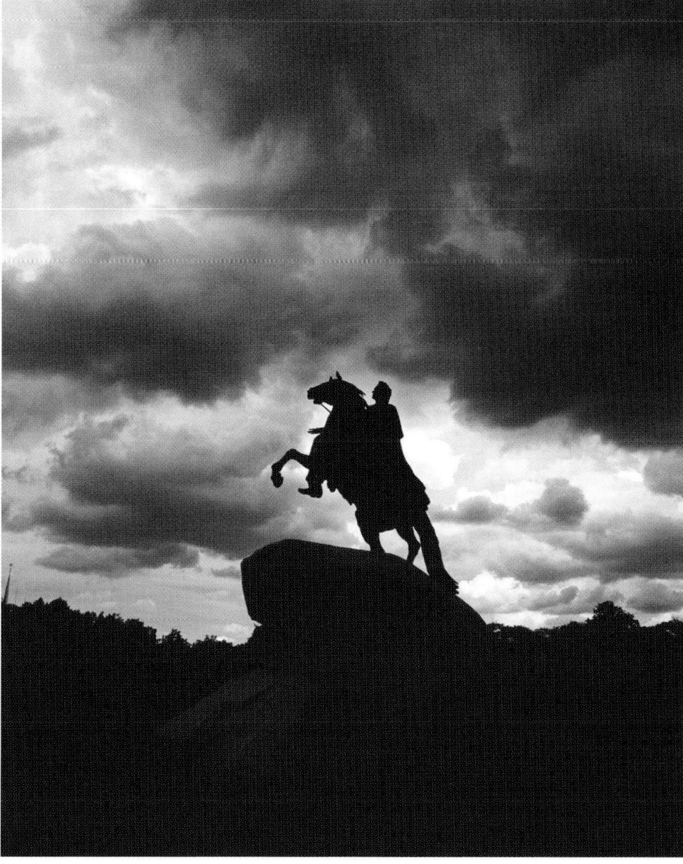

left: A storm approaching from the Gulf of Finland, seen over the statue of Peter the Great in St. Petersburg. Fenton took the first photograph of this statue in 1852.

opposite page top: The raising of the first chains on the bridge was photographed by Fenton during his 1852 visit. In addition to this study, a series of images recently discovered combine to show panoramic views of the works in progress,
opposite page bottom: One of the bridges over the Dnipro River today, photographed from the bell tower of the Great Lavra monastery, showing the post-war expansion of Kiev across the river.

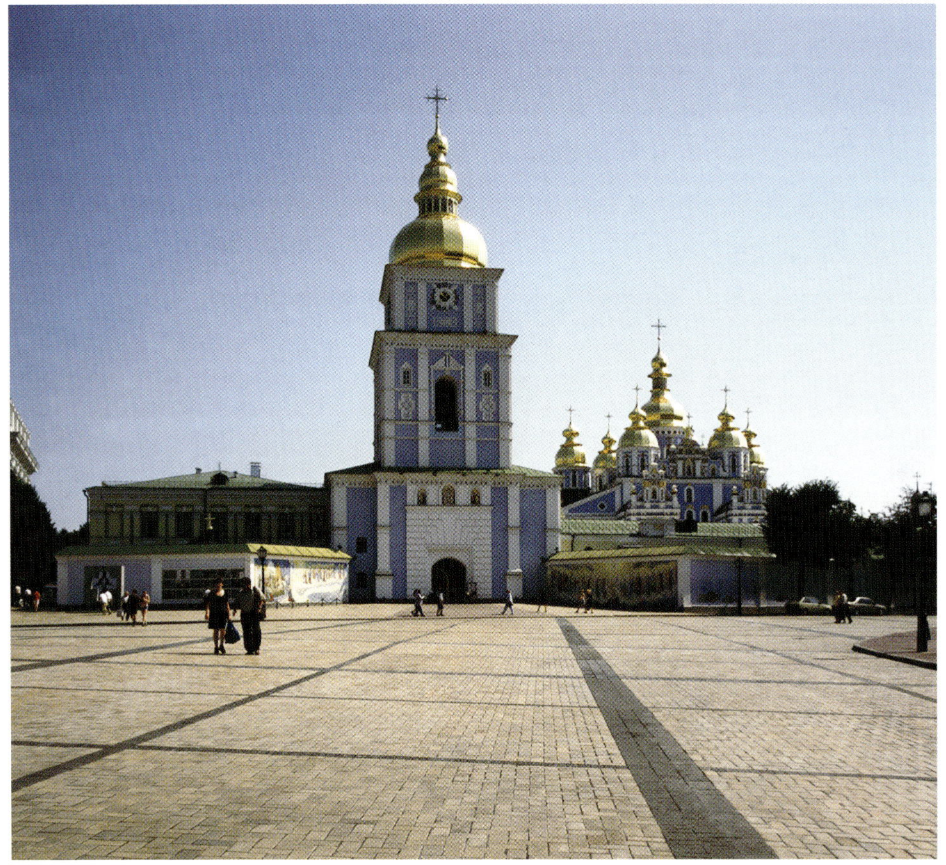

above: The Mikhailovskiy Monastery in Kiev is a complete reconstruction of the original photographed by Fenton in 1852, and destroyed by Stalin in 1937. Inside the precinct is a monument to Professor Nikolei Makarenko, the only academic who refused to put his name to Stalin's document stating that the building was of no architectural or historical importance. He later died in prison. It was here, reputedly, that the monk Grigori Rasputin first met members of the Csar's family, initiating his rise to infamy.

which are slowly becoming familiar to us.

While many of the locations Fenton photographed may seem unchanged to today's visitor, they are, on closer inspection, very different indeed. St Mikhail's Monastery in Kiev, resplendent in its coat of fresh blue paint today is a complete reconstruction of the original photographed by Fenton. Demolished on the orders of Stalin, to make way for a huge civic square and monolithic government buildings which were never built, the monastery has been completely rebuilt since Ukrainian independence. Stalin even persuaded local architects and historians to confirm in writing that the original buildings had neither architectural nor historical importance, and to agree to their demolition. One historian refused to sign, and subsequently died in prison. The citizens of Kiev, almost none of whom remembers the original, are still getting used to the huge tower of the monastery dominating their city skyline again.

Elsewhere in Kiev, another monastery photographed by Fenton has subsequently been replaced by a hotel.

One of Fenton's 1852 images, captioned *Scaffolding for the repair of a Cathedral, Moscow,* in fact showed building work on the Cathedral of Christ the Redeemer, then nearing completion - a huge building which in the 19th century dwarfed every building around it, and completely dominated the skyline along the Moskva River.

It too was demolished by Stalin, this time to make way for a tower block of administrative offices - a plan later abandoned as the lower courses of the new building started to sink into the soft ground of the riverbank. The site eventually became a community swimming pool.

Shortly after the emergence of the Russian Federation out of the old Soviet Union, an almost perfect facsimile of the Cathedral of Christ the Redeemer was created. The huge cross which tops its dome was placed there with the help of mountaineers and a helicopter. Muscovites who were involved with the reconstruction proudly tell visitors that it took forty five minutes to erect the cross - exactly the

right: In 1852 Fenton photographed work on the construction of the Cathedral of Christ the Redeemer shortly before its completion. Erected to commemorate the defeat of the French, only the dome needed to be erected in late 1852. In the rebuit church, elaborate stonework has been replaced with bronzework, but otherwise it is a faithful, if somewhat gaudy, reconstruction on the Moscow skyline.

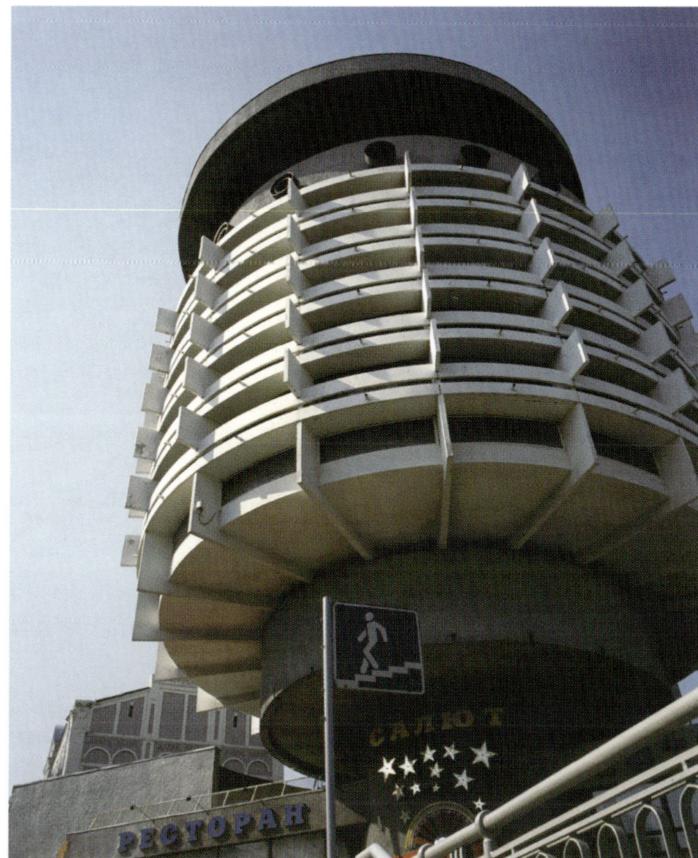

above: Kiev's Hotel Salut occupies part of the site of St Nicholas's monastery, another of the sites destroyed by Stalin in the 1930s. Fenton's 1852 view looked past the monastery's gate tower towards the magnificent Upper Lavra monastery, a view now obscured by trees. While St Nicholas's has gone, the Lavra has survived, and its central cathedral – destroyed under obscure circumstances during the Second World War – has been carefully rebuilt.

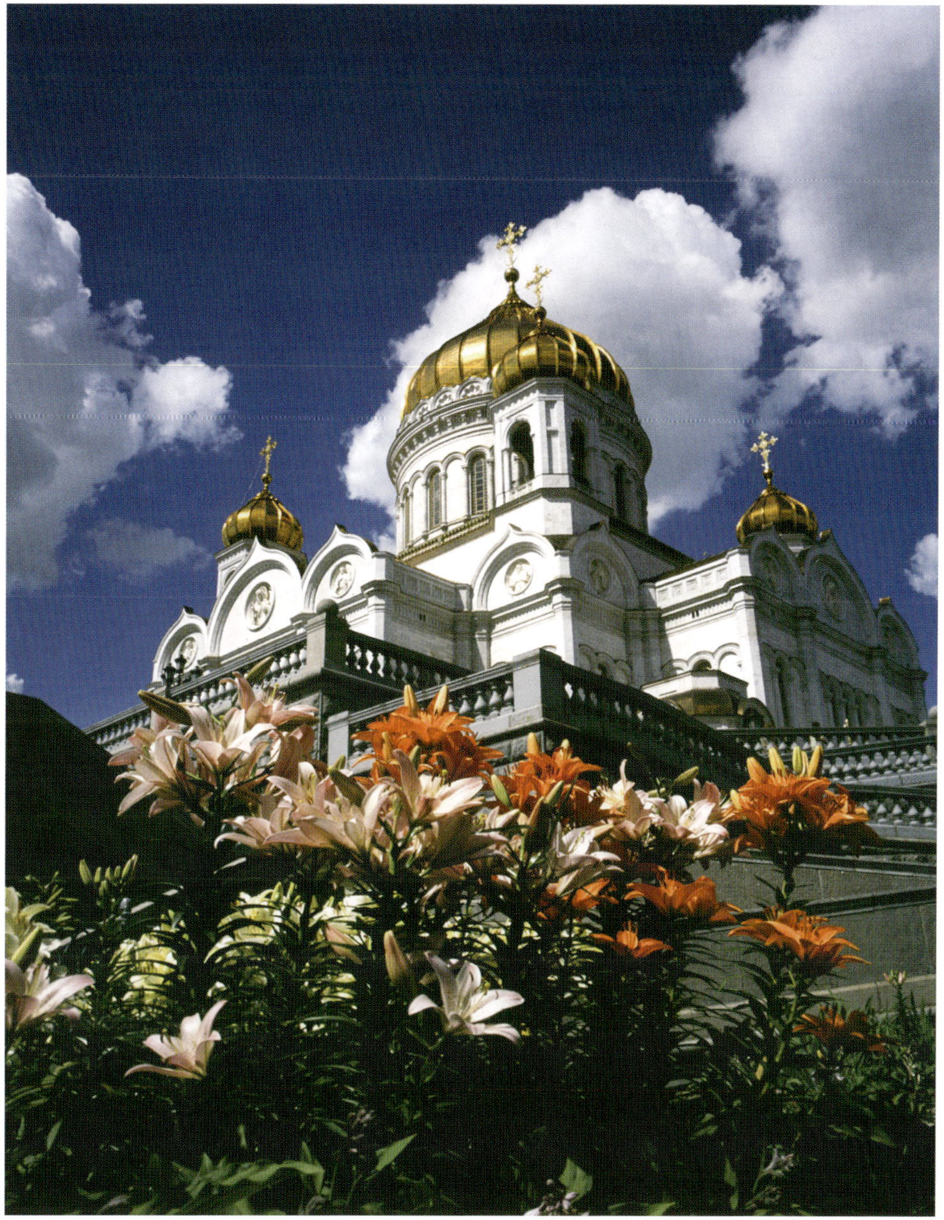

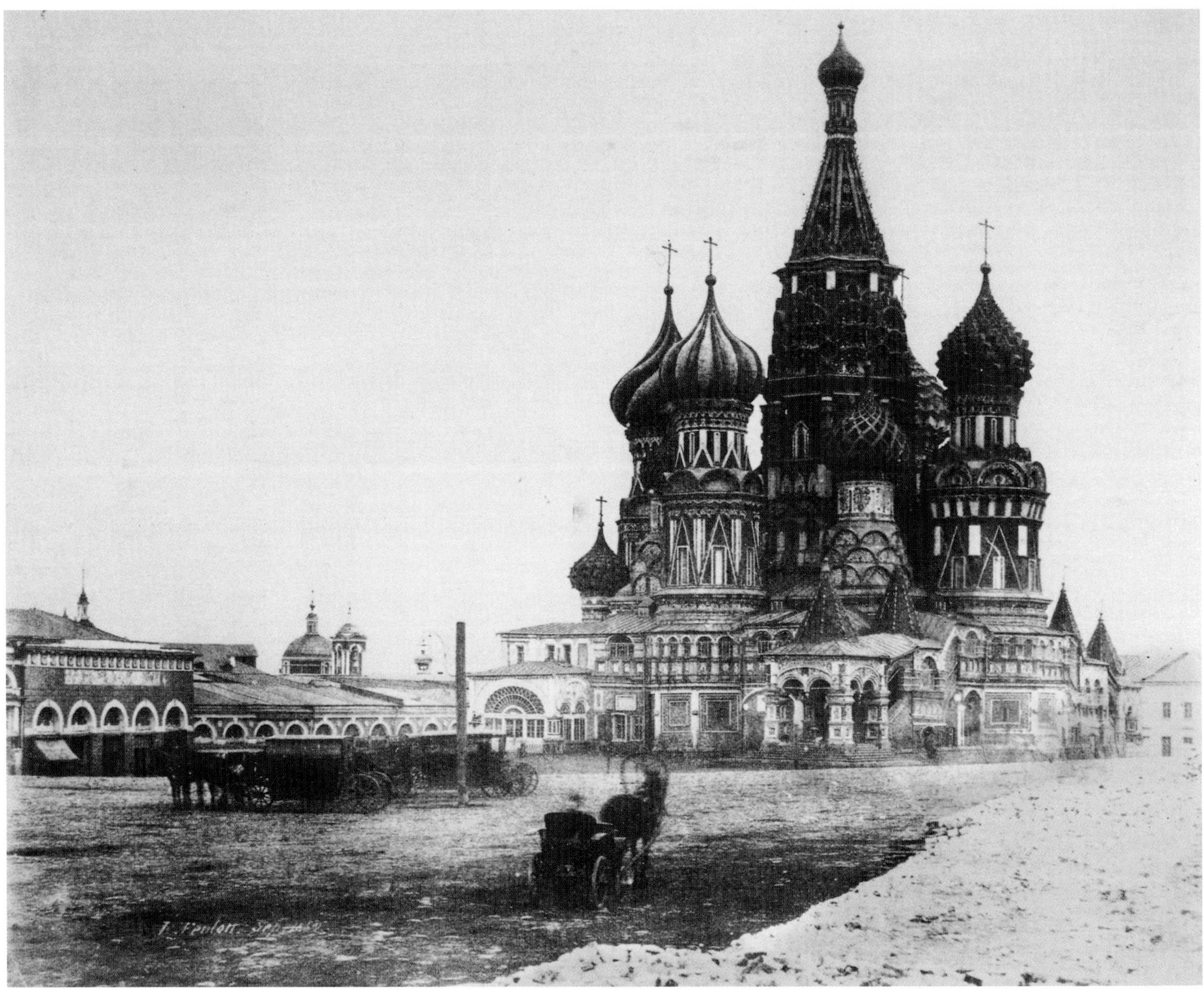

same time that it took Stalin's men to raze the original to the ground.

In Moscow's Red Square, Fenton photographed the wonderful St Vasili's (St Basil's) Cathedral after an unusually early snow, the long exposure required for his waxed paper negative clearly evident from the blurred horses' heads. Work on the cathedral had started three hundred years earlier, and had been completed by 1561.

Undoubtedly one of the most exquisite of the many exquisite buildings in Moscow, it was designed for Ivan the Terrible by Postnik Yakovlev. Ivan, according to tradition, was so enchanted with the building that he ordered the architect to be blinded so he could never design anything more beautiful!

Its beauty has attracted artists and photographers ever since, Fenton being the first person to photograph it. His photograph was taken in mid-afternoon, as was mine, albeit from a slightly different direction.

J. C. Bourne was also in both Moscow and St. Petersburg, but so far none of his views of either city have been located. Of Fenton's work, seven views of St. Petersburg, eighteen of Kiev, and three of unknown locations are known to have survived today, in addition to some twenty-two Moscow images - but out of an oeuvre of how many? Were there many more? The two portraits used in the *Illustrated London News* were surely not the only ones he took. How many others were there?

It is interesting that the *Illustrated London News* captioned the picture of the *Priest of the Greek Church* as being *from a calotype by Fenton.*

While the waxed paper process he was using for his architectural work was not ideally suited to portraiture, it is not beyond the bounds of possibility that Fenton might have employed the more sensitive calotype process which Bourne was using. Might, therefore, the description of the portrait of the priest as a calotype actually be correct? If so, then it would be the first recorded occasion of him having used Talbot's process.

opposite page: St Vasili's Cathedral on Red Square, photographed by Fenton after an early snowfall in late September 1852.
below: St Basil's today, undergoing almost continuous restoration, is a riot of colour – a feature lost on Fenton's pictures due to the limited spectral sensitivity of his waxed paper negative materials.

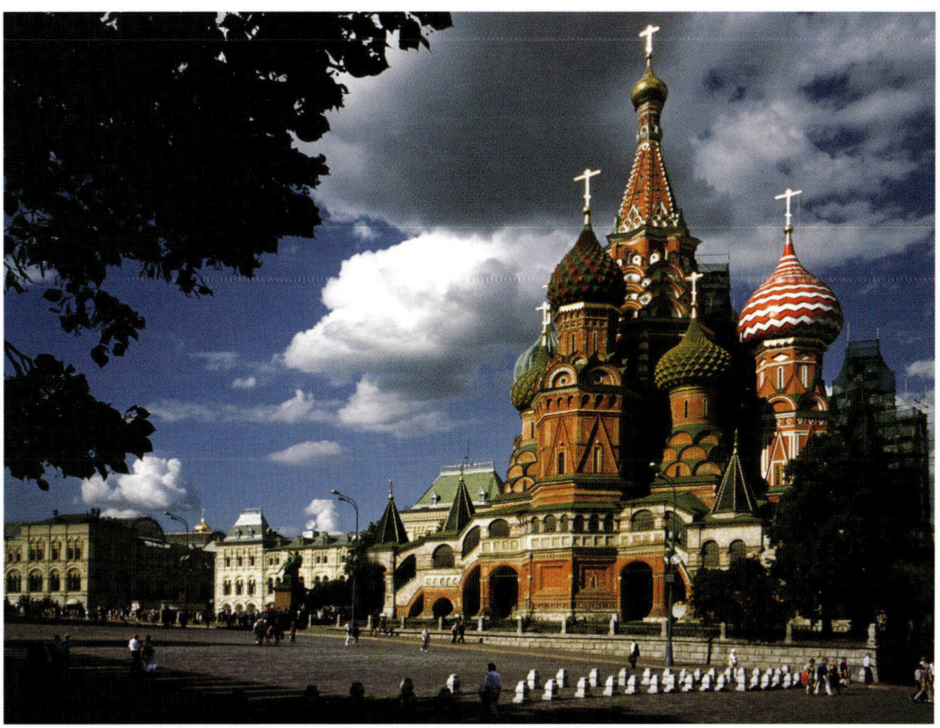

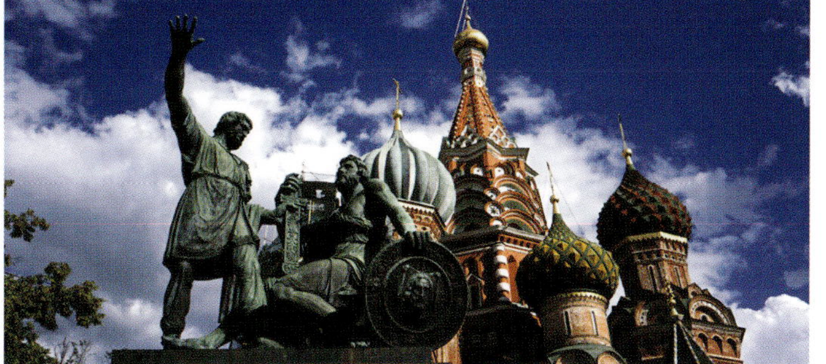

left: In Fenton's day, the statue of Minim and Poharskiy stood in front of the building visible on the far left of the picture above. Today it stands in front of the main entrance to St. Basil's, facing east across Red Square.

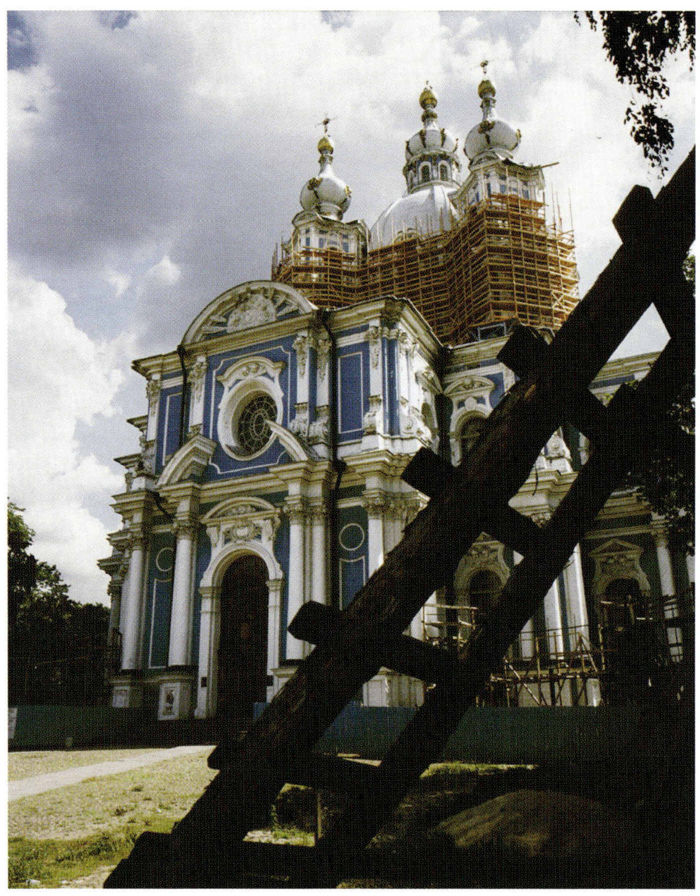

above: The wooden scaffolding encasing the Smolnoyy Convent in present-day St Petersburg would not have seemed unfamiliar to Fenton, being very similar to that which he saw being used during the construction of the Cathedral of Christ the Redeemer in 1852.

Of Bourne's images taken in Kiev, in addition to the two albums known to survive, there is evidence to suggest that others may be located in South America. Further research may eventually bring them to light.

Several of Fenton's views in Moscow and Kiev – and presumably also therefore in St. Petersburg – were stereoscopic or three-dimensional views taken for viewing with the Wheatstone Reflecting Stereoscope.

It is reasonable to conjecture that Fenton, already one of the leading photographers of his day, and with experience of the easier-to-prepare waxed paper process, may have been attracted by the challenge of working so far from home.

At least three of the Moscow views and two from Kiev have been identified as left or right images from stereoscopic pairs – where the two images were taken from camera positions a few feet apart, and then combined for viewing in three dimensions using a system of mirrors.

The Wheatstone Reflecting Stereoscope, invented by Sir Charles Wheatstone, initiated a fascination for 3-D imagery which would flourish in the later 1850s after the development of the smaller stereoscopic format introduced by Sir David Brewster. Fenton himself would go on to become a master of the medium, with many of his stereo images being published in Lovell Reeve's *Stereoscopic Magazine*, the *Stereoscopic Cabinet*, and books such as *The Conway in the Stereoscope*.

St. Petersburg, Moscow and Kiev have, of course, all changed considerably in the century and a half since Vignoles, Bourne and Fenton made their pioneering journey. While many of the views have changed forever, a surprising number remain recognisable. All three cities, emerging from the constraints of the Soviet era, are racing to catch up with the western cities they seem determined to imitate. In doing so, they are suffering the same problems – the stranglehold of the car, the influx of Western and American branded goods, and the appearance of the ubiquitous McDonalds, KFC and Pizza Hut.

At the time of visiting St. Petersburg, the city seemed encased in scaffolding, as the authorities worked towards the restoration of all the city's major historical buildings. The unrealistic target of achieving that goal before the city's tercentenary in 2003 was never achieved!

Much of the scaffolding being used was wooden, and in that respect Fenton might have felt he was in familiar surroundings as it was not dissimilar to the scaffolding he saw encasing the Cathedral of Christ the Redeemer in Moscow a century and a half earlier!

Of course, St. Petersburg has developed considerably since Fenton's visit, and is now a major tourist destination. The quayside is lined with an ever-changing selection of modern cruise ships, while tourist markets, where everything is priced in dollars, punctuate the routes of the popular guided tours.

One of the city's major tourist attractions today - which looks as though it has been there for centuries - was not built until almost half a century after Fenton's visit.

The Church on Spilled Blood, built in a late 19th century reinterpretation of 15th and 16th century Russian church architecture, sits at the end of one of the city's many canals.

It was erected to the memory of Csar Alexander II, who was murdered in 1881 on the instructions of his successor Csar Alexander III. The site now occupied by the great church includes the spot where he died, hence the church's unusual name. The foundation stone was laid less than two years after the murder, but it was well into the 20th century before the building was completed. The church was reopened in 1998 after nearly twenty years of restoration work, and is undoubtedly one of the city most spectacular buildings.

Looking at Fenton's photographs of St. Petersburg, we see an environment with few trees - giving him unrestricted views of the great buildings. Today the city is much greener, and as a result, many of the views he took are completely obscured.

below: By the side of one of St. Petersburg's many canals, the Church on Spilled Blood - built in the Russian Revivalist style half a century after Fenton's visit - is now one of the city's major visitor attractions.

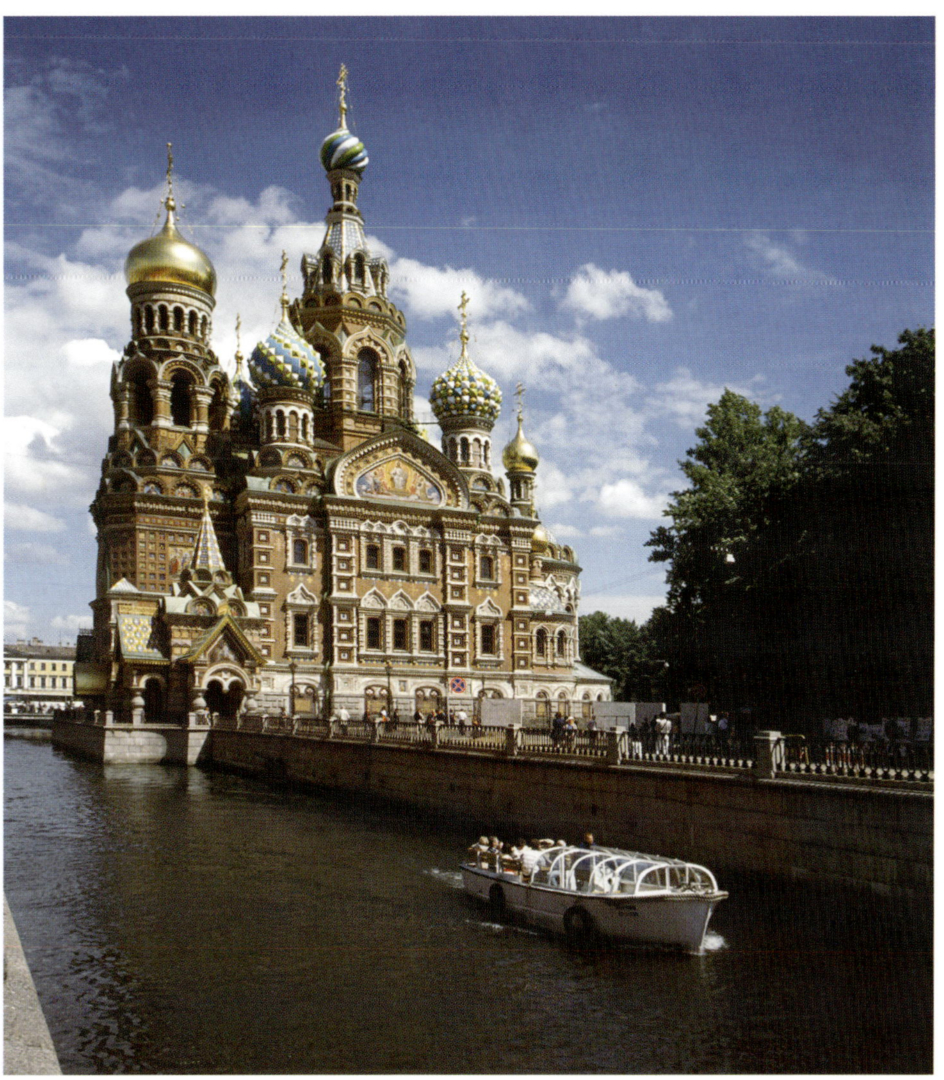

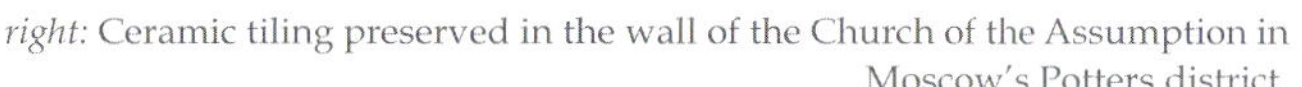

right: Ceramic tiling preserved in the wall of the Church of the Assumption in Moscow's Potters district.

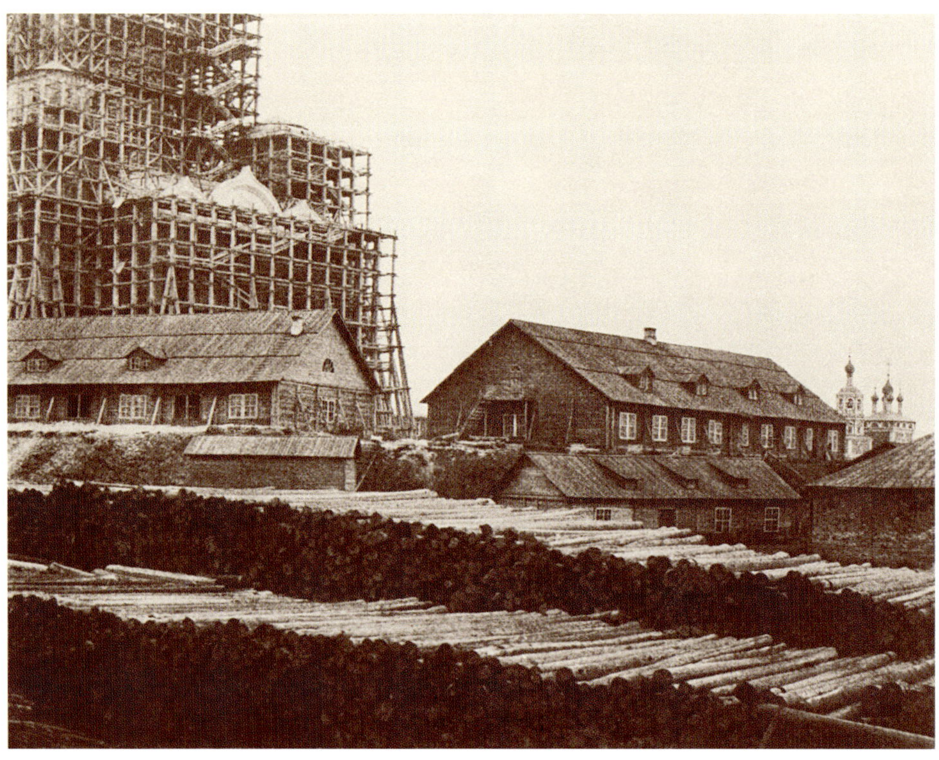

above: The wooden scaffolding piled in front of the partly built Cathedral of Christ the Redeemer in Moscow gives a sense of the scale of the project. Historically, Moscow's cathedrals were usually small, and that gives the group of churchs in the Kremlin's Cathedral Square an intimatcy which religious buildings on this scale can never enjoy. This huge church, outside the Kremlin walls and closer to the river, was built to celebrate victory over the French and was as much a statement about Russian power as it was about religion.

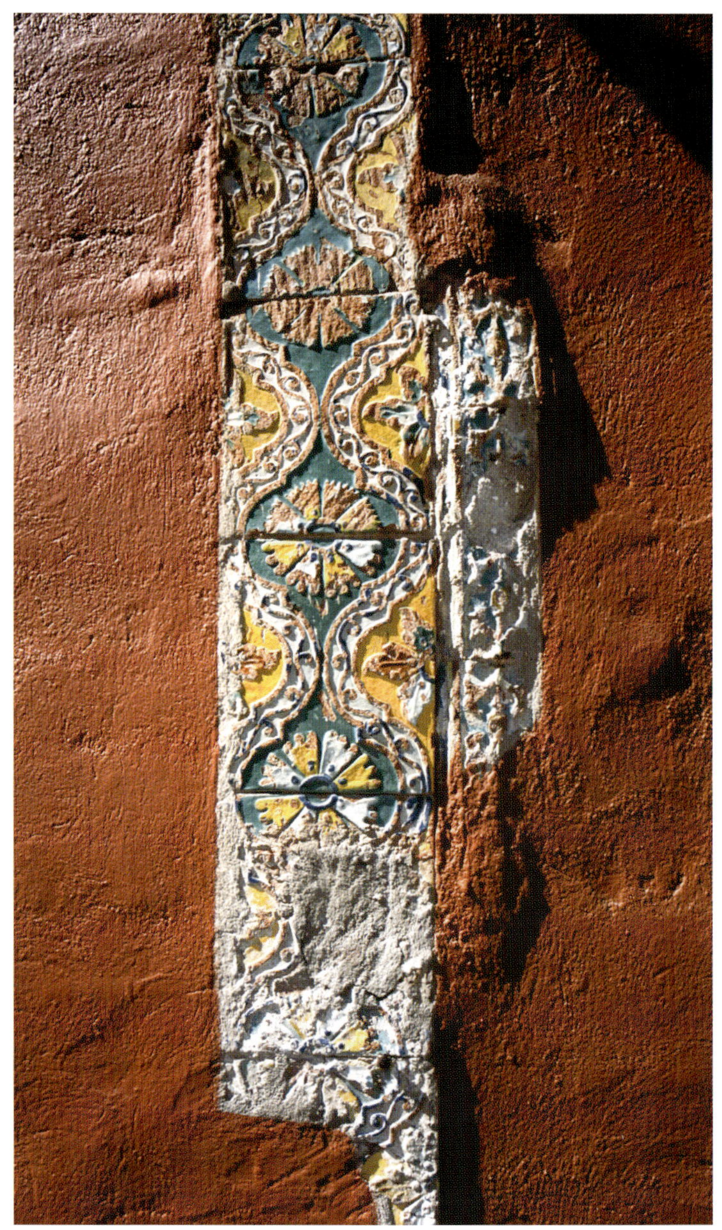

Moscow too has benefited from a century and a half of tree planting, and there too, the fine views afforded to Fenton of the Kremlin walls and towers are now almost all hidden.

With notable exceptions, the centre of Moscow has escaped the developments of the 20th century largely unscathed. The view from Ivan the Great's gatehouse over the domes of the Cathedral of the Assumption is altered only by the huge Samsung neon sign! The few modern buildings inside the Kremlin precinct clash with the historic treasures from the 15th to 18th centuries, and the monstrous Hotel Rossija at the edge of Red Square, with its three thousand rooms, is an horrific legacy of ill-considered 1960s design. From the west end of the square, the huge rectangular bulk of what must be the least hospitable hotel in Russia looms behind the 16th century majesty of St Basil's Cathedral.

Given that the waxed paper process used by Roger Fenton was a relatively slow process, with a maximum of eight or ten exposures in a day being considered a good output, we can assume that he devoted a considerable amount of time to his photography while in Moscow.

At least twelve images have survived from his visit to the Kremlin itself - from a total so far identified of twenty two from Moscow as a whole. Of those twenty two, nine concentrate on religious buildings, including the Kremlin cathedrals, St. Saviour's monastery, and one beautiful image of the lost Seminoff monastery.

Some things in Russia have changed little - the majority of the people in Fenton's day were impoverished peasants, scratching a living under the Csar. Today, in post-Communist Russia, the majority of the people are still impoverished, although there is a large *nouveau riche* able to savour the delights of the Western designer-label outlets in the former GUM department store on Red Square.

Many Muscovites admit that, given the choice of a Soviet state-run store which stocked a limited but affordable range of food and goods, or a post-independence supermarket

below: A glimpse of St Saviour's Monastery, Moscow. When Fenton photographed this church in 1852, he got a clear view from the top of a nearby hill. That view is now obscured by huge utilitarian apartment blocks erected in the Breshnev era.

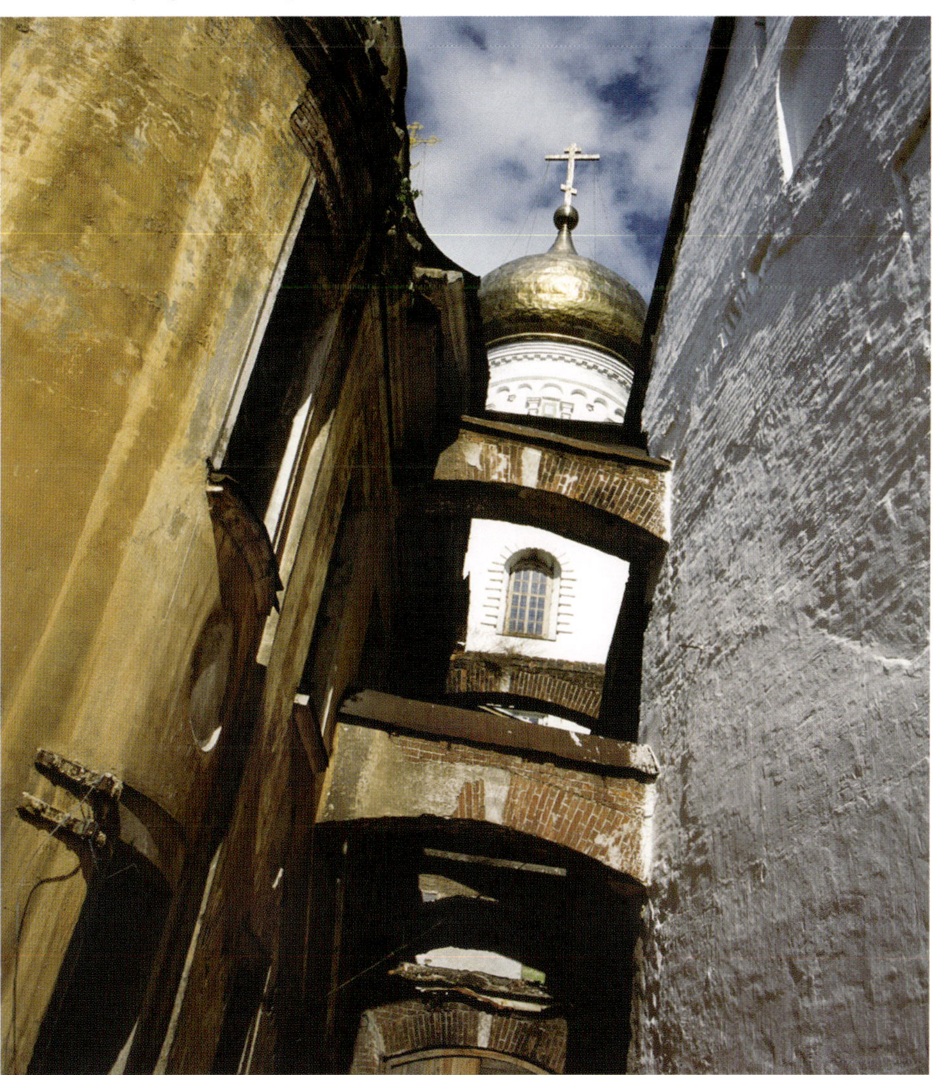

below: Kiev's artists' market runs the full length of Andreyevsky Spusk in the Podol district, selling everything from clothes to paintings, from woodwork to jewelry. Either side of the steep cobbled street are some of the city's finest old buildings, housing some excellent cafés and restaurants. Across the street from this stall, Rastrelli's Andreyevsky Church dominates the hillside.

right: In St. Petersburg's Rykov Suvenirov, situated behind the Church on Spilled Blood, the currency is exclusively American dollars, and the clientele is almost exclusively the city's increasing number of foreign visitors, many of whom arrive on cruise ships as part of a Baltic tour.

below right: Hundreds of paintings by artists of varying talent are offered for sale in St. Catherine's Art Market, off Nevskir Prospekt, St. Petersburg's main thoroughfare. Those with sufficient time to spare, can have their portraits painted while they wait.

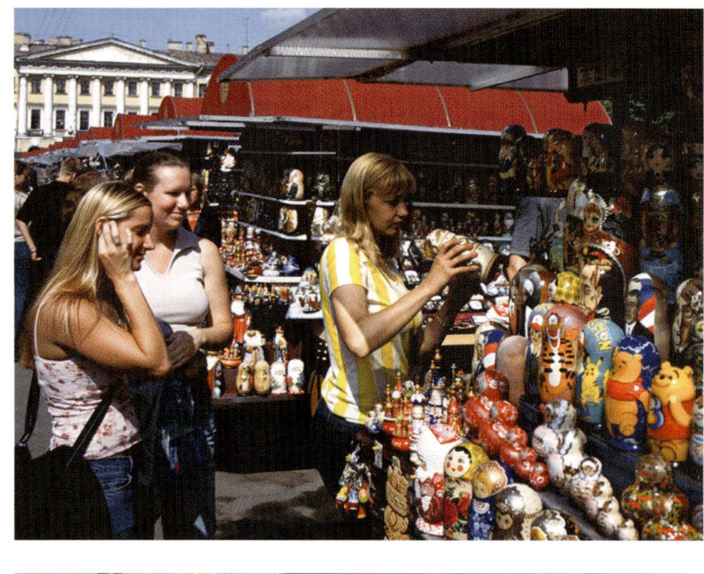

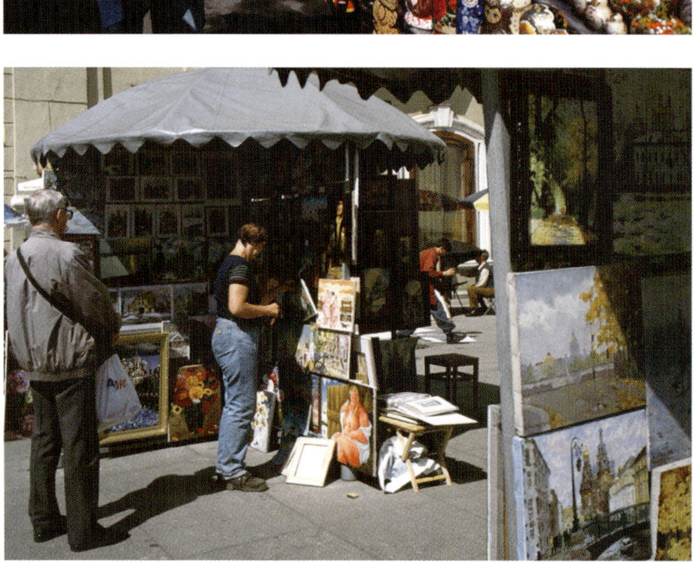

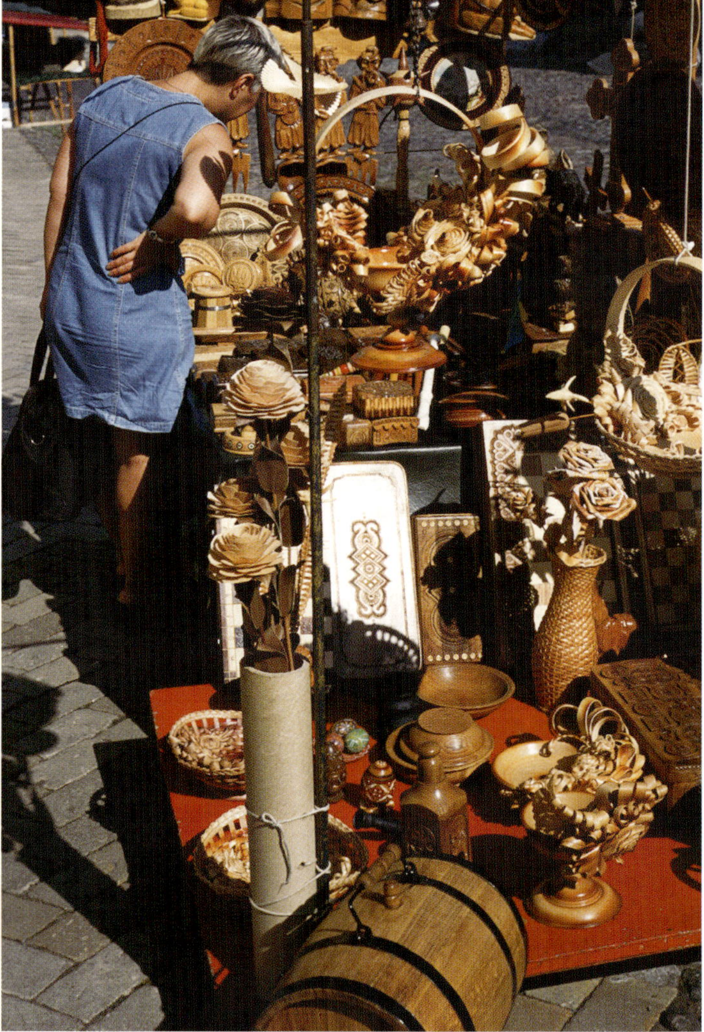

with a wide range of food priced beyond their reach, they find little to commend about that aspect of the new order.

Returning to Red Square by metro one evening, and exiting into the huge cathedral-like structure of the underground station concourse, I came across a group of music students giving in impromptu performance of Vivaldi's *Four Seasons*. The acoustics were sumptuous, the music performed with great skill and sensitivity, but it is perhaps a reflection on present-day Moscow that the money being put in the hat was of very small denomination.

On a train from St. Petersburg to Moscow, other freedoms were more widely appreciated. When asked to single out the most important change since 1991, one Russian businessman immediately reminded me that before the demise of the communist state, nobody would be openly talking to a foreign visitor on a train!

Another obvious change has been the resurgence of religion. Churches closed since the revolution have been restored and reopened. Some of them were reduced to serving as warehouses, prisons, cattle sheds and other secular roles. One was even converted into a museum of atheism in an unusual and individual show of irony by a Soviet official.

Monasteries flourish, and the basic beliefs of the Russian people, often held in secret under the Soviet regime, can now be expressed openly again. Huge amounts of money, much of it from foreign donations, have been expended on giving the church a public face again.

And as the cities have been opened up to tourists, vast industries have blossomed to serve the visitors. Every major city has its tourist market selling trinkets, jewelry and guidebooks. Matryoshka dolls, both traditional and modern, are everywhere. There is even a set in which every doll bears the face of a different former American President!

Amber is popular in Kiev and in the artists' quarter of the city, around St. Andrew's Church, beautiful amber jewelry shares stall space with carved wood, embossed

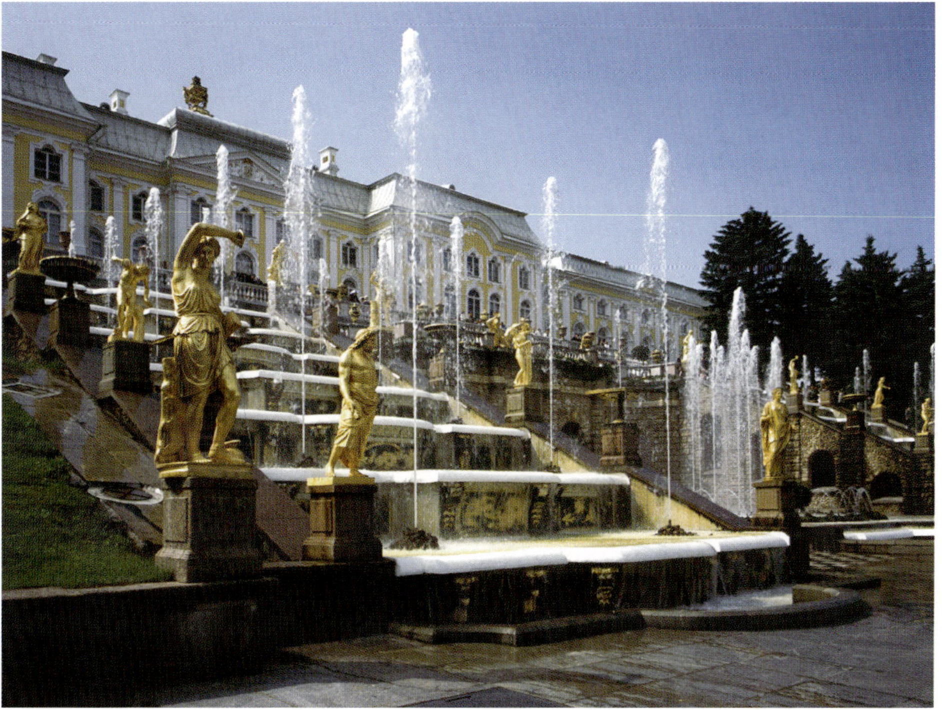

above: In Fenton's day, the huge palace at Peterhof a few miles from St. Petersburg was still a royal residence, and therefore inaccessible. Since then it has seen a great deal of Russian history, including almost total destruction at the hands of the Germans in World War II, and a subsequent complete rebuild and restoration. Built to be even more extravagent than Versailles, the palace is one of the most spectacular buildings in a region renowned for spectacular buildings. The hundreds of fountains at Peterhof are fed by a fourteen mile network of pipes and use thirty thousand cubic metres of water each hour. By comparison, a modern four bedroom house uses about thirty cubic metres in a year!

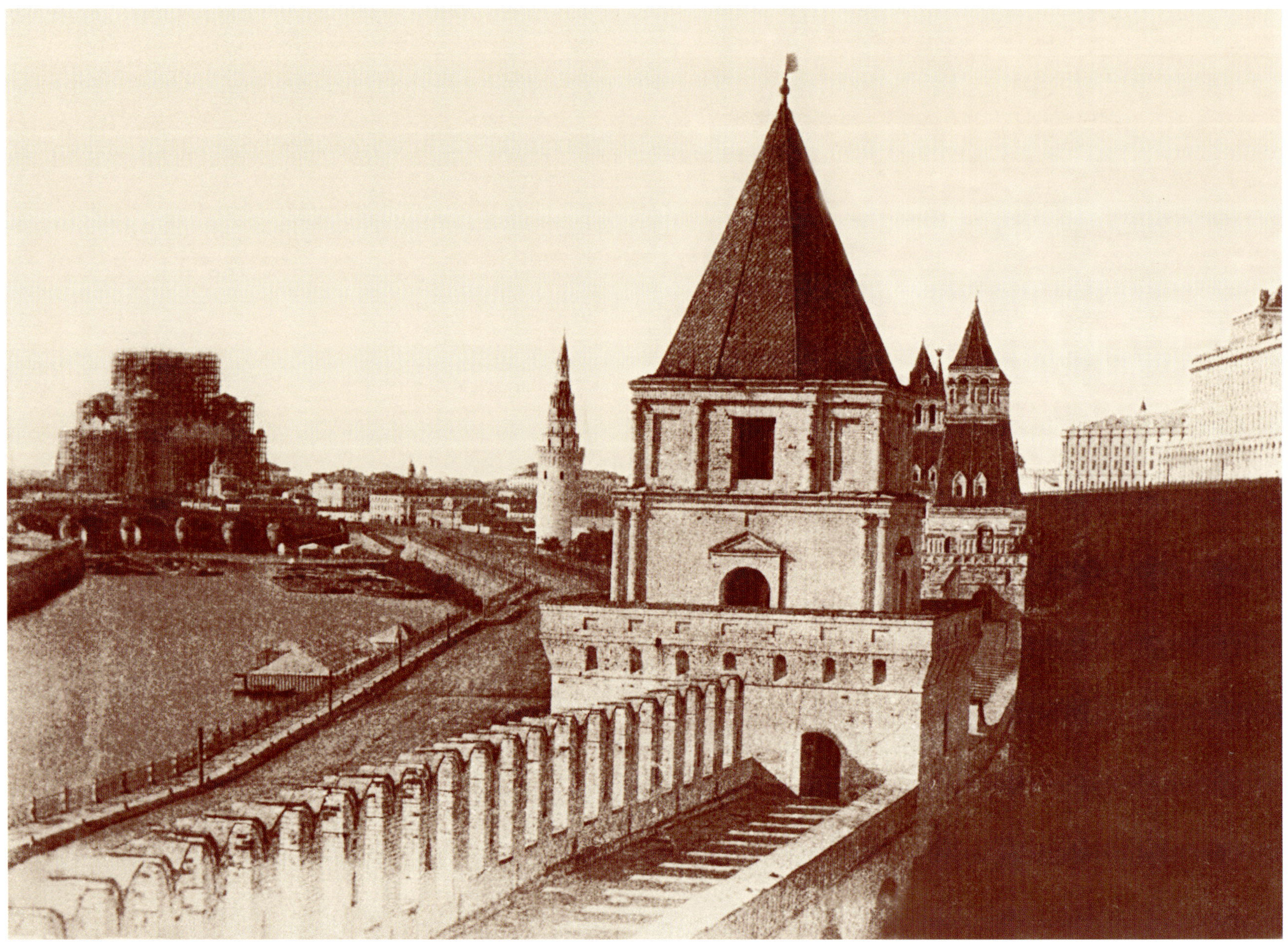

leather, and a host of other creations by local craftsmen.

In Moscow and St. Petersburg, delicate boxes made of birch bark are everywhere. As in any tourist centre, some of the items show exquisite traditional craftsmanship - something the government actively keeps alive - while elsewhere, vendors are catering to a less discriminating sector of the tourist market.

Fenton's photographic account of Russia, of course, is not representative. He was passionate about architectural and landscape photography, and had an especial interest in churches, castles and history.

The Russia seen in his pictures is, by the very nature of the photographic processes available at the time, sparsely peopled. The long exposures necessary meant that Muscovites could walk the entire distance across his field of view while the negative was being exposed and not be recorded. With exposure times sometimes as long as fifteen to twenty minutes, they might have repeated the journey still without interfering with his image. Even with the increased brightness occasioned by the snow, exposures would still require several minutes.

Today, with high-speed emulsions, or highly sensitive digital cameras, capturing the 'feel' of a place as well as its physical appearance is an essential part of any travelogue.

In Fenton's day, however, the blue sensitive materials he used were more ideally suited to dull weather - soft shadows or no shadows giving the best results. So he was perhaps less at the mercy of the weather than today's traveller. With modern colour photography, we prefer to photograph under sunshine and at least a hint of blue sky - dull lighting only really appealing to us if it has a spectacular visual effect.

Fenton was, however, much more at the mercy of the wind - camera movement during the long exposure would have ruined his views. Hence the robust construction of his cameras, and the sturdy wooden tripods he needed to support them. It is perhaps just as well that Moscow was largely treeless in 1852!

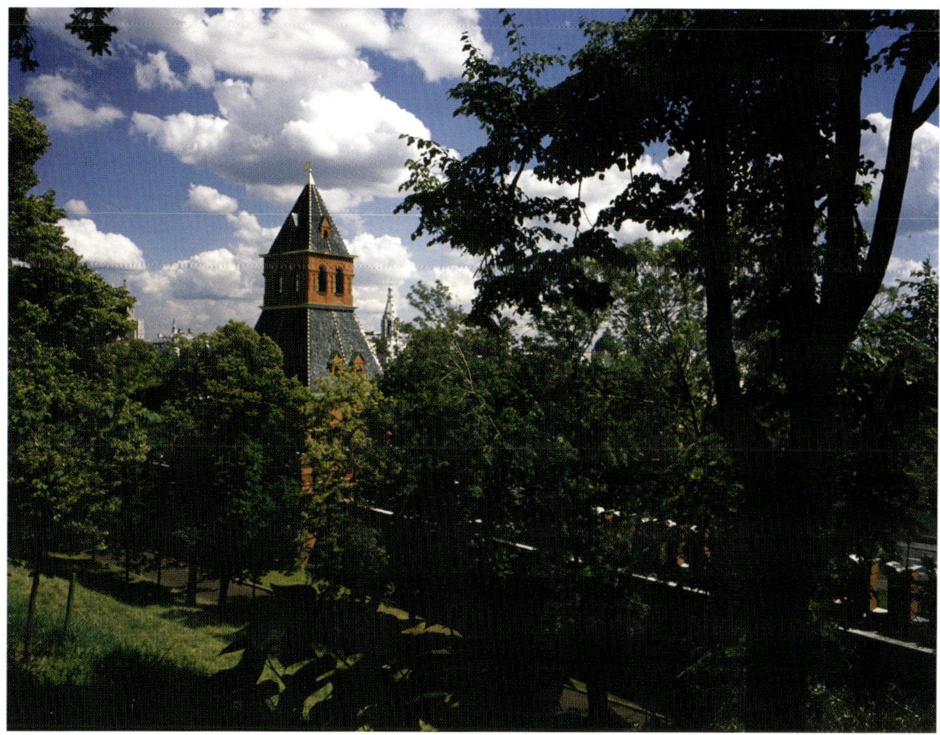

left: The Walls of the Kremlin, one half of a stereoscopic pair of images taken by Fenton in 1852. Then there was not a tree in sight, giving an austere look to the area. The Cathedral of Christ the Redeemer, nearing completion, can be seen encased in scaffolding in the distance.

above: Seen from inside the Kremlin, this is one of a very few views of the walls and towers possible today. This tower is visible to the right and behind the main tower in Fenton's view.

below: An ancient Post House preserved in the museum at Pigorov a few miles from Kiev is typical of the domestic buildings which Fenton saw and photographed near the Dnipro river a century and a half ago. The museum has collected wooden buildings from all over the Ukraine

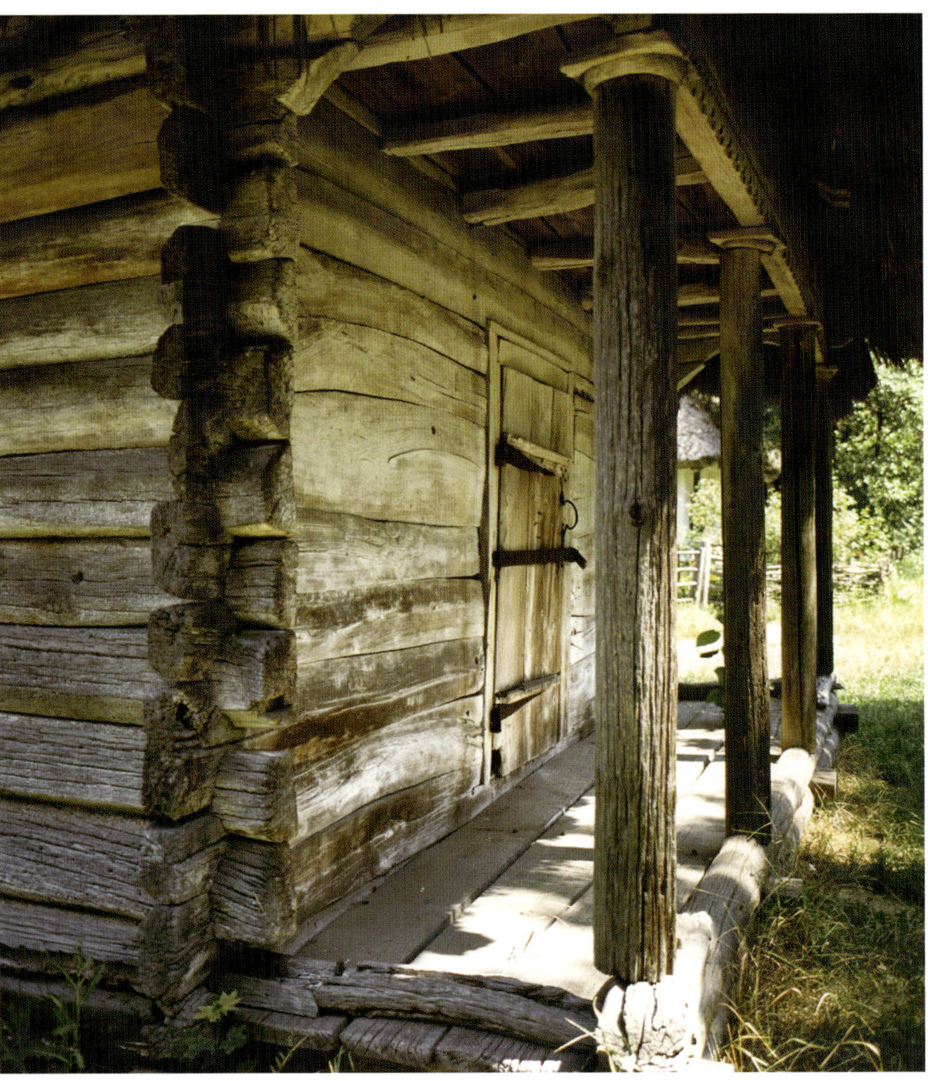

In Kiev - perhaps the most rural and least developed area of Russia that Fenton visited - he did also turn his camera towards domestic architecture. In addition to the imposing churches and monasteries, he was fascinated by the wooden post houses and cottages which still abounded on the slopes above the Dnipro river.

Modern Kiev has swept them all away, replacing them with tall apartment blocks of little character. But a remarkably far-sighted decision by the Soviet authorities to support an initiative by the Ukrainian Society for the Protection of Historic Monuments saved these important aspects of the country's heritage from destruction.

In an outdoor museum at Pirogov on the edge of the Goloseyevsky Forest, examples of these rare and fascinating buildings, together with rural wooden architecture from all over the Ukraine, have been systematically gathered together at a location a few miles from the city.

Wooden churches, farms, cottages, village inns and a rich assortment of windmills have all been rebuilt on a large undulating and wooded landscape to create smallholdings, villages and complete communities which must look very much as they looked two, three and four hundred years ago.

The development of the Museum of Folk Architecture began in 1969. It is remarkable that these buildings survived in their original locations until as recently as then and the site now preserves well over one hundred predominantly wooden buildings on a one hundred and fifty hectare site. It opened to visitors in 1976.

The houses and farm buildings have all been furnished appropriately, and are grouped together according to their age and original locations.

Craftsmen keep ancient crafts alive in some of them, and the inns now serve food and drink to visitors. For the visitor, it offers a unique opportunity to step back in time, and in my case, to experience a little more of the landscape and architecture through which Fenton travelled.

Fenton returned to Russia in 1855 under very different

left: Fenton's view of a Post House, part of an ensemble of wooden buildings, is believed to have been taken in Kiev.
below: This view, simply titled 'Russian Cottage' was one of a pair of stereo images taken for viewing in the Wheatstone stereoscope. Buildings similar to those seen in both these photographs are preserved in the Pigorov open air museum.

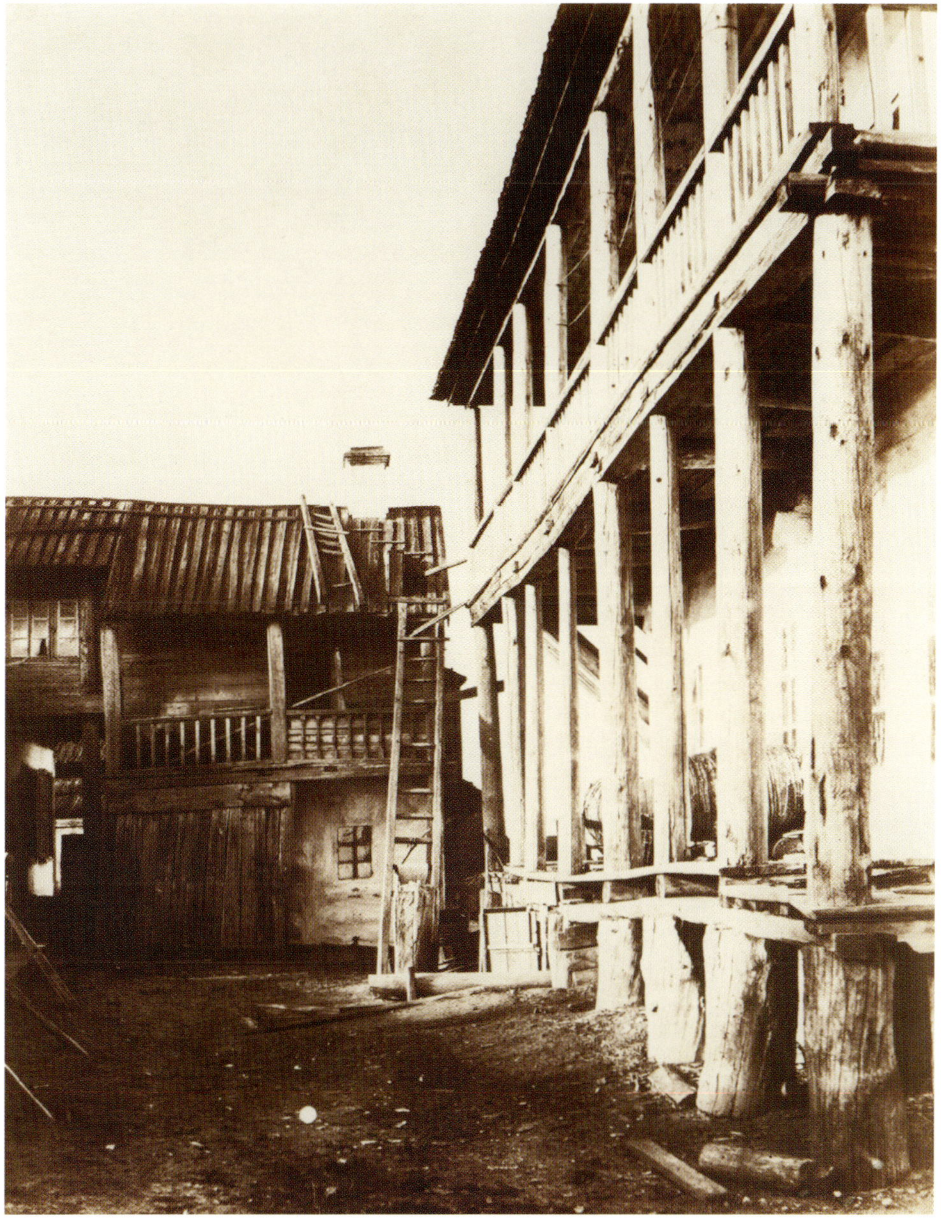

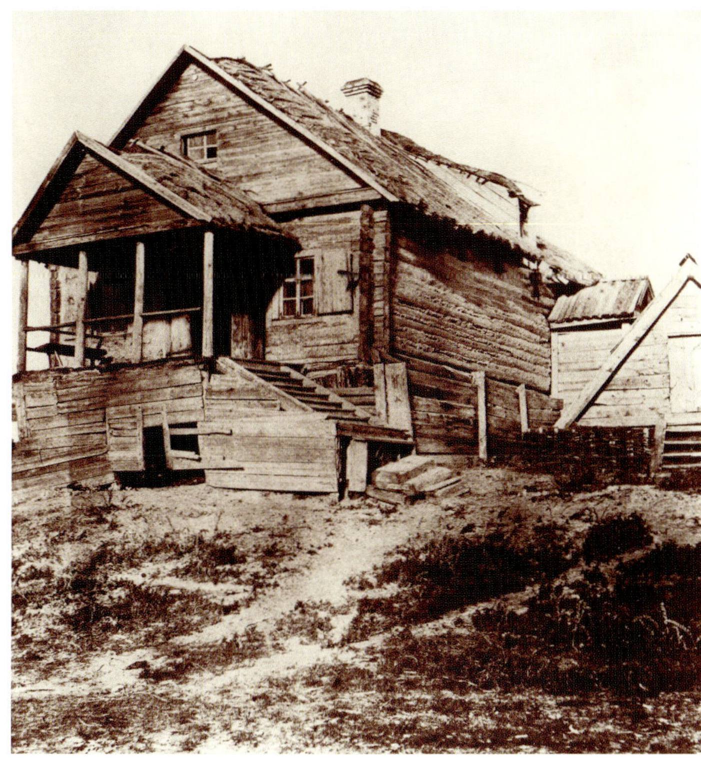

circumstances. For his first visit he had been given access to the Kremlin and treated as an honoured guest, but for his second visit three years later, it was as the semi-official British photographer of the Crimean War where Russia was very definitely the enemy!

By this time, too, he had progressed from the slow waxed paper negative process, to the much more sensitive but somewhat tricky wet collodion glass plate.

By that time too Fenton was a leading light in

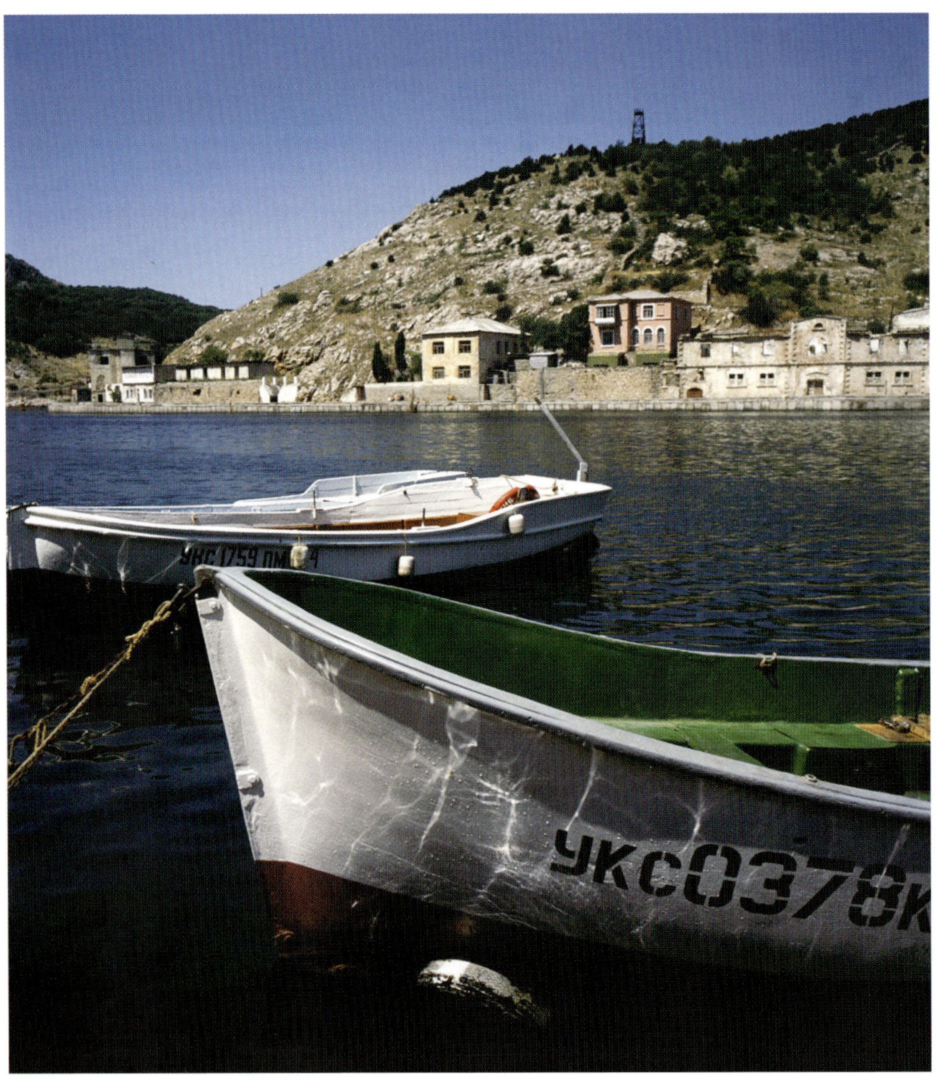

the Photographic Society of London (now the Royal Photographic Society) which had been founded in 1853 with Fenton as its first Honorary Secretary. It was understandable, therefore, that upon his return from the Crimea – and after a suitable period for his recovery from malaria – he should present a lecture to the Society on his experiences. In that lecture he gave a detailed account of the equipment he took with him. Bear in mind that almost a century and a half later, all my equipment and materials were contained in a small shoulder bag!

I took with me, he wrote, *a camera for portraits fitted with one of Ross's 3-inch lenses, two cameras made by Bourquien of Paris, of the bellows construction, and fitted with Ross's 4-inch landscape lenses, and two smaller cameras made by Horne and fitted with their lenses, but in place of which I subsequently employed a pair of Ross's 3-inch lenses with which I had previously worked. The stock of glass plates was, I think 700, of three different sizes, fitted into grooved boxes each of which contained twenty-four plates; the boxes of glass were again packed in chests so as to ensure their security. Several chests of chemicals, a small still with stove, three or four printing frames, gutta-percha baths and dishes, and a few carpenters tools, formed the principal part of the photographic baggage.*[7]

Interestingly, he included printing frames – but there is no mention of paper on which to make the prints! He continued:

I must not forget, however, the foundation of all my labours, the travelling dark-room. The carriage, which has already had an existence chequered with many adventures by field and flood, began its career, so far as its present historian knows, in the service of a wine merchant in Canterbury.

When it entered the service of the art, a fresh top was made for it, so as to convert it into a dark-room; panes of yellow glass, with shutters, were fixed in the sides; a bed was constructed for it, which folded up into a very small space under the bench at the upper end; round the top were cisterns for distilled and for ordinary water, and a shelf for books. On the sides were places for fixing the gutta-percha baths, glass-dippers, knives, forks and spoons. The kettles and cups hung from the roof. On the floor, under the trough for receiving waste water, was a frame with holes in which were placed the heavier bottles. This frame had at night to be lifted up and placed on the working bench with the cameras, to make room for the bed....[8]

As if that was not enough to take with him, there were, of course, the provisions for himself and his assistant Marcus Sparling. That accounted for another thirty-six large chests and, by his own admission, when he saw them stacked up at London's Blackwell Pier, he wondered how he was going to keep track of everything during both the long voyage and the photographic campaign itself!

He arrived in Balaclava in March 1855 and worked for three months before leaving in June, at the height of the Crimean summer. My arrival was in early July, in a hot but not extreme summer, yet nothing could have prepared me for the heat, the humidity, and the exhausting challenge of trying to take photographs under those conditions - even with easy-to-use modern equipment.

In his lecture, Fenton wrote about his collodion drying almost instantly on the glass plates as he tried to coat them in his horse-drawn darkroom, and of only being able to take pictures before 10am because of the intensity of the heat and the brightness of the light. He probably therefore had no more than three and a half hours each day in which he could work. The sun rises above the mountains by about 6.30am in early summer, with photography on the higher plains being possible a little earlier.

The light was so intense that even with weaker sensitising solutions than he used at home, he was able to take what he described as "almost instantaneous" pictures - with exposure times almost too short for him to control.

It is only by experiencing first-hand the conditions under which he worked that the true scale of his undertaking can be appreciated. Working in the fetid conditions of his mobile darkroom, with evaporating ether in a confined

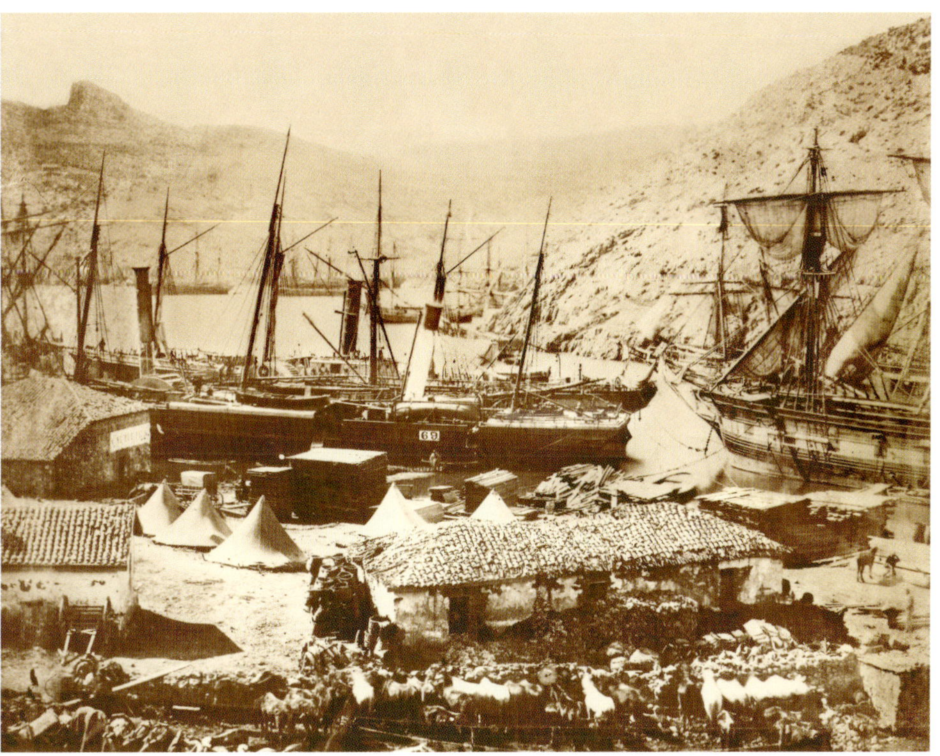

opposite page: Balaclava Harbour today, now host to some small cargo vessels, a few fishing boats and assorted pleasure craft. Empty submarine pens cut deep into the rocks, and a rusting floating dry dock - in which an even rustier submarine was being renovated - offered a tangible reminder of its more recent past as a Soviet naval port.

above: Fenton titled this view of the harbour in March 1855 'Cattle Pier, Balaclava' and it was one of the first photographs he took after unloading his mobile darkroom, his equipment, and his horses. With the sun already high in the sky, the conditions inside his darkroom van where he coated and processed his collodion negative were extremely challenging. In the harbour can be seen all the provisions for the troops which they should have had in the previous winter.

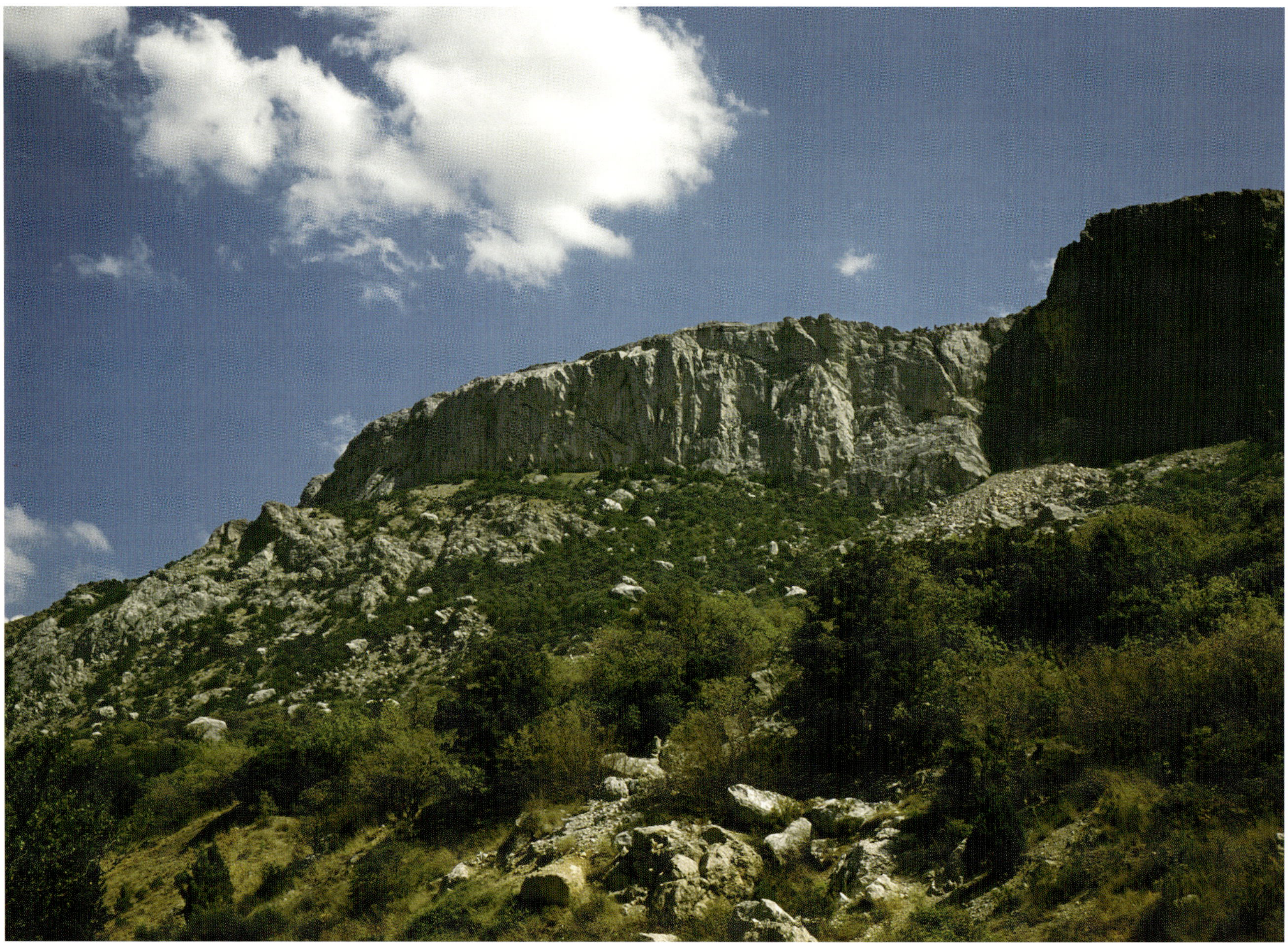

space must have been immensely challenging. The three hundred and sixty Crimean War photographs which he brought back, rather than being read as a somewhat stilted, contrived and politically expedient account of the war, can justifiably be seen as a magnificent achievement with an imperfect process under appalling working conditions.

In addition to his published account of the experience, he wrote detailed accounts of his journey through the war zone in letters to his wife Grace and his publisher Thomas Agnew.

His photographs were a public relations exercise – unprecedented in their day, as nobody had ever successfully used the camera in a war zone. Under a measure of government patronage, his unwritten brief was to produce a series of images which would achieve commercial success and bring a return for Agnew's investment; which would portray the central characters of the allied side of the conflict; and which could reassure the public back home that the war was being successfully prosecuted.

His early photographs of Balaclava Harbour, therefore, were clearly trumpeting the success of the Ordnance Corps, and the successful delivery of plentiful provisions, but his letters home painted a different picture. To his wife he wrote:

> *The whole place is one great pigsty. At present eighty sheep are slaughtered every day in the vessels in the harbour alone, and the entrails thrown into the water alongside. All over the camp, animals wanted for food are killed close to the tents, and the parts not used are left rotting for days… The stench along the waterfront is very bad, but they are taking pains to get rid of the filth. All the dead horses and oxen floating about the harbour are being towed out to sea. Do what they will, there is an immense quantity of putrefying matter which cannot be got rid of.* [9]

An enigmatic character at the best of times, Fenton may even have been concerned that the combination of the photographic process at his disposal, and the job his

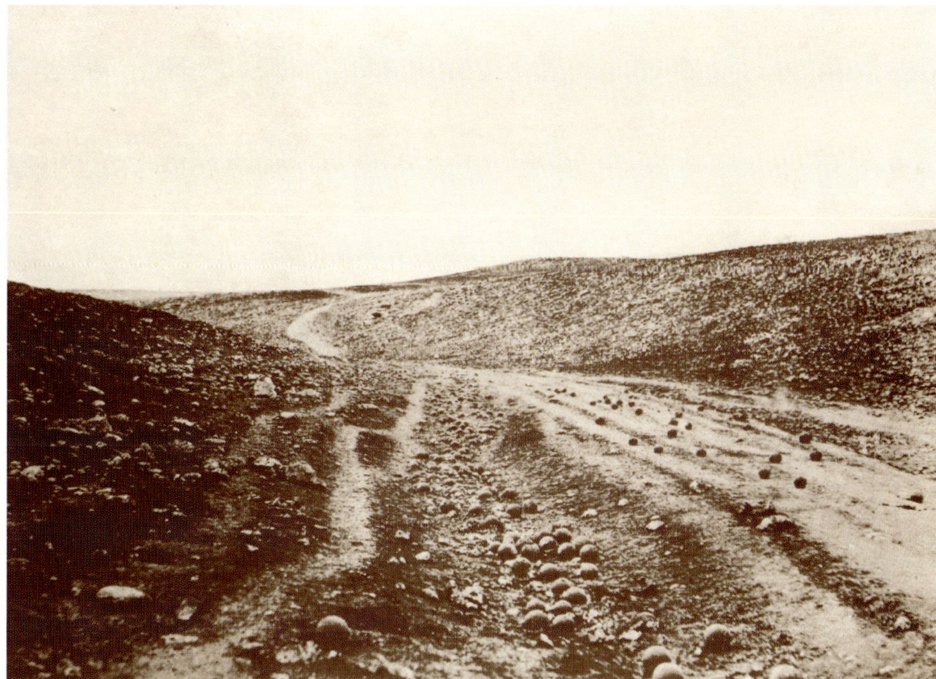

opposite page: The dramatic scenery of the Crimean hills, seen here very early on a June morning, provides a beautiful backdrop to the Black Sea coastline. For the soldiers on both sides, however, who had to negotiate this rocky terrain during the Crimean War – often under terrible weather conditions – it must have seemed anything but beautiful. A landscape less suited to warfare it would be hard to find.
above: Photographed by Fenton in June 1855, 'The Valley of the Shadow of Death', his chosen title resonant with biblical connotations, is the only one of his Crimean images which captures anything approaching the horror of war. This image of the bleak landscape strewn with spent canon balls still echoes the heat and horror of battle which had had raged there only hours earlier. Fenton had, however, waited until the dead and wounded had been carried away before taking his photographs.

below: Balaclava Harbour today, photographed from the former Soviet submarine pens, shows the head of the harbour where the British fleet was tied up and which Fenton photographed on his first day in the war zone (*opposite page*).

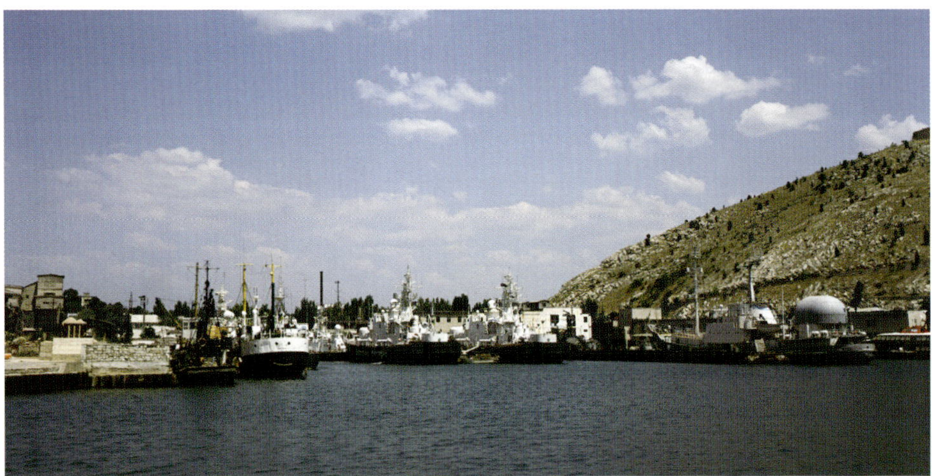

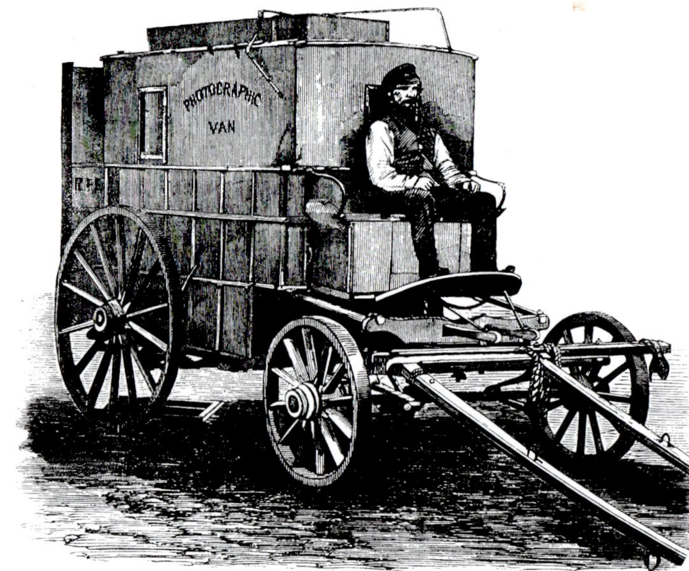

*right:*Fenton's horse-drawn photographic van with his assistant Marcus Sparling on the box. Sparling would later change his name to William when he published his major photographic manual. The van was Fenton's sleeping quarters as well as his workroom - and he slept surrounded by ether and other strong-smelling chemicals. Sparling, and William, the third member of the team, slept on the ground beneath the wheels.

pictures were required to do was irreconcilable with the truth of what was going on in the harbour and the trenches. So he told two stories of the Crimean campaign - one through his images, and the other through his letters. It is almost as if, knowing that his pictures were telling only a very small and selective part of the story, he used his letters and diaries to set the record straight. It is undoubtedly true that the process he was using placed severe restrictions on what was possible to photograph - action pictures were all but impossible. It is also true that, as the pictures were to be sold by Agnew in Manchester and Colnaghi in London, they had to be interesting enough to sell without being explicit enough to disturb. So his pictures stopped far short of presenting a balanced view of proceedings. There were camp scenes on the plains between Balaclava and Sevastopol, endless portraits of the major players from the generals down to lower officer ranks - but very few enlisted men - and a comprehensive series of views of Balaclava harbour.

The picture he presented around Balaclava's quayside was one of bustle, of plentiful supplies and of an efficient working unit all pulling together. Elsewhere, there were railway officials building a supply railway to the front line, sanitary commissioners apparently ensuring that the troops were living in a hygenic environment, and there were the officers themselves, sufficiently relaxed about the whole situation to be photographed enjoying a quiet drink - and drinking from fine glassware. Had such pictures been seen at the time, they would have contrasted vividly with the reports which William Howard Russell had been sending to the *Times* since the previous November.[10] Fenton's letters, while conceding that things were not as bad as he expected, tell a story closer to Russell's than do his pictures. It would be left to James Robertson and others to present a more realistic view of the devastation of war after Fenton had returned home.

Despite the limited scope of his work, working in the Crimea was not easy, and on more than one occasion

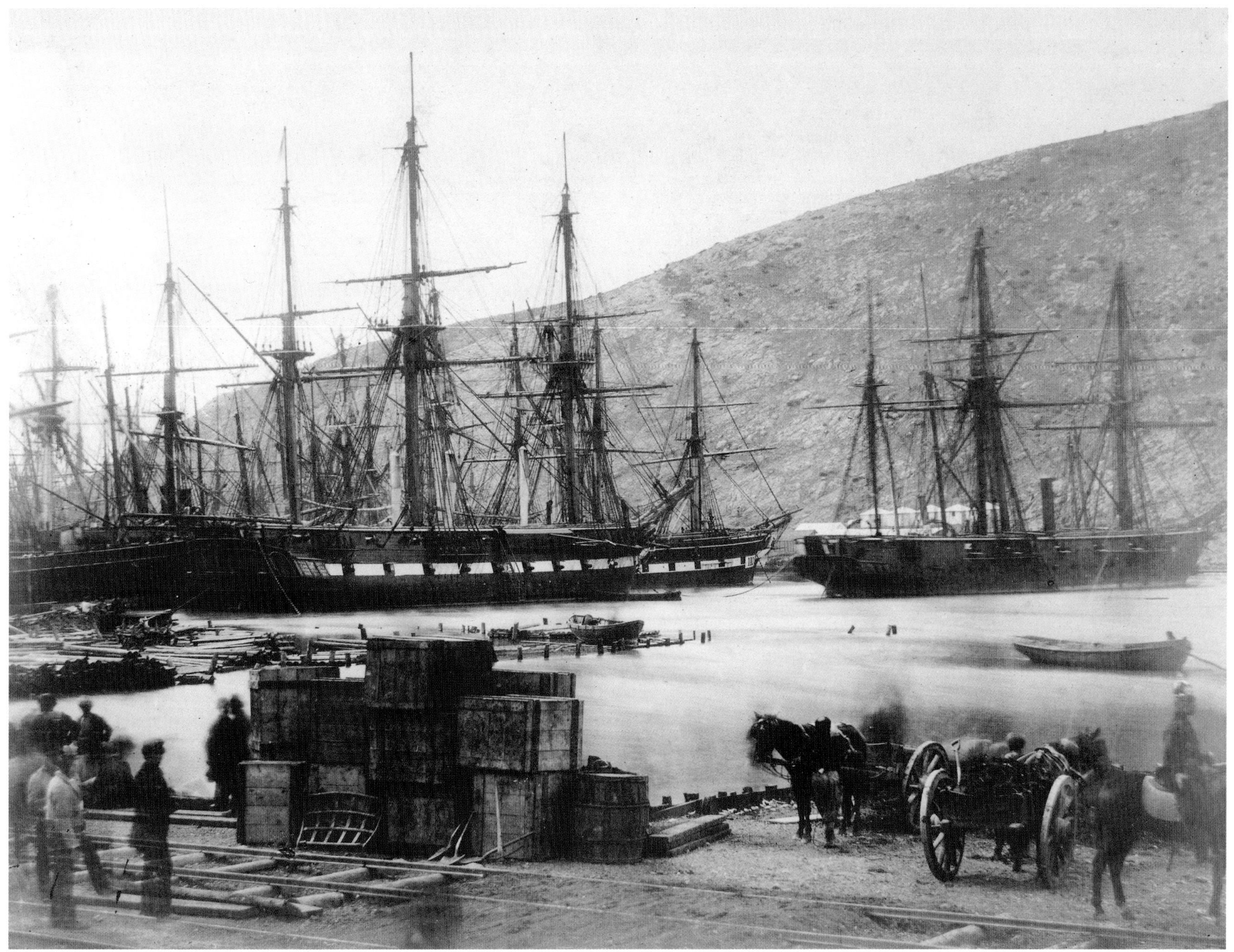

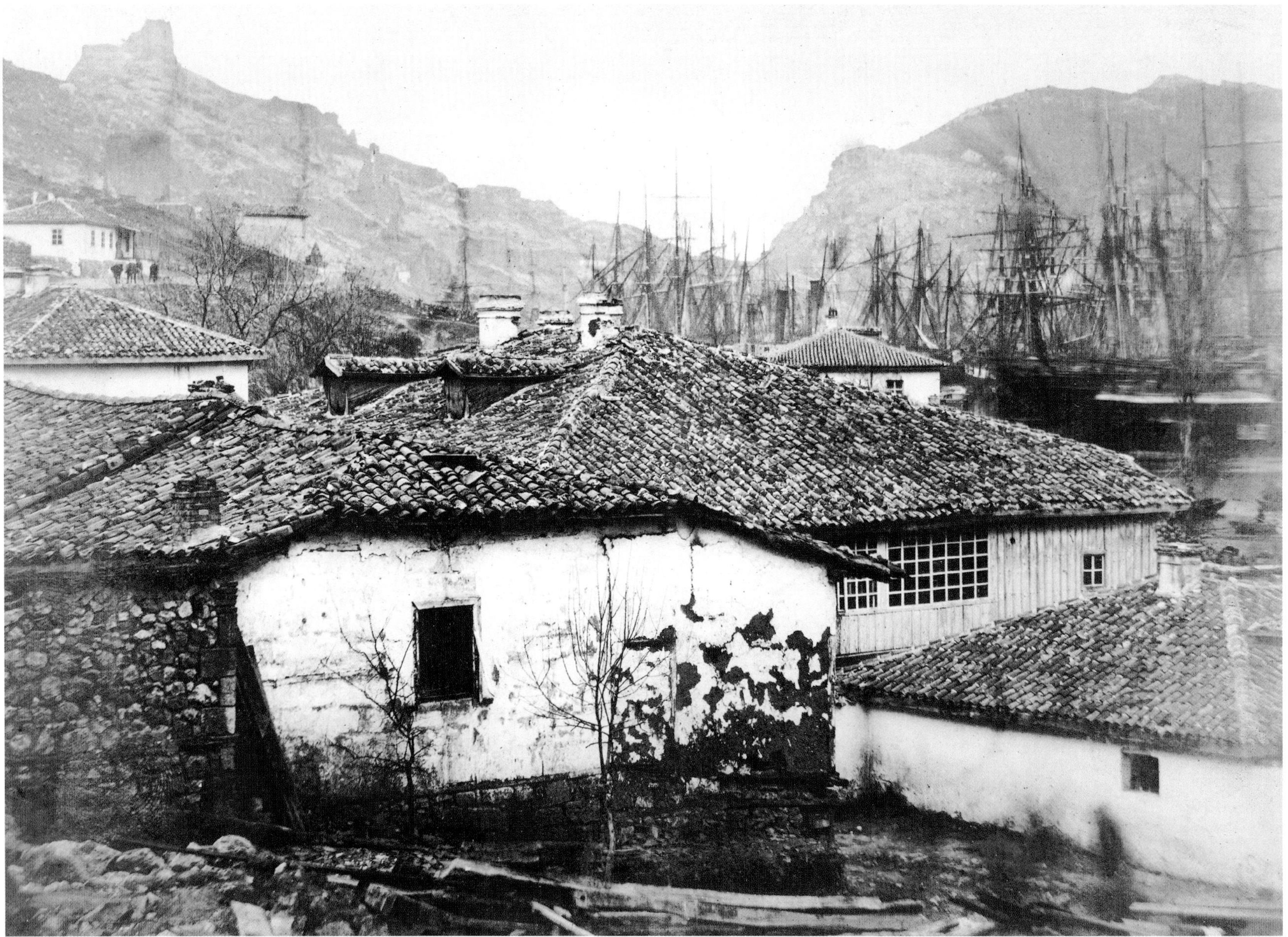

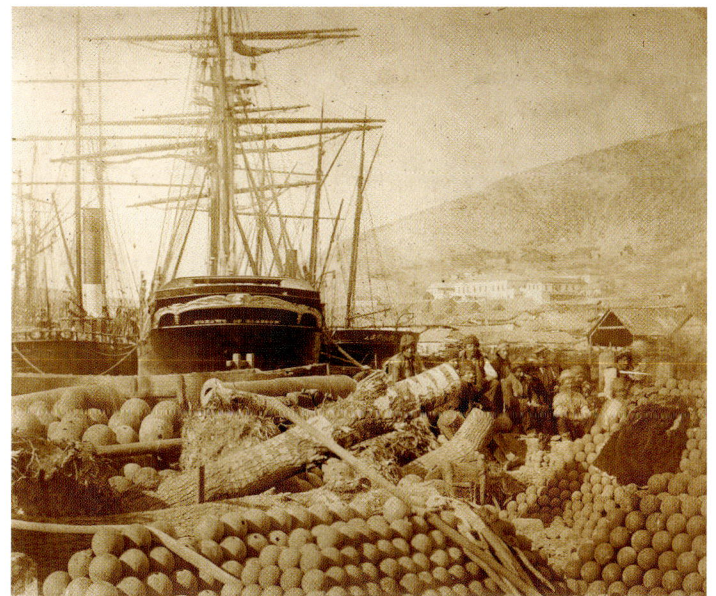

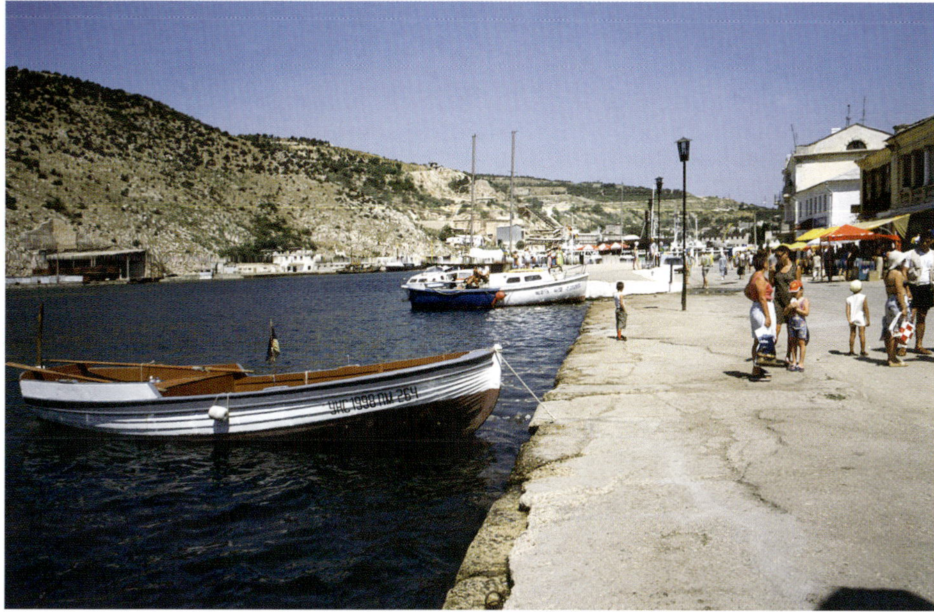

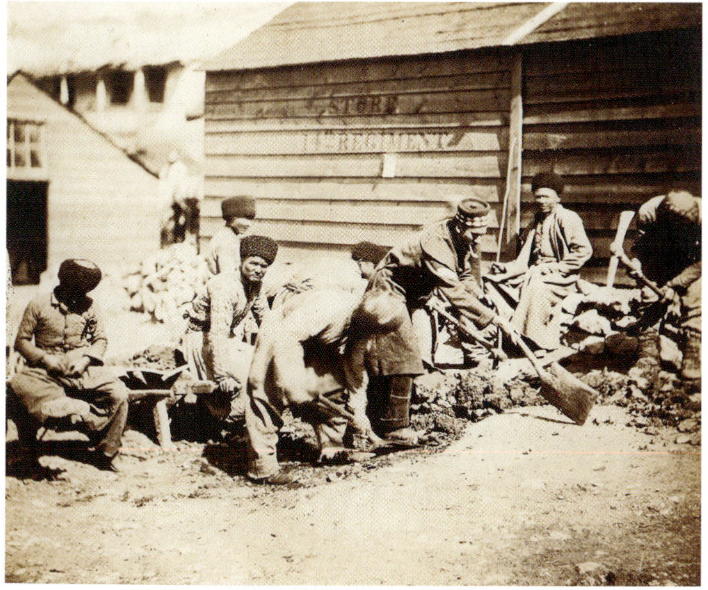

opposite page: Cottages at Balaclava, another of Fenton's earliest Crimean views. The port was a hive of activity with much to be observed and recorded for posterity.

above: Balaclava waterfront today. It is amazing to think that in November 1854, at the time of the great storm, there were over one hundred ships crammed into this tiny space. Many of them were tied so close together that they ground each other to pieces at the height of the storm.

above left: The ordnance Wharf, Balaclava, in June 1855. As part of the propaganda exercise which was implicit in Fenton's brief, photographs showing ships laden with supplies, and quays piled high with ordnance were probably a prerequisite for the publishers who were paying Fenton's salary and expenses.

left: Tartar Labourers. Fenton was fascinated by the many different people who supported the forces. Tartars, Croats and others all posed for his camera.

opposite page: In Sevastopol today, in a huge rotunda, a remarkable 360° panoramic painting celebrates the seige of the city in 1854-55, seen by the Russians as an heroic stand against their enemies. From the central viewpoint, as if on the roof of the Malakoff Fort, a realistic representation of what has been described as the last mediaeval war and the first modern war is all around. Created to mark the 50th anniversary of the seige, the original painting was destroyed by the Germans in 1942, and lovingly recreated in 1955 to mark the centenary of the seige.

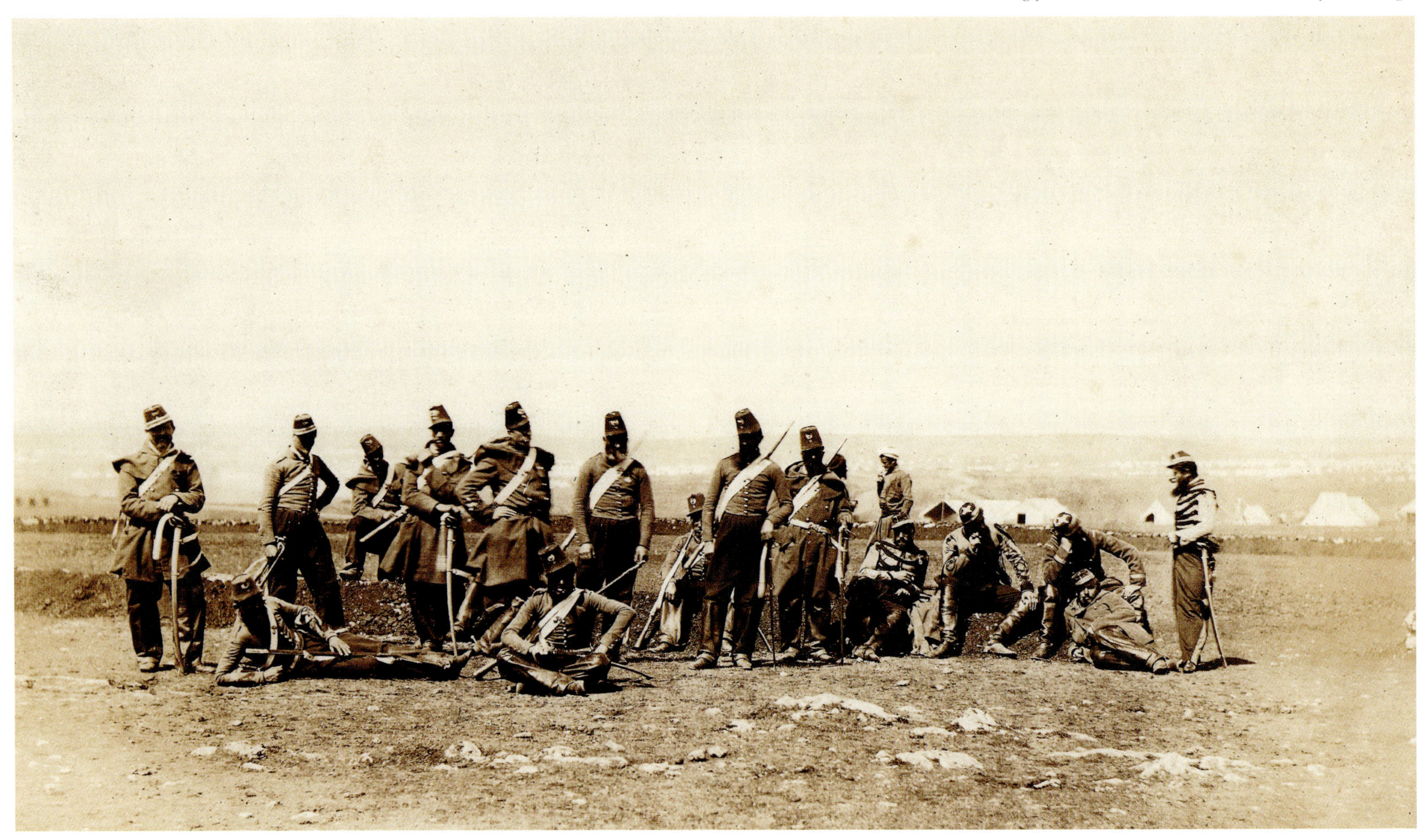

above: Roger Fenton's carefully posed study of 'Chasseurs d'Afrique' is in sharp contrast to the animated battle scene depicted in the great panorama painting in Sevastopol (*opposite page*). Photography was, as yet, incapable of capturing action, so Fenton was restricted to broad panoramic scenes and group portraits. This study was made on the plains above Balaclava, and the British encampment can be seen in the distance.

Fenton's photographic van was fired upon as he made his way closer to the field of battle.

Around Balaclava itself he enjoyed unrestricted access. In trying to replicate some of his views, I was not so lucky. Access was denied to the commercial port where ships were unloading logs and other light cargo but, ironically, good pictures were possible from the other side of the harbour – from the now disused Soviet submarine base!

The terrain around Balaclava harbour was certainly not conducive to waging a war. In the winter of 1854, torrential rain had turned the area into deep mud. What transport there was got bogged down in the mire. There was no way horses could pull loads up the slippery hillsides, and the soldiers found themselves carrying their own supplies to the front line. By the time of Fenton's arrival in March 1855, spring had arrived and with it drier weather. The horrors of the previous winter were no longer in evidence. He did complain about how slowly things happened though, and about how difficult it was to get down to serious work in the field remarking

> *I saw that if I could get none but official assistance, Sebastopol would be taken probably* vi et armis, *but not by photography.*[11]

As it turned out, Sevastopol did not fall until September 1855, by which time Fenton was back home recuperating after the bout of malaria which had cut short his endeavours. It would be left to others to photograph the almost total destruction of that city – some of it at the hands of the Russians themselves as they withdrew. The city was destroyed again in 1942 during World War II.

Fenton did join the armies marching on Kertch near Sevastopol, at the time a largely unpopulated area. Today it is a sprawling suburb of Sevastopol. The target was the Redan Fort.

In his lecture to the Photographic Society, he remarked

> *I had hoped to add to the collection of views which I had formed, photographs of the scenes since so ably depicted by Mr. Robertson, and with that view made everything ready*

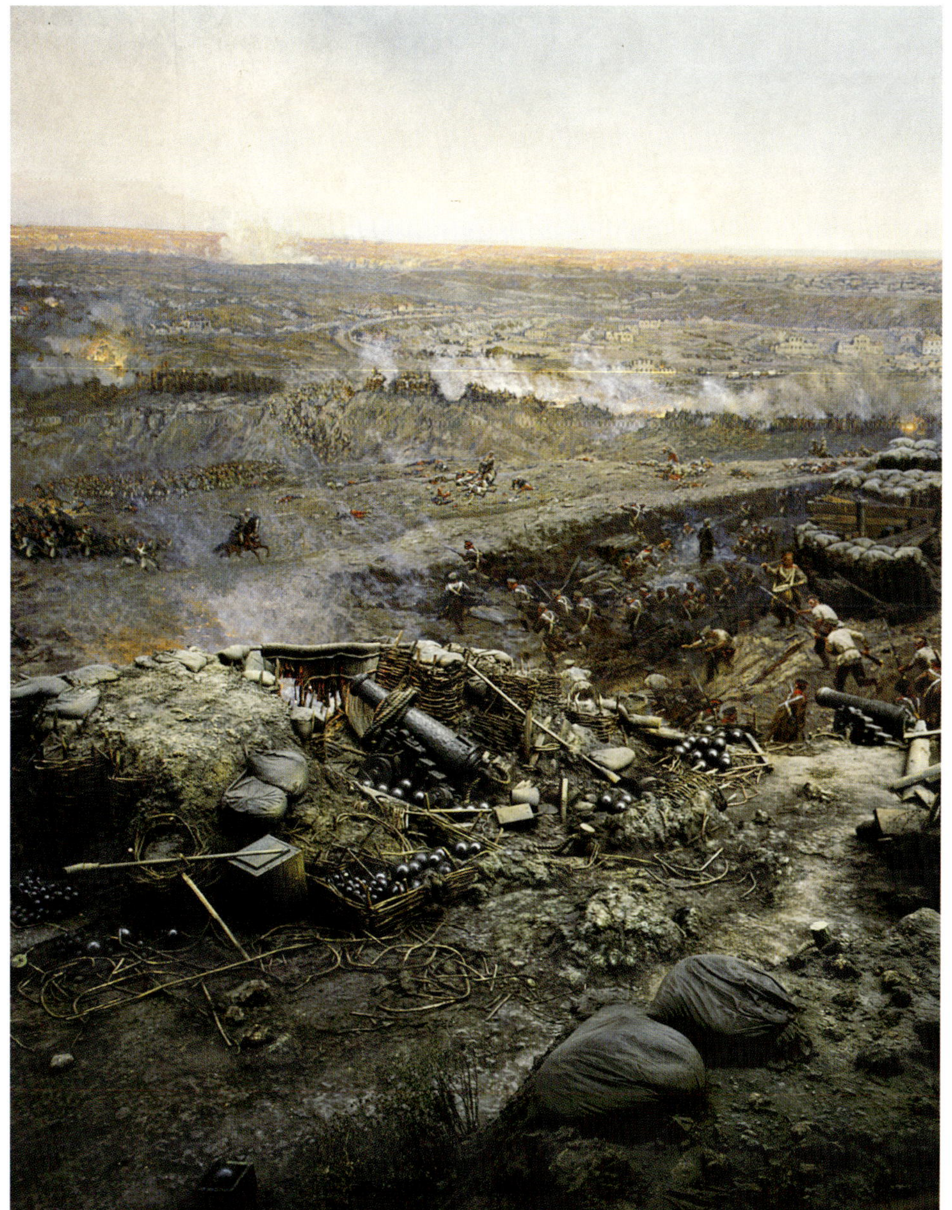

for going into Sebastopol after the attack of the 18th of June, which we all knew to be impending, and which everybody had settled was to succeed so surely, that those who had doubts scarcely ventured to express them. When that attempt failed, and to the list of friends already sacrificed were added new names, I felt quite unequal to farther exertion, and gladly embraced the first opportunity of coming away.[12]

Thus ended Roger Fenton's second and last venture abroad with his camera. Despite becoming one of the leading professional photographers of his day, he confined himself to working within the shores of Great Britain. Unless, that is, persistent rumours of photographs taken in Egypt after he retired from professional photography in 1862 turn out to be well founded.

Today, while Fenton's name is most widely known in connection with his Crimean War images, his fame rests not just on his achievements in Russia, but on the huge body of visually articulate images he produced on the abbeys, cathedrals, castles and great houses of England, and some eloquent landscapes in England, Scotland and Wales. His work for the British Museum pioneered the

below: Sevastopol harbour today is home to the Russian Black Sea fleet. Visible in the distance beyond the ferry are several local ferries, and numerous pleasure craft.

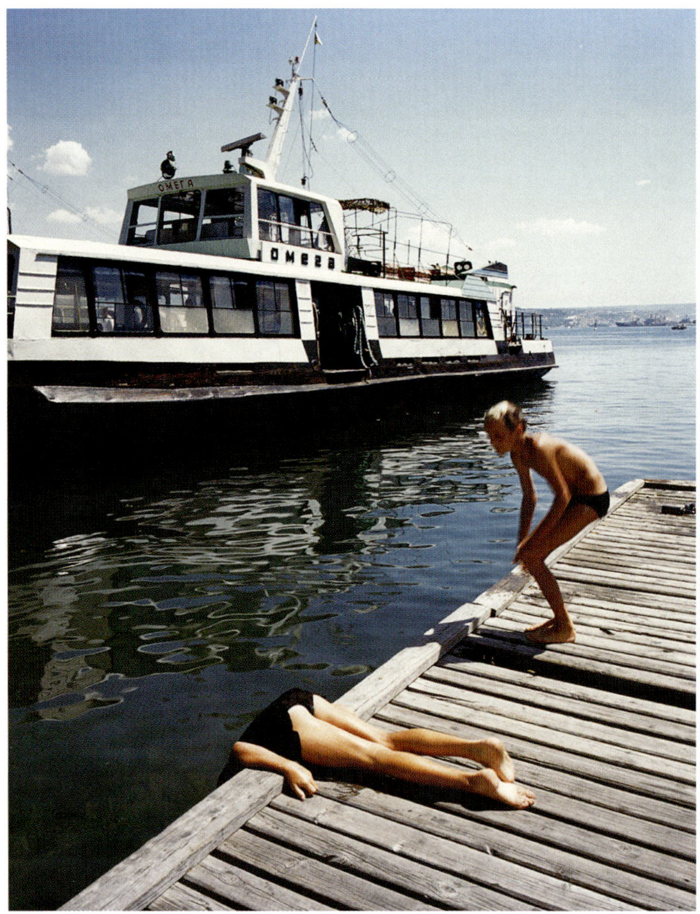

above left: James Robertson's depiction of the Malakoff Fort after the fall of Sevastopol in 1855 – weeks after Fenton's return to England – shows just how fierce the fighting had been. The little fort has now been rebuilt as a museum to various Crimean wars and battles. Its location is taken as the viewing platform at the centre of the panorama on the previous page.

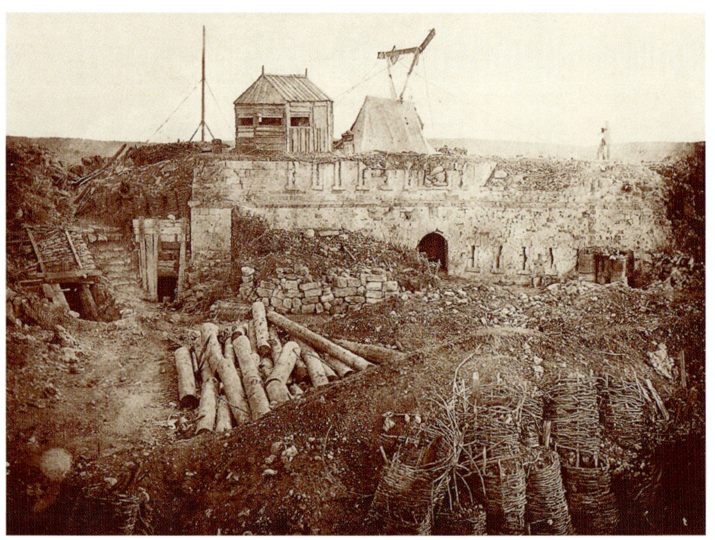

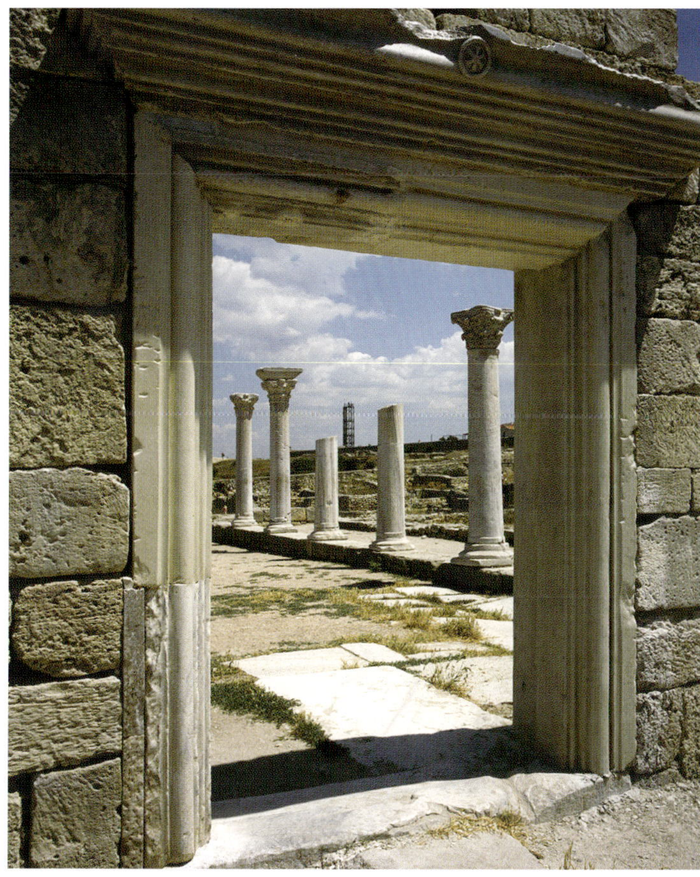

left: One of the many attractions of Sevastopol today is the ancient Greek city of Chersonesus – Khersones to the Crimeans – much of which still lies buried on the clifftops just outside the city.

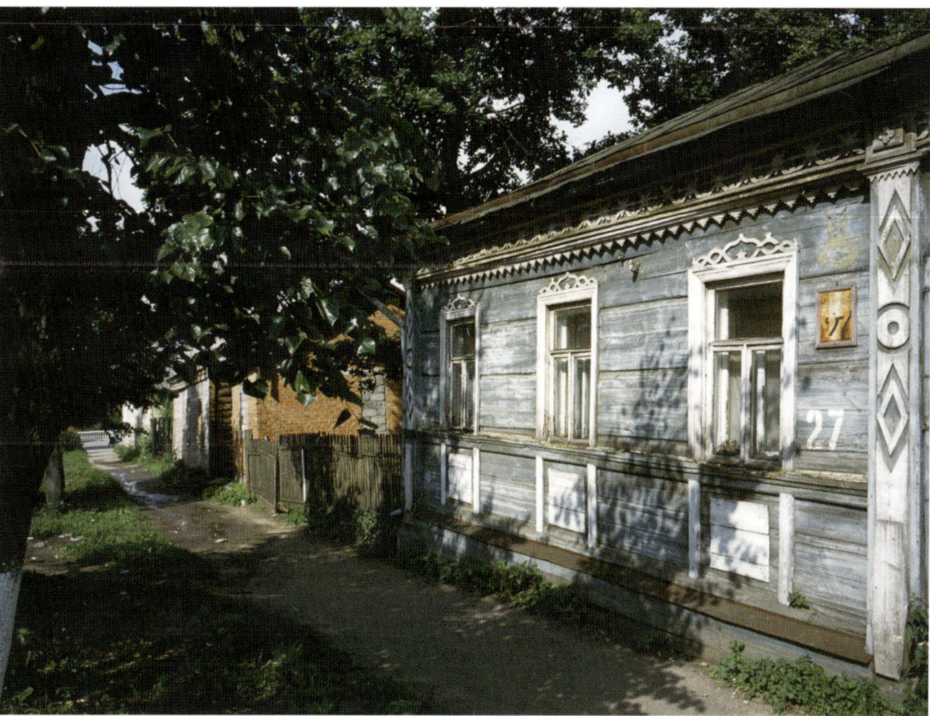

above: Outside the big cities, a considerable amount of traditional Russian wooden architecture still survives. This beautiful house was photographed in the small town of Sergiev-Possad, 75km north-east of Moscow, near the Trinity Monastery of St Sergius.

idea of disseminating photographic images of historic artifacts for study by academics, and his sales booth in the museum foyer predicted the museum shops on which those institutions rely for much valuable income today.

He helped establish the (Royal) Photographic Society in 1853, wrote extensively about photography in the emerging photographic press, and shared his knowledge enthusiastically with his peers.

It is ironic that the Crimean legacy which ensured his fame also hastened his death. He had to leave the Black Sea in July 1856 after become dangerously ill, and the prolonged period of recovery from his ordeal delayed the publication of his Crimean images, arguably reducing their popularity and topical relevance. Despite concerted efforts to sell the images – both as sets in portfolios and as single prints – huge numbers of prints remained unsold and were auctioned off. The publisher, Thomas Agnew, never recouped his considerable outlay.

It was as a result of a recurrence of his Crimean illness that Roger Fenton died in 1869 at the age of only fifty.

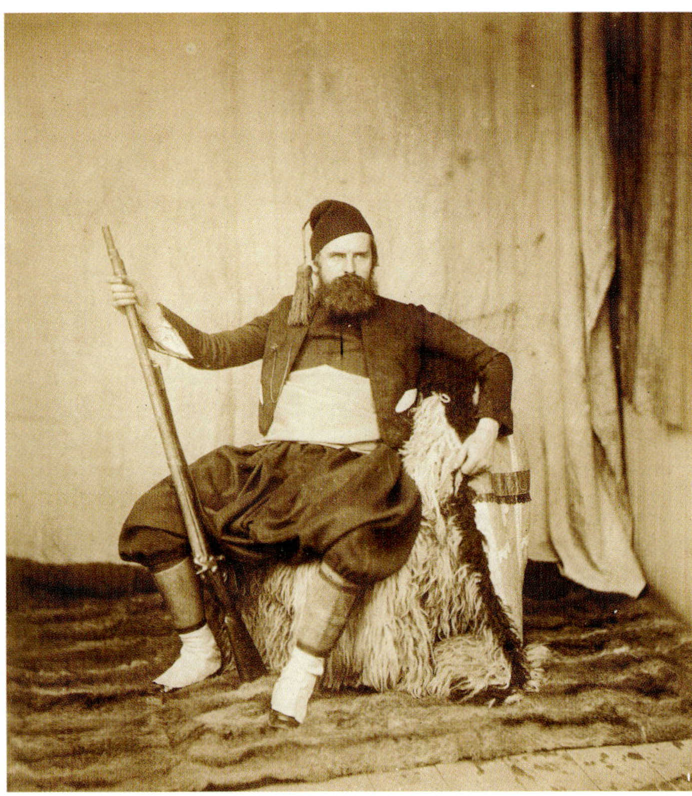

above: Roger Fenton posing in front of his own camera, dressed as 'Zouave, 2nd Division'. The photographer appears in a variety of guises in several of his own group portraits. Despite the fact that, in the 1850s, the absolute truth of the photograph was rarely questioned, images like this were accepted as realistic representations of the war, if not the actual truth itself. The creation of such fictions would be unthinkable under codes of ethics which are applied to documentary photography today.

Notes

1. The Royal Photographic Society Collection is now housed at the National Media Museum, formerly the National Museum of Photography Film and Television, Bradford.
2. Frequent reference in Vignoles' diaries refer to this relationship. Vignoles diaries are in the Department of Manuscripts at the British Museum, catalogue numbers 34.528–34.536
3. The National Museum of the Ukraine, Kiev, has an album containing thirteen salted paper prints, some from calotype negatives, some from collodion, taken by John Cooke Bourne in the weeks before the bridge opened in 1853. The album was presented by Vignoles to the Russian General Subersky at the time. Subsersky's descendants presented it to one of the museums later absorbed into the National Museum of the History of the Ukraine.
4. A printed frontispiece to the Kiev album includes all these statistics.
5. Vignoles diaries, Department of Manuscripts at the British Museum, catalogue numbers 34.528–34.536, and quoted in Vignoles, Keith "C.B.Vignoles and the RPS", *The Photographic Journal*, January 1983, p29.
6. Titles taken from Fenton prints contained in the RPS Collection, National Media Museum, Bradford.
7. Fenton, Roger "Narrative of a Photographic Trip to the Seat of the War in the Crimea" read to the Ordinary Meeting of the Photographic Society held on 3rd January 1856, and subsequently published in *The Journal of the Photographic Society* January 21st, 1856, pp284-291.
8. ditto.
9. Letter from Fenton to Thomas Agnew, quoted in Helmut & Alison Gernsheim *Roger Fenton: Photographer of the Crimean War*, London, Secker & Warburg, 1954, p16,
10. William Howard Russell, the Special Correspondant of *The Times* had been warning of the forthcoming food and clothing shortages in the Crimea, and the gross mis-management of the war, since autumn of 1854. His most compelling report, dated November 25th 1854, read *It is now pouring rain – the skies are black as ink – the wind is howling over the staggering tents – the trenches are turned into dykes – in the tents the water is sometimes a foot deep – our men have not either warm or waterproof clothing – they are out for twelve hours at a time in the trenches – they are plunged into the inevitable miseries of a winter campaign – and not a soul seems to care for their comfort or even their lives.* Quoted in Alan Hankinson *Man of Wars: William Howard Russell of the Times*, London, Heinemann, 1982.
11. From Fenton's letters to his wife and publisher, reproduced in Helmut & Alison Gernsheim *Roger Fenton: Photographer of the Crimean War*, London, Secker & Warburg, 1954, p15.
12. Fenton, Roger "Narrative of a Photographic Trip to the Seat of the War in the Crimea" in *The Journal of the Photographic Society* January 21st, 1856, pp284-291.

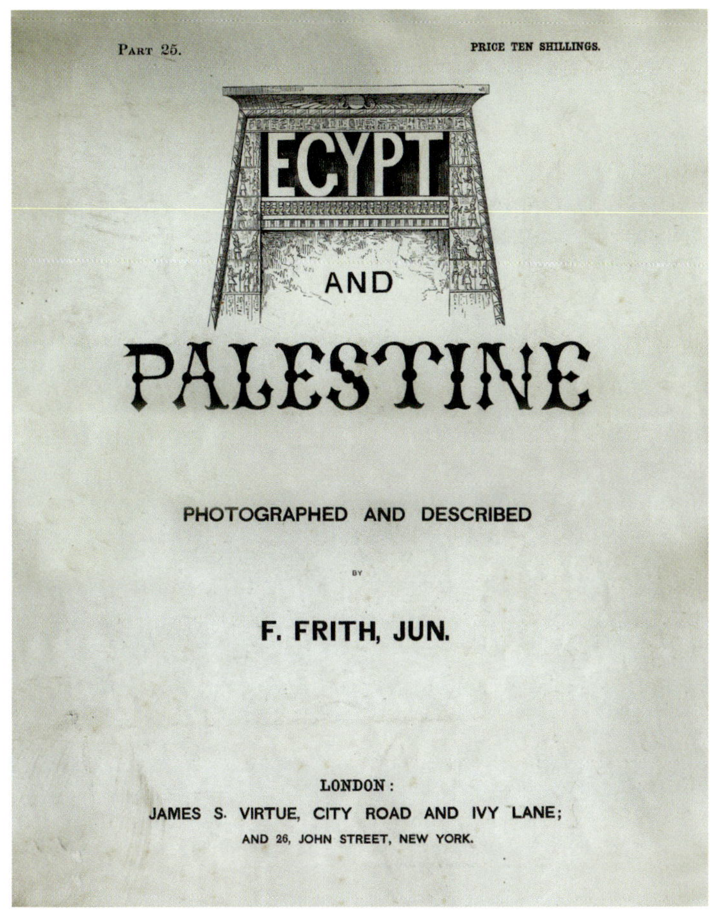

PART 25. PRICE TEN SHILLINGS.

EGYPT

AND

PALESTINE

PHOTOGRAPHED AND DESCRIBED

BY

F. FRITH, JUN.

LONDON:

JAMES S. VIRTUE, CITY ROAD AND IVY LANE;

AND 26, JOHN STREET, NEW YORK.

Francis Frith

Journeys in the Nile Valley 1856-1859

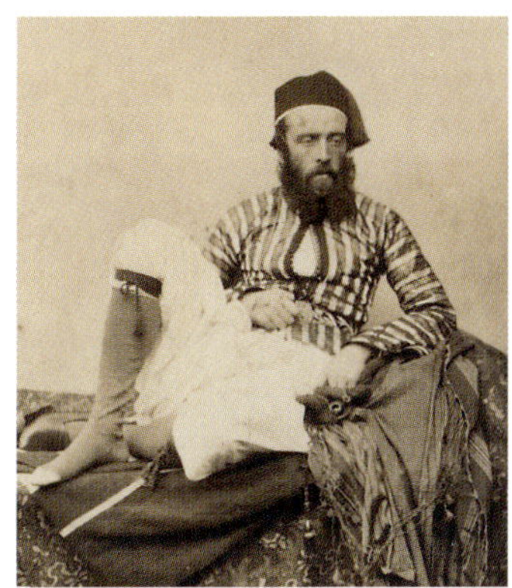

above: Francis Frith, photographed during one of his Egyptian journeys

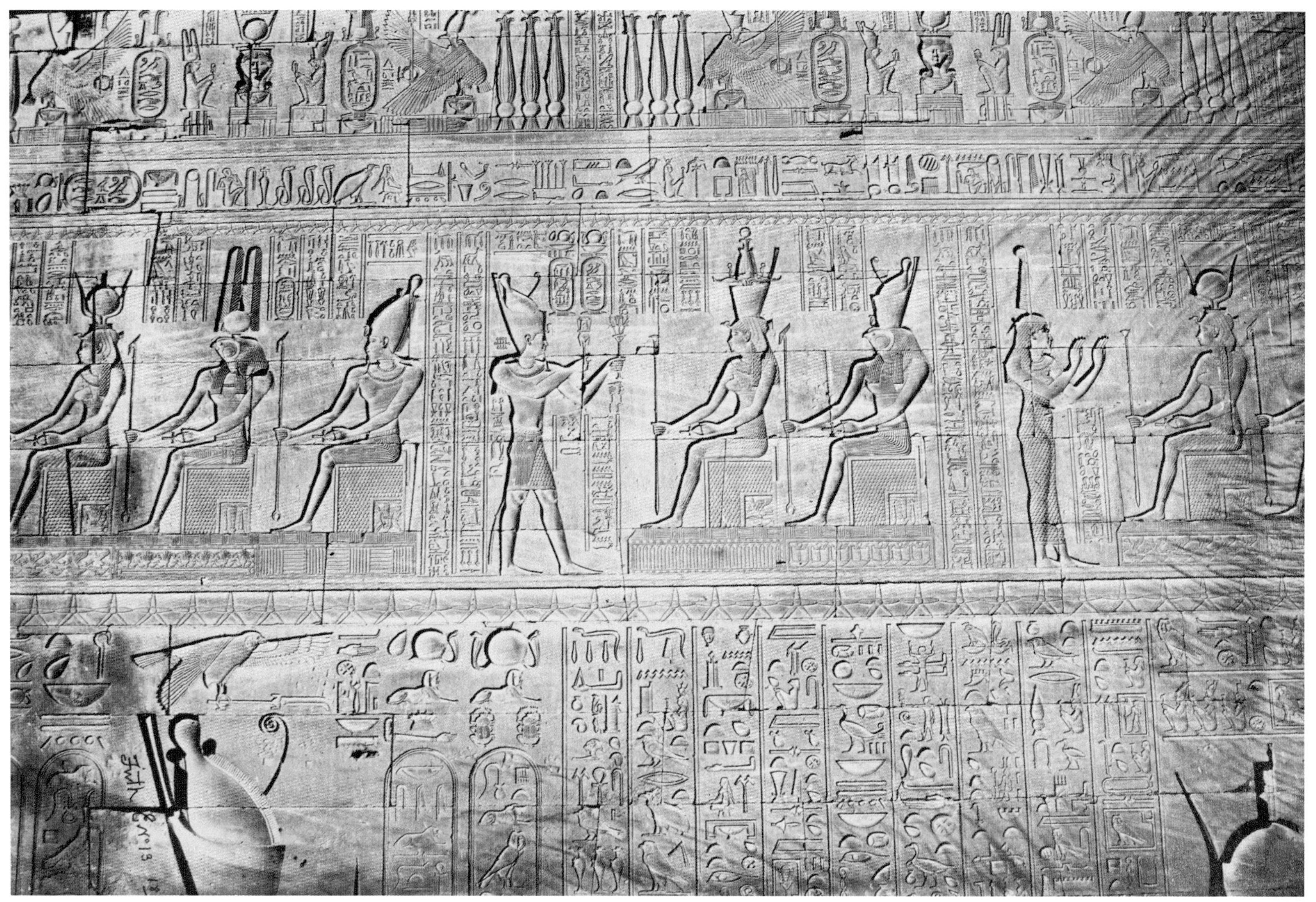

above: Relief sculptures on the walls of the temple at Dendara, Egypt, photographed by Frith in 1857. Under the heat of the Egyptian summer sun, Frith's collodion dried before he could spread it evenly across the plate. As it dried, the sensitivity fell, creating underexposure in the negative and dark streaks in the print.

Writing in the commentary which accompanied his photographs of the sculptures at Dendara, Francis Frith wrote

I do not expect to be able to convey to the mind of the reader any true idea of the strange feeling of interest and wonder which the first views of these Nile sculptures inspire. For myself, I confess that although I was of course prepared to see an abundance of hieroglyphic sculpture, I was, nevertheless, completely taken by surprise. I was not at all prepared to realise such vivid contact with the very minds and feelings of the men of 3000 years ago. Everyone is familiar with the sort of interest one feels in seeing the autographs of great men, long lost to earth: with such a feeling, but with a charming sense of mystery added, do we regard the Egyptian sculptures. To stand in the very footmarks of the first men of time, and look upon their genuine handiwork, is wonderfully suggestive of the men themselves.[1]

The power of the sculptures has not been diluted by time or familiarity, and today's visitors still stand in awe of their beauty when first confronted by them. They may not, however, get to see them in such sharp relief as Frith did. Police escorts to and from the site dictate when you can visit, how long you can stay and when you must leave. The Egyptians depend so heavily on tourism today, that every precaution is taken to avoid an attack on visitors such as that at the Temple of Hatshepsut near Thebes in the 1990s.

Frith's picture was taken very early in the morning, with the sun shining obliquely across the decorated wall. By the time my car, escorted by two police vans, reached the site, the wall was in shadow.

Frith's journeys to Egypt were to take him further up the Nile than anyone before him, and the resulting images were published in a series of partworks, books and sets of stereoscopic cards.

Others had been to Egypt long before him – Jules Itier in the mid 1840s, Maxime du Camp in 1850, Félix Teynard in the early 1850s, and many others, but Frith's travels were by far the most comprehensive. He visited places that no

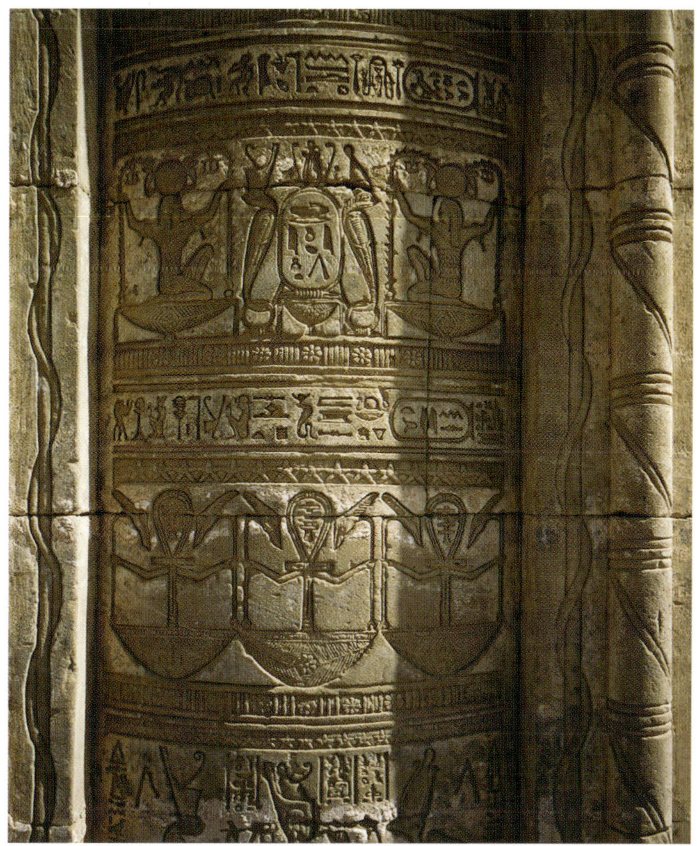

above: Sculptured column, Dendara. A little off the most popular tourist track, Dendara does not have the crowds which flock to other sites, despite having the most complete Hall of Columns in Egypt. Frith remarked that it was *certainly inferior to no existing temple in the perfection and beauty of its masonry, and the mere cutting of its sculptures.* Visitors today join a small convoy with police escort to visit the site!

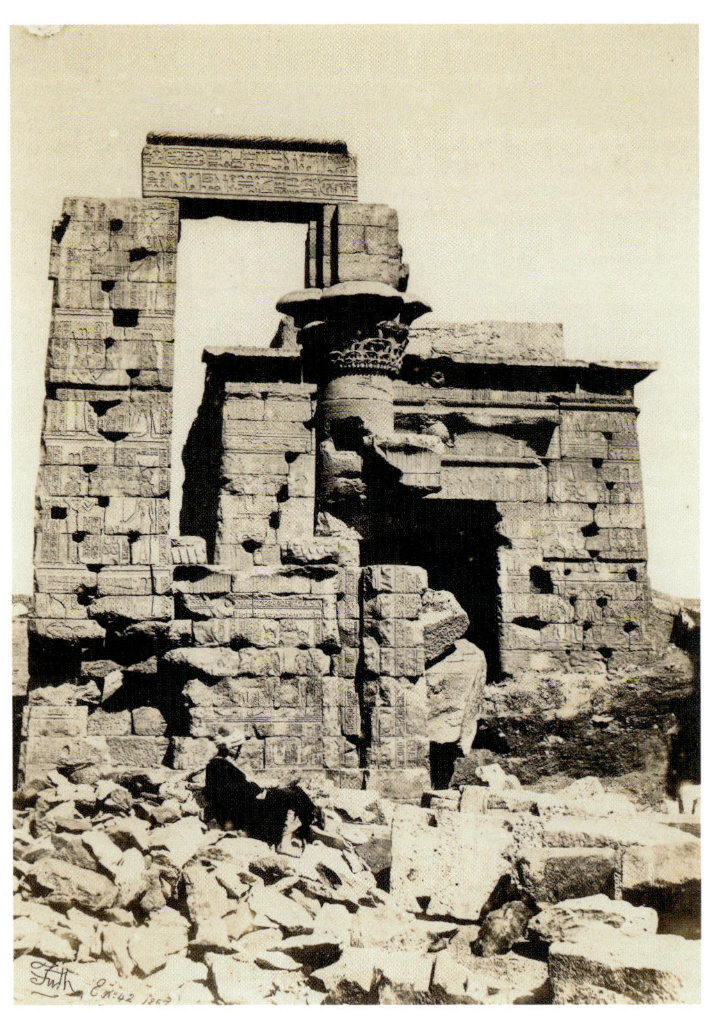

above: The Temple at Erment, a few miles south of Thebes on the west bank of the Nile, photographed by Frith in 1857.

other photographer had, and the decision to publish the pictures in a series of partworks ensured that he reached a wider audience than anyone before him. The photographs would establish his name and reputation, and lay the foundations for the Frith publishing empire which thrived for well over a century.

He arrived in Egypt for his first journey in September 1856 through the port of Alexandria after a long sail from Liverpool, in what he described as a "nearly new screw-ship" and under "a tremendous gale of wind nearly the whole way." He then transferred to a small steam launch for the first stage of his journey up the Nile. He spent ten months exploring and taking photographs before returning home in July 1857. Three months later he set off again, this time spending six months in Palestine, Syria and Egypt. A third trip in 1859 took him further up the Nile than anyone had ever ventured with a camera before, and the fifteen hundred images he brought home caused a sensation.

I flew direct from Manchester to Cairo and arrived in the intense heat of Egypt only a few hours after leaving the unseasonal cold of a British autumn.

The Egypt into which Frith stepped was very different to today's Egypt in some respects, but in others he would find the country today quite familiar. He was, of course, primarily there to photograph the antiquities, then recently celebrated in a series of folios of lithographs by the Victorian artist David Roberts whose illustrations of the great temples and tombs had been published in Britain in the 1840s.[2]

Frith, with a strong artistic background, may have been aware of Roberts' works as soon as they were published, but was certainly impressed by them when he decided to travel to Egypt with his camera.

Roberts' partwork appeared at monthly intervals between 1842 and 1849, and the similarities between some of his painting, sketches and engravings, and some of Frith's early photographs of the same locations cannot just be coincidence.

One of the first important books to give credibility to

the idea of visiting the archaeological sites in Egypt as a tourist attraction – rather than to pillage them for historical artifacts – was William Makepeace Thackeray's *Notes on a Journey from Cornhill to Grand Cairo*, published part way through the publication of Roberts' works.[3]

The re-issuing of Roberts' portfolios in the mid 1850s may well have rekindled Frith's interest in the near East and by that time – with the potential of photography widely recognised – the possibilities of using photography to explore further what Roberts had done with the lithograph must certainly have appealed to him.

It is interesting to observe that while Roberts' views of Egypt include many scenes of daily life, Frith – seeing academia as his prime market – limited himself just to the antiquities, occasionally including himself or his servants as an aid to scale. It would be left to other local Egyptian photographers to portray the Egyptian way of life in pictures they marketed to the growing numbers of people who undertook the Grand Tour from the mid 1870s.

Travel in Egypt in Frith's day was an enormous challenge and, like any other photographer using the wet collodion process, a portable darkroom was an absolute necessity. Frith took with him a darktent – which he sometimes set up on board his riverboat, and at other times set up near the site he was photographing. He also took with him a wicker carriage which doubled up as darkroom and transport for all his equipment and materials. Like any wet plate photographer, he carried with him several hundred kilograms of equipment and materials. When the heat of the day got too much for him to work successfully in the carriage, he sought refuge in the cool interiors of tombs and there, by the light of a candle, set about the task of preparing his collodion plates. I travelled light with only a compact 645 autofocus camera and a supply of modern colour film!

Of his carriage, Frith wrote

This carriage of mine, being entirely overspread with a loose cover of white sailcloth to protect it from the sun, was a most

below: A timeless image in the Nile valley, as a felucca glides along the river at Aswan. A few hundred metres away, Aswan's Corniche is lined with the large Nile cruise ships which bring thousands of visitors to the ancient sites.
bottom: A camel-handler rests with his animal near Saqqara, while a tourist policeman looks on.

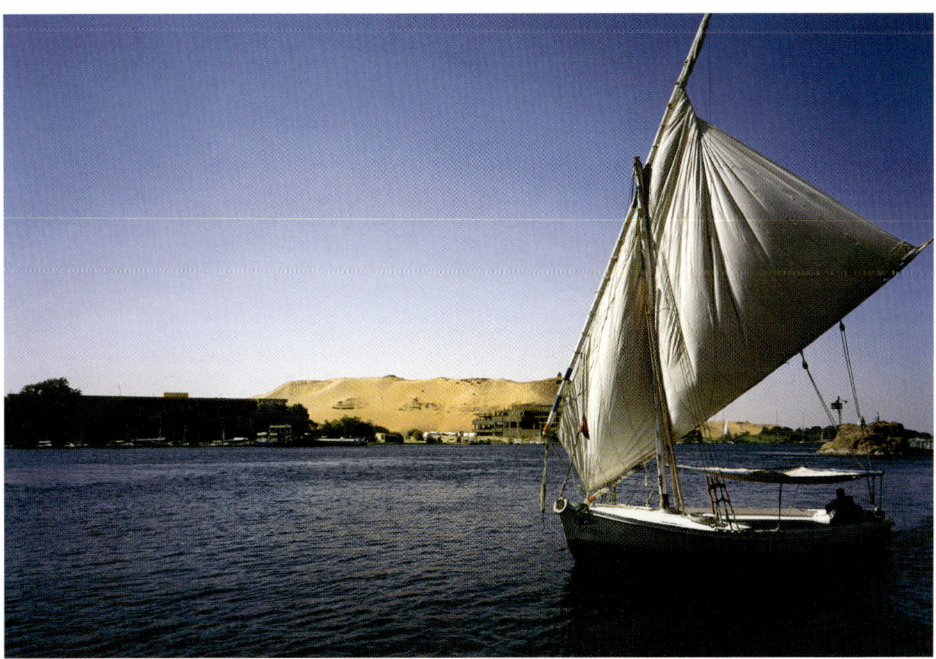

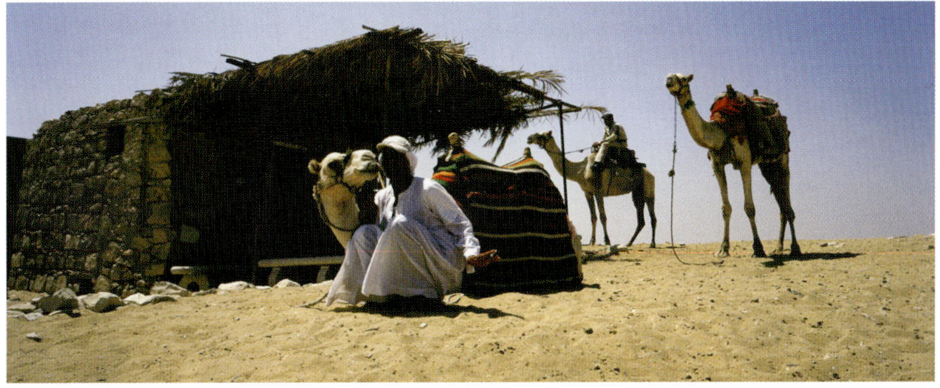

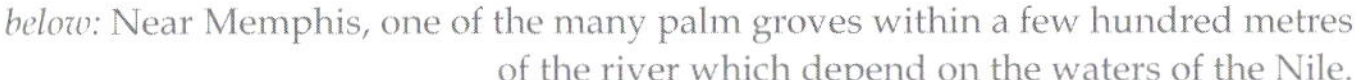

below: Near Memphis, one of the many palm groves within a few hundred metres of the river which depend on the waters of the Nile.

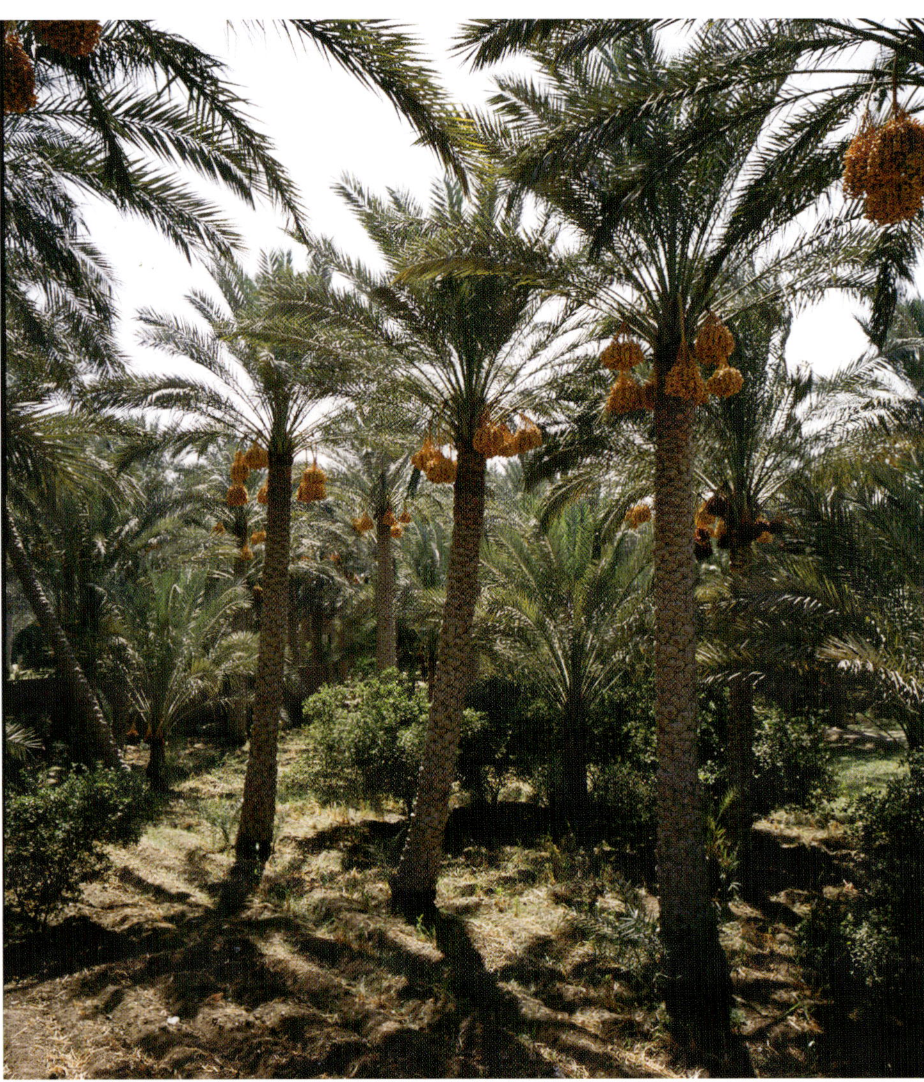

conspicuous and mysterious looking vehicle, and excited amongst the Egyptian populace a vast amount of ingenious speculation as to its uses. The idea, however, which seemed the most reasonable, and therefore obtained the most, was that therein, with right laudable and jealous care, I transported from place to place – my harem! It was full of moon-faced beauties, my wives all! – and great was the respect and consideration which this view of the case procured for me! [4]

For Frith, a lay preacher of the Society of Friends, to recount such a story says much about the man!

The mode of transport for most people in today's Cairo is the taxi – the city is almost overwhelmed by them. The roads are crowded, the air is laden with diesel fumes, and the sound of car horns day and night is unremitting.

Travelling by taxi to the Mosque of Mohammed Ali in the Citadel – which dominates the Cairo skyline, appears on coinage and has become a visual symbol of the city – I tried to open a window to let some of the fumes out of the car. There was no winder handle! Without a word, the driver opened the glove box, passed me a window-winder and while I let some air into the car, he kept his hand over the front passenger seat until I disconnected the handle and returned it to him!

Frith disregarded the buildings of 19th century Cairo, turning his cameras only towards the antiquities. In that respect his work differs from that of David Roberts who was as fascinated by the 'modern' as he was by the antiquities. The huge mosque, built in the Turkish style was under construction when Roberts visited, and had been completed only eight years before Frith's arrival – although its state of repair today makes it look a lot older. A century and a half of Cairo's polluted air has caused extensive corrosion to the exterior stonework. It remains, nonetheless, a remarkable building, dedicated to the man who is credited with uniting Egypt and establishing the nation's identity.

Neither Frith nor Roberts were in Cairo to see the construction of the impressive Gezira Palace, built to accommodate the Empress Eugenie of France when she

below left: The Mohammed Ali Mosque in the Citadel dominates the Cairo skyline. It has become an iconic image of the city, appearing on banknotes, coins and postage stamps.
below right: The elaborate columns of the Gezira Palace, built on the orders of Khedive Ismail to accommodate the French Empress Eugenie during her visit for the opening of the Suez Canal. The Palace is now incorporated into the Cairo Marriott Hotel, and serves as its entrance foyer.

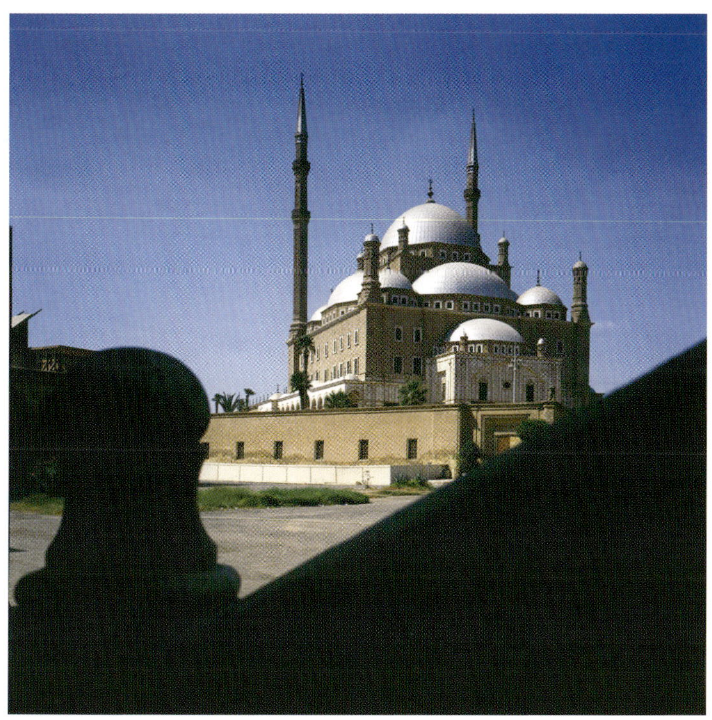

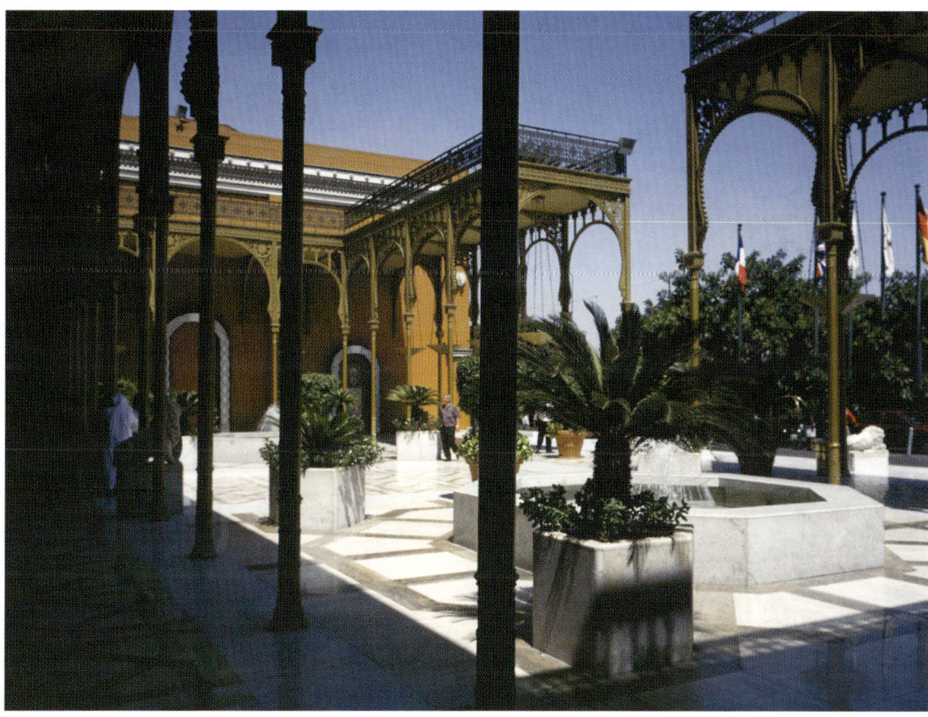

visited Egypt for the opening of the Suez Canal in 1869. Today it has been incorporated into the huge Marriott Hotel, a lavish piece of 19th century Turkish-style architecture hemmed in by two brutal late 20th century tower blocks.

To most travellers in the 19th century, as today, Cairo itself was sometimes overlooked in the haste to see the Pyramids at Giza, sandwiched between the outskirts of the ever-expanding city and the desert. This most popular of tourist attractions is almost overwhelmed by souvenir sellers and beggars, local camel-owners offering – for a fee of course – to pose with their camels for a photograph, and stalls selling film which has been baking in the sun for days on end to unsuspecting tourists. At the edge of the car park, a Pizza Hut and a KFC greet visitors.

Nothing prepares the traveller for the heat of Egypt – and in that respect today's experience is just as overwhelming as was Frith's. In other respects, of course, today's photographer has it easy – lightweight cameras, easy access to film, and much much easier transport. Compare the ease of photography at the pyramids or

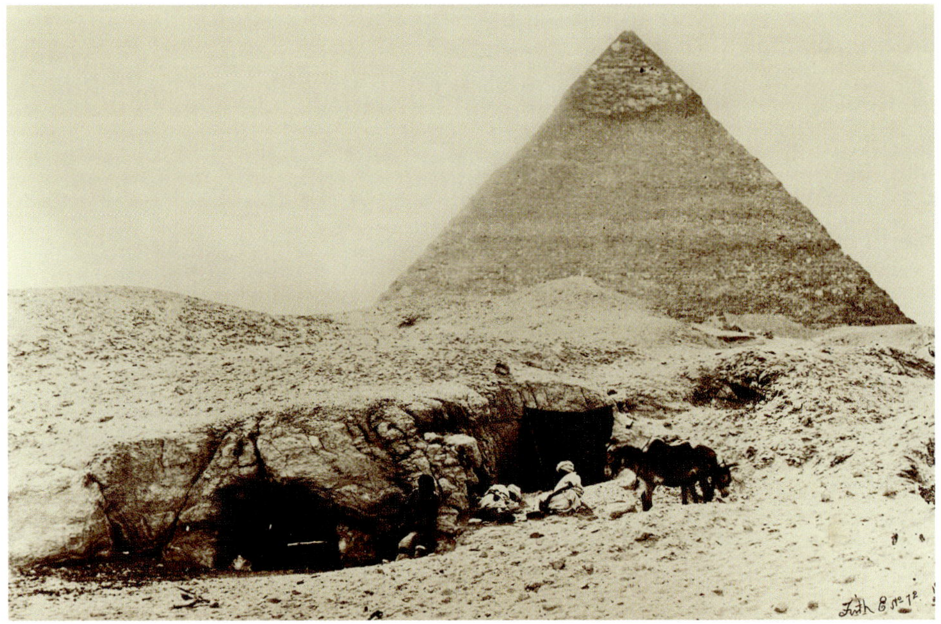

above: Frith captioned this view as 'Belzoni's Pyramid, Gizeh' a name it briefly held in recognition of the Italian explorer and antiquairian Giovanni Belzoni – described by the great Howard Carter as *one of the most remarkable men in the whole history of Egyptology*, and who discovered the entrance on the north face of the pyramid in 1818, and had previously discovered some of the lost tombs in the Valley of the Kings. Today it is known as the Great Pyramid or Khaefre's Pyramid. In front of the left-hand tomb entrance, just visible in Frith's photograph, there is a small tressle table with bottles on it. Might this have been the tomb into which Frith crawled, *pushing my way backwards upon my hands and knees,* to coat and prepare his 10x8 inch collodion plates?

temples today with Frith's account of his labours

> *I prepared my pictures by candlelight in one of the interior chambers of the temple. It was the most unpleasant apartment – the hole in which I worked. The floor was covered to the depth of several inches with an impalpable, ill-flavoured dust, which rose in clouds as we moved; from the roof were suspended groups of fetid bats – the most offensively smelling creatures in existence; in some of the tombs, the odour which they emit is so powerful as to render the place "impossible".*[5]

In another account he recalled setting up what must have been the world's first floating darkroom on the deck of the boat he had purchased for the journey up the Nile. In the concluding essay, he seemed relieved it was all over – yet only a few months later he was tackling an even more daunting journey further up river.

> *My labours with regard to this publication are now at an end. I regret many imperfections of which I am fully conscious. I regret especially that I was so grievously hurried whilst taking my views: most undoubtedly I might have done more justice to my subjects – yet, when I reflect upon the circumstances under which many of the photographs were taken, I marvel greatly that they turned out so well. Now in a smothering little tent, with my collodion fizzling – boiling up all over the glass the moment it touched, – and, yet again, pushing my way backwards upon my hands and knees, into a damp, slimy rock tomb to manipulate, – it is truly marvellous that the results should be presentable at all.*[6]

It is interesting to consider for a moment the adaptability of Frith and the other Victorian photographers who followed in his footsteps. The tombs and temples were, at one moment, their darkrooms, illuminated by candles and littered with the paraphernalia of the wet collodion process, and later – when artificial light from flares or primitive flash came into use – they became their subjects.

The temples and tombs were, at that time, still at least partially buried in the sand. That endowed them with a mysterious quality so much admired by the Victorian painters and photographers who saw them. They were the logical extension of a romanticism which had thrived on the rediscovery and exploration of overgrown ruined abbeys and castles at home.

The Victorian Grand Tour of Egypt was just coming into fashion at the time of Frith's visits, and his photographs, when published back home, fanned that enthusiasm for visiting the ancient sites.

Those who undertook the Grand Tour suffered all the privations one might expect – long overland journeys in searing heat, poor accommodation, and the unwanted attention of wolves and thieves. What would Frith and his contemporaries have made of the souvenir sellers of today? Perhaps they would have concluded that little had changed!

Reading some of the diaries that travellers to Egypt kept in the 1870s and 1880s – illustrated with the work of photographers such as the Zangaki Brothers, Antonio Beato, Pascal Sebah and others who followed in Frith's footsteps – the overwhelming picture is not of the pleasures of a holiday, but of the rigours of undertaking an arduous journey which demonstrated that one had both the money and the leisure time to indulge in such an expedition.[7]

Sadly, too many of today's visitors hardly ever experience the real Egypt. They fly in on air-conditioned planes, stay in air-conditioned hotels or Nile cruise ships, and transfer to the ancient sites in air-conditioned coaches, stepping out into the searing heat for a few brief minutes.

More worrying for a nation so dependent upon tourism, the package holidaymakers benefit the local economy very little. The hotels, ships and coaches are owned by multinational corporations, and even much of the food they eat is imported to suit Western palettes.

From Cairo, Frith travelled up the Nile visiting Thebes, Luxor and Karnak, where the great temples were still largely buried in the sand and silt of the desert and the Nile Valley.

At Luxor, the ground level had risen so much over the centuries that over the temple site, and several metres

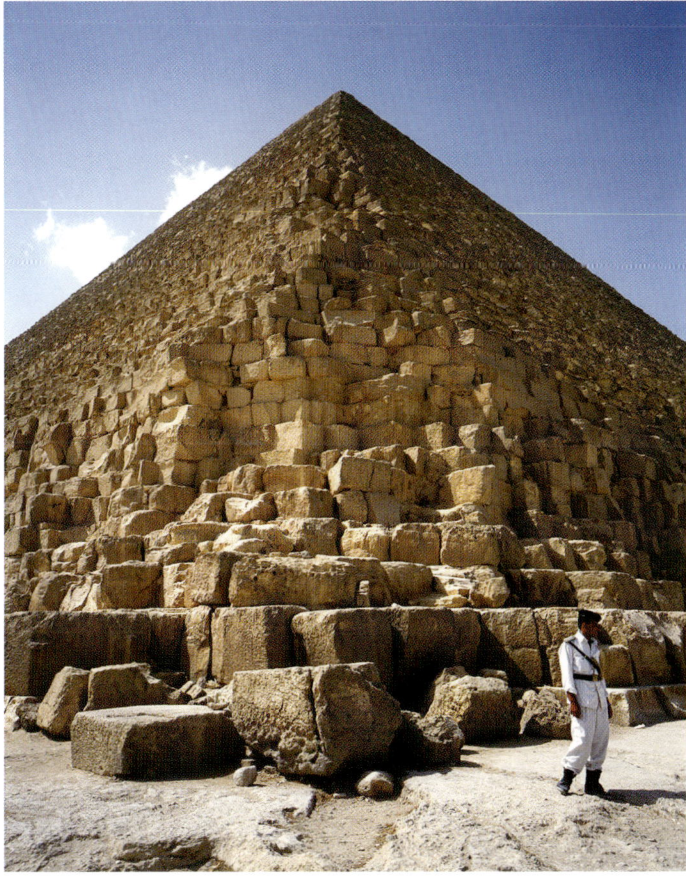

left: Climbing to the top of the Great Pyramid was considered an essential component of the Grand Tour in Victorian times. Not surprisingly, it is forbidden today, and armed tourist police stand guard to discourage the reckless!

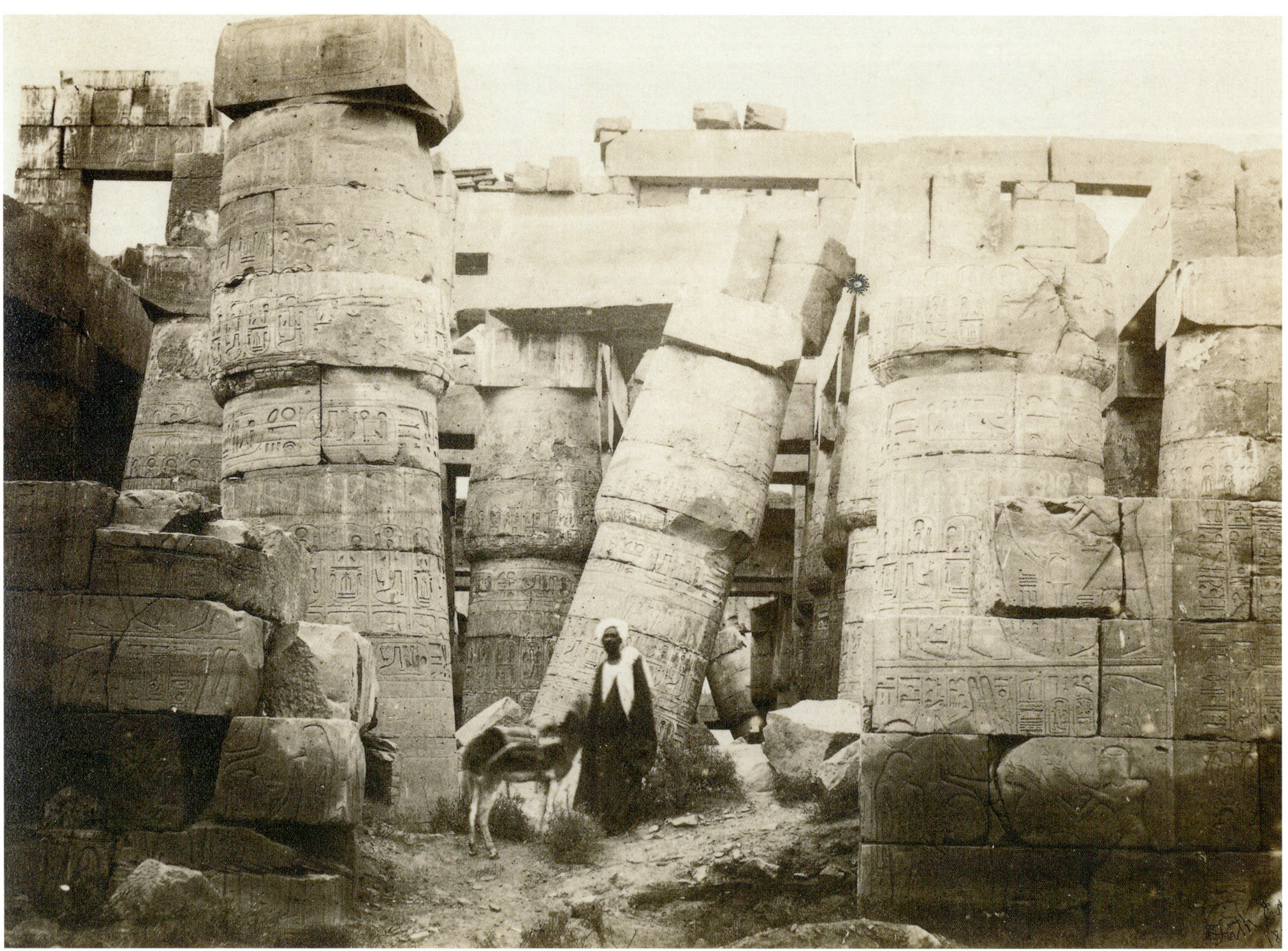

opposite page: The Hall of Columns in the Temple of Karnak near Luxor was still half buried in the desert, its columns toppled and broken, when Frith photographed it in 1857.

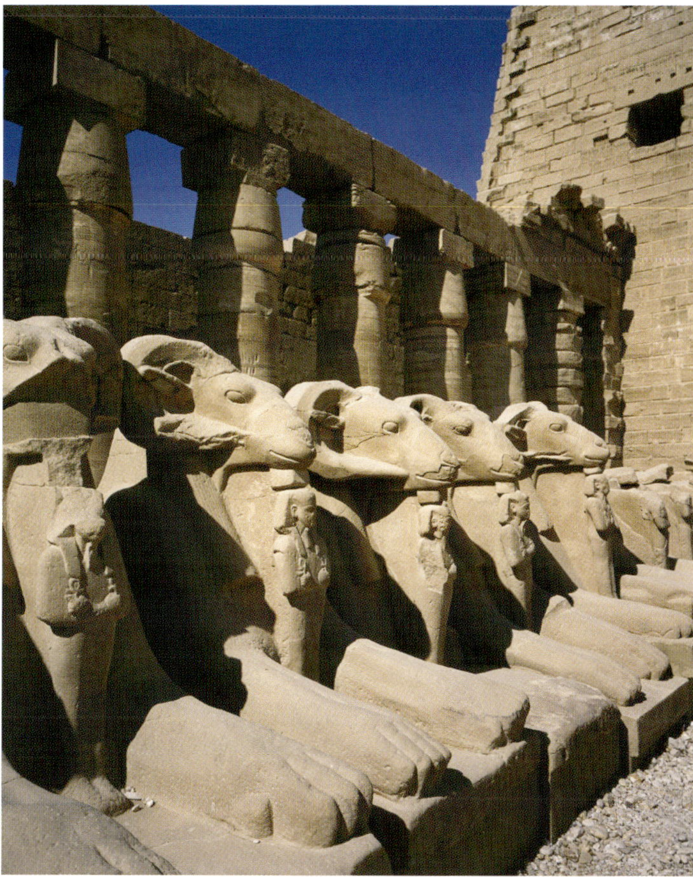

above and right: Today, Karnak Temple has been almost completely excavated, and partly reconstructed. In the course of that work, sadly, some of the romantic magic it held in Frith's day has been lost. Many of the colums, photographed partially collapsed by Frith, have been re-erected and, where stones are missing, concrete sections have been inserted – to be replaced should the original stones ever be found. Excavations continue at the outer edge of the site, which is now one of the busiest tourist attractions in the Nile Valley.

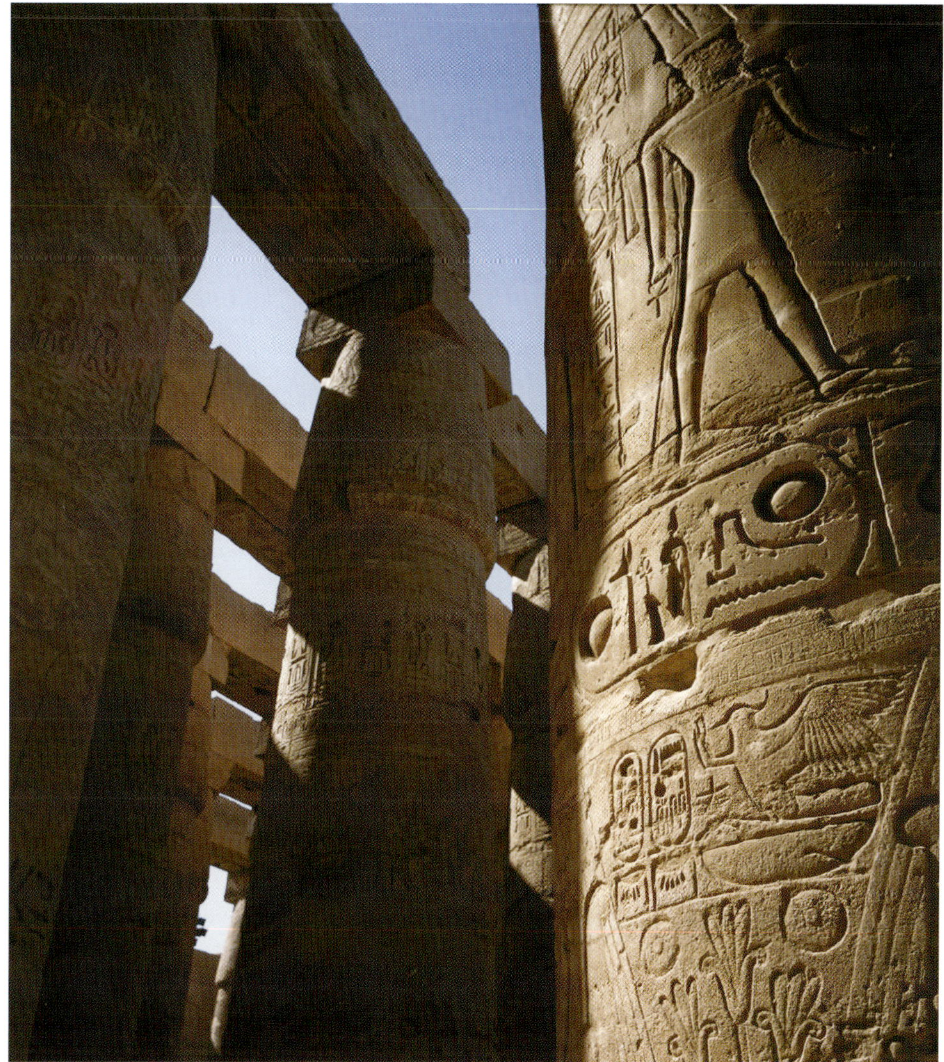

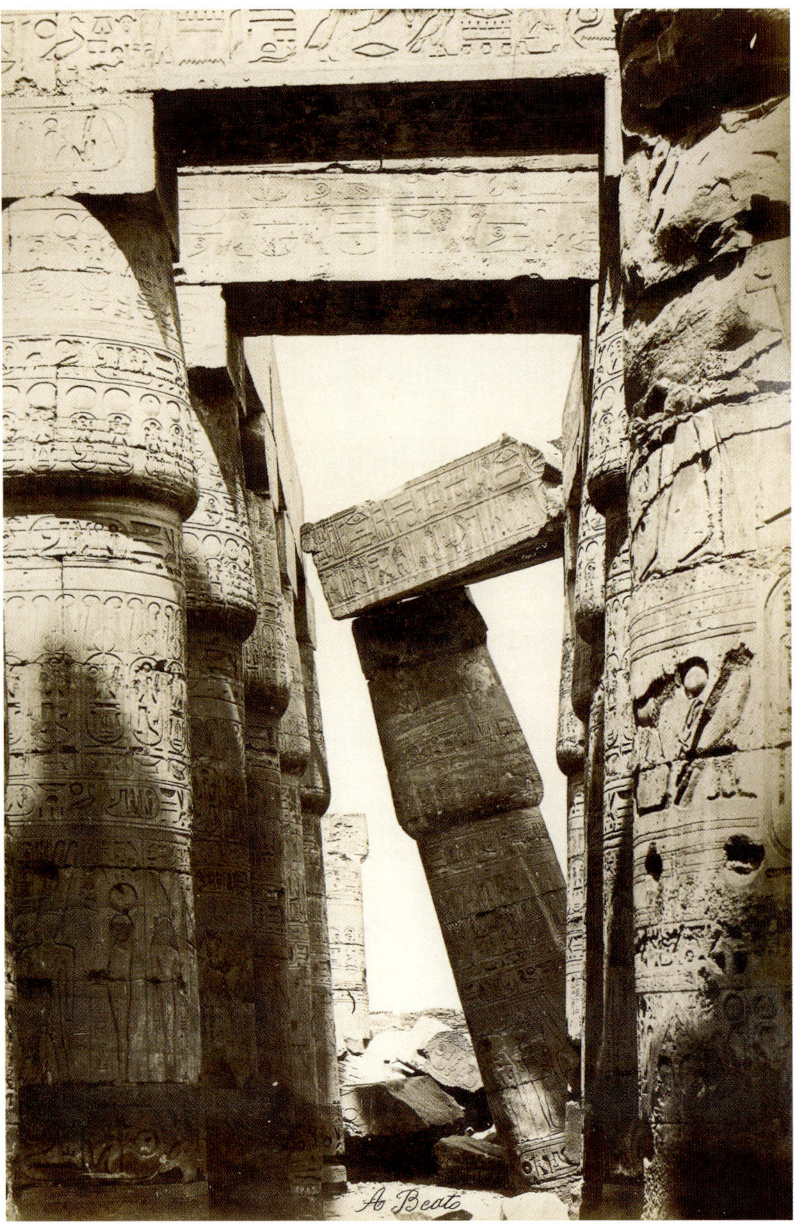

above it, a complete village had grown up. Until 1881, well after Frith's visit, the temple remained largely unknown. When it was eventually cleared and excavations begun, the archaeologists had a particular problem. On the 'new' ground level was a 13th century mosque of considerable architectural and historical interest. Today it stands precariously on top of a mound in the middle of the temple site, some of its doors high up on a wall!

At Karnak, again partly buried, Frith could see only the top half of the pillars, some of them tilted at precarious angles. Now, fully excavated, many of the columns have been re-erected, and where original stonework has been lost, concrete sections have been inserted.

In his diaries, Frith lamented the fact that the pillars in the great Hall of Columns were too close together for him to get any good pictures.

I have taken advantage of the dilapidation of a small part of the outer wall at this point, he wrote, for from the interior of the hall any photographic representation of this wonderful place is simply impossible, owing to the close juxtaposition of its columns.

Twenty years later Antonio Beato would achieve what Frith could not, producing a series of large format images really capturing the majesty of the place. Beato's pictures would find their way into countless albums assembled by subsequent travellers on the Grand Tour of Egypt.

Across the Nile, in the ruins of Thebes, Frith found much to interest him – the Colossi of Memnon, the Ramasseum, and the huge temple complex at Maharakka.

Today, with the exception of the Valley of the Kings, that side of the river gets many fewer visitors than the east bank. Indeed, at the Ramasseum I was the only visitor, with two security police on duty and six guides all trying to get a few pence from me for showing me around. Seeing such a wonderful site without the crowds which are commonplace at Luxor and Karnak came as a total but very welcome surprise. Having spent much of the journey waiting till tourists in brightly coloured clothes either moved out of

opposite page: Antonio Beato produced a remarkable series of views of Karnak Temple in the 1870s. Frith had written in 1857 that he thought photography inside the temple impossible due to the closeness of the columns. Beato proved otherwise with his stunning 16"x12" views of the site.
below: This view of Luxor from the Nile, photographer unknown, dates from the late 1860s or early 1870s, and shows how the village had been built over and around the ruins. The site was cleared in the 1880s under the guidance of the archaeologist Gaston Maspero. Only the Abu al-Haggag Mosque – considered to be of too great a local religious significance to be demolished – was left in place, now standing high above the temple floor.

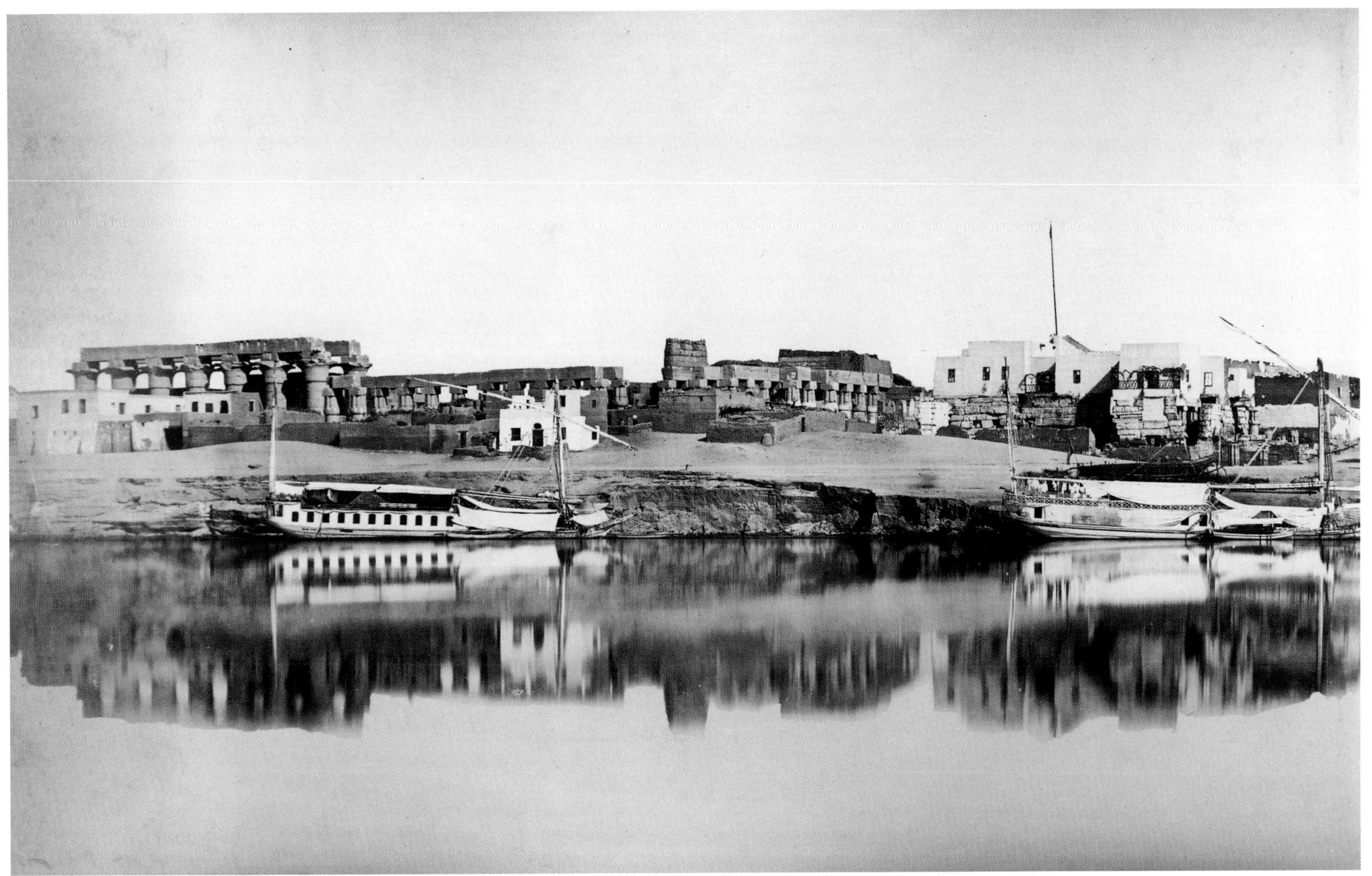

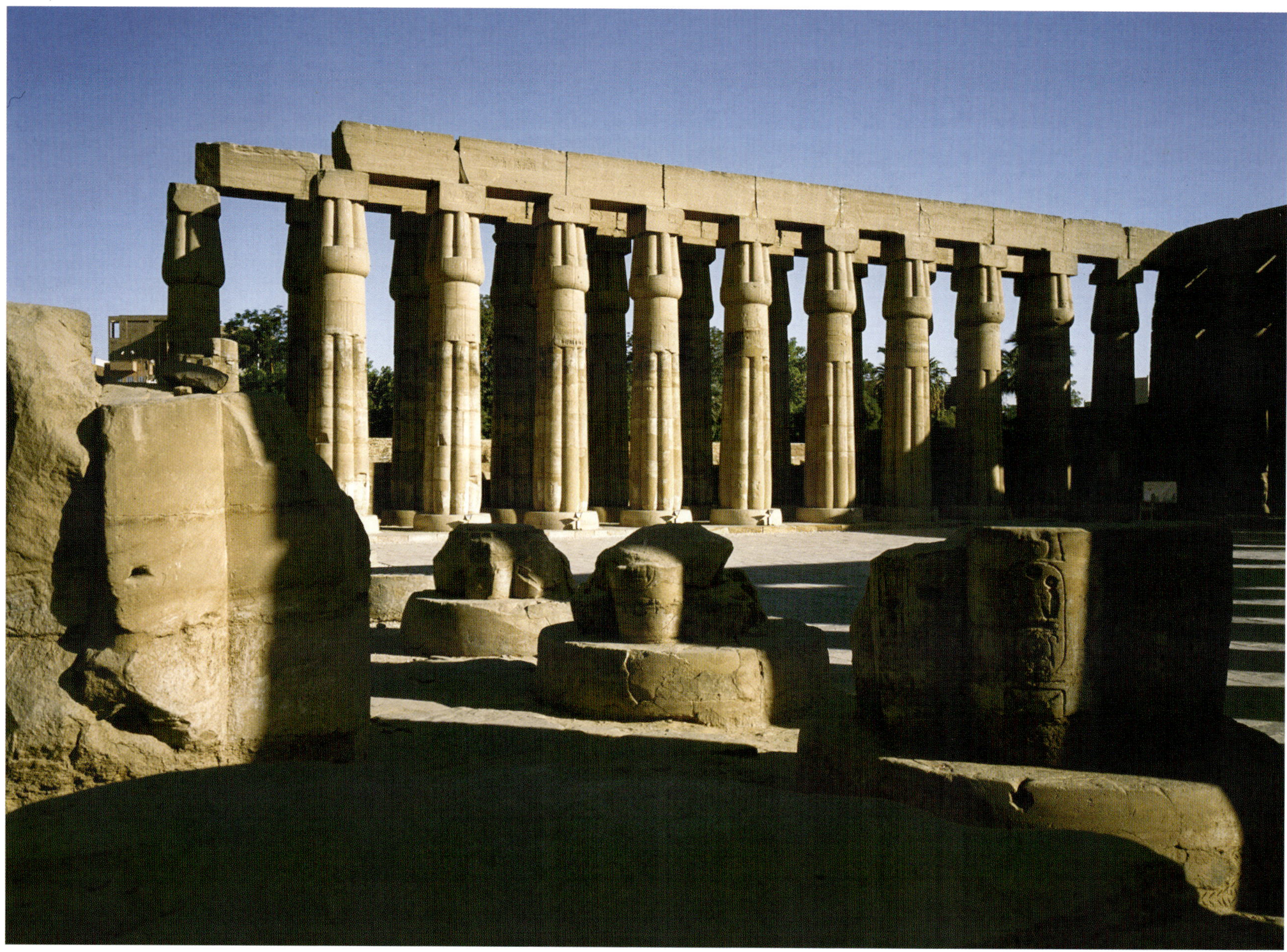

the way or moved into shadows before taking pictures, the Ramasseum seemed like paradise!

Working with a modern autofocus camera and a very wide angle lens really brought home how much more freedom today's photographer has compared with our Victorian predecessors. The limited range of lenses available to Frith and his contemporaries, and perhaps artistic conventions as well, resulted in photographs which have a naturalistic perspective – not dissimilar to the view seen by human eyes. Today's photographer has so much more opportunity to explore and redefine space, thanks to lenses which combine a dramatically wide field of view with truly rectilinear picture geometry.

Add to that the speed at which today's photographer can work, and the real challenge which confronted Frith can be more fully appreciated.

With the wet collodion process, and all the attendant manipulations which the photographer had to go through both before and after taking the picture, work rate was never high. The sheer size of the camera, the weight of transporting it around, and the time taken to set it up each time, meant that six or eight pictures per day even under normal working conditions was considered good. Given the scale of the challenges which Frith faced, his work rate may have been even less than that. Given the work involved in making each collodion negative, the scale of his output from the three trips to Egypt is phenomenal.

Of course taking the pictures was only part of the job. Once home, his staff had the task of preparing the views for publication. The 1857-58 trip alone resulted in a published set of seventy six 10"x8" images of Egypt and Palestine. The prints which had to be produced for this publication alone ran into many thousands.

James Virtue, Frith's publisher for the images from the second journey, also published a list of 'subscribers' to the partwork. It is interesting to reflect on the market for early photography of this type and the subscriber list clearly demonstrates the pioneering nature of Frith's

opposite page: Luxor Temple today, the focal point of the town, and a magnet for visitors. The commercial development of the waterfront now means that the temple is a little further from the river, and safer as a result.

below: The Colossi of Memnon stood in open country in Frith's day. Now they stand by the side of the busy road which leads to the ruins of Thebes.

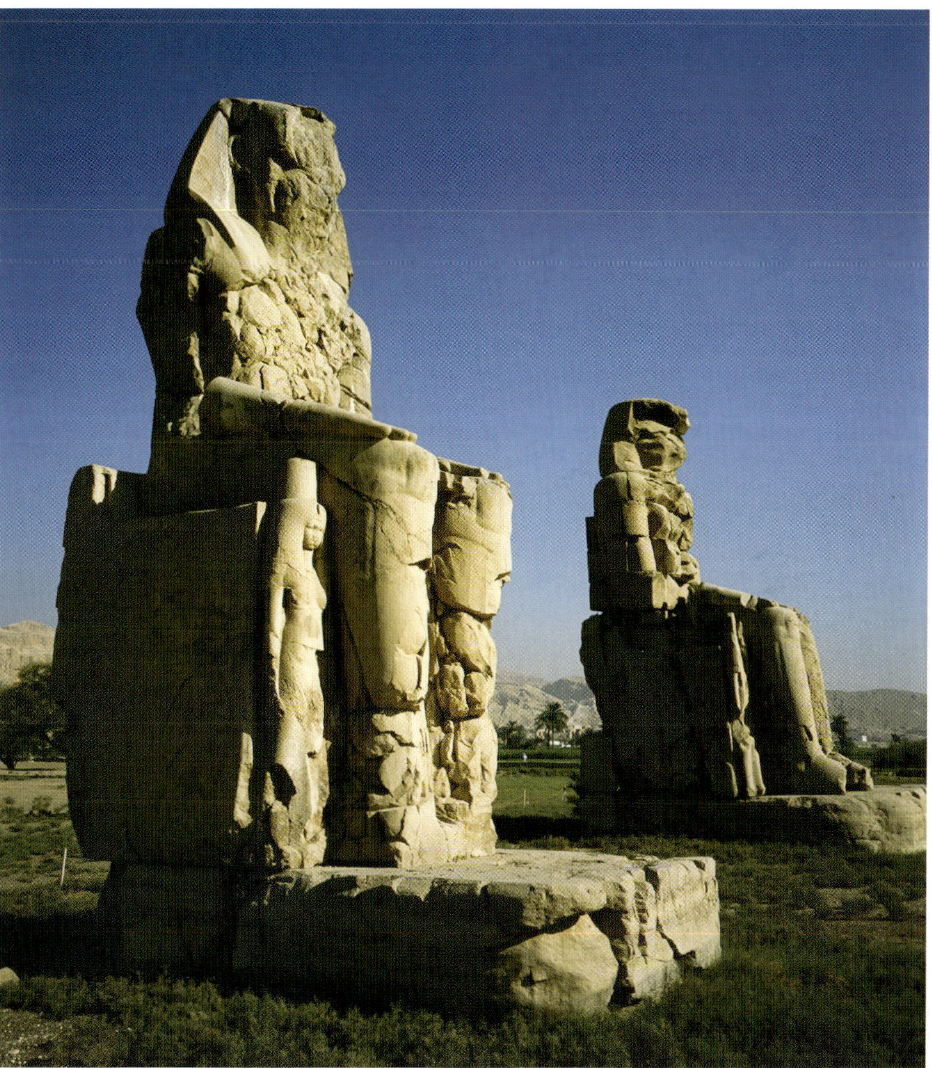

below: The Ramasseum at Thebes, a huge temple site largely overlooked by today's visitors, was once dominated by a huge 18 metre high 1000 tonne statue of Ramses. The site of the shattered remains of this statue inspired Percy Bysshe Shelley to write his famous poem *Ozymandias*. Ramses' huge foot is seen here lying just outside the temple's Second Court.

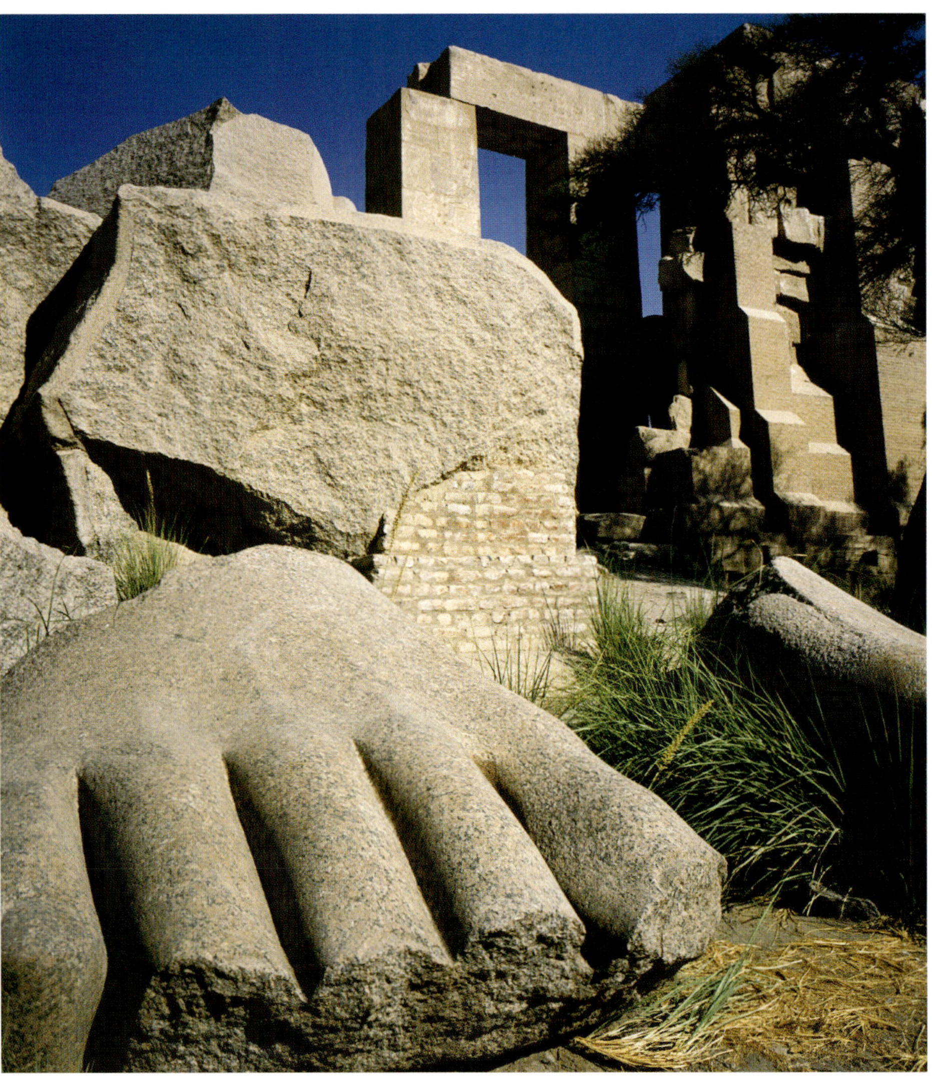

work. Twenty years later, with the Grand Tour established, photographers produced work primarily for sale to tourists, but Frith's work was aimed clearly at academics.

A total of ninety-one subscribers gave colleges in Cambridge as their addresses – and thirty-seven of those were from Trinity College. There were also eight from St John's, six each from Emmanuel and Christ, five from Magdalen, the remainder from Caius, Corpus Christi, Sidney, St Peter's, Jesus, Kings and Pembroke! Only nine subscribers were from Oxford Colleges.

To ensure that their needs were well catered for, Frith and Virtue added texts liberally peppered with quotes from eminent historians, archaeologists and classical scholars.

In the case of the temple at Maharraka, the academic input was supplied by Sir John Gardner Wilkinson who contributed the information that

> *Like most edifices in Nubia, it has been used as a place of worship by the early Christians, and is the last (i.e. the most southerly) that we find of the times of the Ptolemies or Caesars, with the exception of Ibreem, or Primis.*

Frith, however, tended to lapse into the romantic! His commentary on Maharraka concentrated on the apparent fact that it was never completed.

> *When one enters a stupendous temple whose foundations were laid three thousand years ago, he wrote, and after passing from hall to hall and from chamber to chamber, whose walls are all vocal with the quaint language of forgotten time, an apartment is reached in which the artist's hand seems but that instant to have laid aside his chalk – how powerful and strange is the appreciation, as it were, of the momentary lapse of ages! How difficult to realize the fact, that two thousand years ago that hand was stayed, and that the work will never be resumed.*[8]

At Philae, he marvelled at the partly excavated temple sitting at the very edge of the island in the middle of the Nile. Were he to revisit today, he would not recognise the place.

With annual flooding of the Nile even in Frith's day,

below: The Temple at Maharraka, as photographed by Frith in 1857, and about which he wrote *after passing from hall to hall and from chamber to chamber, whose walls are all vocal with the quaint language of forgotten time, an apartment is reached in which the artist's hand seems but that instant to have laid down his chalk – how powerful and strange is the appreciation, as it were, of the momentary lapse of ages! how difficult to realise the fact, that two thousand years ago that hand was stayed, and that work will never be resumed.*

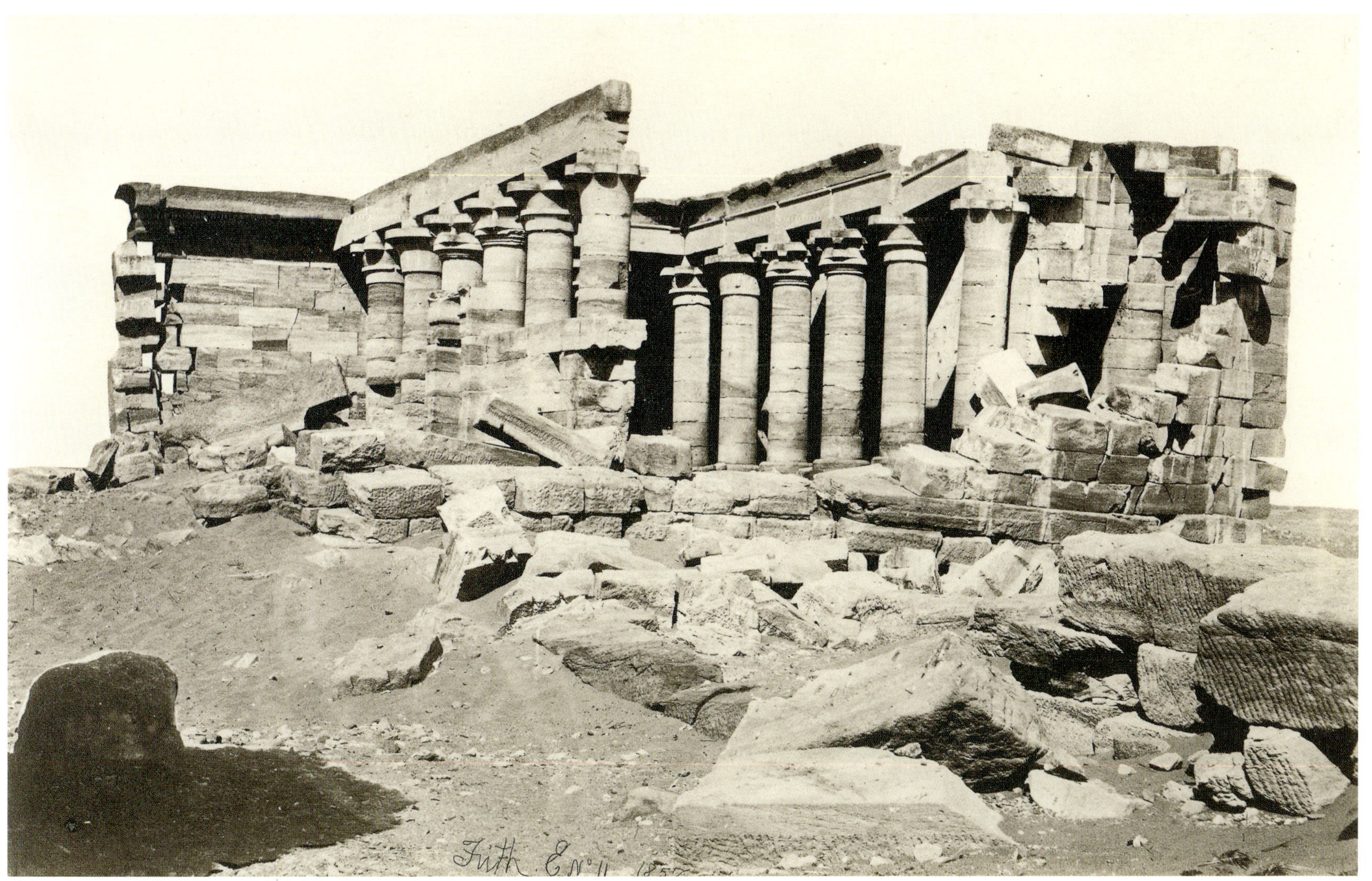

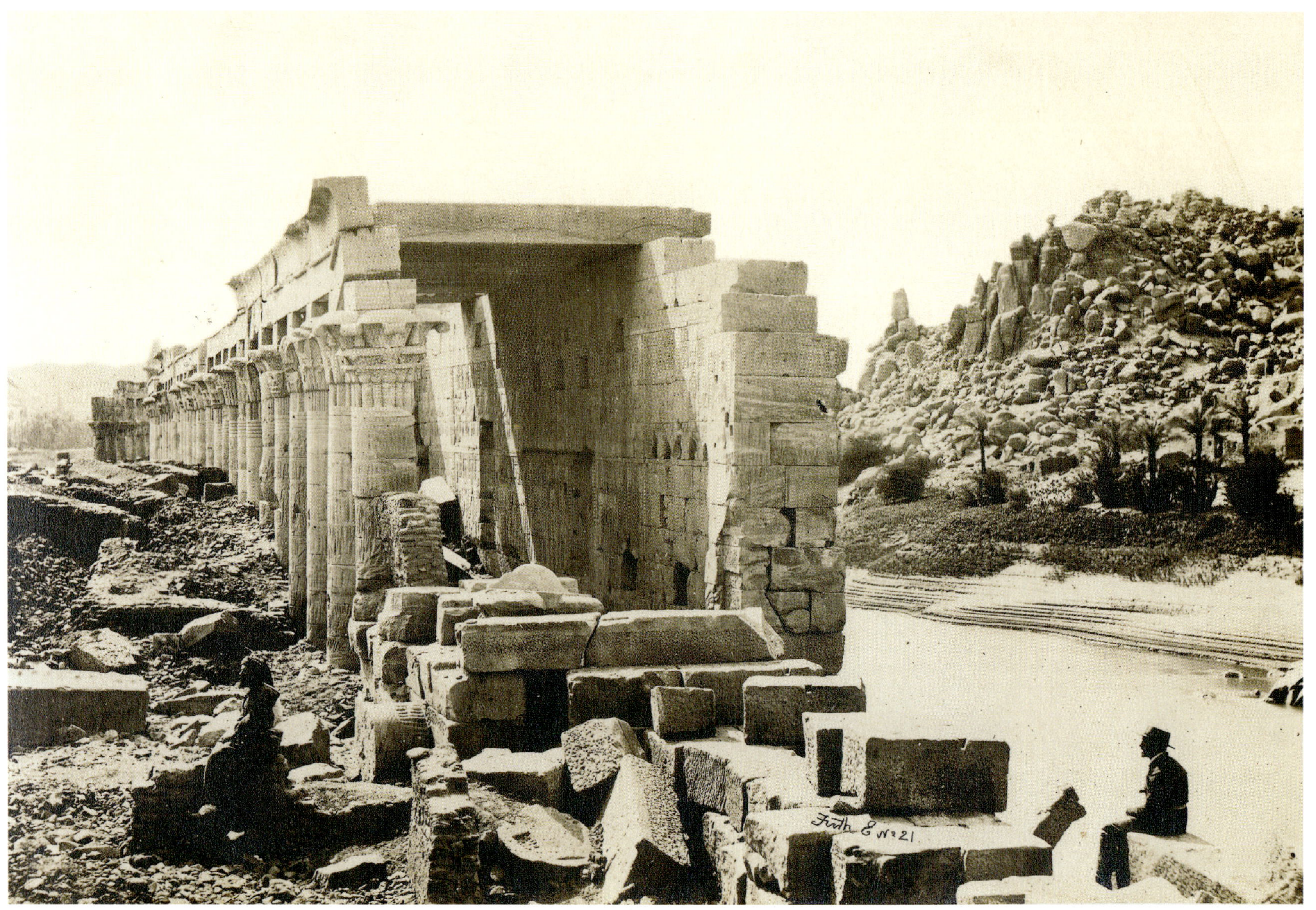

above: In his caption to this view of the West Colonnade of the Temple at Philae, photographed from the north in 1857, Frith commented that the capitols *are indeed exquisitely beautiful; and no two of them are alike.* This was one of several views he made on the island.

the temple suffered from periodic inundation. After the completion of the Aswan Dam in 1902, it spent much of each year partly under water, and visitors to the site sailed through the colonnades and arches.

When the High Dam project was conceived in the 1950s, the certainty was that the temple would be lost forever many metres below the rising waters of the new Lake Nasser. A project was initiated to dismantle the temple and rebuild it above the proposed high water mark on the nearby island of Agilika, itself remodelled and landscaped to look like Philae. Today it is reached by a short boat trip from Aswan, and only a few decades after the rebuilding, it is already hard to believe, when approaching the 'new' island, that this is not the original setting.

The Roman influences on the site are considerable – at Trajan's Kiosk in particular, where the traditions of ancient Egypt meet the imperial hand of Rome.

Frith observed that

> *Upon the nearer columns in the picture may be observed numerous short flutings. Many of the temple ruins, especially the pillars, are mutilated in this manner. I judge that here the Arabs and early Christians have sharpened the tools with which they have so laboriously delved in these mountains of masonry for the treasures supposed to be concealed, or with which they chipped away at the offensive idolatrous images, for many of the colossal sculptures upon the island of Philae are chipped over so carefully, as to be almost obliterated.*[8]

However, Frith's total dedication to making images of the temple sites and tombs meant he overlooked the rich tapestry of life along the length of the Nile.

Given the intensity of the light, exposures would certainly have been short enough to capture animated scenes of daily Egyptian life, but catering for that aspect of the market was left to later, and usually local photographers.

Even then, the portraits and populated views which were published seldom captured the real Egypt. Instead, what often appeared were Westernised stereotypes of what Egyptian life was thought to be like – often contrived and

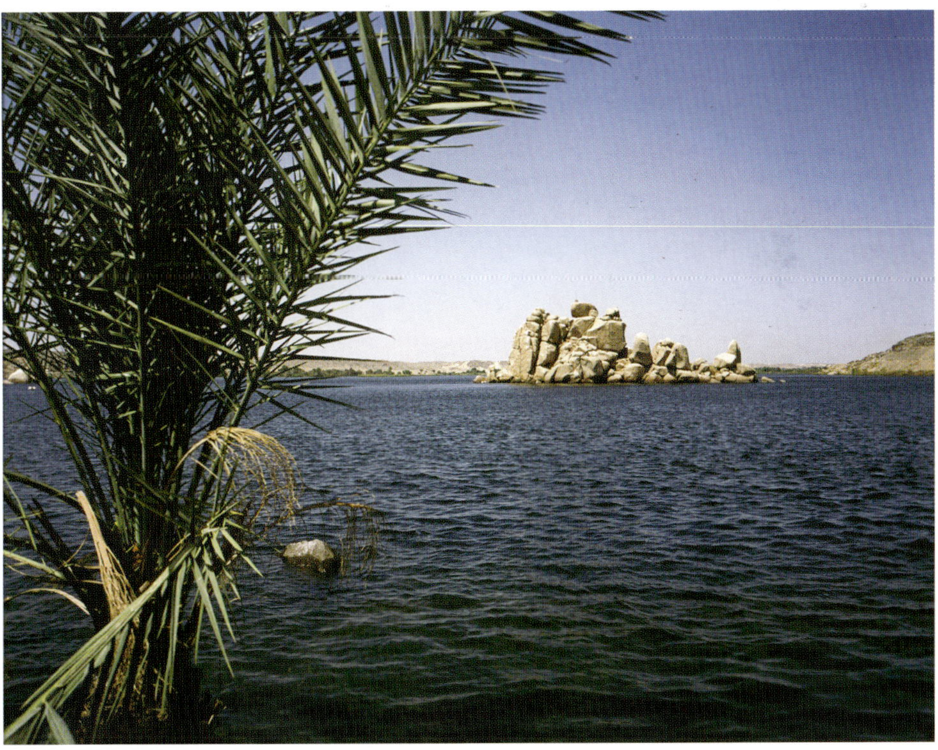

above: This view from the quay below the temple at Philae is very different to that which would have greeted Frith had he stood on the same steps. In place of the nearby banks of the Nile – the view which would have been laid out before Frith – today's visitor is faced with the southern end of Lake Nasser, the artificial sea which covers a vast area of the Nile valley and conceals many ancient sites considered too difficult or expensive to save.

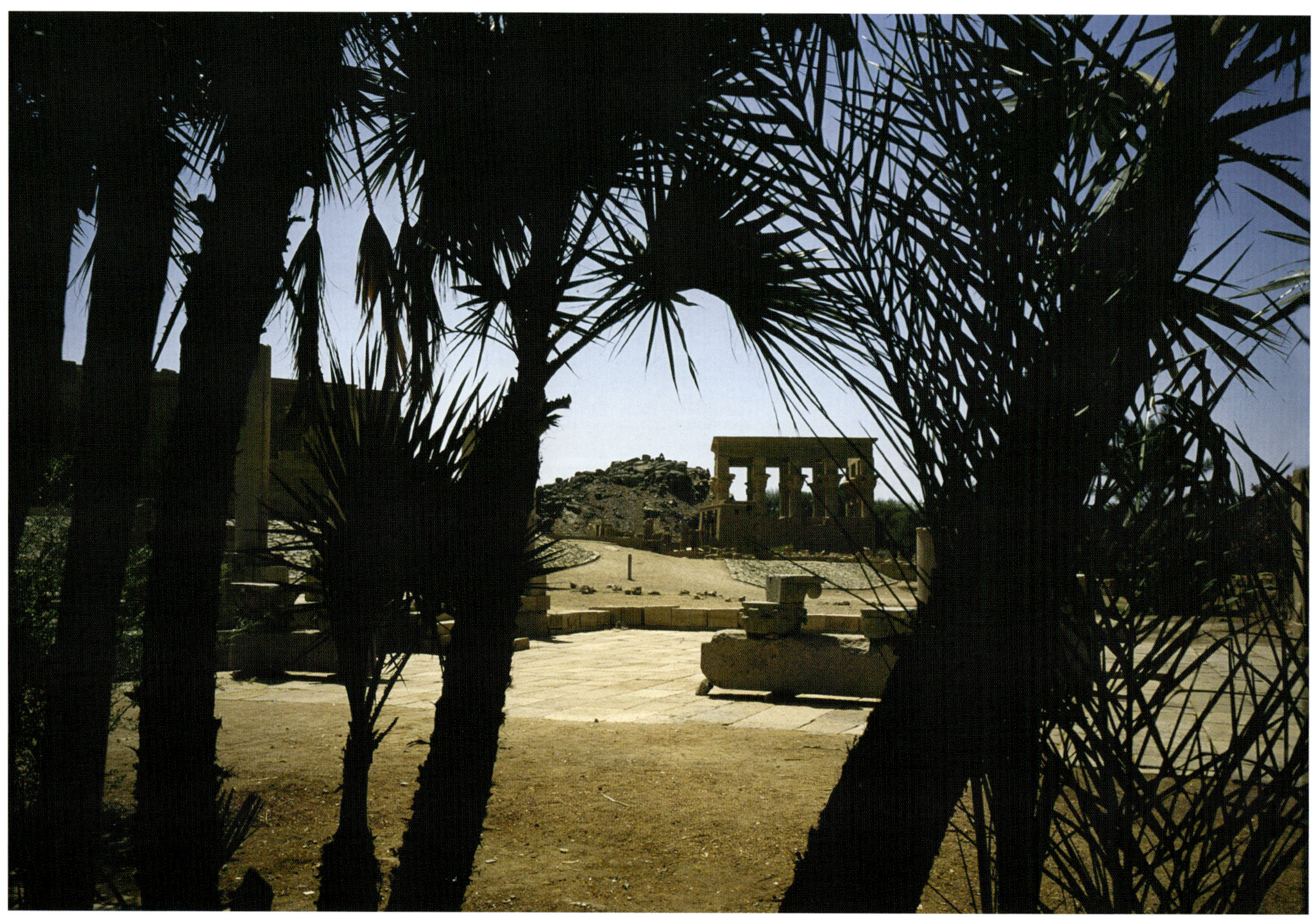

above: The Temple of Philae in its new home on the island of Agilika already looks as though it has stood there for centuries. In this view, the Roman Kiosk of Trajan can be seen in the distance, with its fourteen columns, and its sculptured scenes of the Emperor burning incense before the figures of Isis and Osiris.

photographed in makeshift studios, with stilted poses and very unnatural looking characters!

One of the exceptions was Antonio Beato, who settled in Luxor and operated a very successful business from there. He had already travelled and photographed extensively in Turkey, Palestine and India. Once established in Egypt, he claimed to have photographed every excavation carried out in the Nile Valley over four decades. Many of his photographs are now in the collection of the Egyptian Museum in Cairo, an invaluable account of archaeological methods in the second half of the nineteenth century.

He additionally took his camera out and about in the Luxor area and photographed Egyptians at work and in their leisure time, filling in a considerable gap in the photography available for the growing numbers of travellers to take home with them.

As he lived and worked in the area for so long, his images chronicle a crucial period in the development of the Nile Valley as a tourist destination.

In Frith's pictures, however, the only human presence is that of his servants, his travelling companion, Francis Wenham, or perhaps an assistant. Frith himself, clad in arab dress, appears in several stereoscopic views.

The published *Egypt and Palestine Photographed and described by F. Frith Jun.*, perhaps surprisingly, only contained a single image of the fabulous rock temple at Abu Simbel, hewn out of the solid rock in the thirteenth century BC.

Frith revisited the site during his third and final trip to Egypt, which took him just beyond the sixth cataract, further than any photographer before him. The stereoscopic views he produced during that 1859 journey were eventually published in book form in 1862.

On my trip, Abu Simbel was the undisputed highlight. Like Philae, it was saved from the rising waters of Lake Nasser by a hugely expensive multinational effort under the auspices of the United Nations. The reconstruction is marvellous, and but for the exhibition of images which

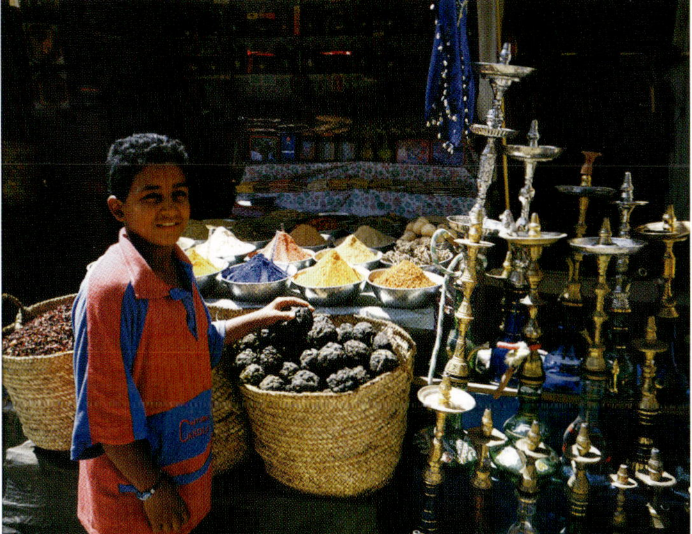

left and below: The souk in Aswan is just a few metres from the Corniche with its wide pavements and quays lined with Nile cruisers. In the souk, every imaginable spice is offered for sale amongst the hundreds of stalls which line the labyrinth of narrow streets and alleyways. While undoubtedly a magnet for visitors eager to be parted from their money, the souk is primarily the general market for the locals.

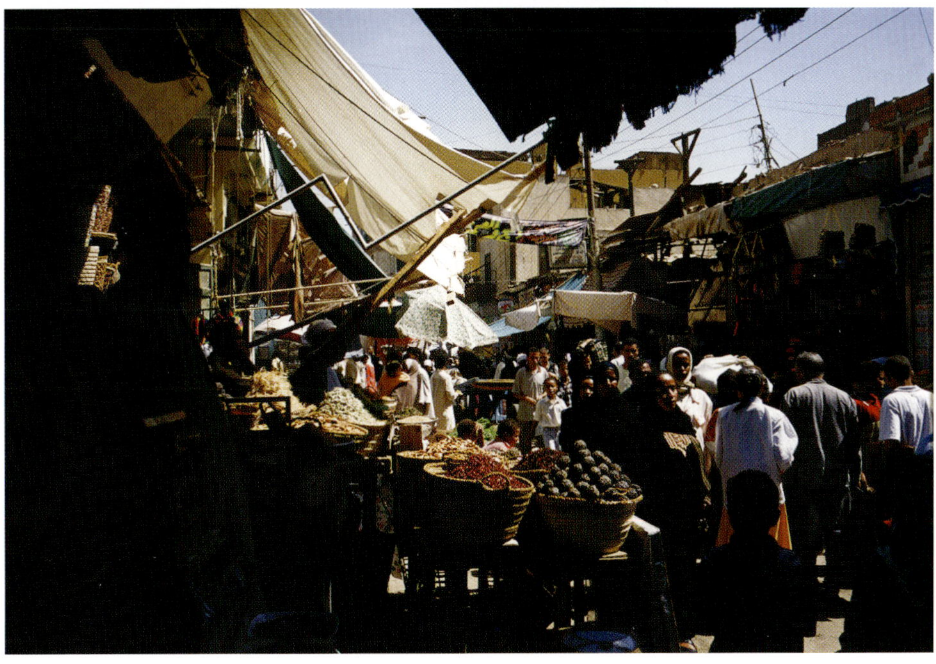

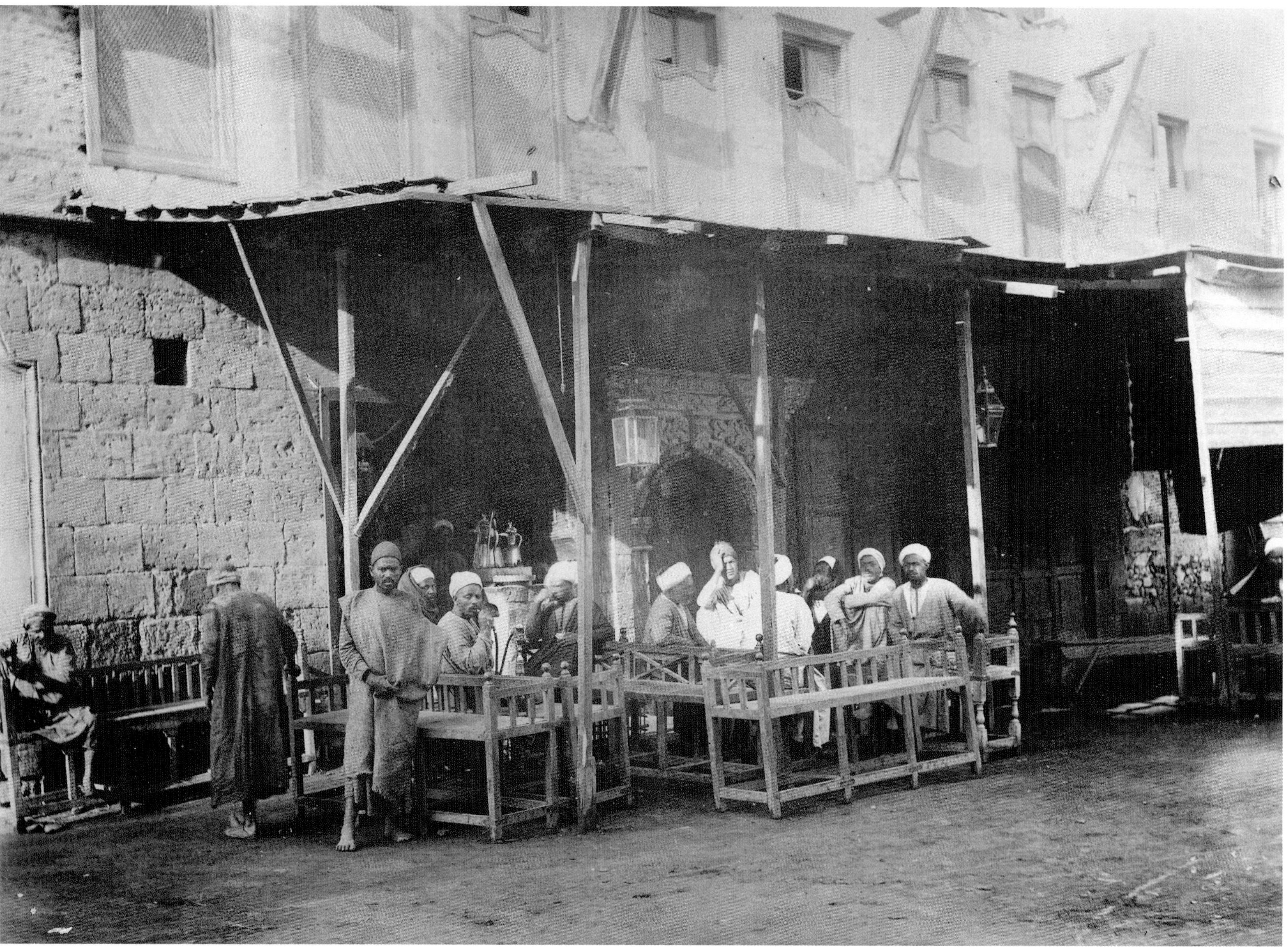

shows how the temple was dismantled and reconstructed under a landscaped concrete dome, few would believe it was anything other than as it has always been.

When Frith and the other early photographers first photographed it, the temple was still well buried in the desert sand, only part of the huge statues which stand in front of the entrance visible above the encroaching desert.

Dawn is the time to see Abu Simbel, as the sun rises over Lake Nasser and illuminates the awesome façade. That does mean leaving Aswan before 5am, to join up with a convoy of cars and coaches and meet the military escort which will guide the modern-day caravan across the desert at high speed – covering just under two hundred kilometres in just under two hours.

Even the journey itself is awesome. On the way out, with no light pollution to spoil the view, the skies are just full of stars, thousands of them visible. On the way back, in the midday heat, the mirages out in the desert are just as memorable, and thankfully seen from the inside of an air-conditioned car or coach. The scale of Frith's undertaking in that searing heat – and of those who carted their wet collodion equipment across that same desert before and after him – is suddenly put into sharp focus.

What Frith and others started has become an enduring aspect of Egyptian life. The country depends heavily upon the tourist trade, and probably could not survive without it. Generations of visitors have since enjoyed its treasures, and bought countless photographs, postcards and souvenirs to remember their visit.

Thirty years after Frith completed his third journey, a

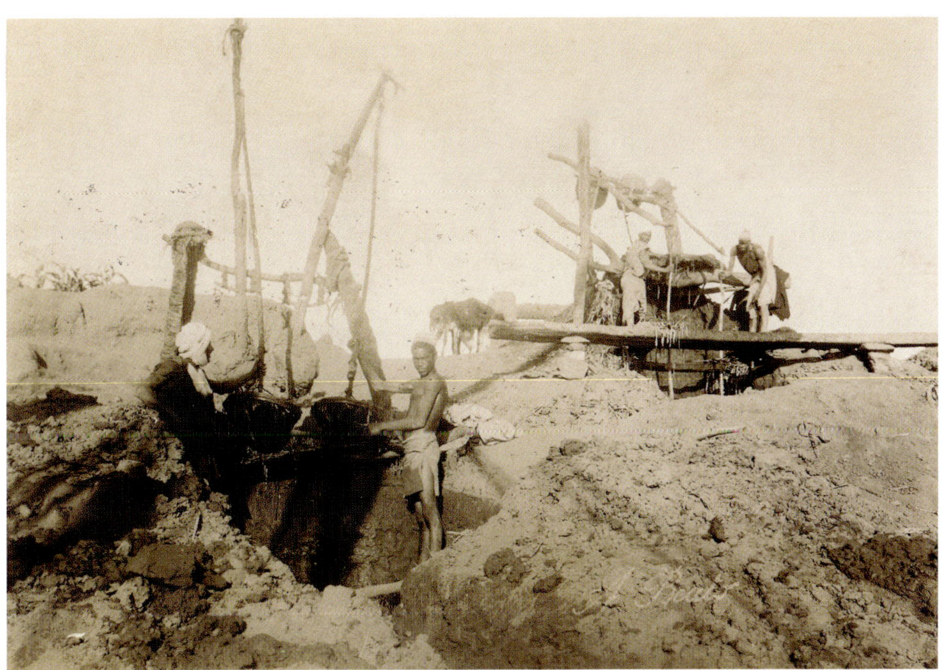

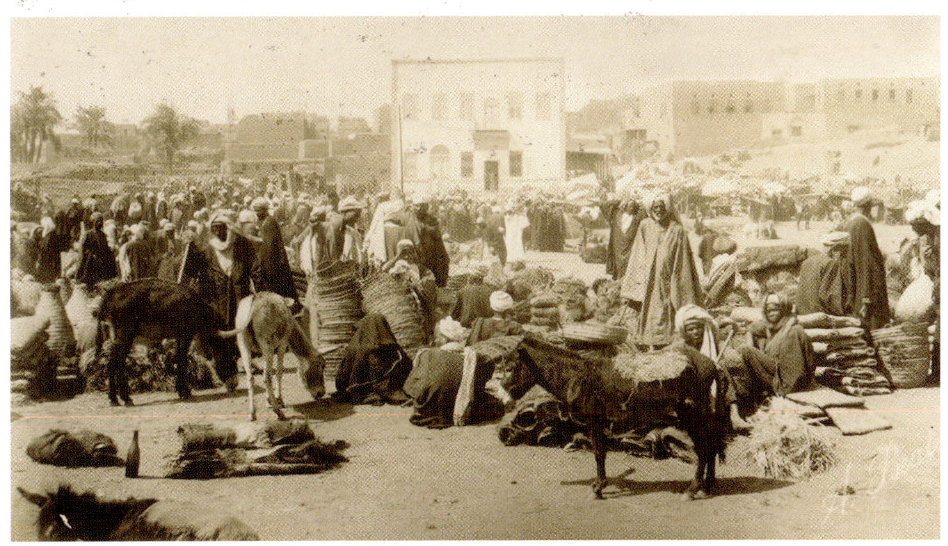

One of the few foreigners whose work captured the character of life in 19th century Egypt was the Venetian photographer Antonio Beato. The three images on these pages are all from his extensive coverage of the Nile valley.
opposite page: Beato's study of an arab café, taken in the 1870s, showed a traditional style of outdoor café seating which can still be found in remote areas today.
this page top: Farmers using 'shadoofs' or simple pumps to raise water for their cattle and to irrigate their fields. A simply hydraulic pump, proposed in the early 19th century had been rejected as it put too many men out of work!
right: Luxor Market, c.1880, was the lively heart of the town

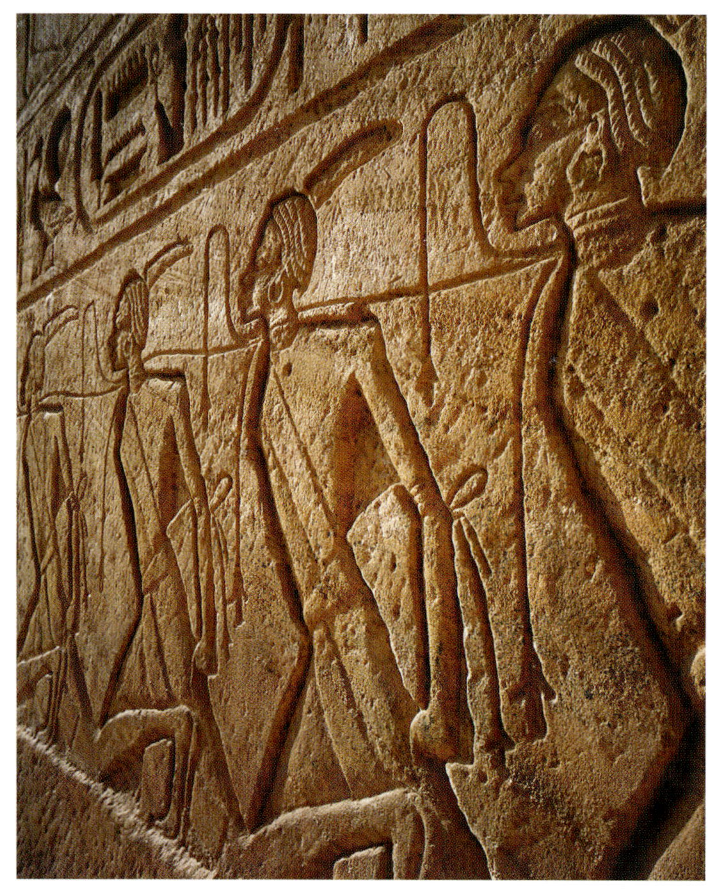

right: Elaborate sculptured panels flank the entrance to the great temple of Ramses II at Abu Simbel.
opposite page: Approaching the huge façade of Ramses' Temple at Abu Simbel, it is hard to believe that it has only been on its present site for forty years. The original location is now deep below the waters of Lake Nasser. The entire temple was cut into numbered blocks, raised several hundred feet and re-assembled with such precision and skill that it appears to have stood by the shores of the lake forever.

wealthy businessman from Warrington in Cheshire, Robert Garnett, with his wife and two friends, unknowingly walked in Frith's footsteps through Egypt and Palestine when they did their first of two Grand Tours. While their friends bought photographs as they went - by Antonio Beato, the Zangaki Brothers, Pascal Sebah, and many others - Robert Garnett sketched all he saw, while his wife, Mary, kept a detailed diary which was eventually published together with Robert's sketches.[10]

At Aswan, Mary recorded

There is not much to be seen, more to be endured, for a horde of children crowded down upon me, and sang the one word "Backsheesh" to a weird dismal tune unceasingly.

The same still happens today! Backsheesh, was once payment for doing a small service. Children have redefined the process by seeking backsheesh simply to stop pestering visitors. Mary Garnett apparently did not yield. Many of today's visitors do!

At the end of her first tour, Mary Garnett ended her diary in deep appreciation of the experience

Egypta! – Our whole being thrills at the sound – it is mystery more than history. More strange than fiction and yet how real, for there we come to the very cradle of the human race, the germ of all civilisations, the alphabet of all science and of all art, the very root and genesis of the earth. There is no past beyond Egypt. Let us sit down reverently before it and take a long breath.

The appeal of Egypt has certainly not lessened with familiarity, and photography is now a part of that experience on a scale which Francis Frith could not have imagined. Indeed, books and TV programmes on Egypt attest to its enduring popularity.

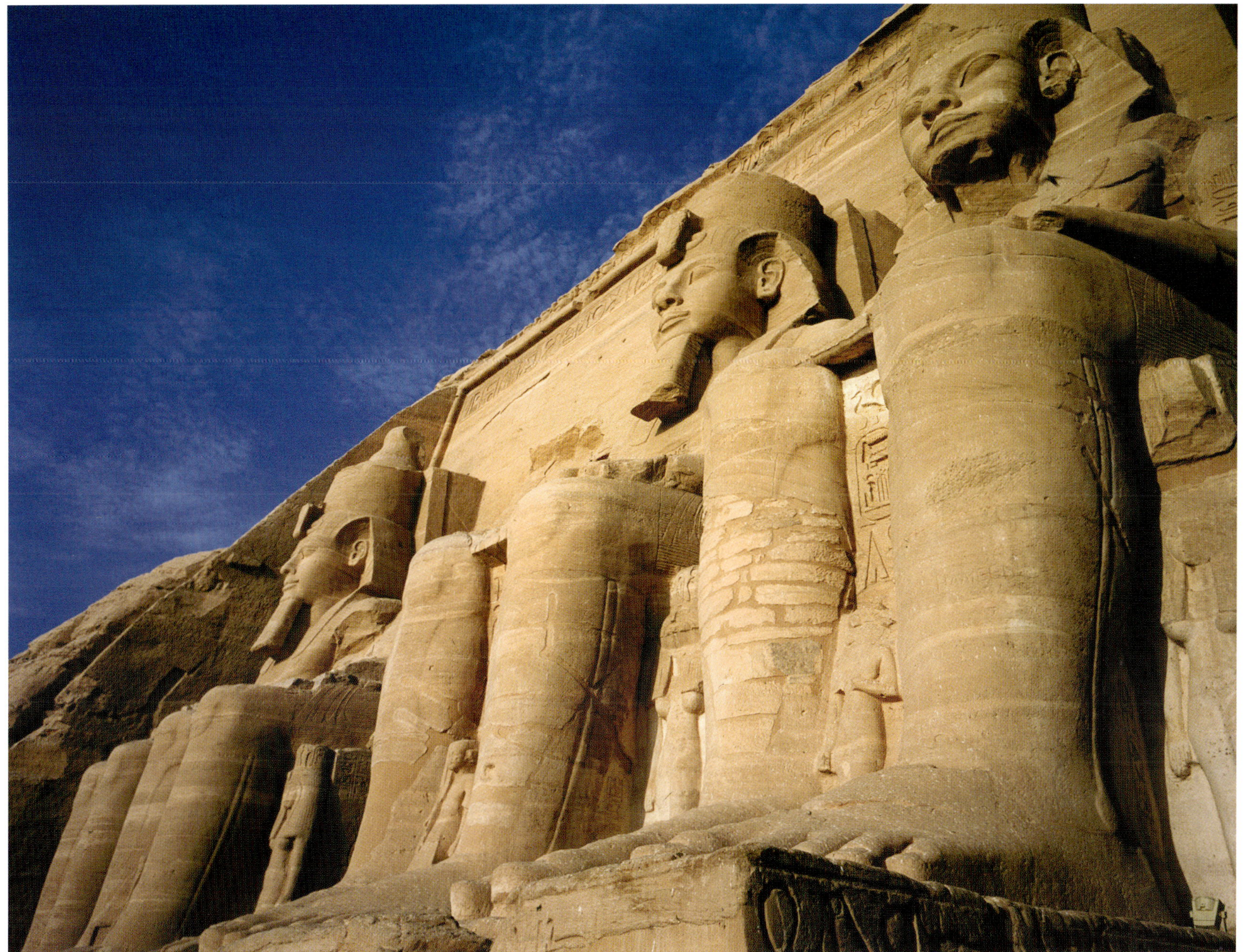

left: The traditional view of Egypt kept alive for tourists - traditionally-dressed Egyptians on camels are happy to pose for visitors – at a price!
below left: The modern face of Egypt – the rapidly expanding city of Cairo seen from the top of the Cairo Tower which dominates the island of Zamalek. A pall of pollution permanently hangs over the place.

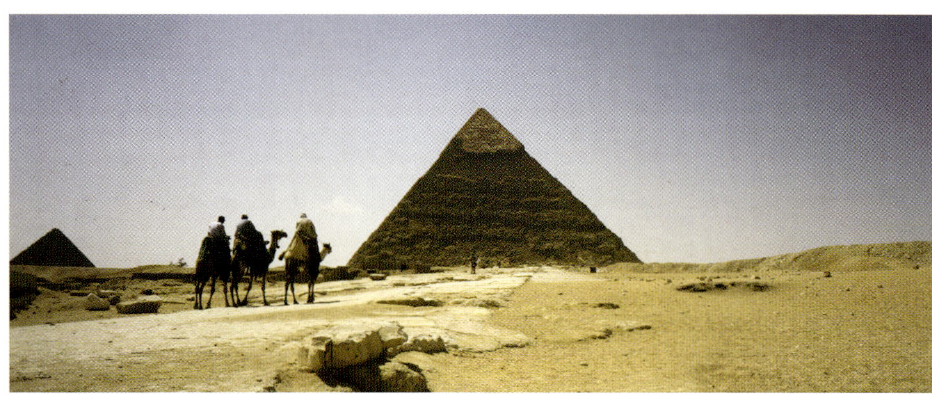

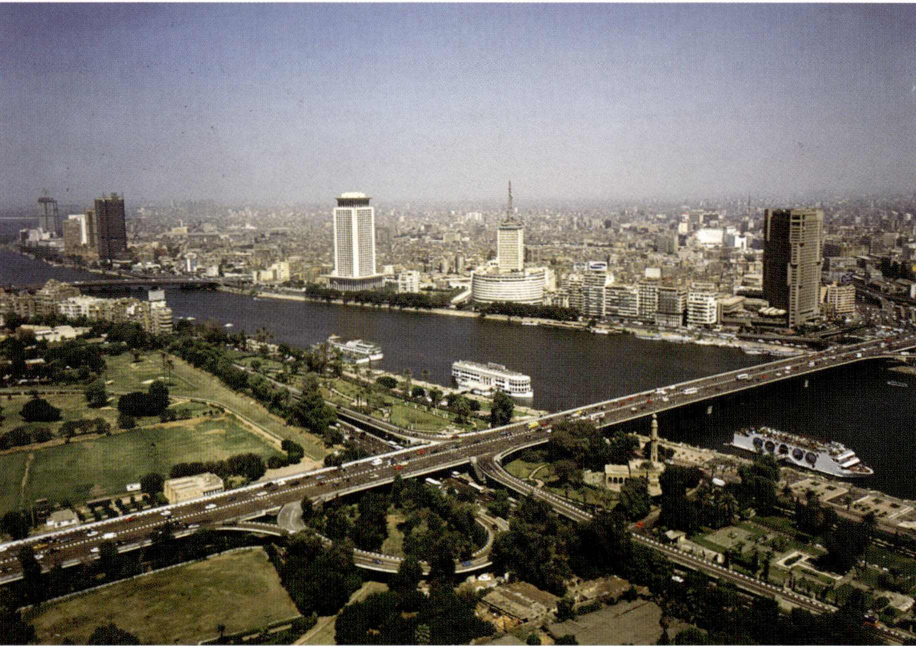

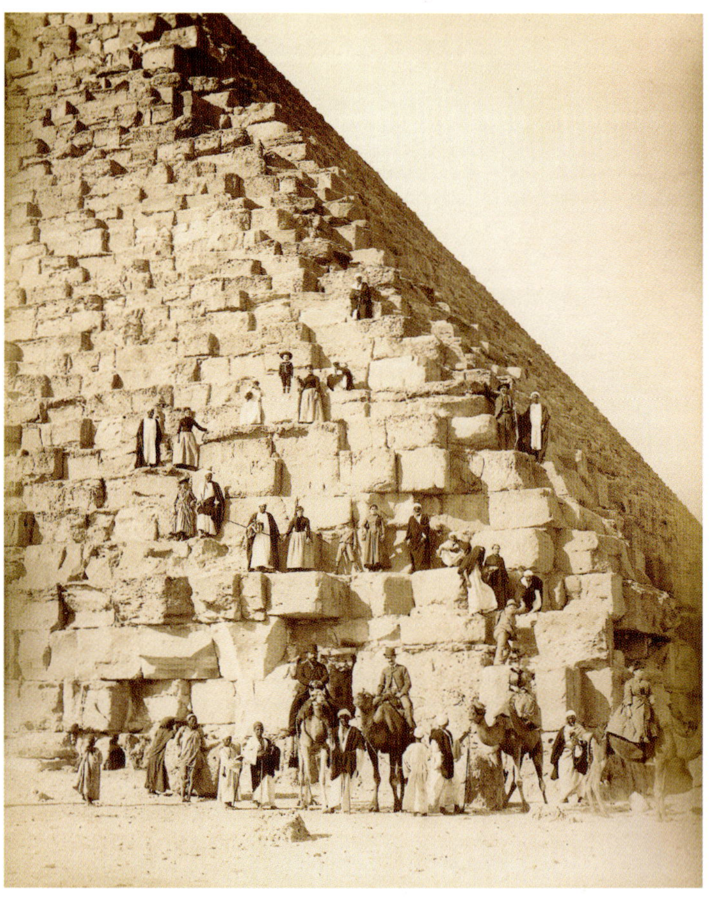

above: 'The Ascent of the Pyramid of Cheops' photographed by the Zangaki Brothers, is a wry commentary on the Grand Tour. At ground level, the normal order is maintained – Europeans on camels, servants on foot – but as the visitors climb up the pyramid, they become more and more dependent on the 'dragomen', even having to hold hands with them. For demure Victorian ladies, this required considerable courage, as they had been brought up to keep foreigners at a distance!

right: The basic design of the twin-lens stereoscopic camera changed very little over a twenty year period – the major difference between the camera illustrated here and that used by Frith being the addition of interchangeable lens apertures. This example was illustrated in Gaston Tissandier's 1878 book *A History and Handbook of Photography*, translated by John Thomson whose travels feature later in this book. The design similarity can be seen (*below right*) in the Bland & Long advertisement which is contemporary with Frith's travels.

below: The Temple at Kom Ombo, photographed by Frith in 1858/9, and seen here in a rare uncut pair of stereoscopic prints. For the mounted stereo views sold to the public, each pair of images had to be cut out and pasted on to either a buff card, or the pages of a book. Like all albumen prints, these were made by contact with the negatives, exposed in daylight in rows of printing frames on outdoor racks. To reduce the printing time for large orders, photographers often exposed a number of identical or similar collodion glass negatives. Duplicate negatives also offered a useful insurance against the almost inevitable breakages which happened during the journey home and in the printing factory. The printing and finishing work was all done by a predominantly female workforce – augmented sometimes by children as well – at Frith's own printing works. As well as being sold as part of a set of stereo cards, this image was published as one of one hundred stereo views in the book *Egypt, Nubia and Ethiopia*, published by Smith, Elder & Co., in 1862. An earlier series of stereos, taken during his first visit to Egypt, was published by Negretti & Zambra.

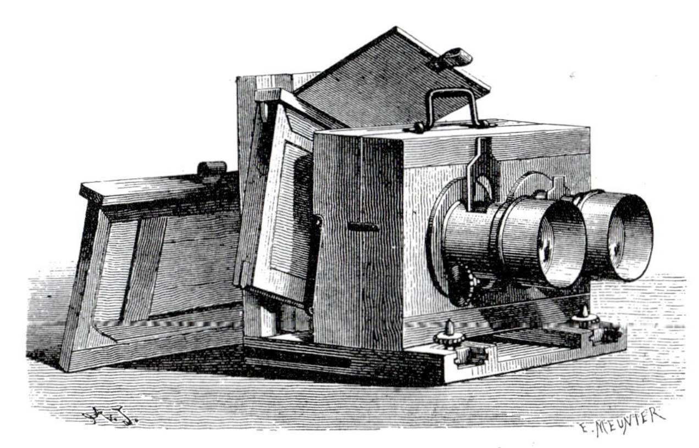

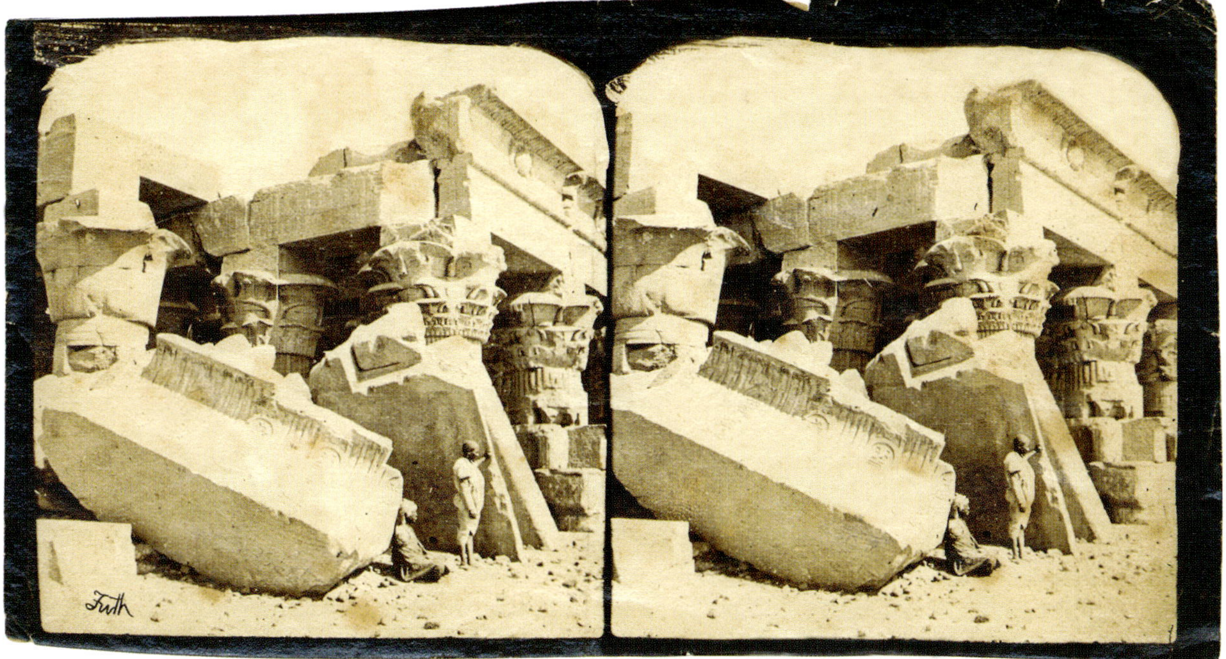

PHOTOGRAPHIC NOTES.

BLAND AND LONG,

153, FLEET STREET,

OPTICIANS AND INSTRUMENT IN ORDINARY **PHOTOGRAPHIC MAKERS TO THE QUEEN,**

BEG to state that the Apparatus and Instruments supplied by them are Manufactured on the Premises, under their Immediate Superintendence, and are of First Class Workmanship, comprising the Latest Improvements.

PHOTOGRAPHIC CAMERAS, RIGID, FOLDING, DOUBLE BODY,

AND EVERY OTHER FORM OF THE BEST WORKMANSHIP.

ACHROMATIC PORTRAIT LENSES,

Giving Pictures of great Intensity and Flatness of Field. The Chemical and Optical foci warranted to coincide. Pictures produced by these Lenses, for Depth and Stereoscopic effect, are unrivalled.

ACHROMATIC LANDSCAPE LENSES,

These Lenses, for Rapidity of Action and perfect Definition, are not to be surpassed. Their range of Chemical focus is also great, so that the foreground and distance are equally in focus.

STEREOSCOPIC CAMERAS, OF THREE FORMS.

	£	s.	d.
No. 1, with Compound Lens, and sample sliding front	3	3	0
No. 2, Bland & Long's Double Lens Camera	5	6	0
No. 3, LatimerClark's Arrangement	6	0	0

PORTABLE TENT, FOR WORKING COLLODION IN THE OPEN COUNTRY. **THE BEST** HITHERTO INTRODUCED, BEING **VERY PORTABLE** AND CONVENIENT IN WORK

SIZE, TO ACCOMMODATE OPERATOR, **SIX FEET HIGH,** Packing, with Stand, &c., complete, into space **24 × 18 × 4.** PRICE: **£4. 4s.**

Elastic Folding Cameras, very Portable. Changing Apparatus for Dry Collodion. Porcelain and Glass Dishes. Camera Stands. Dipping Baths, in Glass, Gutta Percha, and Porcelain. Water-tight Baths for carrying Solutions. **Chemicals of Absolute Purity,** Collodion, Negative and Positive.

The Collodion and Iodizing Solutions can be obtained separate, in which state they will keep for an indefinite period, and can be exported to any climate, without risk of deterioration.

Price of Collodion and Iodizing Solution (separate):—Negative, 12s. 6d., Positive, 9s. per pint.

☞ *Illustrated Priced Catalogue, free in course of Post.*

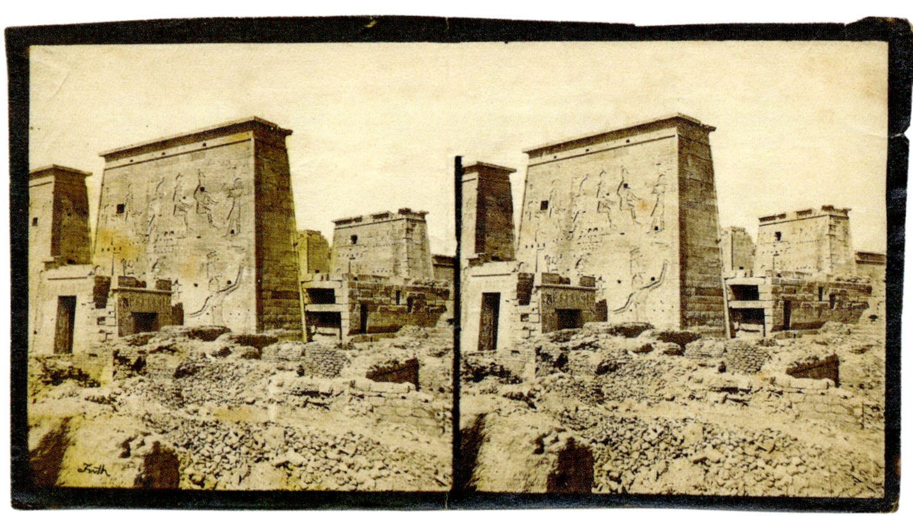

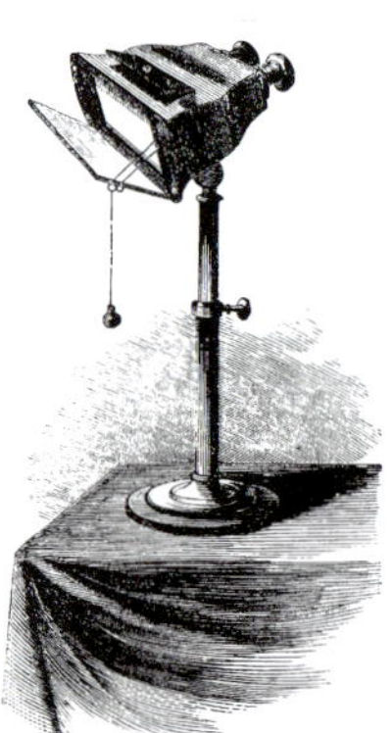

above: The Temple at Philae, from the book *Egypt, Nubia and Ethiopia*, published by Smith, Elder & Co., in 1862. While the negatives of the Kom Ombo view, (*previous page*) had been marked up to be trimmed with an arched top to each image, this view was published trimmed to a square. The survivial of these unmounted images is remarkable and, considering the richness of their print quality, they must simply have been surplus to requirements.

below right: To view stereo images both in books and card-mounted, a special viewer was required. This version could be used hand-held to view card-mounted pictures, or laid on the pages of a book as required. Frith's first published set of stereos was published in book form, so just such a viewer would have been necessary. As an aid to viewing, mirrors in the instrument reflect light back on to the pages of the book.

left: A contemporary illustration of an ornate table-top stereoscope, typical of those found in in many Victorian drawing rooms in the 1860s. This instrument was designed for viewing card-mounted stereos by reflected light, and glass stereo diapositive by transmitted light. Frith's images of Egypt were available in both formats.

Notes

1. Francis Frith *Egypt & Palestine Photographed and Described*, London, James S Virtue, 1857.
2. David Roberts *The Holy Land, Syria, Idumea, Arabia, Egypt and Nubia,* London, F.G.Moon, 1842-1849.
3. William Makepeace Thackeray (writing as M.A.Titmarsh), *Notes on a Journey from Cornhill to Grand Cairo,* London, Chapman & Hall, 1846.
4. Francis Frith *Egypt & Palestine Photographed and Described,* London, James S Virtue, 1857.
5. *ditto.*
6. *ditto,* Introduction.
7. William and Mary Garnett, *Sketches and Letters of Egypt and Palestine with Sketches of other Countries*, Warrington, Mackie & Co., 1904, contains some amusing accounts of Grand Tours undertaken by two Warrington families in the late 1880s and early 1890s. Such journeys were considered to be demonstrations of status and wealth, far removed from our modern idea of an enjoyable holiday. While the Marsdens collected photographs with which to remember their journeys, William Garnett sketched while his wife compiled a diary. Just why it took them so long to publish their accounts is not known.
8. Francis Frith *Egypt & Palestine Photographed and Described,* London, James S Virtue, 1857.
9. *ditto.*
10. William and Mary Garnett, *Sketches and Letters of Egypt and Palestine with Sketches of other Countries,* Warrington, Mackie & Co., 1904.

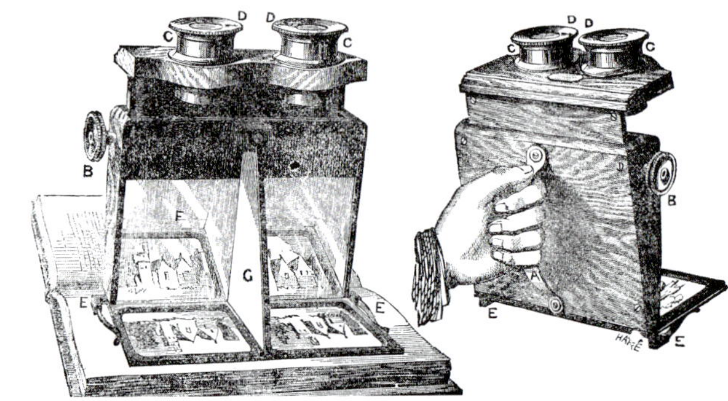

C.G.H. Kinnear & Thomas Melville Raven

Travelling in France in the 1850s

Abstract of an Account of an Architectural and Photographic Tour in the North of France. By C. G. H. KINNEAR, Hon. Sec.

[Read December 15, 1857.]

TOWARDS the end of last August, I set out, in company with two other members of this Society, Messrs. Alexander and James Adam, on an Architectural and Photographic Tour through the Northern Provinces of France. My companions had a folding camera, by Ottewill, taking pictures 11 × 9 ins., and I had a flexible-bodied camera, made according to my directions, by Mr. Bell, of Potterrow. It is somewhat on the principle of Capt. Fowkes' camera, which you will recollect was exhibited here through the kindness of Messrs. Horne and Thornthwaite, last spring; but my camera is stronger than Capt. Fowkes', and so is less liable to be injured by the rough usage to be met with in travelling, and is besides more rigid; and, moreover, it cost only one half the price of the other. It takes pictures $12\frac{1}{2} \times 10\frac{1}{2}$ ins., and folds into a compass of $15\frac{1}{2} \times 13 \times 3\frac{1}{2}$ inches, and weighs 13 lbs., with slide and focusing-glass complete. Both cameras were fitted with Ross's single achromatic lenses.

We were provided with a large stock of iodized waxed paper. That which I took was "Papier Rive," which I had waxed and iodized

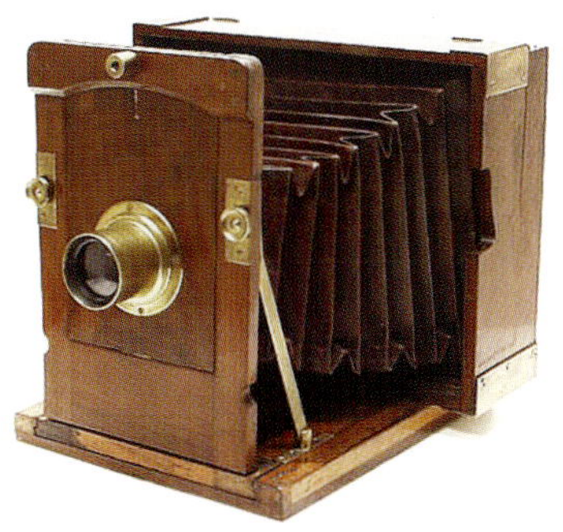

above: Ottewill's Improved Kinnear Camera, 1860s, based on Kinnear's 1857 design.

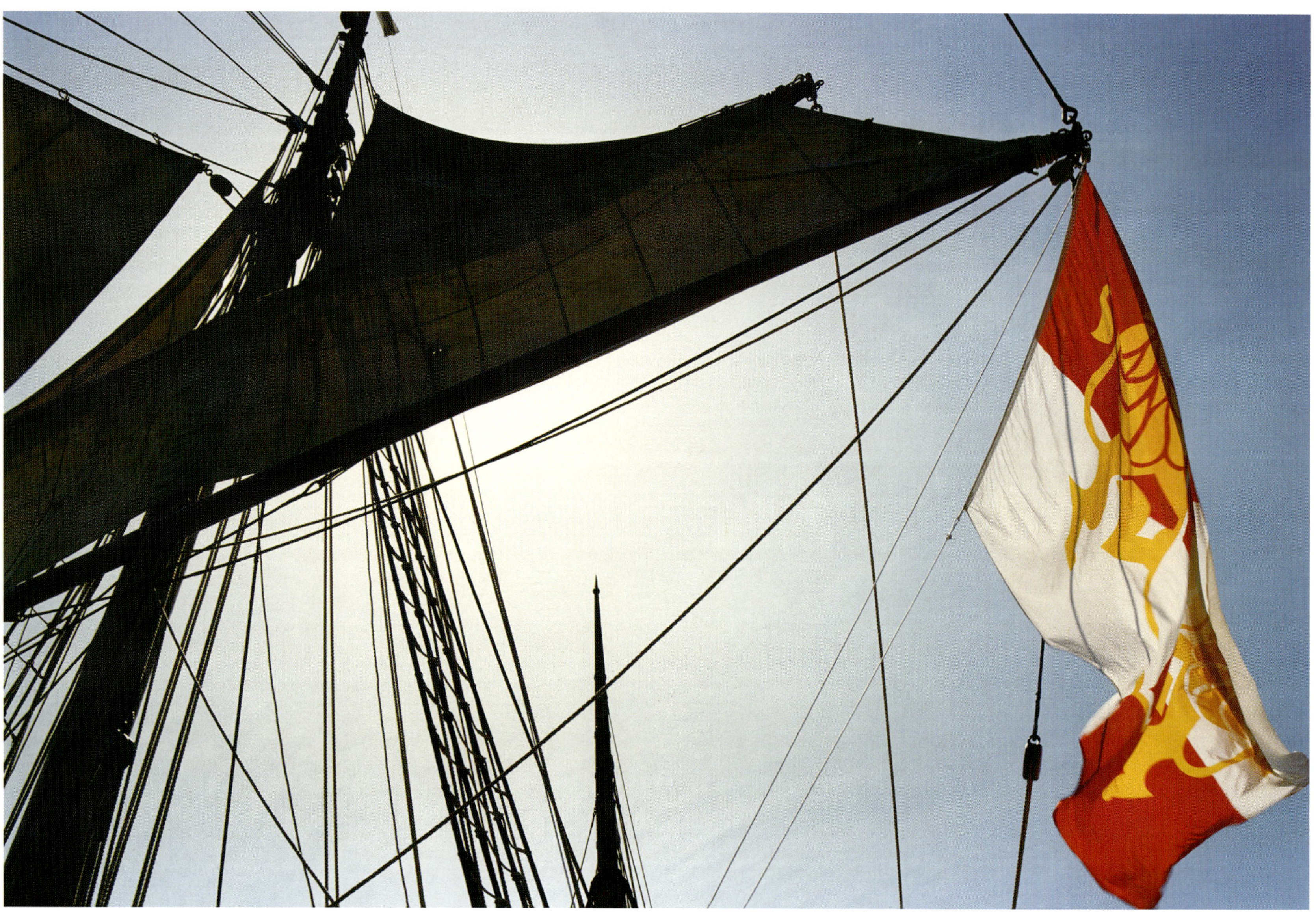

above: In the warm summer breeze, the Breton flag flies from the mast of a sailing ship in the harbour at Douarnenez in Finisterre, north western France. In the mid 19th century, crossing the channel on small sailing vessels with all the paraphernalia of early photography was a major undertaking.

As soon as we turned the corner and looked down the narrow street, we knew we had found the exact spot. No other view matched the description. It was cloudy and raining, and surprisingly cool for a French summer, but the satisfaction of 'being there' was considerable.

Looking towards the twin towers of Bayeux Cathedral, the view was exactly as had been described by Victorian photographer Charles Kinnear in 1857, when recounting his journey through Normandy and Brittany to an enthralled audience of members of the Photographic Society of Scotland.[1]

During the sunny intervals of a day which showed the first clouds we had seen since we began our tour, and which looked threatening for the next day's work, reported Kinnear, *I took the only two views which could be obtained of it in the afternoon; one, of the two spires rising at the end of a narrow street, which, however, hides much of their base, and the other of the south porch which is rich in sculpture.*[2]

The difficulties which had to be confronted by the early photographers in order to get the pictures they wanted were considerable, even when working close to home. For the travelling photographer, those difficulties must at times have seemed almost insurmountable. Despite the scale of the problems of transporting bulky equipment and chemicals, the more intrepid of the first calotypists took their cameras abroad within a very few years of the medium's introduction.

Less than three years after Talbot's first photographic expedition from Lacock to Scotland, members of the Edinburgh Calotype Club had ventured to France, Belgium, and even Italy with their cameras. These pioneering travel images, by George Moir, James Francis Dunlop, Robert Macpherson and others, survive in a remarkable album in the Edinburgh City Libraries collection.

Talbot himself had taken his calotype camera to Paris, Orleans and Rouen as early as May and June 1843.

Calvert Richard Jones and the Reverend George

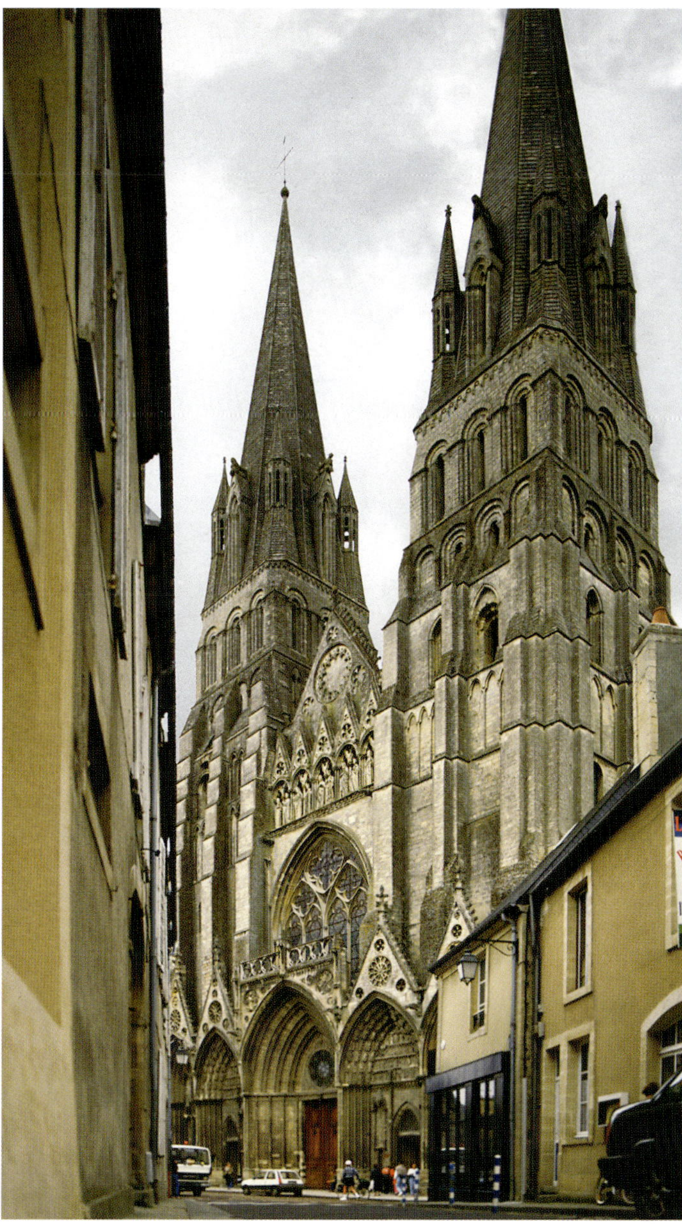

left: The view that started the whole Great Photographic Journeys project. This view of Bayeux Cathedral was taken from a camera position as close as possible to that described by Charles Kinnear in 1857 – and under very similar weather to that which he experienced.

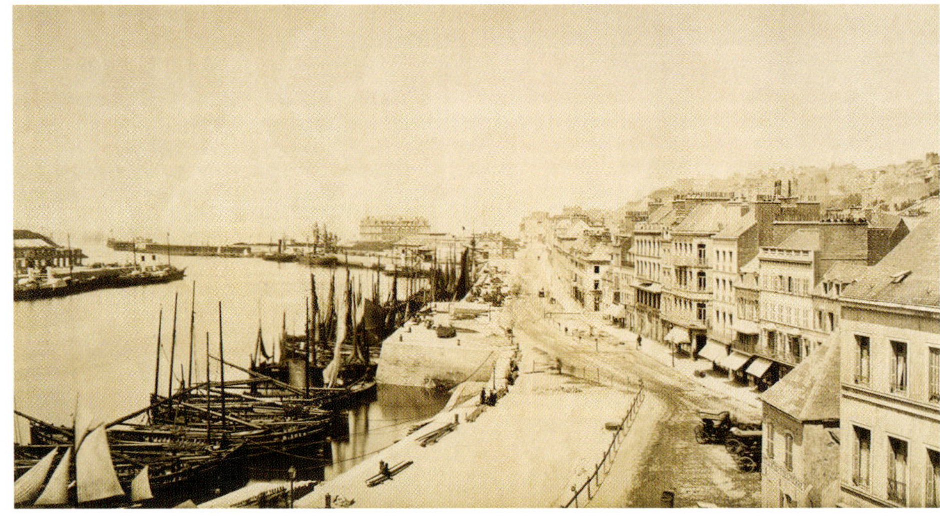

above: The harbour at Boulogne, photographed by an unidentified photographer a few years after Kinnear's visit, with a mixture of sailing ships and steamers tied up at the quayside. For many British travellers, arriving in this port would have been their first contact with anything French.

opposite page left: La Grande Rue, the narrow main street in St. Malo, photographed in the 1870s.

opposite page right: The Port St. Vincent, St. Malo, c.1870. Both of these pictures date from after the introduction of much more sensitive glass plates, permitting shorter exposures than were possible in Kinnear's day. Had he chosen to use wet collodion plates, he would have experienced exposures a fraction of those he had to use, but by the time dry plates were introduced, exposures were down to a fraction of a second. In this view, the image of a small dog has been captured as it made its way across the road, and the trotting horses have been captured without the blurring so typical of images taken two decades earlier.

Bridges brought some fine calotypes back from Rome and Pompeii in 1846. There were others - invariably wealthy landowners, doctors, lawyers, and others able to take a prolonged period of time away from their work, and meet the considerable cost of getting their equipment and materials to mainland Europe.

Those early travellers, however, were the exception rather than the rule, and fifteen years later, such journeys still proved popular subjects for lectures, and for essays in the growing number of photographic magazines.

In 1857, Charles G. H. Kinnear crossed the Channel at the start of a journey through northern France, armed with a large format camera and Waxed Paper negatives.

My journey was, in part, a recreation of Kinnear's August 1857 journey, and part recreation of another journey - by the Reverend Thomas Melville Raven two months later in October 1857.[3]

Perversely, while we know the subjects of many of their pictures, and the exact camera locations of some, and while we have their detailed accounts of their experiences and the challenges they faced, very few confirmed examples of either man's photography have yet been found. A number of images by unidentified photographers survive in major collections, taken from the right places, and taken at the right time, but while these might be by Kinnear or Raven, further research is still desperately needed before any acceptable degree of certainty can be claimed. The majority of the Victorian images which are used here to illustrate their journeys are, regrettably, by other photographers.

While I travelled with my rollfim camera, a case of lenses and a supply of colour transparency film, Kinnear and Raven both had rather more to transport. They both used the Waxed Paper process, invented by Frenchman Gustave le Gray in 1850, and which despite giving the travelling photographer more freedom than wet collodion, still needed a fair amount of chemistry and materials to accompany the photographer.

Just as Roger Fenton had done when using Waxed

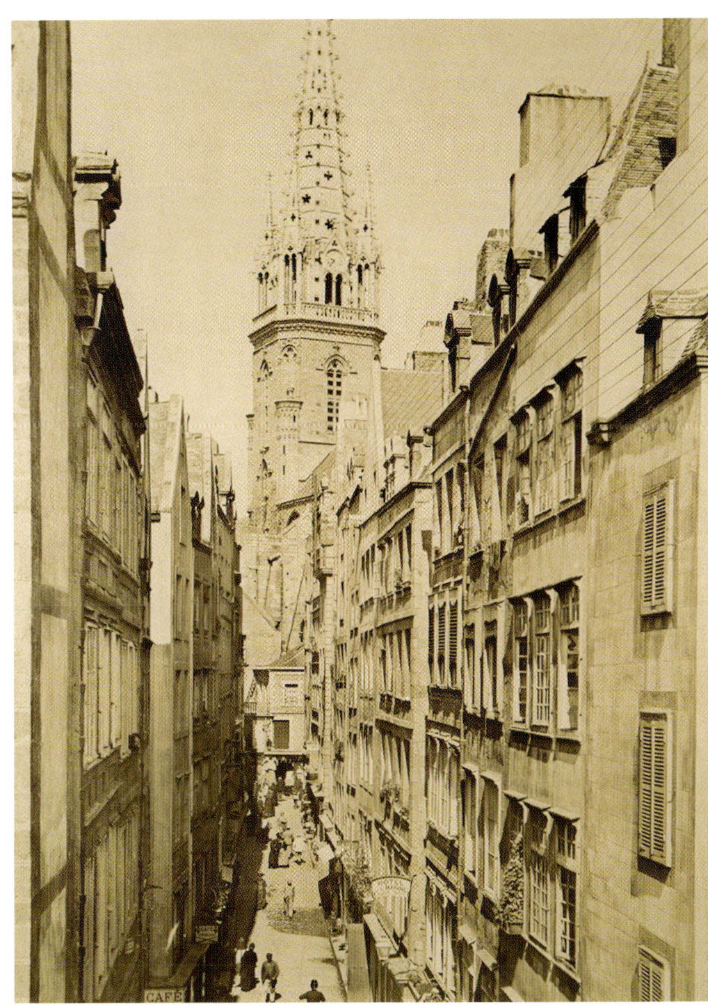

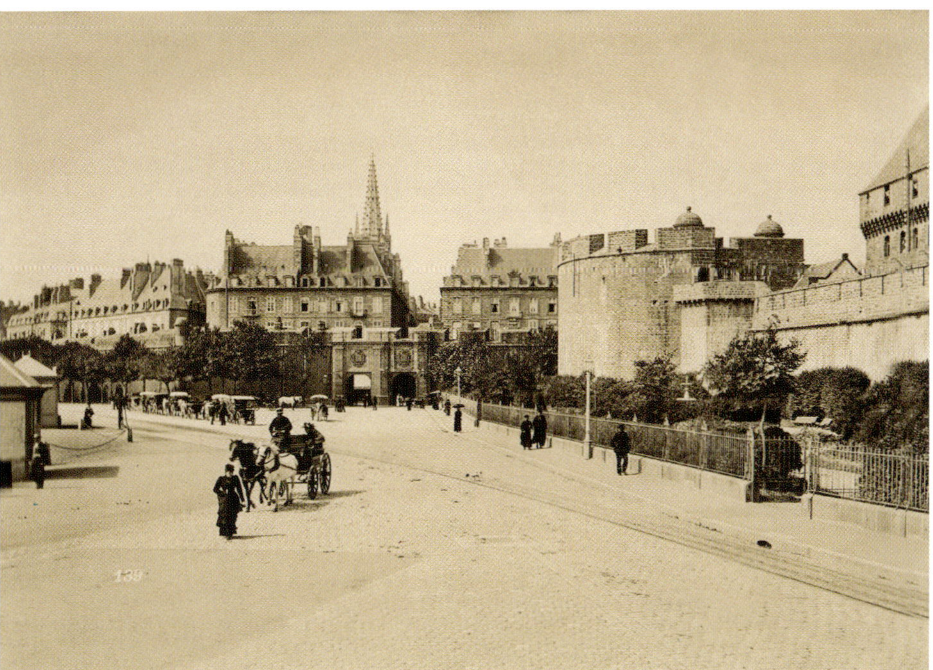

Paper in Russia five years earlier, both Kinnear and Raven could prepare their materials a few hours or a few days in advance, and process them a few hours or days later. Usually, however, they were processed the same evening.

In his diary Reverend Raven lamented the problems of getting his materials into France, never mind the problems of using them! When he arrived in St. Malo – just as we did – he recalled that

> *The Customs House officers made a great piece of work with some of my chemicals, and the camera completely puzzled them.*
>
> *I had three or four pounds of hypo-sulphite of soda, very carefully wrapped up in several folds of paper, in my portmanteau, which I had placed there to be out of the way of everything appertaining to photography, which they pounced on, and away two officers went with it, I followed protesting that it was not tea, or coffee, or even tobacco,*

right: The quayside in the little port of Dinan as it looked when the Reverend Raven stepped ashore from his steamer.
below right: The port today is largely deserted, save for a few pleasure craft.

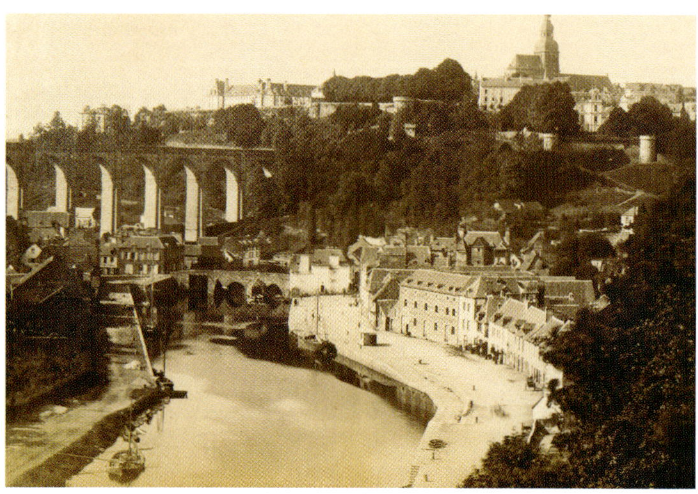

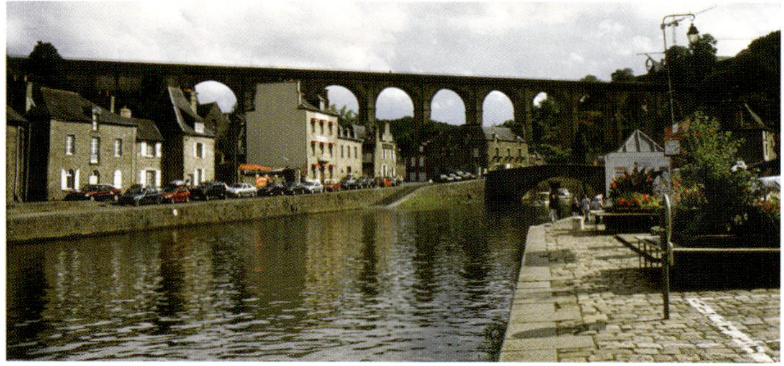

opposite page: Landscape near Poitiers. Although both Kinnear and Raven seem primarily to have been attracted by the photographic potential of the buildings they visited on their travels, the wide open French landscape has inspired photographers since photography's earliest days. However, to users of all early blue sensitive processes, and especially slow processes like Waxed Paper, capturing the majesty of France's wonderful skies was difficult. The blue sensitive chemistry, and long exposures, meant that on early prints, the sky was reproduced as a uniform white or grey. Rev. Raven evolved a techque to remedy this deficiency.

each one of which it seems they were certain it must be; at last I got the parcel into my own hands, and opening it up, offered to each of them a crystal to taste, which did not satisfy them in the least, and away I had to march with them, and it, to a superior officer, who pulled out a long paper, then a large book, and having looked over them most carefully for the words 'hyposulfite de Soude', under the head 'acides', he allowed me to take possession of the parcel once more; the only conclusion I could come to was, that he was no chemist, but his opinion of me seemed much more undefined. Then followed the examination of every chemical case, every bottle of which was regarded with strong suspicion, and held up to the light as if it would tell some awful tale.

It was beginning to get dark, and I was the last in the room; the case in which my iodized papers were kept had still to be examined, but they were sick of photography and allowed it to pass unopened, much to my satisfaction.[4]

In today's relaxed travel regime within the EU, of course, my kit entered St. Malo uninspected! Indeed on that first occasion my cameras passed through St. Malo unused as it rained persistently. Perhaps Raven was right when he told his readers that

There is nothing picturesque in St. Malo, I left the following afternoon, sailing up the river to Dinan.

We had left Portsmouth in late evening sunlight on board Brittany Ferries' *Bretagne*, and doubtless had enjoyed a much less traumatic crossing than the Reverend Raven.

St. Malo today is largely a reconstruction of the ancient city. Destruction during the Second World War was almost total, but today's visitor sees what looks like the original walled mediaeval city.

Being familiar with the photographs of wartime St. Malo taken during the assault on the city in 1944 by the great American model-turned-photographer Lee Miller – she was caught up in the middle of the final battle for control of the area – today's restored city seems a quite remarkable achievement.

The ancient city within the walls – the Intra-Muros –

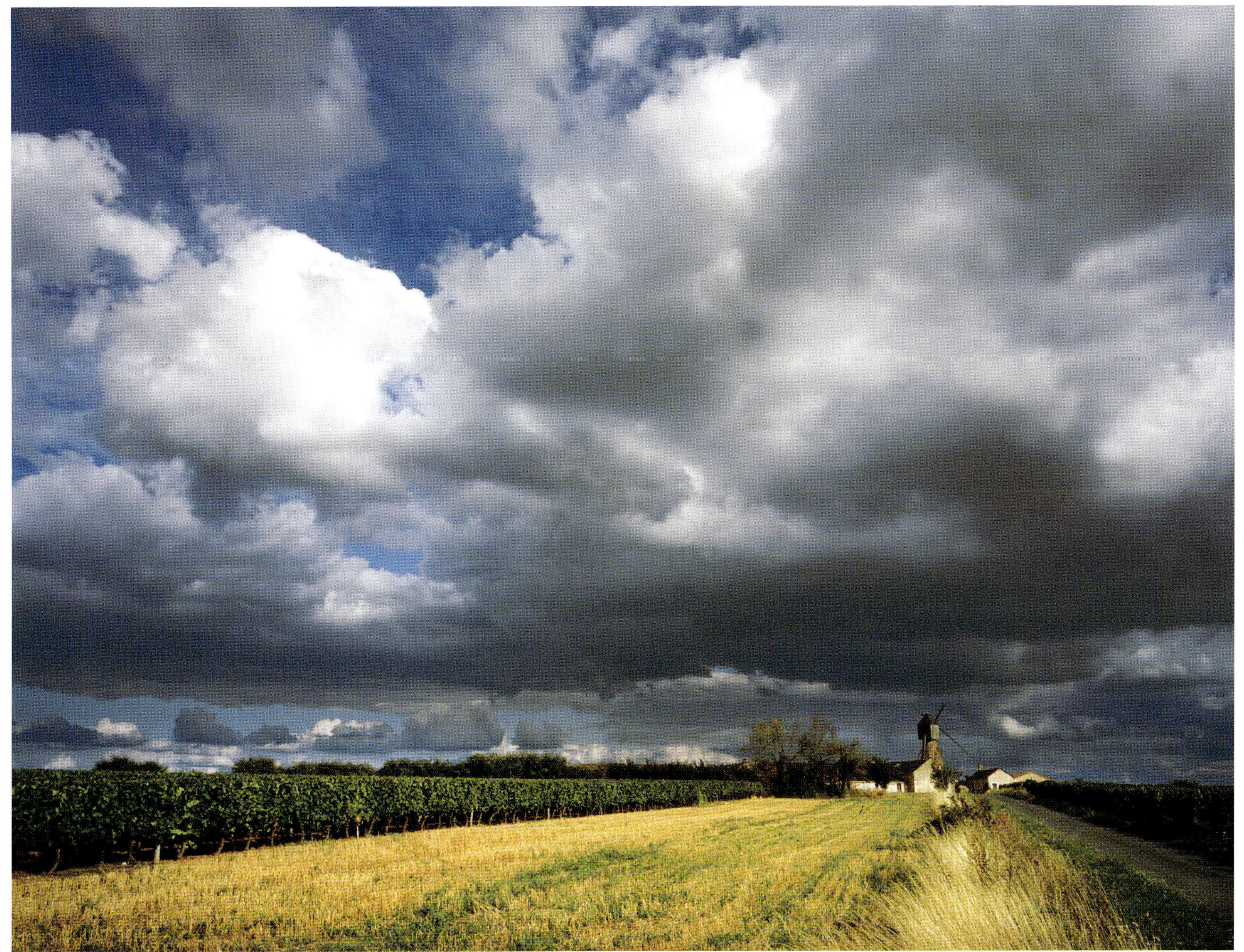

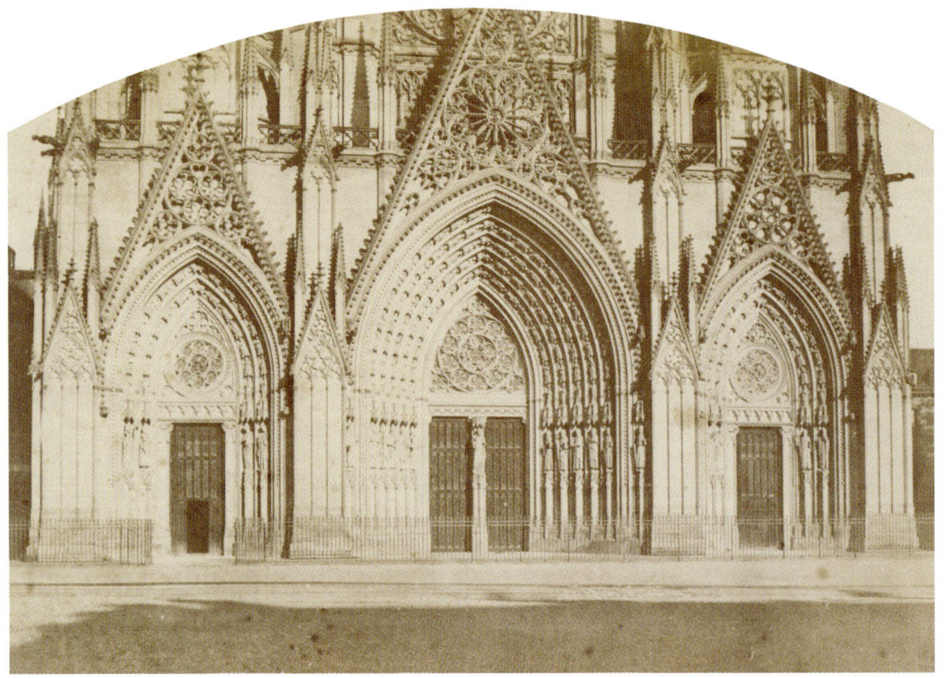

above: The West Door, St Ouen, Rouen, photographed on Waxed Paper by Charles Kinnear on his first outing with his new camera in France, in late August 1857. Like Fenton before him, he had waxed and iodised his papers before leaving home. The west front of the 13th-15th century former abbey church had been extensively renovated - some would say rebuilt - between 1846 and 1851. Kinnear enjoyed Rouen, but warned his audience that any photographer '*must make up his mind to a good deal of annoyance when he plants his camera in front of any building in the principal streets or squares. The town is more bustling and crowded than almost any other which we visited on our tour, and though cameras must be sights more common in Rouen than almost any other city in the world, they excited a disagreeable amount of sensation in its streets.*' Interestingly, although he had 'rising front' on his new camera, he has failed to fully correct the verticals in this image.

dating from the 14th to 17th centuries, has been completely rebuilt, and is still served by its two major gates - the Porte St. Vincent and the Grande Porte. The expanding modern city all but surrounds the ancient walled town, and has now incorporated the seaside resorts of Paramé and Rothéneuf.

The harbour is still used by fishing boats and cargo vessels as well as Brittany Ferries' vessels, and until relatively recently was only accessible at certain points on the tide. It is not all that many years ago, that ferry passengers were regularly held up waiting for enough water to enter or leave the port. Parts of the inner harbour are still dry at low tide.

Charles Kinnear crossed to France with two fellow photographers, Alexander Finlay Adam, and James Adam. All three were users of le Gray's Waxed Paper Process, and Kinnear at least had journeyed abroad with his camera before - having previously photographed in France, Italy and Germany - and probably elsewhere as well.

Their journey was described - by Kinnear in his lecture to the Photographic Society of Scotland on December 15th 1857 - as an *Architectural and Photographic Tour in the North of France* and they had set out in late August 1857. All three were from Edinburgh, so the journey was a major undertaking. It had been well planned, and the challenges of travelling long distances had been taken into account. Kinnear told his audience

> *As our route was to embrace a district in which there are as yet no railways, and only small and incommodious diligences, it was of importance to reduce the bulk and weight of our luggage as much as possible. My photographic outfit was composed of –*
>
> *A Portfolio for carrying the iodised paper, with a division for the pictures.*
>
> *Four quires of thick white blotting paper.*
>
> *Two papiér maché dishes nesting into each other, contained in a wooden dish which protected them, and also served for washing the pictures in.*
>
> *A 12-oz. bottle for the sensitising solution.*

5-oz of nitrate of silver (crystallized).
8-oz of glacial acetic acid.
1/4-oz of gallic acid.
1/4-oz of citric acid.
Each in a wooden case.
A packet of animal charcoal.
A gutta-percha funnel.
A pair of horn-forceps
Scales and measuring glass in a case.
Two large pieces of yellow calico,
and some large pins and a couple of towels.
All these went into my portmanteau.[5]

Their first destination for photography was Rouen, because, as Kinnear told his audience[6]

There is plenty of work for the photographer there, and he might easily employ himself for a week, taking either the purely architectural subjects, or the equally tempting picturesque bits with which the town abounds.

From Rouen, they went on to Caen, further west along the coast about half way between Dieppe and St. Malo. We moved east from St. Malo to pick up his route, and then followed the itinerary he described in his lecture.

From Caen, a forenoon's drive along a level road, with a slight detour to visit and photograph the fine spire of Norrey, took us to Bayeux, as dull and melancholy a town as any cathedral town in England. It contains absolutely nothing of interest but its cathedral and the famous tapestry.

Bayeux today is a tourist city strangled by cars. The old city around the magnificent 13th century cathedral - Notre-Dame de Bayeux - is made up of narrow streets where both walking and photography are difficult but well worth the effort. With today's hand-held cameras, the challenge is considerably less than that which must have faced Kinnear with his large unwieldy bellows camera and tripod.

Both he and Raven recounted, to their separate lecture audiences, lovely stories about how hoteliers dealt with travelling photographers, their special needs, and their chemicals in the early days! After returning to his home in

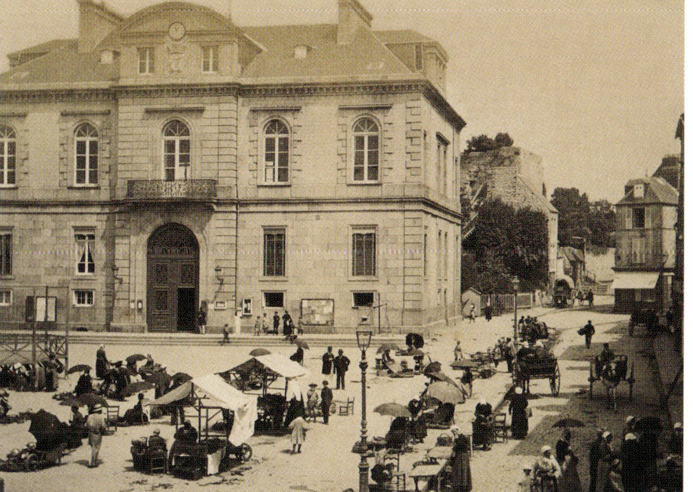

left: The Hotel de Ville and Market, Avranches, photographed on collodion by an unknown photographer. A remarkably animated scene for its day, such a view would not have been possible with Kinnear's slow paper negatives. Only those people who stood absolutely still for the duration of the exposure would have been captured by his camera. Most of the time, his camera would have captured what one photographic magazine of the day described as empty 'cities of the dead', with only the occasional ghostly image to suggest that anyone other than the photographer had been present.

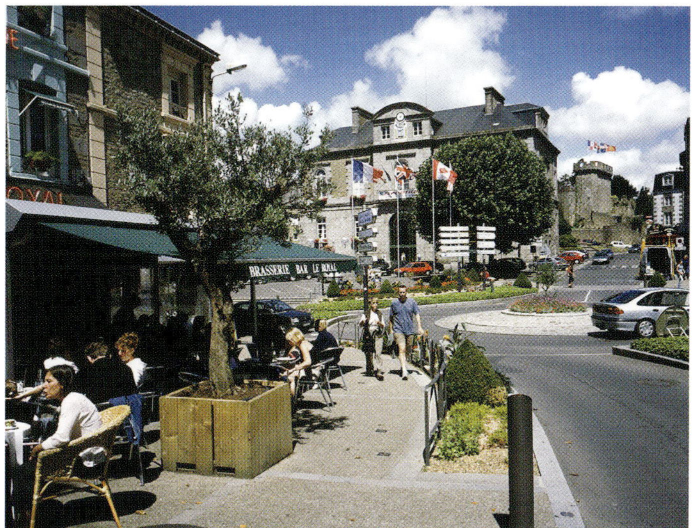

below left: The Hotel de Ville and main square in Avranches has today been sacrificed in the name of modern traffic management, and is now a car park.

Jersey, Raven wrote in *Photographic Notes* in early 1858 that

I go upon the principle that 'fortune favours the brave,' (say nothing about it) take my rooms and work in them as I like. In one hotel my camera was seen, and when I went into my room at night, I found, by the towels and the toilet covers, unmistakable traces of there having been a worker of the same art before me, and as I had no desire to receive the credit due to him, I suggested that as I had all the necessary drying materials with me, I could apply them myself, if I wished to do so, on fresh towels and covers – they were immediately changed but I was told "they were quite clean until they had been used by a Monsieur Anglais".[7]

Looking at the towel on the back of my own darkroom door, I cannot imagine what he meant!

When we read his account of his processing methods, the concerns and implied criticisms of the hotel concierge were hardly surprising! In February 1858, long after the wet collodion process was in the ascendancy, he wrote

I am quite convinced by every day's experience of one thing, and that is, that glass is quite out of the question for this country. Had I been working with collodion I should not have had one negative to show twenty miles from the place at which it was taken. In the waxed-paper process, I sensitise my paper in my own room just before going to bed; if the following day should not be fine, I am still ready for the first fine hours that should come, though I may have to wait for it for three or four days. I develop at night, and when the negative is fully out, wash it well and leave it in clean water til the following morning. I then clean the dishes thoroughly, put them by, and excite fresh paper for the next day, place it when finished in the dark slides, clean the dishes and put them by, and then make ready for fixing the negatives just developed by the first dawn of daylight. As soon as this appears, I get up and immerse the negatives in the hypo bath, take to my bed again for half an hour; when it is time to get up, I examine the pictures, and if finished, wash them thoroughly. There is little satisfaction in taking unfixed negatives about with one, as their delicacy and fineness of

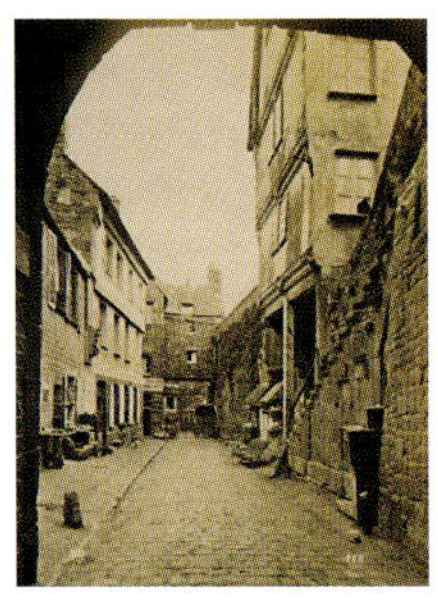

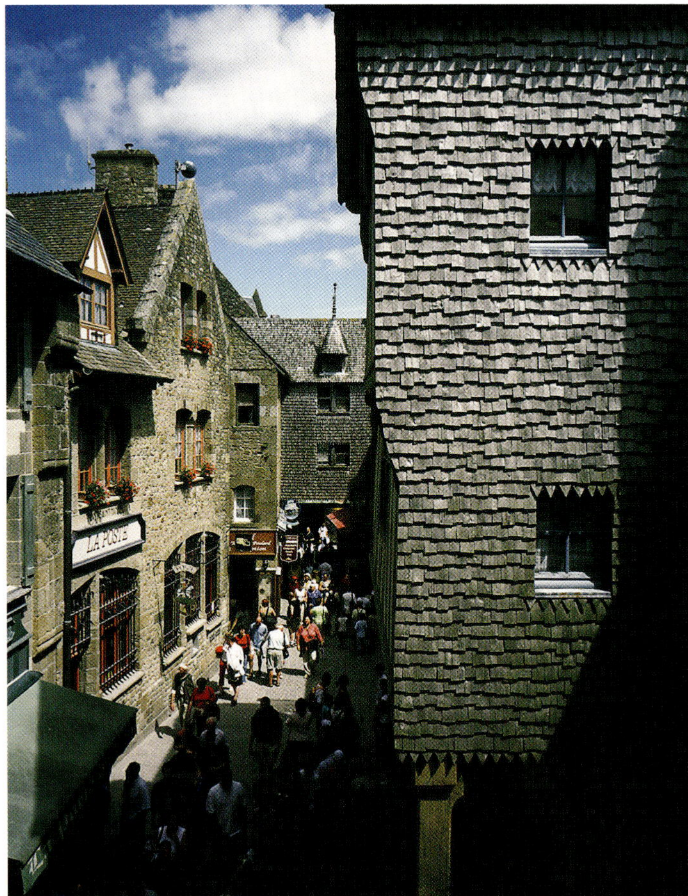

above: A narrow alleyway off la Grande Rue, Mont St. Michel, c.1870.
right: Every day in the summer thousands of tourists make their way up the winding streets from the car park to enjoy the spectacular views from the courtyards around the abbey.

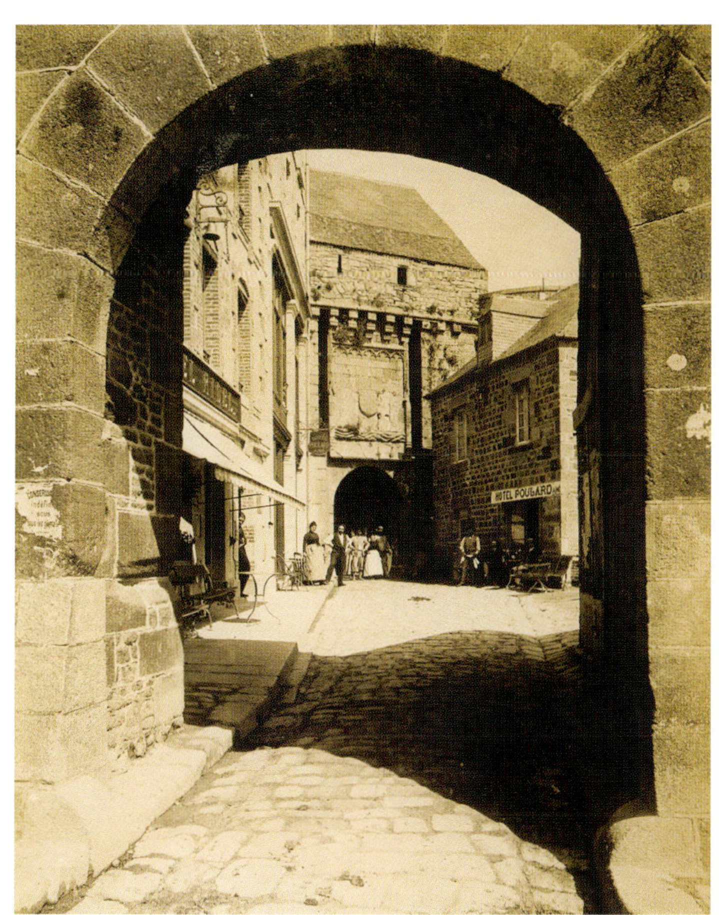

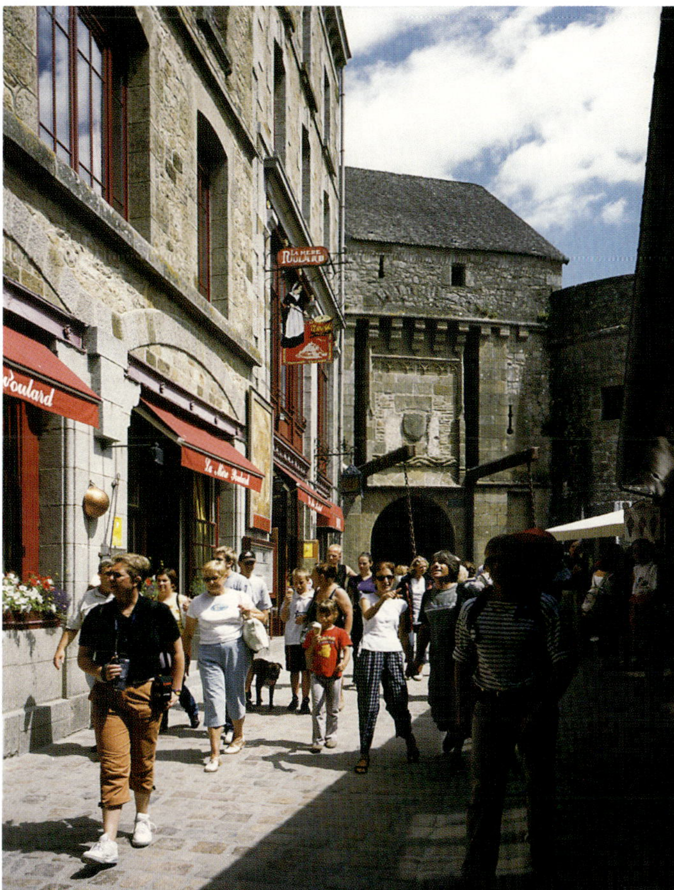

left and far left: Almost a century and a half separate these two views of La Grande Rue, although today's crowds would have been undreamed off. While the presence of a camera was once a rare event – for which the hotel and shop staff posed to have their picture taken, today's crowds are oblivious to the fact that they are being photographed.

detail are invariably lost by doing so, and if I am unable to wash the picture thoroughly before leaving the place at which it was taken, I manage to do so at the next place at which I stay.[8]

Even in the middle of the 19th century, the eccentric ways of the English seem to have been a staple subject of conversation in France. Nothing changes.

In Bayeux in August 1857, Kinnear, while promoting the advantages of waxed paper for the travelling photographer, also recognised its limitations. He was impressed by the tapestry, and hoped that it would one day be photographed, but knew that the slowness of Waxed Paper would turn such a challenge into an ordeal. To his audience, he urged the next photographer using collodion who visited the tapestry - which at the time *was exhibited under a glass case in the public library* - to make an attempt to photograph it. A series of photographs of it, he declared *would still possess much interest*, despite Charles Stothard's engravings already being well known.

Today's highly dramatic presentation - a far cry from a glass case in the library - shows how far museum display has evolved over a century and a half - and the huge market for photographs of the tapestry today underlines the wisdom of Kinnear's words.

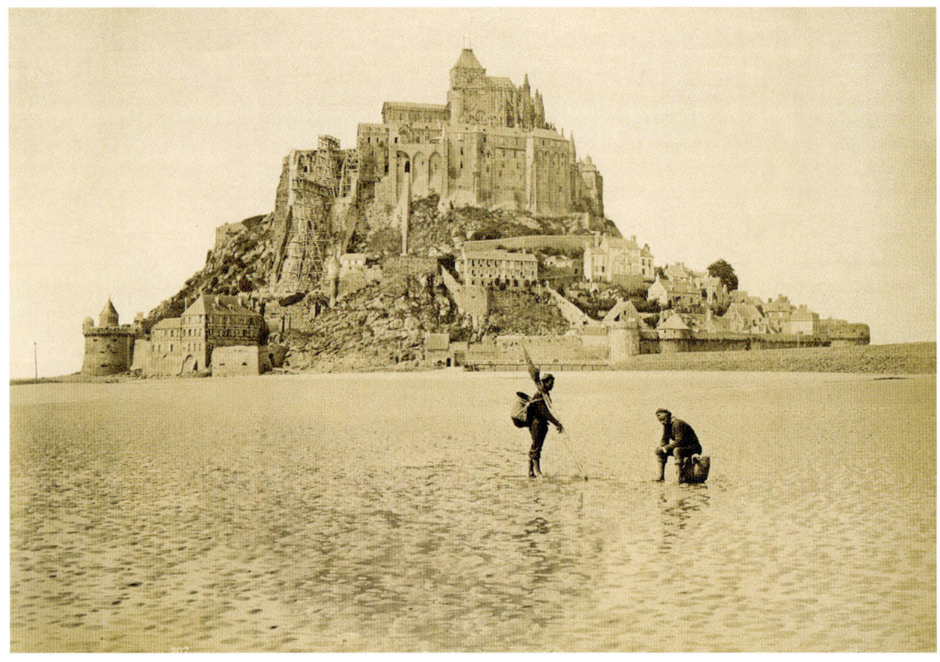

above: Mont St. Michel photographed about a decade after Kinnear's visit. Images of the rock were produced for tourists from the late 1850s, and by the time this picture was taken, the tourist market was growing considerably as a greater enthusiasm for travel, and easier transport, gripped the British and European middle classes. In this view, the tide is just starting to rise through the sand - creating the soft sinking conditions which had bedevilled Kinnear's attempts to photograph the place.

From Bayeux, Kinnear and his friends travelled to Norrey where they took a number of pictures. For us, the heavens opened, and photography had to be abandoned.

The party's next stop was Avranches which, according to Kinnear, contained no remarkable buildings, but gave them their first view of Mont St. Michel, the place he most wished to visit and photograph.

Like us he arrived there in dull and gloomy weather, but to his audience he concentrated on the fine view of the rock which was afforded by the town's ancient walls.

That evening, in his hotel bedroom, the trio prepared and sensitised their paper negatives for the challenge which lay ahead of them the following day. Again, like them, we arrived at the rock just before noon, and again,

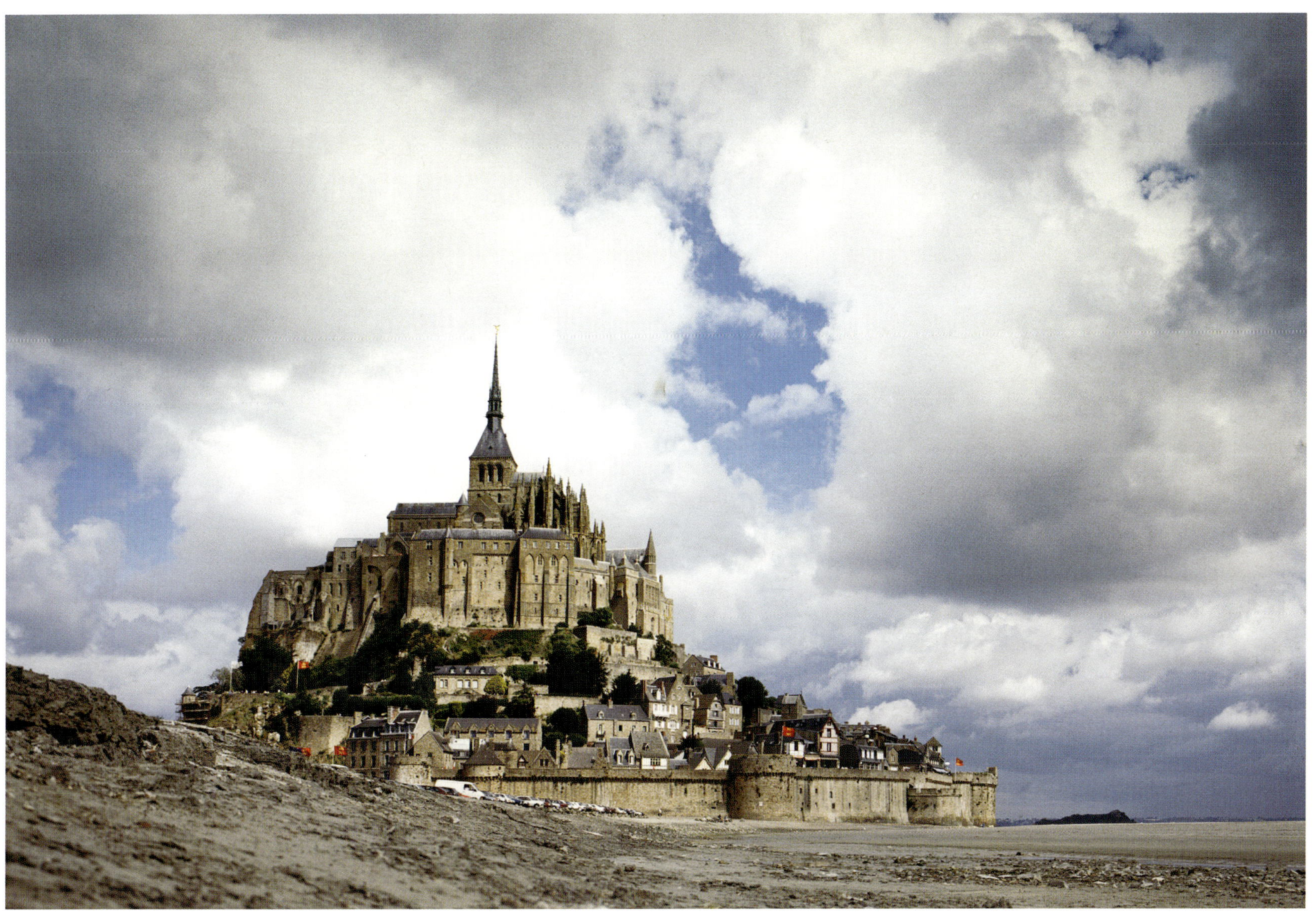

above: Mont St Michel todayis approached via a long causeway to the car and coach park below the rock, but plans are afoot to remove it. Within the next few years the causeway will be replaced by a bridge, traffic will be restricted to a car park on the mainland, and the tide will once again be free to flow around the rock.

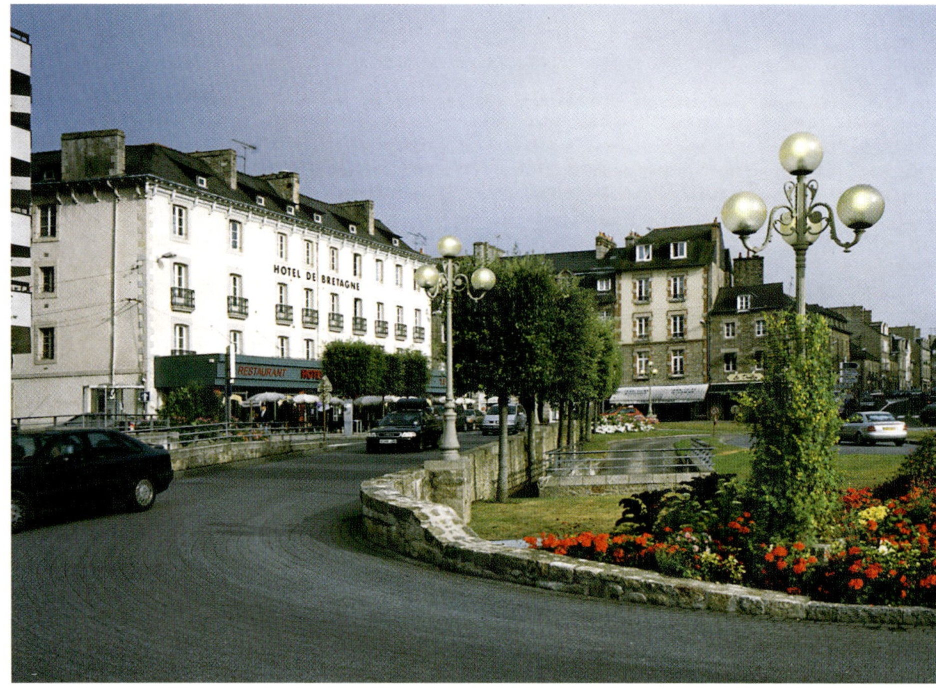

above: Dinan's Hotel de Bretagne was chosen by Thomas Melville Raven as the ideal base for him and his family during their stay in the town in October 1857, primarily because of the 'imposing looking pump' which stood at the front door, and promised a supply of fresh water. He was rather less than charitable towards the use of English in the hotel, noting that "the salle-a-manger was ornamented with a framed print of an hotel in the neighbourhood, under which was printed in French, German and English, its chief recommendations. The English translation states that there are pleasant 'graves' in the grounds for visitors." There may no longer be a pump by the door, but the hotel still offers a fine welcome, and is an ideal base for exploring the town.

the heavy cloud was just breaking as we made our way across the causeway. Unlike us, Kinnear and his party did not have the challenge of taking pictures without including the hundreds of cars and coaches which marred the view. Indeed, in Kinnear's day there was no causeway. He was dependent upon a carriage and driver.

Standing on the causeway looking towards Mont St. Michel today, with endless rows of coaches, and hundreds of cars, or being jostled in the narrow winding streets which zig-zag up to the Abbey at the top, it is impossible to believe that this was ever the peaceful place described by Kinnear in his lecture.

> *My first view was taken from the firmest sand I could find as near the rock as would admit of my getting the whole view in my camera. I planted the legs as firmly as I could, spreading the legs well out, and pressing them into the sand as far as possible. After focusing quickly, I put in the paper slide, pulled up the shutter and retired to a respectful distance as the water was rapidly rising through the sand, and soon it stood some inches deep where my dry spot had been. I feared the picture would be lost. We developed our pictures in the evening in the small town of Doll, and I had the satisfaction of seeing that out of my four views, three were completely successful. The first one taken would perhaps have been the best of all, but the camera had sunk to the extent of, I should think, three or four inches – and so made the picture so indistinct as to be worth nothing.*[9]

While the Reverend T. Melville Raven may have been a little surprised by the dirty reputation earned by *les messieurs Anglais*, Kinnear was certainly much less than pleased by what he was to discover about a quite different group of *messieurs Anglais*.

Believing himself and his colleagues to be the first British photographers to undertake such an adventurous journey, Kinnear recalled how he learned from his coachman, as they crossed to the rock, that they were not.

Just like discovering that someone had beaten a 21st century climber to the summit of a newly discovered mountain, Kinnear later recalled that all had not gone quite according to plan:

> *We happened to stop for a few seconds when our carriage began to sink in the sand... A bad prospect for our camera legs! But the guide assured us that it was all right for two 'messieurs Anglais' had been photographing there last week! This was rather a disappointment, but we were partially consoled afterwards by the soldiers who came to look on, telling us they were stereoscopic pictures that the English gentlemen had been taking.*[10]

But he put his disappointment behind him, and moved on to offer processing advice to other would-be travel photographers. This included carrying a syphon, a small barrel and a length of hosepipe, by which means to collect rain water – the closest to the distilled water recommended for mixing the sensitising and processing chemistries.

Raven, however, was less critical of the local water supplies, suggesting that he had chosen the Hotel de Bretagne in Dinan in consequence of its having an imposing-looking pump before the door.

Despite several criticisms of his own he did agree it was the best hotel in the area.

> *It is necessary for the photographer to make a very strict bargain with 'Mademoiselle', for if he does not, he will find on leaving that she is not 'fair' and the hotel is comfortable for one in Brittany, but like them all has a host or hostess who would skin you if they could realize anything by the operation*[11]

Not least of its attractions was the fact that processing in the bedrooms, if not actually encouraged, was apparently tolerated, and the servants never tired of carrying water and cleaning dishes while he processed his negatives.

From Charles Kinnear's lecture notes, we know a lot about his cameras, and the size of images he and his companions produced. Having already read the list of materials and processing equipment he deemed essential, and then considering the bulk and weight of the cameras, it is worth remembering that one of the Waxed

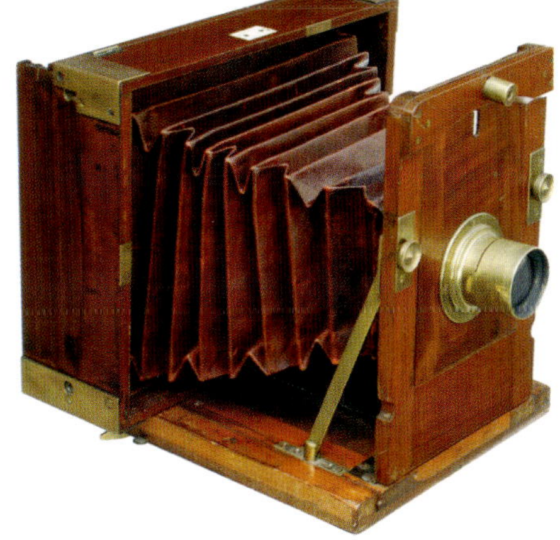

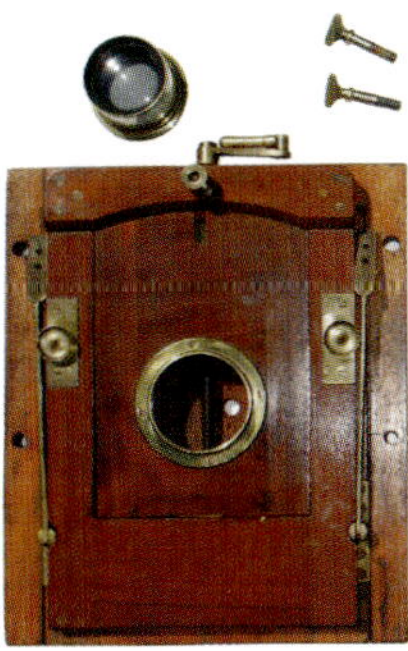

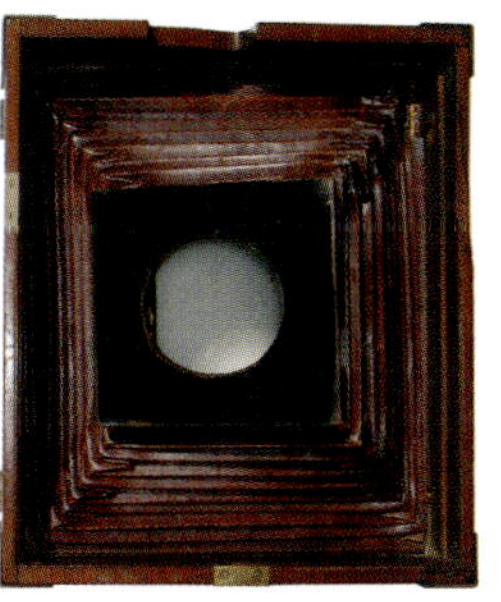

above: No surviving examples of the original Kinnear camera have so far been discovered, but his original design was subsequently modified, refined, strengthened, and marketed by Ottewill & Co., as their 'Improved Kinnear Camera' from the early 1860s.

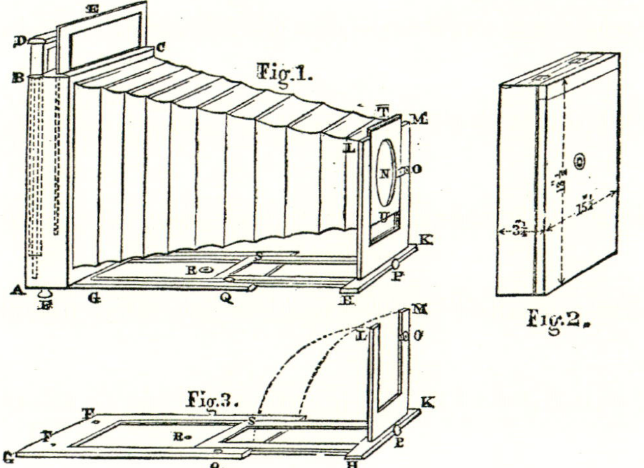

above: This diagrammatic representation of the Kinnear camera accompanied a description in *The Journal of the Photographic Society*, February 22nd 1858.

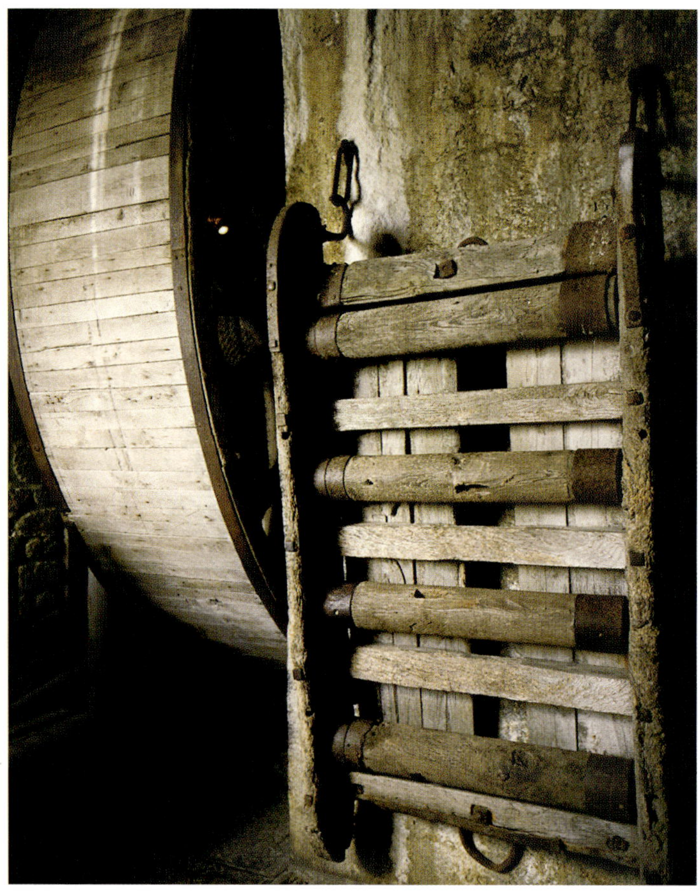

above: The treadmill at Mont St. Michel, a reminder of its years as a prison in the 19th century, is preserved in the Monks' Ossuary, one of the Abbey's many vaulted chambers built into the sides of the rock. The wheel raised and lowered a hoist which ran up and down a steeply sloping inclined trackway and was used for the delivery of large and heavy objects and materials to the prison. A similar mechanism had been used by the monks who built the Abbey centuries earlier.

Paper process's perceived advantages was that with it the travelling photographer could forget the additional burden of the portable darkroom or darktent and 'travel light'!

> *My companions had a folding camera by Ottewill, taking pictures 11x9ins., and I had a flexible bodied camera, made according to my directions, by Mr. Bell of Potterrow. It is somewhat on the principle of Capt. Fowkes' camera… but my camera is stronger than Capt. Fowkes', and so is less liable to be injured by the rough usage to be met with in travelling, and is besides more rigid; and, moreover, it costs only one half of the price of the other.It takes pictures $12^{1}/_{2}$ x $10^{1}/_{2}$ins., and it folds into a compass of $15^{1}/_{2}$ x 13 x $3^{1}/_{2}$ins., and weighs 13lbs., with slide and focusing-glass complete. Both cameras were fitted with Ross's single achromatic lenses.*
>
> *We were provided with a large stock of iodized waxed paper. That which I took was 'Papier Rive' which I had waxed and iodized myself…* [12]

Kinnear was somewhat modest in his description of his camera – it was, in fact, of a ground-breaking design, and one which established and defined the outward appearance of the field camera for decades to come.

Capt. Fowkes' camera, to which Kinnear referred, was one of the first practical camera designs for outdoor use to reduce the weight and bulk to be carried by dispensing with the rigid wooden body. Fowkes replaced the sliding boxes with short square bellows which linked a tapered wooden box – like a pyramid on its side containing the lens panel – with the large negative holder. The wooden pyramid could be collapsed for transportation – but the same extension could have been achieved at lower weight with longer bellows. Fowkes was, like Kinnear, an architect by profession, so the two men may well have been acquainted with each other, and Kinnear had clearly investigated the Fowkes camera design.

His ingenuity was to replace both the pyramid and square bellows with tapered bellows. He thus achieved a greater extension and greater operating flexibility in a camera which, when collapsed, took up no more room than Fowkes' design.

Of course, there had been bellows cameras before – since 1851 in fact – but not tapered bellows. Indeed, for his large-format scenic views, Roger Fenton had taken French-designed bellows cameras (by Bourquien of Paris) to the Crimean War in 1855.

The original bellows camera designs had all used square bellows, but with tapered bellows the camera could be folded into a much smaller volume for easier transportation – when the camera was folded down, each pleat nestled neatly into the one beneath it. Kinnear's camera, at $3^{1}/_{2}$ ins. deep when folded, reduced the closed volume of the camera by about half compared with the square bellows alternative.

Kinnear must have hoped that the stability of his lighter-weight camera would not have been compromised. At Mont St Michel, he faced an alternative hazard, which he recounted to his audience.

> *A smart breeze, too, was blowing in gusts around the rock from the sea, so between the vertical and horizontal motions of the camera, I feared the picture would be lost.*

He was not wrong in his assumption. Given the lighter weight of his camera, it is perhaps surprising that his first picture at Mont St. Michel was ruined by the tripod slowly sinking in to the sand. But then again, as the tide rises quickly through, rather than over the sands, perhaps not. That lighter weight, however, would have increased the likelihood of lateral movement in the wind. He moved to firmer ground for the subsequent exposures!

He later noted that during the long exposure required for the relatively insensitive Waxed Paper process – sometimes as long as twenty minutes – the tripod had sunk three or four inches! By the time of his fourth and last exposure, the tide had apparently turned, the sands were drier and firmer, and he felt assured of success.

Mont St. Michel, in Kinnear's day, was being used as a prison, and he observed on his way to the top – to take

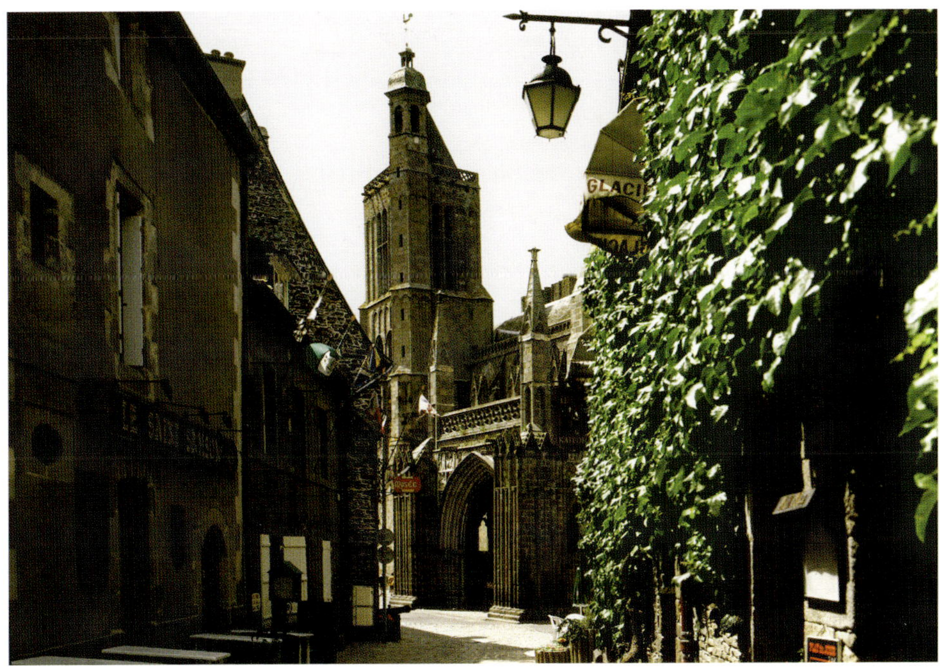

above: Kinnear's only remark about Dol de Bretagne was that *we developed our pictures that evening in the little town of Dol, and I had the satisfaction to find that out of my four views* [of Mont St., Michel] *three were completely successful.* He did not apparently stay long enough to photograph the beautiful 13th century St Samson's Cathedral.

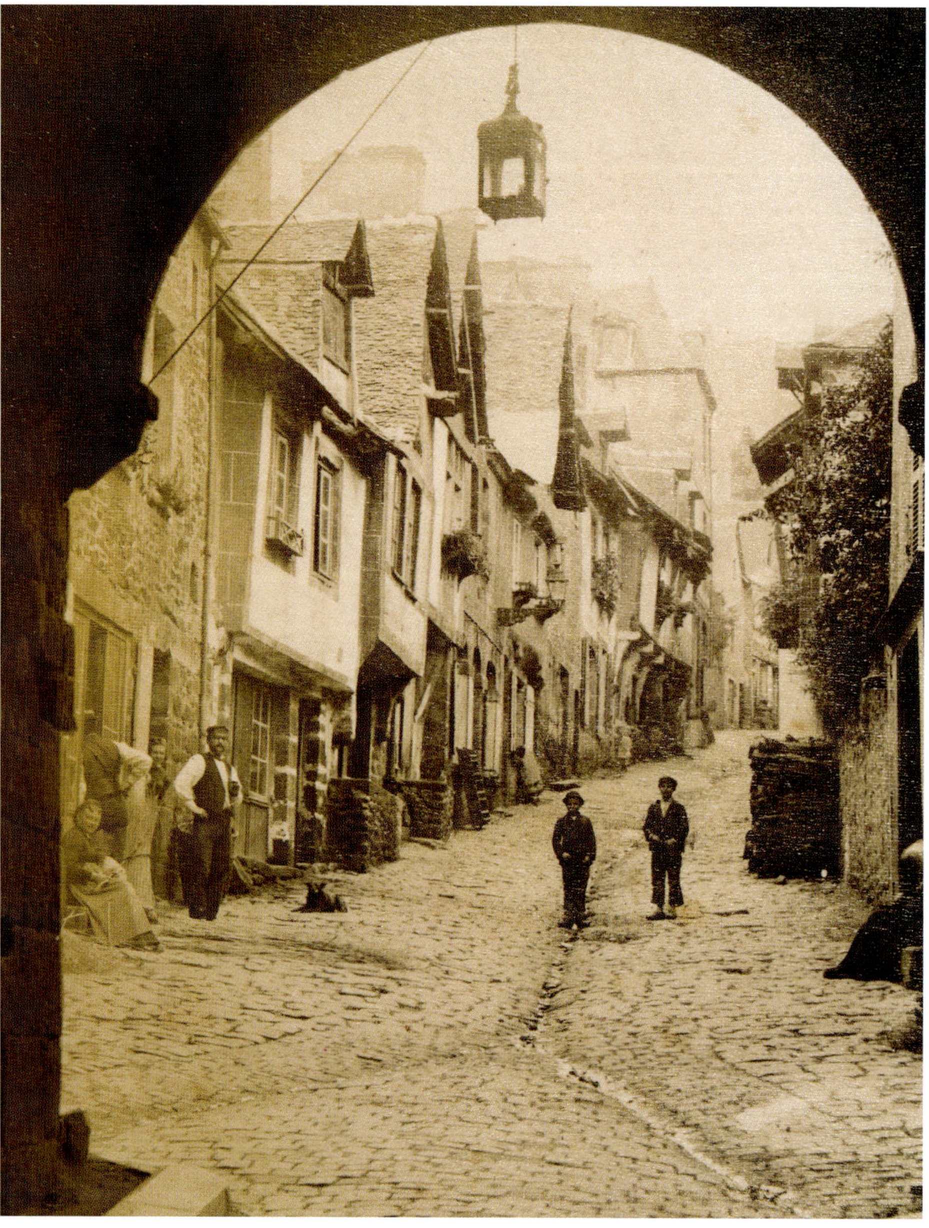

a spectacular view – that the fine old Gothic *chambre des chevaliers* was filled with prisoners working at looms.

He and his companions moved on to Dol de Bretagne, a small town a few miles distant, where another hotel room served as a makeshift darkroom. Surprisingly, perhaps, he made no mention of the town's magnificent 13th century cathedral – St. Samson's – although he certainly did photograph it. *The Cathedral, Dol, Normandy* was the title of two of the catalogue entries of the Waxed Paper images he exhibited at the 1858 Exhibition of the Photographic Society of Scotland in Edinburgh – alongside images from Rouen, Angers and Beauvais.

Until relatively recently, Dol was a regular traffic bottleneck on the way west into Brittany – with long traffic-jams blocking the approaches – but now by-passed, it has regained the quiet composure which must have greeted the intrepid photographers.

Kinnear's travelogue ended with his account of developing his negatives in "Doll", the remainder of his lecture concerning itself with the intricacies of photographic manipulation.

> *I brought home with me between forty and fifty negatives,* he wrote, *not a great number certainly, but as I had thrown away at the time any that were not were not satisfactory, they were all what I considered really good; and although I was exactly a month abroad, there were at least ten days of this time during which I had no opportunity of using the camera, partly because I was engaged in travelling through districts which afforded no photographic subjects, and partly on account of the badness of the weather. If, however, I did not bring back a great many negatives, I did bring back a good deal of experience, which I trust will be profitable to myself on some future occasion....*[13]

A detailed description of the camera appeared in the *Journal of the Photographic Society*[14] but, surprisingly, in neither essay was the performance of this ground-breaking camera design evaluated.

Of the total of *between forty and fifty negatives* which

Kinnear *considered really good*, he had, however, probably exhibited no more than nine by the end of 1859.

That number included five images exhibited at the 1858 Photographic Society of Scotland exhibition in Edinburgh – alongside fourteen Scottish views and two taken in Oxford. In April/May 1859 he exhibited one of his Mont St. Michel views, a study of the Chateau de Blois, and a view of the Palais de Justice in Rouen at the Glasgow Photographic Society exhibition, held at the Gallery of the Crystal Palace in Buchanan Street[15], where he also showed a view of Bayeux Cathedral, which he saw as one of only two saving graces in a city which, he said, contains absolutely nothing of interest but its cathedral and the famous tapestry.

His experience of photographing the cathedral would be little changed today. His 1857 description could just as easily have been written almost a century and a half later!

> *But, unfortunately for photography, the cathedral is so hemmed in by buildings that no view can be obtained that will convey a proper idea of the whole, or the elegance of the twin spires which terminate its western end. During the sunny intervals of a day which showed the first clouds we had seen since we began our tour, and which looked threatening for the next day's work, I took the only two views which could be obtained of it in the afternoon; one, of the two spires rising at the end of a narrow street, which, however, hides much of their base, and the other of the south porch, which is rich in sculpture. These pictures... came out beautifully....*[16]

Beautifully enough for him not only to exhibit one of them in Glasgow, but also at the British Association exhibition in Aberdeen in September of the same year. Indeed, the same four images were shown at both venues.

Just a few months after Kinnear and the Adams brothers returned to Britain the Reverend Thomas Melville Raven's plans seem to have been extremely flexible and, like all dedicated photographers, dictated by the weather, the quality of the light, and the sights which greeted him upon arrival. It was as he sailed up river from St. Malo towards Dinan that he decided to stay there awhile. His

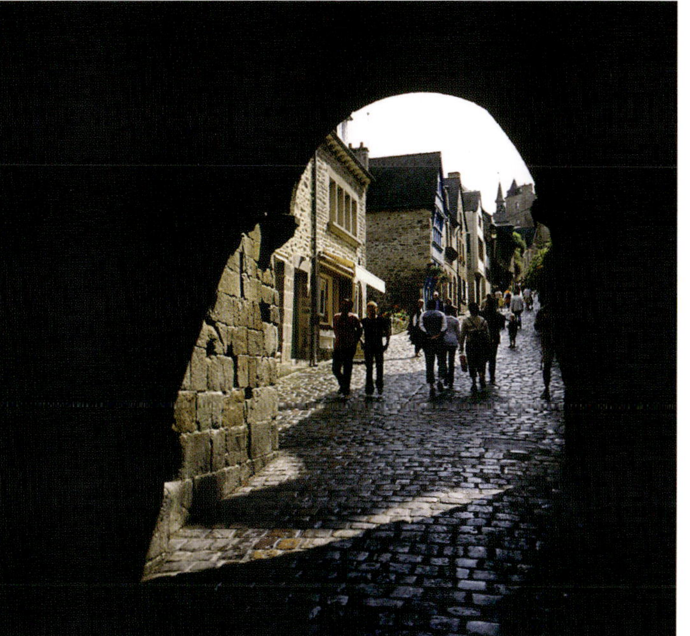

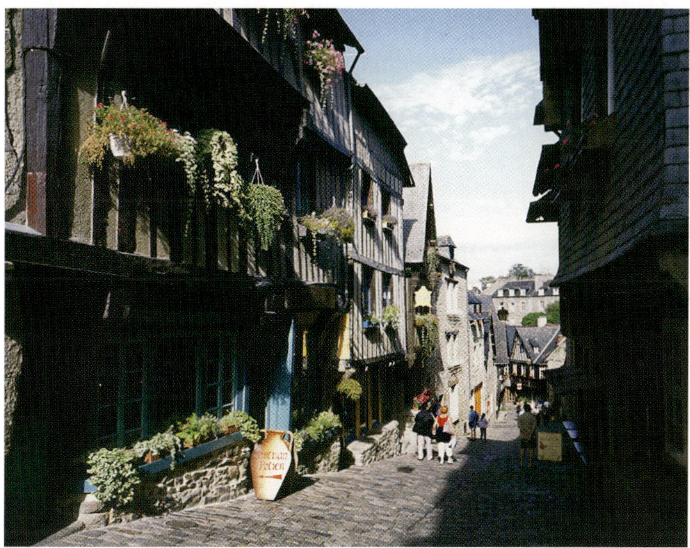

opposite page: The Rue du Jersual, Dinan, seen through the Port du Jersual. It would have been up this hill that the Reverend Raven and his family would have made their way to the Hotel de Bretagne.
left: the same view today, little changed in a century and a half.
below left: Seen from the Old Town at the top of the hill, the Rue du Jersual leads down to the quayside.

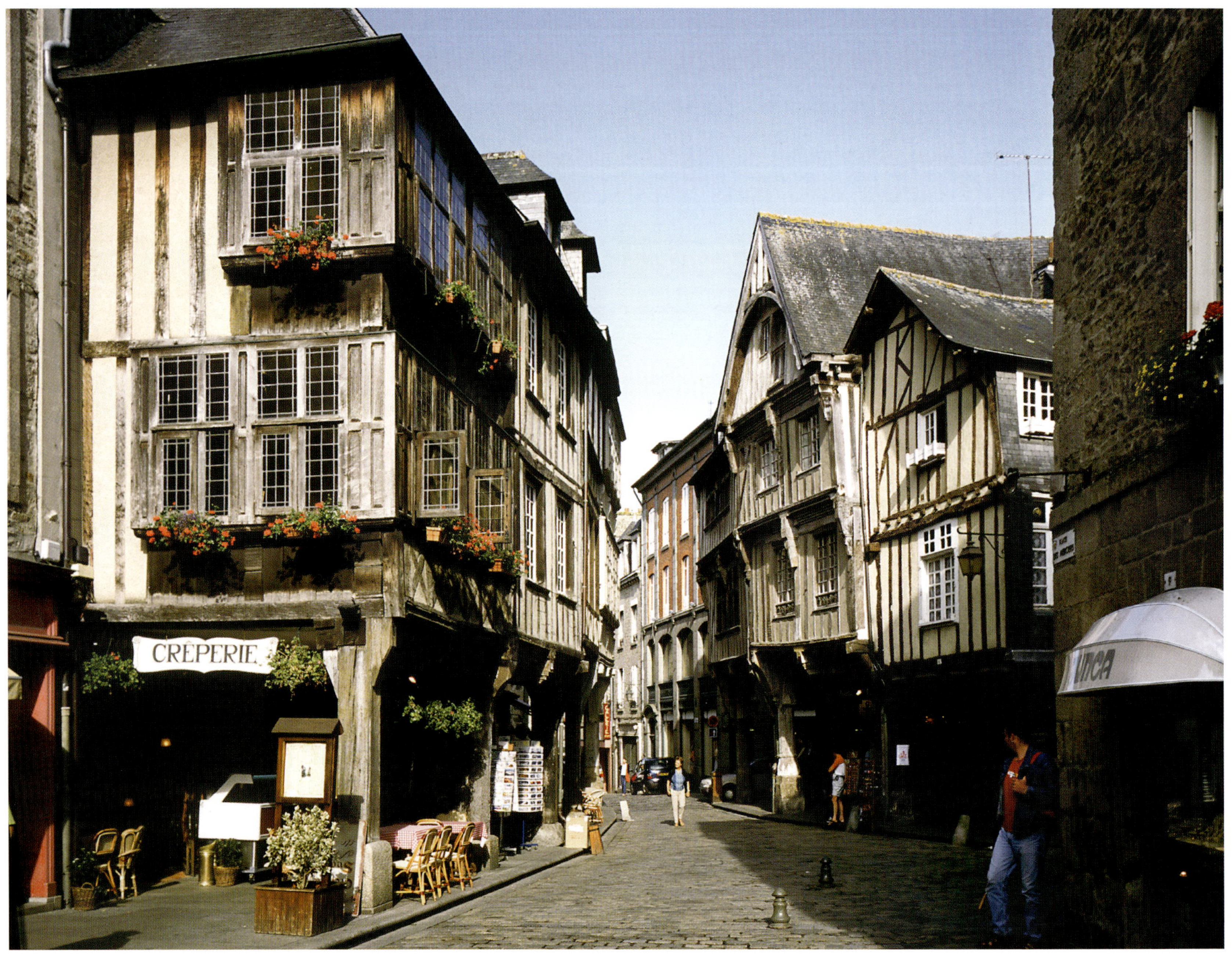
CRÊPERIE

notes don't reveal anything of Mrs. Raven's thoughts about these arrangements, or for that matter how she entertained herself while the good Reverend waited for sunshine!

> *In passing from the steamboat into the town, I saw so many subjects for the camera that I decided to stay there a few days, and fixed on the Hotel de Bretagne as the proper resting-place for a photographer.* (because, he said, it had an imposing-looking pump before the door).

Had he arrived in the port of Dinan today, Raven would still have recognised much of what greeted him. Certainly the flotilla of pleasure craft would have surprised him, but the route along which he and his party made their way up the Rue du Petit-Fort, through the Porte du Jersual and up the steep incline of the Rue du Jersual into the town has changed little. The character of the mediaeval city remains undiminished. Dinan is a mediaeval town par excellence and it is hardly surprising that Raven immediately recognised its photographic potential. As he recalled, however, all did not go according to plan.

> *The weather was wretched, with the exception of a few hours, during the week we spent in the place, of which, however, I made the most.*

He must have been pleased with at least some his pictures, for he illustrated his lecture to the Photographic Society of Scotland with no less than sixty of them in December 1858, and two of his views entitled *Old Houses, Dinan* were exhibited at the 1858 Exhibition of the society – alongside twenty-nine other photographs from his journey. As has already been suggested, for most photographers using the Waxed Paper process, six or eight pictures was considered a good day's work – the papers being prepared the night before use and developed the night afterwards. So the sheer number of images Raven felt worthy of use during his lecture implies a highly successful expedition! If they shared a hotel room, Mrs. Raven would have had to put up with it being turned into a makeshift processing laboratory each night before they could go to bed!

As Raven's technique was unusual, locating a number

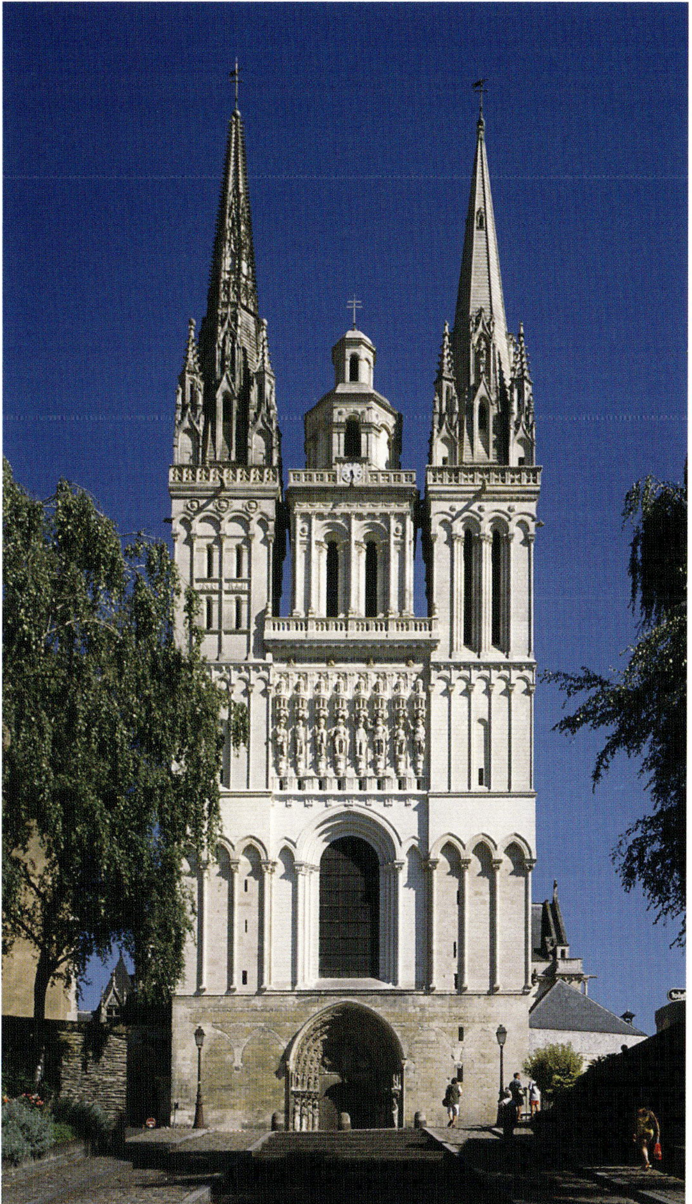

opposite page: The Place des merciers in Dinan is one of the architectural treasures of the old town. Here, and in the nearby market place, a host of early timbered buildings survive. Exhibition catalogues confirm that Raven took several pictures in the old town, producing images which he subsequently exhibited at the Photographic Society of Scotland in Edinburgh, 1858 and Glasgow Photographic Society, 1859.

left: Since Raven's day, many of the old buildings to the west of the cathedral at Angers have been cleared away, revealing wonderful views of the west front for today's photographers, and offering a panoramic vista of the river from outside the great west doorway.

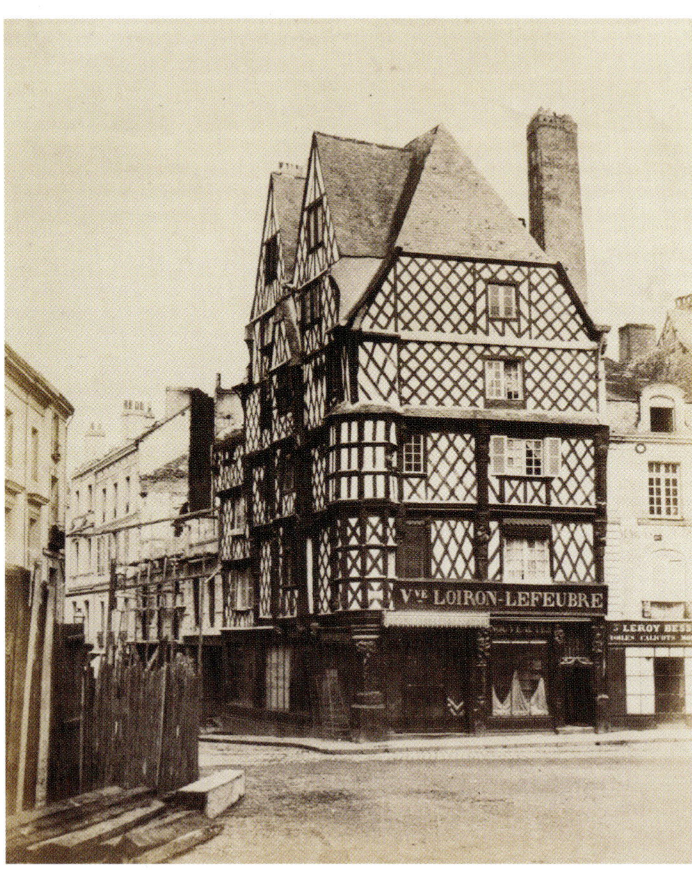

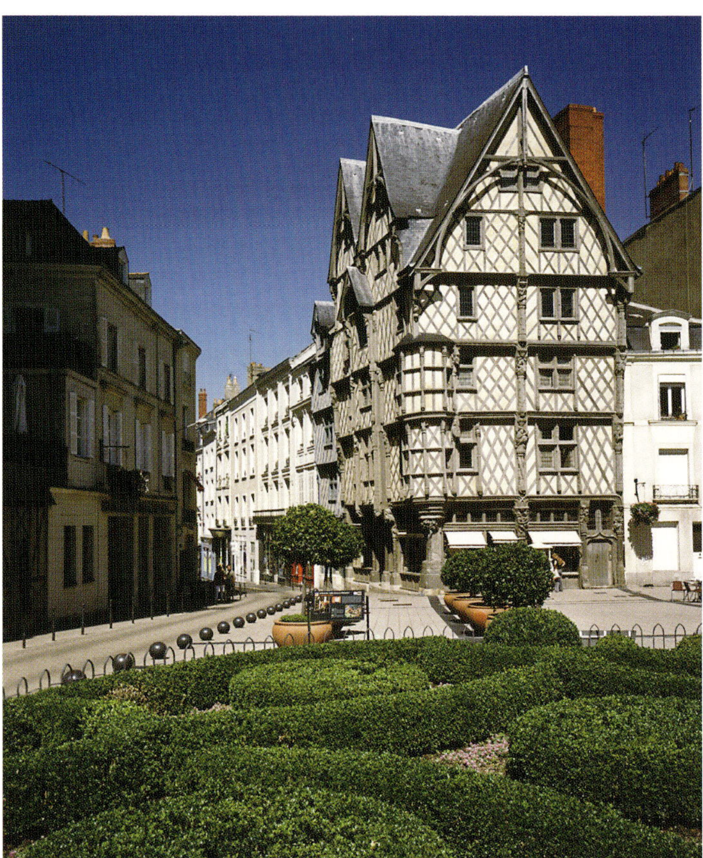

right: The Maison d'Adam is the most striking timbered building in Angers, and has long been a magnet for photographers and visitors. This view, credited to Charles Kinnear in an album in the National Media Museum. Bradford, must date from an earlier visit to France, as Angers was not on his 1857 itinerary. Interestingly, when Raven visited Angers, he must have taken an almost identical picture – the only view available – which he titled 'Old Wooden House, Angers' and subsequently exhibited at the 1858 exhibition of the Photographic Society in London.
far right: The Maison d'Adam today. Extensively rebuilt since Kinnear and Raven's day, it now houses a shop selling the work of local artists and craftworkers.

of these pictures would be a revelation. As has already been observed, the Waxed Paper process required long exposures which, combined with the limited sensitivity of the paper negatives – sensitive only to blue light – meant that skies reproduced either completely dark on the negative (white on the print) or a muddy grey colour. Several of Raven's pictures were described engimatically in exhibition catalogues as having been taken by *Waxed Paper/Collodion*, but one entry, in the catalogue for the Photographic Society of London's 1859 exhibition, suggests what his technique actually was. It seems that the Reverend Raven sometimes took separate exposures of interesting skies, using the much faster wet collodion process – where the sky could be exposed in a fraction of a second – and combined this with a photograph of a scenic view or a building at the printing stage. His study of *River Rance, Brittany*, the river up which he sailed to Dinan, is described in the exhibition catalogue as *Waxed Paper/Collodion Sky*.

From Dinan the party travelled to Rennes and then on to Nantes, where Raven admitted to his Edinburgh audience that he had been unable to take any pictures as he had not prepared any papers the night before. He was, in any event, unimpressed by either city noting that

> *We went on to Nantes, passing through Rennes. In the latter place I saw nothing to make me regret that we were so soon going to leave it. To the former place the ladies of my party took such an aversion, in consequence of a very dirty hotel at which we stayed to breakfast, that we determined to go on that very evening to Angers.*[17]

In Angers, however, he found much to interest him, although the equipment available to him – none of today's ultra-wide-angle lenses – placed some restrictions on what was possible. And with developments in the century and a half since Raven's visit, the layout of parts of the town has changed considerably. He found the magnificent cathedral hemmed in by other buildings, making a full view of it impossible. In the small square to the west of the cathedral, he could only photograph the west doorway. The creation of the flight of steps leading up to the cathedral from the river in the closing years of the 19th century has opened the view up for photographers ever since.

While none of Raven's views of Angers has yet been located, a view of the Maison d'Adam taken by Kinnear survives in the Edinburgh Exchange Club Album in the National Media Museum in Bradford – an album which contains a further two of Kinnear's French images and three by Raven. So far, this is the only confirmed source of their French work.

Like Raven and Kinnear, today's visitors are drawn to the timbered houses in the neighbourhood of the cathedral – the Maison d'Adam being the most impressive.

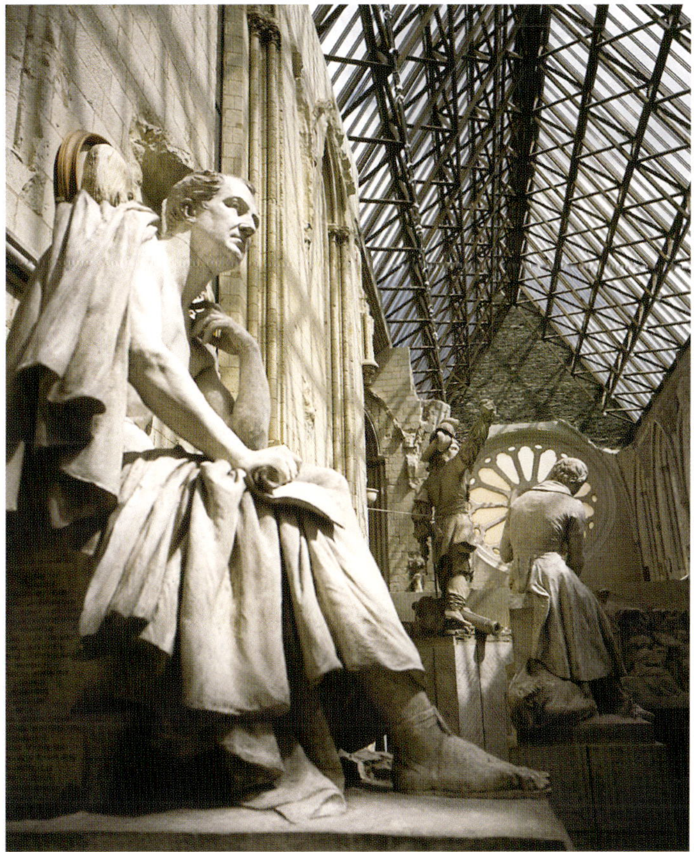

left: The Abbaye de Toussaints was in ruins when Thomas Melville Raven briefly visited it in 1857, and so it remained until the 1980s. Then a striking modern roof was erected over the ruined church, and the interior turned into a spectacular museum showing the works of David d'Angers.

The abbey church of Toussaints was a 'must' on our itinerary, if only because Raven lamented how little time he had been able to spend there. What we found was not the overgrown ruin of the 1850s, but possibly the most inventive and inspirational recycling of a medieval

below: The dramatic outer fortifications of the huge chateau at Angers. Inside, the magnificent 14th century Apocalypse Tapestry is housed in a specially constructed climate controlled building.

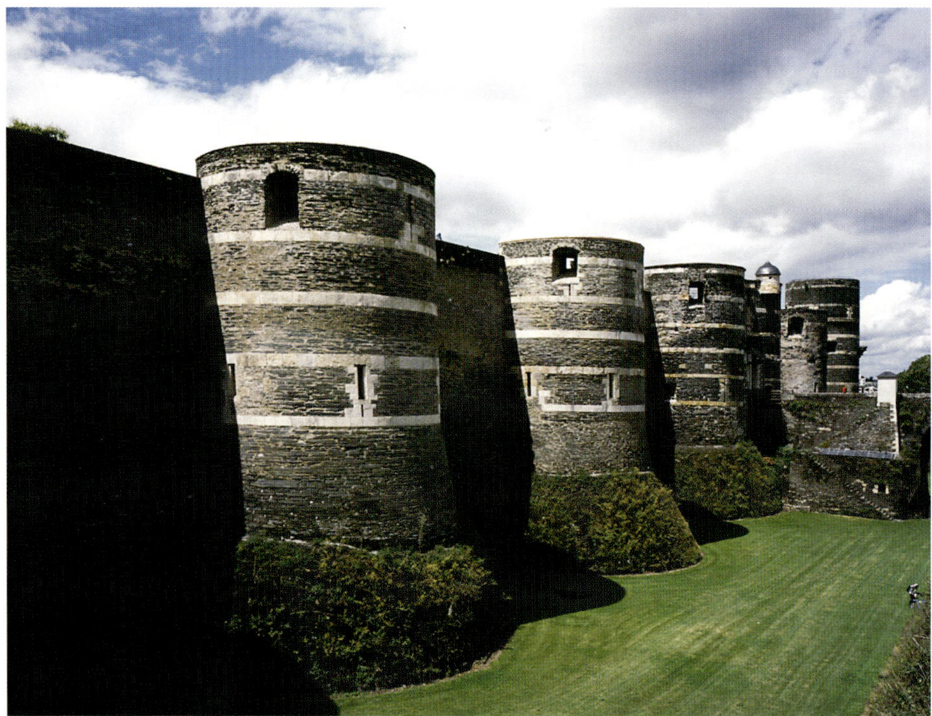

church. Now fitted with a strikingly modern glass and steel roof, the church has been turned into a museum of the works of Pierre-Jean David, who had died in 1856, a year before Raven's visit. He is better known as David d'Angers, perhaps the most eminent of France's 19th century sculptors, and his major public works include the pediment of the Panthéon in Paris. He donated the maquettes for many of his works to the city of his birth - whose name he had adopted in 1828. A visit to the museum is a 'must', both for the building itself and for its contents.

For today's visitor, *the* visit in Angers is to the huge chateau and the 14th century Apocalypse Tapestry. The tapestry is housed in a building reminiscent of some of the monolithic office blocks erected within the Kremlin walls in Moscow - and while the tapestry is magnificent, the building is hideous! The huge tapestry survived intact from the late 1300s until an ill-advised bishop of Angers in the 1820s decided it was no longer fashionable and cut it up into 'manageable' sections! Horrific stories, some of them probably apocryphal, tell of sections of this wonderful tapestry being used as bedside mats and horse blankets!

Canon Joubert, a local priest, spent many years from 1848 trying to locate all the sections and reassemble the tapestry - and at the time of Raven's visit, was fully engaged in his quest. Today over 80% of the amazing hundred-metre-long tapestry has been reassembled and is on view. After seeing it, the Bayeux Tapestry seems rather small-scale!

From Angers, Raven and his party caught the train to Saumur, while we of course did the journey by car. Saumur is on the line from Angers to Tours, and after a brief visit to the chateau and what he described as the 'druidical Temple of Saumur'- but was in fact a prehistoric chambered tomb without its covering earth mound - they were back on the train again to Tours.

Travelling by train must have posed considerable logistical problems for Raven, as even with the lightweight Waxed Paper negative process, the weight of equipment and chemicals which he had to transport, in addition to the family's luggage, must have been considerable. This necessarily restricted his photography - if a location was too far from railway station or hotel, then carriage-hire had to be arranged.

He never exhibited his Saumur views, despite obviously being pleased with them, one of which was

> *taken from the top of a neighbouring hill, which commanded an extensive view of the charming Loire, with the old castle and pretty town.*

Of what he termed the *druidical remains* he wrote

Not far from the main road stand these pierres couvertes as they are called, in all their mysterious concealment, puzzling the mind and exciting the imagination with their rude forms and simple contrivances. The temple of Saumur is not a quarter of the height of Stonehenge, but is entirely covered in, and apparently of ruder construction.[18]

After giving a detailed description of the chambered tomb, and another smaller one nearby, he admitted to his readers that

these interesting remains are not suited to photography, so we determined to take the next train to Tours.

After a stay of two or three days in Tours, the party moved south to Poitiers where he was drawn – as have been generations of photographers ever since – to the remarkable church of Notre Dame, which has one of the most magnificent west fronts of any medieval church in Europe, and an interior which is as near perfect as can be imagined. Whilst he was impressed by the churches, the state of the town itself did little to impress.

The churches in this place were all under repair with the exception of that of Notre Dame. It was impossible, therefore, to attempt to take many pictures in Poitiers, which is one of the dirtiest of dirty places. It is at the same time one of the most interesting towns on the Continent. The churches are extremely curious, although in general so battered and worn as to present the aspect of a heap of ruins at first sight. This is particularly the case with Notre Dame. I never saw a church the appearance of which was so striking, not from its beauty or grace, but from the singularly devastated, ruined state in which it towers above the buildings around, as if it belonged to another world.[19]

Pictures of the church taken in the few years before his visit show it dirty and in need of a bit of attention, but hardly in the *devastated, ruined state* that he describes.

It would be fascinating to have Raven's interpretation of the scene for comparison. Perhaps he was disappointed by the results of his attempts to photograph this amazing

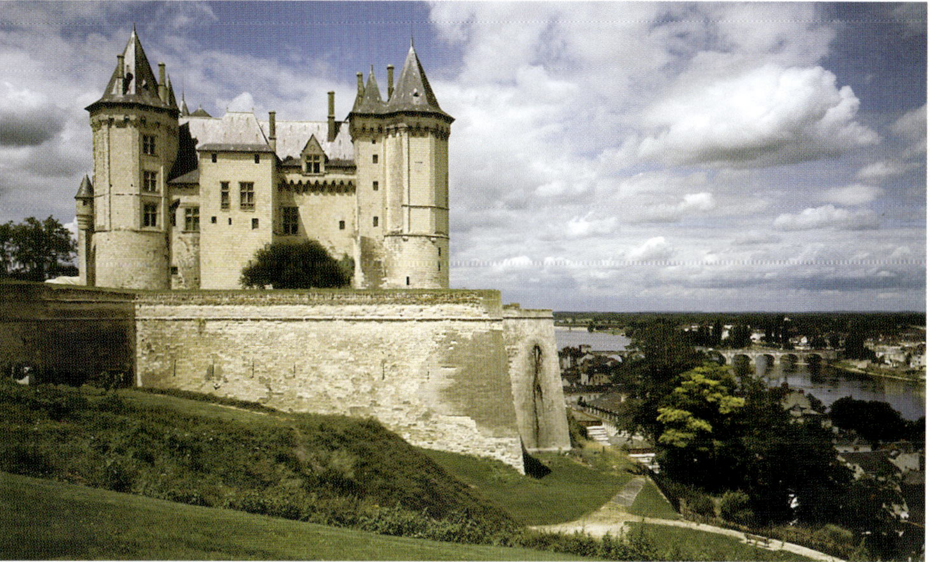

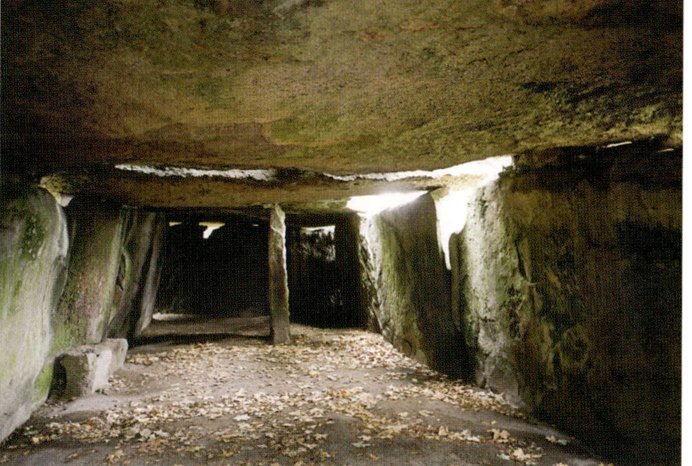

above: Saumur's imposing chateau dominates the town. From his description, Raven photographed the chateau from a very similar viewpoint, but, despite being pleased with the result, does not appear to have exhibited it.
left: The interior of Saumur's Grande Dolmen, which Raven described as a 'druidical temple', stands in the garden of a bar and brasseries in the suburb of Bagenux.

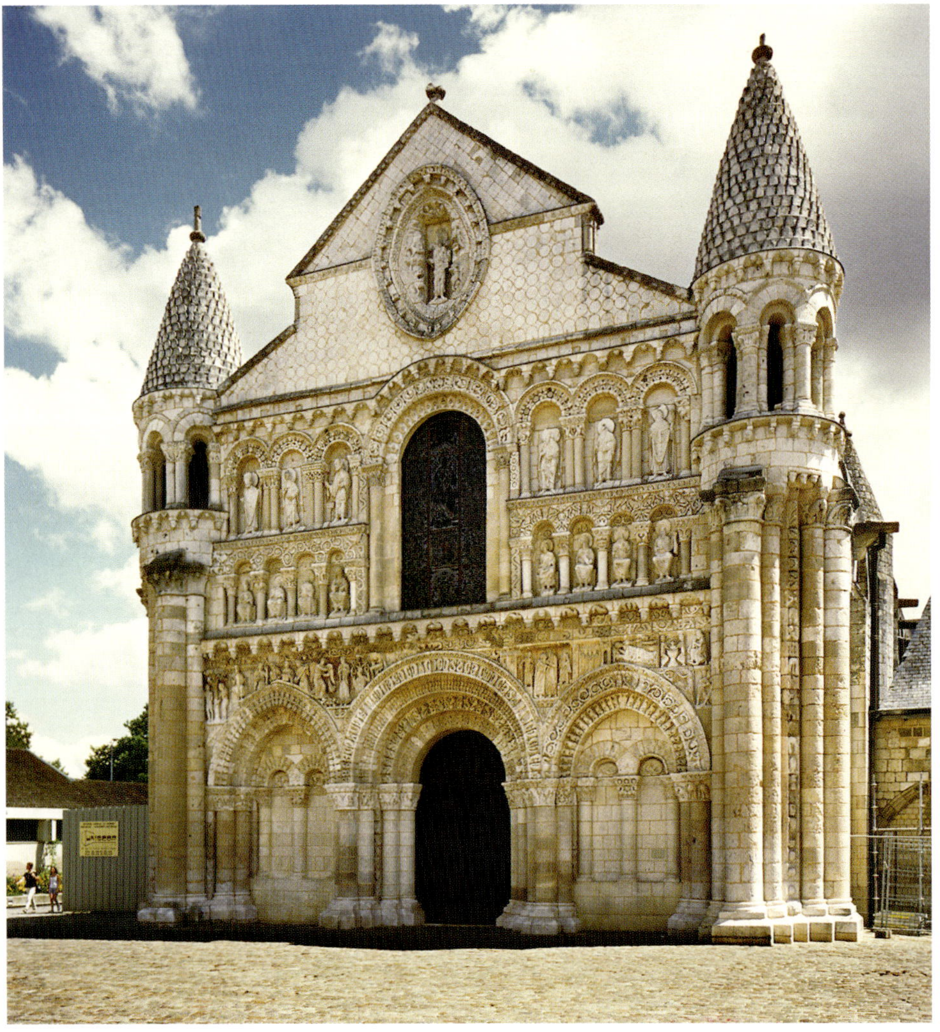

above: The 12th century Romanesque west front of Notre Dame de Poitiers.

building, for he exhibited only a single picture of the Church of Notre Dame, and as far as can be ascertained, he never exhibited his images from Tours, or from Bordeaux - his next-but-one stop.

From Poitiers he moved to Angoulême where, he noted that he

> *had just time the following morning to expose one piece of paper in my camera before we started for Bordeaux.*

He was clearly pleased with the result, for it too appeared in the Glasgow exhibition.

From Angoulême to Bordeaux and then, after a detour to Bayonne and Biarritz, to Pau - the party's intended destination where, probably to the delight of Mrs Raven, they had a long and relaxing holiday.

The Reverend Thomas Melville Raven produced many photographs during the family's stay in Pau - which were well received and widely praised and exhibited on his return to Britain - but, just as with most of the locations he photographed on the trip, not one of his pictures of Pau has been located in the course of the research for this book.

The *British Journal of Photography* carried a notice of Kinnear's death in its issue for November 16th 1894 in which it was noted that

> *We are sorry to have to announce the sudden death of Mr Kinnear of Edinburgh, a gentleman whose name is so intimately associated with the Kinnear Camera, of which he was the inventor. Professionally, he was an architect of high eminence in Edinburgh. He was an Associate of the Royal Scottish Academy, and also Colonel of the Midlothian Volunteer Artillery, being the oldest volunteer artilleryman on the active list in Scotland. We had a visit from Colonel Kinnear only a short time ago when he was up in town, and found that his love of photography had suffered no diminution but that he was, if possible, still more attached to it than ever.*[20]

That abiding enthusiasm for photography makes the apparent loss of so many of Kinnear's images all the more surprising.

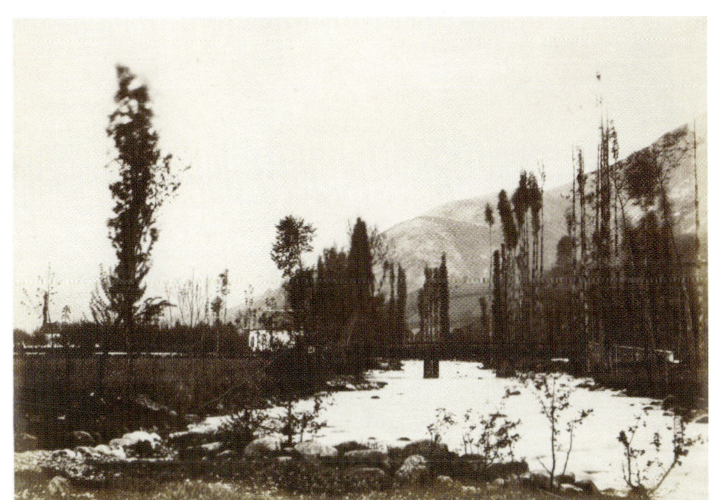

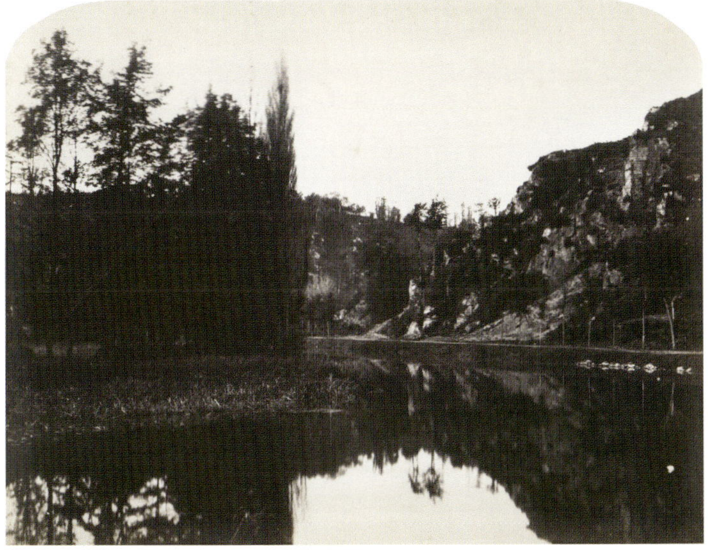

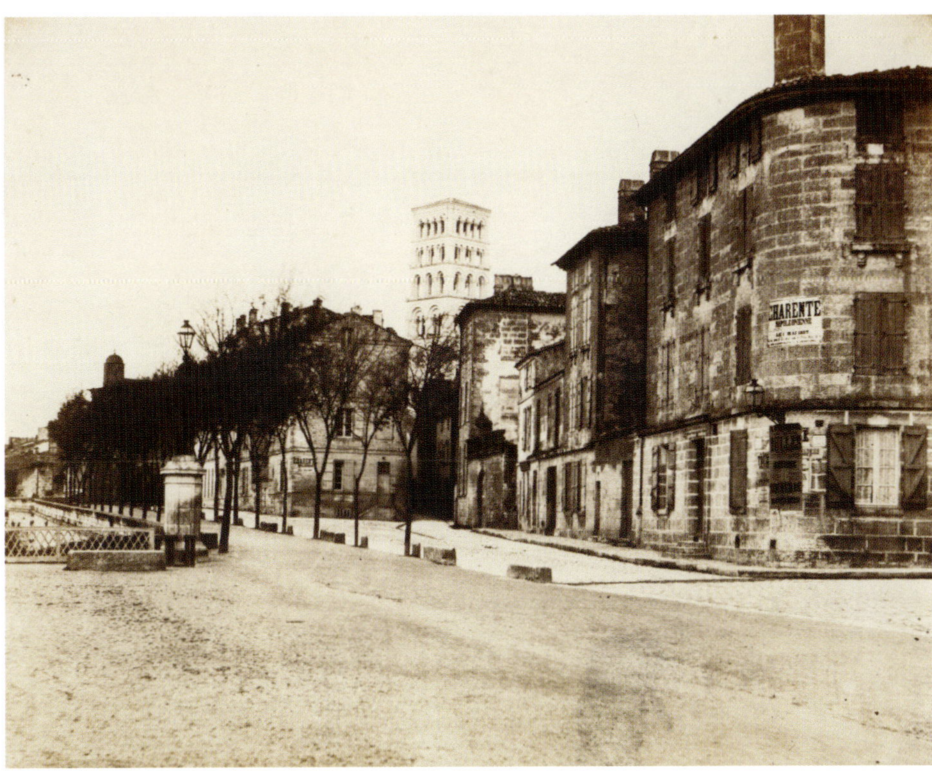

above left: Bagnères de Bigorre, photographed by Raven in October 1857. He exhibited several views in and near the town at the Edinburgh Photographic Society's 1858 exhibition, and Glasgow Photographic Society's exhibition in 1859. Intriguingly, they appear as 'Bagniers de Bigorre' in the catalogue to the Edinburgh exhibition!

left: Simply titled 'Pyrenees', this comes from the end of the journey when the family was enjoying a holiday.

above: Street Scene, Angoulême. A print of this image – from the 'one piece of paper' which Raven exposed in the town – was also exhibited in the 1859 Glasgow exhibition. Given his statement that he only took the one picture, the print entitled 'Angoulêmée' exhibited in the 1858 Edinburgh Photographic Society exhibition must have been from the same negative.

below: Within a few years of the journeys made by Charles Kinnear and the Reverend Raven, a considerable market had developed selling photographic mementos to tourists. In addition to large format prints, visitors to the great attractions of France could buy cartes-de-visite, stereoscopic cards and stereo diapositives like this view of the great Loire chateau at Chenenceau, c.1860. A significant impetus to the tourist market had been given in 1855 by the prominence given to photography at the Exposition Universelle in Paris. A considerable number of British visitors had made their way across the Channel to Paris to see the exhibition, and additionally, the work of several British and French professional photographers had been exhibited there, and offered for sale.

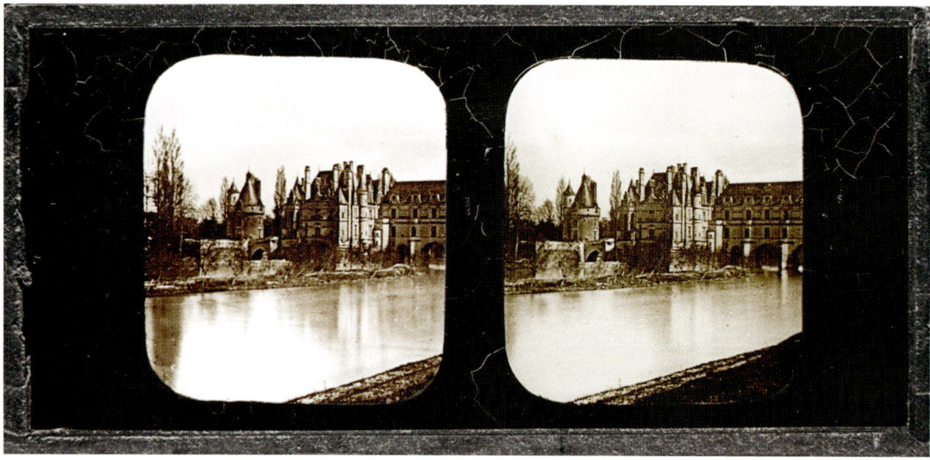

Notes

1. C.G.H. Kinnear: "Abstract of an Account of an Architectural and Photographic Tour in the North of France", *Journal of the Photographic Society*, Dec.21, 1857, pp116-121. Kinnear, at the time Honorary Secretary of the Photographic Society of Scotland, read his paper to his Edinburgh audience on December 15th 1857. It is a testimony to the currency of the stories covered in the *Journal of the Photographic Society* that it was published less than a week later.
2. *ibid*, p118.
3. Raven's account of his October 1857 journey was published under the title "Account of a Photographic Tour from Jersey to the Pyrenees" in *Photographic Notes*, Feb. 1st, 1858, pp 42-45. A second paper - "Pau and the Pyrenees, with a slight Sketch of a Photographic Tour made to them through the west of France" - appeared in the *Journal of the Photographic Society*, Dec. 21st 1858, pp104-108.
4. T. Melville Raven, "Account of a Photographic Tour from Jersey to the Pyrenees" in *Photographic Notes*, February 1st, 1858, page 43.
5. C.G.H. Kinnear: "Abstract of an Account of an Architectural and Photographic Tour in the North of France", *Journal of the Photographic Society*, Dec.21, 1857, pp116-117.
6. *ibid*, p118.
7. T. Melville Raven, "Account of a Photographic Tour from Jersey to the Pyrenees" in *Photographic Notes*, February 1st, 1858, page 42.
8. *idem*.
9. C.G.H. Kinnear: "Abstract of an Account of an Architectural and Photographic Tour in the North of France", *Journal of the Photographic Society*, Dec.21, 1857, pp119.
10. *idem*.
11. T. Melville Raven, "Account of a Photographic Tour from Jersey to the Pyrenees" in *Photographic Notes*, February 1st, 1858, page 43.
12. C.G.H. Kinnear: "Abstract of an Account of an Architectural and Photographic Tour in the North of France", *Journal of the Photographic Society*, Dec.21, 1857, pp116-117.
13. *ibid*, p119.
14. "Mr. Kinnear's Portable Camera", *Journal of the Photographic Society*, Feb.22, 1858, pp165-166.
15. For a listing of Kinnear's work exhibited between 1856 and 1859, a useful reference is Roger Taylor *Photographs Exhibited in Britain, 1839-1865*, Ottawa, National Gallery of Canada, 2002, pp442-443. The material in this listing is drawn from surviving exhibition catalogues of the period, and while it may not be fully comprehensive, it does suggest that Kinnear ceased to exhibit in 1864, although his passion for photography endured for the rest of his life. Indeed, his exhibition record has a gap between 1859, when he last exhibited photographs taken with his beloved Waxed Paper process, and 1864, when he exhibited three images of views in Fife taken with Dr Hill Norris's dry plates.
16. C.G.H. Kinnear: "Abstract of an Account of an Architectural and Photographic Tour in the North of France", *Journal of the Photographic Society*, Dec.21, 1857, p118.
17. T. Melville Raven, "Pau and the Pyrenees, with a slight Sketch of a Photographic Tour made to them through the west of France", *Journal of the Photographic Society*, Dec. 21st 1858,, page 106.
18. *idem*.
19. *idem*.
20. "Death of C.G.H. Kinnear" in *The British Journal of Photography* November 16, 1894.

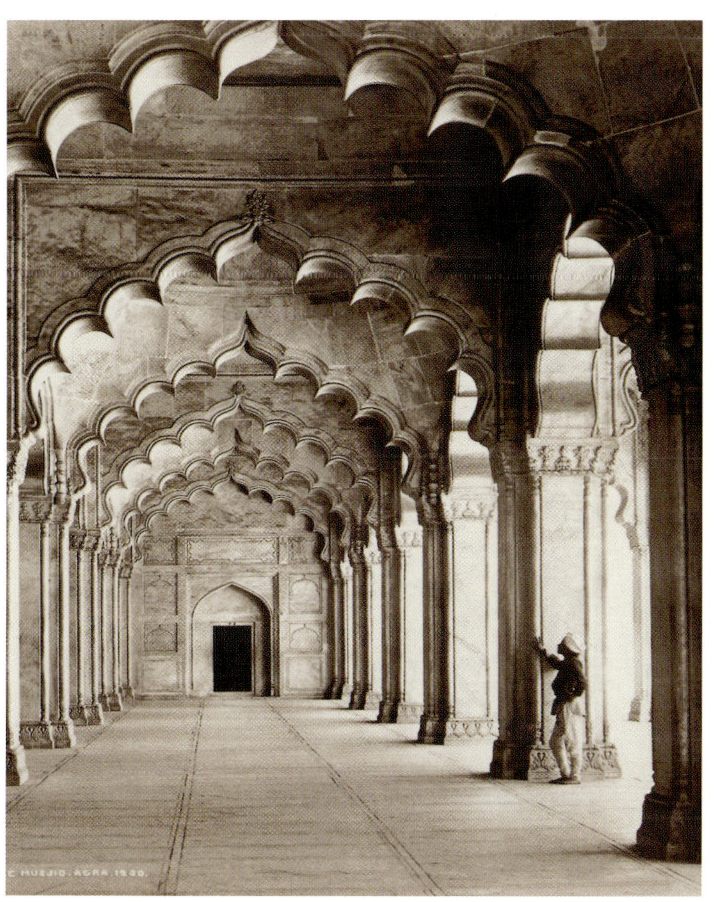

Samuel Bourne

'Photography in the East' Travels in India 1863-70

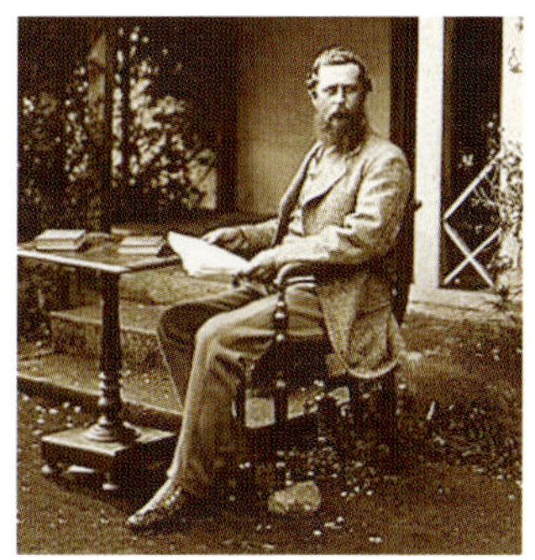

above: Samuel Bourne at home, photographer unknown

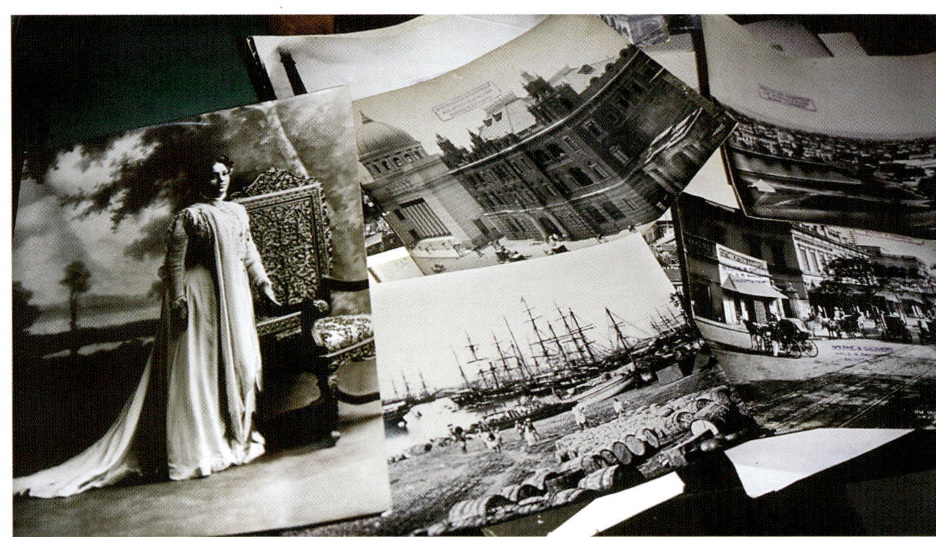

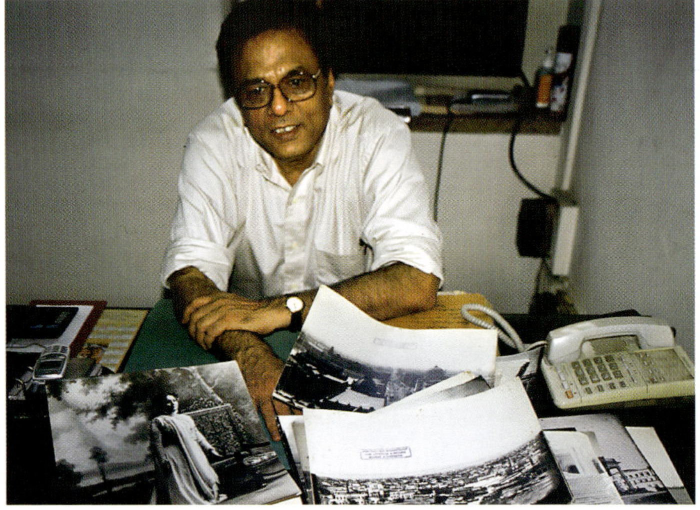

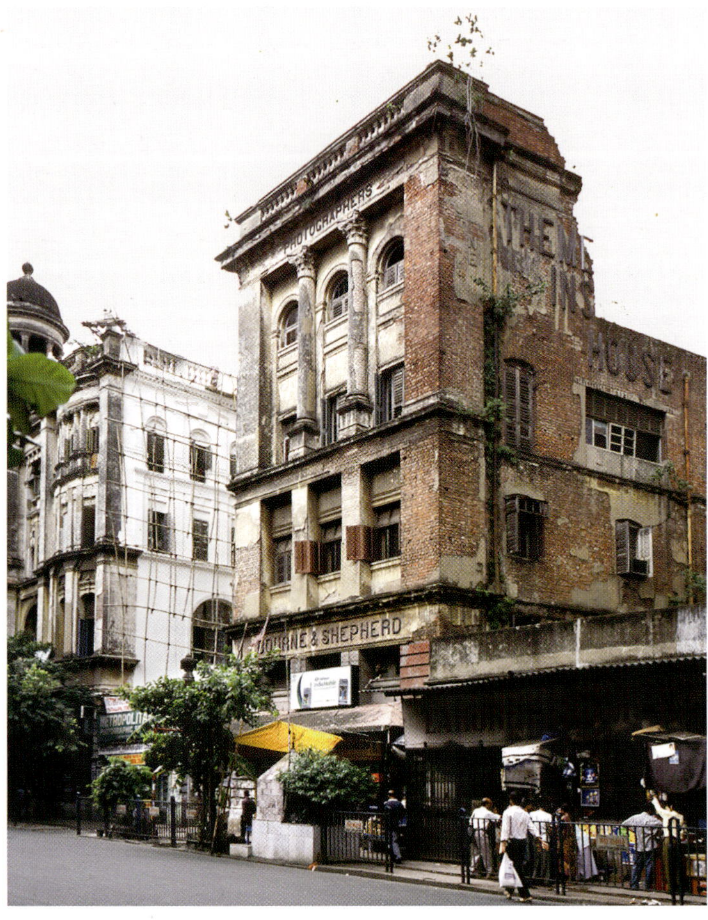

above: The Bourne & Shepherd studio in Kolkata's Banerjee Road, showing the partial demolition of the top floor. The building was erected in the 1920s, when the company moved around the corner from its premises next to the Grand Hotel in Chowringhee Road.

above left: Only a few prints survive from the once-huge Bourne & Shepherd archive which was stored in the upper floor of the Kolkata studio. The studio advertised that they made prints to order from the original glass negatives. The prints seen here include works by Samuel Bourne, Bourne & Shepherd, Charles Murray, and the last European to operate as sole owner of the studio, Arthur Musselwhite.

right: Jayant Ghandi, the present owner of the Bourne & Shepherd studio with some of the surviving prints. These examples cover a period of over sixty years of the studio's one hundred and forty year history.

The exterior of the old building was crumbling, succumbing increasingly rapidly to the destructive effects of the Kolkata climate. Inside, it had fared a little better, and the bare wooden staircase barely creaked as I made my way up to the second floor studio where an old 1920s Watson 15x12 camera and an even older ornate studio posing-chair stood in one corner. The chair was familiar - it had featured in many of the lavish portraits of Princes, Maharajahs, officers of the Raj and their wives, which had established the studio's reputation as one of the most fashionable place to be photographed in the British Empire well over a century before.

Above my head, three of the five 1kw floodlamps in a ceiling recess burst into life, revealing a studio with little of the glamour it had once known, or the great reputation it had once enjoyed. A Pentax K1000 - battered but not bowed - stood on an old tripod flanked by two Multiblitz Minilites. This was the studio of Bourne & Shepherd in Kolkata's Banerjee Road, home since the 1920s of the longest-surviving photographic studio in the Indian sub-continent.

Such is the legendary status of Bourne & Shepherd in Kolkata, that my driver knew immediately where I was looking for. No need to check telephone books or maps. Bourne & Shepherd has been a part of the city's social scene since the late 1860s, and the reputations of the two men whose names the studio still bears go back further than that.

On the front of the building is the fanciful claim 'Established 1840'. Bourne did not arrive in India until 1863, and Shepherd a few years earlier. The two men probably did not meet until 1864, and it is likely that their partnership was formed early in 1865, a quarter of a century later than the 'established 1840' claim, but still a significant time ago. That was when the partnership of Shepherd & Robertson - with studios in Agra and Shimla - was apparently dissolved, and Charles Shepherd welcomed Samuel Bourne and his newly established partner in the

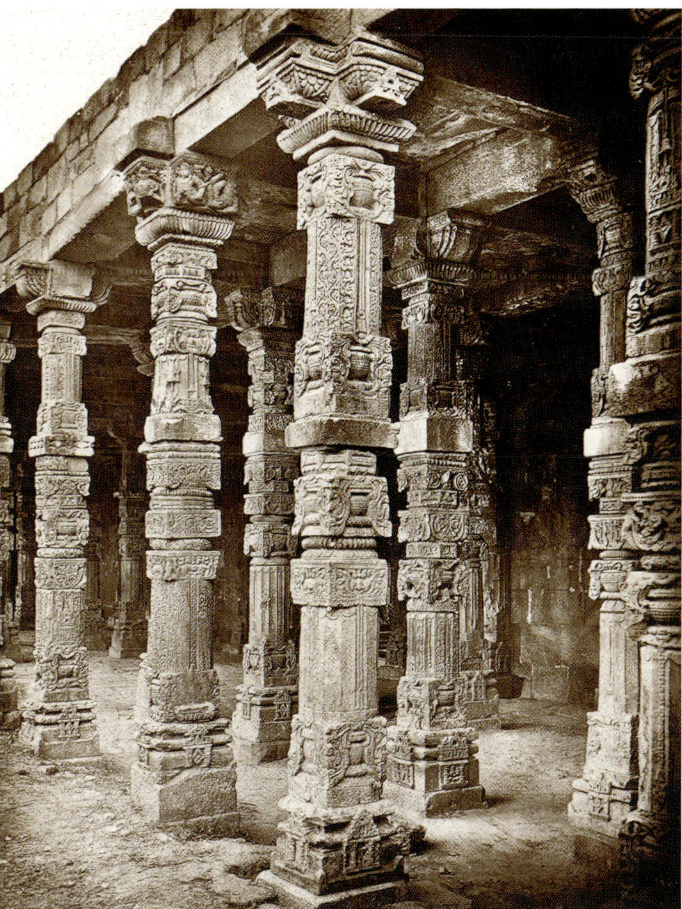

left: While Bourne's reputation has, justifiably, grown steadily over the years, Charles Shepherd is often portrayed as just a junior partner. The partnership was, however, one of equals. Both men had a highly developed talent for both landscape and architectural photography, and their work was much in demand. This study of the Quwwat-ul-Islam Mosque, which he titled 'Masjid-I-Kutb-Al-Islam', appeared as one of the plates in Walter Bentley Woodbury's 1875 'coffee-table book' *Treasure Spots of the World.*

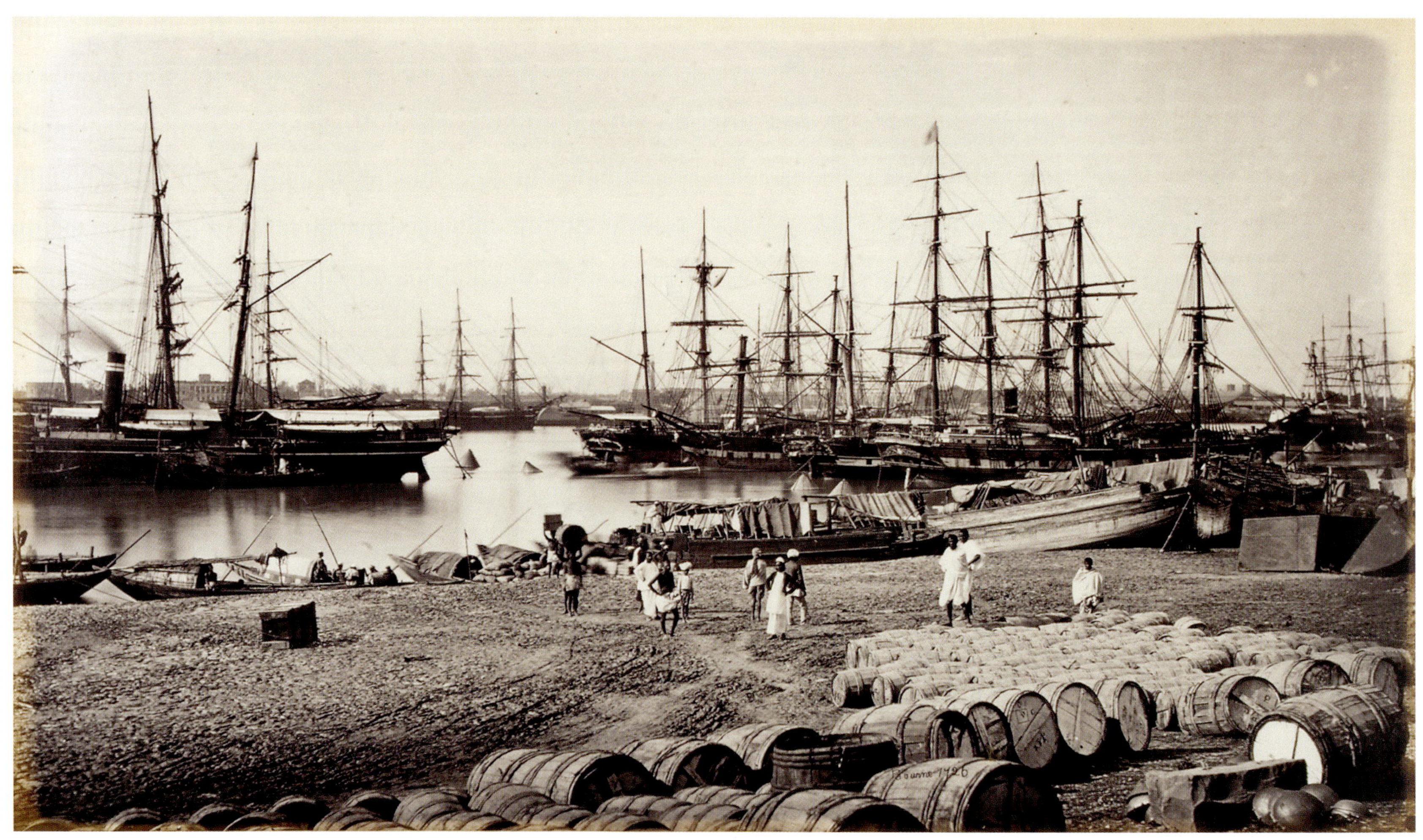

above: The Custom House, Calcutta, photographed by Bourne in the mid-1860s. It is a remarkably animated scene, considering the limited sensitivity of the wet collodion process at the time. The movement evident in the small boats at the water's edge cofirms the long exposure, and makes it clear that Bourne must have enlisted the total total compliance of the Indian workers – but one has to feel sorry for those required to hold heavy crates and barrels on their heads!

Shimla studio of Howard & Bourne, to join him in a new business to be known as Howard, Shepherd & Bourne. The Bourne & Shepherd Shimla studio was ideally positioned to cash in on a lucrative portrait market - Shimla was, after all, the Raj's summer capital chosen because of the almost British weather conditions enjoyed in that part of the western Himalayas.

Howard left the company in 1868, but the Bourne & Shepherd name had been in use since 1866 when the company issued its first catalogue of 1500 Indian views. There can be few, if any, photographic businesses still in existence with a longer pedigree than this. By the time the men joined forces, both had established enviable individual reputations, Bourne as the finest architectural and landscape photographer in India, and Shepherd both as an architectural photographer and as a portraitist.

Interestingly, given the fact that the studio still bears their names, both Bourne and Shepherd had left the company and returned to England long before the studio's elegant new premises in Banerjee Road were constructed in the 1920s. Bourne returned to England in 1870, and was replaced by Kenneth Murray. Shepherd left in 1885 The studio's original location had been round the corner on Chowringhee Road, next to the Grand Hotel, which opened its doors to the rich and famous of Calcutta society about the same time as the studio. Chowringhee Road, at that time and for half a century afterwards, epitomised everything that was considered stylish, fashionable and good about Victorian Calcutta. High-ranking officials of the British Raj rubbed shoulders with princes and their retinues in the foyer of the Grand as well as in the waiting room of the studio next door.

In the years before establishing the studio in Calcutta and another in Bombay, Bourne had made several important and demanding journeys with his cameras, bringing back several hundred images which, from the British perspective, revealed the architecture and landscape of the sub-continent.

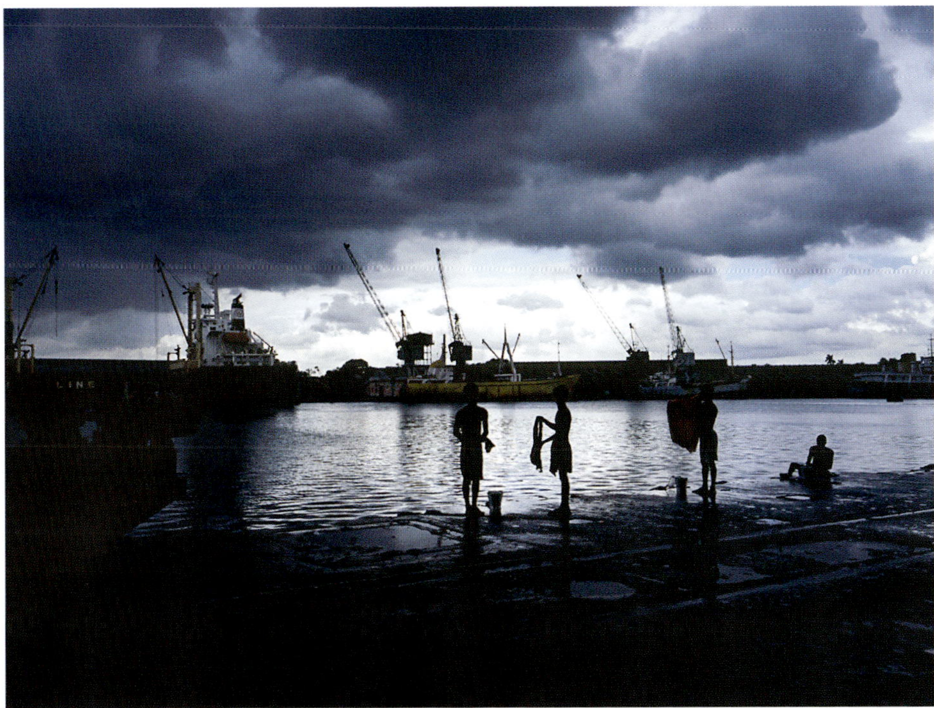

left: Kolkata Docks today, after a late monsoon cloudburst - with only a few ships in a vast expanse of desolation, and a group of children diving and swimming in the filthy water. Since Bourne's day, the docks have expanded considerably, and are now, once again, contracting as the largest container ships can no longer gain access. As designated 'security areas' photography is not usually permitted in docks, harbours, railway stations and airports, but thanks to the Deputy Commissioner of the Docks Police, who made one of his commanders, and a jeep, available, that restriction was waived.

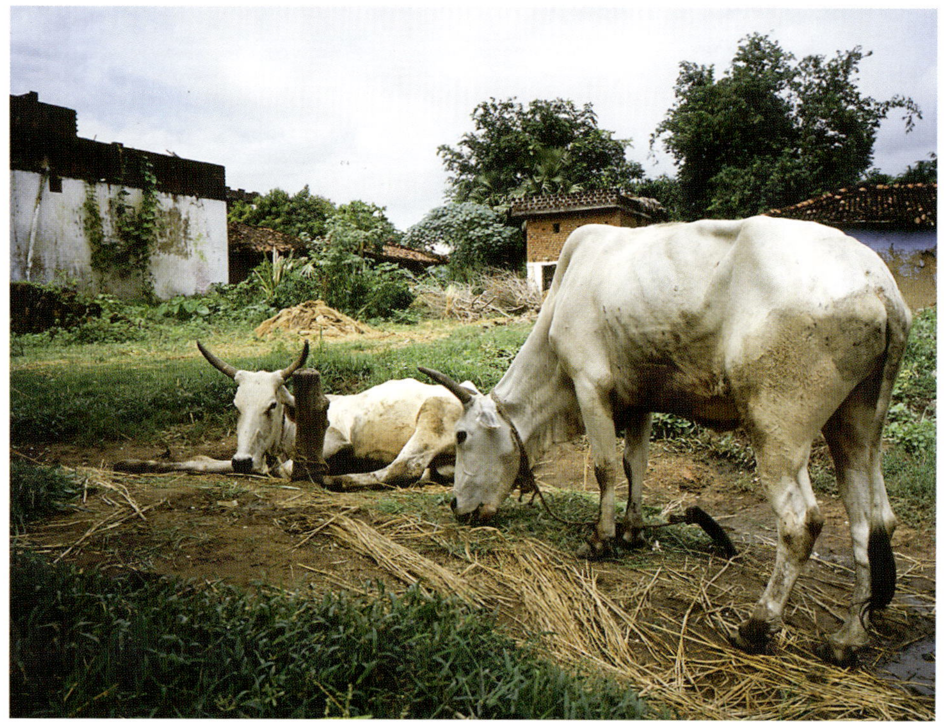

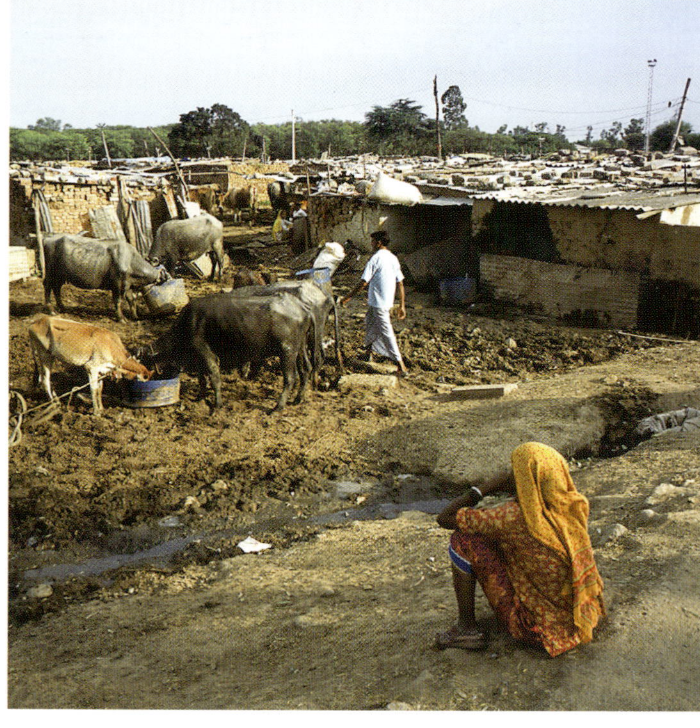

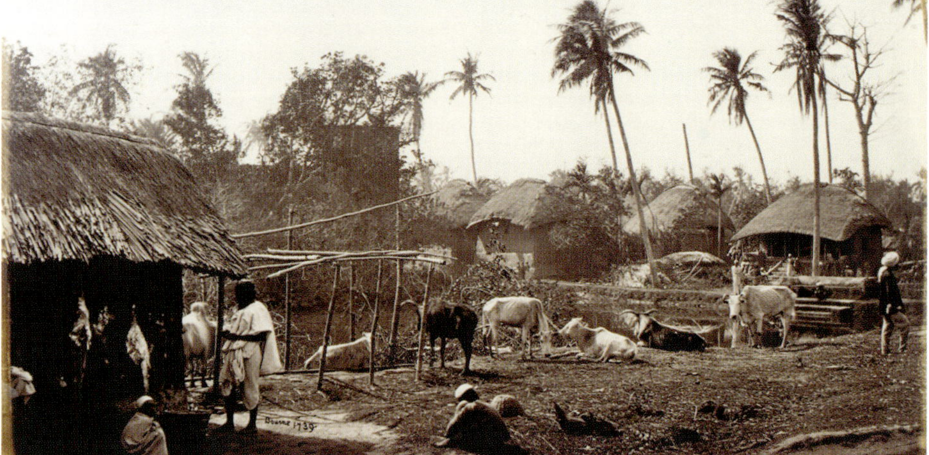

left: A farmyard scene, photographed by Bourne c.1865 shows, if anything, farm workers living in better accommodation than many of them enjoy today. The straw-roofed houses seem in much better condition than today's corrugated-iron roofed shanty town outside Chandigarh (*above right*).

above left: A rural farmstead a few miles from Gaya presents a scene which is largely unchanged since Samuel Bourne's first journey in the spring of 1863. While the metropolitan centres of Mumbai and Delhi are rapidly taking on the mantle of modern cities everywhere, conditions in the Indian countryside remain very primitive, the roads remain poor, and the living conditions of the rural community are hardly less harsh than they have been for centuries.

above right: Primitive living conditions are not restricted to rural areas. This photograph was taken only a very few miles from the centre of the city of Chadigarh in northern India. A woman sits in the evening sunlight watching the daily ritual of feeding the cattle. In areas like this there is no readily available grazing land, so the food has to be transported to the cattle. It is not uncommon to see women walking along the road carrying huge quantities of hay on their heads.

India was the jewel in the crown of the British Empire, and the British presence on the sub-continent was considerable. It is not surprising, therefore, that amongst the many people sent to India to support British rule, there were many with a keen interest in photography - some professional, many amateur. From an historical point of view, therefore, there is today a rich heritage of early photography of the country available for study, but at the time, relatively few of those images were widely disseminated in Britain.

Some do stand out, though most of them are connected with the military. For example, the work of Captain Linnaeus Tripe, who served with the army of the East India Company, was published widely in India and Britain in the second half of the 1850s. Other soldier photographers included Colonel Henry Greenlaw of the Madras Native Infantry, Captain Henry Dixon, Captain Thomas Hesketh Biggs, Captain Eugene Clutterbuck Impey of the Bengal Native Infantry, and the many photographers from the Royal Engineers who systematically photographed British progress across the continent

Dr John Murray's work with large paper negatives, much of which was published in Britain, remains one of the most significant of the early photographic coverages of the architecture of India, while Dr John McCosh, a military surgeon attached to the British Army during the Sikh Wars is given the accolade of having been the first person to take photographs while taking part in a military campaign.

Writing in 1856 in *Advice to Officers in India*, after he had retired from the army, McCosh wrote

> *I would strongly recommend every assistant-surgeon to make himself a master of photography in all its branches, on paper, on plate glass, and on metallic plates. I have practised it for many years, and know of no extra professional pursuit that will more repay him for all the expense and trouble (and both are very considerable) than this fascinating study - especially the new process by Collodion for the stereoscope. During the course of his service in India, he may make such a faithful collection of representations of man and animals,*

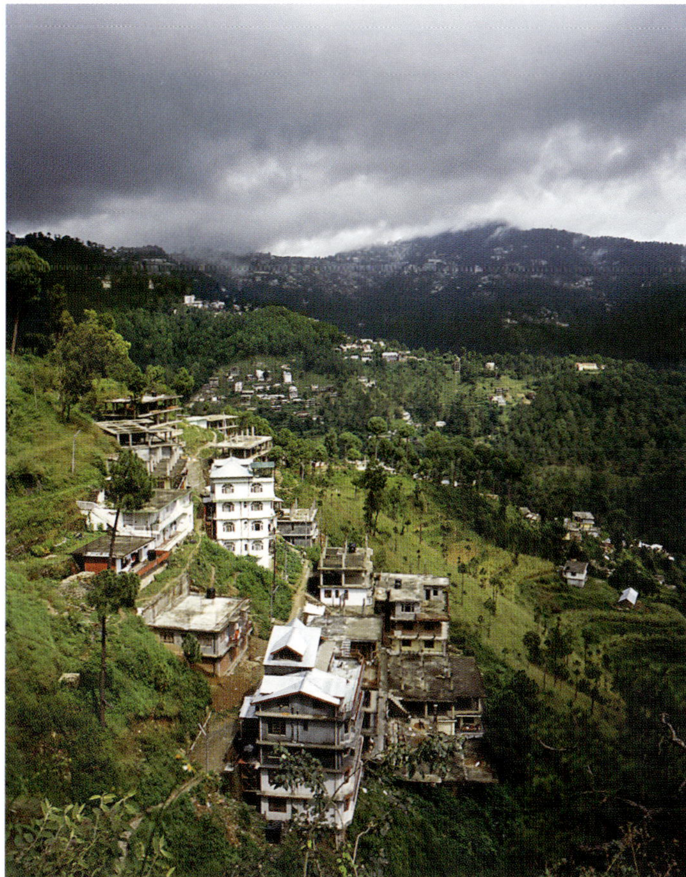

left: Shimla - Simla in Bourne's day - seen here, shrouded in cloud, built on the hillside in the distance, sits over 7500 feet up in the foothills of the Himalayas. It was here in 1863 that Samuel Bourne embarked on his new career as a professional photographer, in partnership with a Mr. Howard on Simla's Mall Road.

or architecture and landscape, that would be a welcome contribution to any museum.

Bourne's great contribution to photography in India would be that he went well beyond representation. His quest for the picturesque resulted in a body of remarkable images, albeit showing India through obviously British eyes, and his published account of his travels - from which is borrowed the title of this chapter - regularly appeared in the pages of the *British Journal of Photography*.

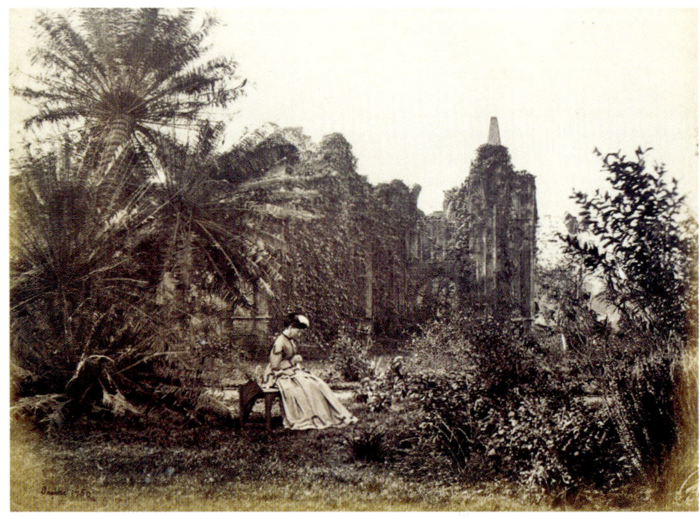

right: Gothic Ruin, Barrackpore Park, Calcutta. Bourne's obvious love of the picturesque is given full rein in this romantic study of his wife, Mary - whom he had married in May 1867 in Nottingham, before returning to India a few months later. Apart from the luxuriant Indian undergrowth, this image could have been taken at any ruined site back home.

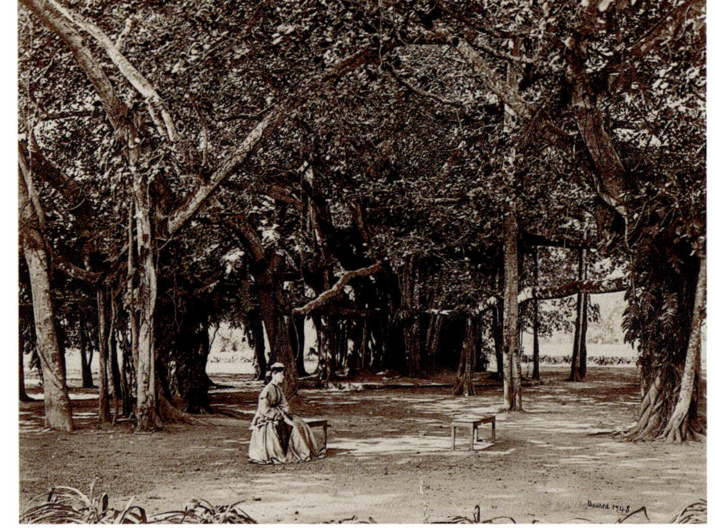

below right: The ancient banyan tree in Calcutta's botanic gardens at Barrackpore Park, photographed by Bourne in the late 1860s. Although signed 'Bourne' in the negative, the image carries a Bourne & Shepherd catalogue number of 1748. The figure of Mary seated under the tree gives a wonderful sense of scale. Bourne & Shepherd's first Calcutta studio was opened in 1868, and these two images may date from that time.

His journey started, as did mine, in Kolkata - Calcutta in Bourne's day and until relatively recently - but while he seems to have completed his twelve hundred mile journey into the mountains without ever unpacking his cameras, my journey was punctuated by frequent photographic detours and stops. That 1863 journey to Shimla (then known as Simla) predates any of his major photographic journeys for his purpose was to get there to take up his first job as a professional photographer in Howard's studio. The former bank clerk from Nottingham had arrived in India to embark on a new and rather risky career!

Bourne arrived in India in January 1863, aged 29, having had a growing interest in photography for at least ten years. He had become a founder member of the Nottingham Photographic Society, formed in autumn 1858[1], and had exhibited some of his photographs in the Society's first exhibition - of over two thousand images - early in the following year.[2]

His work was immediately noticed by the eminent writer - and one of the competition judges - George Shadbolt, editor of the *British Journal of Photography*, who expressed concern that the high technical excellence of Bourne's work was not matched by any apparent creative ability! It was, Shadbolt remarked,

very questionable whether the application of so much skill to the delineation of a mere street view… is not labour thrown away.

He went on to suggest that the reason why Bourne's work had not picked up the top prize was because they were *somewhat deficient in the artistic element.*[3]

That comment was probably unwarranted, and it seems clear that Bourne's reputation was greater than Shadbolt gave him credit for – indeed he was invited to deliver an important lecture to the Nottingham Photographic Society in January 1860, and his paper "On Some of the Requisites Necessary for the Production of a Good Photograph" was eventually published in *The Photographic News.*[4]

As early as 1860, Bourne knew what successful photography demanded of him. He exhorted his audience, and his readers that

> *In the first place, no photographer will ever travel very far in the pathway of success, unless he devotes to the pursuit of his art a considerable sacrifice of time, and no small amount of hard and laborious exertion.*

His remarks included several, almost prophetic, comments on his future life as a travel photographer.

> *And when, with sore and weary feet, we have travelled far over hill and dale, searching for the picturesque, in the broiling heat of a summer's sun, we return home with our burden to commence the long and tedious work of development, many a sigh must we expect to heave as we see, perhaps, the result of our labour in nothing but a mass of dirty stains and patches, with only here and there a perfect bit of the lovely landscape we so much wished to perpetuate. Or, if we wish to make sure of our pictures on the spot, and lug about a huge tent and a score or two of bottles, in addition to what is required for a dry process, the thing absolutely becomes the work of a slave.*[5]

Writing in the *British Journal of Photography* just a week after that lecture, Shadbolt expressed his delight at the artistic progress Bourne had made in his work.[6]

All the while he had been working in Nottingham in Moore & Robinson's bank, which he had joined at the age of nineteen. He apparently lived with the Robinsons for at least some of that time.[7] Bourne's own belief in his photographic prowess had never been in doubt, and he determined to make photography his career. It is one

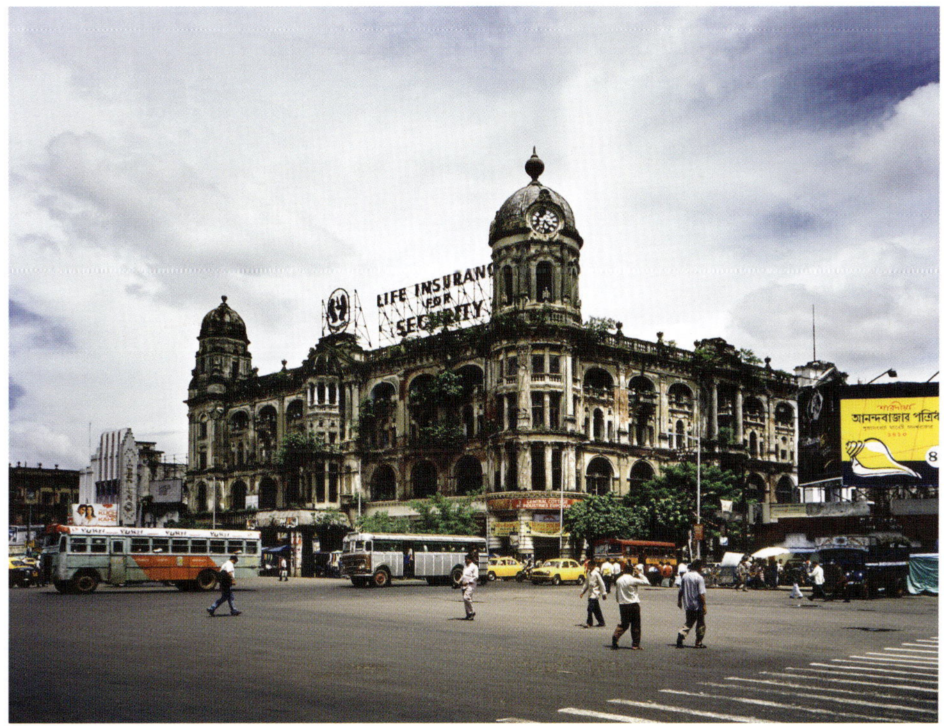

above: The busy junction of Chowringhee Road and Banergee Road in central Kolkata. in Bourne's day, this was the most affluent part of the city centre, and the fine buildings reflected its status. With the buildings decaying and crumbling, India is only now starting to recognise the need to preserve the architectural heritage of its cities. However, Kolkata's other problems place such considerations well down the priority list, and if this fine architecture is to be saved, international help will be needed.

right: Although his reputation rests largely on his romantic and picturesque interpretation of India, Bourne was equally adept at the formal architectural record. On the journey during which he took this study of the Sumeree Temple, Ramnuggur, he took at least two cameras with him. His second camera was left set up on the platform at the base of the tower, and can be seen set up on its tripod just between the tower and the tree.

opposite page: Cut into a dark cleft in the rocks below the fort at Gwalior, these giant sculptural figures - part of a group of twenty-one - date from the 7th -15th centuries, when the pacifist Jain religion held sway in large areas of India. Photographed in fog and rain, in their dark and heavily wooded location, even modern photographic materials were pushed to the limit!

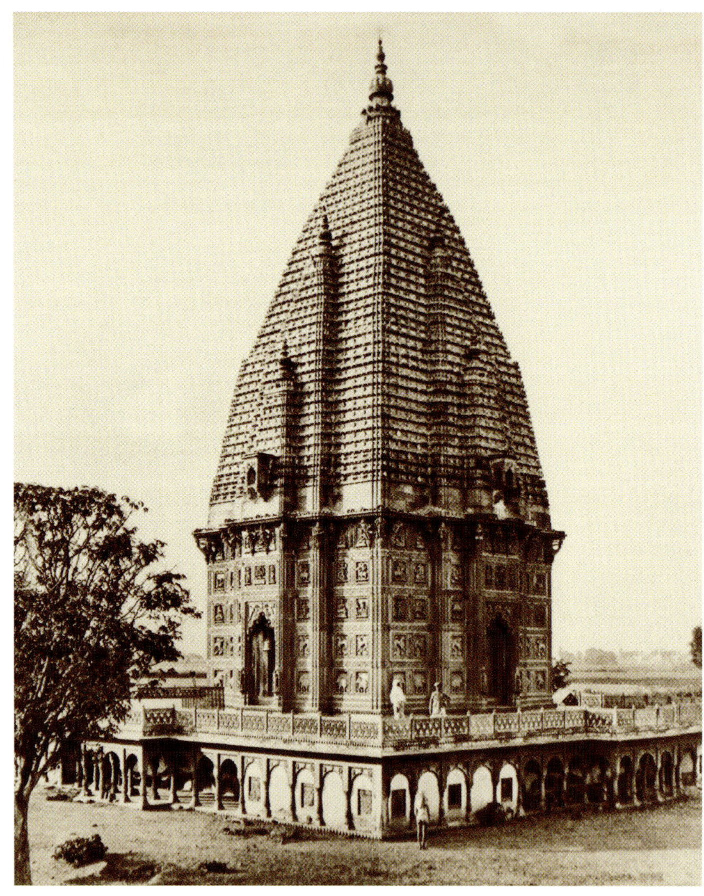

thing to decide to change careers, but Bourne's decision to do so in India was unusual. Whatever the reasons for this dramatic change of direction, Bourne had clearly mapped it all out very carefully before resigning from the bank. He had already made contact with Howard in Shimla, and apparently undertaken to move to the Himalayas for a planned two years. In the event, he stayed for seven.

He appears to have left England from Gravesend in October 1862, arriving in Calcutta on board the steamer *Queen of the South* on January 29 1863.[8]

By the middle of February 1863, he was on the move again en route for Simla, this time on a train bound for Varanasi, then known as Benares, a holy city on the Ganges several hundred miles north west of Calcutta.

My journey took a slightly different route - for while Bourne was intent on getting to Simla/Shimla as quickly as possible, my plan was to visit as many historic sites as possible along the way. While Bourne would have the opportunity, in the years following his arrival in India, to explore and revisit the places he simply travelled through in February 1863, I would not. So I left the train at Gaya station, to be met by a car and driver for the short drive to Bodhgaya, the holiest Buddhist site in India. The car was a Hindustan Ambassador, based on a British design over half a century old - the 1948 Morris Oxford - and still in production, a rugged and robust vehicle ideal for the roads we would encounter over the weeks which followed. The only sign that this was a 'modern' car rather than an antique was the provision of eminently welcome air conditioning, although we eventually switched it off as the cameras took too long to acclimatise to the temperature and humidity when I stepped out of the car. It only went back on after the day's photography was over, and we were making our way to the next overnight stopover.

Bourne's images of India are remarkable. His ability to capture the essential majesty of the buildings was matched only by his talents for grouping the people into wonderful animated studies wherever he went. The only

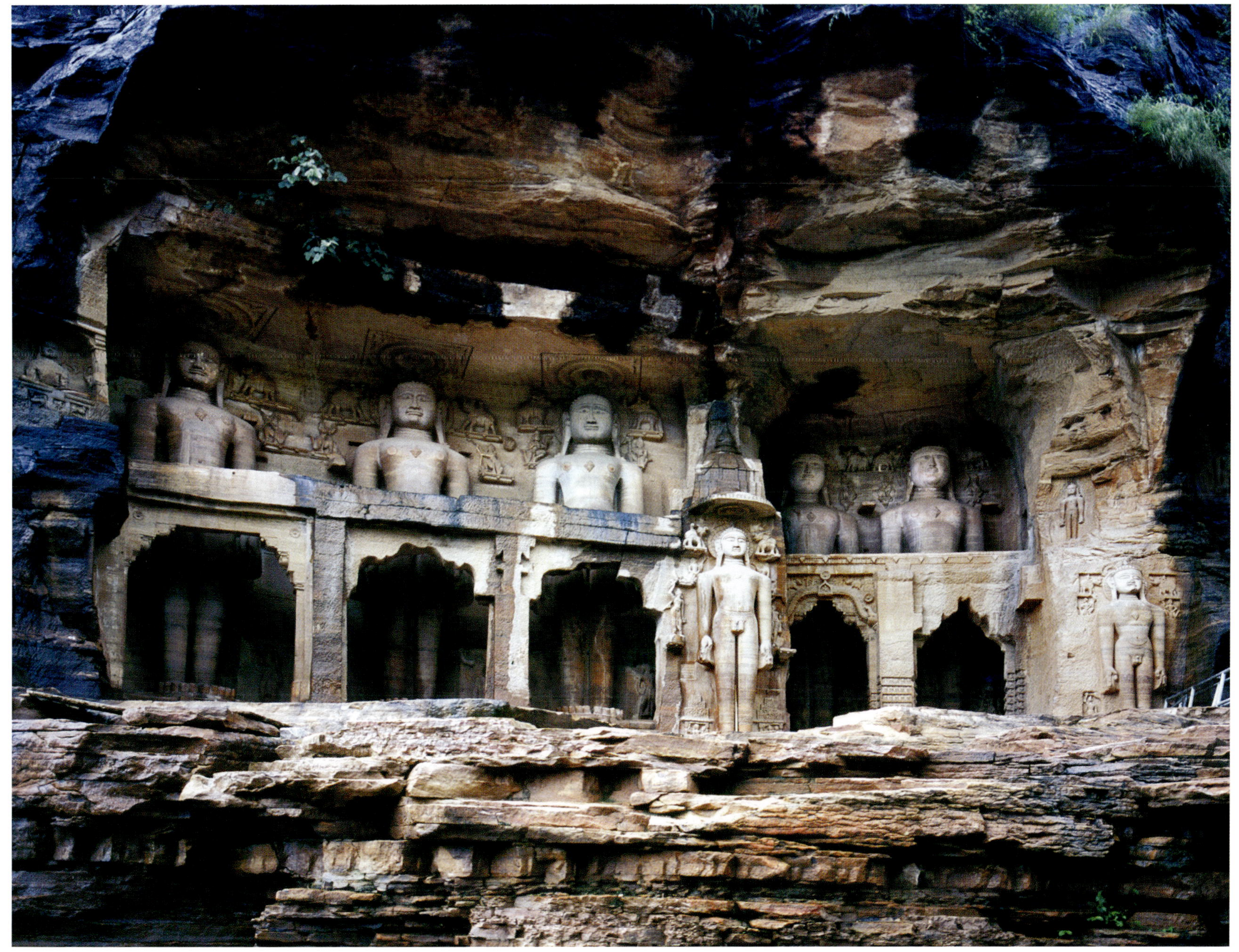

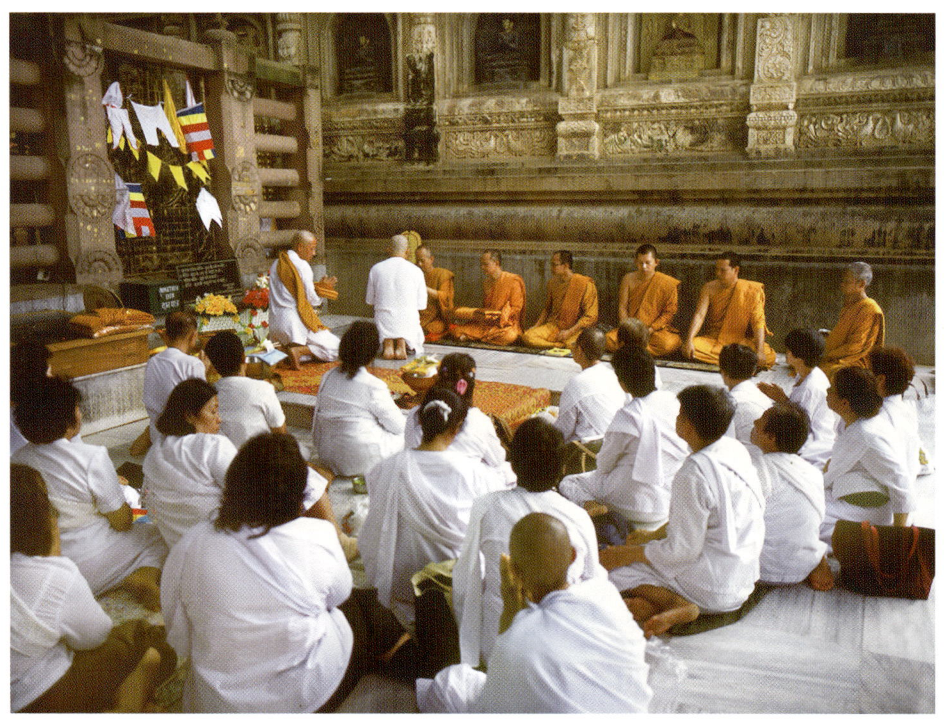

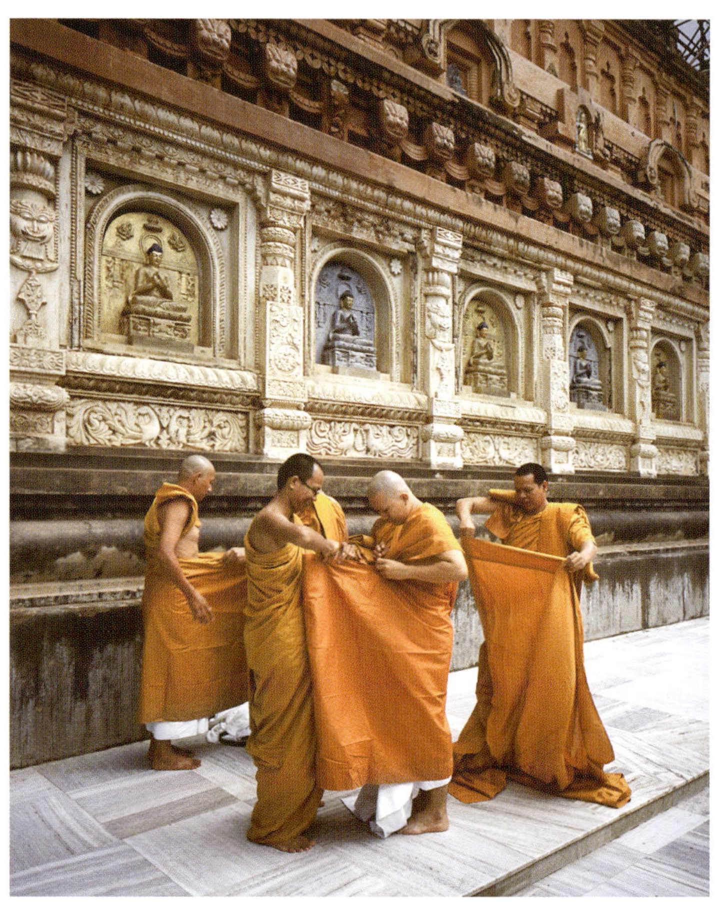

above: At Bodhgaya, in the shadow of the Mahabodhi Temple, and near the Bodhi Tree under which Budha is believed to have received enlightenment, a group of Budhists observe novices being inducted into the monastic life.
right: Away from the gaze of their friends and supporters, the novices are wrapped in the familiar orange monastic robes, allowing their white robes to fall to the ground, before returning to the group.

thing he could not capture was the wonderful colour of the places, the peoples, the costumes, and the rituals he would observe.

Some of the locations on my itinerary were not available to him either – the magnificent Mahabodhi Temple at Bodhgaya and the sacred Bodhi Tree, the site of Buddha's forty-nine day fast, had been flooded, ruined and lost long before Bourne's arrival. Buddhism had gone out of fashion centuries earlier, and the site had simply been forgotten until it was sought out when the religion enjoyed a revival in the 19th century. It was eventually rediscovered by Burmese Buddhists working with British archaeologists and restored. Today, it is, once again, undergoing major restoration while crowds of pilgrims gather in its shadow alongside the Bodhi Tree. The site is now a major international centre for Buddhism, and while all the different Buddhist sects have their own temples within a few hundred yards of the Bodhi Tree, the Mahbodi temple is sacred to them all.

From Bodhgaya, we travelled by road to Varanasi. In Bourne's day Benares, as it was then known, marked the end of the railway line from Calcutta, and the point at which he too had to take to the road.

The Ganges, calm and benign for much of the year, becomes a raging torrent when the monsoon rains swell it and raise its level by several metres. Already ten metres above its normal level when the pictures on the following pages were taken, it rose another two metres overnight and boat trips were suspended.

In the first of his series of articles in the *British Journal of Photography*, Bourne wrote

> *This place is well worth the attention of the photographer. It stretches for two or three miles along the banks of the sacred Ganges, and, seen from the opposite bank, its temples and mosques with their minarets and gilded domes glittering in the sun, looks truly magnificent and imposing. A bridge of boats spans the river, which adds greatly to the picturesqueness of the effect. While waiting here for the arrival of my luggage,*

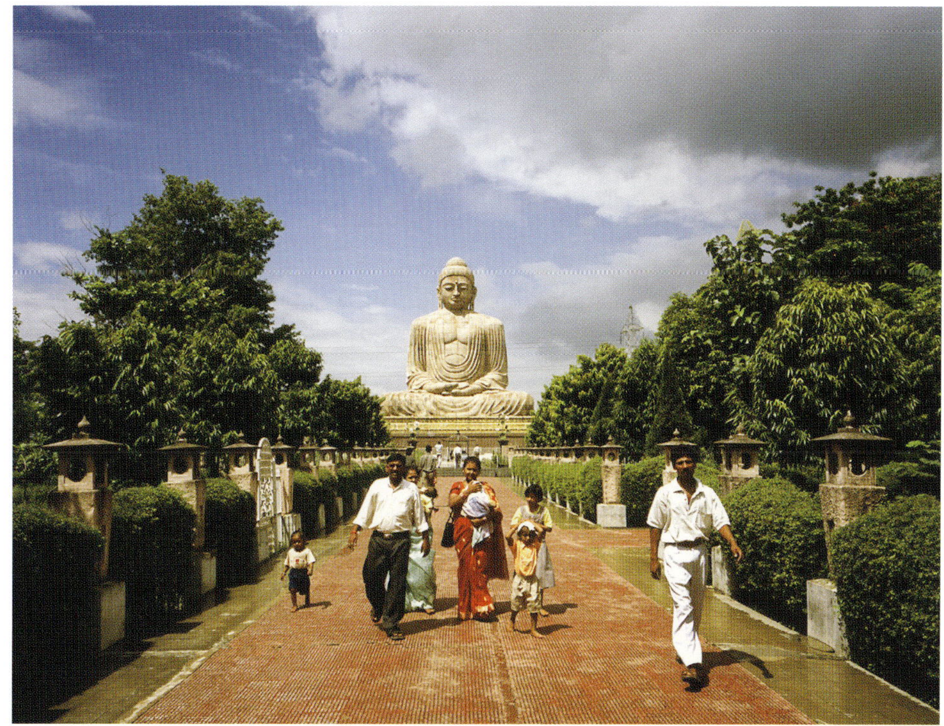

above: The most recent addition to the Bodhgaya skyline is the Great Budha built by the Japanese Daijokyo Buddhists in 1989 and unveiled by the Dalai Lama in September that same year. Only minutes before this picture was taken, torrential rain had soaked everyone walking up the avenue but, within minutes of the rain ceasing, the intense heat of the September sun had all but dried the place. The statue stands twenty five metres (82 feet) high.

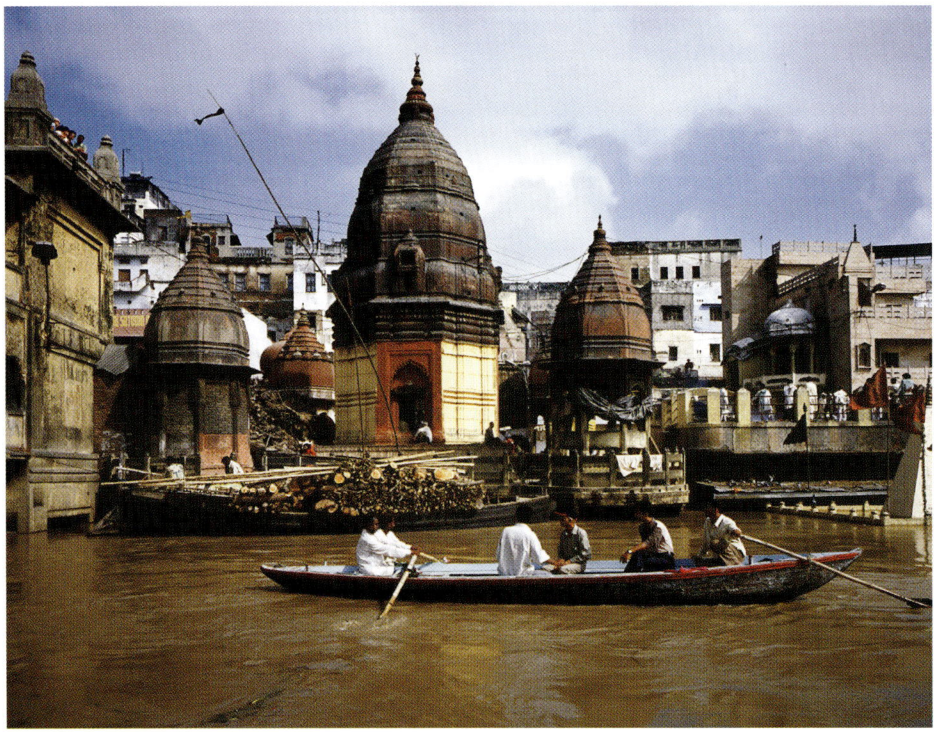

above: Manikarnika Ghat, one of the Funeral Ghats at Varanasi, almost inundated by the swollen waters of the Ganges. A heavily-laden barge carrying wood for the fires is tied up at the ghat awaiting unloading. Walking through the laybyrinthine lanes and alleyways from the ghat, we passed a number of bodies being brought for cremation – men wrapped in yellow shrouds, women in red. A few hundred metres away, the 'electric crematorium' does in forty-five minutes what takes the traditional timber funeral pyre five or six hours. In the centre of Bourne's view of the riverside ghats, taken c.1865, the building in the centre of the modern colour view (*above*) can be seen – standing about twenty metres above the river level, and about fifty metres back from the water's edge. Comparing the two photographs gives a real sense of just how much additional water floods down past Varanasi during the monsoon season. The annual inundation of these buildings, and many others along the city's lengthy waterfront is just an accepted part of life.

I had the opportunity of inspecting this ancient eastern city, The streets are so narrow and so crowded that it is difficult to get along them; and as you wind about through these narrow defiles, turning sharp angles, entering dark and obscure passages, threading your way through crowded and interminable bazaars, you are lost and confused in the intricate labyrinth.[9]

Walking through the city is much the same today, except a bridge replaces the bridge of boats, and perhaps there are more people. And at dawn, in the early morning sunlight, people in their hundreds and thousands make their way through those labyrinthine lanes and alleyways down to the Ganges for their ritual bathe, or just to wash their clothes in the river. Here, Bourne's itinerary and mine were the same – he wrote

At length, your guide leads you to the foot of a flight of steps which land you on the platform of the great Mohammedan mosque by which Benares is known, and which forms so conspicuous an object from the river.

He was also able to photograph the Golden Vishwanath Temple, dedicated to Shiva, a privilege denied to today's visitors, as the use of cameras anywhere near the temple has been banned in recent years!

More than forty years before Bourne arrived in Benares for the first time, another Englishman, James Prinsep had been posted to the city as Assay Master of the Benares Mint. Prinsep was fascinated by the city, and set about mapping the streets and producing the first accurate plans of the narrow lanes and alleyways. He also set about improving the city's drainage, instigating a programme of limited street widening – where such was possible – and installing a sewage system.

A keen artist, Prinsep also set about the task of producing detailed drawings of the important aspects of the city, and these were published with accompanying descriptive notes in a portfolio, first in England in the late 1820s, and later republished in India in 1830 under the title *Benares Illustrated in a Series of Drawings by James*

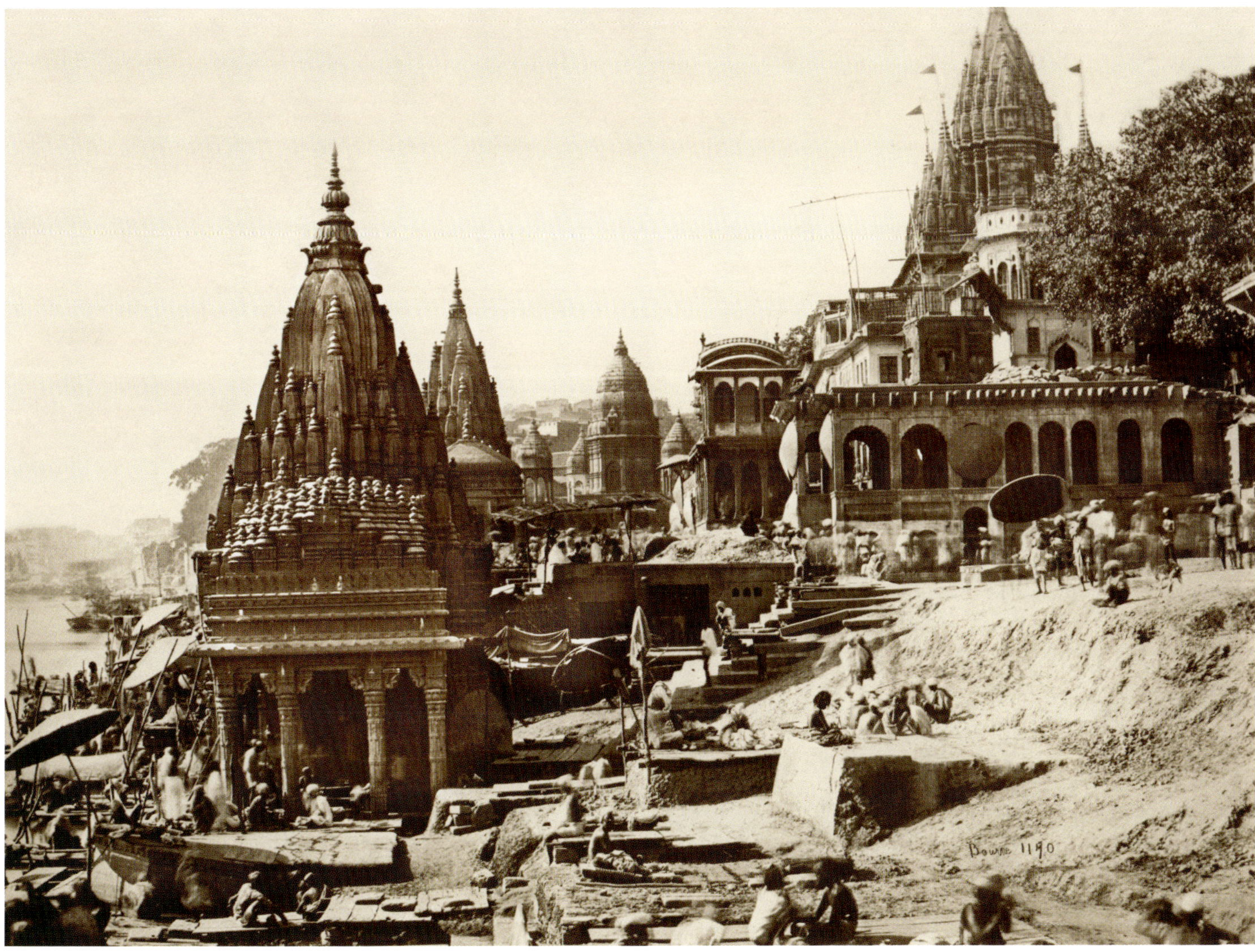

left: Vishnu Pud and Other Temples near the Burning Ghat, Benares, photographed by Bourne 1865, and numbered '1170' in the Bourne & Shepherd catalogue.

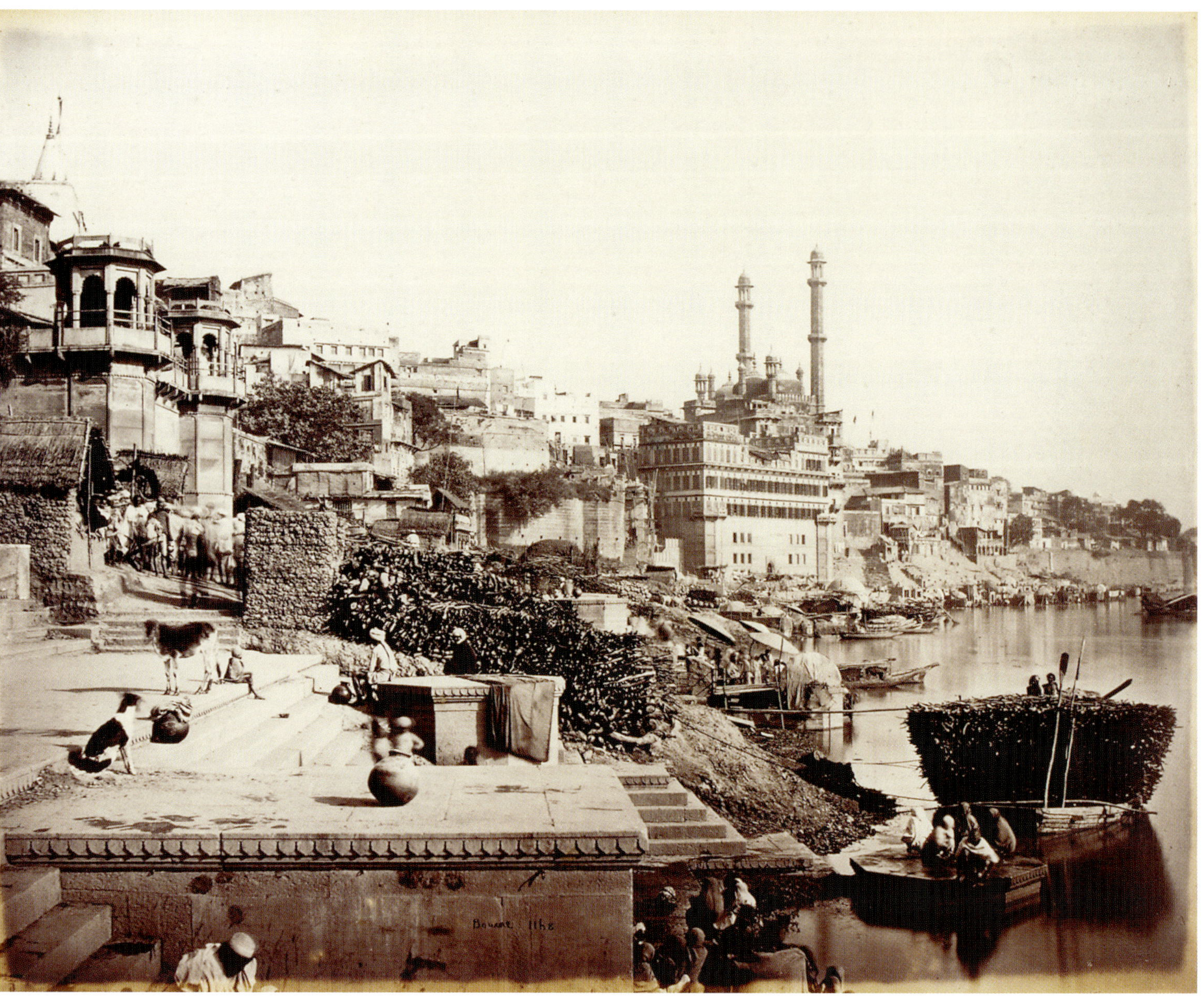

right: The Burning Ghat at Varanasi, photographed by Bourne c.1865. A barge heavily laden with wood for the funeral pyres is tied up and awaiting unloading. Bourne's pictures were taken either in early spring or early winter when the waters of the Ganges are at their lowest.

Prinsep FRS. Lithographed in England by Eminent Artists. The volume was printed at the Baptist Mission in Circular Road, Calcutta, and sold widely. Several of the views in it are so similar to Samuel Bourne's later photographs - including the Bourne image on opposite - that it is tempting to suggest that he may have been aware of, and perhaps an admirer of, Prinsep's work.

Although he took no photographs on his first visit in February 1863, Bourne clearly viewed the city with the photographer's eye, and recognised the potential of certain key viewpoints. He was also fascinated by the 'Burning Ghats' where cremations were carried out daily in huge funeral pyres.

> *Descending from this elevation to the banks of the river he wrote, I witnessed the ceremony of the burning of two dead bodies. Five or six savage-looking men were heaping wood on the blazing piles, but I could discern through the flames the roasting skull and feet of one of the bodies. One of them was that of a woman whose husband stood by evidently regarding the horrid spectacle with the highest satisfaction.*[10]

As we left the funeral ghat, and started to walk through the narrow streets back into the city, we were passed by processions bringing several bodies down to the ghat for cremation - a sight as old as time, the male bodies wrapped in yellow shrouds, the females in red.

Bourne returned to Varanasi on several occasions producing a number of fine images which were listed in Bourne & Shepherd's 1867 catalogue.

Widespread redevelopment of the waterfront in the late 19th century swept away many of the ancient buildings which are seen in Bourne's pictures. Many of those which survive are slowly deteriorating from a mixture of neglect and the annual inundations of the river. If the city is to survive, it requires the immediate instigation of a major restoration project.

In the foreword to Prinsep's book, he quotes an ancient saying which, apparently summed up the city of Benares, *"Ranr, sanr our scerhce"*, which acknowledged the three

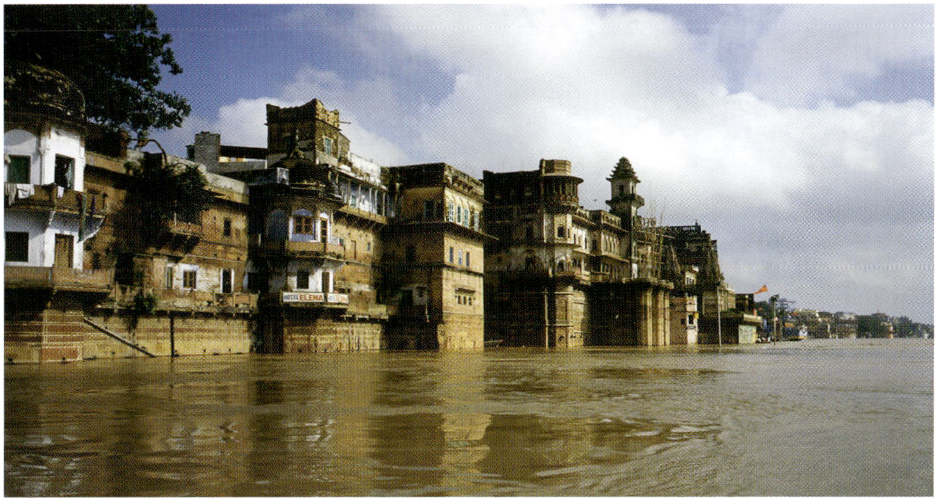

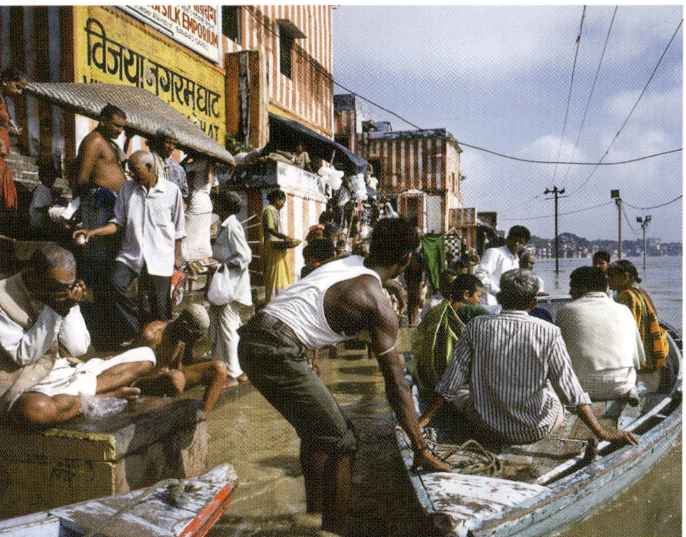

above: The heavily flooded Ganges with high water levels cutting off access to many of the ghats used for ritual bathing. The half-submerged 30 foot high Greek columns of Darbhanga Ghat, centre, are normally reached by a flight of fifteen steps from the river

left: A colourful early morning scene on the river as ritual bathers vie for space with boatmen taking visitors and pilgrims for a river trip.

most instantly recognisable features of the city - prostitutes, bulls and broad stairs. Today, the bulls - or at least the cows - are highly visible, walking and 'decorating' the streets, but the broad stairs were all under water!

For his journey north from Benares, Bourne had arranged a *dâk* at Benares, a wooden-bodied coach which, apparently, was without suspension. His seventy six mile journey to Allahabad must have been a rather less comfortable experience than the train journey from Calcutta. By car a hundred and forty years later, the journey took three and a half hours, but in 1863 it would have taken more than twice as long.

Of Allahabad, Bourne had nothing positive to say, save for the view that,

> *from the number of barracks built and building there, the city was not likely again to suffer so fearfully at the hands of the mutineers.*

The 1857 Indian mutiny had been well reported in Britain, and the importance in the campaign against the mutineers of Allahabad - a sacred location at the confluence of the Ganges, Yamuna and Saraswati rivers - would have been well known to Bourne.

In the five or six years before his arrival, India can hardly have ever been out of the news. The mutiny was directly responsible for the East India Company effectively losing governance of India, and the country passing to the authority of the British crown in the following year, 1858. So the British had only officially been in control for five years when Bourne saw it for the first time.

One of the heroes of the British forces at Allahabad during the 1857 mutiny, Sir Henry Havelock would feature on the designs of two thermoplastic 'union cases' in the early 1860s. The union case, one the world's first mass produced uses of moulded thermoplastic, became a popular casing for early daguerreotype and ambrotype photographic portraits from the late 1850s.

From Allahabad, Bourne returned to the comfort of the recently opened railway for his two hundred and eighty

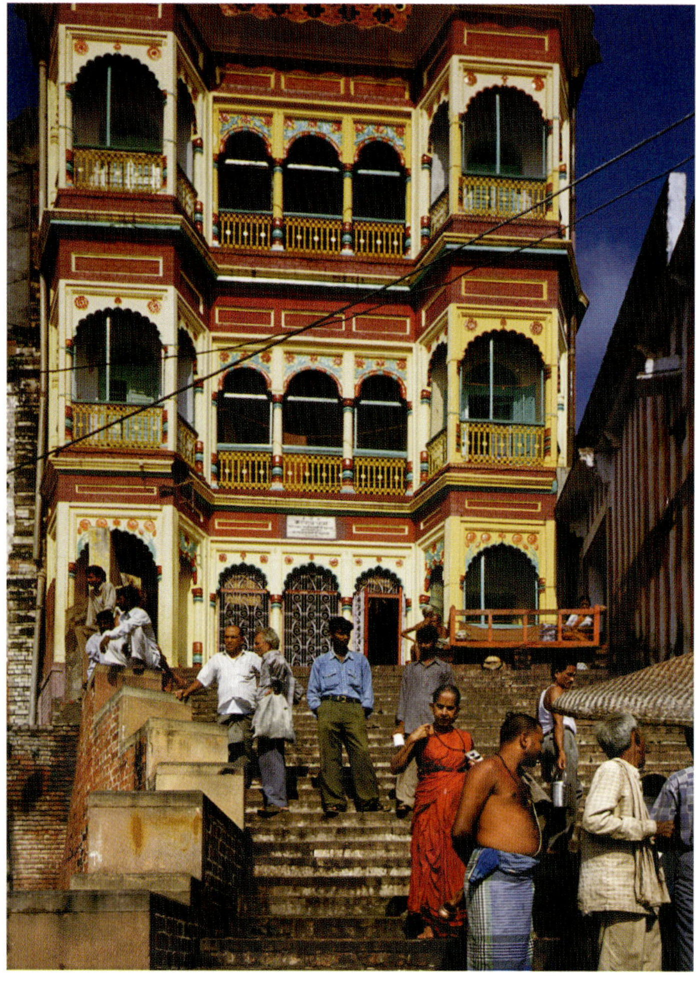

above: Varanasi's stepped ghats line the waterfront for over six kilometres - four miles. From dawn to dusk, crowds of people visit the river as part of their religious rituals and devotions.

mile journey to Agra while, for the second time, our routes diverged and I made my way to Khajuraho by car, over roads which defy description.

In places washed away by the monsoon floods leaving only deeply rutted mud and mud-filled potholes, and in others no more than tracks, the route was punctuated by abandoned lorries, sitting at improbably eccentric angles in the mud. One bore the legend 'Super Fast Goods Carrier' but with an axle in pieces and tilting at an angle of 45°, it would not going anywhere fast in the foreseeable future.

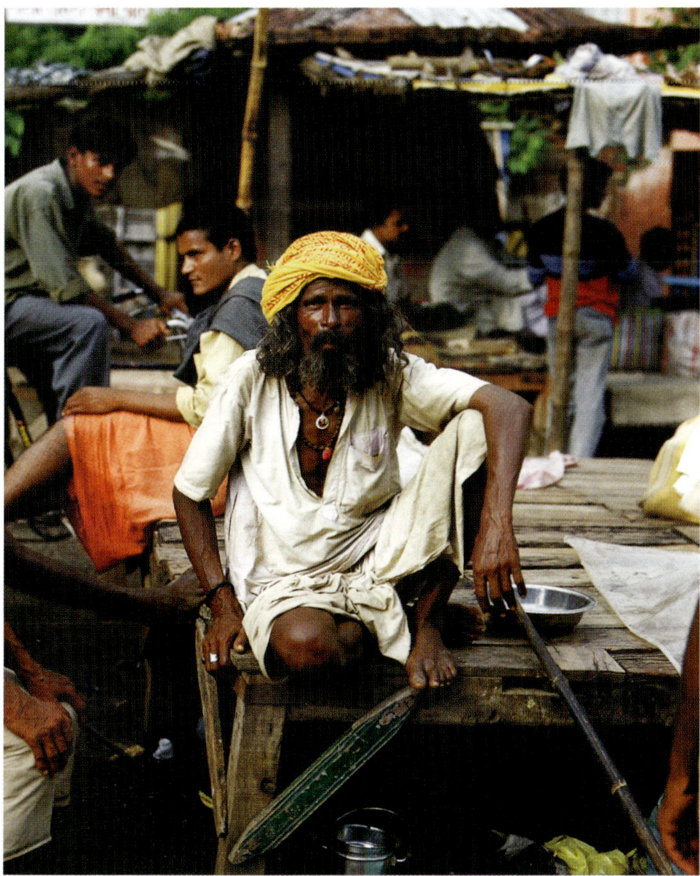

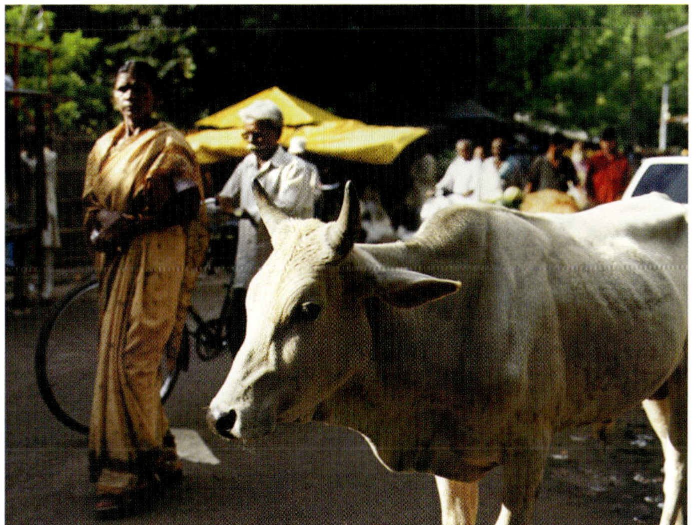

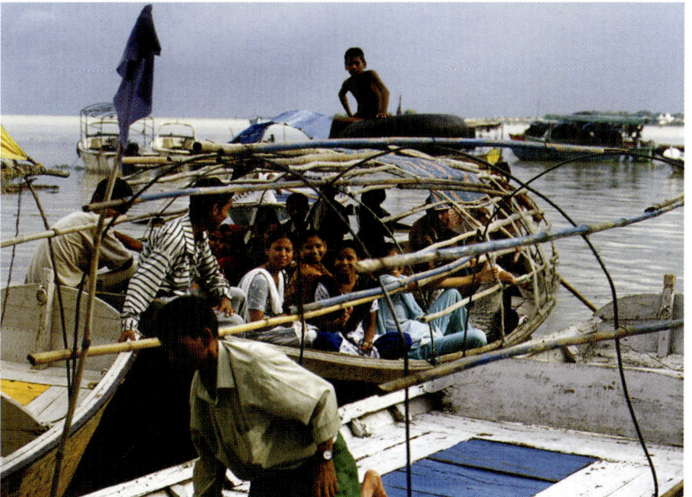

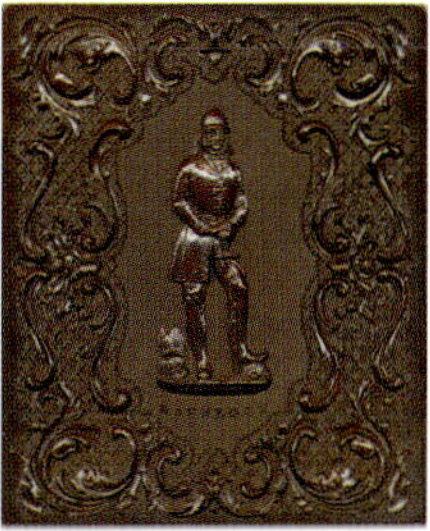

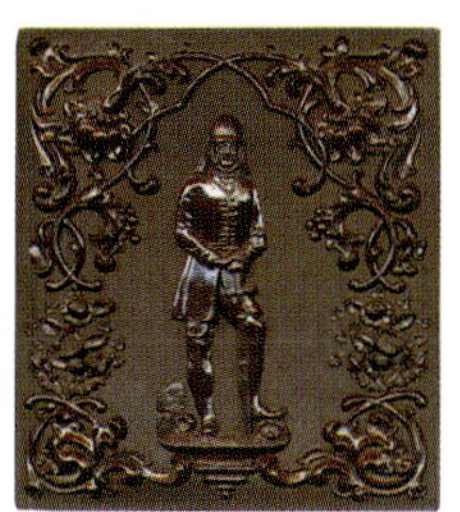

far left and left: At the water's edge at Allahabad, near the 'sangam' where the three holy rivers meet, pilgrims, holy men and souvenir sellers mingle in the narrow street.
above left: Traffic, pilgrims and visitors have to negotiate their way around the cattle that roam the Allahabad streets.
above: Sir Henry Havelock, a British officer during the Indian Mutiny is featured on two thermoplastic photographic portrait cases from the 1850s.

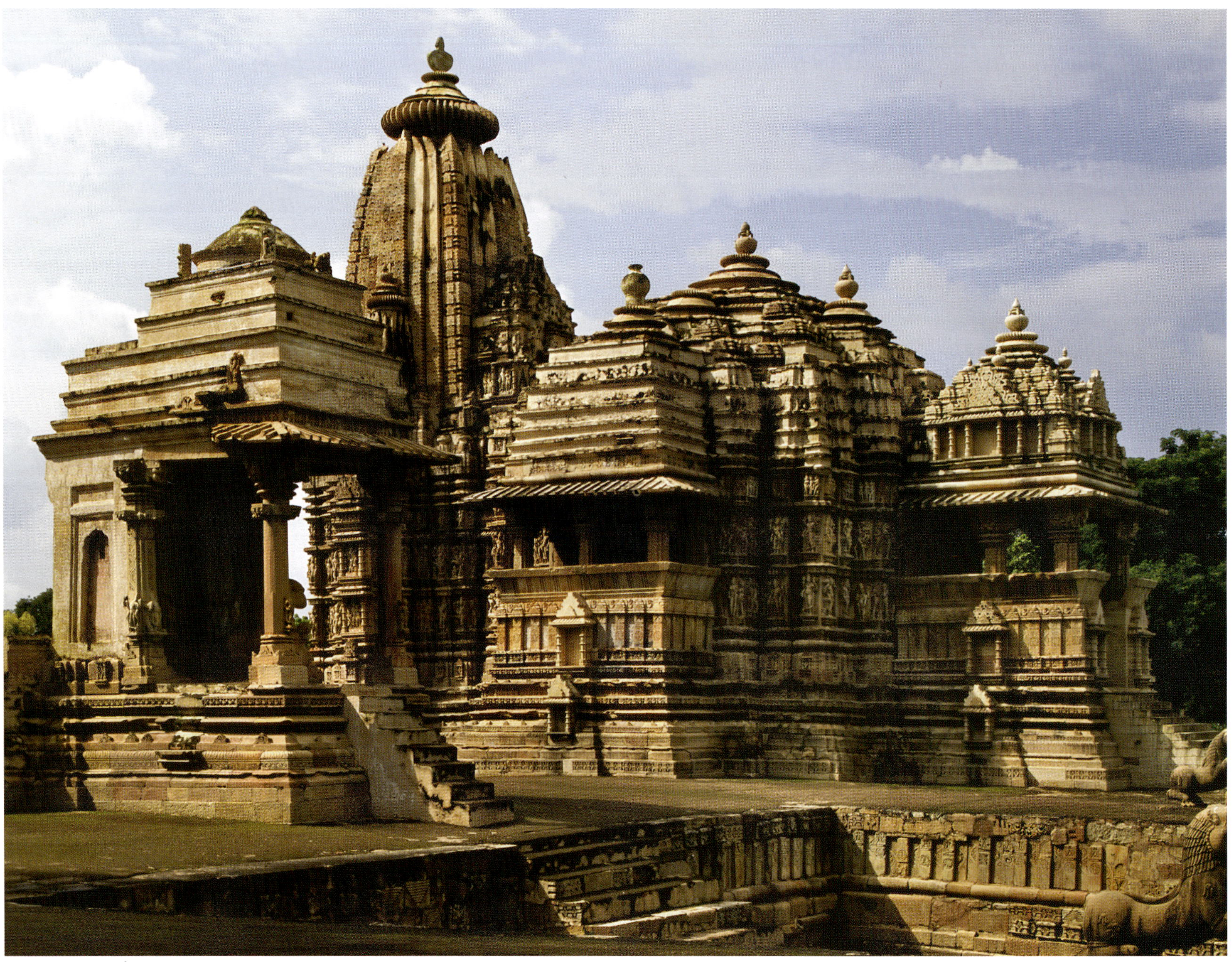

At one point we, too, succumbed to the mud, and had to seek the help of some local farmhands to get us out of the deep rut into which we had sunk. After some negotiations between my driver and the farmers, a fee of 20 rupees, about 30 pence, between the five of them was agreed and we continued on our way. Eventually we arrived in Khajuraho in darkness, after eleven hours on the road and covering just 150 miles!

Bourne visited Khajuraho within a couple of years of arriving in India, although the magnificent temples in his day were not quite as well cared for as they are today.

The huge temple site had been all but lost until its rediscovery in 1838, by an engineer with the British army, Captain T. S. Burt. Once rediscovered, interest in the complex of twenty-five surviving temples - from an estimated original eighty five - grew rapidly, and persists to this day.

Elsewhere in India, it is not uncommon to find that when the Hindu religion declined and Islam was in the ascendancy in mediaeval times, Hindu temples were dismantled, and their intricate stonework reused in the construction of mosques.

The little village of Khajuraho has its own airport, and is surrounded by a large number of hotels, ranging from simple guest houses to international quality five star hotels, which cater for the huge numbers of visitors who arrive every year - pilgrims, tourists and historians.

The temples were built using interlocking stones - without mortar - and the complexity of the structures is amazing. Time and the damaging effect of the Indian climate have caused erosion of the intricate sculptures, however, and a group of masons is permanently involved in replacing worn and damaged stone.

India is a country where labour is abundant and cheap, and even simple flat-faced stones are cut and dressed by hand, much as they would have been a millennium ago when the temples were originally built.

The temple site is a rocky plateau, well above the water

opposite page: The magnificent Devi Jagdambi Temple at Khajuraho, part of the Western Temple complex which comprises one of the finest groups of Hindu Temples in India. The site was developed over a period of five hundred years, with the majority of the spectacular buildings dating from the 9th-11th centuries. Rediscovered only in 1838, the temples are believed to have survived largely because of their remoteness.

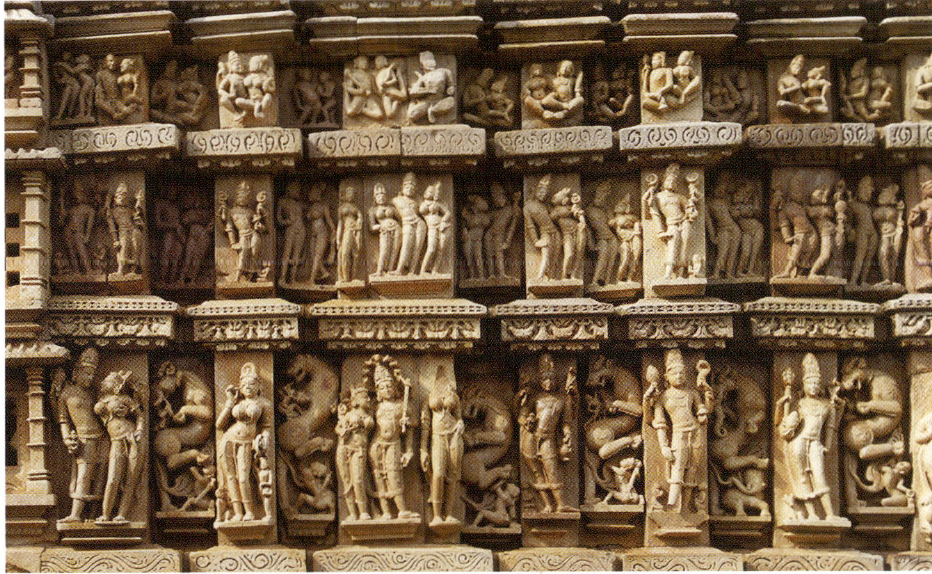

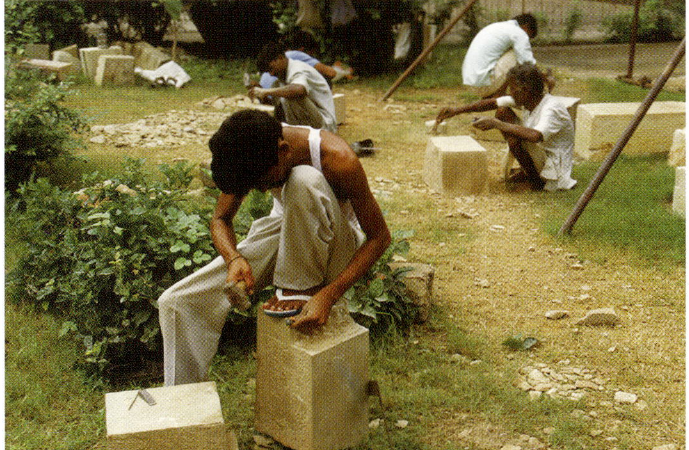

above: Detail of the ornate carving on the Parsvanatha Temple, in the Eastern Group of Temples at Khajuraho.
left: The stillness of the temple site is broken only by the sound of chisels on stone, as masons work cutting new stones to replace eroded sections of the Lakshmana Temple.

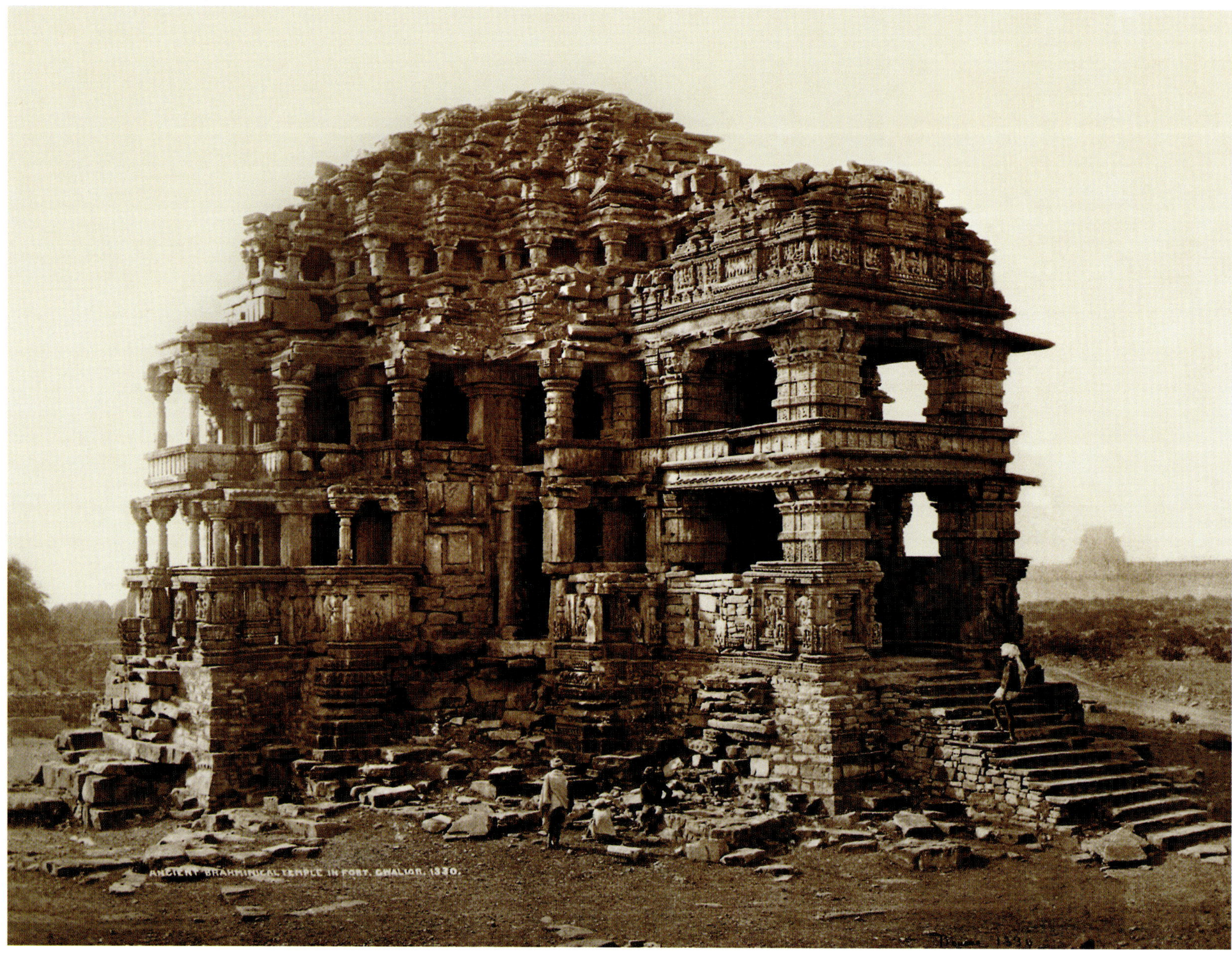
ANCIENT BRAHMINICAL TEMPLE IN FORT, GWALIOR. 1330.

table and the flood plains - a good job, as the torrential rains which frequently punctuated my visit quickly turned the hotel lawns into an extensive lake! It quickly became clear that, in India at this time of year, it is wise to carry an umbrella!

From Khajuraho, a long drive of 175 miles in yet more torrential rain took us to another location Bourne would visit later in his time in India - Gwalior, where the huge Mughal fort dominates the skyline and contains within its walls some remarkable temples.

The height of the fort above the town meant that, for the duration of my visit, it was shrouded in cloud, as were the temples within it. Bourne during his 1866 visit found lighting conditions much more conducive to photography!

It is interesting to reflect on George Shadbolt's criticisms of a few years earlier that Bourne's work was somewhat deficient in the artistic element, when considering the images produced between 1864 and 1866, as he travelled extensively in India in search of the picturesque. The Sas-Bhau temple at Gwalior is a classic example of Bourne's ability to combine the picturesque with the informative, creating images which both inform the viewer of the great richness of Indian heritage and culture, and yet also pander to exactly the same romantic ideals as the overgrown images of British abbeys and castles with which he would have been familiar back home.

It is also, perhaps, typical of 19th century British arrogance that the architecture of India should be defined and explored within a Western aesthetic, but his market would have predominantly been ex-patriots working in the British-Indian administration and allied organisations.

It is also worthy of mention, however, that this romantic, reflective approach to photographing India did not occupy his time completely. As his understanding of India matured, he did frequently turn away from the architectural heritage picture, and turn his attention to ethnographic studies of the peoples he encountered.

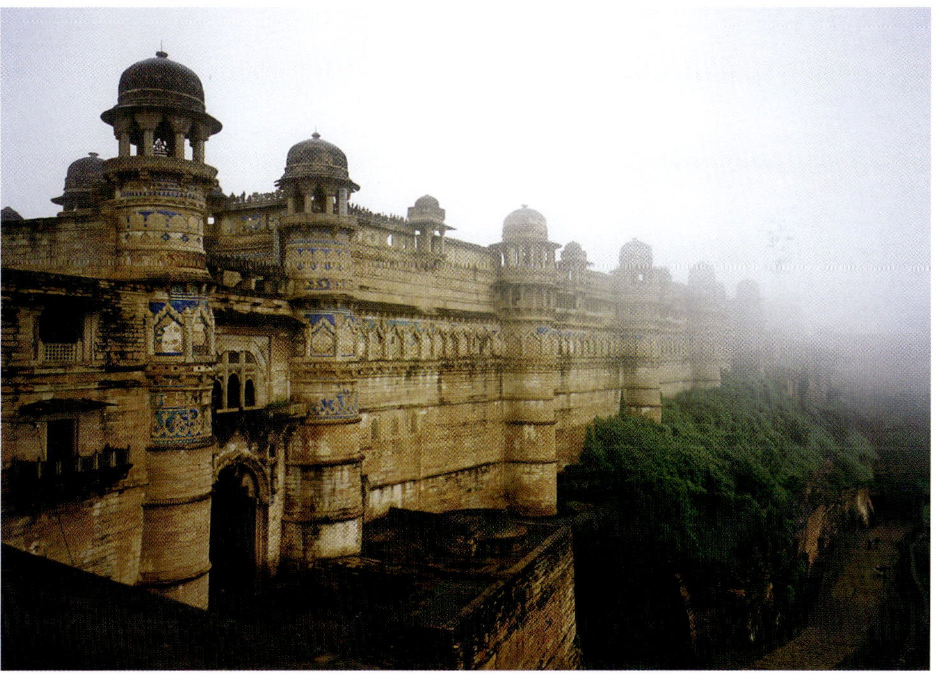

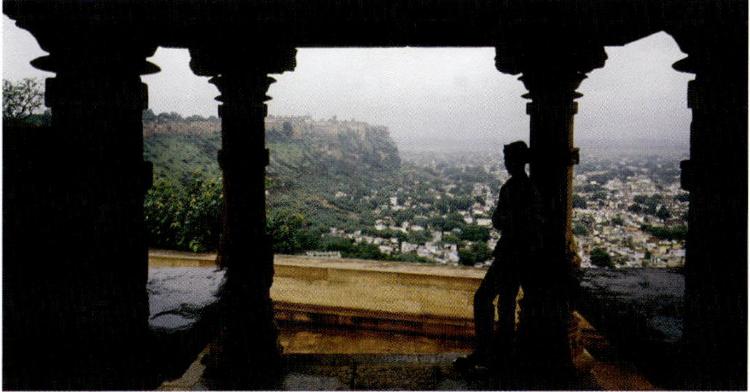

opposite page: Bourne's magnificent study of the Sas Bhau Temple inside Gwalior Fort, 1866.
above: The perimeter walls of Gwalior Fort shrouded in mist, cloud and rain.
left: From inside the small temple on the site, the perimeter walls of the huge fort can be seen on the distant escarpment, with the city laid out below.

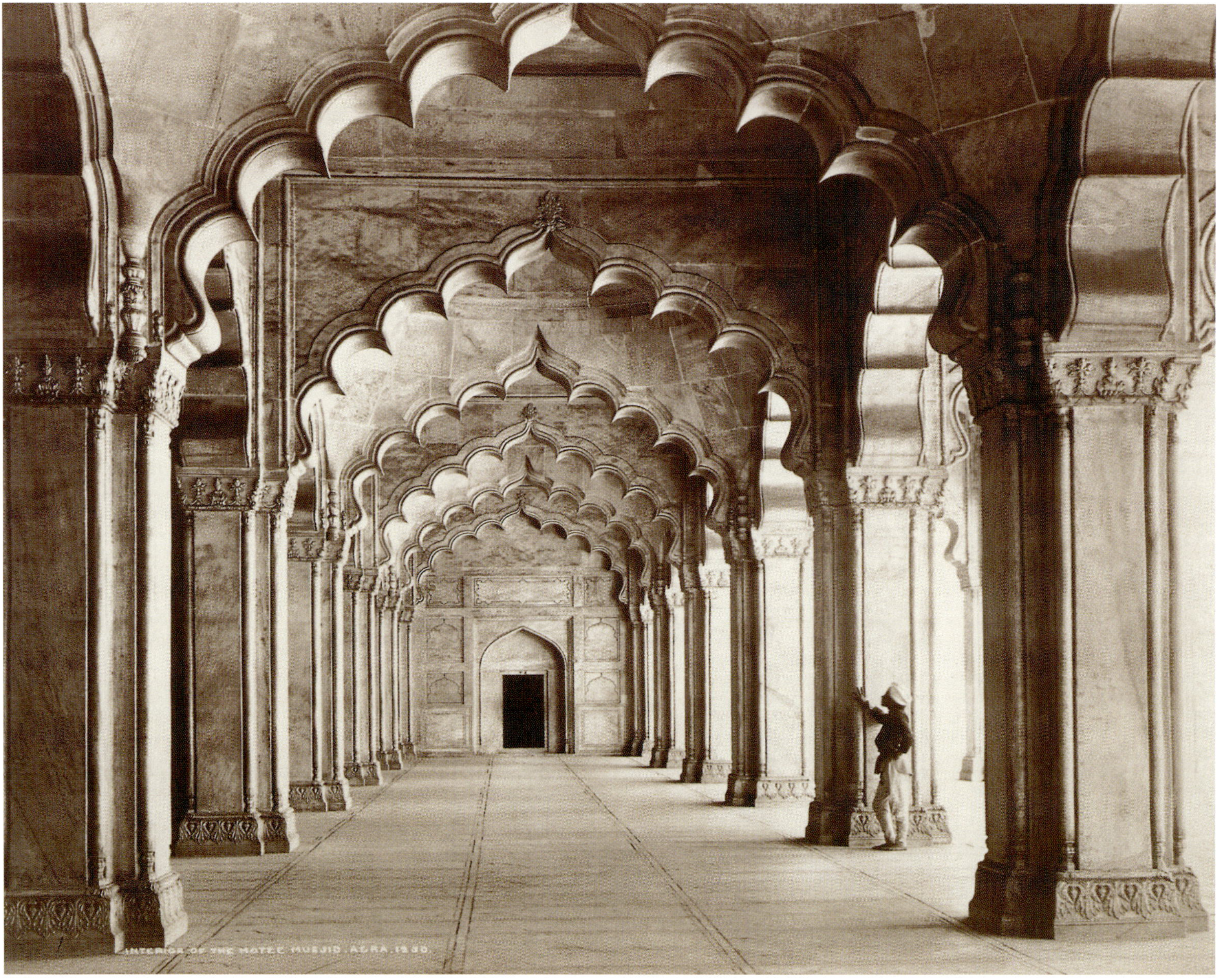
INTERIOR OF THE MOTEE MUSJID. AGRA. 1230.

From Gwalior, a relatively short drive - in torrential rain of course - brought us to Agra, where we rejoined Bourne's 1863 itinerary.

Agra impressed and moved him, as it has done to generations of visitors before and since. The Taj Mahal, the surrounding buildings, Agra Fort and the other architectural treasures of the area became popular subjects from the Bourne & Shepherd catalogue after he photographed them comprehensively in 1864-65. He described his first sight of the Taj Mahal to his *British Journal of Photography* readership in 1863, asking

> *Shall I attempt to describe it? If I do undertake a task which I must of necessity fail, since the ablest pens have pronounced it indescribable... It is one of the things which every photographer who sees it tries to reproduce, but in which, I am sorry to say, he so often fails... How much I regretted when I visited it that my cameras were not accessible... I, however, hope to have the pleasure of photograping it shortly... So I left this dreamlike though solid object behind me, with the conviction that I had seen another of those things which are 'a joy forever'.*[11]

On my first visit, in overcast conditions, fine rain and flat grey light, the Taj looked almost ordinary, but the following day in soft but full sunlight it glowed, and the intricate inlaid detail on the marble was revealed in all its glory.

The Taj Mahal stands as a model of how a heritage site should be managed. Mobile phones are banned, as are cigarettes, sweets, food and any drinks except a bottle of water. The result is that the place is quiet and clean. Electric buses ferry visitors from the car park about a mile away and, despite the huge numbers of people who visit the place every day, the atmosphere is peaceful and almost serene. Indians can visit for a token charge, foreign visitors pay the equivalent of admission to any stately home back in Britain.

Before photography, lithographs and paintings of the Taj Mahal often distorted the spatial relationships between the buildings on the site - the great gateway, the

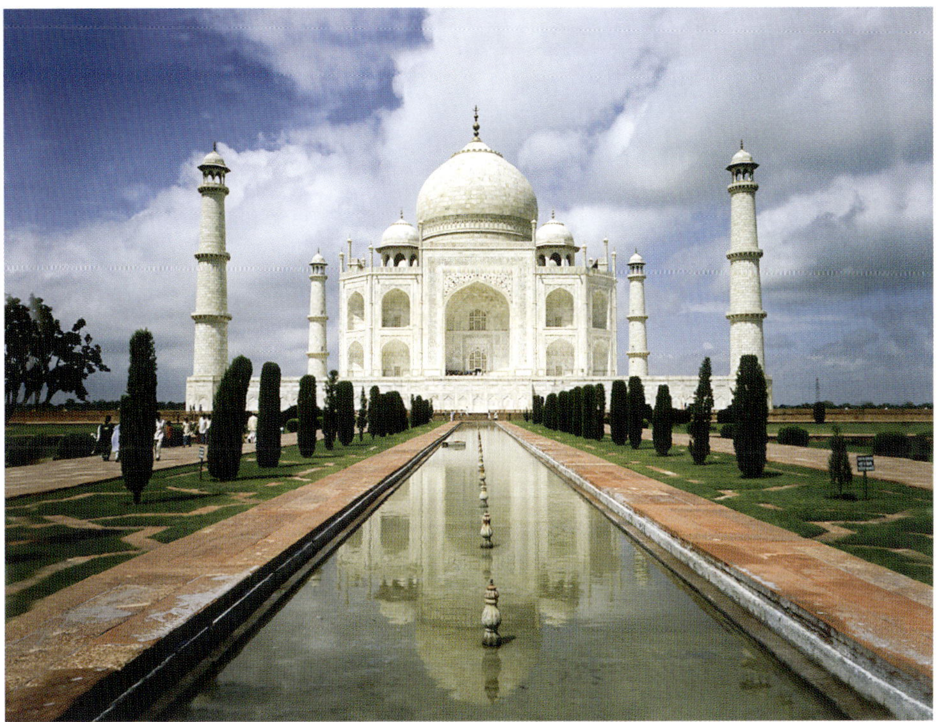

opposite page: The Interior of the Motee Musjid, Agra, photographed by Bourne c.1865 and catalogued at number 1230 in Bourne & Shepherd's 1868 catalogue, is better known as the Pearl Mosque. It is one of his most elegant compositions, the soft light of the interior being ideally suited to the wet collodion negative and albumen printing paper.
above: The classic, timeless view of the Taj Mahal, probably the most photographed and instantly recognisable view in the world.

below: Agra Fort, with the Taj Mahal in the distance. This unusual view probably dates from Bourne's 1865 visit to the city.
left: The colours of a sleeping dog harmonise with the the intricate inlaid marble backdrop of Intimad-ud-Daulah's Tomb, known locally as the "Baby Taj".
bottom: The Diwan-i-Aam, the Emperor's Audience Hall, Agra Fort.

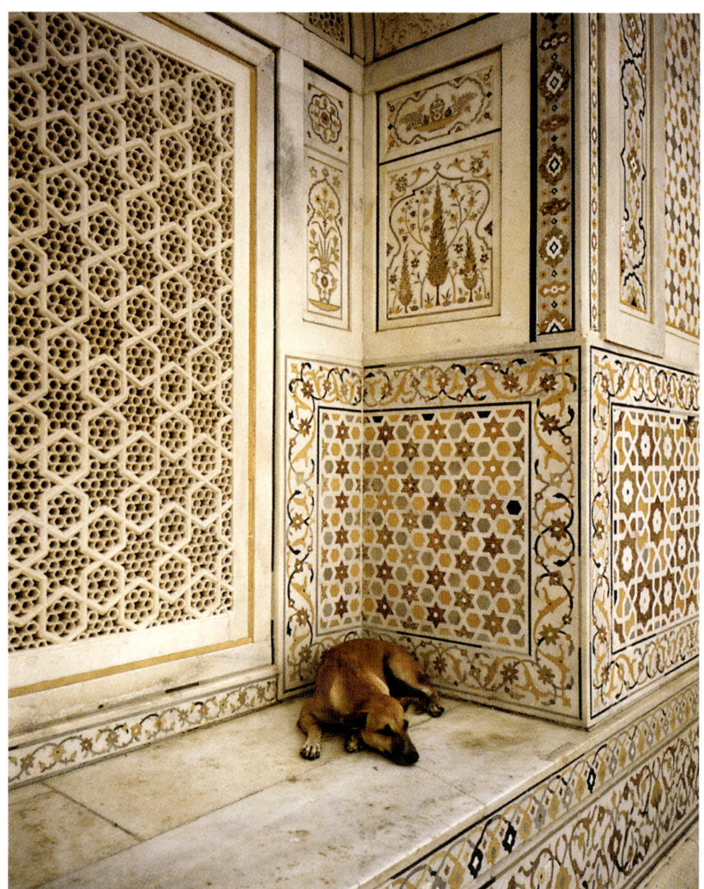

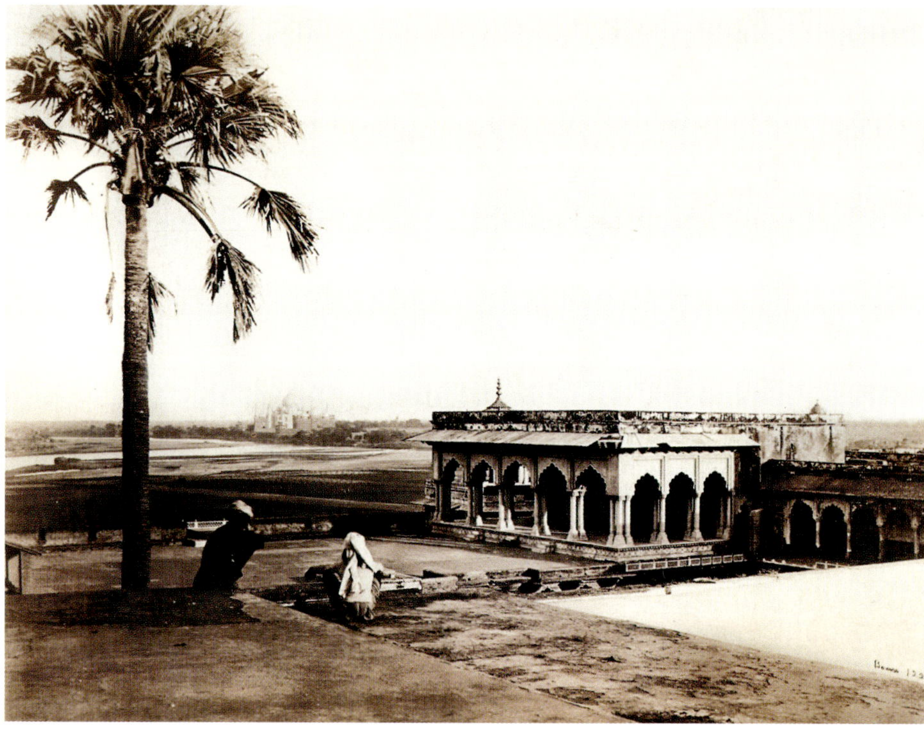

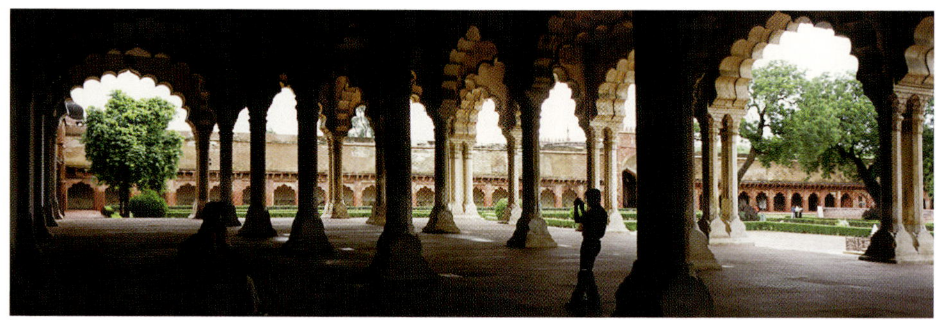

below right: The beautiful red sandstone of the Mehman-Khana, or Assembly Hall, which stands to the right of the Taj Mahal, and is in perfect symmetry with the mosque to the left of the Taj.
below: The ruins of Emperor Jahangir's 17th century Palace, Agra – 'Jehangeer' in Bourne's catalogue – photographed c.1865.

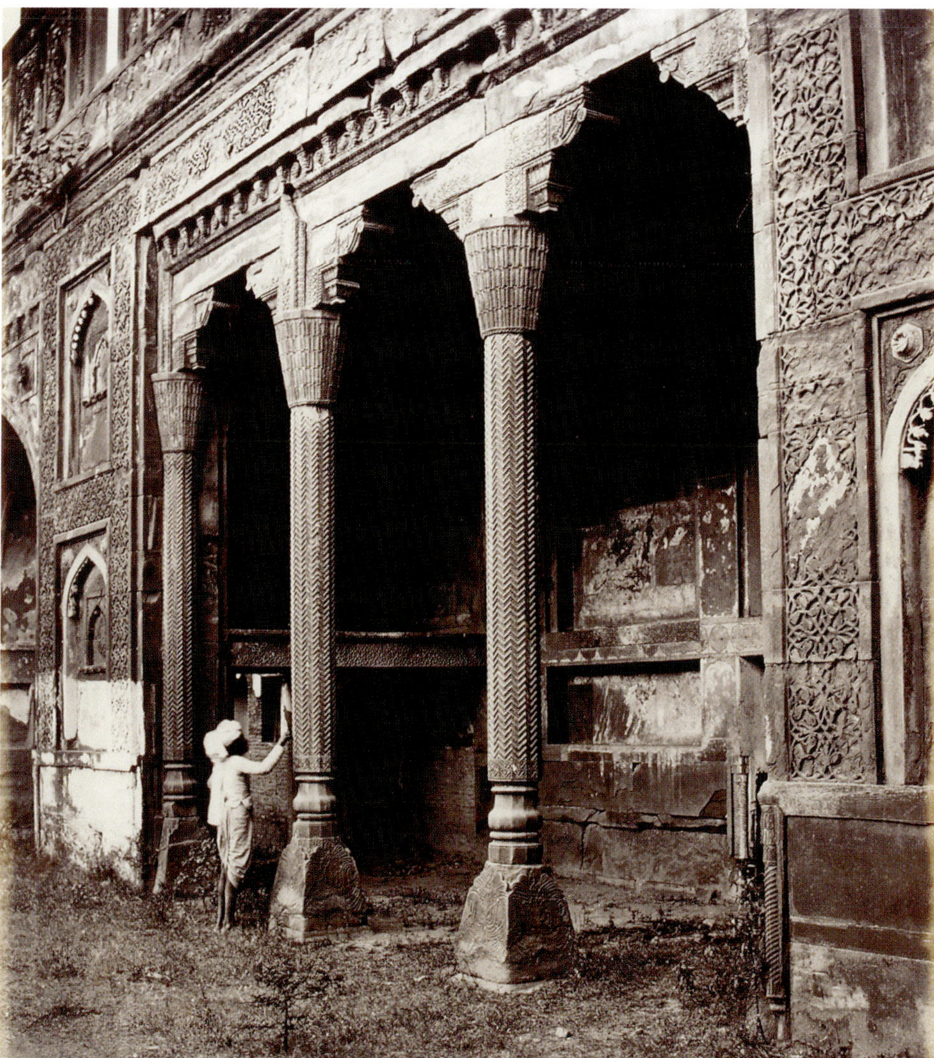

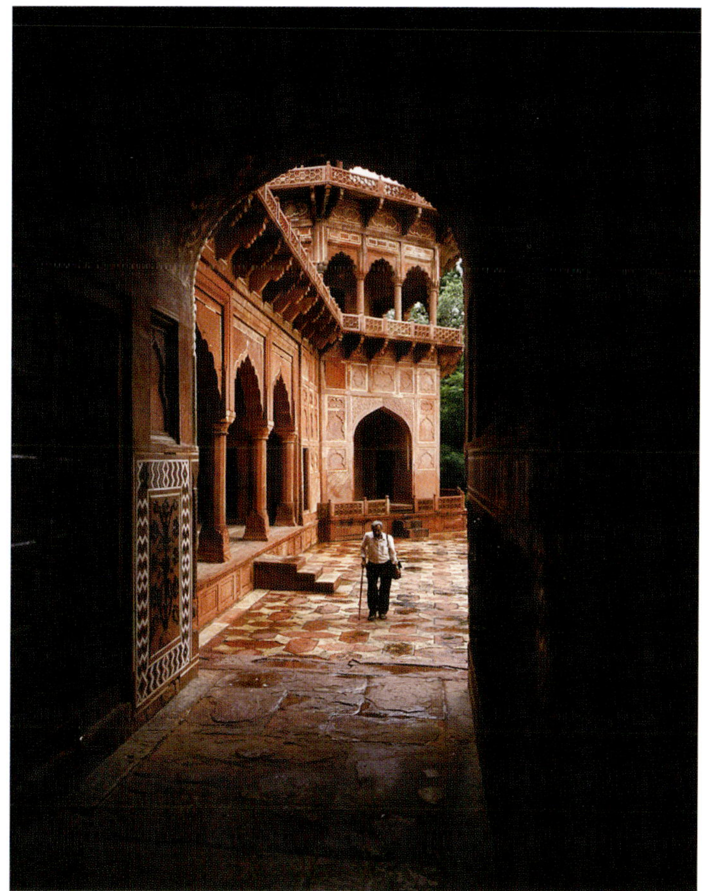

below: The brightly coloured painted brick and plaster astronomical instruments which formed part of Sawai Jay Singh's 18th century observatory now stand in a Delhi park, against a backdrop of the modern city.
right: The ruins of the 12th century Quwwat-ul-Islam mosque was build using carved stonework from an earlier Hindu temple.

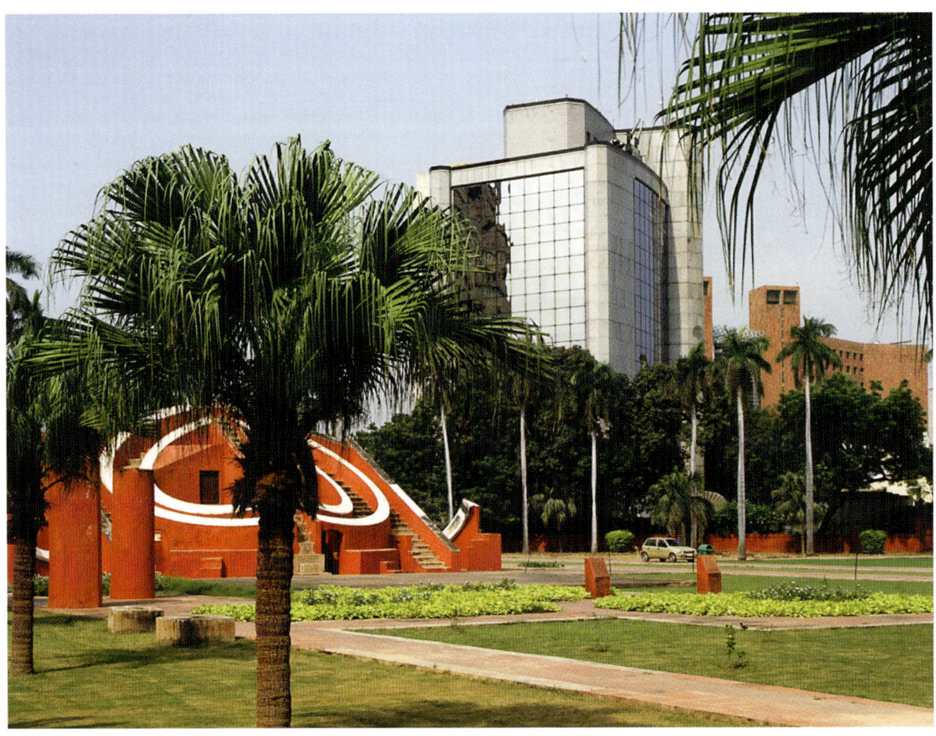

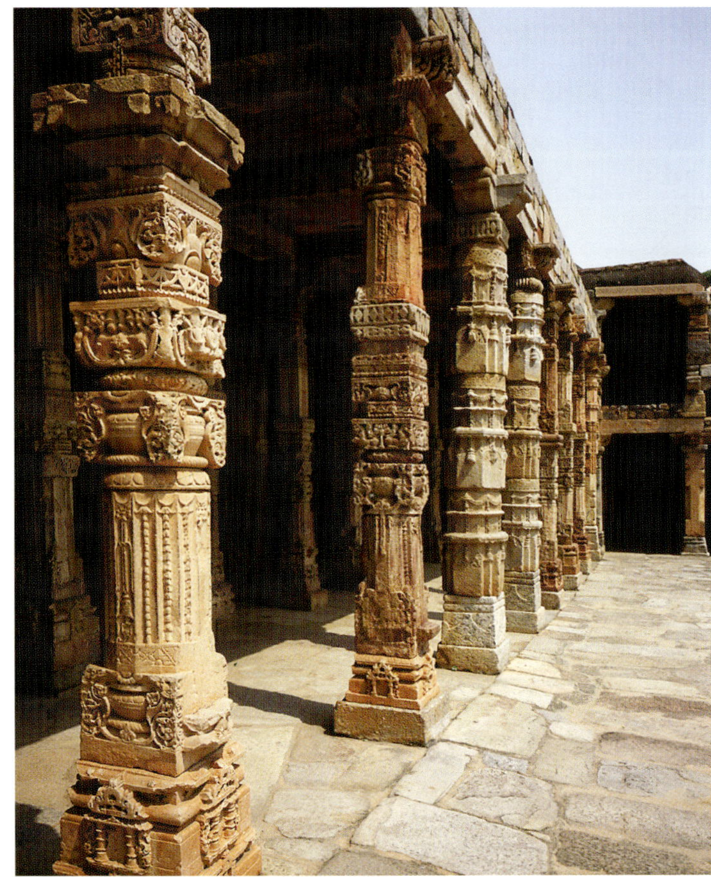

mosque, the assembly hall and the Taj itself. Photography presented it, accurately for the first time, in all its glory, and defined the 'classic' views which are imprinted on the mind of every visitor before they ever get there. They are not disappointed - visiting the Taj Mahal is, truly, a unique experience. At Agra, Bourne noted

> *We must now bid farewell to the railway, and betake ourselves to the rattling clattering dâk – and the two day journey to Delhi.*

In Bourne's day the road from Agra to Delhi was poor - a description which can still be applied to most of the country's roads today. An exception is the Agra to Delhi highway - a modern four-lane dual carriageway, albeit still with roaming cattle to contend with. The contradictions which clearly exist as India struggles to become a modern society are epitomised on such journeys - the progress of cars and the endless stream of lorries being tempered by the constant need for vigilance on roads where cattle graze the central reservation, and modern traffic shares the road with ox-carts, camels and the occasional elephant.

Today's journey from Agra to Delhi takes about four and a half hours in real terms, but in many respects the journey seems as though we are travelling from the medieval living conditions of the countryside into the 21st century.

Delhi is a city in transition - part shanty town on the perimeter, part the old city Bourne would have recognised, part the Lutyens' architectural masterpiece that is New Delhi, and part today's cosmopolitan capital, with increasing numbers of glistening glass-fronted office blocks.

In his June 25th 1863 letter to the *British Journal of Photography*, Bourne wrote

Of course Delhi can't fail to be interesting to the photographer. The Cashmere Gate, the fort, and other noted places must *be taken, while its mosques and similar buildings will be photographed for their own merits. About eleven miles from Delhi is the famous Kootub, of which many of my readers have doubtless seen Beato's large photograph, published by Hering, of Regent Street. But we cannot afford to spend more than the day in this great and interesting city, as we are bound for Simla, and anxious to see the mighty Himalayas.*[12]

He did, of course, return to Delhi on several occasions, as did Charles Shepherd, and their photographic catalogue eventually offered a comprehensive series of illustrations of the old city.

His reference to Felice Beato is the only time he acknowledges another photographer's work in his essays. Beato had spent just over two years in India, arriving in February 1858, photographing everything from the aftermath of battles to the great buildings of Lucknow and elsewhere. Photographs of Qutbuddin Aibak's spectacular 12th century tower known as the Kootub in Bourne's day but usually spelled Qutb today, were popular in the late 1850s and early 1860s, apparently enjoying considerable sales. Beato was just one of several photographers to attempt to photograph it.

The next place of importance we come to, wrote Bourne, *is Umballa, a large military station, from which we get our first view of the hills. After travelling for a whole fortnight*

below: A Sikh gentleman in Ambala's busy fruit market - who insisted on being photographed!
bottom: A poignant reminder of British rule, Ambala's overgrown and seemingly abandoned Christian cemetery remains one corner of this particular foreign land that is forever England.

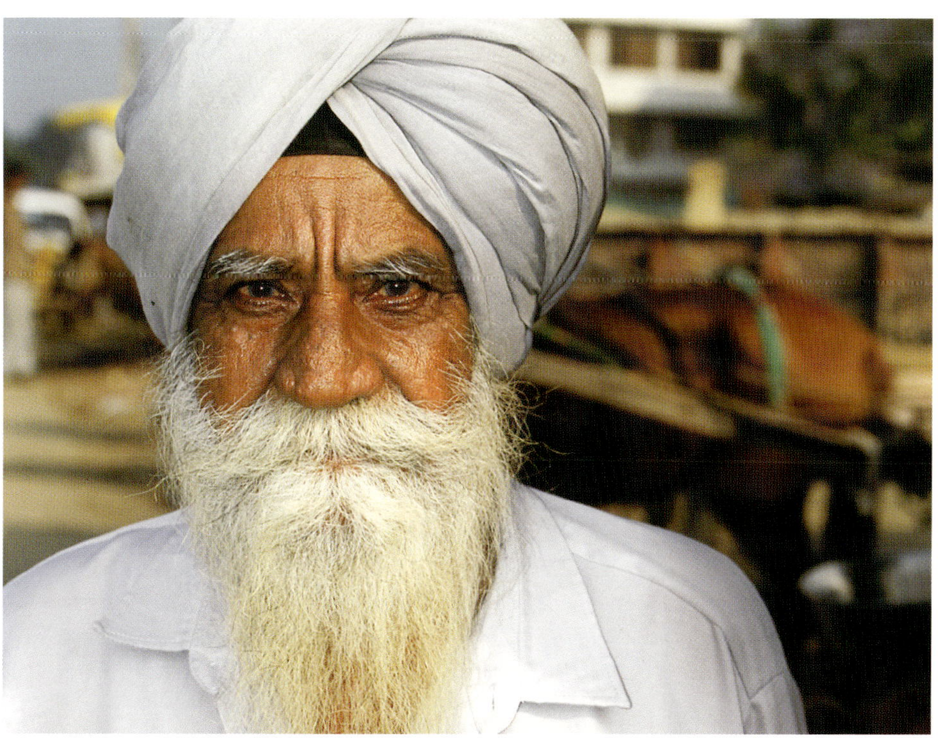

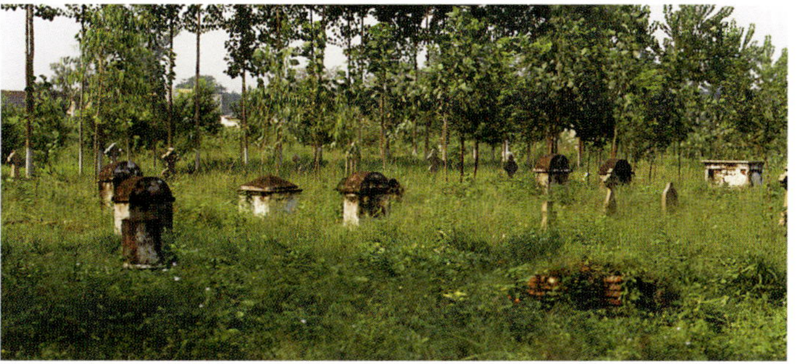

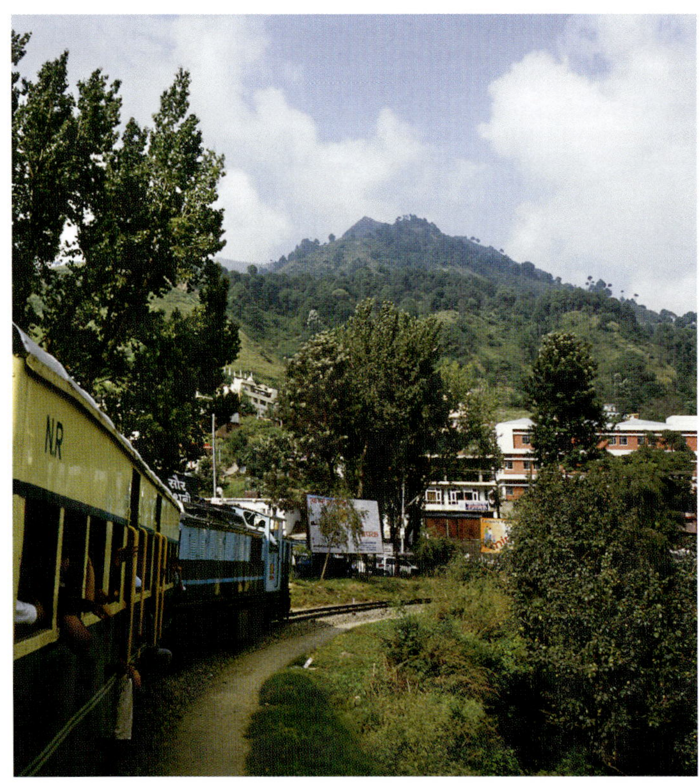

above: The narrow gauge railway approaching the town of Sohan on its way up through the mountains. The distance from Kalka to Shimla is relatively short as the crow flies, but sixty miles by train, a journey time of five and a half hours.
right: As the train climbs up towards its destination at Shimla, the temperature drops dramatically. Towards the end of the rainy season, the mountains are invariably shrouded in clouds.

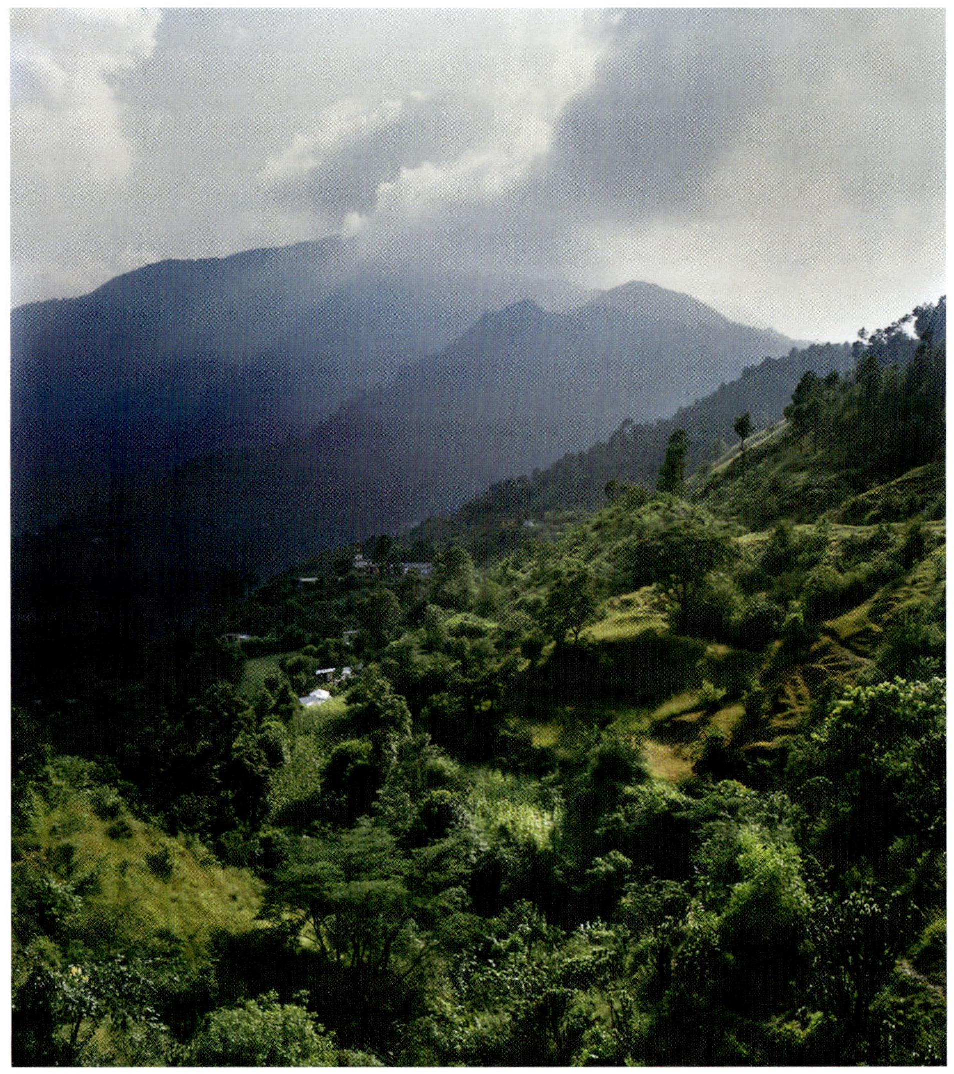

through a country flat as a cricket ground, and devoid alike of hill and dale, picturesqueness or beauty, you may imagine the delight with which a photographer sees once more ranges of blue mountains, lifting their summits to the clouds; or better still, crowned as was one of these, with glittering snow.[13]

Ambala is still dominated by its huge military station, and it carries some poignant reminders of both a hundred years of British presence, and the turmoils which have blighted the country since Independence.

The 19th century Cathedral of St John, recently built when Bourne first passed through the town, survived until the 1965 Indo-Pakistan war. The bombed out shell - in the midst of the military compound - stands as a reminder of relatively recent unrest. Nearby, and almost suffocated by the undergrowth, the gravestones in the Christian cemetery - many of them broken, some of them upended - carry a brief history of the people who once lived and worked there so far from home. That 'corner of some foreign land that is forever England' seemed almost forgotten.

Ambala is well off the tourist trail and not used to many foreign visitors, but the welcome from the local people was very warm. Like Bourne, I merely looked around briefly, stayed overnight and then moved on, for my destination was also the moutain city of Shimla, one-time hill station, and former summer capital of the British Raj.

A journey of forty miles brought me, as it had Bourne before me, to the little town of Kalka - Kaeka in Bourne's diary - at the foot of the hills. At Ambala the mountains had seemed still so far away, but as Kalka came nearer, the height of even the foothills dwarfed anything Bourne or I had ever experienced in Britain. Shimla, the end of both our journeys, sits almost eight thousand feet up in the mountains, at almost twice the height of the highest peak in Britain.

Bourne exchanged his coach for some horses for the final ascent up to the hill station, while today's traveller has the option of car or narrow gauge mountain railway. Had the railway pioneers had their way, Bourne might

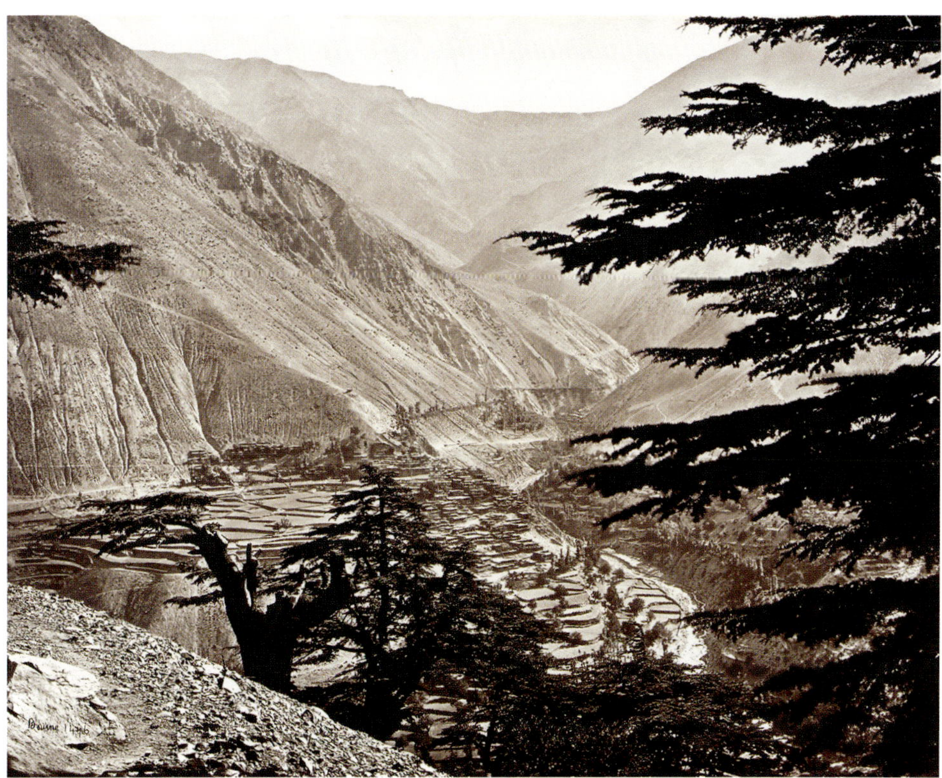

above: Despite his original misgivings about the scenery which he encountered upon his arrival in Shimla, Bourne subsequently used the mountain town as the starting point for several ambitious expeditions further north through the Himalayas and into Kashmir. Transporting a huge weight of household goods as well as his equipment - on one trip taking his dining table and chairs with him in order to retain a sense of civilised life - Bourne returned with a spectacular series of images of breathtaking scenery no other photographer had ever seen. He frequently, however, encountered resistance from the servants who had to transport everything over difficult terrain.

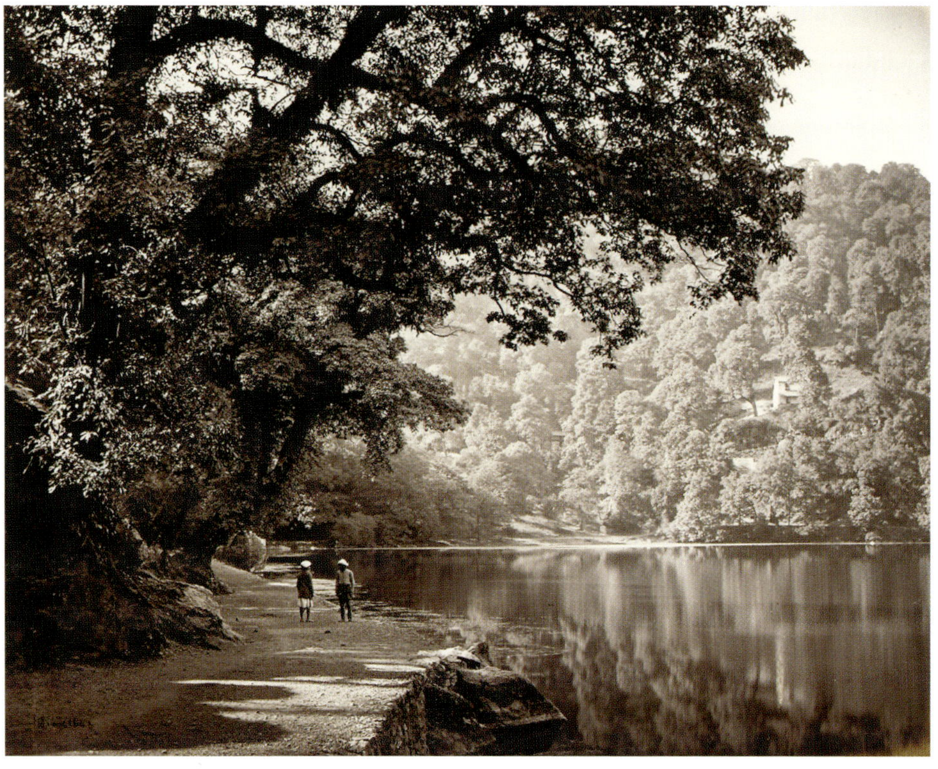

above: River Scene, Srinagar, c.1864, the epitome of the picturesque landscape he had been seeking. Originally despairing the lack of lakes and rivers when he arrived in Shimla, Bourne discovered plenty on his travels into Jammu and Kashmir.

even then have been able to travel by train – for the idea of a railway from Kalka to Shimla had first been proposed as early 1847. It was, however, almost forty years before the first serious survey of the terrain was completed, and 1903 before the line finally opened to the public. My journey over a century later is a testament to the quality of the construction, and the vision of its designers.

Sometimes described as the most daring railway project in the world, in places the track runs perilously close to the edge of the narrow ledges cut in the rock, with sheer drops below, making the experience both unnerving and spectacular. With one vista almost immediately surpassed by the next, the five and a half hour journey passes very quickly. The journey by road is also spectacular, which makes Bourne's casual dismissal of the scenery he discovered at Simla somewhat surprising. Perhaps it was the fact that it took him two days to get there.

> *We spend a night at the hotel* [in Kalka] *and having procured ponies, start early next morning on our mountain journey.* he wrote *On turning the sharp angle of a mountain when about half way on our journey, we catch our first glimpse of Simla. It seems no very great distance as the crow flies, but such is not our course: we must round many a corner, and circumvent many an off-shoot before we reach this coveted spot. Another night spent in one of the staging bungalows where a bedstead is all the accommodation you can get, and an early start next morning brings us about four p.m. in full view of the place we so much wish to see.*
>
> *I must confess to disappointment on my first view of Simla... and I naturally began to wonder where I should find the series of views for which I had undertaken this long journey.*[14]

That remark is interesting both because of his apparent inability to appreciate the beauty of the location, and because it clearly sets out an early agenda for his time there. Despite having made a two year commitment to work in a portrait studio with Howard, the taking – and presumably the marketing – of a series of picturesque scenic views was clearly uppermost in his thinking.

> *Its great defect for the photographer is its lack of water; I do not mean for the purpose of carrying on his manipulations, but for introducing into his views. There are no lakes, no rivers, and scarcely anything like a stream in this locality, neither is there a single object of architectural interest, no rustic bridges, and no ivy clad ruins; trees and mountains, and the beautiful play of light and shadow around them are, therefore, all that the photographer has to compose his pictures.*[15]

The reference to the rustic bridge and the ivy-clad ruin

– both of which echoed remarks made by Manchester photographer James Mudd in his advice to landscape photographers published in 1858, and which Bourne no doubt had read before leaving Britain, firmly locate Bourne's aesthetic in the traditional mid-Victorian understanding of the picturesque.[16]

He went on to make, and report on, two epic journeys into the Himalayas, and he also made several journeys criss-crossing India and photographing every major monument.

In the Himalayas, he took his cameras further and higher into the mountains than anyone before him and, along the way, found rivers, lakes and streams in abundance; more than enough to satisfy his quest for the picturesque.

But travel photography had undoubted hardships. Bourne was, it would seem, not one who easily adapted to changing circumstances. He was one who always insisted that the requirements of the social order be observed. Thus, as he left for a lengthy expedition into the mountains with a retinue of servants, six bearers, a team of coolies, and a caravan of supplies which stretched some several hundred yards behind him – including his dining table and chairs, considered essential to maintain a civilised lifestyle – we find him reporting to his *British Journal of Photography* readers that sometimes he might go for two months without speaking to another European – overlooking the fact that in addition to forty two local coolies, he had taken his own man-servant and several others. Conversation with servants, it seems, hardly warranted consideration as conversation, and he claimed to have no interest whatsoever in learning to speak what he dismissively described as *barbarous Hindustani, and a hundred local compounds thereof.*[17]

By contrast my journey, over one hundred forty years after Bourne's, relied for its success on the active participation and support of the local people, and on their knowledge and their experiences. Perhaps that is the greatest social and cultural distinction between today's

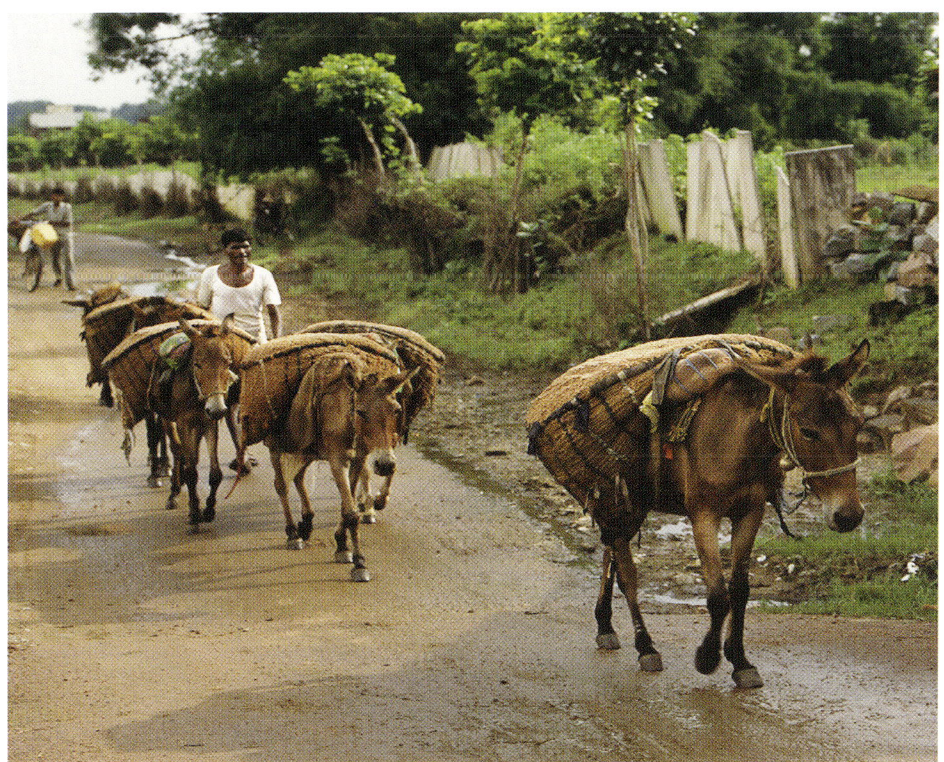

above: The traveller today is often confronted with scenes which would not have been unfamiliar to Bourne one hundred and forty years earlier. Given the poor condition of the roads, and the terrain which has to be traversed, the pack mule is still the most effective means of transporting small quantities of materials. These mules are delivering sand to the on-going restoration of the temples at Khajuraho.

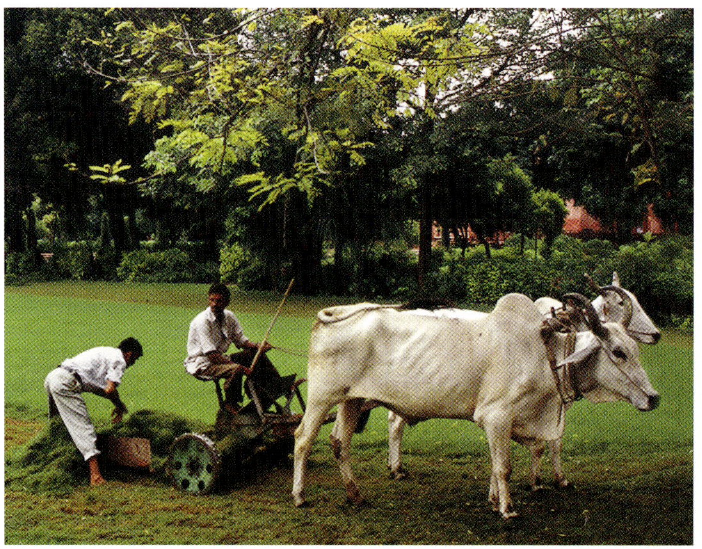

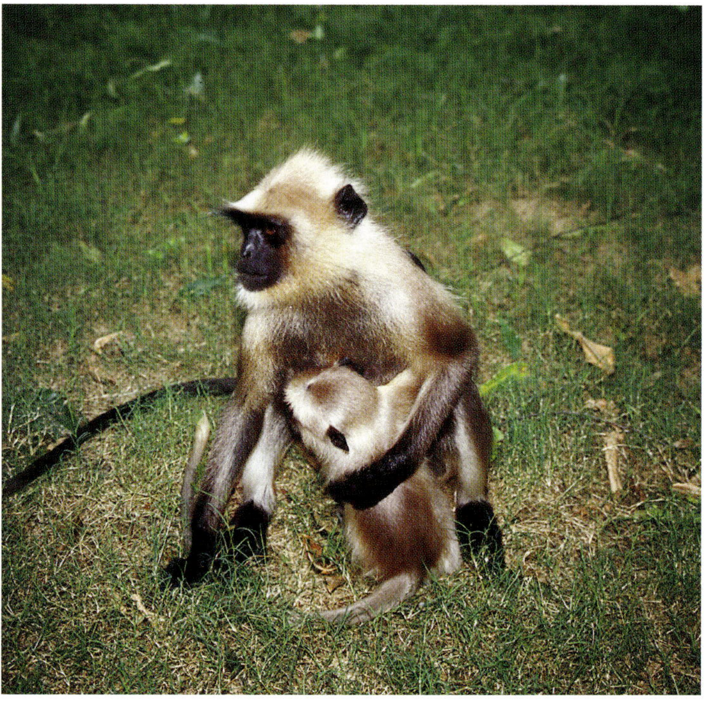

right: Cutting the grass at the Taj Mahal using animals to pull the mower may look quaint and rather old-fashioned, but it is all part of a policy not to allow any oil-burning equipment or vehicles anywhere near the World Heritage Site. Electric buses and both bicyle-powered and hand-pulled rickshaws transport visitors from the car park about a mile away.

far right: The park surrounding the mausoleum at Sikandra is home to both antelopes and monkeys. Monkeys live throughout India, but their natural lifestyle has been modified to embrace being fed by visitors, and scavenging amongst the huge quantities of vegetable waste discarded in the towns and villages.

traveller and the Victorians. Bourne was travelling in India at the height of Britain's imperial power, when arrogant dismissal of the culture and heritage of the nations which made up the Empire was the order of the day. His 1866 account of how he hunted down coolies, who had rebelled against his authoritarian ways and gone home, is a case in point.

Taking a stout stick in my hand I set out in search of them, in a mood not the most amiable. After searching several houses unsuccessfully my attention was attracted to another, where two women stood at the door watching my proceedings. I fancied they looked guilty, and at once charged them with concealing my coolies."Nay, sahib; koee admee nahe hy mera ghur pur; coolie nahe hy." (No sir; there is no man in my house; there is no coolie.) [So he did understand a little of the language!] *Not satisfied with this answer, I walked in, and soon discovered my friends hiding beneath a charpoy or bed, and dragging them forth made them feel the "quality" of my stick, amid the cries and lamentations of the aforementioned females.*[18]

He did, however, also share with his readers a detailed account of his equipment - and despite having been an enthusiastic user of Fothergill's dry process back in England, he used wet collodion for all his Indian trips.

My photographic requisites consisted of a pyramidical tent ten feet high by ten feet square at the base, very simple in construction, having merely a bamboo rod at each of the four corners, and opening and closing like an umbrella. This, though only one man's load, will seem like a ponderous article when compared with the tents used in England; but in this country I could not work in one of those little suffocating boxes without any elbow room and without ventilation. I like to have plenty of both, as I am jealous of the bloom which I have hitherto retained on my cheeks, and of the hale and robust constitution with which nature has blessed me. My stock of glass consisted of 250 plates 12x10 and 400 plates 8x4 1/2. I had two boxes of chemicals divided into compartments, each bottle fitting into its own compartment – one box being a duplicate of the other – so that if one should "come to grief" down some precipitous mountain, I might have the other to fall back upon. Besides these I had my field box, and a "khilta" full of stock or spare chemicals. My cameras, two in number, were of the square bellows form, very light and portable, fitted with Grubb's aplanatic and Dallmeyer's triplet lenses; the doublets and triple singlets were not then out. One box contained my two mounted glass baths, which were absurdly heavy, camera top, and sundry loose articles. Another contained four Winchester quart bottles – two for bath solutions, one for spirits of wine, and the other for distilled water. The lids of all these boxes were padded, so that when closed they fitted moderately tight on the stoppers of the bottles, which were all of the same height, thus preventing them from shaking loose, and obviating the necessity of typing them down every time after using. In all, my photographic requisites formed about twenty loads; the remainder consisted of personal baggage, tents, bedding, 'batterie de cuisine', hermetically-sealed stores, a good supply of Hennessy's brandy in lieu of "Bass" and "Allsopp", sporting requisites, books, camp furniture, &c., &c.[19]

After his second major expedition into the mountains, Bourne returned to England for his marriage in 1867, returning to Calcutta where he supervised the opening of the new Bourne & Shepherd studio there. It seems probable that he and his new wife lived at least part of the year in Calcutta, but he is unlikely to have expected her to endure Calcutta summers.

In 1870, with the business hugely successful and studios operating in Bombay as well as Simla and Calcutta, Bourne and Shepherd went their separate ways, with Bourne returning to England with his wife and child for yet another change of career – running a business in the cotton industry with his brother-in-law. The passion for photography which had provoked him to give up his career in banking and go into partnership with Howard in Shimla had lasted little more than a decade.

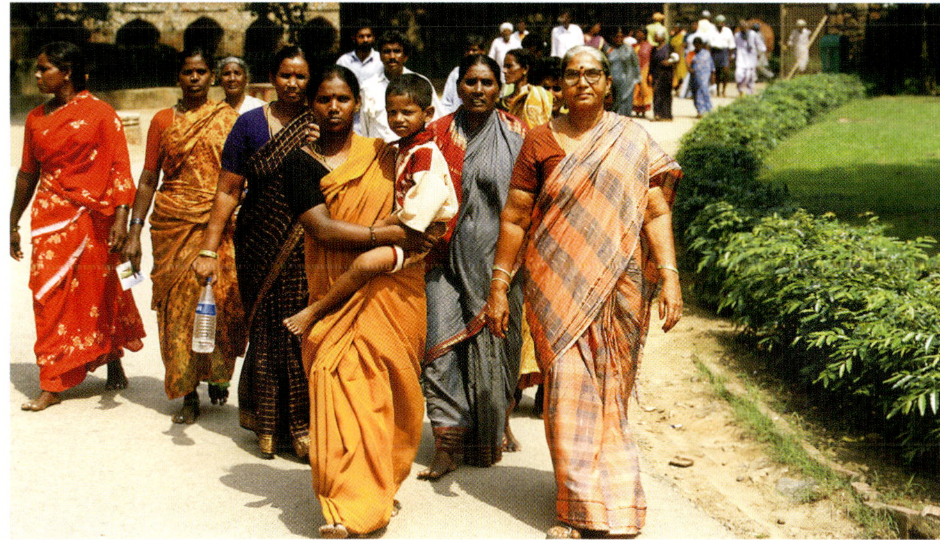

above: These women walking towards the ruined Quwwat-ul-Islam Mosque in Delhi epitomise one of the most enduring images of India – rich bright colours.

Before Bourne's departure, he and Charles Shepherd had welcomed Charles Murray into the business, initially as an employee, but from 1872 as a partner effectively in charge of the company's new studio in Bombay.

Murray's talents as an architectural and landscape photographer were at least matched by his abilities as a portraitist and with Shepherd, he and others took the business into new directions and new heights of success.

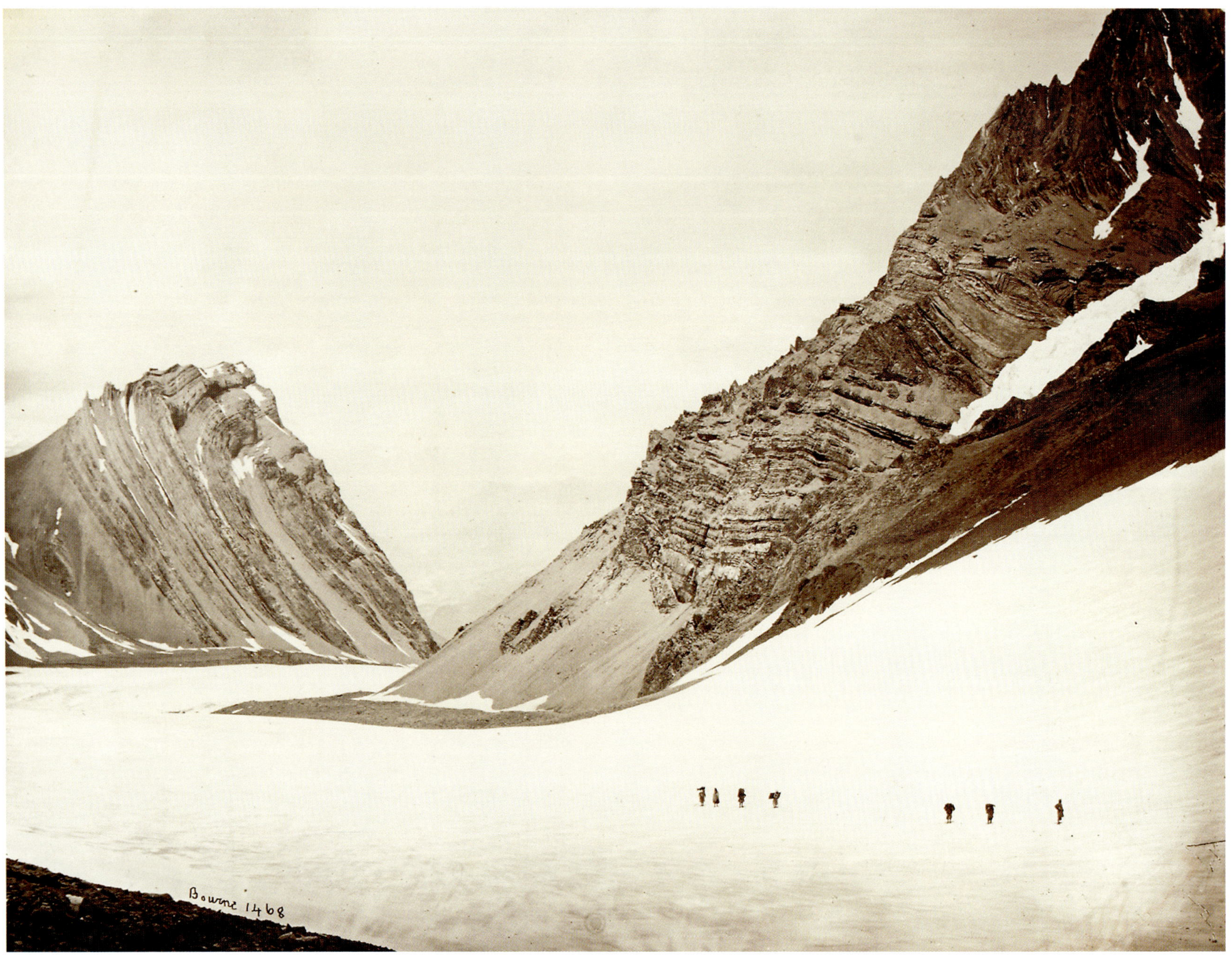
Bourne 1468

Bourne finally severed all ties with the company in 1874, and by the time Shepherd left India in the mid 1880s, the Calcutta studio was being managed by one J.E.Shirmer, and by 1888, the wonderfully named W. McClumpte was listed in trade directories as the general manager of all the company's studios.

A number of changes of ownership followed, before the individual studios were established as separate 'associate' companies.

During the Royal Visit of 1911, King George V and Queen Mary were photographed by Bourne & Shepherd photographers during the *Durbar* held to mark the King's Coronation. It was at that event that the King-Emperor announced the moving of the capital from Calcutta to New Delhi. Old Delhi had been the capital before the British arrived.

By the 1920s, when the new premises were opened in Banerjee Road, only the Calcutta operation retained the 'Bourne & Shepherd' name which it still uses today.

According to the present owners, the studio was bought by Arthur Musselwhite in the early 1930s, and he continued to operate the business throughout the Second World War - during which time lucrative contracts for photographing British, American and Indian military personnel contributed to a period of considerable success. But by the 1950s, with the British gone, Musselwhite had seen his business contract considerably, and he put the studio up for auction. It was bought in 1955 by William Walker, Varjivan Jaitha and S.J.Suraiya but they operated it only for a few months - making Walker the last European owner of Bourne & Shepherd.

By 1957 Qimat Jindal was the sole proprietor, diversifying into developing and printing services, and the present owners, Jayant Gandhi and others, bought the Bourne & Shepherd name and the Banerjee Road premises in 1964.[20]

With hindsight, they bought a potential goldmine, for in the upper floors of the building was an archive of a century's

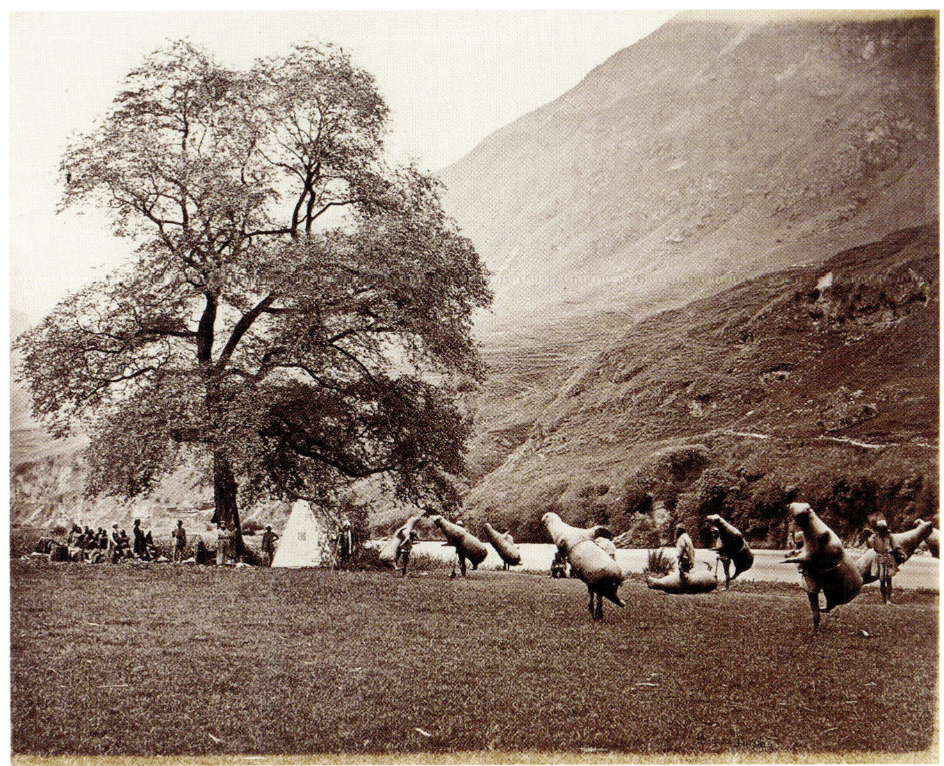

opposite page: This remarkable view was taken in the autumn of 1866, during Bourne's third trip into the Himalayas in search of the source of the Ganges - a journey which took him and his camera further and higher into the mountain range than any photographer before him. This image superbly captures the beautiful emptiness of the landscape of Northern India.

above: Mussocks Crossing the Bea River, August 1866. Under the tree what is believed to be Bourne's yellow calico dark tent can be seen and, to the left, part of his retinue of servants and coolies, waiting to cross. The 'mussock men' used inflated buffalo skins to cross the river, sitting astride the skins while they ferried both passengers and goods across the waters.

images by Bourne, by Shepherd, and all their successors – hundreds of original glass plates including many dating back to Bourne's first photographic expeditions in the 1860s.

It is, perhaps, a reflection of India's relative disregard for its Victorian past that the true value of that holding was never fully understood. It remained unconserved, incompletely catalogued, and stored in far from ideal conditions in the attic of a hot and humid building. It was, in fact, little more than an occasional additional source of income, with prints being made on demand from a relatively small number of selected negatives. Bourne & Shepherd did advertise this service locally, but there is little evidence that demand was ever very great. Surprisingly, and sadly, the logic of passing the archive to a museum where it could be conserved appropriately was apparently never considered. While elsewhere in the world, the surviving output of the greatest Victorian photographers was being avidly sought and preserved, the world seems to have been sadly unaware that the Bourne and Shepherd negative archive had survived at all.

Then, as recently as 1991, disaster struck. A devastating fire gutted the upper floors, destroying all the original negatives, leaving only the small collection of contact prints Mr. Gandhi kept downstairs. All of Bourne & Shepherd's immense and irreplaceable output had been lost in the space of a few hours. Part of the top floor of the building was subsequently declared beyond repair and was demolished. The state of the building today might suggest that the remainder will follow it soon.

Notes

1. The setting up of the Nottingham Photographic Society was reported in *Photographic Notes*, December 15, 1858, p291.
2. *Photographic News*, January 14 1859, p226. The exhibition was open to the public from January 7-15 1859.
3. Quoted in *The Photographic Journal*, January 15 1859, p23-24.
4. Samuel Bourne: "On Some of the Prerequisites Necessary for the Production of a Goof Photograph" in *The Photographic News*, February 24 1860, pp296-298.
5. Quoted in the *British Journal of Photography*, February 1 1860, p42.
6. Samuel Bourne: "On Some of the Prerequisites Necessary for the Production of a Good Photograph" in *The Photographic News*, February 24 1860, pp296-298. Further extracts appeared in subsequent issues. The lecture was also published in the *Nottingham Atheneum Society Magazine*, in August, October and December 1860 pp5-42 and 68-73.
7. Pauline F Heathcote: "Samuel Bourne of Nottingham" in *History of Photography* Volume 6 No.2, April 1982, p100.
8. Suggested in Gary D Simpson: 'Samuel Bourne in India' in *History of Photography,* Volume 16 No.4, winter 1992, p13.
9. Samuel Bourne, "Photography in the East", in the *British Journal of Photography*, July 1 1863, p269.
10. *ditto*
11. Samuel Bourne, "Photography in the East", in the *British Journal of Photography*, July 1 1863, p270.
12. Samuel Bourne, "Photography in the East", in *the British Journal of Photography,* September 1 1863, p345.
13. *ditto*
14. *ditto*
15. *ditto*
16. James Mudd"The Artistic Arrangement of the Photographic Landscape" in *The Liverpool & Manchester Photographic Journal*, 1857, p43. Mudd's comments about the pursuit of the picturesque included *What delightful hours we have passed in wandering through the quiet ruins of some venerable abbey, impressing with wondrous truth, upon the delicate tablets we carried, the marvellous beauty of Gothic window, of broken column, and ivy-wreathed arch. How pleasant our visits to moss-green old churches, and stately castles, and a thousand pretty nooks, in the shady wood by the river side or in the hedge rows, where the twining wild convolvulus, the bramble, the luxuriant fern, have arrested us.*
17. Samuel Bourne, "Narrative of a Photographic Trip to Kashmir (Cashmere) and Adjacent Districts", in the *British Journal of Photography*, October 5 1866, p474.
18. Samuel Bourne, "Narrative of a Photographic Trip to Kashmir (Cashmere) and Adjacent Districts", in the *British Journal of Photography*, October 19 1866, p499.
19. Samuel Bourne, "Narrative of a Photographic Trip to Kashmir (Cashmere) and Adjacent Districts", in the *British Journal of Photography*, October 5 1866, p474.
20. This short history of the studio since 1870 was compiled with the help of the present owner, Jayant Ghandi, who gave generously of his time and knowledge during the early days of my Indian journey.

THE STRAITS OF MALACCA,

INDO-CHINA, AND CHINA;

OR,

TEN YEARS' TRAVELS, ADVENTURES, AND RESIDENCE ABROAD.

BY J. THOMSON, F.R.G.S.,
AUTHOR OF 'ILLUSTRATIONS OF CHINA AND ITS PEOPLE.'

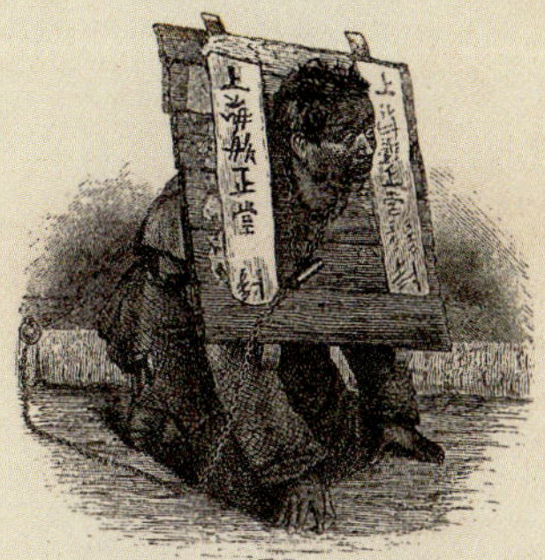

ILLUSTRATED WITH UPWARD OF SIXTY WOOD ENGRAVINGS BY J. D. COOPER,
FROM THE AUTHOR'S OWN SKETCHES AND PHOTOGRAPHS.

NEW YORK:
HARPER & BROTHERS, PUBLISHERS,
FRANKLIN SQUARE.
1875.

John Thomson

Illustrations of China and its People

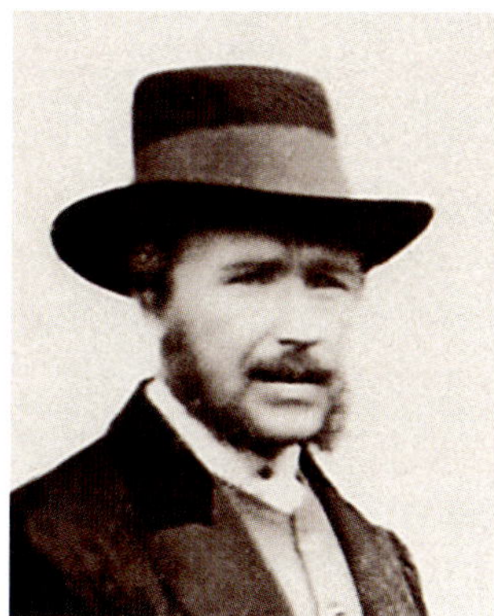

above: John Thomson F.R.G.S., self-portrait, China, 1871

below left: Physic Street Canton – now known as Guangzhou – one of Thomson's evocative illustrations from the book *Illustrations of China and its People*, published in four volumes between 1873 and 1874. Physic Street was one of a maze of narrow trading alleys in Canton, just a few yards from the city's busy harbour on the Pearl River. While the street itself no longer exists, trading is still carried on in many similar streets nearby. The harbour was filled in many years ago, and its location is now covered by a wide dual carriageway. In his caption to this picture, Thomson wrote "Physic Street or, more correctly, Tsiang-Lan-Kiai (our Market Street) as the Chinese term it, is one of the finest streets in Canton, and, with its array of brightly coloured sign-boards presents an appearance no less interesting than picturesque."

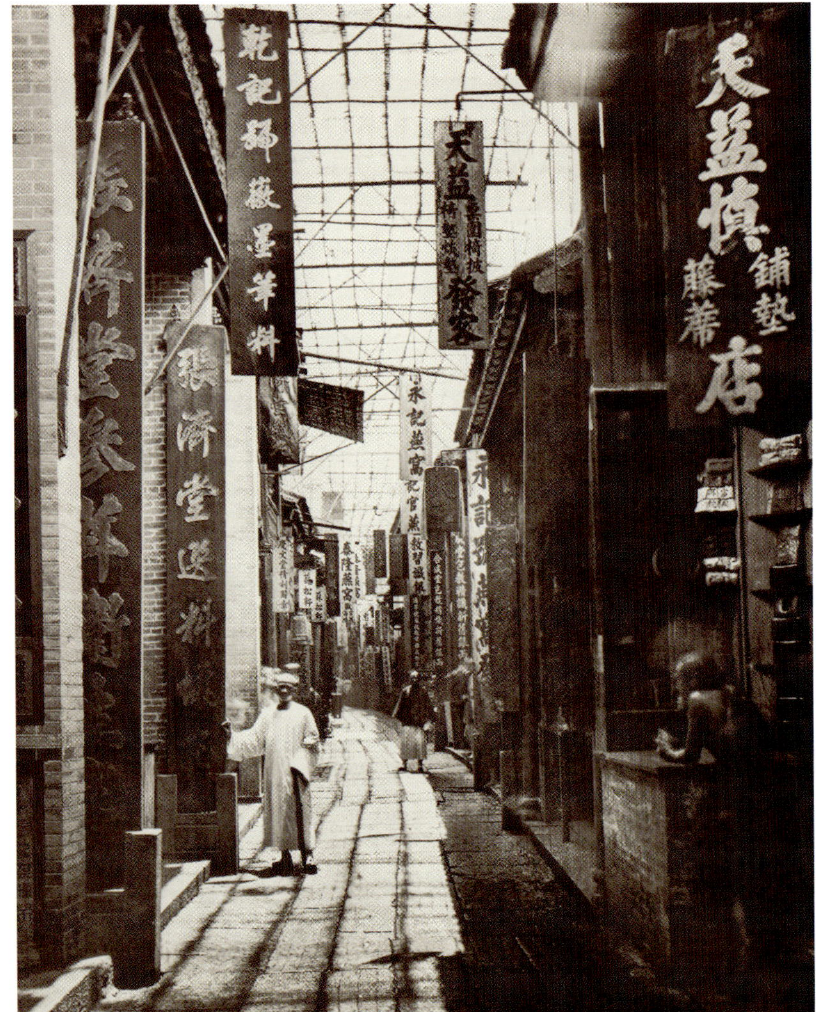

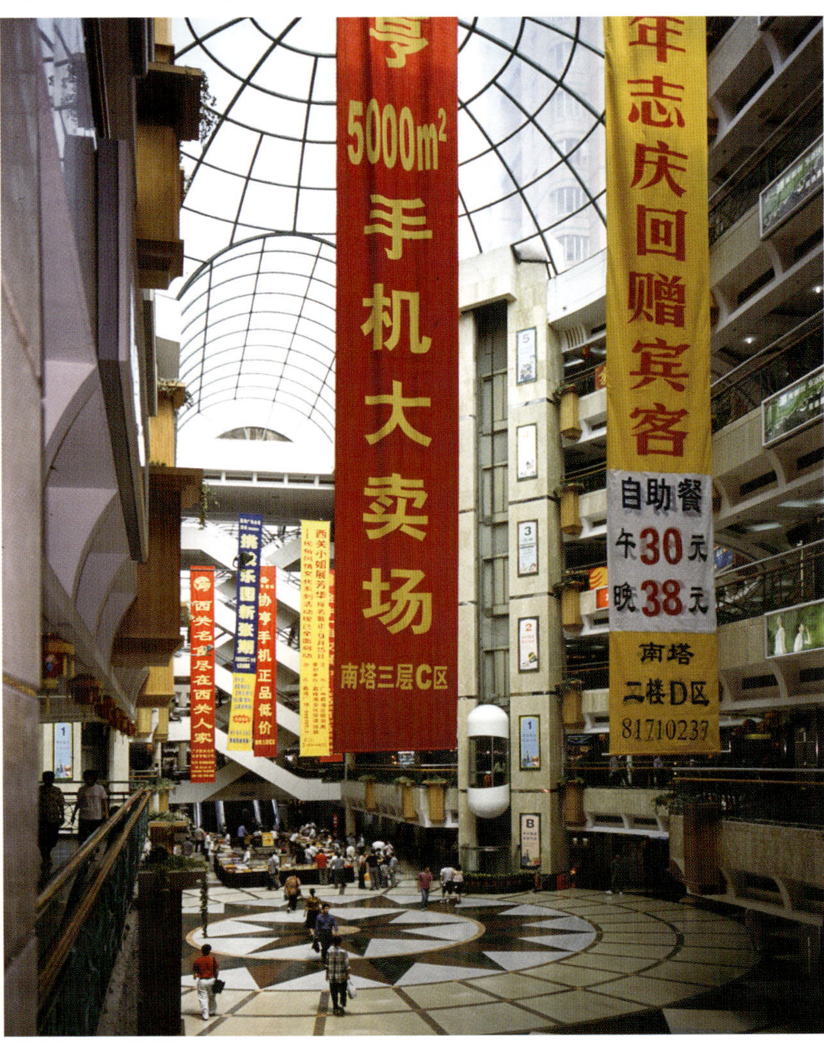

above right: The spirit of Physic Street lives on in a modern shopping mall only a short disance from where the old street once stood.

The Scottish photographer John Thomson was by no means the first to visit China with a camera - that honour goes to the Frenchman Jules Itier some twenty five years before him - but Thomson's book *Illustrations of China and its People* published in 1873/4 was a first.[1] It was the first to present a photographic view of the country which combined architectural images with pictures of the people, their activities and their lifestyles.

In that respect, it was a true travelogue in the modern sense, seeking through words and pictures to capture that often-elusive 'sense of place' which brings good travel books to life.

He took his camera to places where no other photographer had been, and in the introduction to the book he noted that

> *I therefore frequently enjoyed the reputation of being a dangerous geomancer, and my camera was held to be a dark mysterious instrument, which, combined with my naturally, or supernaturally, intensified eyesight gave me the power to see through rocks and mountains, to pierce the very souls of the natives, and to produce miraculous pictures by some black art, which at the same time bereft the individual depicted of so much of the principle of life as to render his death a certainty within a very short period of years.*
>
> *Accounted – for these reasons – the forerunner of death, I found portraits of children difficult to obtain while, strange as it may be thought in a land where filial piety is esteemed the highest of virtues, sons and daughters brought their aged parents to be placed before the foreigner's silent and mysterious instrument of destruction.*[2]

Today's children demonstrated no such fear, invariably positioning themselves directly in front of the camera, waving and shouting 'hello'.

With an almost journalistic approach - way ahead of its time - Thomson's book explored a country about which the people back at home in Britain knew little or nothing.

To a degree, we still know relatively little about China today, although that situation is changing rapidly.

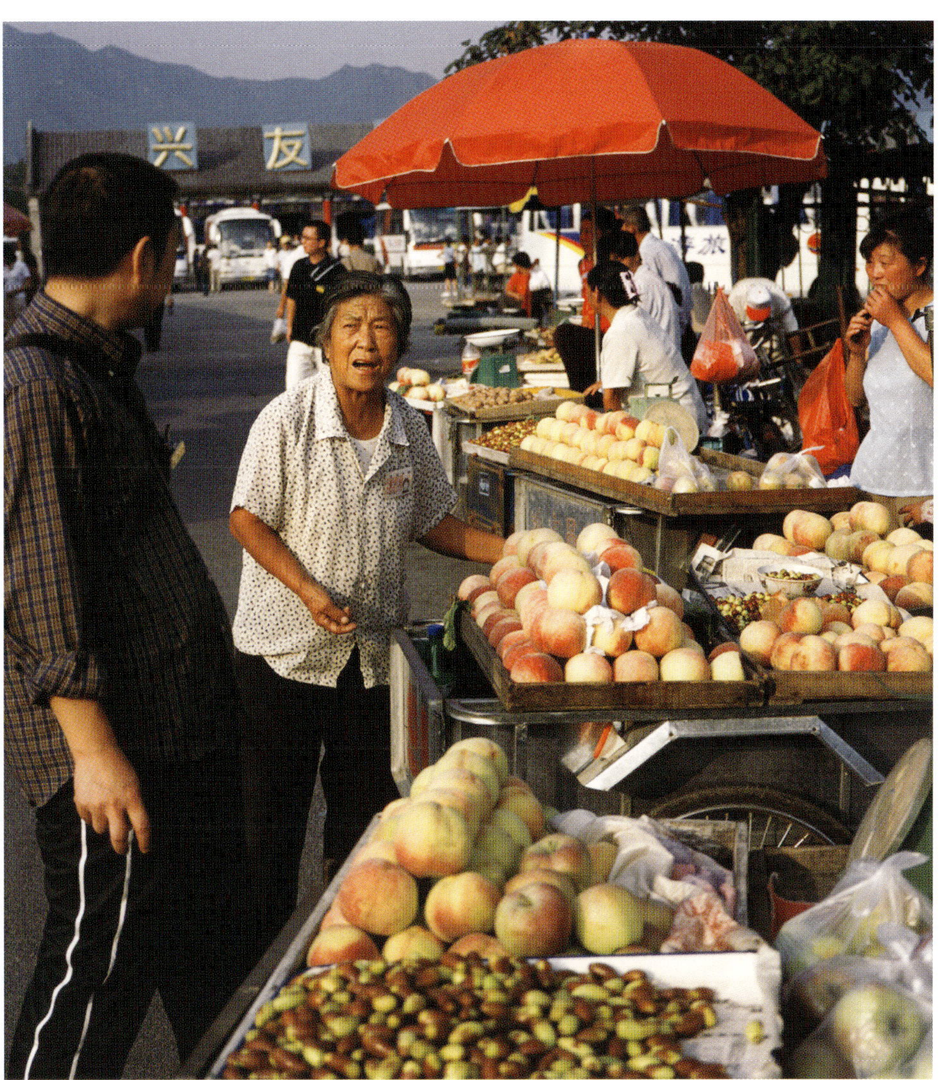

below: At Shisan Ling, near the Ming Tombs, in an open-air market, traders work well into the evening, staying open as long as the car park remains well supplied with tourist coaches.

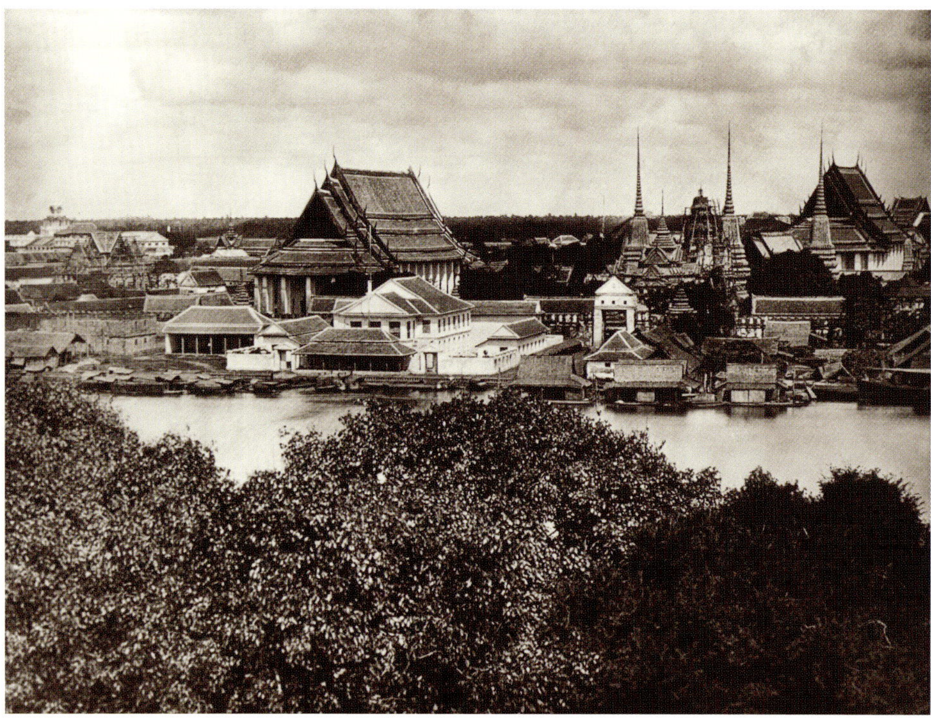

above: View of Bangkok from the River Menam, 1865/66, one of the Siamese series which was later published in Walter Bentley Woodbury's *Treasure Spots of the World* in 1875, and titled *Bangkok, Capital of Siam*. It was one of two views Thomson contributed to the book, the other being *Amoy Harbour, China*, taken in 1871 or 1872. Thomson also wrote the accompanying texts for both pictures.

Thomson was fascinated by travel and by what he recognised as the immense power of photography to educate and inform.

He moved to the Far East in the early 1860s, first visiting Singapore, and then living for almost a year in Penang. In 1863 he opened a successful studio in Singapore, from where he made several journeys to neighbouring countries - including China, Ceylon and India. He sold the studio after only two years, and then travelled extensively in Siam (Thailand) in 1865, and in Laos and Cambodia in the spring and summer of 1866, spending a few weeks in Vietnam before temporarily returning home to Edinburgh in the late summer.

In 1866 he was elected as a Fellow of the Royal Geographical Society, and proudly thereafter always styled himself 'FRGS', maintaining an almost lifelong association with the Society, lecturing, advising, instructing members in the challenges of expedition photography, and otherwise supporting the Society's many activities. He became an Honorary Life Fellow in 1917.

Shortly after returning to Scotland in 1866, he wrote about his experiences as a photographer in the Far East in an illuminating series of articles for the *British Journal of Photography*[3], offering advice to any other photographers who might wish to tackle the wet collodion process under the extreme conditions he had experienced in Singapore and elsewhere.

Through those articles, we know a great deal about his techniques, and about the way in which the photographer had to be ever-willing and able to modify the already-tricky process to cope with the demands which extreme conditions of heat and humidity placed upon him

He was, by 1866, absolutely convinced of the value of publishing his photographic essays in book form, with accompanying explanatory texts, and in 1867 his first travel book, *The Antiquities of Cambodia* was published.[4]

Returning east later that year, he visited Vietnam along the way, arriving in Hong Kong in 1868.

A royal visit to Hong Kong by the then Duke of Edinburgh in 1869 gave Thomson the opportunity to take a fine series of images of Victoria Harbour full of ships, a vivid contrast from today's scene. The local Chinese, who came to see the Duke were disappointed at finding him, as Thomson described,

> *only a man after all, attired in the simple uniform of a captain; with no display of purple and fine linen, and with none of the mystic emblems of royalty to hedge his dignity around. A very different being this, surely, from the offspring of their own great Emperor, who is brother of the sun, and kinsman to the moon, on whose radiant countenance no common mortal can look and live.*

Within the harbour, he noted that

> *Ships of all nations vied in the splendour of their decorations; long lines of merchant boats guarded the approach to the wharf; and on a thousand native crafts, adorned with flags and shreds of gaudy cloth, appeared the dusky multitudes of the floating population, swarming over the decks, or clinging to the rigging of their vessels.* [5]

Today the scene between the Kowloon peninsula and Hong Kong Island is much less animated but none the less interesting – the fifty-year old Star ferries ply their way across the narrow strip of water, while cargo ships and cruise liners make their through the narrow waterway. The main commercial activity has now moved west to the huge container ports. And of course the harbour is much narrower than it was in Thomson's day – as more and more land has been reclaimed from the sea and built upon.

At the time of his visit, Hong Kong had been a British colony for less than thirty years, having been ceded to Britain by the Treaty of Nanking in 1842 – ratifying a state of affairs which had effectively been in existence since the previous year.

Thomson noted that there were no cabs in Hong Kong – sedan chairs being the only public conveyances. In today's city, red and white cabs in their thousands compete for space in the narrow streets with elderly tram cars – and

below: The Hong Kong waterfront today is unrecognisable as the location for Thomson's 1868 view, yet Thomson's accompanying text would still apply!
bottom: The same view, the Praya, photographed by Thomson from the Parade Ground. He described the architecture then as 'massive and strong'.

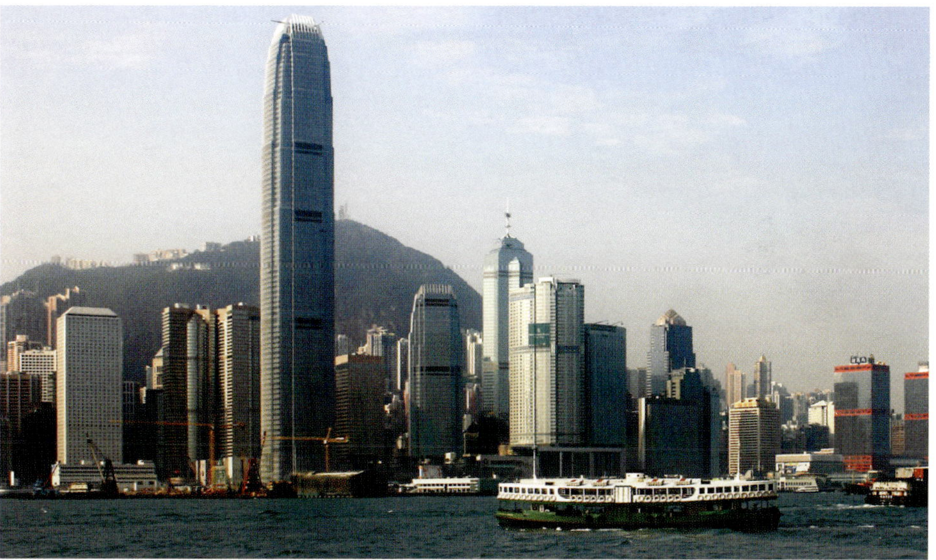

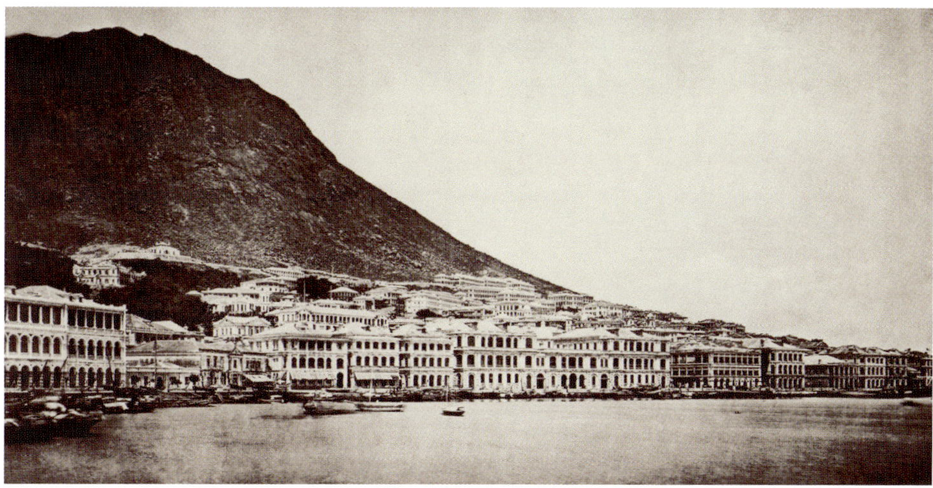

right: The Hong Kong Sedan Chair, as photographed by Thomson in the early 1870s, was the only form of public transport at the time, and popular amongst all but the poorest classes of local society.

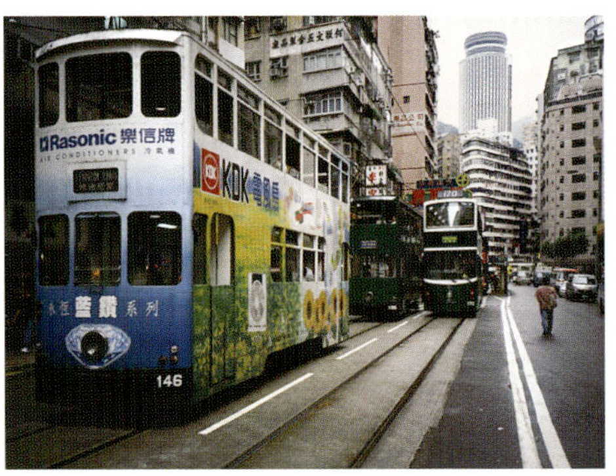

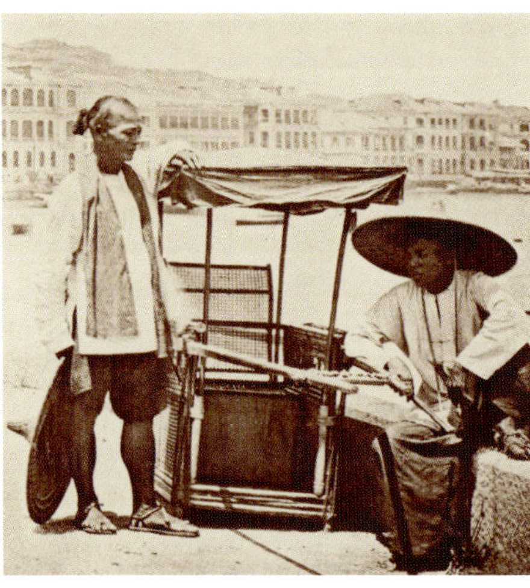

above: Elderly trams trundle back and forth along streets only a few minutes walk from the waterfront – some of them once ran along the streets of Glasgow more than half a century ago!
right: A busy street in Hong Kong. The city today offers some striking visual contrasts between the old and the new.

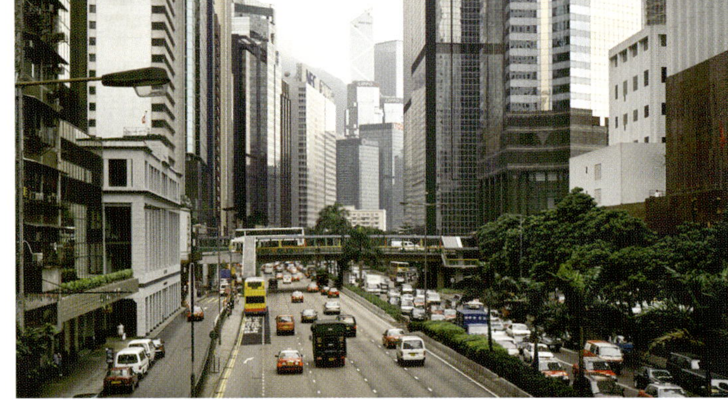

a few modern ones – and endless queues of huge double decker buses.

In Thomson's day, the sedan chair was also a means of identifying rank – the more chair coolies you had in attendance, the higher your social standing. British military officers, Thomson noted in his description of the sedan chair, were specifically barred from using such conveyances and, if they were unwilling to walk, they were expected to ride around Victoria city on horseback.

Just like today's taxis, even in the early 1870s public chairs were licensed, and each carried a card with the tariffs clearly explained – from ten cents for a short journey, to two dollars for the entire day.

The Hong Kong equivalent of today's white Rolls Royce – as the ultimate wedding transport – was the Bridal Chair, a specially ornamented and gilded sedan with red silk curtains which, as Thomson noted

> *screen the blushing fair one, on the day of marriage from the intrusive vulgar gaze.*

From Hong Kong, Thomson journeyed to the Portuguese colony Macau – reached by a four-hour steamer crossing. He found little to please him. Only one picture appeared in *Illustrations of China and its People* – as plate XXIII in the first of the four volumes – and his text mentions none of the striking buildings which can still be seen there today.

Surprisingly, the great 17th century Jesuit Cathedral of Sao Paulo merits not even a mention, let alone a photograph. Sao Paulo had been burned down during an enormous typhoon in 1853, and the ruin must have dominated the old city – as it still does today. Curiously he does observe that

> *There is now hardly a sign of trade in these once busy streets – or, indeed, of active life in any form – save at noon when tawny worshippers hasten in crowds to the cathedral.*

Macau today is a strange mixture of European and Chinese styles, and the Portuguese influence is evident everywhere. The old buildings are predominantly Portuguese in style, but the increasing number of modern skyscrapers is changing the face of the city completely.

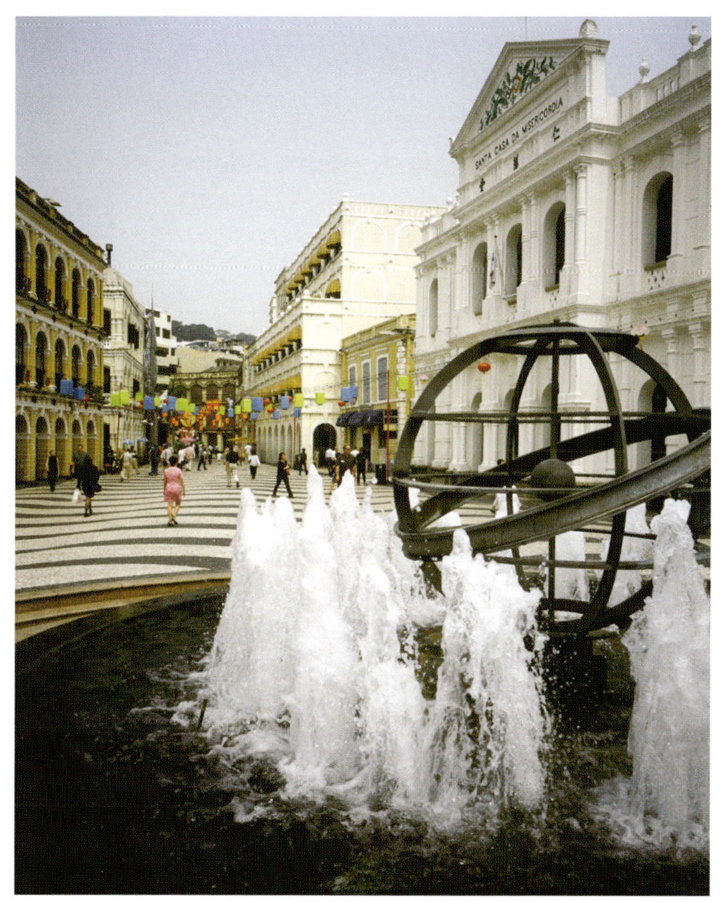

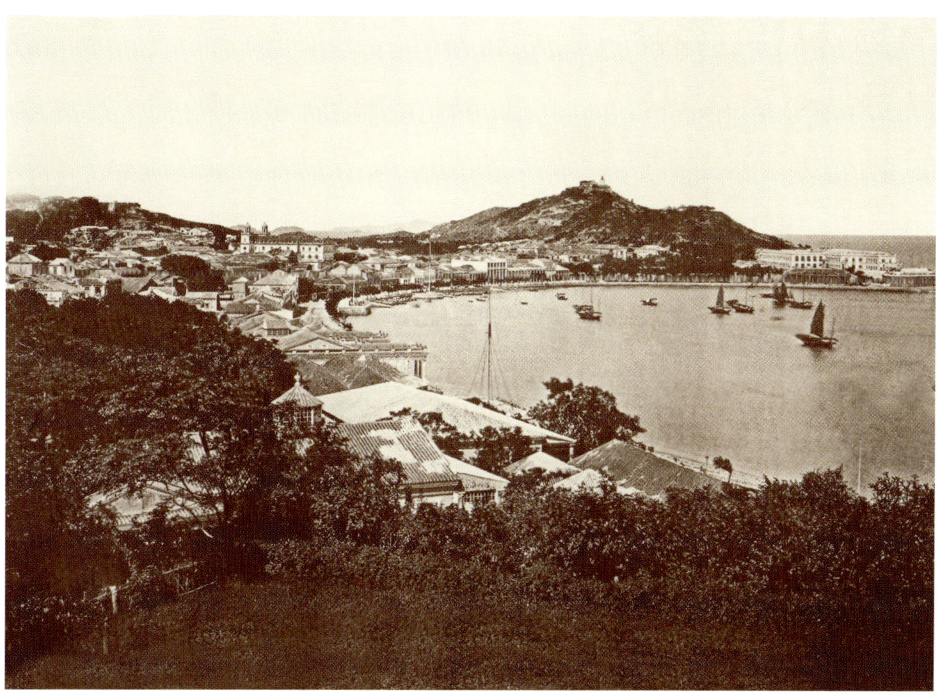

above: The Macau waterfront, as photographed by Thomson. Of this small Portugese colony, he had little to say of merit, except that it was a pleasant location for residents of Hong Kong to visit for a brief holiday!.
left: Today Macau is coming to terms with its status as a Special Economic Region of the People's Republic of China under the "One Nation, Two Systems" policy now in place in both Macau and Hong Kong. The street signs are still in both Portugese and Chinese, and Chinese passport-holders still need a visa to enter either region – so in practical terms little has changed for the average Chinese.

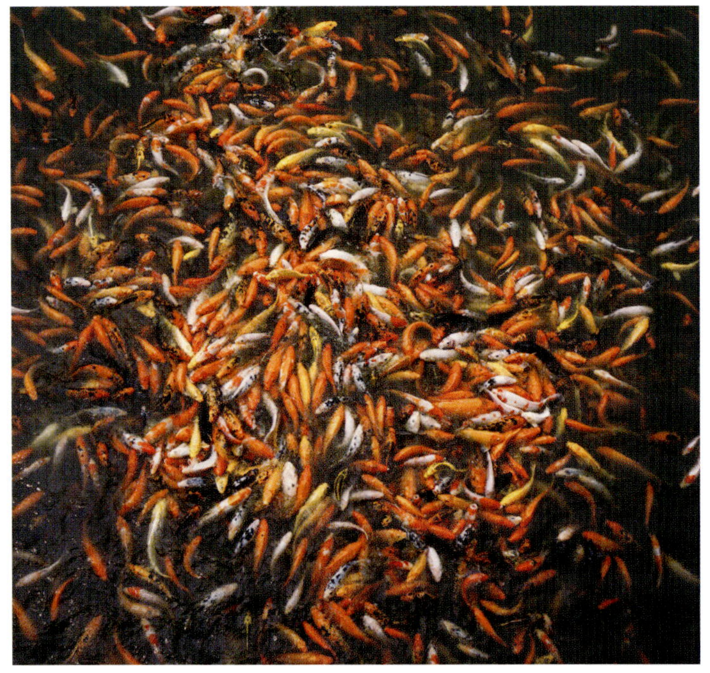

right: Koi in the lake at Liang's Garden, Foshan. Traditional gardens can still be found all over China. They survive as havens of peace and tranquility in an increasingly hectic world.

below: Lou Lim Leoc's Garden, Macau, follows a general pattern for private town gardens which can be traced back centuries. Today it is open free to visitors.

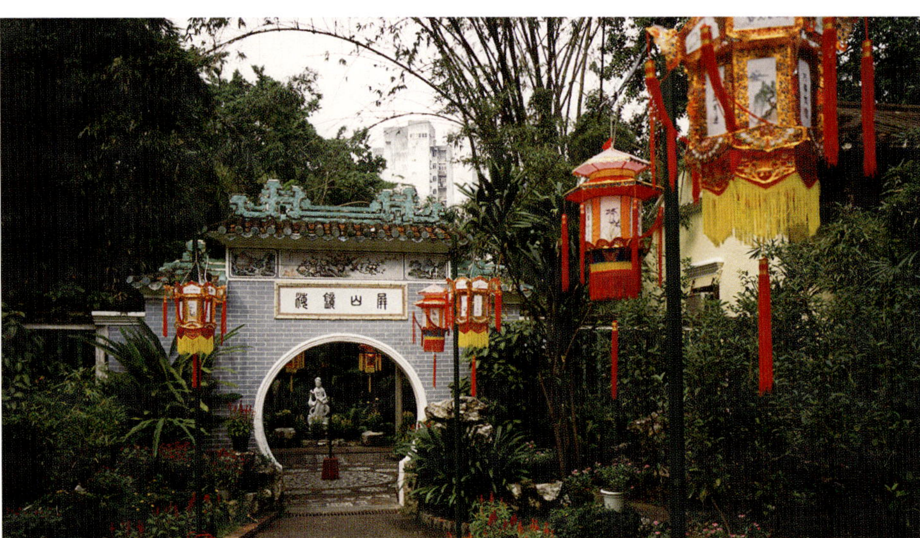

While the Portuguese influences are apparent in the winding streets up to Sao Paulo and the old fortress – now the Macau Museum – reminders of Chinese traditions are never far away. Just a few moments' walk from the ruined cathedral, Lou Lim Leoc's Garden transports the visitor away from the bustle of noisy humid city life and into a quiet oasis of natural beauty, pavilions and lanterns. At the time of visiting, the lake in the centre of the garden was filled with brightly coloured paper lanterns in the shape of birds and other creatures, in celebration of the Chinese mid-autumn festival.

Macau is made up of the main Macau peninsula, and two islands – Taipa and Coloane. Modern bridges and causeways now link the islands with the peninsula, and the new airport's runway has been built on reclaimed land to the east of Ka Ho Bay, linked to the terminal on Taipa by two causeways. It is a curious sight to watch aircraft as they taxi along these narrow causeways out to the runway in the sea.

Macau itself is separated from mainland China by nothing more than a customs post. Once through customs, visitors emerge into the city of Zhuhai. The customs barrier will remain in place until 2047, under the fifty-year promise made when it was returned to the People's Republic of China by Portugal in 1997. From there, a short journey by car took me to Guangzhou – Canton in Thomson's day.

Canton was still a walled city when he arrived, and although he noted that there was little of antiquity in the city, he did find it a good source of subjects for his camera.

As his subjects were China and its people, and the city of Canton had a wide range of industries and occupations, he was able to produce a fascinating series of working portraits, views of temples, factories and other buildings.

In one of the city's temples, he photographed the Buddhist Abbot, a venerable old man who had spent more than half his life in the temple, and whom Thomson had met on his first visit three years earlier.

below: The Queen of Heaven Temple at Ningpo was used as Plate 1 of Vol. III of *Illustrations of China and its People.* It was the meeting place of the Fukien Guild, as well as being a notable Buddhist shrine. Thomson wrote *"I have chosen this edifice as the frontispiece of this volume because it affords one of the finest examples of temple architecture in the Empire, and partly because the subject of Chinese guilds and trades unions is exceedingly important in connection with the social economy of the people. There are masters' guilds, where, at stated times, the current price of products and manufactures are fixed, and there are servants' guilds where, in like manner, the wages of labour are regulated. Judging from the great antiquity of some of these guild houses, trades unions and combinations which are of recent development in our own land, have been in operation in China for centuries."*

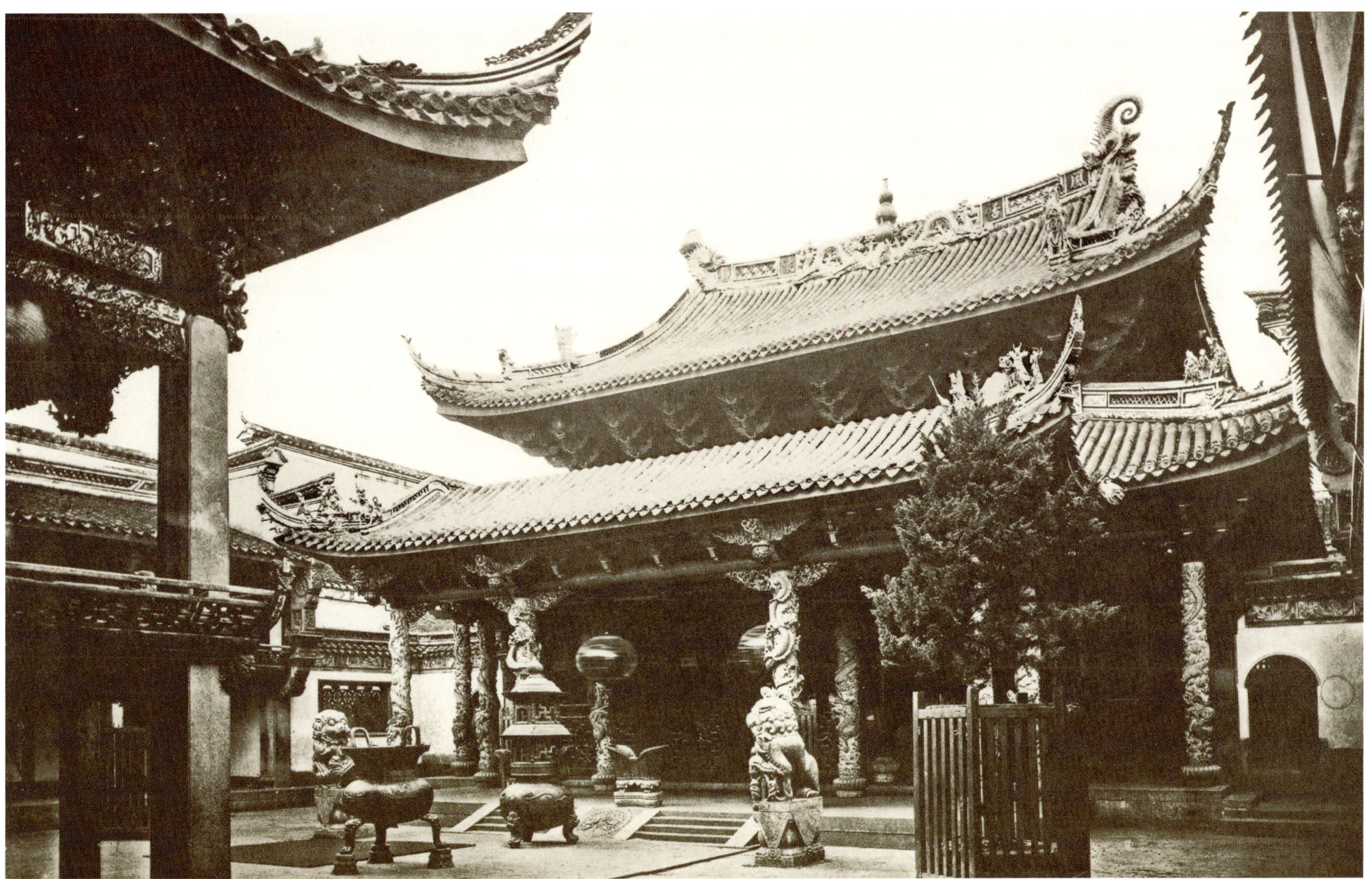

He was, said Thomson

greatly devoted to his flowers, discoursing on their beauty with an eloquent fondness, and expressing his delight to discover in a foreigner kindred sentiments of admiration.

When I visited the city's largest and most important Buddhist shrine, I too met a monk who had spent over half his life in a religious house. But this man's life had embraced everything from farming to fighting for his country in the 1930s and 1940s.

We sat in the warm shade beneath the temple's tall pagoda and talked for over an hour. He had left the mainland for Taiwan in 1960, where he had subsequently spent over forty years in a monastery. This was his first return to the Chinese mainland. He had the appearance of a man completely at peace with himself. At eighty-two years of age, he had a long and fascinating life story to relate and, through an interpreter, we talked of many things. He was as fascinated about life in the West as I was about the changes he had seen in his lifetime, and about his life as a Buddhist monk. After about an hour, he rose, bowed deeply, wished my interpreter and me a long and happy life, and returned to the temple.

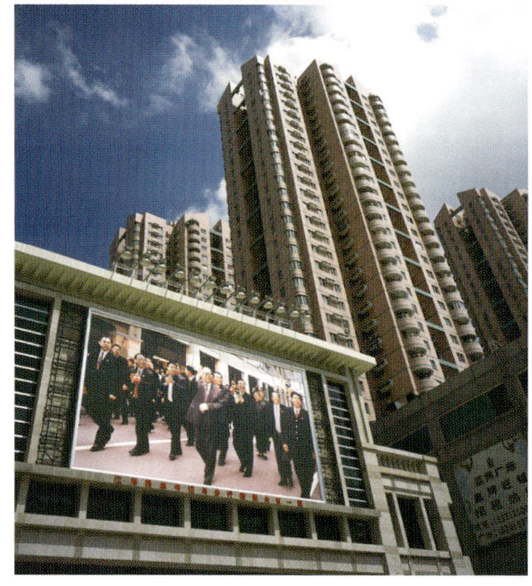

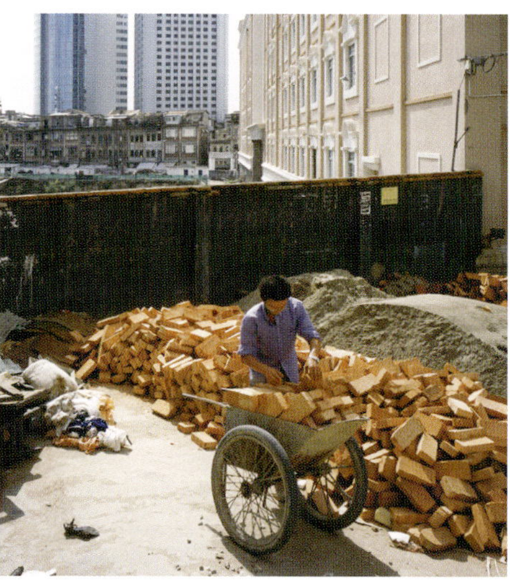

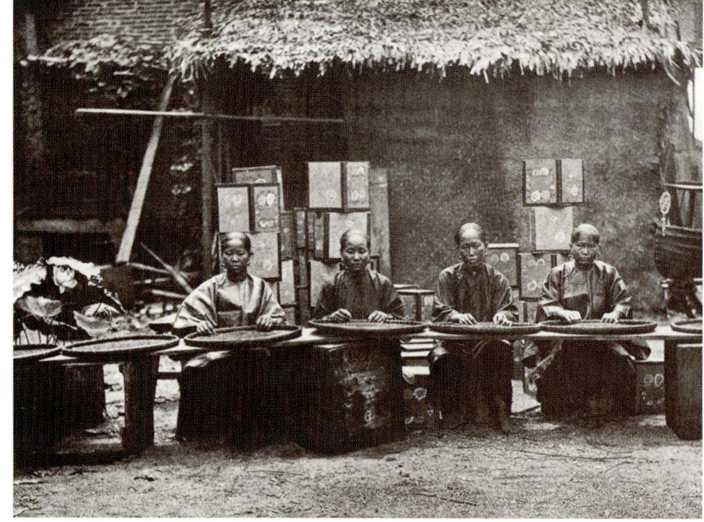

above left: Party officials smile benignly from a large billboard in Guangzhou. *above right:* A bricklayer on a Guangzhou building site – the contrasts between old and modern building practices is striking. In the middle of the building site, a few old houses stand lost amongst the rapidly rising new city. *right:* Tea-pickers, Canton – one of Thomson's many evocative studies from the early 1870s of the Chinese at work.

Like every other city in China, Guangzhou today is a constantly changing mixture of the old and the new. Tall apartment blocks and office blocks are going up everywhere, dwarfing the older low-level housing until it too is swept away.

There are contrasts in scale as well, with huge mechanised building sites operating side by side with others where wheelbarrows and shovels are as common as giant cranes and excavators – the primitive and the modern existing, sometimes uneasily, on opposite sides of a simple wooden fence.

Canton, in Thomson's day, was a major centre of the China tea industry, with plantations in the surrounding countryside, and numerous factories large and small where the tea was dried, blended and prepared for export through the port of Macau. Today that industry is no longer a major

below left: Thomson's photograph of his friend, the Abbot who loved gardening, shows a man who had spent over half of his life in his monastery. *"He received us with great courtesy:* wrote Thomson, *"conducted us to his private apartments, and there refreshed us with tea-cakes and fruit."*
below right: Over one hundred and thirty years later, another Buddhist monk – who had, like Thomson's Abbot, spent over forty years in monasteries – walked in the same temple garden in Guangzhou. The parallels between the lives of the two men brought Thomson's experiences a little closer. This was the man's first return visit to the Chinese mainland after four decades in Taiwan. He had joined the Chinese army as a teenager, and had fought against Japan, returning to his farm after the war and spending fifteen years on the land before becoming a monk.

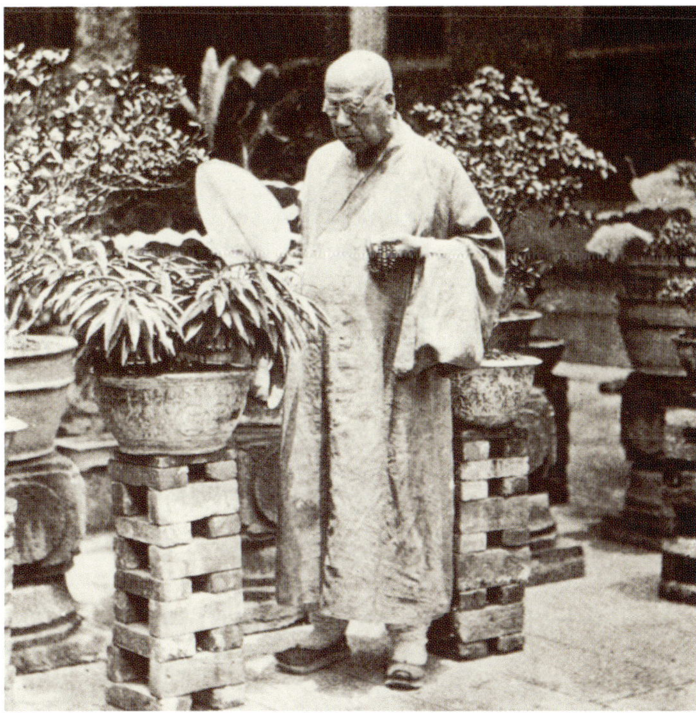

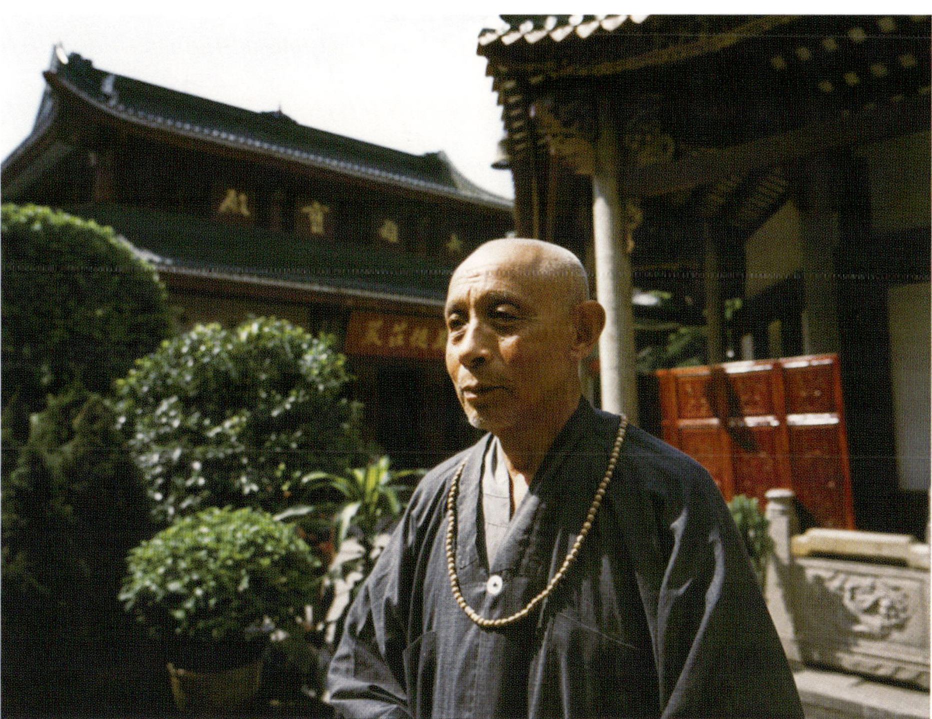

employer in the city, although the local teas are still widely available.

Canton was especially known for its black teas. In the caption to his photograph of tea-pickers, Thomson reported that

> *Black teas, after being partially dried in the sun, and slightly fired, are rolled either by the palm of the hand on a flat tray, or by the foot in a hempen bag. They are scorched in iron pans over a slow charcoal fire, and after this spread out on bamboo trays that the broken stems and refuse leaves may be picked out. It is this operation which is performed by women or children that is shown in the photograph.*[6]

Thomson closed his first volume of words and pictures with his arrival on the island of Formosa, now Taiwan, and in the first few plates of Volume II he explored the island, before sailing back to the Chinese mainland, arriving at the port then known as Swatow, but today as Shantou.

In the 1870s, Swatow was the port for the important city of Chao-Chow fu, a few miles further inland on the Han River, and was the smaller of the two cities. Today

right: Beneath the trees, near the harbour at Shantou, handmade parasols lie open in the dappled sunlight in one of the many stalls which line the waterfront. Although all the larger commercial enterprises in China are joint ventures in which the government retains a stake, small independent operators are allowed to sell their wares wherever they wish. Most small shops and all market stalls are private ventures, selling everything from the essentials of life to luxuries – and, of course, an assortment of souvenirs aimed predominantly at the country's growing tourist market.

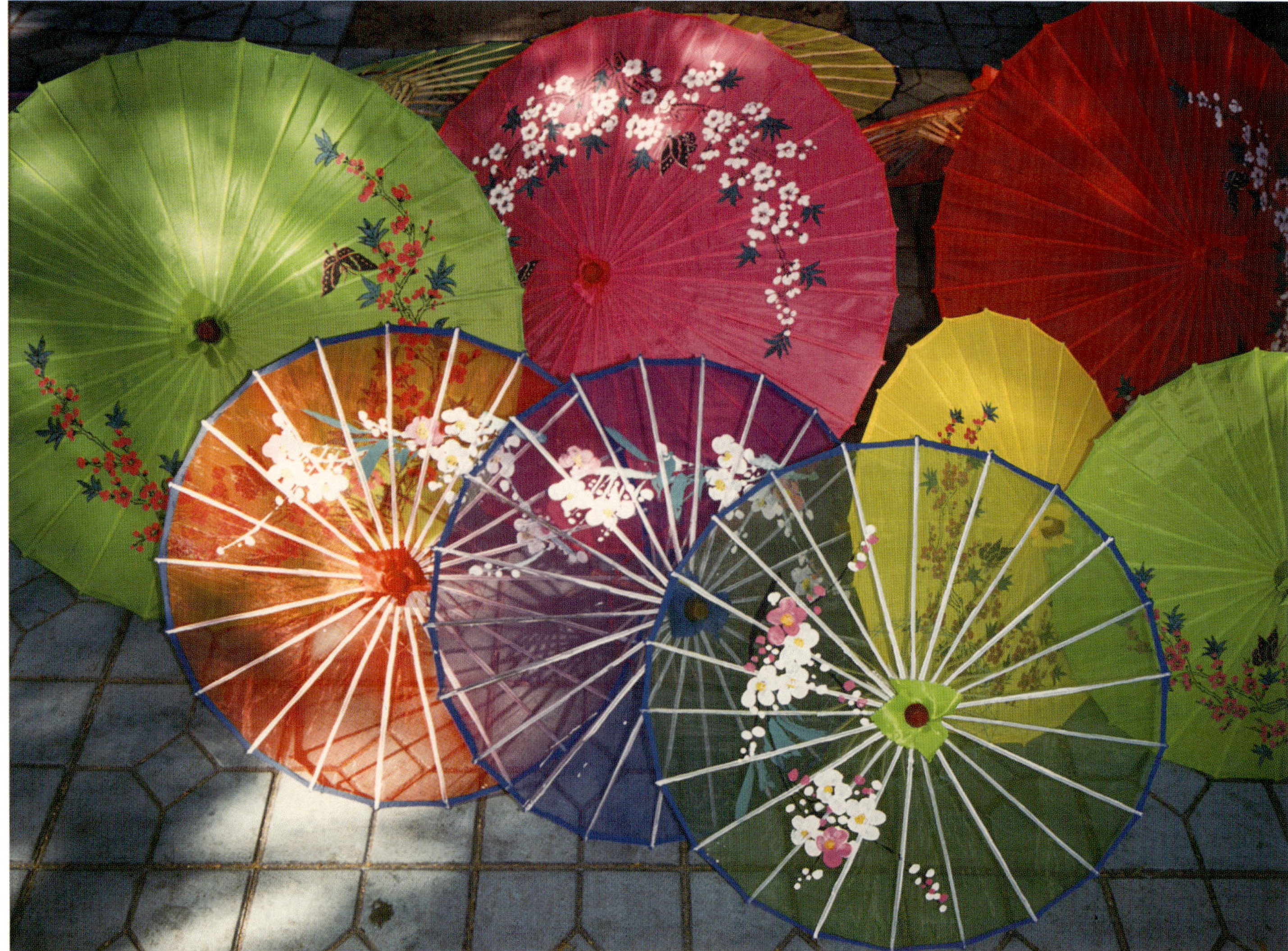

Chouzhou as it is now known, is dwarfed by the city of Shantou.

In Chao-Chow fu he photographed the ancient bridge over the Han River - with houses balanced precariously on top of it - and the riverside Guxi Pagoda, then out in the country, some miles from the city. Today the foundations of the old bridge can still be seen at the waterline of its 1950s replacement - itself sidelined by a bridge more capable of dealing with modern traffic.

Swatow, closer to the mouth of the river, had been one of the first ports to be opened to foreigners, in 1858, so by the time of Thomson's visit, there were already Western influences evident in the houses and other buildings.

In less than ten years, the amount of trade through the port had doubled and, in his account of the place, Thomson listed sugar, rice, paper, chinaware, pottery and grass-cloth as the main exports. Opium was the major import. Over two and a half million pounds worth of trade, both imports and exports, passed through the port in 1870.

The other major export was people, and he noted that twenty thousand Chinese had emigrated through Swatow

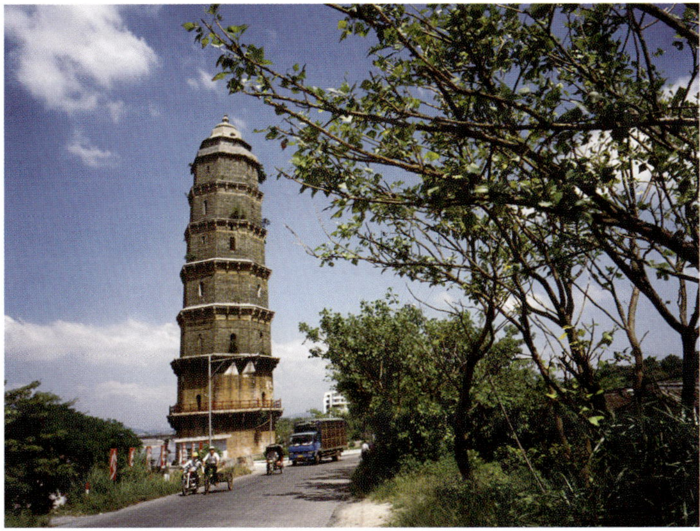

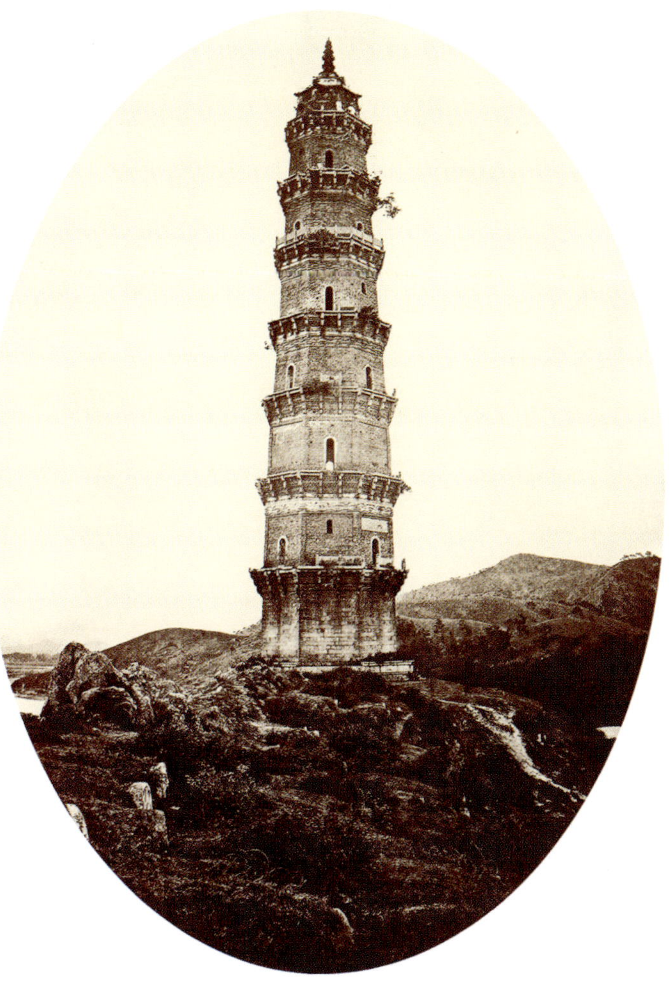

left: Thomson wrote that the Chao-Chow-fu pagoda *"commands an extensive view of the river and the country around"* and surmised that such structures had evolved from defensive look-out towers.
below left: Today it stands by the side of a busy road.

in 1870 alone, looking for something better than the wages they could earn at home. And those must have been low, for Thomson recorded that

> *Wages from two to three dollars a month are all the inducement held out to emigrants, and that such a sum as this is esteemed by the toiling poor sufficient to enable them to save money to invest in farming on their return to their own country.*

By the time he reached Shantou, Thomson had already travelled a considerable distance with his camera, and it is easy to overlook the logistical challenges a journey like his must have posed. As with Roger Fenton, Francis Frith and Samuel Bourne, the physical challenge of transporting equipment was matched by the physical endurance needed to work in the high temperatures which prevailed. While Fenton and Frith both worked in relatively dry heat, Thomson, like Bourne in an Indian summer, had the additional challenge of high humidity, requiring quite different chemical formulations to be experimented with and mastered.

To overcome the problems of heat, Thomson like others before him worked in the early morning.

> *In any part of the east where I have travelled, I have generally found the early morning to be the best time for photographic purposes. There are cloudy days occasionally, when a fine sky may be obtained and good photographs taken any hour. The early morning has, however, many advantages. The temperature is lower, and for an hour or two nature enjoys the most perfect repose; there is not then a breath of wind to stir even the restless leaves of the 'people' tree, and the most delicate stem of long grass bending under the weight of its feathery flower may be photographed without a head-rest;*[7]

Further up the coast, the city of Amoy was Thomson's next port of call. Today, Amoy is known as Xiamen (pronounced Shahmen), and what was a quiet little port more than a century ago, is now a large, modern, and rapidly developing city.

The old centre of Xiamen has been sidelined, and a new modern city built. Street trading traditions of old

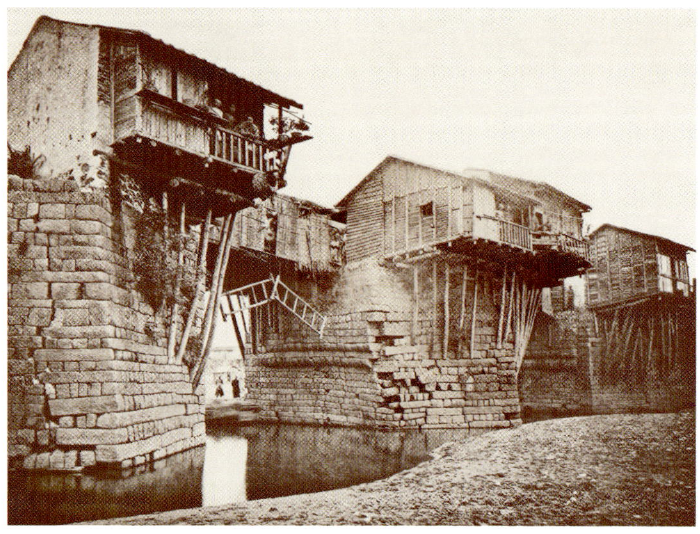

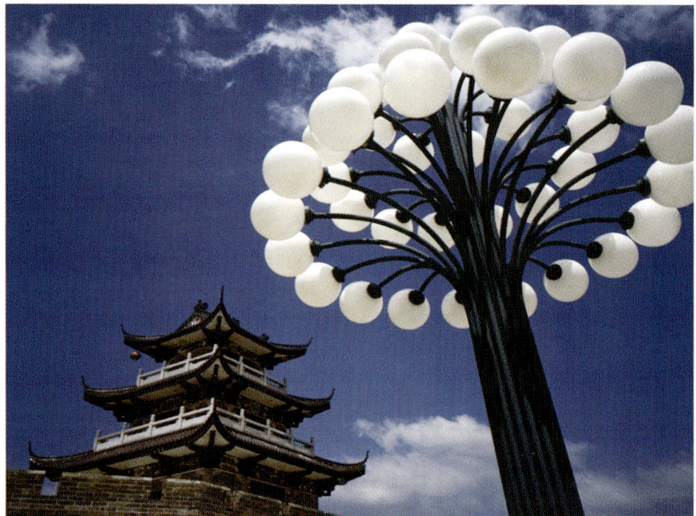

right: The Chao-chow-fu bridge, c.1870. *"When taking the illustration,"* wrote Thomson, *"I endeavoured to avoid the crowd by starting to work at daybreak, but the people were astir, and seeing my strange instrument pointed cannonwise towards their shaky dwellings, they at once decided I was practising some strange outlandish witchcraft against the old bridge and its inhabitants."* The foundations of the old bridge can still be seen in the river today. *below right:* Modern streetlighting contrasts vividly with one of the restored gates into the walled city of Chouzou. The city walls look out over the Han River and on to the 1950s bridge which stands on the site of the old Chau-chow-fu bridge.

still continue in the narrow streets and markets of the old city, while the new centre offers a much more westernised face.

In John Thomson's day, the port of Amoy was a staging point for exports from Formosa and other parts of Fukien province, with sugar and tea accounting for the greatest volume of trade. Sail was just giving way to steam at the time, with steamers offering shorter voyage times, and bringing other ports along the coast within easier reach. Amongst them was Hong Kong and he noted that the import trade from Hong Kong was, by then,

> *in the hands of local Chinese merchants who, if persons of respectability and standing, find every facility afforded to them by the banks in carrying on their commercial undertakings, however small their own capital may be.*

Xiamen itself is an island city, and its landscape fascinated Thomson, although he illustrated his visit with only a single panoramic view of the harbour. He wrote:

> *Historically, this part of the province has a deep interest attached to it, in so far, at least, as European intercourse is concerned. If not the earliest, it was one of the first ports resorted to by European traders – a fact which may be gathered by an inspection of the ancient foreign gravestones bearing Latin inscriptions that are still to be found on the hills of Amoy. The harbour at Amoy is one of the safest and most accessible to be found along the coast of China, nor does its position lack picturesqueness, as it is guarded by an array of bold granite rocks, upon which the natives look with awe and reverence, while the hills around present a multitude of gigantic granite boulders, wearing the most grotesque shapes, and perched in strange disorder on their summits.*[8]

In the old city, street markets sell every foodstuff imaginable. To the western eye, one of the more unusual sights was undoubtedly a harvest of large jellyfish laid out to dry on the pavement in the sun.

With the major shopping streets now some way away, the old centre was almost deserted – in sharp contrast to the bustle in the modern shopping malls. Along the

below: At low tide, the shore of Gulang Yu island plays host to local women scraping limpets from the rocks. This laborious and back-breaking work yields a small harvest of shellfish to flavour a popular local stew served with noodles.

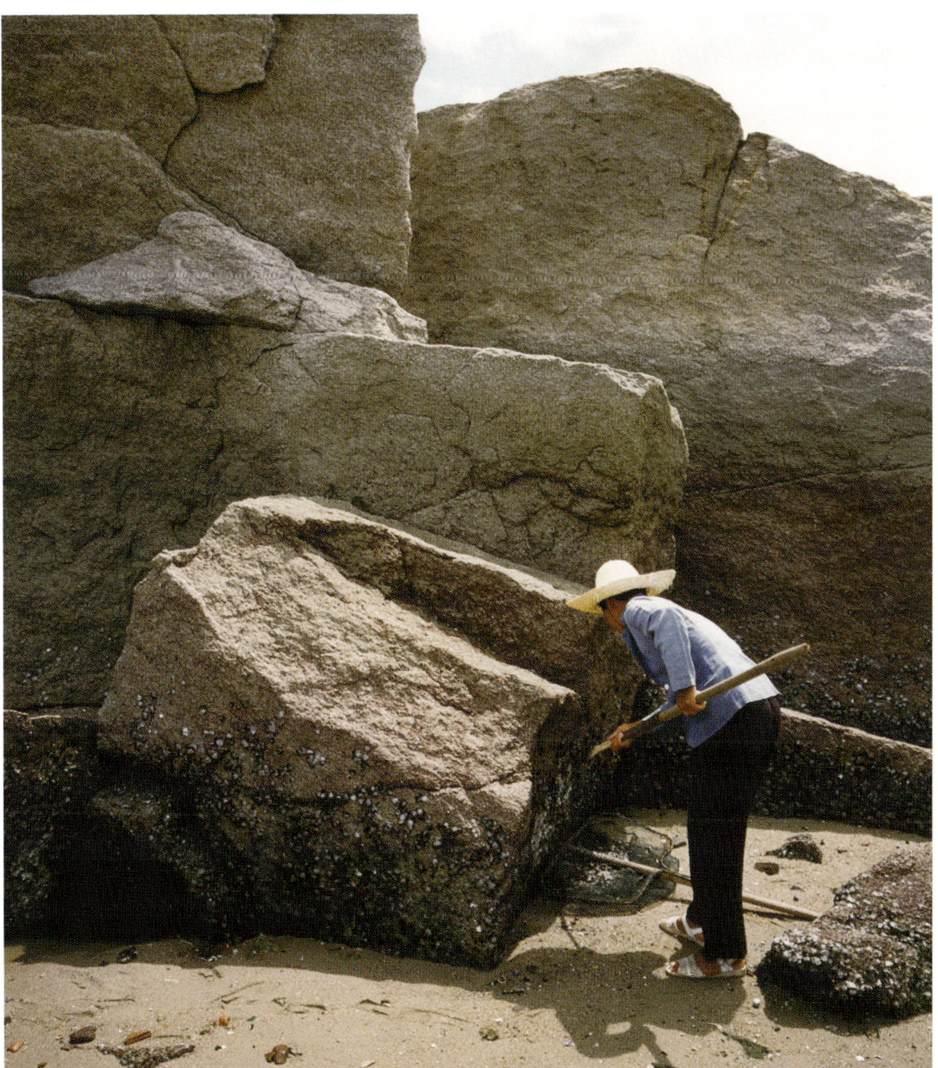

below: The skyscrapers of Xiamen, seen from the shores of Gulang Yu island. Whilst Gulang Yu retains much of its old Chinese and Colonial-style architecture, Xiamen is rapidly developing as a vibrant modern city.

bottom: Thomson's view of the same scene, titled 'Amoy Harbour', showed a safe anchorage in almost rural surroundings. In his description of the place which accompanied the photograph used in Woodbury's *Treasure Spots of the World*, Thomson acknowledged that Amoy was not the local name of the island city – "*the native name of the island is Hia-mun, and it forms one of a group of many such islets that stud the coast of Fukien.*" Hia-mun is not far removed from today's pronunciation of Xiamen.

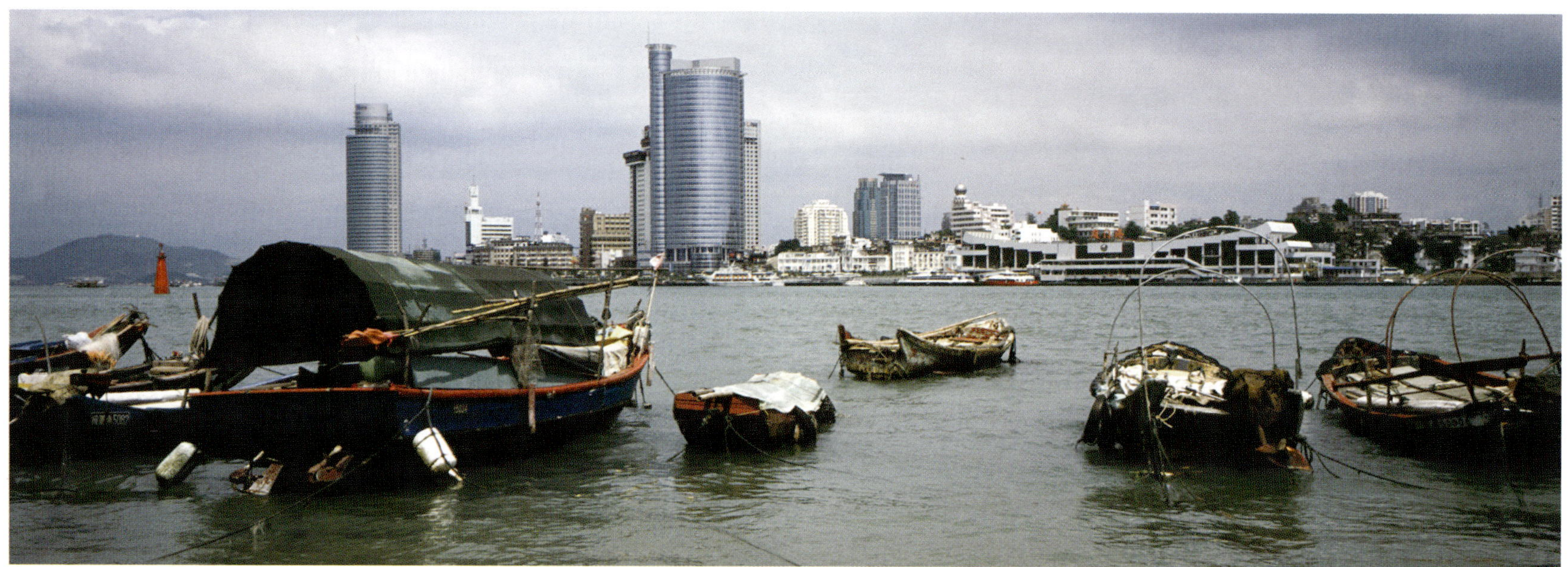

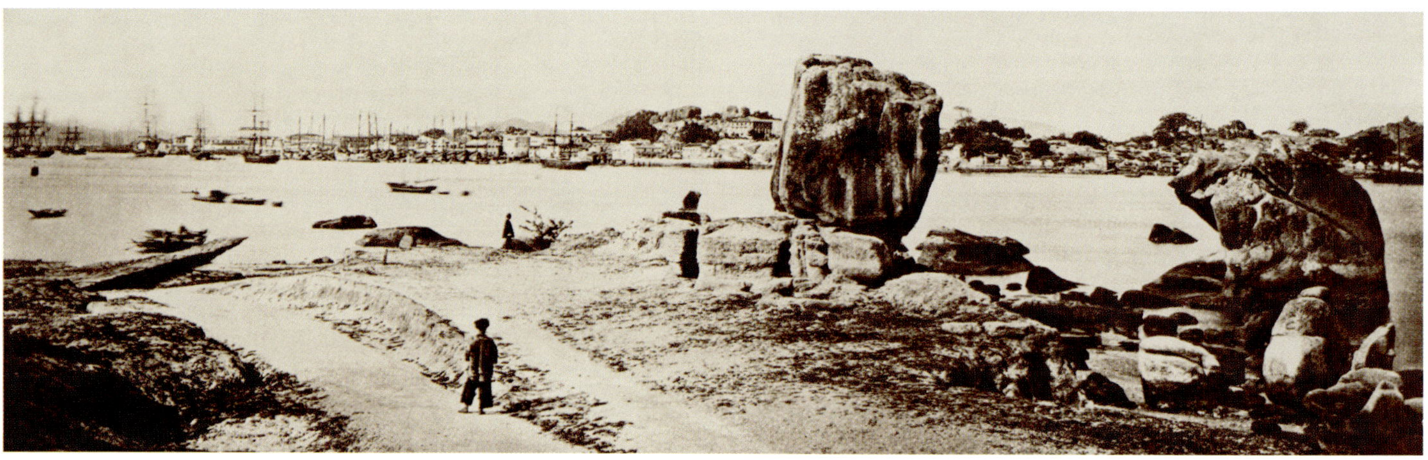

below left: Rows of jellyfish laid out to dry in the early autumn sun.
below right: Half way up the winding street from the ferry jetty on Gulang Yu island, a fish merchant prepares his merchandise for the day. The fish, all alive, may now be in brightly coloured plastic basins rather than wooden troughs, but that is probably all that has changed since Thomson's day. An elaborate array of hosepipes keeps the water cool and the fish fresh until they are sold.

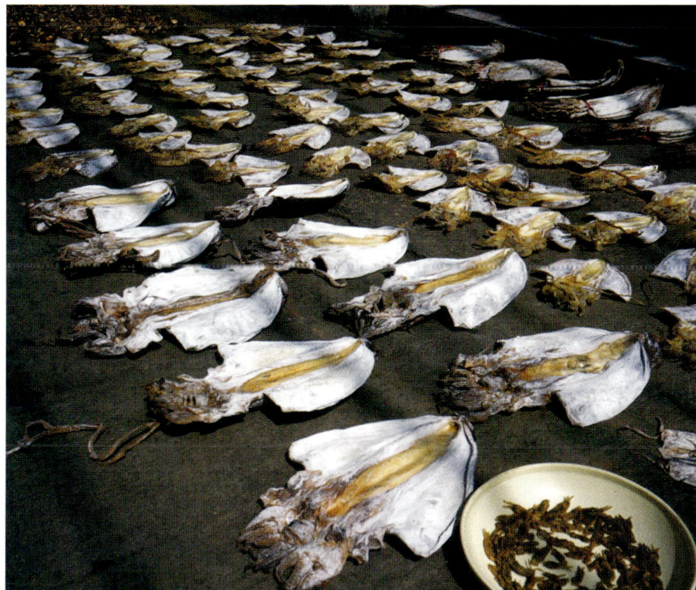

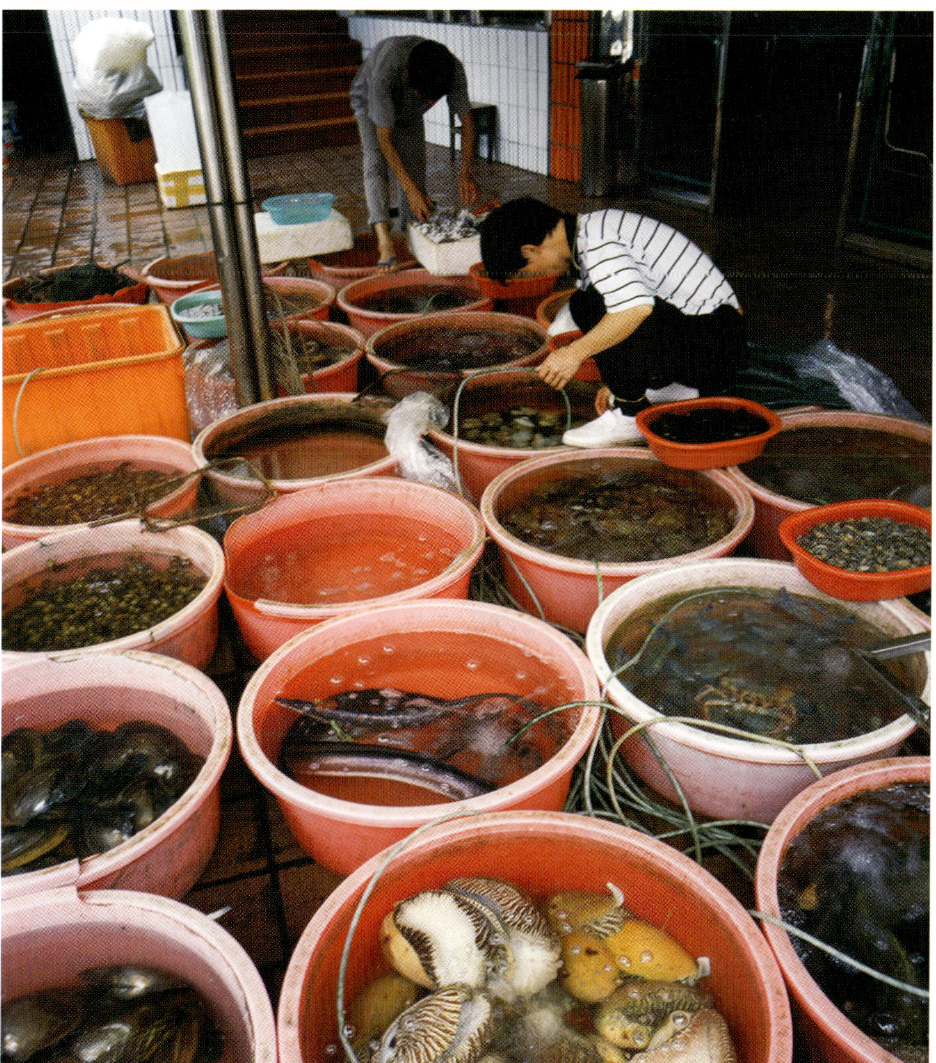

waterfront, the tall glass and concrete towers looking across the harbour seem out of place.

On the nearby island of Gulang Yu progress has been a lot less rapid, and many colonial buildings survive alongside ancient Chinese houses. Perhaps Thomson would still recognise much of the island today, and still be able to find his way around.

In his series of articles for the *British Journal of Photography*, published in August 1866, Thomson used his own experience in the Far East to offer guidance to those who would follow in his footsteps.

> *A few words about the description of the camera I have found most suitable, and I am done for the present. The camera must be strongly made, and the wood of the driest, so as not*

below: Thomson first photographed the Shanghai waterfront in 1869. Returning three years later, he was amazed by how much the place had developed.
bottom: On the Bund today, the oldest buildings are less than a century old, and Shanghai is China's fastest developing city

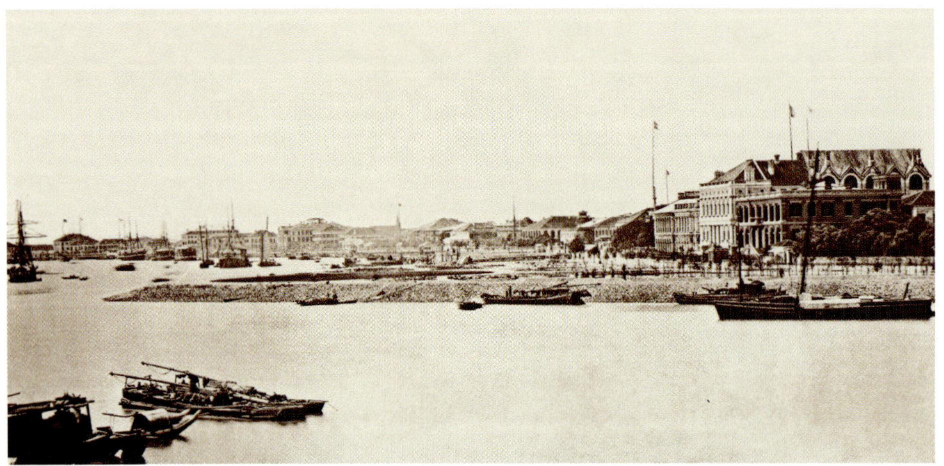

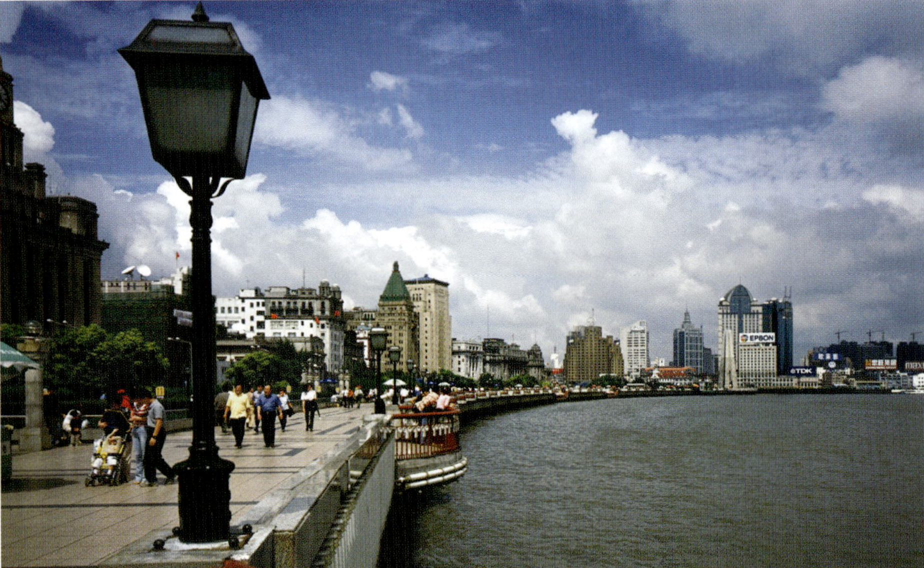

to warp in the hottest sun. It should be portable, and of the 'Kinnear' form. I may state here that I have had such a bellows camera in use for about two years, during which time I have carried it with me on my travels through jungle, swamp, and forest, and still, though battered and worn, it is a serviceable instrument. The bellows has never suffered from damp, or the attack of white ants, or insects of any description. The only improvement I can suggest on this form of camera is that the sliding front should be capable of being depressed, so that objects below the line of sight may be photographed without altering the level of the camera.[9]

This shows a clear understanding of the advantages of 'drop front' which later became standard in field cameras.

The 'Kinnear' camera was, of course, that designed and used by Charles Kinnear during his journeys through France in the 1850s. It enjoyed immense popularity, and from it evolved a century of camera designs.

Of the practicalities of working cleanly in such extremes conditions, he also exhorted his readers to take good care of their equipment and especially their 'frames' or plate holders. With the plates being loaded wet into the frames, the availability of clean and dry holders was a major restricting factor in the number of negatives the photographer could take in a day's work.

It is therefore of the greatest importance that an Eastern photographer should always have two or three good frames in reserve. For further security the under part of each frame should be bound at the corners with silver and not brass, as brass is liable to be destroyed by drops of silver solution. I have also found it a great protection to the frame to sponge it out immediately after use, and to open back and front and set it up to dry.[10]

With today's easy-to-use digital cameras, it does us no harm at all to pause for a moment and reflect on the simple fact of Victorian photographic life that plate holders needed to be washed and dried after every single exposure.

Thomson opened the third volume of *Illustrations of China and its People* with images of Amoy, Foochow and

below left: The centre of Shanghai today is crowded day and night. It really is a city that never sleeps – the streets are a blaze of neon and shops stay open until late into the night.
below right: The vibrant colours of a kite shop in the old quarter of the city. This photograph was taken in the days leading up to the mid-autumn fesatival, when shops are full of lanterns, kites, decorations and the very rich 'moon cakes' which are a special delicacy associated with the holiday.

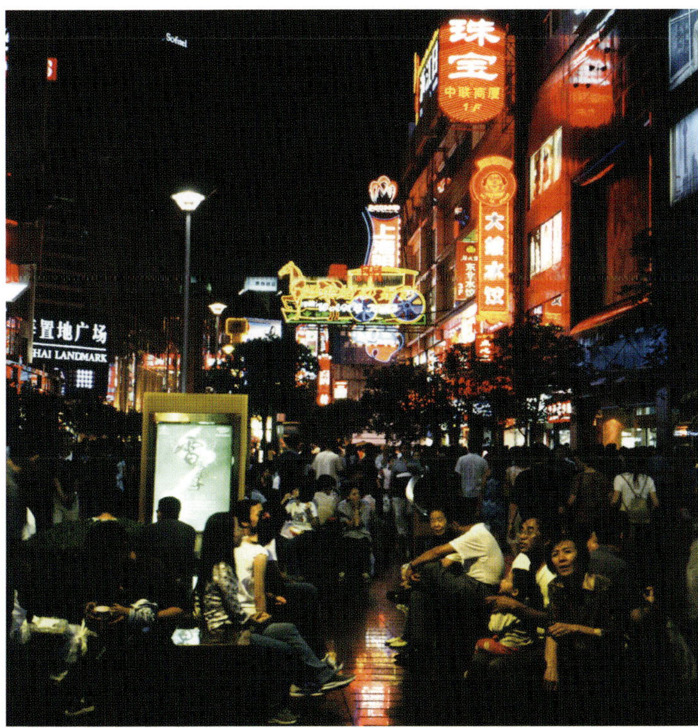

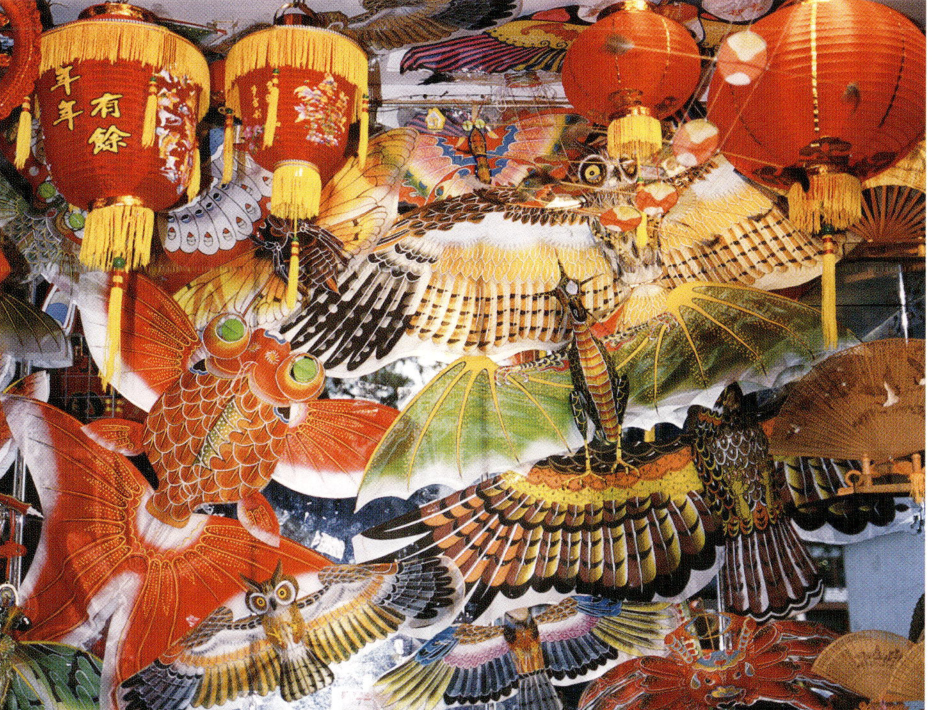

Ningpo, illustrating temples, actors and tea plantations. I rejoined his itinerary at Shanghai, already the premier trading centre in China by the late 1860s.

He visited the city first in 1869 and again in 1872, remarking on his second visit that

> *Since 1869, the date at which the illustration was taken, the foreign settlement at Shanghai has been steadily improving.*

Today Shanghai is developing at a phenomenal rate. Everywhere new glass and steel tower blocks are being erected, and the architectural landscape is already rivalling that of Hong Kong. For a few years at the end of the 1990s, a surprisingly large proportion of all the tall cranes in the world were in use on both banks of the Pearl River. From the window of my city centre hotel – one of the city's finest before the last war but now itself likely to be scheduled for demolition in the not too distant future – the few remaining old houses seemed overwhelmed by the concrete monsters rising both all around and over them.

Remarkably little of any antiquity has survived this drive towards regeneration, but several of the magnificent

below: In Shanghai's Hu Xing Ting Teahouse, drinking tea is somewhere between a ritual and an art form. Taking tea, which is accompanied by quails' eggs and an assortment of savouries, can last a long and very relaxing period of time.

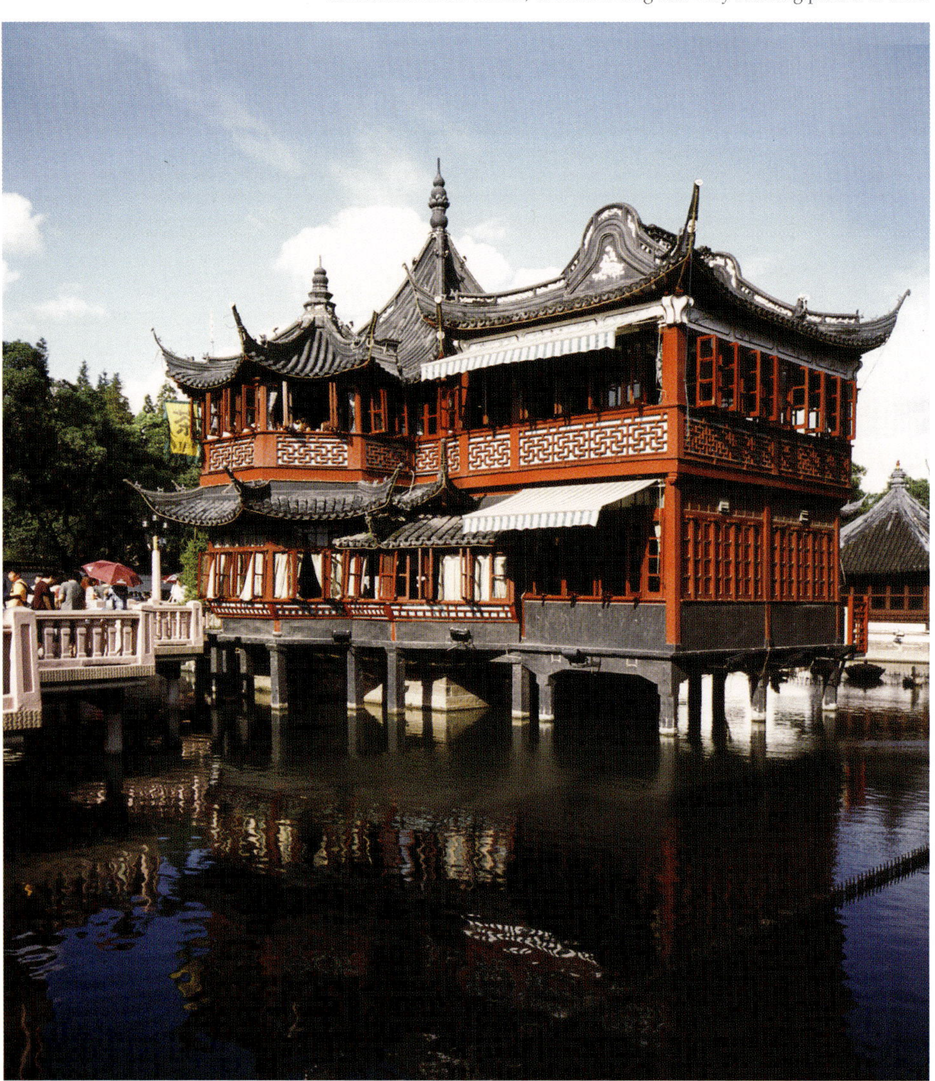

early 20th century buildings on the Bund - including the former headquarters of the Hong Kong & Shanghai Banking Corporation which now houses the Bank of China - have been carefully restored to their former splendour.

However, efforts are now being made to preserve other significant reminders of the character of the old city. In an area called Xintiandi (New Heaven on Earth) a group of early 19th century Shikumen houses, or at least their frontages, have been preserved and converted into a fashionable pedestrian area, home to a surprisingly large number of restaurants, galleries and cafés.

The old centre of Shanghai - a labyrinth of narrow streets and alleyways around the Yu Garden - has been preserved and restored as both a tourist attraction and as a market for the locals. Although many of the buildings are relatively recent, they retain and celebrate the character and decoration of old China. Past a profusion of wonderful restaurants catering for every taste, the visitor eventually arrives at a small lake, in the centre of which - and reached by a zigzag bridge - is the extraordinary Hu Xing Ting Teahouse. Drinking green tea in the upper floor of this teahouse is a unique experience. I was brought a glass of jasmine tea with a dried flower head in the bottom, surrounded by leaves. The waiter poured boiling water over it and filled the glass to the top. Before my eyes, as the water was absorbed, the flower blossomed and grew in the glass. The smell and the flavour were wonderful, but watching the flower grow and bloom in the glass as it was repeatedly refilled with water was a wonderful visual experience. Traditionally, many of the varieties of China tea got their flavour from being bagged with flower blossoms of various types - Thomson mentioned *chroanthus, olea, aglaia and other flowers* to his readers. The blossom actually being in the glass while the tea infused added considerably to the flavour.

In this, and every other teahouse in China, tasting the teas before buying remains a tradition Thomson would still recognise. In his book he refers to many of the varieties

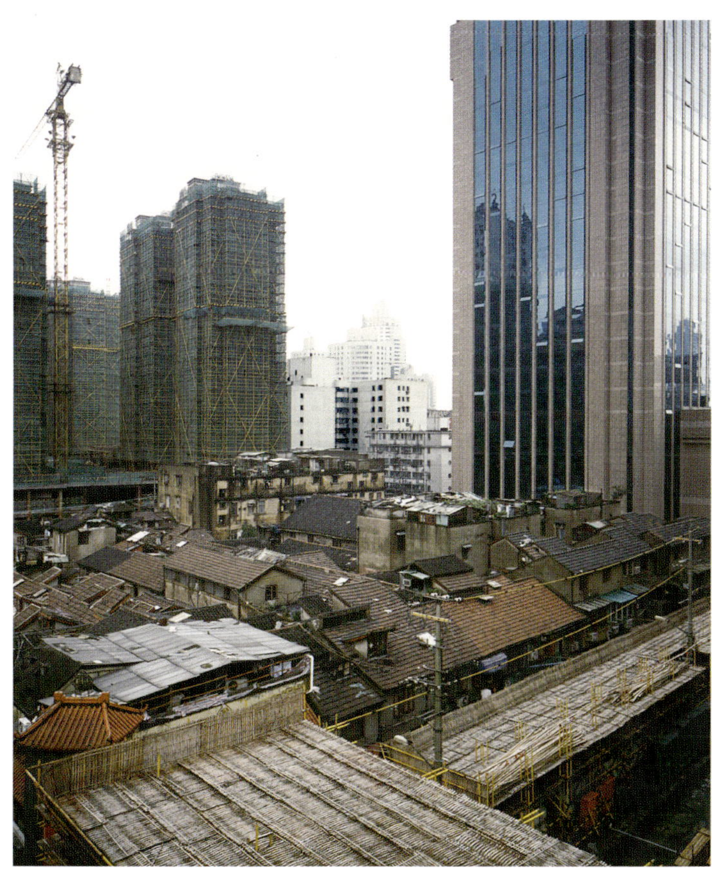

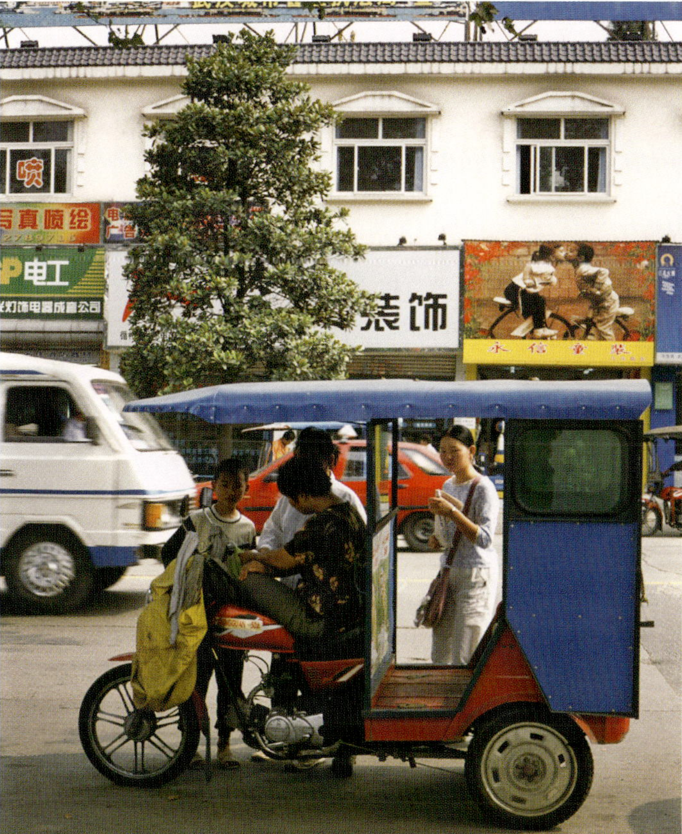

far left: Shanghai's love of the tower block is rapidly overwhelming the old low-rise city. This view taken from a balcony on the Yangtse International Hotel, built in 1934 and once one of the largest hotels in the east. The old houses in this picture have already been demolished to make way for yet more modern office buildings.
left: One of over fifty thousand 'ma-mo' or 'drunken taxis' in the city of Wuhan. This cheap form of transport is ideally suited for negotiating the narrow streets and alleyways in the old parts of city. They earned their name from the ease which which their drivers weave them around market stalls and pedestrians, and reach places inaccessible to the fourteen thousand genuine taxis – all of them Citroen BXs. built in a joint-venture factory in the city.

available to him – green tea, black tea and even gunpowder tea, all of which are still readily available today. He was especially fascinated by the preparation of the small pellets of gunpowder tea – made by a team of agile young men who continually rolled and tossed bags of tea leaves using only their feet while they supported their body weight by holding on to wooden beams above their heads! One would like to think that they now have a machine to do all that.

As befits a city reinventing itself – some say as a rival to Hong Kong – Shanghai opened a stunningly beautiful new airport in 2002. From a distance, the terminal looks

below left: The crew at breakfast. Getting them up in the morning was, said Thomson, very difficult as they smoked themselves to sleep each night with tobacco or opium, *'according to their means and choice'*.
below right: Wang, Thomson's interpreter, standing against the ship's cabin as they made their way against the Yangtse current. The exposure must have been very short indeed as there is absolutely no sign of movement whatsoever.

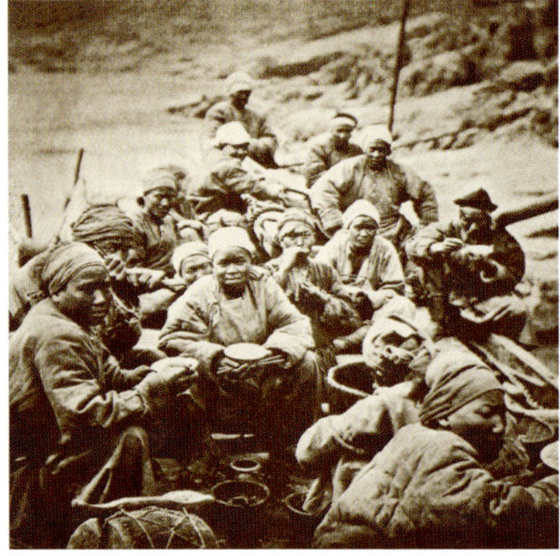

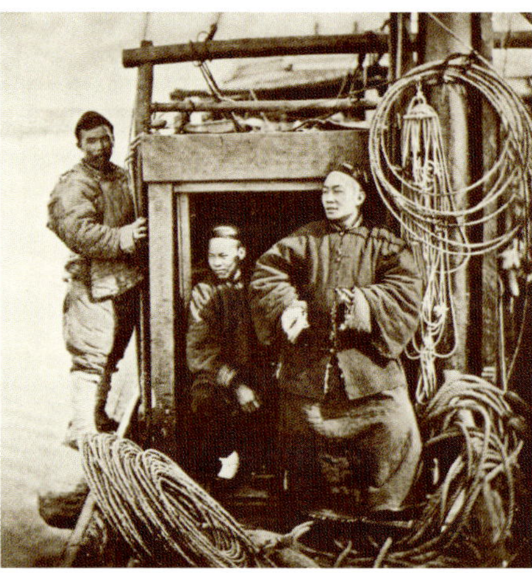

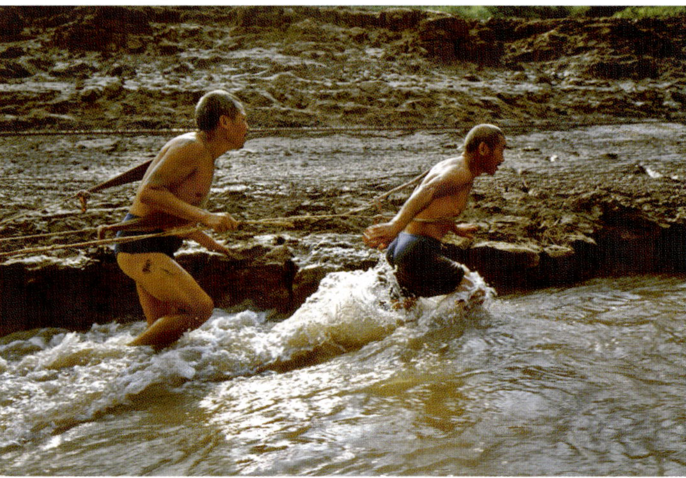

above: Two 60-year old Shennong boatmen hard at work hauling boats up the fast moving stream, just before the Yangtse's rising waters put them out of work. They used to work naked, until asked to cover themselves up 'in the name of decency'!

like a giant seagull spreading its wings ready for flight – a far cry from the old airport on the edge of the city, where the planes took off and landed so close to the houses that you could almost reach out and touch the roofs!

The new airport is connected to the city by the world's first long distance 'maglev' overhead railway, with the trains reaching speeds in excess of 250mph. The journey time from airport to city has, at a stroke, been reduced to only a few minutes!

Turning towards the Chang Jiang, the Yangtse River, John Thomson's next stop was the city of Wuhan. Three separate townships in his day – Hankow, Wuchang and Hangyang – it is now one large modern city but with the old heart still very visible.

From there he set out on the long journey to the Wushan Gorge on the Yangtse in the company of two Americans. Moving upstream from Wuhan, the river widens considerably, and at one point is well over a mile wide. While Thomson chartered two boats – a large single-masted boat with a comfortable cabin for himself and his companions, and a smaller craft to house his servants and crew of about twenty for the journey – I took a bus along the toll motorway between Wuhan and Shashi.

On the river today, tourist ships regularly make the journey between Shashi and Chongqing and back, passing through the three great gorges, the locks at the Gezhou Dam, and at the new Three Gorges Dam. It seems a little incongruous in once-classless China to discover that there are at least five classes of riverboat to choose from – offering everything from a very low cost and somewhat basic cruise through the gorges, to ships which are nothing short of floating five star hotels, with prices to match.

In contrast to today's sophistication, Thomson's sailing boat embarked from Wuhan on 20th January 1871 – with both British and American flags fluttering in the breeze. By the end of their first day, they dropped anchor only ten miles upstream.

The conditions on the boat, especially the rich aroma

below: The fast-moving Shennong stream is a tributary of the Yangtse, and the settlements up stream have long been supplied by a flotilla of small boats and the men who work them. The boatmen used a combination of poles and ropes to physically haul the craft up against the current. As they make their way through narrow gorges, the poles were also used to keep the boats in the centre of the stream and away from the jagged rocks. On the return journey, the boats ran the rapids at exhilarating speed. While, in recent years, many of the journeys have been made for the benefit of tourists, the villages upstream are totally dependent on the river for their supplies. As the water levels rise behind the new Three Gorges Dam, a fleet of motor boats replaced the rope-hauled craft, and many of the men, several of them still doing this arduous job into their sixties, lost their jobs. This scene is already part of the Yangtse's history.

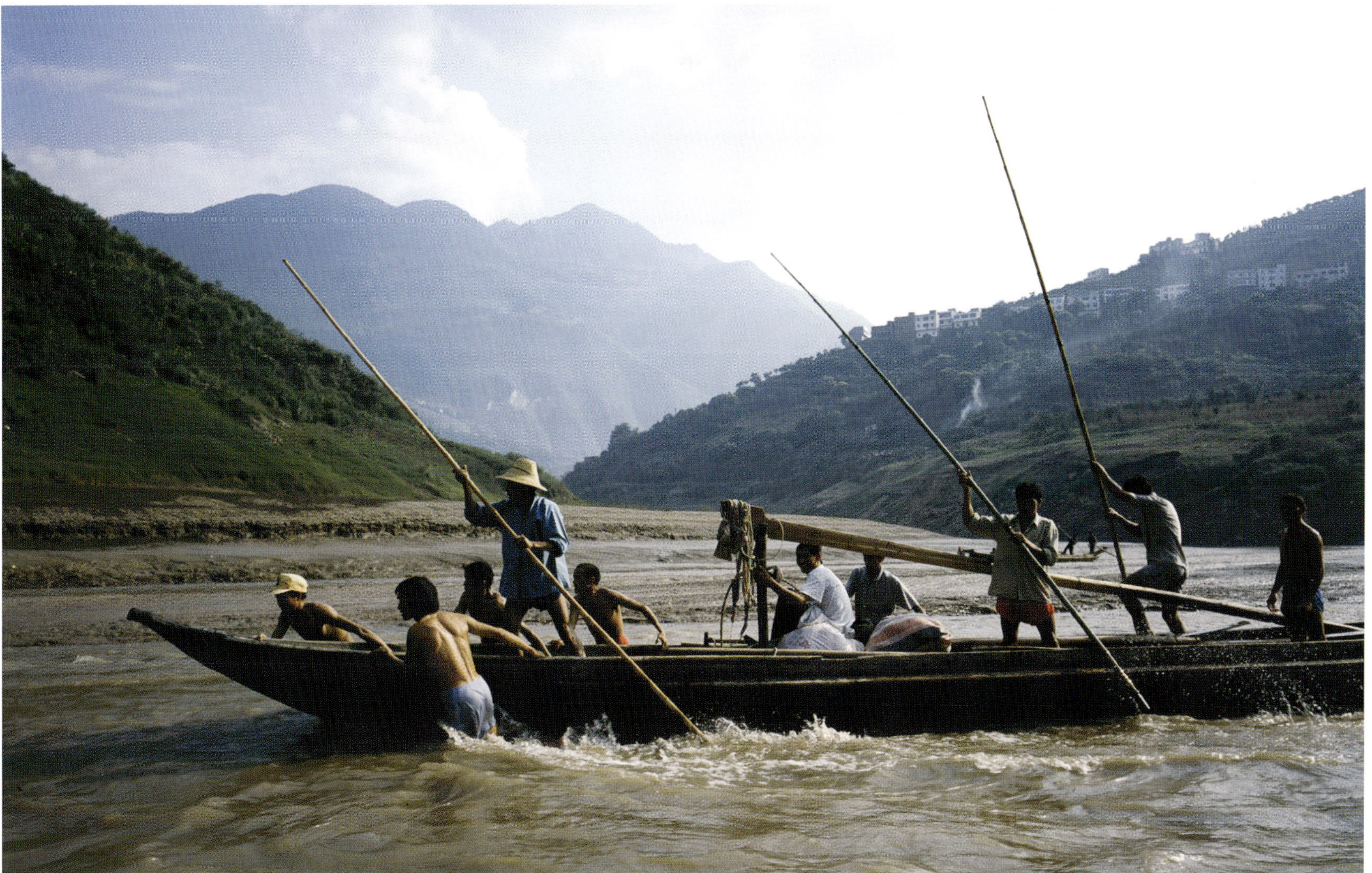

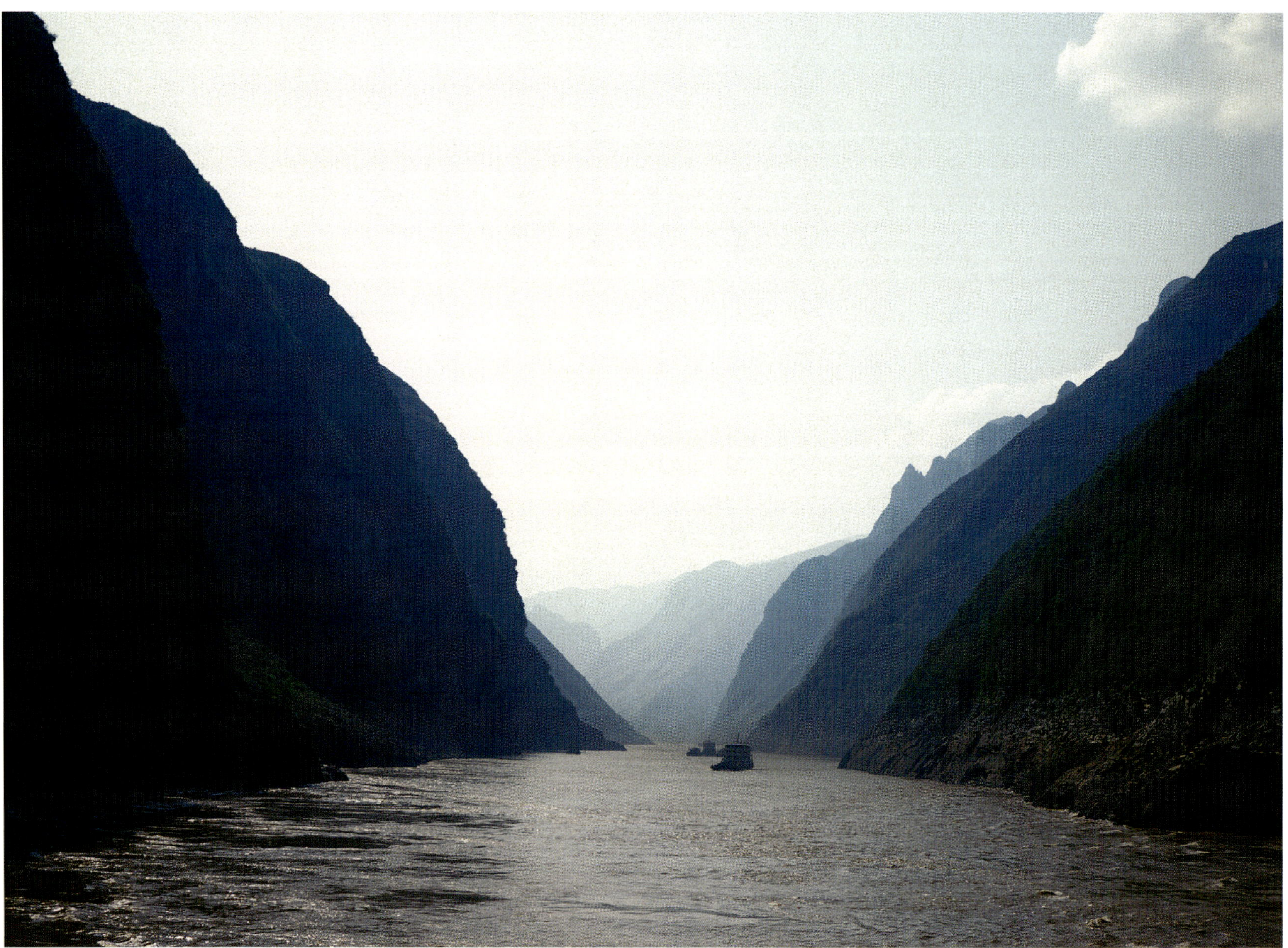

from the crew, figured in Thomson's account of the journey. Nine of the crew apparently slept in one part of the boat's hold - no more than five and a half feet square - with the hatch closed, and apparently they only changed into fresh clothes when the winter came to an end! The boat on which I travelled, by comparison, had one hundred and eighty berths, and a crew of almost half that number.

Surprisingly, reading Thomson's account, his mastery of the intricacies of the collodion process was such that he even took photographs on board the boat while it was underway. Of one such picture - of his interpreter, Wang, who apparently did not understand the local dialects - he noted

> *There he is, presented to the reader in No.35, just after he had been droning, in an obscure corner of the cabin, over a whole classical commentary. The figure to the left is one of the boatmen, while a Ningpo boy is looking from the cabin door; the characters are faithfully rendered, and are engaged in the several occupations with which half their time was engrossed. The boat was underway in mid-stream when I executed this picture.*[11]

Thomson's little convoy arrived at Shashi, three hundred miles sailing from Wuhan, on February 2nd. By coach today, the journey - just over half that distance by road - takes just about three hours!

Three days later, at Yichang - referred to as I-Chang by Thomson - the boats which had brought them from Wuhan were left behind in favour of boats and crews more used to dealing with the currents found in the gorges.

On February 8th 1871, a few miles from Yichang, snow fell, covering the mountaintops, and freshening the air at river level. In striking contrast, as our ship slowly made its way through the gorges in early autumn, the sun tried in vain to penetrate the haze created by both exceedingly high temperatures and unusually high humidity.

Where Thomson found the river as smooth as a mirror, we sailed through muddy brown water which swirled and eddied around us.

opposite page: Wu Gorge today, looking into the misty morning sunlight. The Changh Jiang today is a heavily commercialised river, with cargo vessels and barges making their way from Shanghai and the sea as far west as Chongqing. When Thomson's boat moored here for the night, they were set upon by pirates. Today's cruise ships suffer no such indignity.

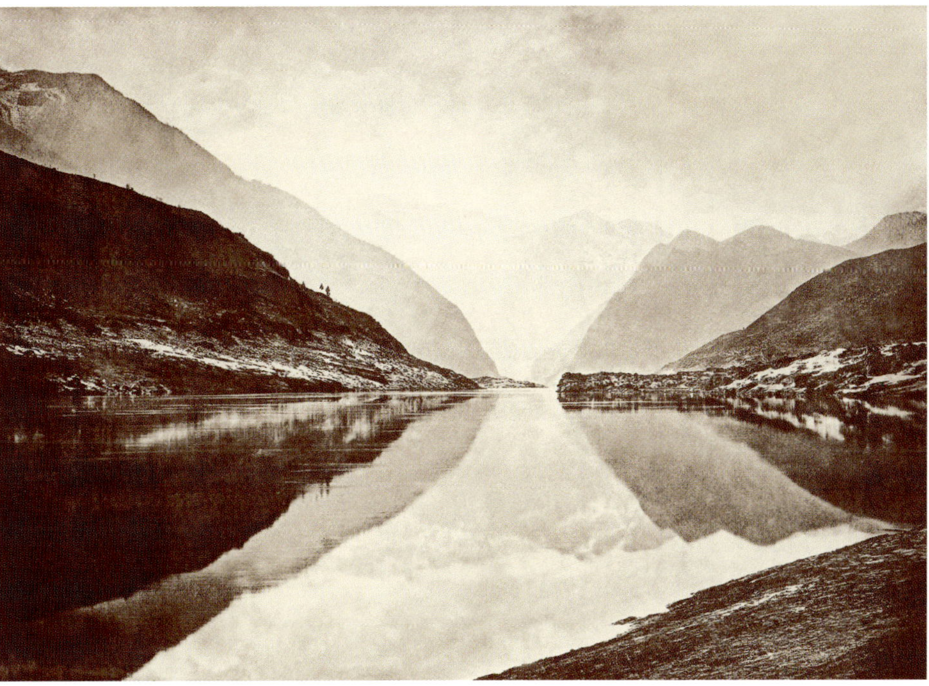

above: Thomson and his party reached Wushan Gorge on 18th February, four weeks after leaving Wuhan. The gorges then were much narrower and more difficult to navigate. In his account of his journey, he notes that when the river was high, steamboat navigation through the gorges would be possible. Of this scene he wrote '*The river here was perfectly placid, and the view which met our gaze at the mouth of the gorge was perhaps the finest of the kind that we had encountered. The mountains rose in confused masses to a great altitude, while the most distant peak at the extremity of the reach resembled a cut sapphire, its snow lines sparkling in the sun like the gleams of light on the facets of a gem. The other cliffs and precipices gradually deepened in hue until they reached the bold lights and shadows of the rocky foreground.* Thomson's view, of course, has been lost for decades. With the opening of the Gezhou Dam in the 1980s, the water levels were raised considerably, and more changes are still to come. When the lake behind the Three Gorges Dam is full to capacity - something which will take several more years to realise - the waters will have risen a further hundred and twenty five metres!

above: The 'Ghost City' of Fengdu, high on Mt. Minshan above the river and reached by a cable car, used to overlook the city of the same name. The old city of Fengdu, clinging to the river's edge, was completely demolished by the end of 2003 in readiness for the rise in river levels. Forward-thinking boatyards even constructed vessels high above the water level, to be floated off when the river rose! A complete new city was construced on the opposite hillside, well above the projected high water level.

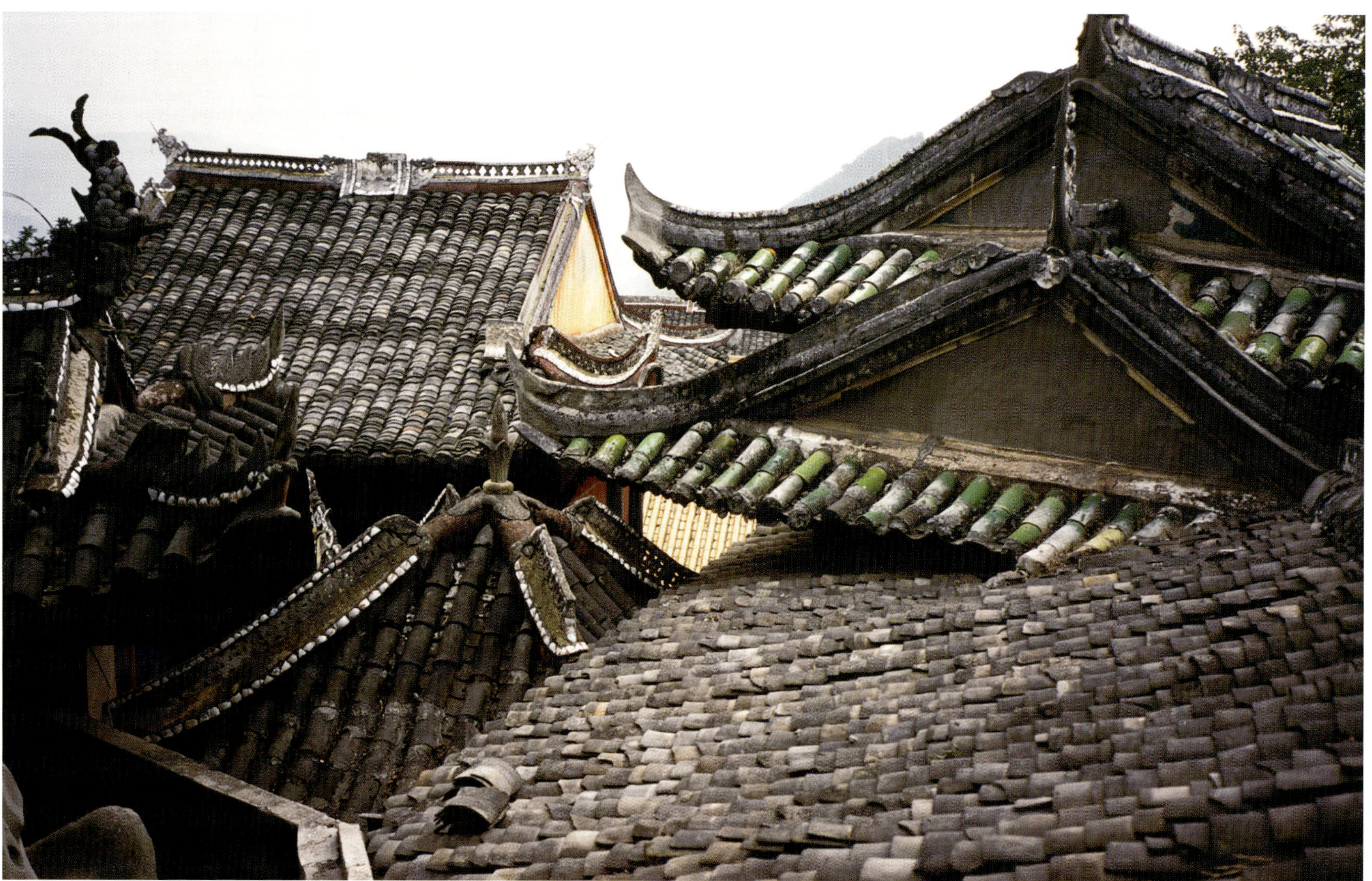

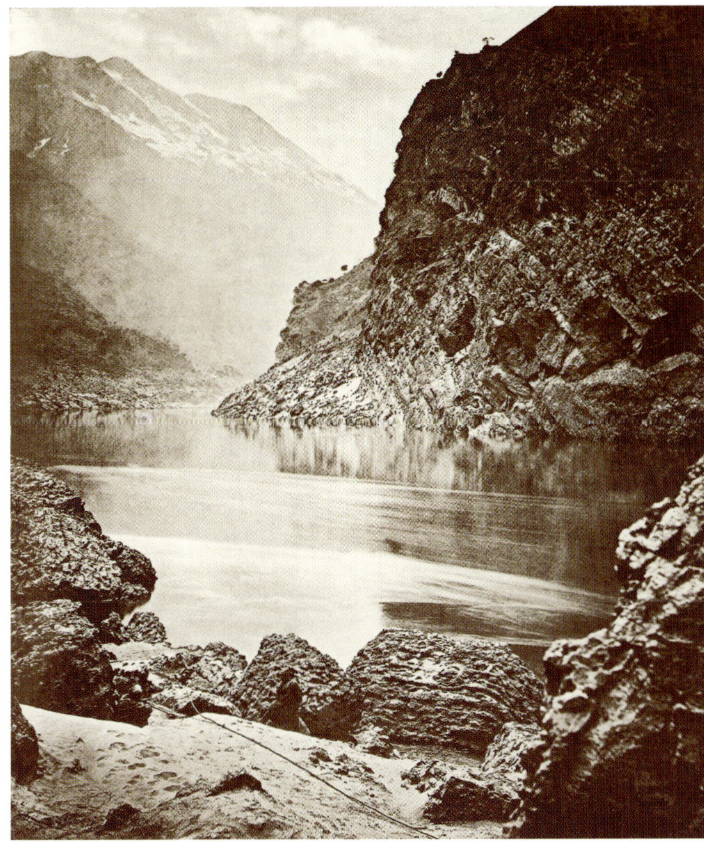

left: Having chartered his own boat and crew, Thomson had the advantage that he could ask to be put ashore with his camera and darktent wherever he saw the potential for a strong photograph. The boat's mooring rope can be seen across the foreground of the picture.

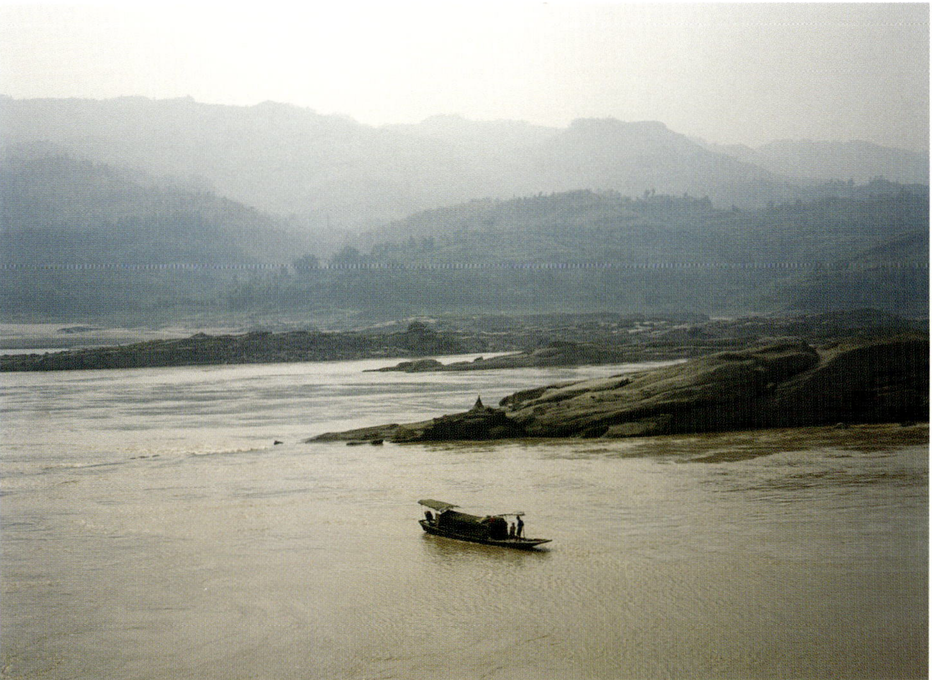

above: Small boats criss-cross the river taking supplies to small villages on the Yangtse and its tributaries. They keep a keen lookout for approaching cargo ships or cruisers, and seek safety in shallower waters.

Severe rain a few weeks earlier had almost breached the banks of the Dongting Lake near Shashi and although levels had dropped considerably upstream, the water was anything but still.

All along the river, we saw the impact of the new Three Gorges Dam project – new cities being built higher up the hillsides and old towns being demolished. Roads were being re-sited up above the proposed water levels, and spectacular new bridges were being constructed across the widening river – widening, of course, as the water levels crept ever higher.

Thomson ended both his upstream journey and his narrative near Zhongzhou, writing that he was

> *leaving the incidents of our downward voyage untold for fear lest my readers may already have grown weary of my narrative.*

And that also brought Volume III of his book to a close. He never made it as far as the city of Fengdu – further west, between the gorges and Chongqing – which has long been known in Taoist legends as the 'Ghost City'. As the dam project neared completion, Fengdu became a ghost city in fact – and as the new city rose on the opposite bank

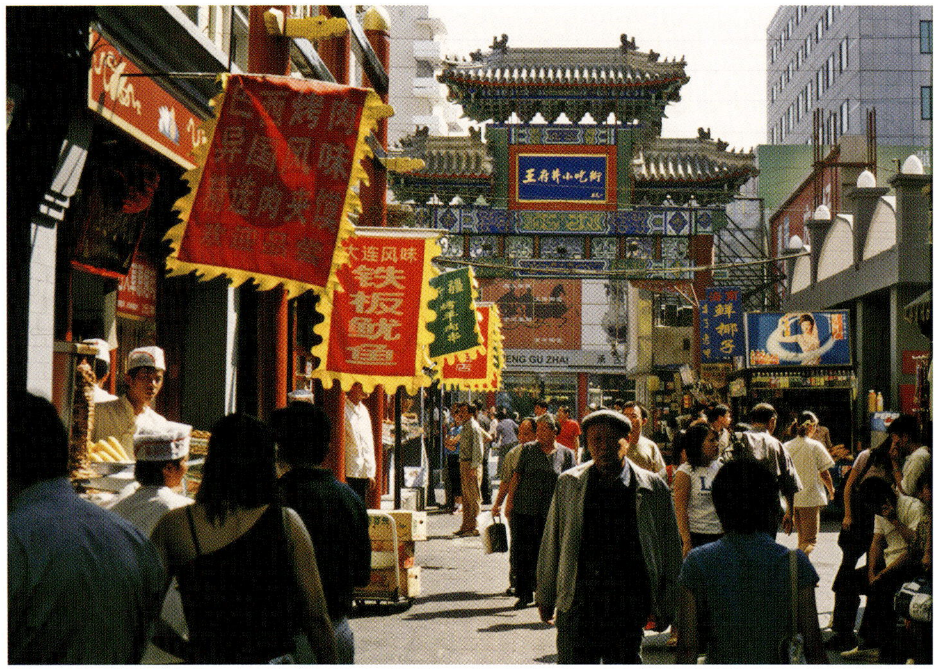

above: Only a few yards from the modern main streets, it is possible to savour something of the character and colour of old Beijing in the narrow lanes and street markets. The range of smells from the kerb-side food stalls is wonderful. Thomson might still recognise aspects of these markets – not unlike one he visited one hundred and thirty years before this photograph was taken, and of which he wrote '*close by was a cook's shed, with a series of brick ovens and fire-places in front. From these, a powerful savour of roasting meats arose. Above a reeking cauldron, puddings spread on a clean board were temptingly displayed.*' Those attractions have not changed, the smells were still tempting, the food looked very appetizing, and every vendor seemed to be doing a brisk trade.

of the river, the old town was systematically demolished and the rubble removed from the site just before the water levels rose. Only the temple complex high on Mt. Minshan remains. Seeing the extent of the rebuilding put the scale of the dam project in context. Well over a million people were relocated and rehoused before the dam was completed.

Fengdu Temple, the origin of the 'ghost' stories, sits at the top of the mountain and has for years been a magnet for visitors from the many cruise boats. As the water levels rise to their final height, it will be virtually alone on the north bank of the river.

Thomson's fourth volume dealt with dignitaries in local and national government, Manchu women, merchants and customs, and finally, with a written and visual account of Peking, the pictures having apparently been assembled from a number of visits to the capital.

Beijing was, in Thomson's time, a walled city containing many fine traditional buildings. Amazingly, the city walls survived until the time of Chairman Mao when they were demolished to make way for a new ring road. Only two or three of the ancient gateways were retained and restored to mark the historic entrances to the city.

It was also a city in some turmoil, thanks to the campaigns which had been waged against the country during the then relatively recent Opium Wars. The Old Summer Palace had been destroyed by the attacking British forces, the Summer Palace had also been partially destroyed and all but abandoned, but Thomson still found aspects of the place which endeared it to him, and even reminded him of home. He wrote

There are a great number of stalls scattered along the principal streets, some of which are built like the old booths of the High Street of Edinburgh!

Aspects of the city which draw visitors today from all over the world were, of course, inaccessible to the late 19th century traveller. The Forbidden City, home of the Emperor was just that – forbidden! Today it is a world heritage site, beautifully cared for and awesome to visit.

Awesome but surprising – turning a corner deep within its precincts, today's visitor can happen upon an ancient pavilion displaying the sign *We sell Starbuck's Coffee* – as incongruous as finding a Little Chef in Hampton Court, or a Pizza Hut at the Pyramids – except that you will find both a Pizza Hut *and* a KFC at the Pyramids! At the time of writing, the presence of Starbucks in such an important location is at last being questioned, and there is a groundswell of opinion calling for its removal.

By the time of the 2008 Olympic Games, Beijing intends to present itself to the world as one of the world's most elegant and modern capital cities, and judging by the buildings already completed, it certainly will.

Some aspects of Thomson's experience have changed little. Tall western visitors are still sufficiently rare even in Beijing to attract attention, and for a photographer, trying to be inconspicuous is an almost impossible task. The natural curiosity of the locals, and their enthusiasm for greeting visitors with a cheery wave and a call of 'hello' makes an immediate impression.

Taking photographs in Beijing streets today, however, is a far cry from the experiences Thomson reported more than a century and a quarter before me, when he wrote

> *I was looked upon as a forerunner of death, as a sort of Nemesis in fact; and I have seen unfortunates stricken with superstitious dread, fall down on bended knee and beseech me not to take their likeness or their life with the fatal lens of my camera.*[12]

In sharp contrast today, photography is everywhere, and cameras are an essential part of the visitor's dress code. While sitting relaxing in a park one afternoon, with all my equipment by my side, I was approached on several occasions by Chinese visitors who handed me their cameras and asked me to take their photographs!

Walking along central Beijing streets today, however, the foreign visitor is more likely to be enticed into buying something. I felt I was constant prey to students keen to entice me into upstairs studios and galleries to show

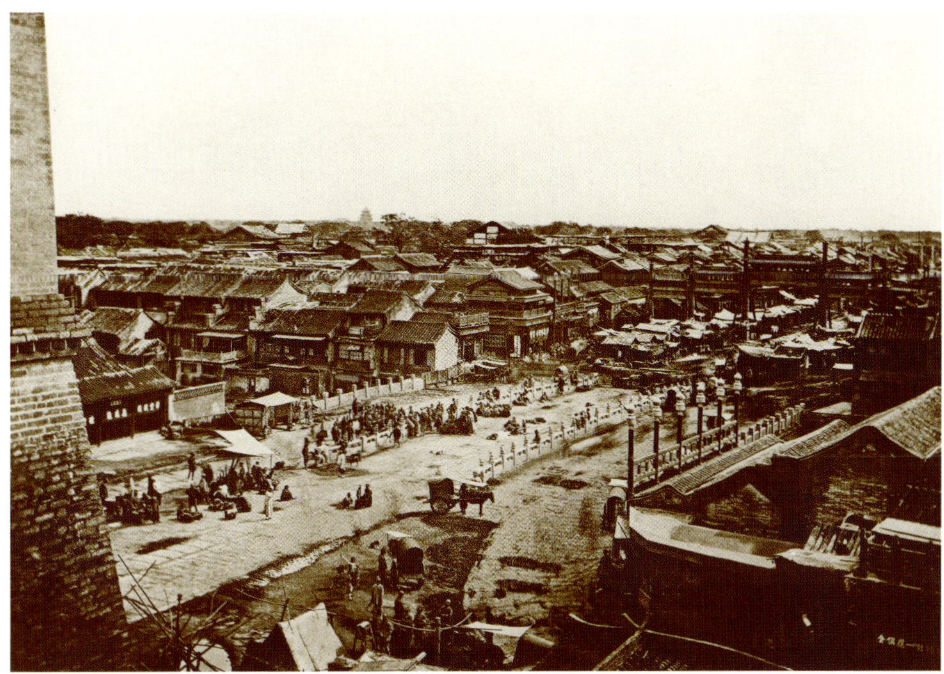

above: 'View of the Central Street in the Chinese Quarter of Peking' appeared as Plate IX in the fourth volume of Thomson's book. The picture was taken from the city walls, near to what he described as the Central Gate between the Chinese and Tartar Quarters. Pools of stagnant water lay alongside the road, being used daily to keep dust down, and to mix into mud to repair nearby buildings. Thomson described how the smell from these pools assaulted his senses, but noted that *'One of my most disagreeable experiences during my visit to Peking was a ride along the road whilst the mud from these putrid pools was being ladled on to the highway to lay the dust. It would have been worse still had I, as some native had done, lost my footing in a dark night and been drowned in the mire'.*

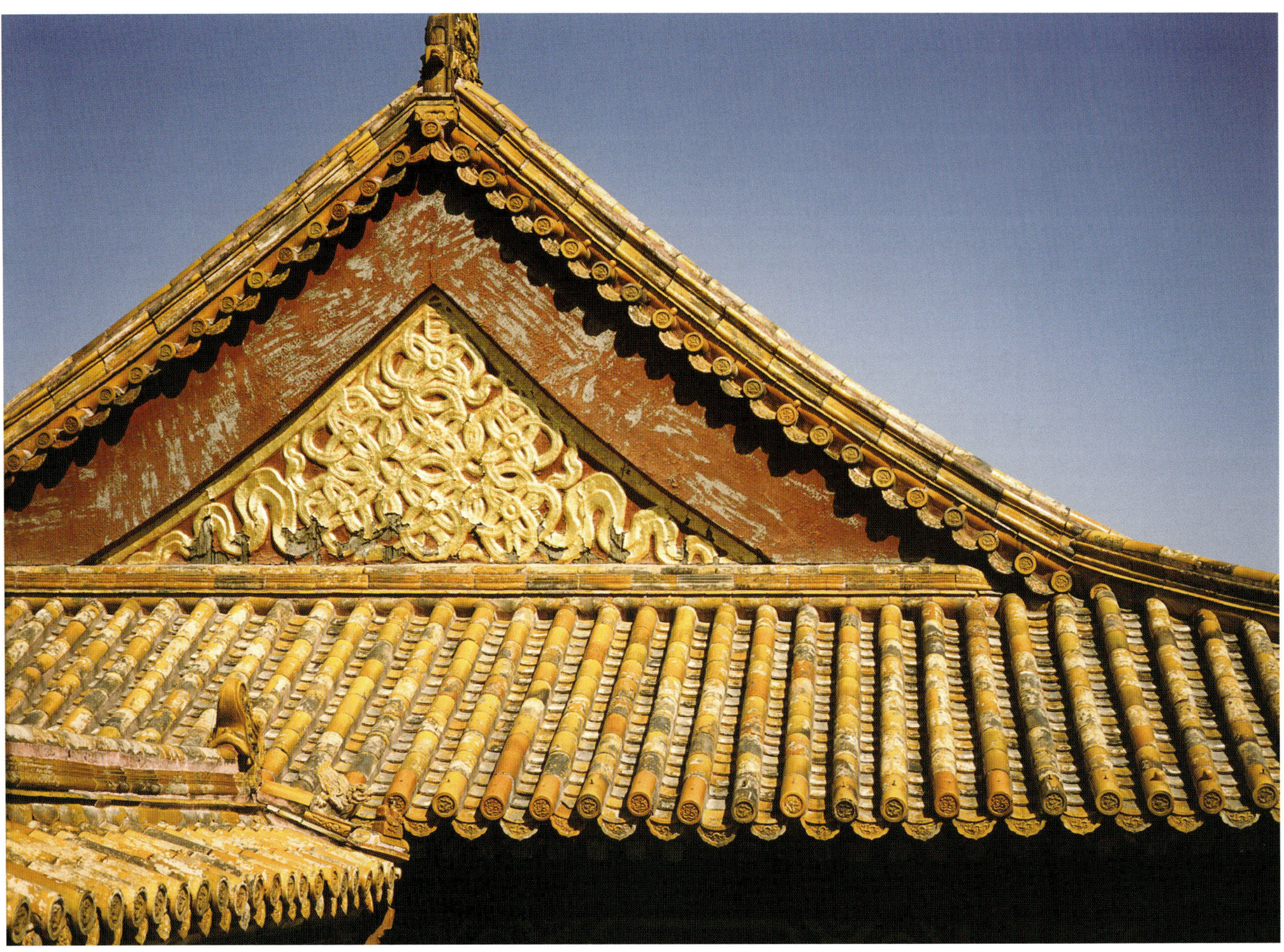

examples of their calligraphy and their painting.

Sitting in city centre squares, yet more young people strike up conversations to practice their English. They are a wonderfully friendly people, who go out of their way to make the visitor feel completely welcome.

While other areas of China had been busy, the crowds in Shanghai and Beijing were almost overwhelming. The streets seemed crowded day and night, and at the major heritage sites the numbers almost defy description.

Writing of his visit to the Summer Palace, semi-abandoned in his day but now happily restored to its former splendour, Thomson marvelled at the extravagance and beauty of the Imperial pleasure grounds.

> *The whole presents us with a Chinese landscape garden; white marble bridges span lakes bedecked with lotus flowers where summer pavilions rise among the islets on every side. The hills, too, are crowned with temples and pagodas, and herds of deer and other sorts of game wander in the woods that shade many a ruined palace.*[13]

Today it is enormous crowds of people who wander the site, and climb the hundreds of steps up to the main vantage point at the top of the Summer Palace itself. The view is spectacular.

Only two of Thomson's pictures made it in to *Illustrations of China and Its People* – one showing the beautiful seventeen-arch marble bridge which gave access to a temple on a small island in Kumming Lake, and the other of the ruined bronze pavilion high on the hill above the lake. The bridge, remarkably, had escaped destruction, as Thomson noted in his text.

> *The bridge has been left almost uninjured… but the whole place remains as it was left by the allies. Nothing has been attempted by way of restoration. Indeed, I suppose that the Chinese have had neither the spirit nor the funds to enter upon such an arduous undertaking, or that the place if left ruinous and desolate designedly as one means of keeping the hostility of the nation active, and as an ever-ready witness to the wanton barbarities to which foreigners will resort. Many*

opposite page: Thomson would only have been able to marvel at the wonderful ceramic-tiled roofs of the Forbidden City from outside the walls. Today, the secluded home of the Qing and Ming dynasties is a World Heritage Site enjoyed by visitors from all over the world. The majority of the buildings were constructed during a twenty year period in the early 15th century by Emperor Yongle, and it is said that more than a million people were compelled to work on its construction.

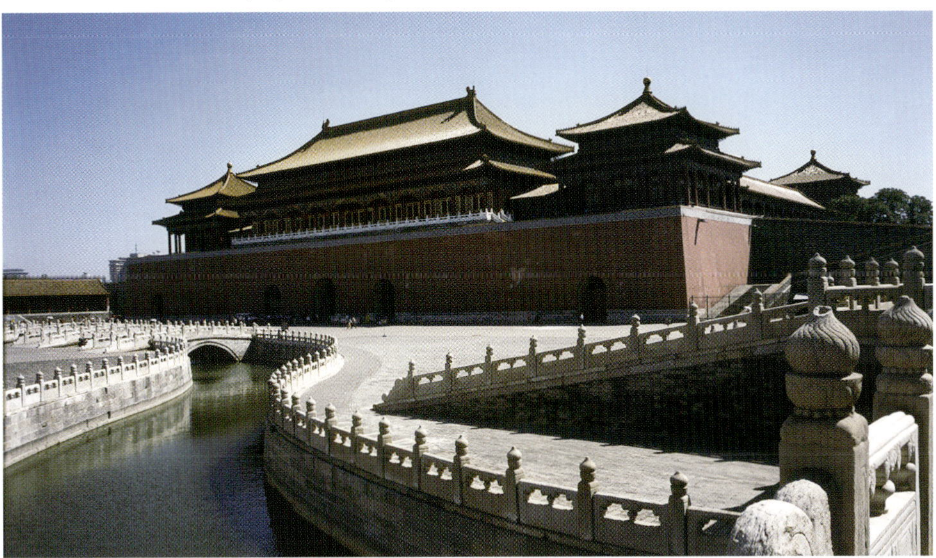

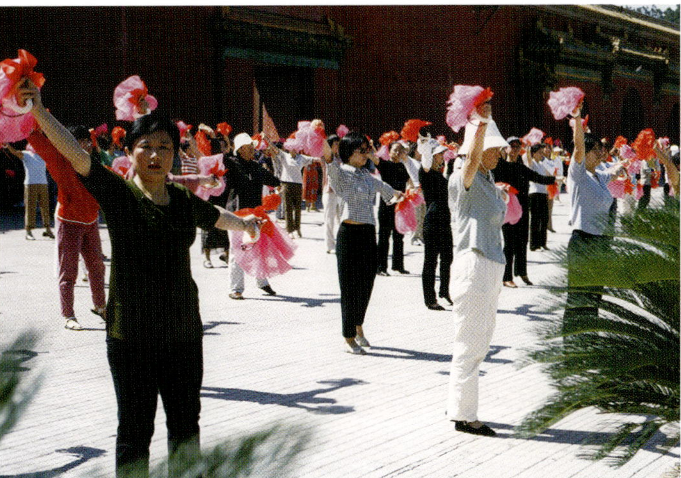

above: The Forbidden City is surrounded by many other palaces, ornate canals and walkways
left: An aerobics session under way in one of the many sheltered courtyards.

below left: The Bronze Pavilion, one of many unusual buildings which sit in the parklands surrounding the Summer Palace.
below right: When John Thomson visited the Summer palace, many of the buildings surrounding the Bronze Pavilion had been destroyed, and the pavilion itself was in a state of considerable disrepair.

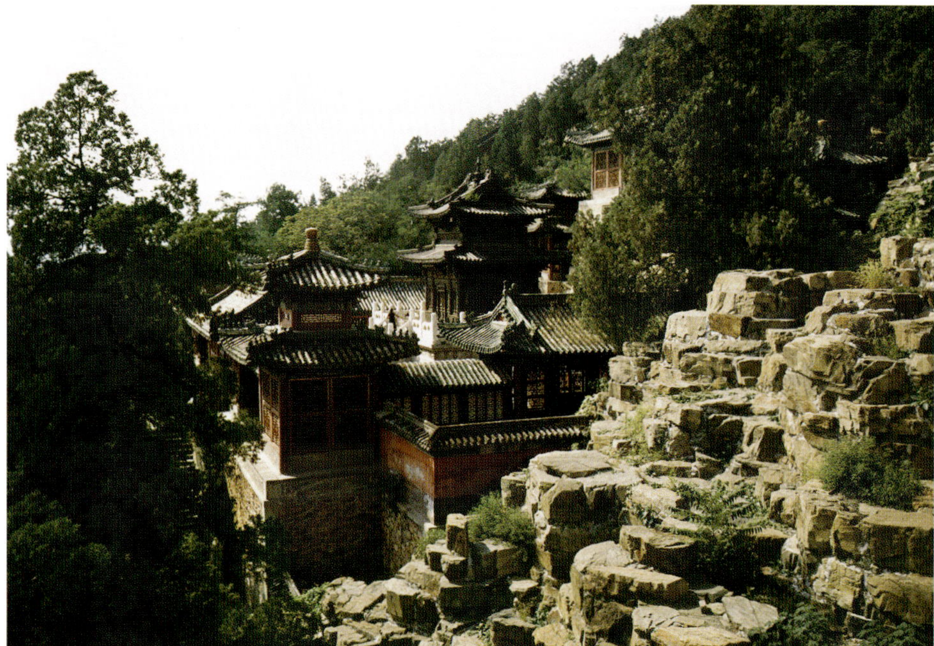

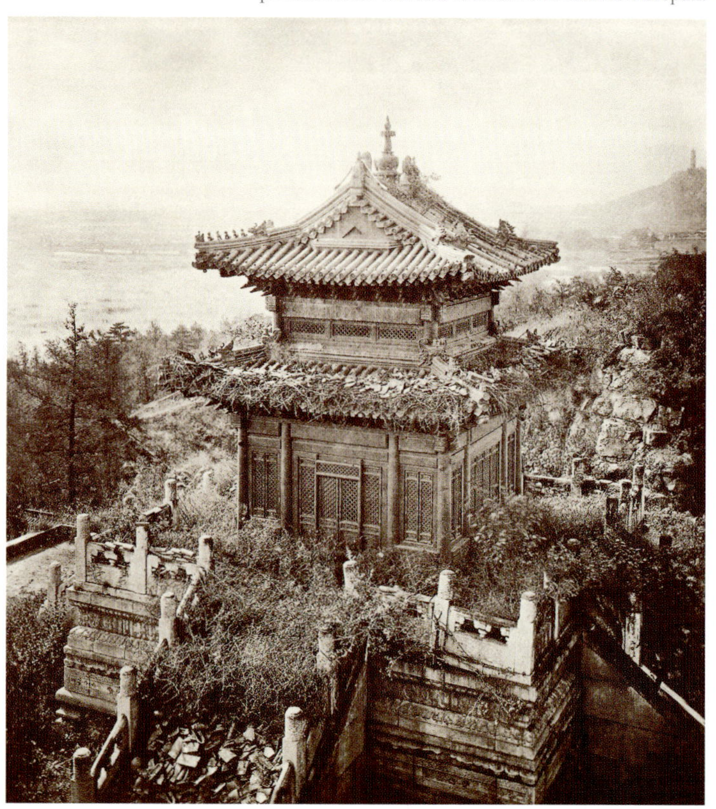

of the educated Chinese have this feeling, and look upon our conduct as an act of heartless vandalism, and say we might have brought pressure to bear upon their government in some way more worthy of our much vaunted civilisation.[14]

And well they might! This one paragraph stands as Thomson's most critical comment on his native country. Even in ruins, however, he found beauty and poetry.

Ivy had cast a mantle of green over the charred and battered walls, creeping in and out of the broken balustrades and wreathing many a marble ornament with its tender leaves.[15]

– a phrase reminiscent of the James Mudd's 'broken column and ivy-wreathed arch' and of the Victorian photographer's seemingly endless quest for the picturesque, and equally descriptive of the place today!

While the Summer Palace was eventually restored, the Old Summer Palace ruins still stand as a reminder of that vandalism. The remains of the once-elegant waterworks and foundations at Yuanming Yuan – which must have rivalled Versailles or Peterhof in splendour – offer a glimpse of just how lavish and ornate the buildings must have been.

below and below right: The remains of the Old Summer Palace stand as a stark testimony to the colossal damage inflicted by the British army in the 1860s, a few years before the first of Thomson's visits to Beijing. The ruins stand in a popular park at Yuanming Yuan on the north west outskirts of the city, originally laid out in the 13th century. The great fountain ruins (*below right*) date from a major building programme in the 1760s.

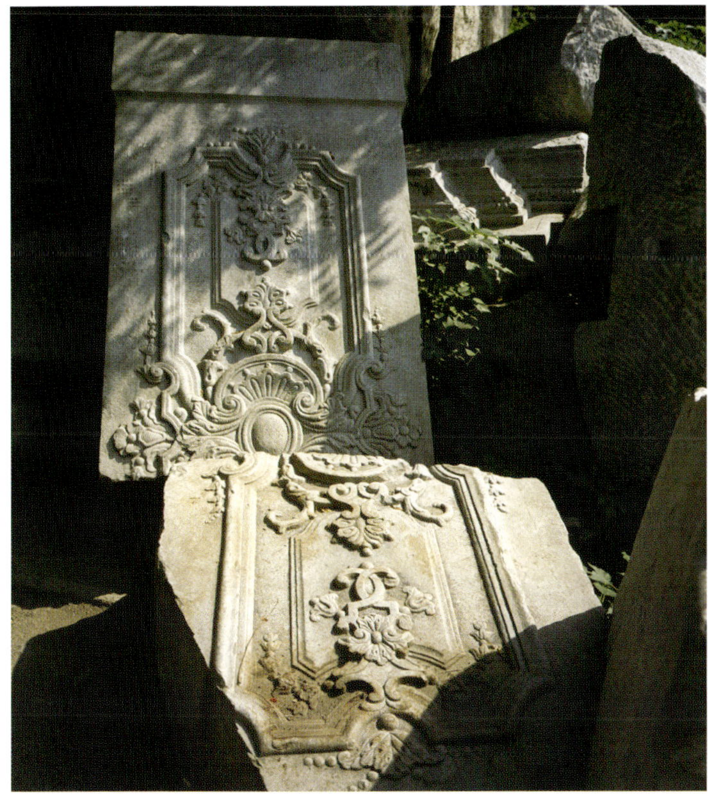

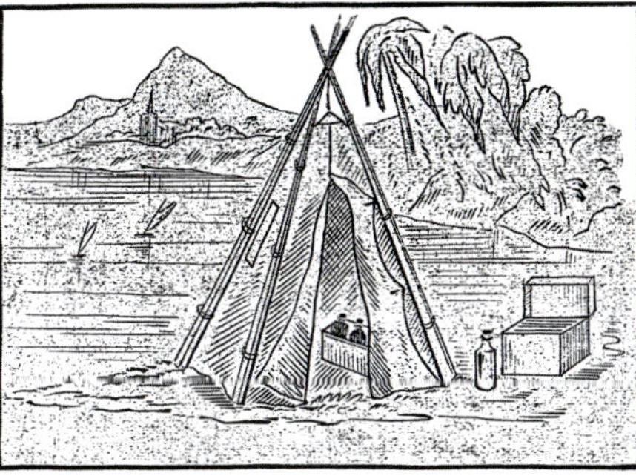

left: The British Journal of Photography published this wood block illustration of Thomson's original design for a lightweight photographic dark tent which could be folded into a very small package for easy transport across the demanding terrain of China. The teepee-like construction could also be assembled or dismantled in a matter of a few minutes.

At the Ming Tombs just outside Beijing, Thomson found further signs of neglect amidst the ancient splendour. He offered his readers only two views - one of the funerary halls at the Tomb of Ming-Lo, and one of the amazing limestone animals lining the approaches to that tomb.

Thomson closed the final chapter of his journey with a rather dismissive account of his visit to the Great Wall of China.

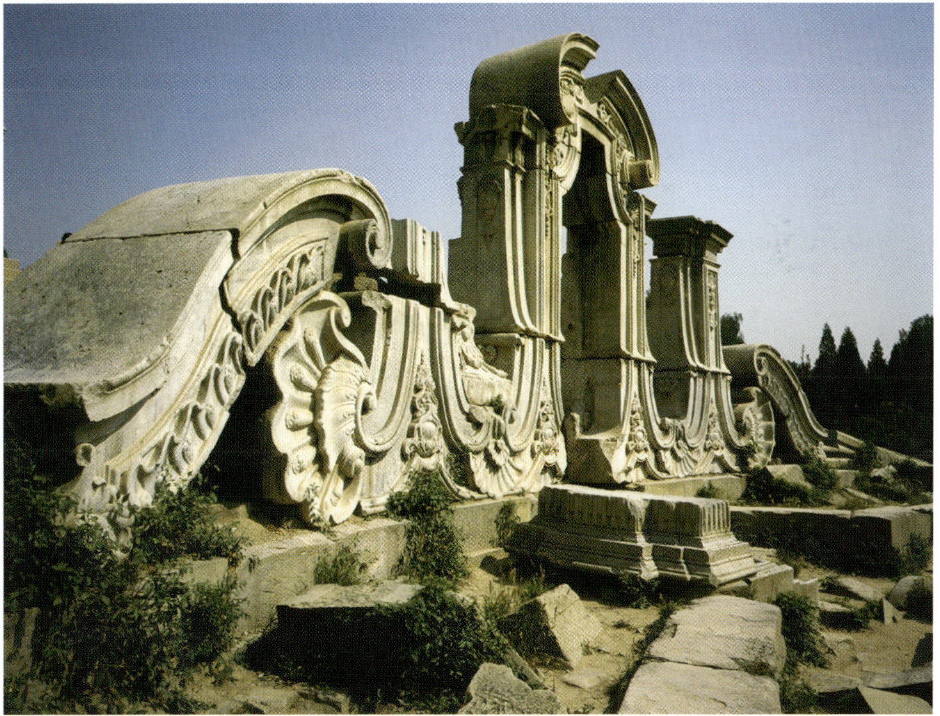

below: From the top of the tower which protects the Emperor's Tomb at Shisan Ling, this view looks back towards the entrance pavilion. The site is dotted with small temples and pavilions, and shaded by cypress and oak trees. Behind the pavilions and temples, a grass-covered mound – the Chinese equivalent of the Egyptian pyramids – contains the remains of the Emperor.

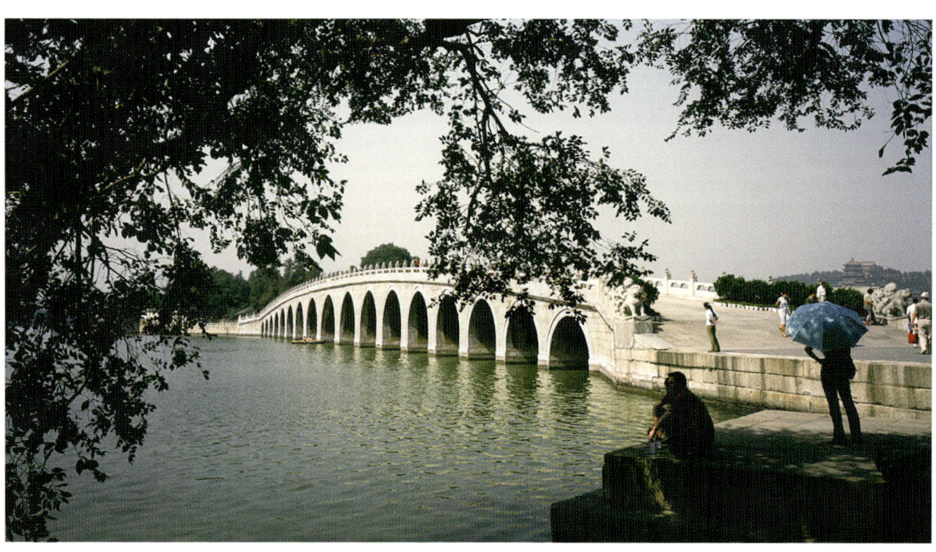

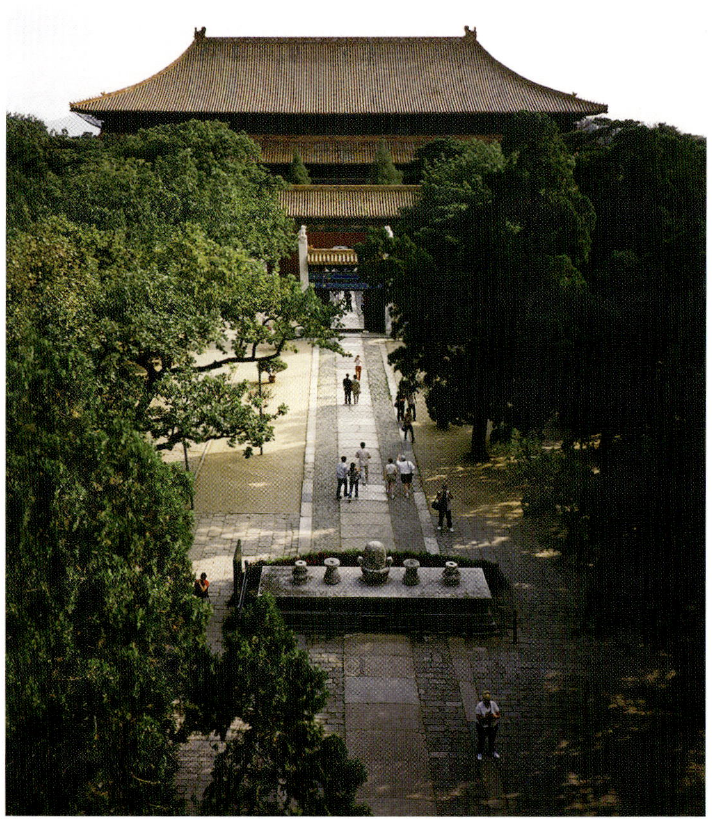

above: In a scene little changed from when Thomson stood his camera on almost the same spot, locals enjoy the autumn sunshine by the marble bridge which leads to a small island in Kumming Lake.
right: The Mable Boat on Kumming Lake is one of the many elegant architectural features in the parklands which surround the Summer Palace.

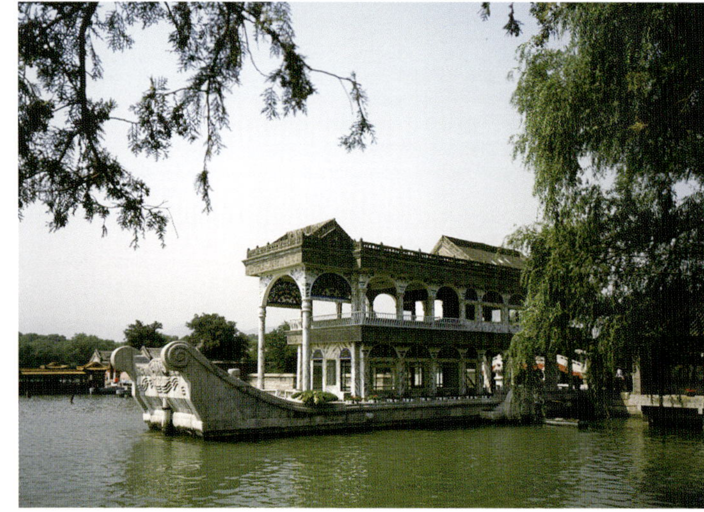

My readers, doubtless share with me in feeling that no illustrated work on China would be worthy of its name if it did not contain a picture of some portion of the Great Wall. This wall is an object neither picturesque nor striking. Viewing it simple as a wall, we find its masonry often defective, and it is not so solid or honestly constructed as one at first sight might imagine. Not a few travellers regard this wall as the greatest

below left: One of the many gargoyles which decorate the balustrades surrounding a pavilion at the Ming Tombs. Here, thirty miles north of Beijing, thirteen Ming Emperors are buried.

below right: The Great Sacrificial Hall at the Tomb of Emperor Yung-Lo was Plate XXI in the fourth volume of Thomson's travels. Like most of the ancient sites he visited, he found the place much in need of attention. *'The Manchu Emperors'*, he wrote, *'though we find them sacrificing to the departed spirits of the Ming sovereigns, bestow little attention upon the buildings of their tombs. Weeds grow in rank luxuriance over the marble pavements, on the steps, the balustrades, and the roofs. Notwithstanding all this, the substantial nature of the structure has defied all the ravages of time.'*

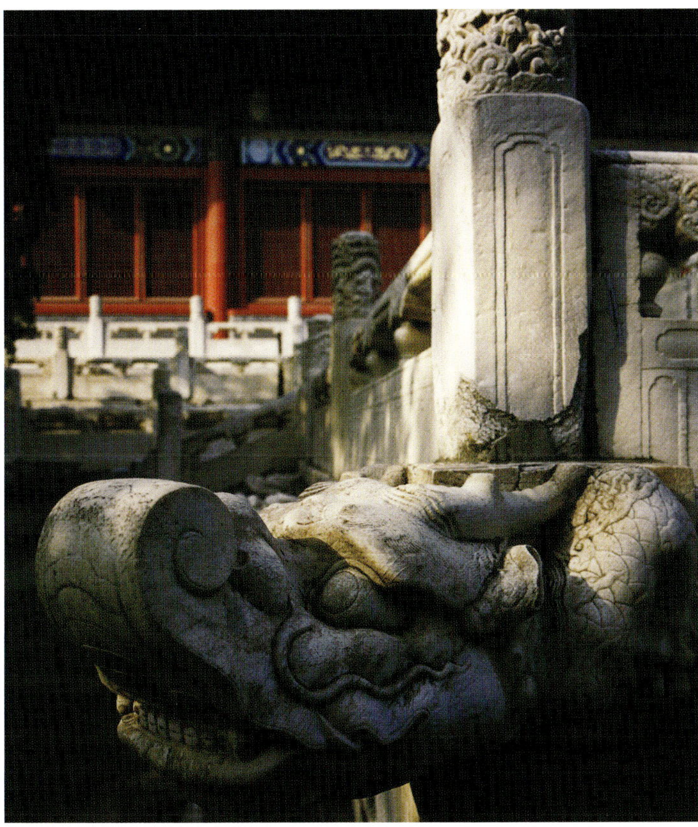

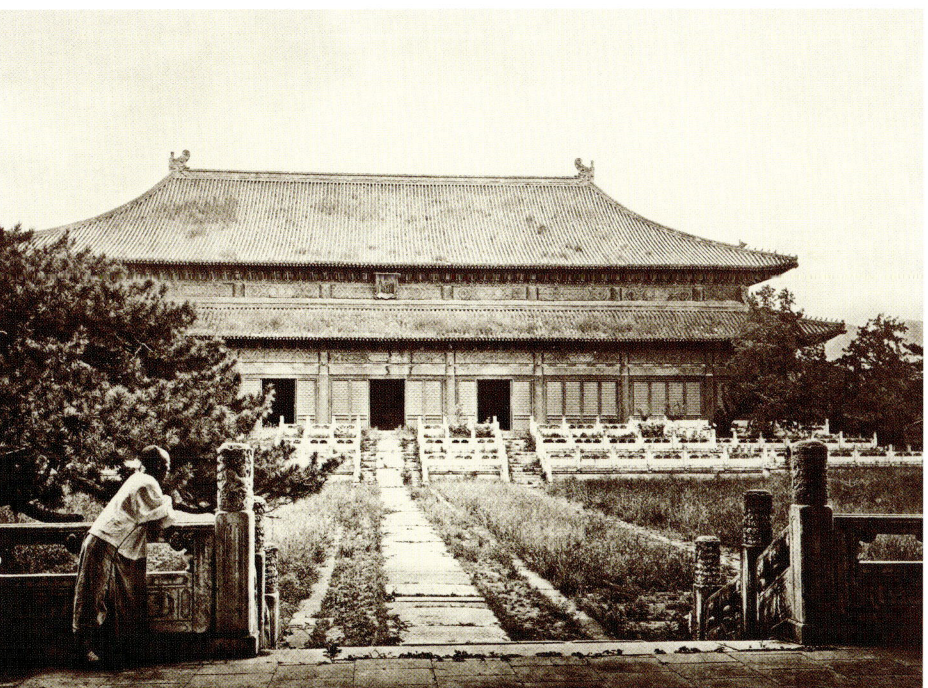

monument of misdirected human labour to be met with in the whole world…[16]

To dismiss one of the acknowledged wonders of the world in such terms is remarkable, and expresses an opinion hardly shared by the millions who visit it each year. Claimed to be the only work of human endeavour visible from space – though it is not in fact visible – the wall, winding its way over mountain peaks as far into the distance as the eye can see, rivals the pyramids in terms of magnificence.

Climbing the pyramids is no longer allowed, and some might say climbing the Great Wall of China might usefully be banned as well – if for no other reason than the toll it takes on one's limbs. The wall follows the natural contours of the landscape, so when the mountainside is extremely steep, so is the wall. Yet the crowds climbing it on an autumn Saturday defied description. Half way up one of the less severely steep climbs, padlocks decked

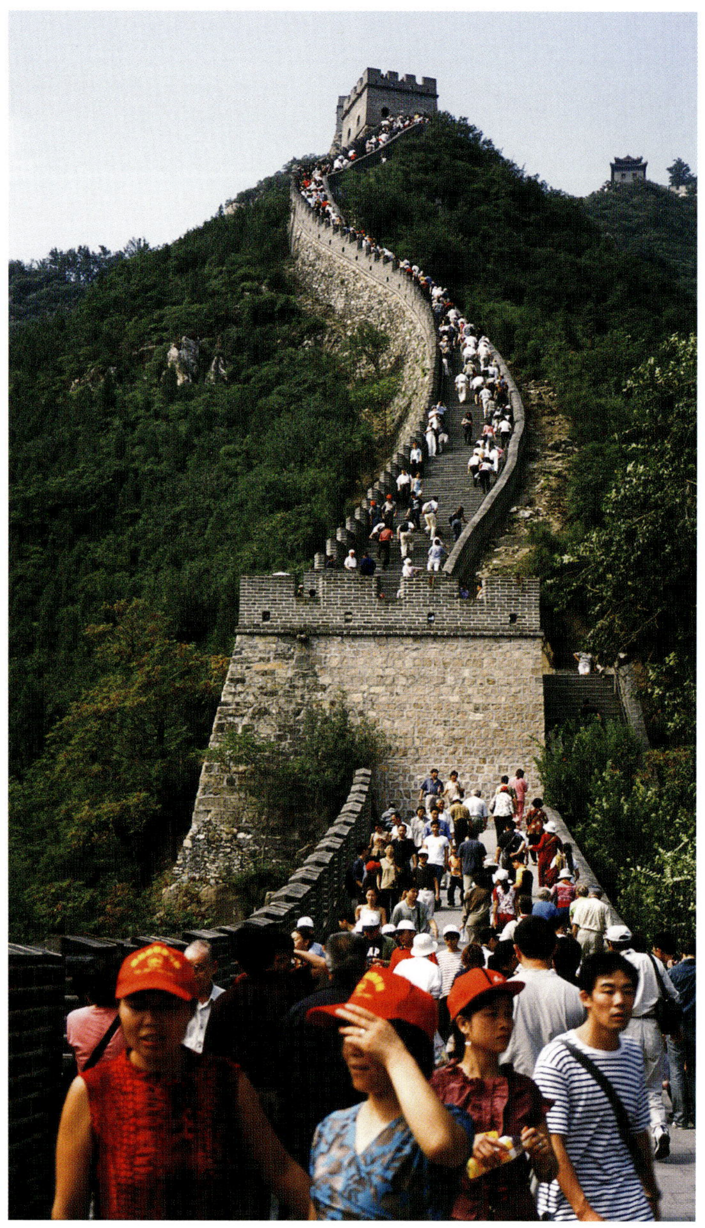

right: Crowds of visitors climbing a section of the Great Wall of China at Baddaling, a few miles north of Beijing on an autumn Saturday morning. This being one of the most accessible sections of the wall, it is one of the busiest. From the top, the views of the wall winding its way into the distance across the mountains are spectacular.

with red ribbons are attached to a chain along one side. Here Chinese couples mark their enduring love for each other by leaving a padlock as a symbol of their union.

Beneath the wall, photographers with open-air studios, replica thrones, and live horses and camels, offer the opportunity to be photographed in a variety of ancient costumes and settings. On the day we visited, they were doing little business. In Beijing a few miles away on the previous day, photographers similarly equipped - except that their horses and camels were stuffed - had been doing a roaring trade.

The Great Wall, originally built to keep people out, has ironically become one of the major attractions which now brings increasingly large numbers of visitors into the country. There are even charity walks organised on stretches of the wall. Times have changed completely.

Thomson's journey was a major undertaking, and his book was groundbreaking in its ambition and scale. In the introduction, he wrote

> *It is a novel experiment to attempt to illustrate a book of travels with photographs, a few years back so perishable, and so difficult to reproduce. I feel somewhat sanguine about the success of the undertaking, and I hope to see the process which I have thus applied adopted by other travellers.*[17]

It was adopted by other travellers, Mr Thomson, it was, and I am simply the latest in a long tradition of travellers with cameras.

Thomson's account of his journey through China has, at times, a slightly superior air to it - perhaps concentrating too often on negative aspects of Chinese culture and civilisation. But then, in his *Street Life in London*, he took exactly the same approach to London's East End.

Despite the fact that his photography is firmly rooted in the western Victorian aesthetic, Thomson probably approached China with a completely open mind. He did not know what to expect, and responded spontaneously to what he found. That gives his work a freshness and a documentary value untypical of the era.

below: A victim of its own popularity, the Great Wall now needs an army of cleaners to pick up litter and keep it tidy.
below right: A photographer's outdoor studio beneath the wall, on a quiet day for business. Here visitors can be photographed wearing a variety of traditional costumes, or posed sitting on a throne or a camel
bottom: Padlocks and ribbons on the wall are a symbol of everlasting love.

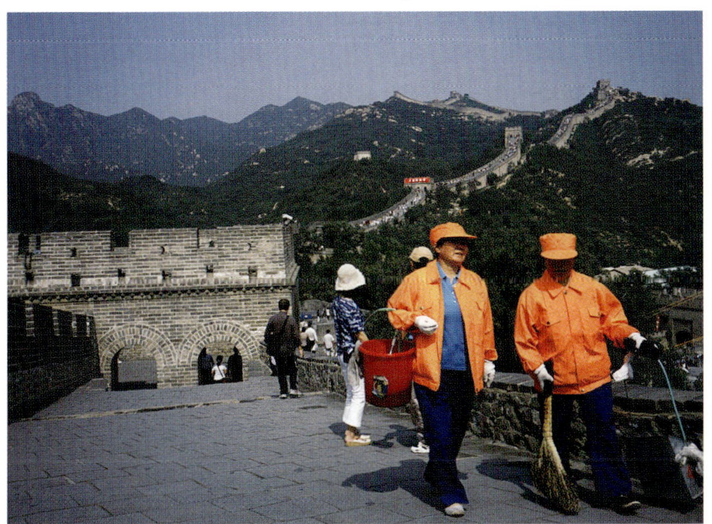

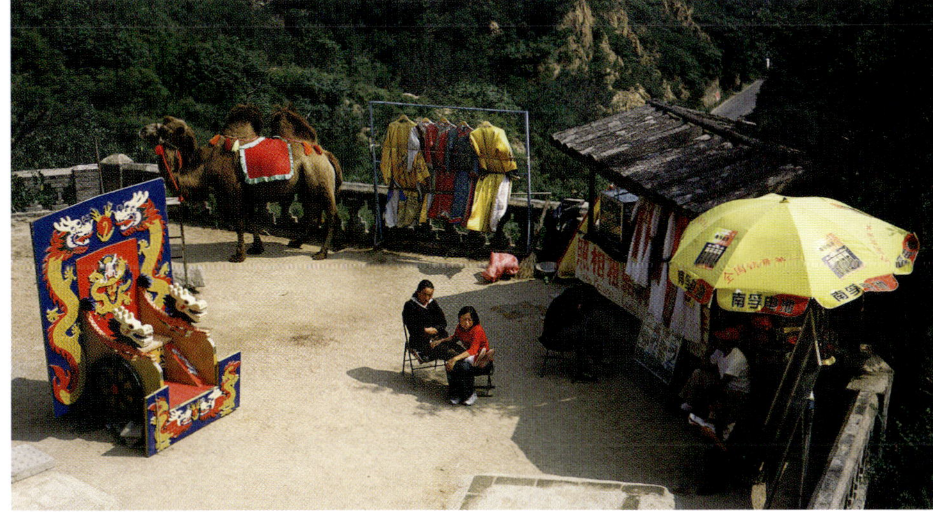

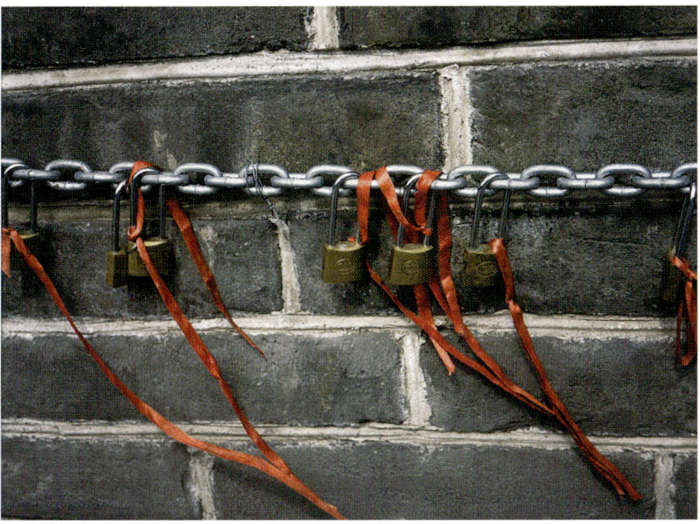

Despite undertaking the usual research before embarking, China surprised me in unexpected ways. Discovering that the city of Chongqing, a place I had never heard of before planning the trip, is one of the world's largest and most heavily industrialised connurbations (and polluted) came as a real surprise.

And on more than one occasion, the country proved it still had the ability to unnerve the traveller. On the coach from Shashi to Wuhan, we were stopped at a checkpoint, while police gave the coach and its passengers a quick, but by no means cursory, check-over.

My interpreter informed me that a few weeks earlier, a coach on the same route had been stopped by a gang of bandits, and the passengers robbed. By way of intended reassurance, I was told that the police were taking steps to make sure it did not happen again. For my part, I would

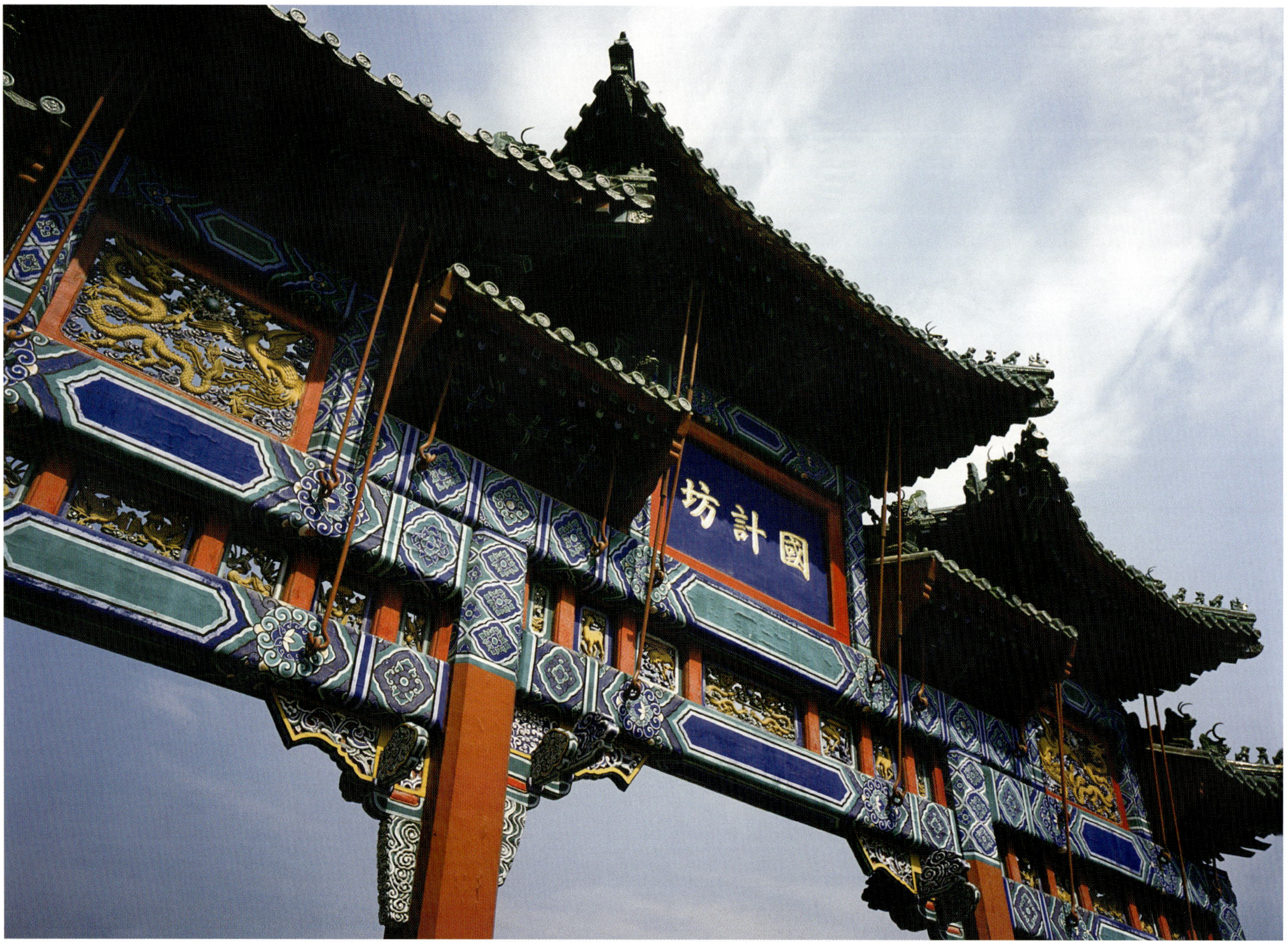
國計坊

probably have been happier knowing nothing about it!

The China through which I travelled had changed significantly since Thomson's day. His journeys, spread over several years, each required him to be effectively 'on the road' for several months at a time, traversing difficult terrain with the huge bulk of his equipment and materials. In that respect, today's traveller recreating his itinerary has life a lot easier. If one thing marks out the advances recently made within China, it is the increasing ease of transport – particularly air travel – and the modernity of the jet fleet.

While he laboured over steep mountain passes with mule trains and ox carts, my journey was largely completed by air in modern Boeing 737s and 767s, by road in comfortable modern cars and coaches, and by river in a surprisingly well-appointed cruise ship.

Even Thomson, writing in 1866, could not resist a final comment about the transport available to him

> *Since my return to England, I have been frequently asked the question – "How did you manage to carry your glass plates such a distance over rough roads, and in rude, springless, jolting conveyances?*[18]

Even the simple choice of wording for that statement suggests just how uncomfortable his experiences must have been. For him, strongly made plate boxes was the answer.

For me, it was a lightweight camera, a padded camera bag, a small cool bag for the film, and the undeniable comfort of assorted Chinese airlines!

opposite page: The brightly coloured great arch at Baddaling, at the entrance to the wall, is a symbol of Chinese culture now recognised and found in Chinatowns the world over. Thomson photographed several similar arches in Beijing and elsewhere throughout China in the 1870s.
below: In a Beijing park, during the mid-autmn festival, brightly coloured balloons sway in the warm breeze.

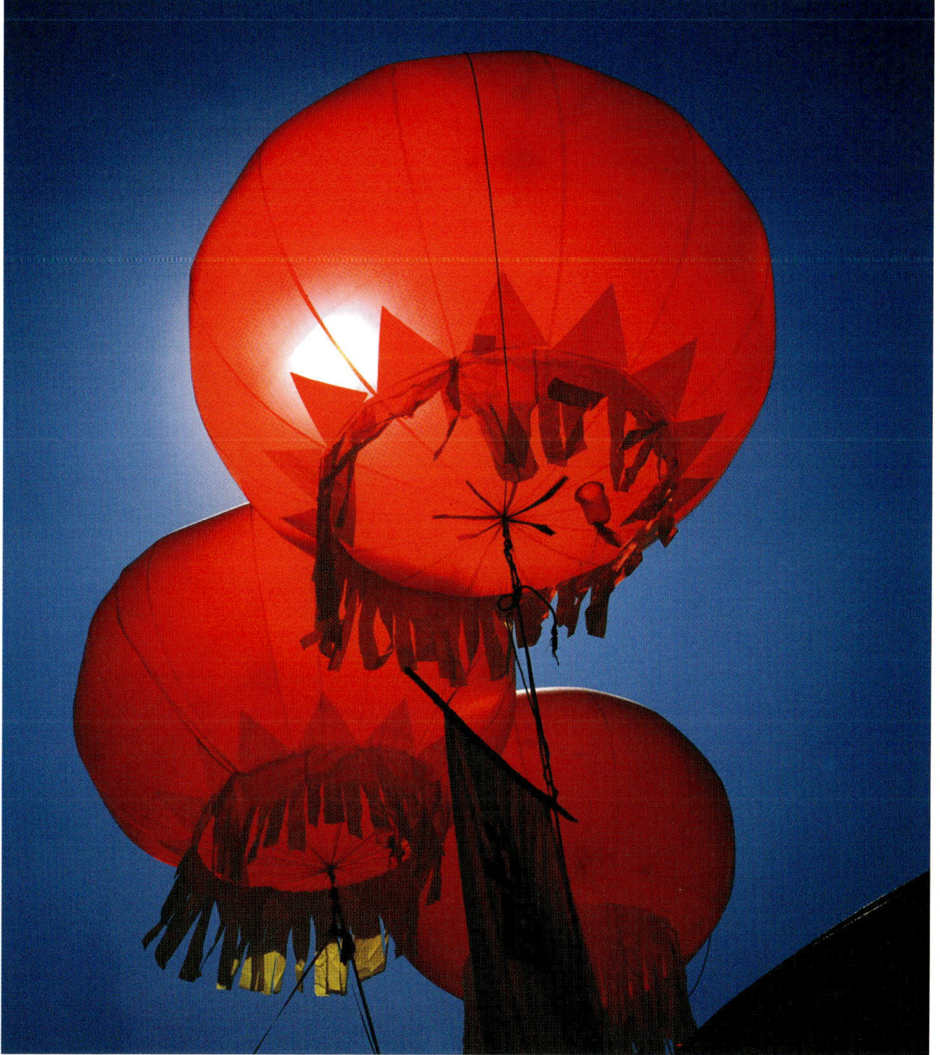

below: The area around the Forbidden City is rich in sculptural decoration.
right: A brightly painted dragon decorates one of the inner chambers in the mountain-top temple at Fengdu on the Yangtse.

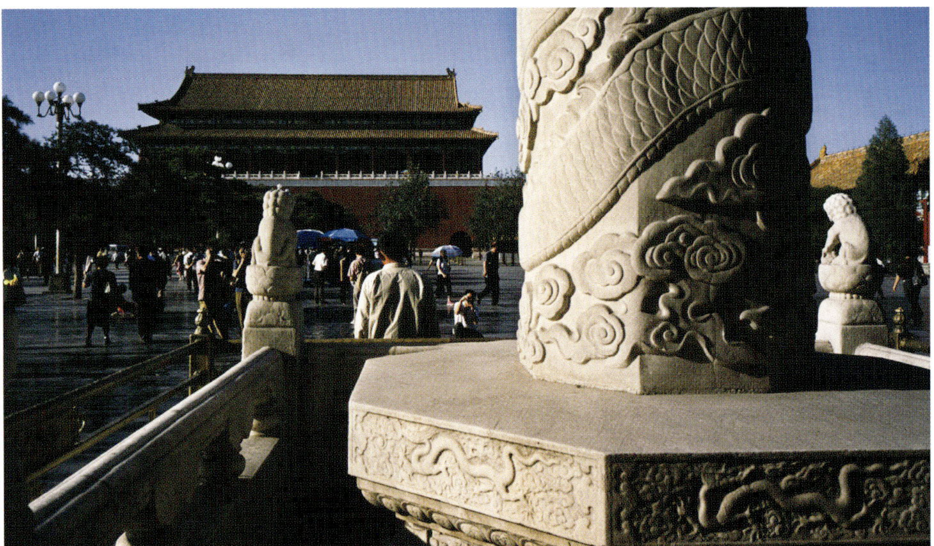

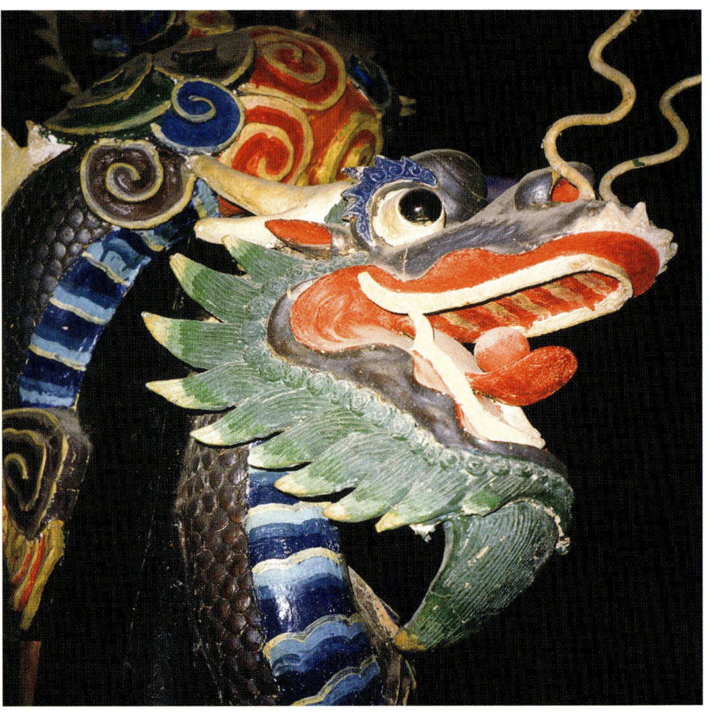

Notes

1. John Thomson: *Illustrations of China and its People. A Series of Two Hundred Photographs with Letterpress Descriptions of the Places and People Represented,* London, Sampson Low, Marston, Low, and Searle, Vols I & II 1873, Vols III & IV, 1874.
2. *ibid*. Introduction.
3. *British Journal of Photography*, August 10th 1866, p380; August 17th 1866, p393; August 24th 1866, p404; October 5th 1866, pp472-3; October 12th 1866, p487.
4. John Thomson: *The Antiquities of Cambodia: A Series of Photographs taken on the spot, with letterpress descriptions,* Edinburgh, Edmonston and Douglas, 1867.
5. John Thomson: *Illustrations of China and its People*, description accompanying Vol. I plate III.
6. *ibid*. Vol I Plate XIX.
7. *British Journal of Photography*, August 10th 1866, p380.
8. Walter Bentley Woodbury: *Treasure Spots of the World*, London, Ward, Lock, and Tyler, 1875. Thomson's description accompanying his view of Amoy Harbour.
9. *British Journal of Photography*, August 10th 1866, p380.
10. do.
11. John Thomson: *Illustrations of China and its People*, description accompanying Vol. III plate XVII.
12. Quoted by Janet Lehr in the introduction to the Dover edition of *China and its People in Early Photograph*s, New York, Dover Publications Inc. 1982.
13. John Thomson: *Illustrations of China and its People*, description accompanying Vol. IV plate XVIII.
14. *do*.
15. *ibid*. Vol. IV plate XIX.
16. *ibid*. Vol. IV plate XXIV.
17. *ibid*. Introduction.
18. *British Journal of Photography*, August 24th 1866, p404.

THROUGH CYPRUS

WITH THE CAMERA,

IN THE AUTUMN OF 1878

BY

JOHN THOMSON, F.R.G.S.,

Author of "Illustrations of China and its People," "The Straits of Malacca, Indo-China, and China," etc.

IN TWO VOLUMES.

WITH SIXTY PERMANENT PHOTOGRAPHS.

VOL. I.

London:

SAMPSON LOW, MARSTON, SEARLE, AND RIVINGTON,

CROWN BUILDINGS, 188, FLEET STREET.

1879.

John Thomson

Through Cyprus with the Camera

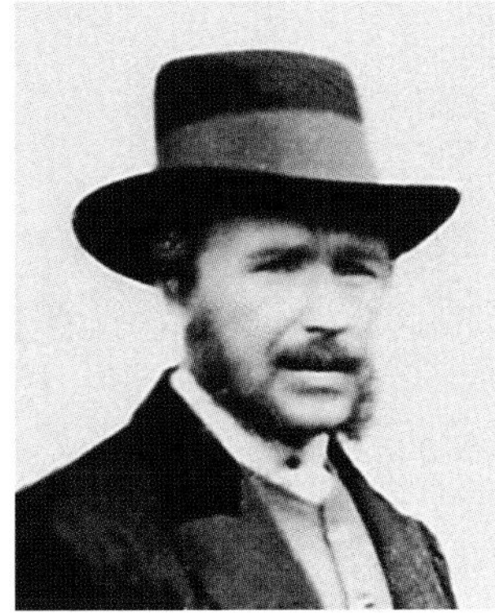

above: John Thomson F.R.G.S., self-portrait, 1871

below: A street in Larnaca. One of the first pictures Thomson took after his arrival on the island, and used as Plate 5 in his 1878 book *Through Cyprus with the Camera in the Autumn of 1878,* published in two volumes by Sampson, Low, Marston, Searle and Rivington, of Fleet Street, London, in the following year. The houses were, according to Thomson, built of stone taken from the ruins of 'Citium' – the Graeco-Roman coastal city of Kourion a few miles west of Larnaca.

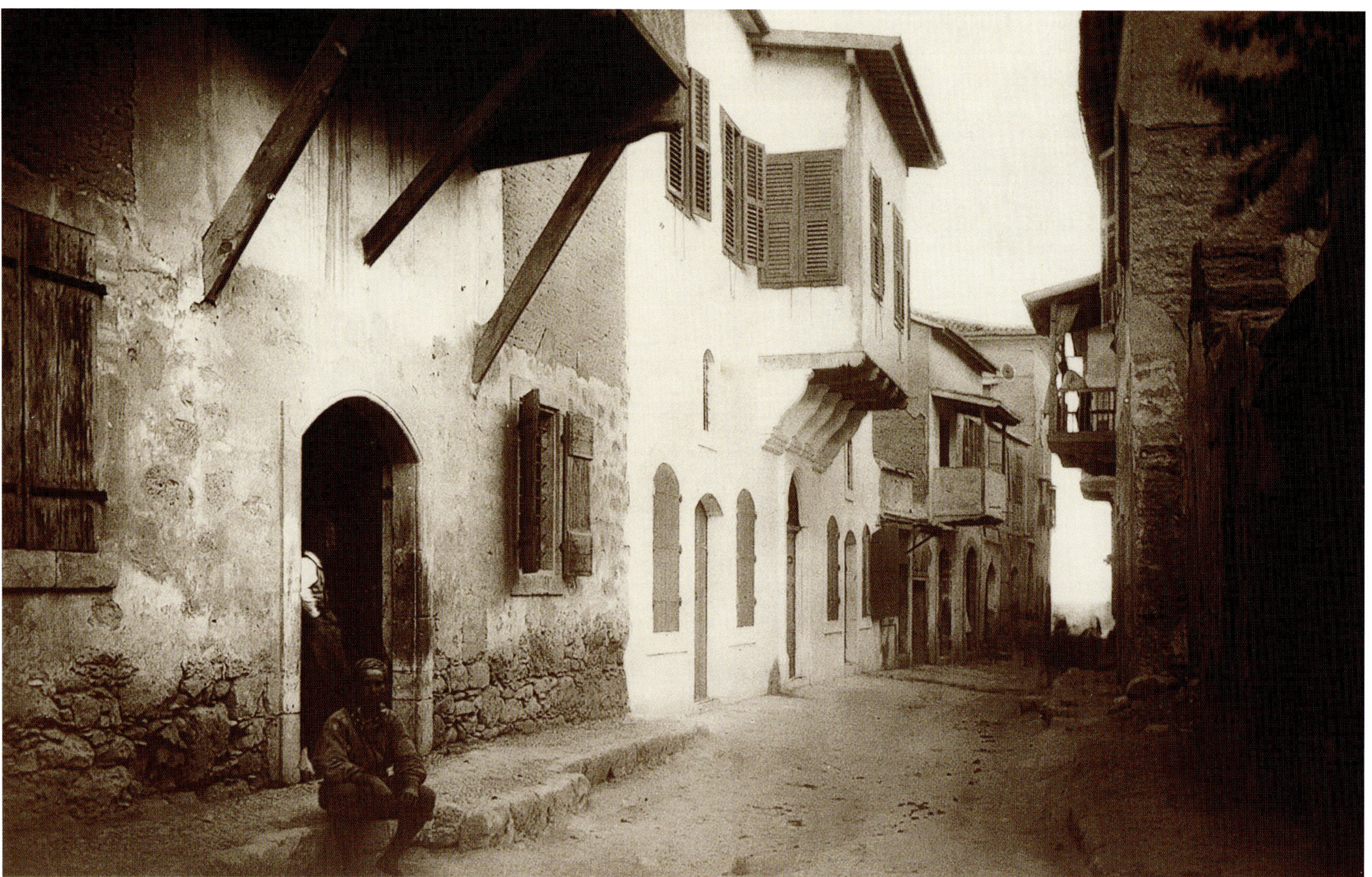

Standing by the Green Line, the UN-patrolled border which separates the Republic of Cyprus from Turkish-controlled Northern Cyprus – a border which has existed now for over thirty years – I realised that if I was to recreate John Thomson's journey around the island, two visits rather than one were going to be necessary. Going through the border to visit Bellapais Abbey for the first time had been neither easy or pleasant. That had been more than ten years ago. A decade later little had changed.

Because of the uneasy military situation, it was going to be difficult, if not impossible, to gain access to some of the places he visited. And yet, so much of the beauty of the island, which Thomson celebrated through his photographs, was along the north coast. Writing in the introduction to his 1879 book *Through Cyprus with the Camera in the Autumn of 1878*, Thomson had been equally uneasy a century and a quarter before me, when he wrote

> *The objects I had in view when – in spite of dangers, some real, some imaginary – I determined to visit Cyprus were two-fold. The first was to obtain a series of photographs of the island and its people; and the second to so supplement these pictures by personal observation as to present to the public a faithful reproduction of what I saw and heard during my travels.*[1]

Why dangers? Well, Cyprus had gone through one of the many turbulent periods in its history. Only a few months earlier, it had come under British control, and that change may well have been one of the triggers for Thomson's journey.[2] While in China and Hong Kong he had developed a considerable reputation as a travel photographer – bringing his unique combination of journalistic approach and ethnographic enthusiasm to his work. The increased accessibility of the beauties of Cyprus under British control, and his continuing passion for travel probably proved too much of a temptation.

The island to which he journeyed was impoverished, backward and largely unchanged for centuries. It was a remarkable opportunity to document a lifestyle and a

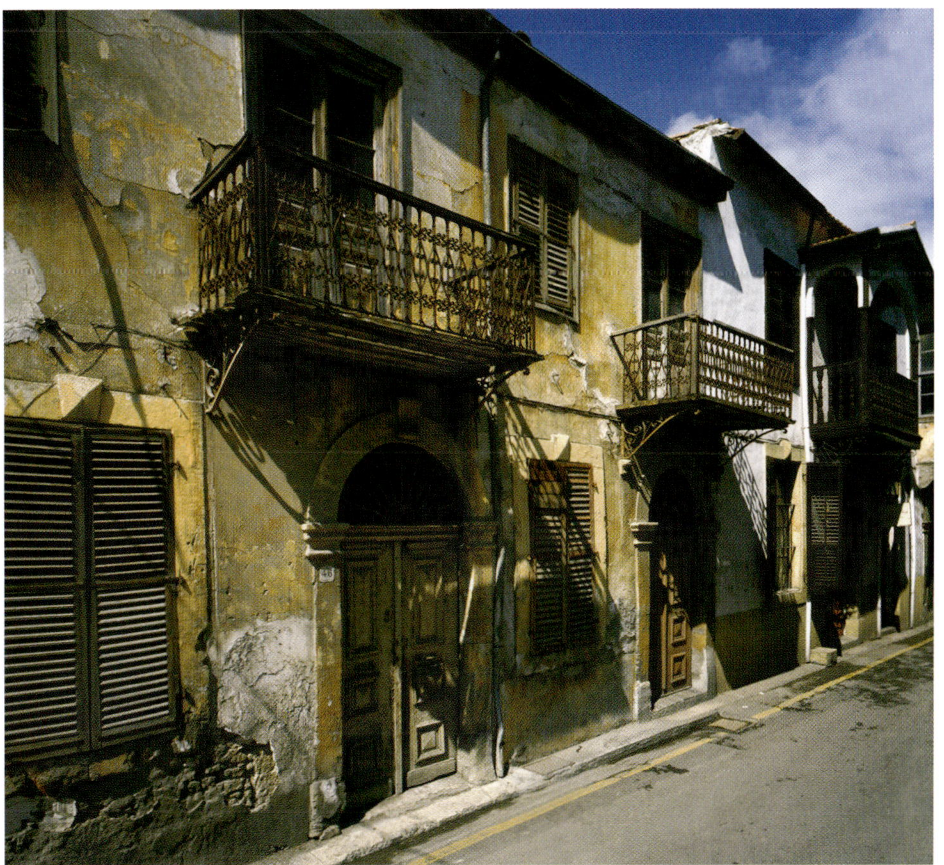

above: A back street in Nicosia still retains the character of the architecture which Thomson photographed in 1878.

right: An open-air fruit and vegetable market in Nicosia. The island abounds with citrus groves, vineyards and olive groves, and the plentiful supply of fresh fruit can be found for sale on hundreds of roadside stalls, as well as in large markets like this.

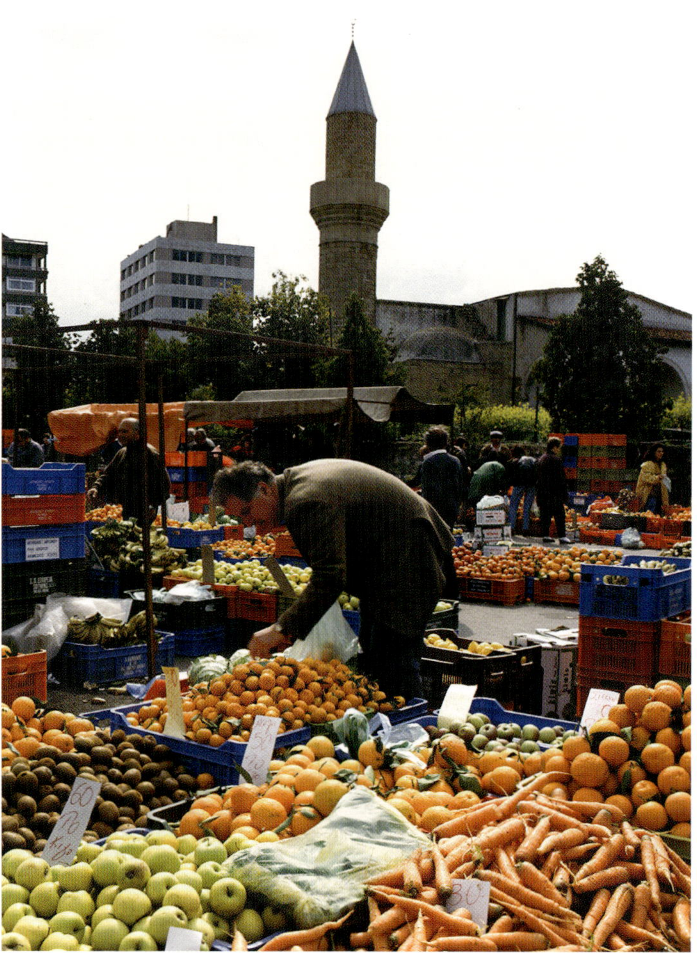

culture about as far removed from Victorian Britain as he could have imagined.

In some respects the island, away from the tourist haunts, still offers that opportunity. In the foothills of the Troodos Mountains, some village communities still live their lives in something like the simple self-reliance of centuries ago.

Driving up a dirt track towards the village of Fikardou, I came across two old ladies, swathed in black from head to foot and resolutely unwilling to be photographed. They were leading two equally ancient mules laden with firewood up the same track. I had got lost some miles earlier and driven off the metalled road. They were simply going about their daily business.

Cyprus today is still an island of extreme contrasts – an uneasy mixture of affluent and peasant lifestyles, of local farmers trying to eke out a living on the land while a few miles away on the south coast, the ever-growing number of hotels and resorts cater for the ever-increasing number of holidaymakers whose pounds and euros skew the economy disastrously.

The island's economic divide is still exacerbated by the 'Green Line'. While there is greater freedom of movement across the border now than there was when I first attempted to recreate Thomson's odyssey a decade ago, that border marks more than just a political divide. For however difficult life inland might be south of the border, the standards of living endured by the rural inhabitants of the breakaway north are much lower.

The border runs through the capital, Nicosia – Lefkosia to the predominantly Greek southerners, Lefkosa to the Turkish north. Ironically, the Turkish name is the older one, while the internationally accepted spelling of Nicosia is a 'reading' of the Greek name largely imposed by the British.

Just as in Thomson's day, however, Cyprus is an island of immense beauty, with interesting architectural juxtapositions brought about by the many cultures and peoples who have influenced its development. The primary influences are Greek, Turkish, Venetian and British, while archaeologically, important Roman and Graeco-Roman sites are scattered along the north and south coasts, and draw visitors in their tens of thousands each year.

John Thomson's pictures were a mixture of architectural views, and portraits of local people - not as heavily biased towards the people as was his oeuvre in China, Vietnam and elsewhere in south east Asia, but nonetheless capturing something of the character of the towns, villages and monasteries he visited. This was to be his last great journey - as indeed it was mine, at least as far as this book is concerned - and his pictures perhaps reflect his waning enthusiasm for being so far from home for so long.

Many of the images of local people which he did include were captured as surprisingly straightforward portraits, endowing them with a formality which was at odds with their humble lifestyles - though they did show a greater willingness to pose for the camera than proved to be the case in the more remote villages today.

There was a reason for the rather more static nature of the portraits - Thomson was, by 1878, using pre-coated dry collodion plates which, while they gave images of equivalent quality to their wet collodion counterparts, had only a fraction of the sensitivity to light. Thus, for his studies of Cypriot people he had to resort to the style of carefully posed formal portraiture which had been universally commonplace two decades earlier.

Because of its reduced sensitivity, photographers had been quite reluctant to change over to the dry process, despite it having been available in various practical forms for well over a decade.[3]

Freedom from the challenges of coating his plates just before use and exposing them wet must have made this journey substantially less physically demanding than his journeys through China a few years earlier.

With dry plates, while there was not the rigid requirement that the plate be processed immediately after

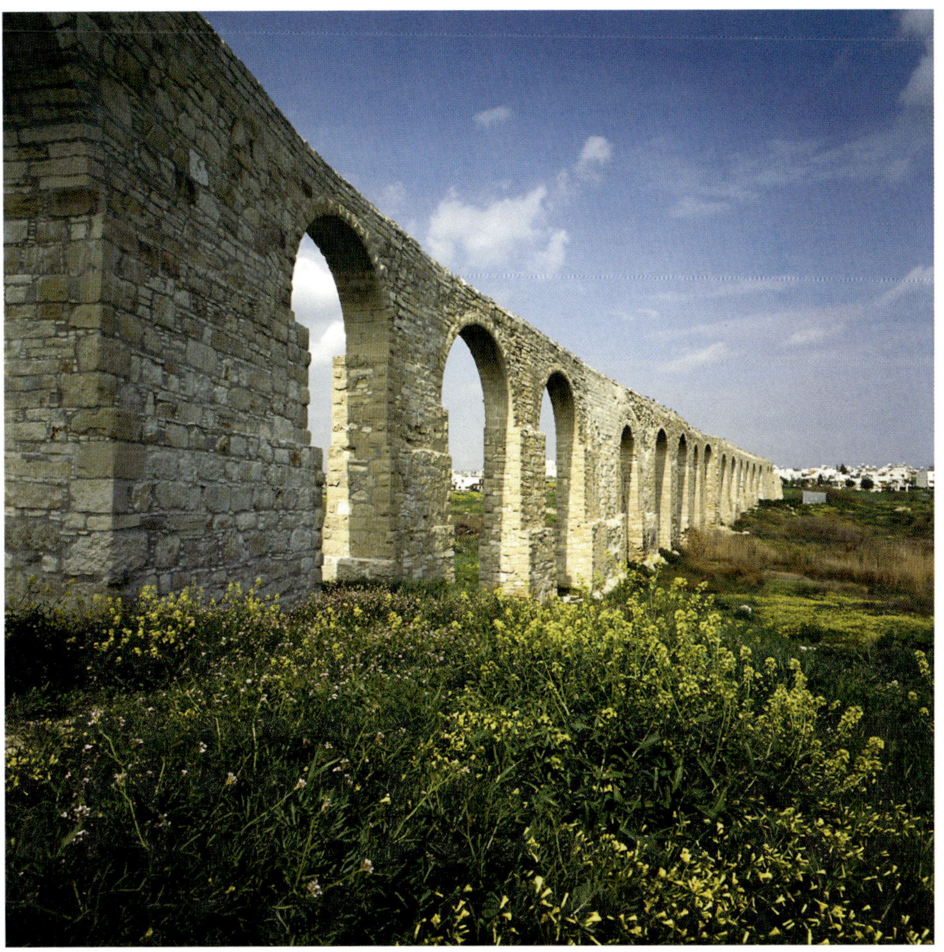

above: A springtime view of the 18th century Venetian aquaduct which brought the first fresh water supply to Larnaca. This elegant structure dominates the Kamares district of the city.

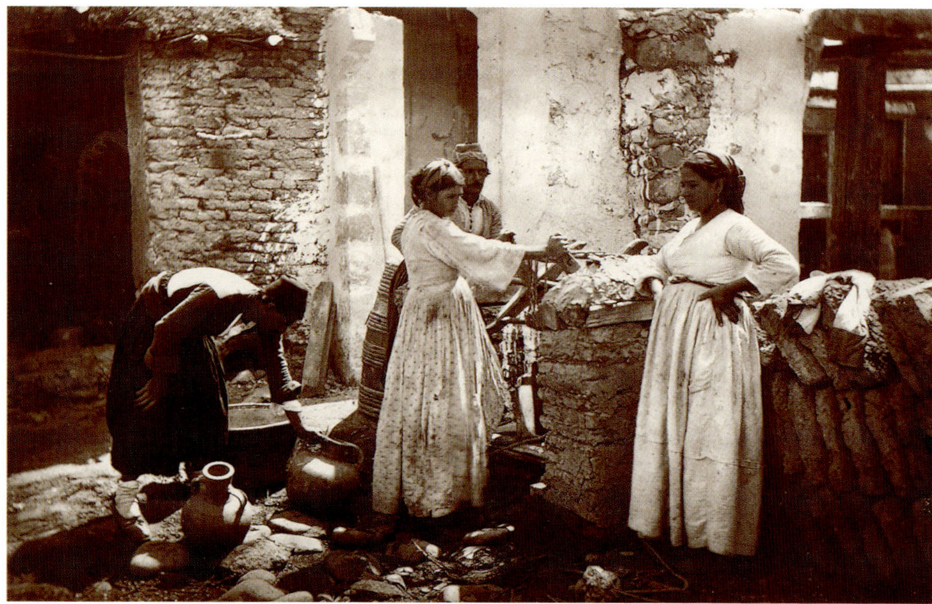

above: Women at the Well, Levka, was one of Thomson's most eloquent group portraits of the Cypriot people. '*It is astonishing*', he wrote in his extended caption for the picture, '*to see how deftly the drawing of water is managed even by children, although the women among Cypriot peasantry form the recognized drawers of water. Still, the heat and the labour are made light of, and these wells form as they did in Jacob's time, pleasant meeting-places where young men and maidens gather together, and where leisure is found for discussing topics more engrossing than the vulgar gossip of every-day life. It somehow happens that young and pretty women are to be found filling their jars just at the moment when men may be expected from the fields, or when a troop from some distant village has halted for refreshment. Then it is that the rope gets entangled with the spokes of the windlass, or the bucket flirts with the water and refuses to be filled, and so the sun declines beneath the horizon before the jars are fairly poised and born away.*'

exposure, doing so was a reassurance that the pictures were successful before moving on to the next location, so he probably did have a darktent with him. Many of his plates, however, would probably have been developed in hotels and inns each evening - a freedom photographers had not enjoyed since the abandonment of the Waxed Paper process at the end of the 1850s.

The increase in exposure time over the wet collodion - with which he had been familiar for years - would have been considerable and not aided by the size of the camera he took with him. From an engraving based on one of Thomson's own sketches which appeared in the *Illustrated London News*, it may look as though he was working with a very large instrument indeed, but from the surviving images and negatives, we have to accept that a bit of artistic licence was used! However, the large 15"x12" plates would have required substantially longer exposures than he had needed in China.

Thomson and I both entered Cyprus through Larnaca. While in my case it was through the international airport after a direct flight from Manchester lasting only about five hours, he arrived by ship into what was then a small port. He set foot on Cypriot soil on September 7th 1878, after a long voyage on the steamer *Arethusa*, arriving only three months after the British had officially taken control of the island.

However, while he was able to tour the entire island, I would only have been able to travel through the border on a day visa, so to recreate the northern part of his journey, I had to make a separate trip from Manchester to Geçitcale via Istanbul!

Thomson's first impressions were not good! After the brief explanatory statement with which this chapter opened, he went on to remark

> *Had I allowed first impressions to influence me, I should have set my face homeward soon after landing at Larnaca; for in that town I found a number of assembled immigrants bewailing the want of forethought that had brought them and*

below: In the ancient amphitheatre of the city-state of Kourion – referred to as 'Citium' by Thomson – children from local schools re-enact a Greek tragedy in the warm spring sunshine, watched by a few tourists visiting the island out of season. In the summer the theatre is the setting for a programme of performances. The amphitheatre was completed in the 2nd century AD, replacing a Hellenic theatre of four centuries earlier. The theatre can seat 3,400 people, and was excavated and restored in the 1960s. In the 1870s, the local people prophesied to Thomson that the British would soon demolish the remains of 'Citium' and build a fine new city on the site!

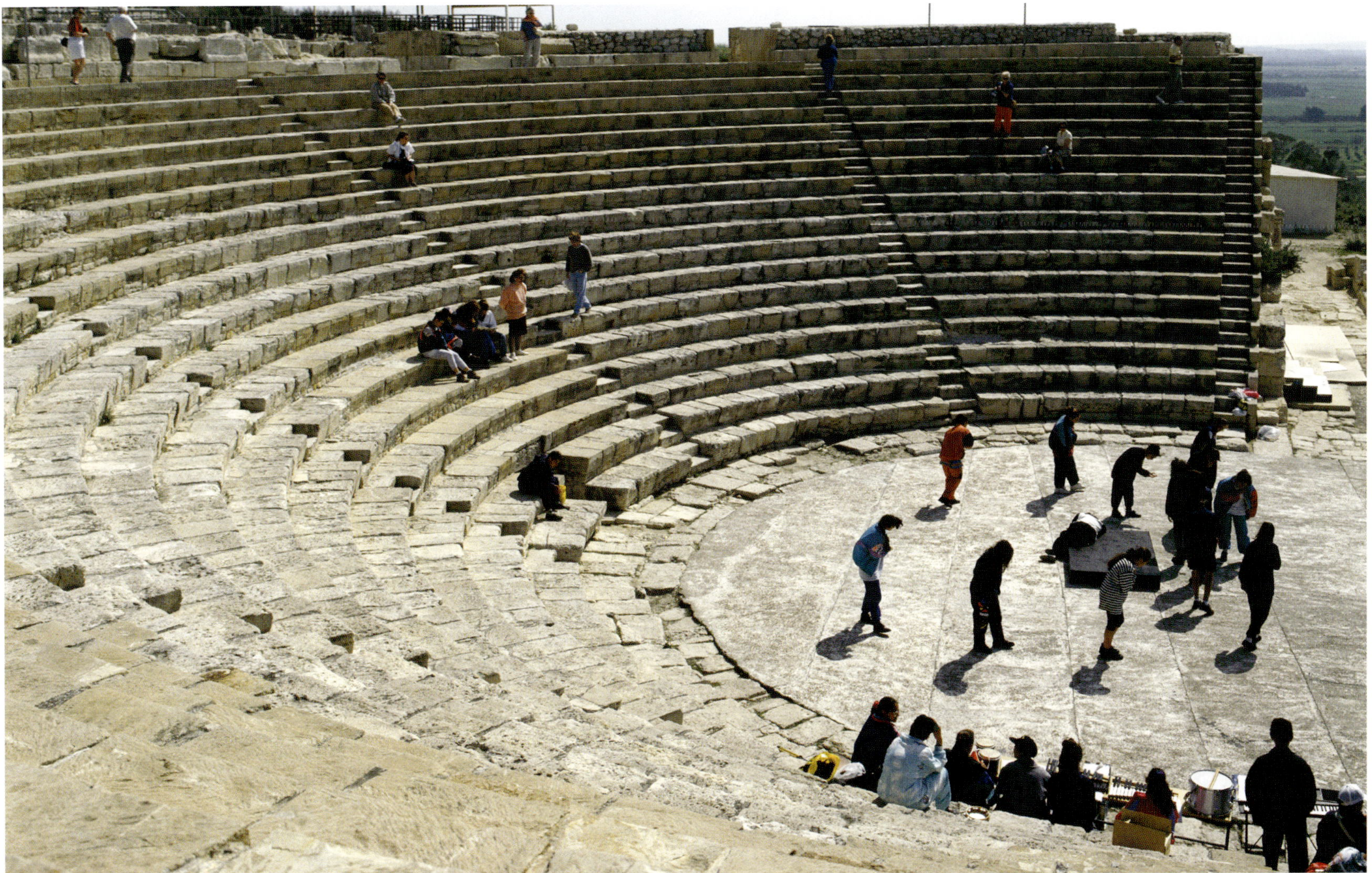

their wares to an "exhausted island' never free from pestilence, and to a poverty-stricken people.

Gloomy forebodings thus greeted me on all sides; but in the end I took what turned out to be the right course. I thought that, after all, I could wait and see things for myself, and pursue my original plan of exploring Cyprus with the "camera" taking views (as impartial as they were photographic) of whatever might prove interesting on the journey.[4]

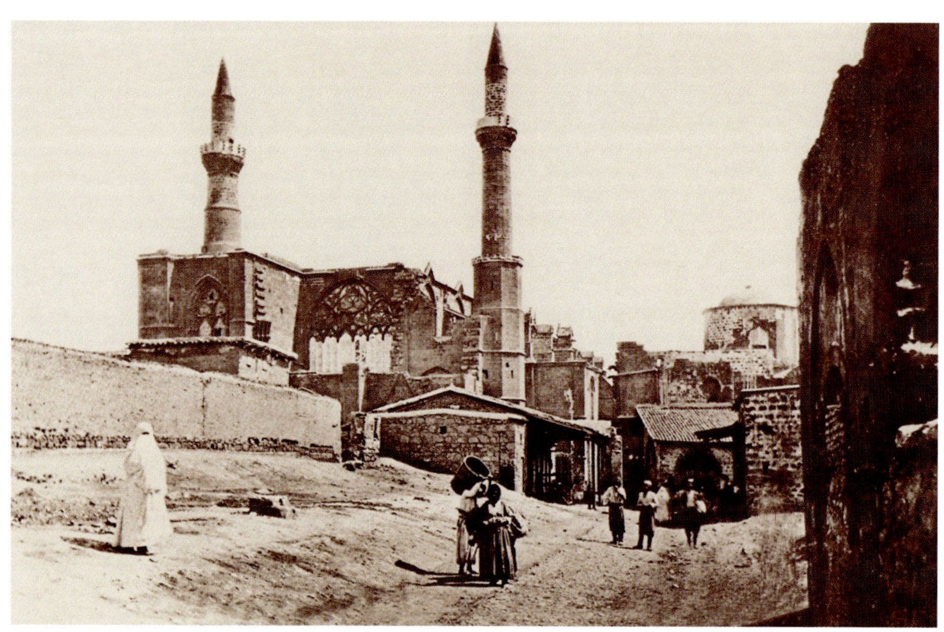

above: A group of people posed in front of the former St Sophia Cathedral in Nicosia. Thomson, who had a great fondness for Gothic architecture noted '*It is fortunate that Moslem* [sic] *economy, or, perhaps, lack of fanatical zeal, has preserved to us so much of this fine specimen of early Gothic architecture. The tower, which once crowned the edifice, has given place to galleried minarets; the old sonorous summons of the cathedral bell has been exchanged for muezzins, which each morning and evening call the faithful to prayer.*' The area where the cathedral stands is now in the northern, Turkish, quarter of the city. The Selimiye Mosque – Thomson never referred to it as anything other than St Sophia's – is today hemmed in by an assortment of buildings, making a recreation of his view quite impossible

The sense of Thomson 'stepping into the unknown' is clear from his choice of words. Cyprus had endured a turbulent past, but we might be forgiven for expecting someone with Thomson's experience of travel to have been able to put such trepidation behind him!

The pictures, which would eventually be published in a two volume set of books entitled *Through Cyprus with the Camera in the Autumn of 1878*, were reproduced by the autotype process[5] as had been the illustrations to his earlier publication, the four-volume *Illustrations of China and Its People*.[6]

Heading north from Larnaca, Thomson spent his first night in the village of Athienou, before proceeding onwards to Nicosia. Arriving late at night, I went directly to Nicosia, staying in a modern hotel close to the UN Green Line.

From Nicosia, Thomson made the journey north to the coast and Kyrenia. On my first visit, I did too, but my journey involved passing through the UN checkpoint at the Ledra Palace Hotel, leaving the Republic of Cyprus, and entering the Republic of Northern Cyprus.

The Green Line is a veritable no-man's land, still time-locked in 1974 with, so the stories go, streets of shops untouched since the day their owners fled from the advancing Turkish army. The Ledra Palace Hotel, and the adjacent buildings still bear the scars of the conflict.

All along the northern side of the line, a sense of the border's impact can be seen in derelict buildings, uninhabitable and unsaleable.

Once through the border, I left one capital city and entered another – Lefkosa – and passed the great Selimiye

Mosque which now occupies the former Cathedral of St. Sophia. The mixture of Gothic architecture and minarets is one of the most unusual and fascinating combinations of church architecture I have ever seen. Thomson was unimpressed, simply suggesting that the poverty of the island had probably stopped the cathedral's demolition and replacement by a more traditional design of mosque, and had thus

> *...preserved to us so much of this fine specimen of early Gothic architecture.*

Thomson was, however, able to get a picture of the west front of the great building - something not possible today as buildings and narrow streets make a clear view impossible.

Between Lefkosa and Kyrenia, Thomson passed through plantations of olives, vineyards, and fields of cotton before making his way through the narrow line of the Besparmak Mountains and up towards the north coast. I chose to make my way up to the ruined Crusader castle which sits precariously on top of one of the hills. From our high vantage points a century and a quarter apart, we both caught tempting glimpses of Cyprus's magnificent northern coastline.

If Thomson did ascend the heights to St. Hilarion Castle with his camera, the pictures did not make it into his published account of the journey, but a number of fine portraits did - of the locals he met along the way. All he said of the mountains was that

> *The way across the hills from Mesorea is simply a mule track, which climbs with a gentle gradient the glens on the southern face of the mountain range, but falls in steep declivities towards the northern plain of Kyrenia.*[7]

Had he reached the castle heights, it is hard to imagine him not taking photographs of it, and commenting on the magnificent views it afforded of the town of Kyrenia itself.

So, perhaps, the explanation for such an omission - and the absence of views of several other of the island's most

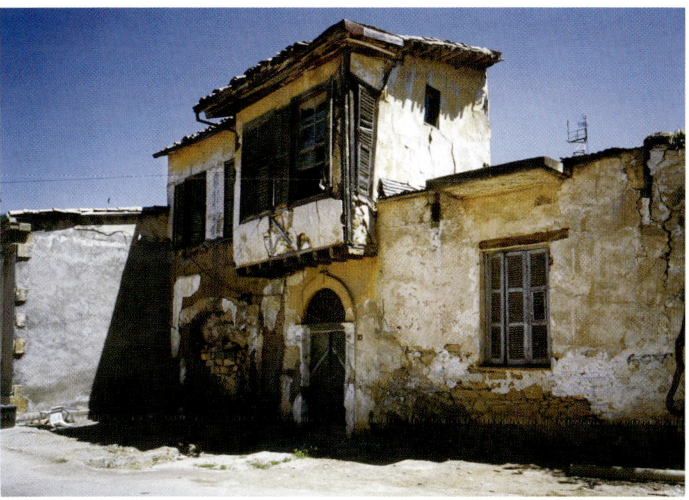

left: Buildings near the Green Line border in the divided city show signs of decades of neglect. The border runs only a few metres from this house in Lefkosha.

below: The minarets of the Selimiye Mosque seen over the rooftops of small workshops in a narrow Lefkosha street.

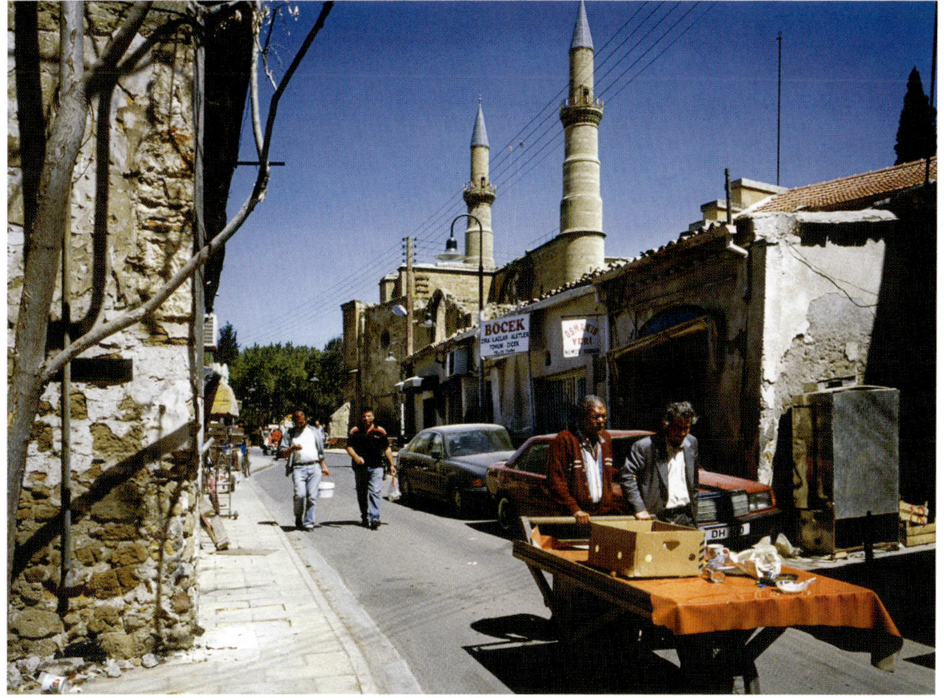

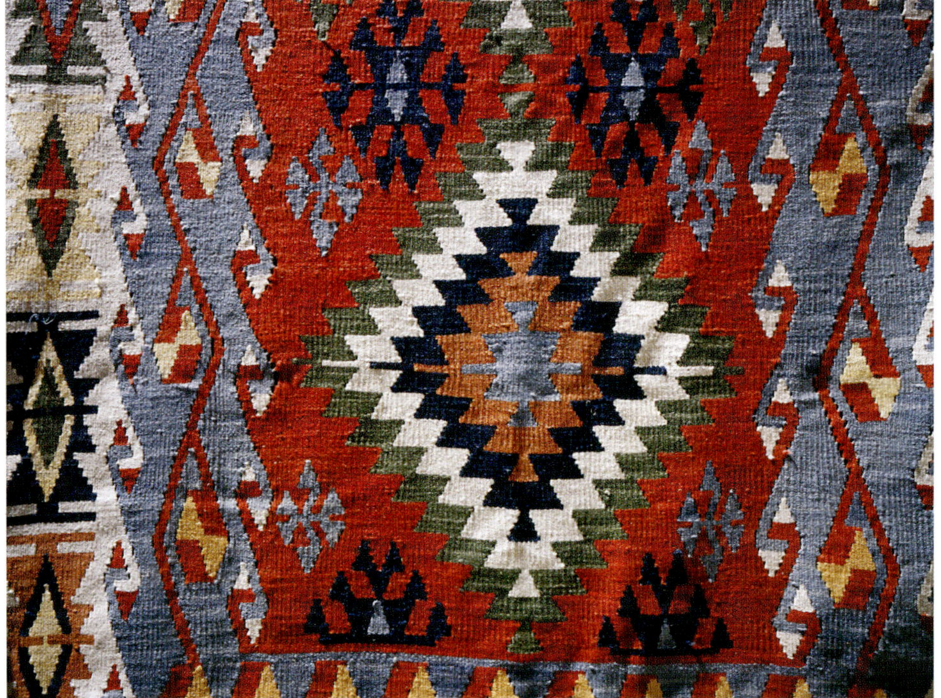

above: A brightly coloured carpet in an outdoor stall near the Semiliye Mosque, Lefkosa. Hand made fabrics and carpets are being manufactured in increasing numbers in the Turkish quarter, to be sold to the growing numbers of tourists able to visit the area since a relaxation of border controls.

magnificent monuments – is more practical than aesthetic. It is not impossible, with the logistics of carrying his large camera and glass plates by mule over such rough terrain, that some of his plates might have been broken and therefore unusable. Using dry plates, he may have been able to travel lighter than in his earlier journeys with the wet collodion process, but as his own sketches of the journey show, his transport arrangements were not the most ideal for carrying delicate glass plates.

The largest surviving negative from Thomson's journey through Cyprus measures 15″x12″.[8] A camera of the dimensions illustrated (*right*) would have been capable of taking negatives of at least 20″x24″! When this sketch was published, the text which accompanied it noted

There are plenty of clouds and sometimes mist or rain upon the high mountain [Mount Olympus] *visited six weeks ago by Mr. Thomson, who has favoured us with a couple of sketches, and the following note:- "We made the toilsome ascent of Olympus on our mules in the morning, accompanied by the headman of the village... Our approach to the summit was heralded by an ominous peal of thunder, that made the earth tremble beneath our feet. It sounded like a terrible protest against the sacrilege of photographing, for the first time, the ruins of the ancient shrine. Dismounting, we clambered through stony debris to the summit. The storm increased and was accompanied by a deluge of rain, such as one can only experience in high regions... Shelter there was none, save that represented in the sketch... Worst of all, my umbrella, of thin calico, proved useless; my pith hat became limp and pasty; while my shoes gave way entirely as I made the descent on foot".*[9]

Even at such heights, rain of such severity as described by Thomson is highly unusual.

Reaching the north coast, and arriving in Kyrenia, his notes suggest that the small town did not immediately impress him.

The view of Kerynia in this plate [illustrated overleaf] *is one of the most imposing that can be obtained from the shore, and yet the place looks no better than many of the small fishing stations common in Southern Europe. It may here be noted that the pursuits of the people are so purely agricultural that few fishing villages are to be found on the coast of Cyprus.... It surprises us, in this quarter, to remark the extent to which some of the houses have been suffered to fall into disrepair; while the lower walls and foundations present a solid front to the sea, the verandahs, holding wind and waves in contempt, are the most flimsy structures in the world. The house in which the Author lodged was adorned with a verandah which had lost its front railing, and had contracted a dangerous dip shorewards. On this frail platform, the family used to sit, undisturbedly, to enjoy the evening breeze, but to me its pleasures were alloyed by the apprehension lest in a moment of weakness the structure might dip still deeper and launch its occupants into the darkness.*[10]

The photograph depicts a Kyrenia largely undeveloped, with a less developed and protected harbour than it had enjoyed since the Roman occupation. The port had clearly fallen into considerable disrepair, despite having a reasonable depth of water – two fathoms according to Thomson – and being the only port on the north coast of the island. An earlier plate titled *Kerynia Harbour* shows the shore sloping gently down to the water's edge, no sign of a constructed quayside. According to Thomson, the remains of a sea wall could be seen offshore, but the port enjoyed relatively little commercial trade. Development later in the century completely remodelled it.

The importance attached to the town in olden times, wrote Thomson, *is seen in the massive fortifications that guard the entrance to the port. It is supposed to have been founded originally by Dorian colonists under Praxander and Cepheus, and, even at a late period in its history, it was jealously guarded and kept open for the reception of food supplies from the mainland to support the garrisons in the mountain forts of St. Hilarion, Buffavento, and Cantara.*[11]

Today, the long history of the port, and its importance as a trading stop in much earlier times, is remembered in the specially built gallery within Kyrenia Castle which houses a beautifully preserved cargo vessel, dating from the 4th century BC, retrieved from the bottom of the Mediterranean by American archaeologists in the late 1960s. The boat was found a mile offshore, in over a hundred feet of water by a sponge diver, and after it was successfully recovered, a specially built museum was opened in 1976.

Historians have deduced, from the cargo it was carrying, and other sources, that the ship regularly plied between Samos and Cyprus, by way of Kos and Rhodes,

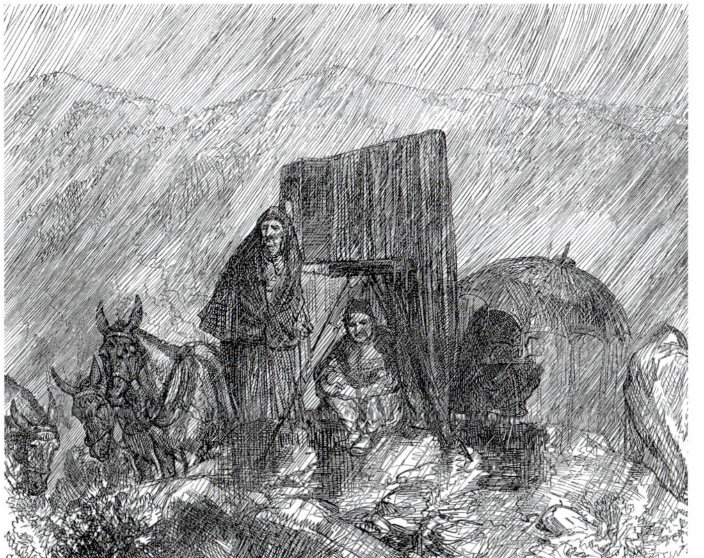

left: Thomson's own, rather fanciful, sketch of himself sheltering underneath his camera during a storm on Mount Olympus.
below: St Hilarion Castle, one of a line of castles built along the ridge of the Besparmak Mountains south of Kyrenia, was not included in Thomson's book, although he did comment on the view from the mountain top looking towards Kyrenia.

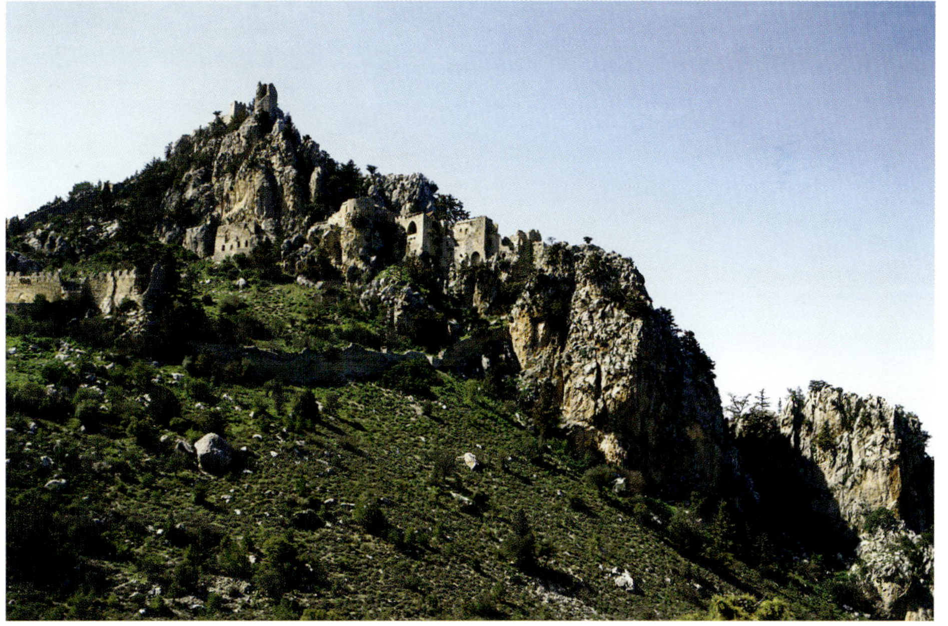

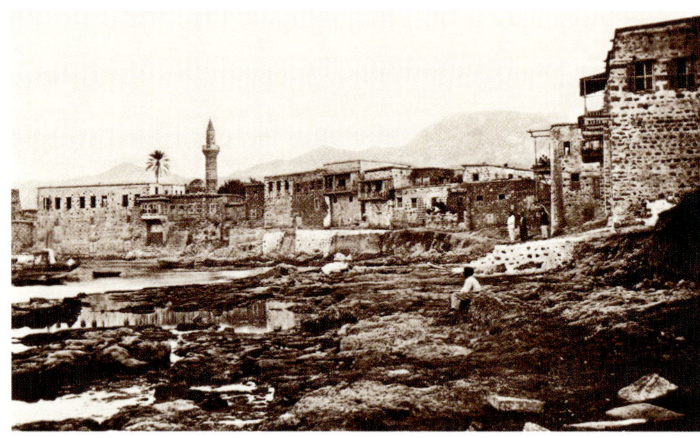

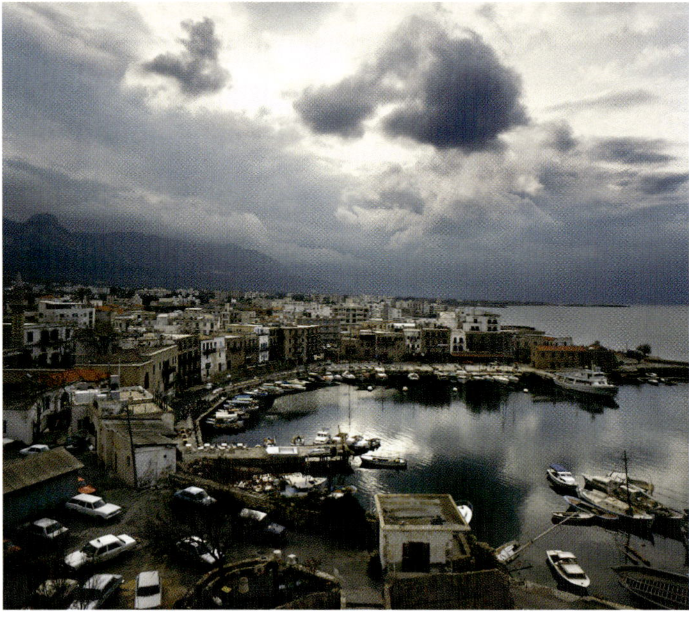

right: In the caption for this view of 'Kyrenia facing the Sea', Thomson wrote '*The picture was taken at low water and it seems evident from the construction of the houses that a great rise in the tide occurs at certain times of the year*'. This waterfront is now entirely made up of restaurants.

below right: Kyrenia Harbour, after a severe thunderstorm, photographed from near the castle in the 1990s. Since this dramatic view was taken, the commercialisation of the harbour and waterfront has been considerable.

and was over eighty years old and crewed by four men when it sank. Its cargo included amphorae full of oils and wines, jars of almonds and other produce.

Such trading links were well in the past by the time Thomson arrived, and he dismissed it with the comment that

The trade at this pygmy port is so insignificant that it has never been referred to in the consular commercial reports, a circumstance to be accounted for by the greater facilities offered for the anchorage of large vessels, by the roadsteads of Larnaca, Limassol, and Paphos, to which places, indeed, part of the produce of the plains of Kerynia finds its way across the island for shipment.[12]

From Kyrenia, today known as Girne, Thomson briefly turned south again, towards the village and ruined abbey of Bellapais - or *Belle Paix* as he referred to it - undoubtedly one of the most beautiful places on the island, and one which he would certainly have been drawn to in his quest for the picturesque. From his first distant view of the abbey sitting at the foot of lush hills, he was captivated.

It may be truly said of the monks of old (as, indeed, of their modern representatives) that "their lines have fallen in pleasant places". Thus the greatest care, aided by monastic taste and experience, seems to have been exercised in selecting the site for the Abbey of Belle Paix. While the surrounding scenery embraces one of the finest panoramas of the shores of the Mediterranean, the crystalline purity of the mountain springs hard by could only have been rivalled by the excellence of the wines that the neighbouring vineyards once supplied.[13]

Presumably the making of fine wines had ceased by the time Thomson arrived. It can, however, be reported that Cyprus wines today offer the visitor a robust and thoroughly enjoyable experience.

In Britain, abbeys like Bellapais would, long ago, have been over-manicured, leaving them somewhat clinical and much less romantic, but the Abbey, nestling in the wooded valley near the little village of the same name - where Lawrence Durrell once lived and where he got the inspiration for his book *Bitter Lemons* in the 1950s - exists in a delightful timewarp. It remains strongly redolent of a time in Britain before obsessions with manicured lawns and health and safety destroyed the picturesque beauty of buildings which had previously been allowed to mellow and age gracefully.

The abbey was founded by the Augustinian Canons in the late 12th century, and by the early 13th century they had converted to the Premonstratensian Order of Canons Regular, an offshoot of the Augustinians. The history of the monastery - the single most impressive Gothic structure to survive on Cyprus - is relatively obscure, but most of the buildings to be seen today date from the second half of the 13th century. Additional fortifications from the 14th century, and a few other minor alterations have left a complex of buildings which has an architectural unity typical of a convent designed and constructed in no more than fifty or sixty years.

The architectural gem on the site, however - the magnificent refectory - dates from the first quarter of the 14th century. It was this building that the British initially contemplated turning into an infirmary in the 1880s.

Looking at Thomson's 1878 pictures, Bellapais Abbey is, indeed, remarkable in how little it has changed in over a century and a quarter. A little excavation work has lowered the ground level down to something closer to the mediaeval floor, much of the fallen masonry has been removed and the masonry still standing has been consolidated, but its charm as a crumbling ruin has not been diminished in the process.

From Bellapais, Thomson returned to Kyrenia, before turning west towards Lapithos and St. Panteleimon, a monastery of Orthodox monks where, he noted:

> *In no part of Cyprus could one hope to enjoy more genial society, or more refined courtesy than within the walls of St. Pantalemoni; and should the reader ever visit the spot, the author commends him to the acquaintance of the venerable Archimandrite and his subordinates in office.*[14]

below: The inner courtyard of Bellapais Abbey, photographed by Thomson - a study in which he included three of his retinue of helpers to give a sense of scale.

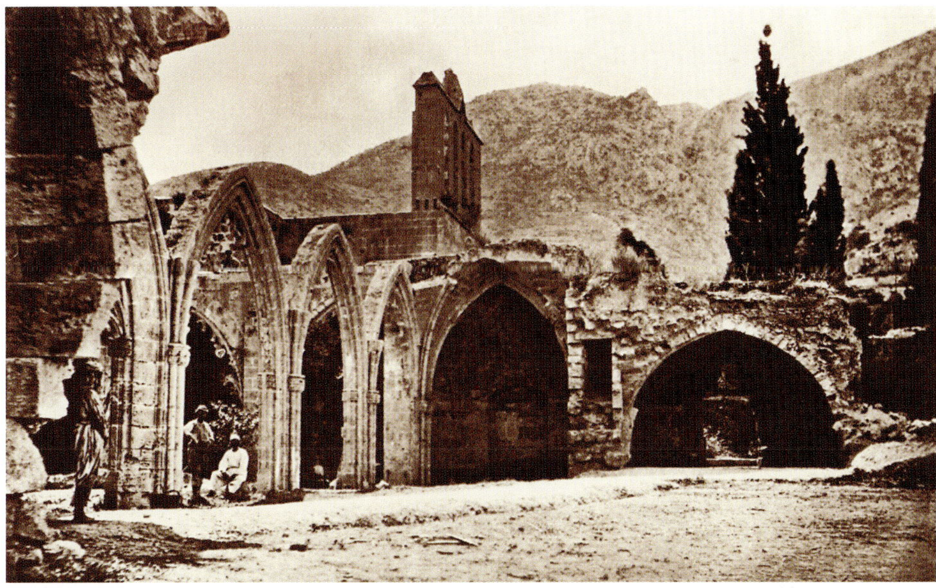

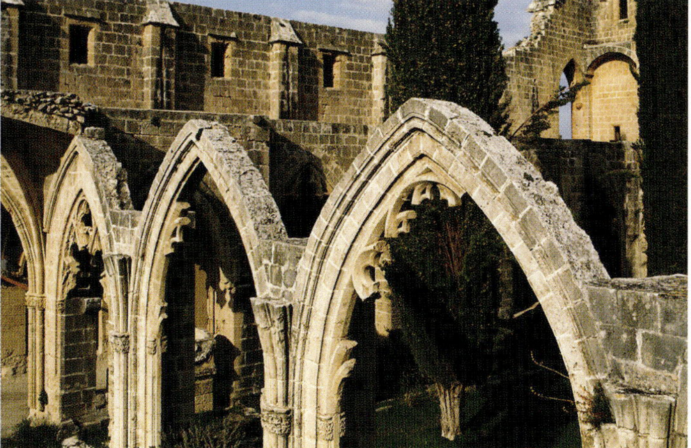

left: The cloisters of Bellapais Abbey today, seen from the roof over the west doorway of the church. What the abbey might look like today had the occupying British forces had their way in the late 1880s, one can only imagine. Not long after Thomson's visit, plans were afoot to turn it in to a military hospital. Luckily for this unique site, those plans were later abandoned before any great damage had been done to the ruins.

below: The monks of St Panteleimon near Myrtou, as photographed by Thomson. When the chapter reduced in size, their successors moved to a smaller monastery.
right: The Agios Panteleimon today is located just outside the village of Agrokipia, about twelve miles south west of Nicosia.
below right: The architectural style captured in Thomson's view is echoed at Agios Herakleidos, five miles south west of Agios Panteleimon.

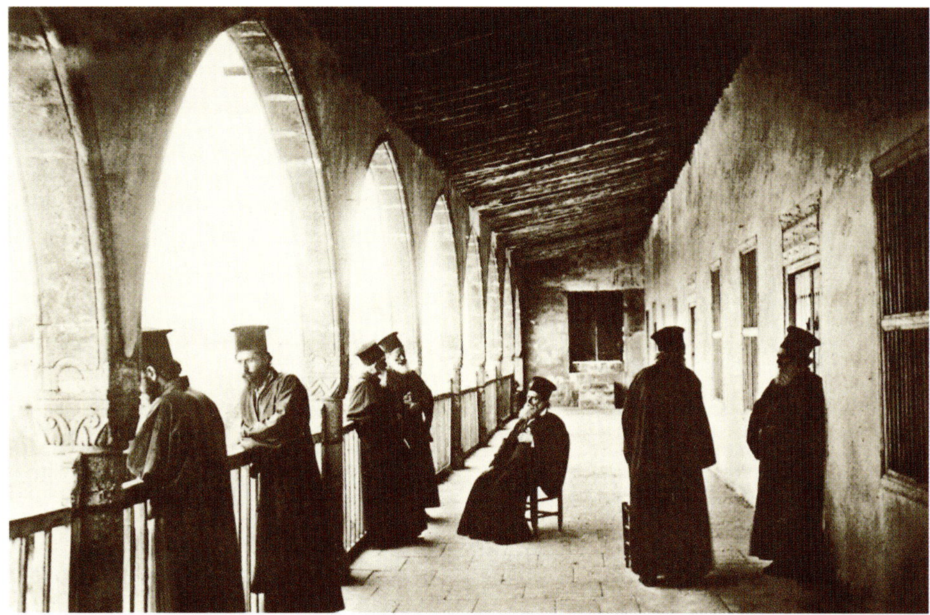

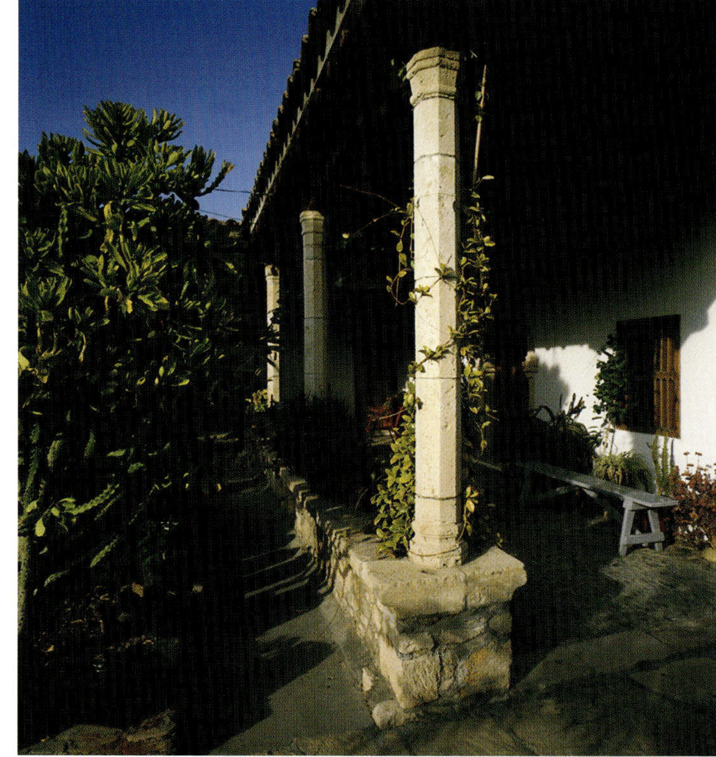

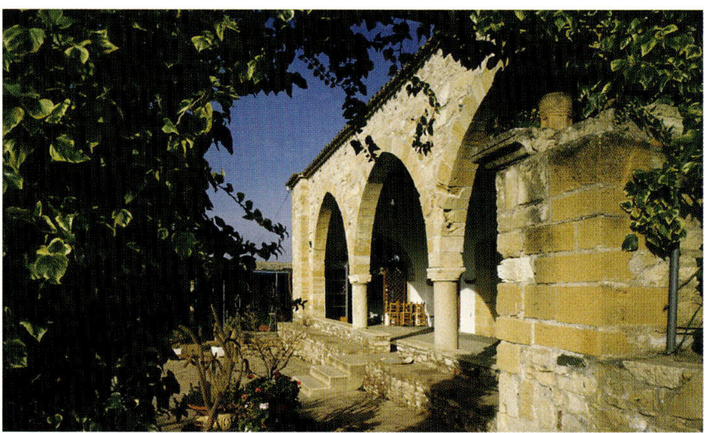

Now inaccessible to visitors, the Turkish army occupies the Myrtou site which Thomson visited in 1878. Relocated south of the border in the midst of arid countryside about twelve miles from Nicosia, today's St. Panteleimon monastery supports a much smaller fraternity.

Thomson's journey continued southwards, to Lefka, and on into the mountains, where they climbed Mount Olympus, the highest peak. In a note to *The Illustrated London News* published in early November 1878, he wrote that

Accompanied by an Arab dragoman, Habib Kuri, and my muleteer, I rested at Prodromus for the night. It is the village nearest to the summit of Mount Olympus, built on the crest

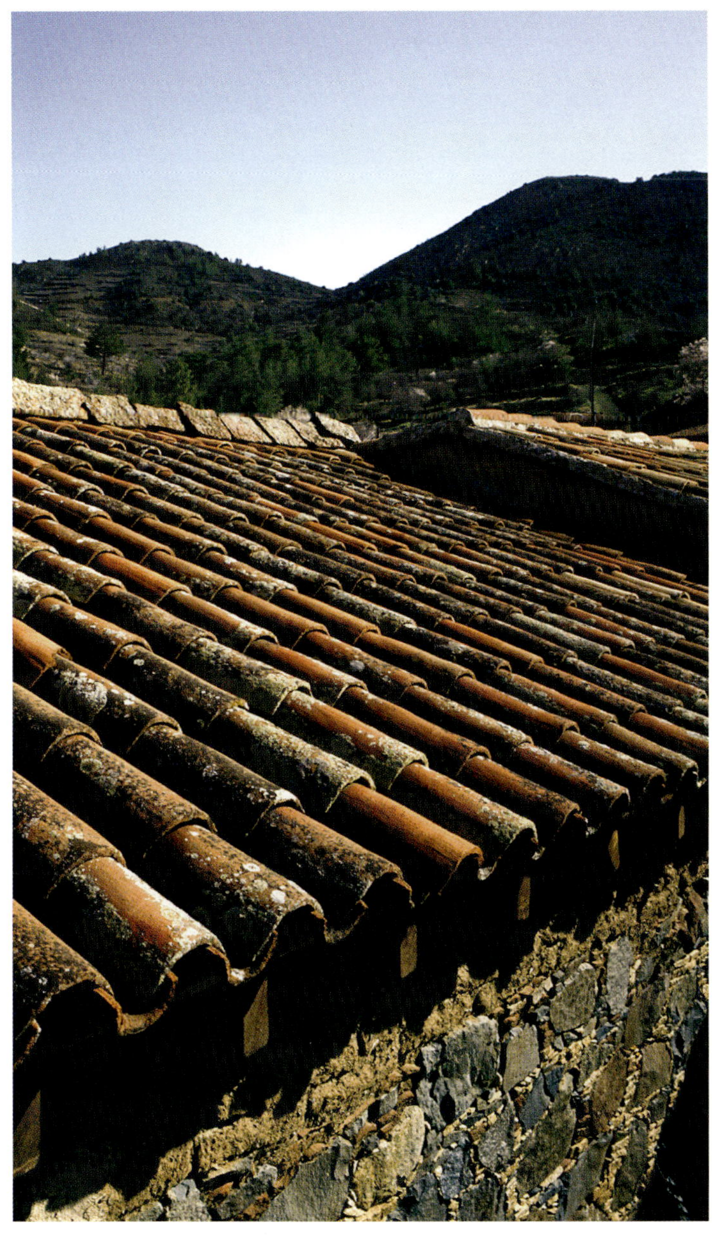

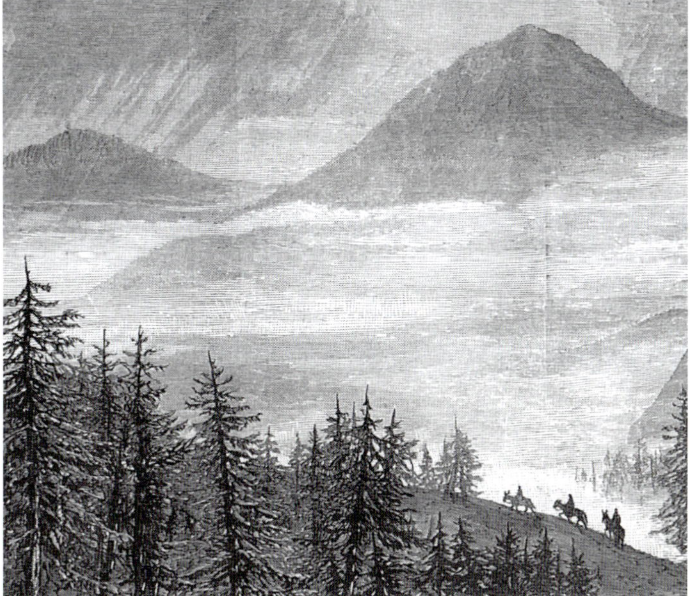

far left: As he travelled through the Troodos Mountains, Thomson visited a succession of villages, remarking on their simple architecture. The village of Fikardou, to the east of the Troodos, has been preserved as a typical example of the building style which could once be found throughout the island.
left: From the *Illustrated London News* November 9th 1878, one of Thomson's own sketches which he supplied to illustrate his journey. It shows his party on their mules, making their slow ascent into the mountains from the village of Prodromus where they had spent the night. *'The accompanying sketch'* wrote Thomson, *'pictures the apex of the classic mountain as it appeared, partially wrapped in a robe of clouds and mist'*.

of one of the lower spurs of the range. The temperature fell perceptibly as we made the ascent during the day, and at night could not have exceeded 40 deg. Fahrenheit.[15]

The head man of the village of Prodromus organised an enthusiastic welcome for the climbers, and offered his own services as mountain guide – an offer which Thomson was delighted to accept, and rewarded him by taking his portrait! He agreed that despite the conditions on the mountain, it was a memorable experience.

It is one of the delights of Cyprus in spring and autumn that it is possible to sunbathe on the beach in the morning, and, later in the day, watch skiers above the snow line.

Coming down from the mountains, and turning south-

right: This fine formal portrait of the head man of the village of Prodromus, was taken by Thomson – as a gift for the man – in recognition of his help as the party's guide on the mountain. *far right:* The Tombs of the Kings – seen here with Paphos in the distance – were only fully excavated long after Thomson's visit, but enough must have been visible in 1878 for Thomson to observe that '*this must have been the family sepulchre of a great personage, or possibly one of the Kings of Paphos*'.

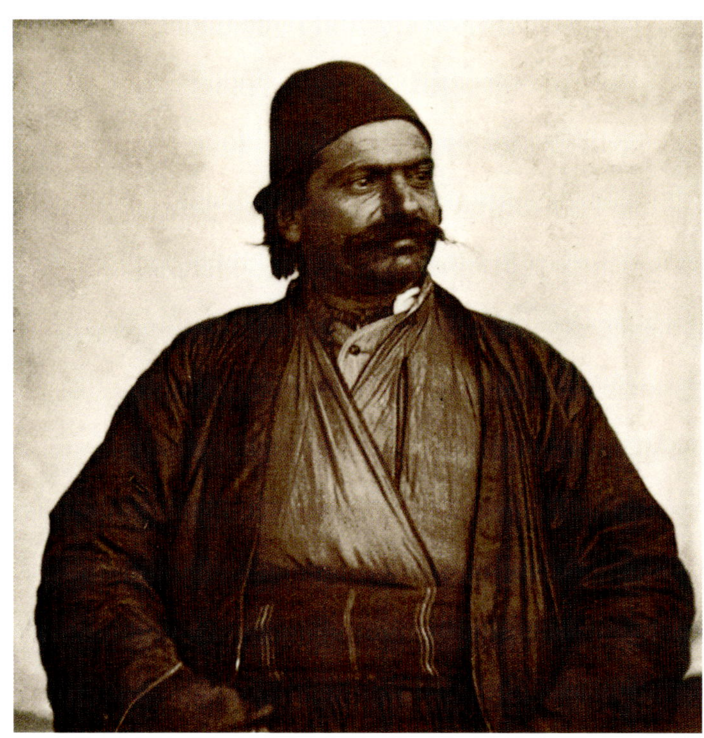

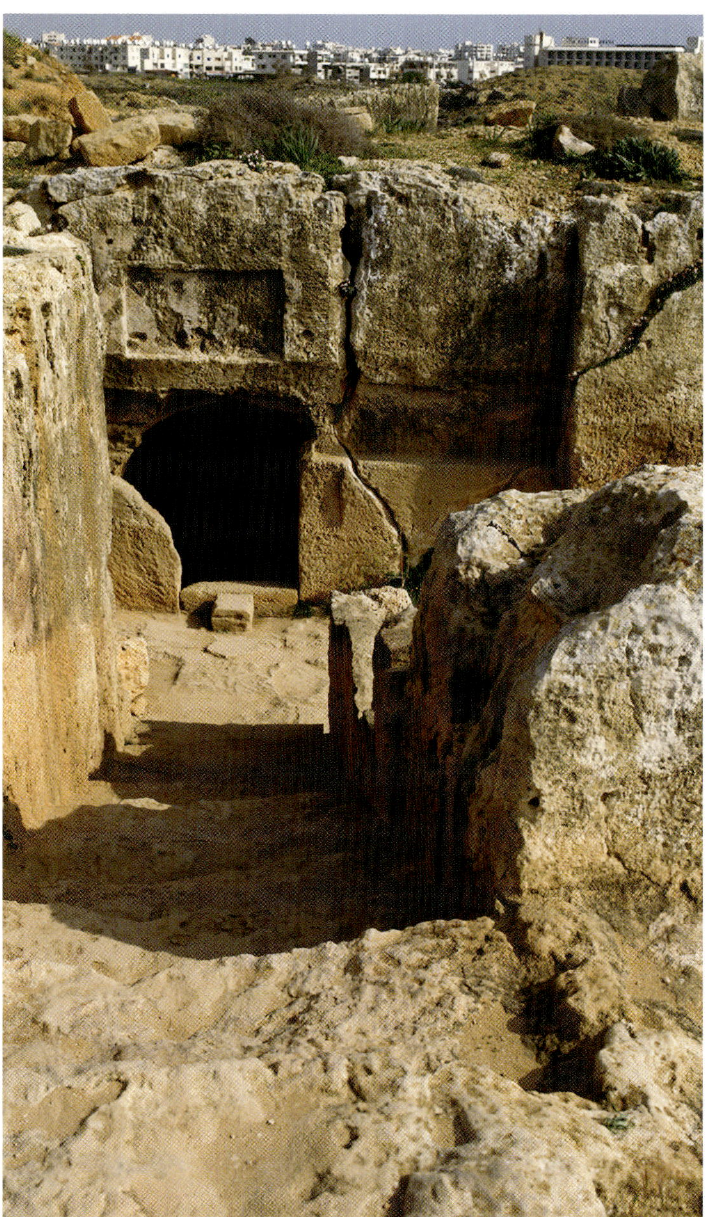

west, the party crossed the plain of Paphos and reached the village of the same name, with its rock tombs. A century and a quarter later, Paphos is one of the island's premier holiday resorts, with high-rise apartment blocks and hotels dwarfing and overshadowing the earlier buildings. Fed by its own international airport, Paphos annually welcomes visitors in their tens of thousands. An uneasy mixture of the brash and gaudy with the ancient and beautiful, the town today bears no resemblance to the sight which would have greeted Thomson and his friends.

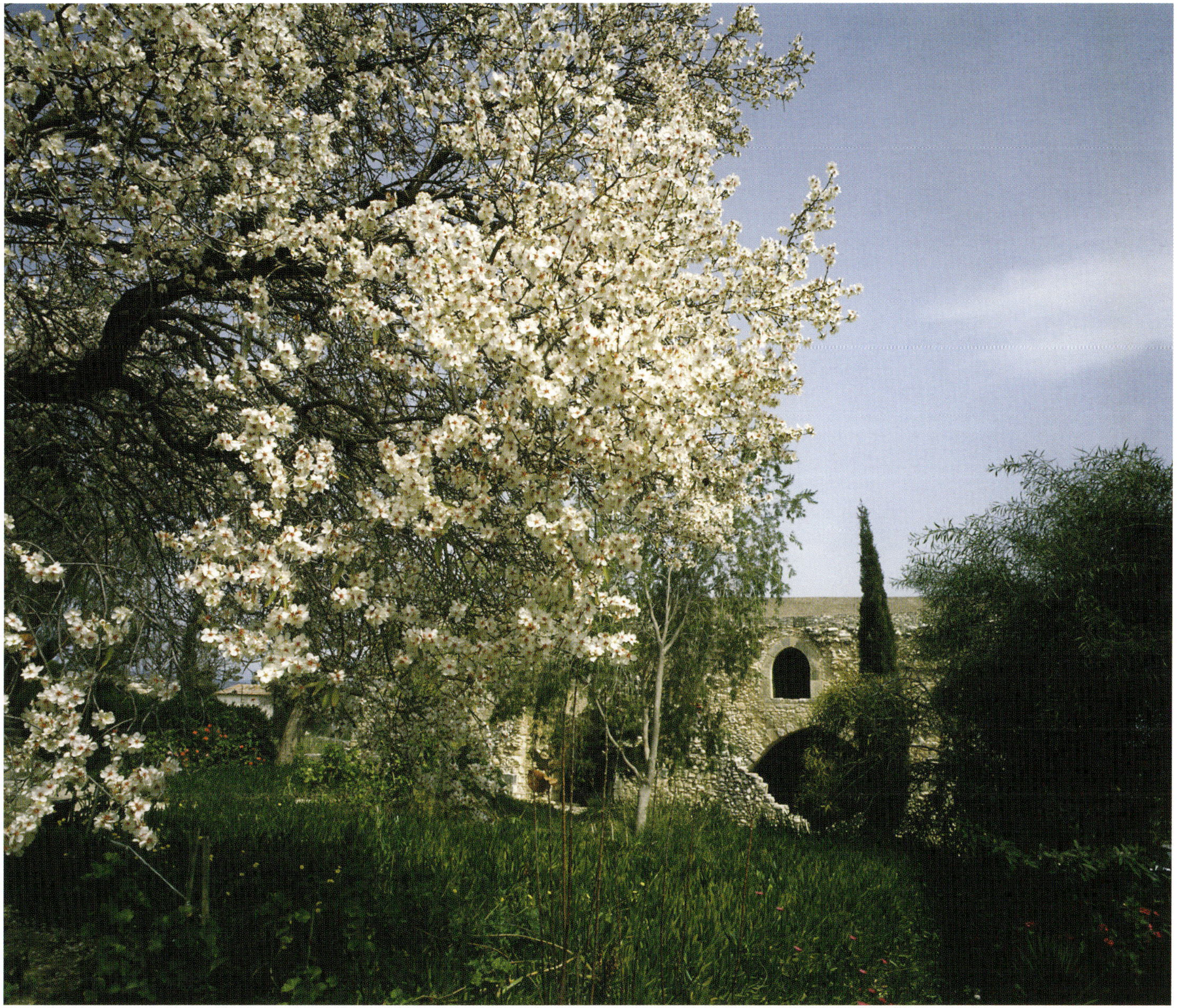

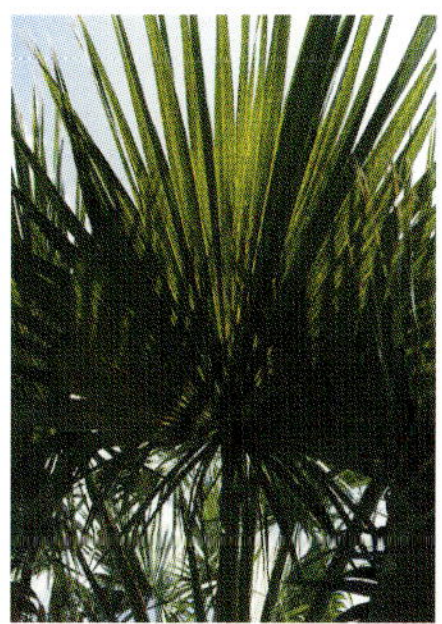

above: The ubiquitous palm tree reminds the visitor that Cyprus is a Mediterranean island.
left: Kolossi Castle, near Limassol, seen here surrounded by spring blossom, was built in the 13th century as the headquarters of the Knights of St John, better known as the Knights Templar.

below: Thomson mistakenly identified the Cathedral of St Nicholas in Famagusta as St. Katherine's. Falling ill during his visit, he declared his intense dislike for Famagusta, describing it as the most unhealthy place on the island!
bottom: Wild anemones flowering in the spring sunshine.
opposite page: The former cathedral, one of the island's great 14th century Gothic masterpieces, has been the Lala Mustafa Pasa Mosque for centuries now.

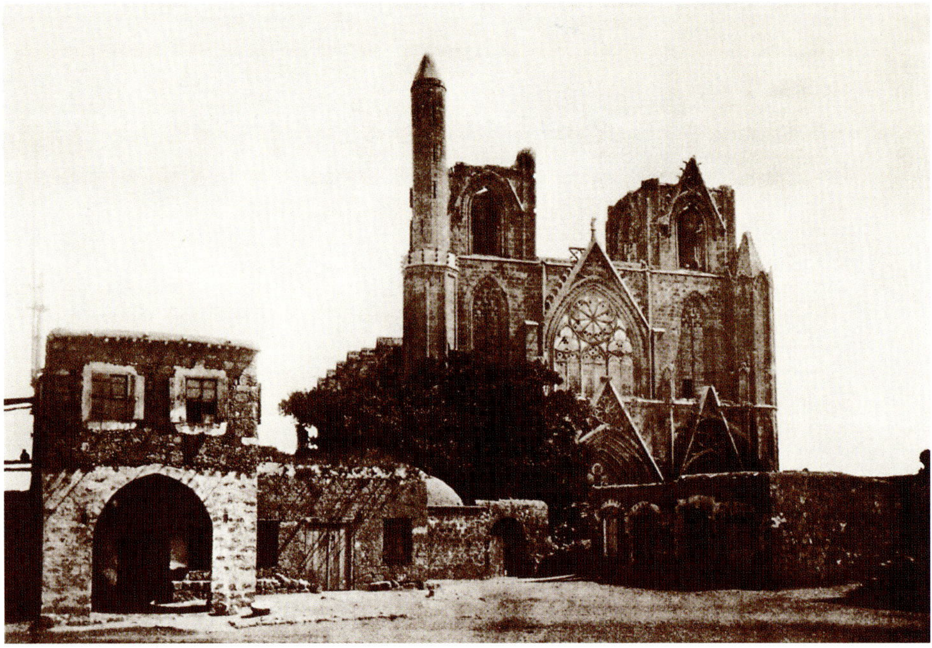

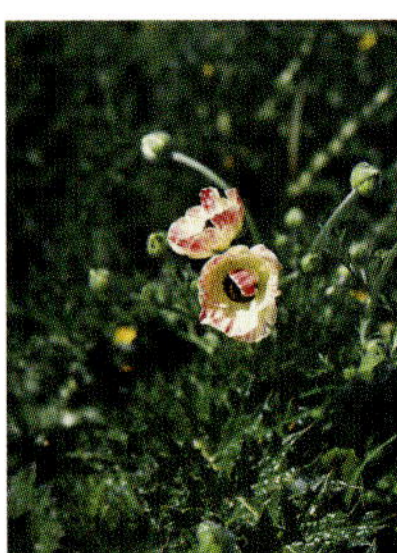

From Paphos, the group moved east towards the ruins of Kourion, and the town of Limassol. That Thomson felt it was important to remark that the make-up of the population of Limassol was one third Turkish suggests that even after only a very short period of time on the island, he was aware of the tensions between Greek and Turk which have dogged the history of Cyprus for centuries. The island had, of course, been under Turkish rule until very shortly before Thomson's visit. The rest of his account of the town was, however, written with tongue firmly in cheek.

In commercial importance, he wrote, *Limassol ranks next after Larnaca itself; and its trade, which falls far short of that of Larnaca, is set down in the Consular reports for 1876 as: Imports, £50,920; Exports: £59,895. The chief exports are wine and carob beans, although a number of other products appear in the list, while in the corresponding catalogue of imports, cotton manufactures and tobacco hold the most prominent places. Playing cards and cigarette papers also figure as articles of import, and are not unworthy of mention as affording some clue to the pastimes of the people.*[16]

The coastline either side of the old town of Limassol is today lined by hotels and high-rise apartment blocks almost at the water's edge, with private beaches and all the paraphernalia expected by the affluent holidaymaker. The old town, however, still retains some of the narrow streets and ancient buildings which greeted Thomson in 1878. He saw a town which was, apparently, relatively prosperous, but in his opinion, at the same time insecure.

There is no sign of insecurity along the south coast of the island today. It is inland, where people are leaving the farms for the greater job opportunities in the resorts, that the insecurity is increasingly evident.

The final destination in Thomson's tour was the town of Famagusta on the east coast, today known by its Turkish name of Gazimagusa, or Magusa for short.

Since the Turkish invasion of 1974, parts of Famagusta have become a ghost town. Before 1974, the old walled city was largely inhabited by Turkish Cypriots, while the new town - known as Varosha - was largely Greek. As another irony in the island's history, Varosha, a village in Thomson's day, was populated by Christians who had been expelled from their houses in Famagusta by the Muslim Turks.

That Greek quarter, which offered over ten thousand hotel beds in the early 1970s, was abandoned with such haste at the time of the invasion that washing was even left hanging on washing lines, where it has remained slowly rotting away for more than three decades. Modern high-rise hotels, which have stood empty and decaying since 1974, in what the Northern Cypriots call Maras, remain off-limits in an area controlled by the Turkish military. Signs

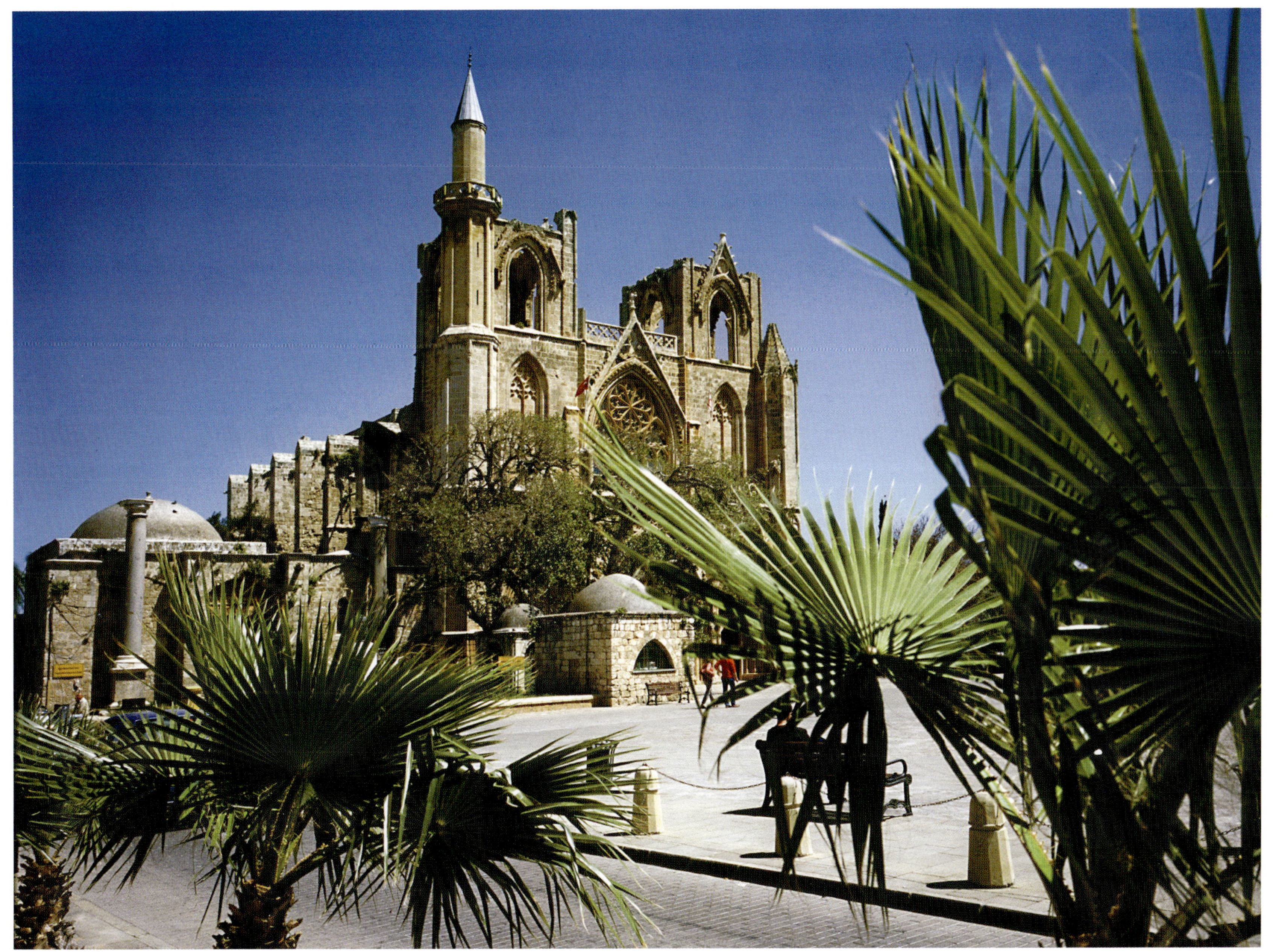

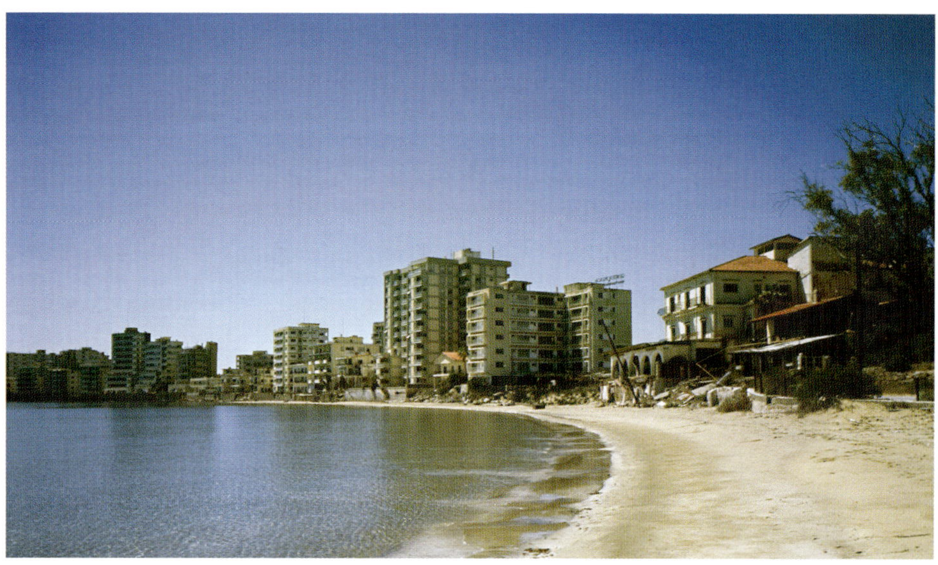

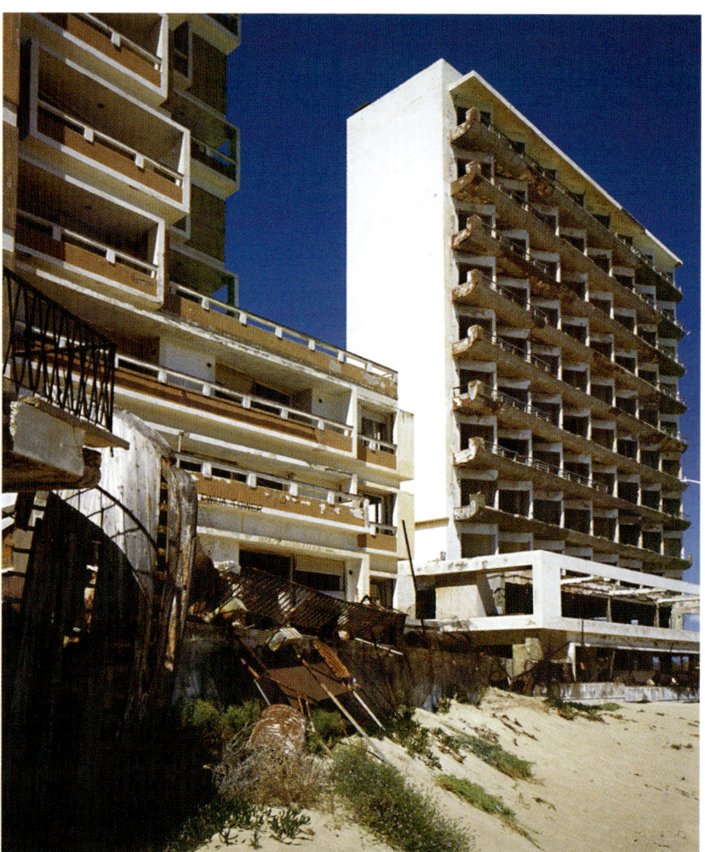

above and above right: Varosha is a ghost town - as much a 'city of the dead' as was Famagusta in Thomson's day. From the Palm Beach Hotel - the last occupied building before miles of waterfront dereliction - the view is eerie. While holidaymakers play on the beach on one side of the high wire-mesh fence, everything on the other side is deserted and still, except for a few armed guards patroling, a veritable 'no man's land'.

along the high mesh fence warn the curious to keep out, and soldiers in watchtowers ensure that nobody enters this strange, eerie and rather bizarre legacy.

While everywhere else I travelled in the footsteps of these great photographers, governments and civic authorities made it possible for me to visit just about anywhere I asked, the government of the Turkish Republic of Northern Cyprus could not be persuaded to let me into Varosha, even escorted, and even with a promise that I would cooperate with any conditions they might see fit to impose. Their total embargo on foreign visitors entering Varosha proved insurmountable - as if by keeping people out, the problem and the embarrassment might go away.

From the perimeter fence, Varosha stands as a crumbling reminder of the island's tormented past and present. It is all the more ironic, therefore, to read John Thomson's impressions of the city of Famagusta in 1878 - change a word here and there, and he might well be talking about Varosha today.

The city was overthrown by the Turks in 1571 he told his readers *and was so left by the invaders that the siege appears to have been an event of yesterday. It is a place of ruins, a city of the dead, in which the traveller is surprised to encounter a living tenant.*[17]

He was less than impressed with the conditions under which the six hundred Turkish residents lived who remained in Famagusta, and equally unimpressed with the *malarious fever* he picked up while there - in the final days of his visit - blaming the marshes around the city. Describing it as *akin to the malarious maladies of the Nile Delta*, he suggested that its eradication could probably be effected by the draining of the marshes and the planting of trees.

Particularly difficult for him to understand or appreciate was the conversion into mosques of the great Christian churches of St. Sophia in Nicosia and the Cathedral Church of St. Nicholas (which he refers to as St. Katherine's) in Famagusta. Of the latter he wrote that

the lofty interior has had to undergo much spurious alteration and spoilation ere Moslem tastes fitted it for the purpose of a mosque.

What would he have had to say - in his blunt and direct manner - about the place today?

Thomson's visit to Cyprus was his last great journey, and he returned to a life in Britain with his wife and family, where he continued to write and lecture about his experiences for many years.

I returned to Manchester from Northern Cyprus having heard countless people in the north speak of their hope that change and reunification would eventually happen - but three years after they voted in a referendum to bring separation to an end, the two communities, while talking to each other at street level, remain divided.

But the overwhelming memory I brought home from all of these 'Great Photographic Journeys' is that the world today remains, as it was in Victorian times, a beautiful, exciting, vibrant and complicated place, filled with wonderful, fascinating and complicated people.

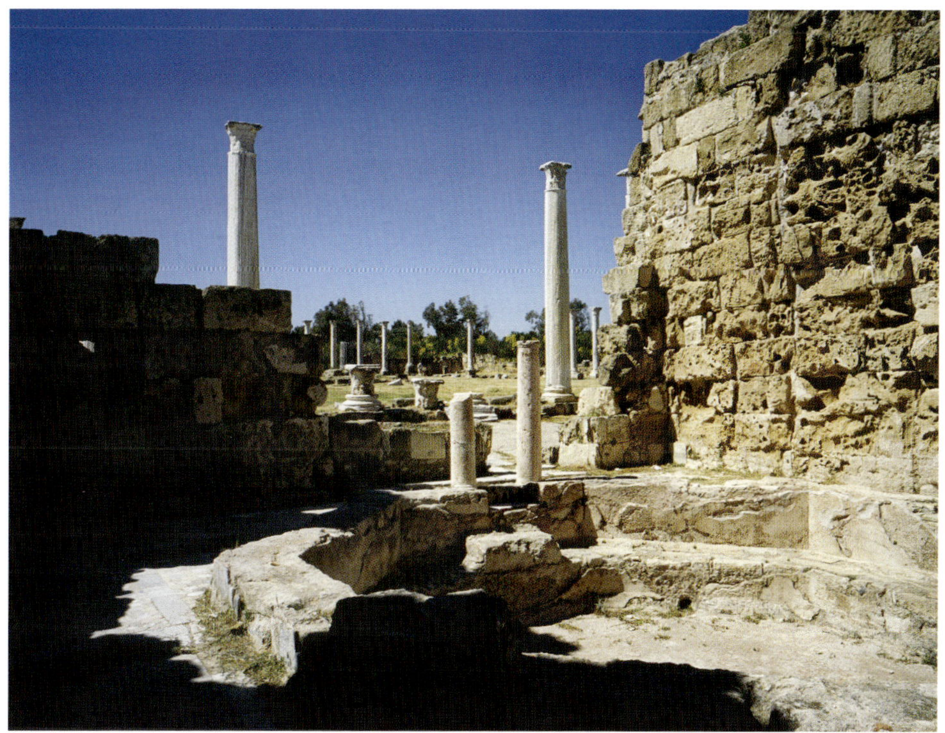

above: The ruins of the ancient city of Salamis occupy a vast tract of land by the coast just outside Famagusta. All Thomson wrote about the place was that it had been used as a quarry eight hundred years earlier to build Famagusta itself.

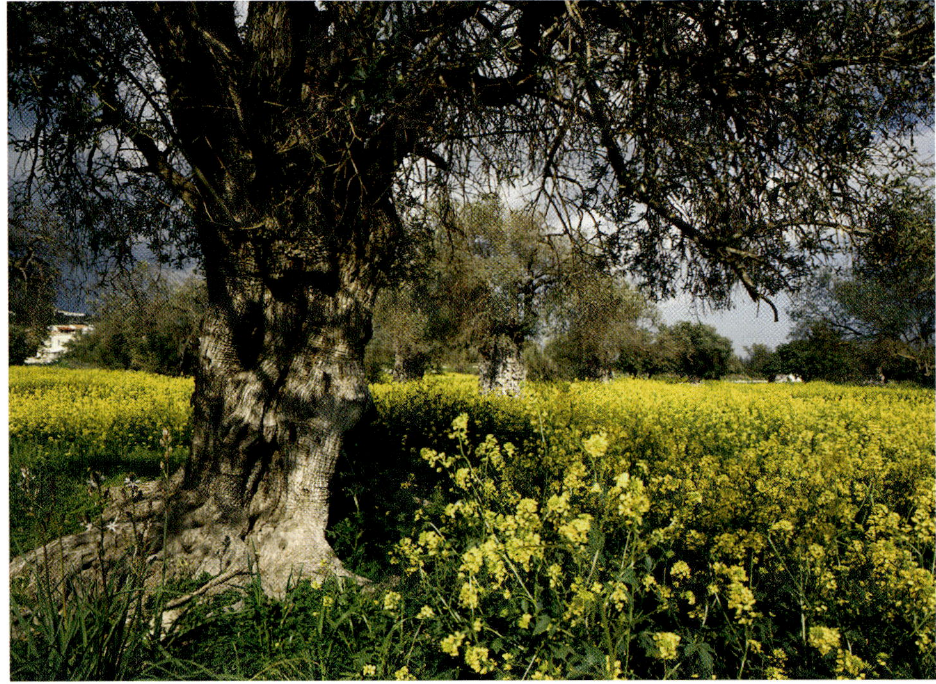

above: A splash of spring colour in Olive Groves near Skarinou.

Notes

1. John Thomson, in the introduction to *Through Cyprus with the Camera in the Autumn of 1878*, London, Sampson, Low, Marston, Searle and Rivington, published in two volumes, 1879.
2. Cyprus had passed from Turkish control into British administration as a result of the Treaty of Berlin in June 1878. It was formally annexed by Britain thirty-six years later at the outbreak of the First World War.
3. Dry collodion plates had first been successfully manufactured in the 1850s, and introduced commercially as early as 1856. The first commercially successful dry collodion emulsion was that introduced by William Blanchard Bolton and B. J. Sayce in 1864. By the time of Thomson's journey to Cyprus, gelatin dry plates, pioneered by Dr. Richard Leach Maddox and introduced in 1872, had already started to relegate collodion - wet or dry - to the history books. Thomson's decision to use dry collodion rather than faster and more reliable gelatine emulsions is unusual and unexplained.
Writing in the *Scottish Geographical Magazine in 1907*, almost thirty years after his visit to Cyprus, and perhaps drawing on slightly clouded memories, Thomson wrote "Dry collodion emulsion, introduced in 1864 by Messrs Sayce and Bolton, greatly reduced the weight of essentials. I employed plates coated with this emulsion later in Cyprus. They were developed with an alkaline solution, and were in no way inferior in point of speed or quality."
4. John Thomson, in the introduction to *Through Cyprus with the Camera in the Autumn of 1878*, London, Sampson, Low, Marston, Searle and Rivington, 1879.
5. The Autotype process was introduced in 1868 by the London-based Autotype Printing and Publishing Company. It was a modification of the Carbon process, and as such ensured that the prints were not susceptible to the fading and discolouration which dogged large production runs of silver albumen prints destined for pasting on to the pages of books and albums. Until atmospheric pollution became an issue, the interaction between the silver print, the glue, and the card or paper on to which it was mounted has been the single most significant factor in the deterioration of early prints.
6. John Thomson, *Illustrations of China and its People*, London, Sampson, Low, Marston, Low and Searle, published in 4 volumes, 1873/4.
7. John Thomson, *Through Cyprus with the Camera in the Autumn of 1878*, London, Sampson, Low, Marston, Searle and Rivington, 1879, caption to the plate 'Kerynia Plain from the Hills'.
8. Remarkably, and unlike those produced by the majority of the great 19th century photographers, Thomson's negatives still survive. They are preserved in the collection of the Wellcome Library in London. Most of the negatives for the plates in both *Illustrations of China and its People*, and *Through Cyprus with the Camera in the Autumn of 1878*, are amongst in excess of six hundred glass plates in the collection. The catalogue numbers go as high as 1200, perhaps suggesting that at one time there may have been nearly twice as many. The largest of the suriving plates measures 15"x12".
9. *Illustrated London News* , November 9th, 1878.
10. John Thomson, *Through Cyprus with the Camera in the Autumn of 1878*, London, Sampson, Low, Marston, Searle and Rivington, 1879, caption to the plate 'Kerynia Facing the Sea'.
11. *ibid,* caption to the plate 'Kerynia Harbour'.
12. *ditto*
13. *ibid,* caption to the plate 'Ancient Abbey, Belle Paix, Distant View'.
14. *ibid,* caption to the plate 'Greek Monks, St. Pantalemoni'.
15. John Thomson in a communication to *The Illustrated London News,* published 9th November 1878, p434.
16. John Thomson, *Through Cyprus with the Camera in the Autumn of 1878*, London, Sampson, Low, Marston, Searle and Rivington, 1879, caption to the plate 'Limassol'.
17. *ibid,* caption to plate 49 'Famagosta'.

Selected Bibliography

William Henry Fox Talbot - Sun Pictures in Scotland

Schaaf, Larry: *The Photographic Art of William Henry Fox Talbot*, Princeton: Princeton University Press, 2000

Buckland, Gail: *Fox Talbot and the Invention of Photography*, Boston: David R. Godine, London: Scolar Press, 1980

Travel Photography - Opening a Window on the World

Buckman, Rollin: *The Photographic Work of Calvert Richard Jones*, London: Science Museum/HMSO, 1990

Fabian, Rainer, and Hans Christian Adam: *Masters of Early Travel Photography*,London: Thames & Hudson, 1983

Hershkowitz, Robert: *The British Photographer Abroad - the first thirty years* London: Robert Hershkowitz, 1997

Khan, Omar: *From Kashmir to Kabul - Photography 1860-1900*, London: Prestel: Ahmedabad: Mapin Publishing, 2002

Lyons, Claire L., et al,. *Antiquity & Photography Ancient Views of Early Mediterranean Sites*, London: Thames & Hudson, 2005

Zannier, Italo: *Le Grand Tour in the photographs of travelers of 19th century* Venice: Canal & Stamperia Editrice, Paris: Canal Editions, 1997

Roger Fenton - Travels in Russia

Baldwin, Gordon, et al, *All the Mighty World - the Photographs of Roger Fenton 1852-1860*, New Haven & London: Yale University Press, 2004

Gernsheim, Helmut and Alison, *Roger Fenton Photographer of the Crimean War*, London: Secker & Warburg, 1954

Hannavy, John: *Roger Fenton of Crimble Hall*, London: Gordon Fraser, Boston: David R. Godine, 1975

Lloyd, Valerie: *Roger Fenton, Photographer of the 1850s*, London: South Bank Board, 1986

Francis Frith - Travels in Egypt

Howe, Kathleen Stewart: *Excursions Along the Nile - The Photographic Discovery of Ancient Egypt*, Santa Barbara: Santa Barbara Museum of Art, 1994

Garnet, Robert & Mary: *Sketches and Letters of Egypt and Palestine*, Warrington: Mackie & Co, 1904

Hudson, Roger: *Travels of a Victorian Photographer, the Photographs of Francis Frith*, London: The Folio Society, 2001

Nickel, Douglas R.: *Francis Frith in Egypt and Palestine*, Princeton and Oxford: Princeton University Press, 2004

Roberts, David: *From and Antique Land - Travels in Egypt and the Holy Land*, New York: Weidenfeld & Nicholson, 1989

Wilson, Derek: *Francis Frith's Travels*, London: J.M.Dent, 1985

Samuel Bourne - India: 'Photography in the East'

Dehejia, Vidya: *India Through the Lens: Photography 1840-1911*, London &

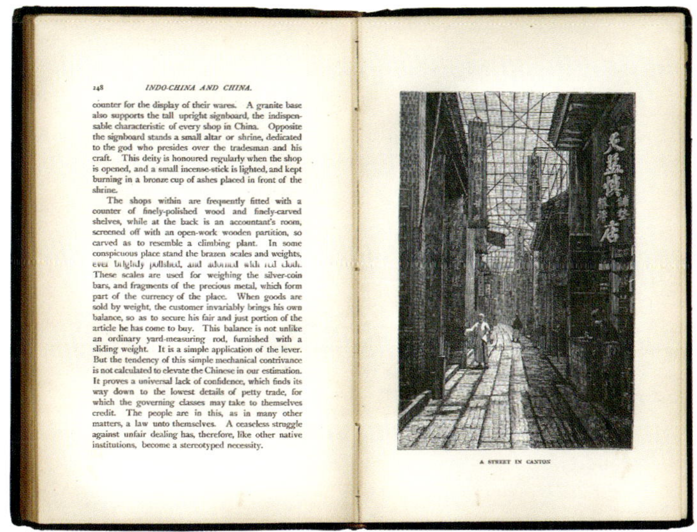

248 *INDO-CHINA AND CHINA.*

counter for the display of their wares. A granite base also supports the tall upright signboard, the indispensable characteristic of every shop in China. Opposite the signboard stands a small altar or shrine, dedicated to the god who presides over the tradesman and his craft. This deity is honoured regularly when the shop is opened, and a small incense-stick is lighted, and kept burning in a bronze cup of ashes placed in front of the shrine.

The shops within are frequently fitted with a counter of finely-polished wood and finely-carved shelves, while at the back is an accountant's room, screened off with an open-work wooden partition, so carved as to resemble a climbing plant. In some conspicuous place stand the brazen scales and weights, ever brightly polished, and adorned with red cloth. These scales are used for weighing the silver-coin bars, and fragments of the precious metal, which form part of the currency of the place. When goods are sold by weight, the customer invariably brings his own balance, so as to secure his fair and just portion of the article he has come to buy. This balance is not unlike an ordinary yard-measuring rod, furnished with a sliding weight. It is a simple application of the lever. But the tendency of this simple mechanical contrivance is not calculated to elevate the Chinese in our estimation. It proves a universal lack of confidence, which finds its way down to the lowest details of petty trade, for which the governing classes may take to themselves credit. The people are in this, as in many other matters, a law unto themselves. A ceaseless struggle against unfair dealing has, therefore, like other native institutions, become a stereotyped necessity.

A STREET IN CANTON

left: The photographs from *Illustrations of China and its People* were reduced to line engravings for Thomson's 1875 book *The Straits of Malacca, Indo-China and China; or, Ten Years Travels, Adventures, and Residence Abroad*, published in New York by Harper & Brothers. The page at which the book is opened shows the engraving based on Thomson's study of Physic Street, Canton. Bizarrely, the spine of the book identifies the author as 'W. Thomson', although the title page confirms the author to be – styled as he preferred it – 'J. Thomson F.R.G.S.' Thomson was not the only author to suffer such an indignity. In 1856, Marcus Sparling, Roger Fenton's assistant during the Crimea War and for some time after their return to London, was identified as 'W. Sparling' on the title page of his book *Theory and Practice of the Photographic Art*, published in London by Houlston and Stoneman.

New York: Prestel, Ahmedabad: Mapin Publishing, 2000

Ollman, Arthur: *Samuel Bourne - Images of India*, San Francisco: Friends of Photography Bookstore, 1983

Pelizarri, Maria Antonella: *Traces of India*, Montreal: Canadian Center for Architecture, New Haven & London: Yale University Press, 2003

John Thomson - Illustrations of China and its People

Goodrich, L. Carrington, and Nigel Cameron: *The Face of China 1860-1912*, New York: Aperture, 1978

Thomson, John: *China And Its People in Early Photographs*, New York: Dover Editions, 1982

Thomson, John: *The Straits of Malacca, Indo-China and China*, New York: Harper & Brothers, 1875

White, Stephen: *John Thomson Life and Photographs*, London: Thames & Hudson, 1985

John Thomson - Through Cyprus with the Camera

Thomson, John: *Through Cyprus with the Camera in the Autumn of 1878*, (reprint) London: Trigraph, 1985

Index